Making Global Society

Barry Buzan proposes a new approach to making International Relations a truly global discipline that transcends both Eurocentrism and comparative civilisations. He narrates the story of humankind as a whole across three eras, using its material conditions and social structures to show how global society has evolved. Deploying the English School's idea of primary institutions and setting their story across three domains – interpolity, transnational and interhuman – this book conveys a living historical sense of the human story whilst avoiding the over-abstraction of many social science grand theories. Buzan sharpens the familiar story of three main eras in human history with the novel idea that these eras are separated by turbulent periods of transition. This device enables a radical retelling of how modernity emerged from the late eighteenth century. He shows how the concept of 'global society' can build bridges connecting International Relations, Global Historical Sociology and Global/World History.

Barry Buzan is Emeritus Professor in the Department of International Relations at the London School of Economics and Political Science, and a Fellow of the British Academy. He has authored, co-authored and edited over 30 books and 170 chapters and articles including *Re-imagining International Relations* (with Amitav Acharya, 2021), *The Making of Global International Relations* (with Amitav Acharya, 2019) and *From International to World Society? English School Theory and the Social Structure of Globalisation* (2004).

CAMBRIDGE STUDIES IN INTERNATIONAL RELATIONS

Cambridge Studies in International Relations is a joint initiative of Cambridge University Press and the British International Studies Association (BISA). The series aims to publish the best new scholarship in international studies, irrespective of subject matter, methodological approach or theoretical perspective. The series seeks to bring the latest theoretical work in International Relations to bear on the most important problems and issues in global politics.

Series list continues after index

Making Global Society

A Study of Humankind across Three Eras

Barry Buzan

London School of Economics

CAMBRIDGE
UNIVERSITY PRESS

Shaftesbury Road, Cambridge CB2 8EA, United Kingdom

One Liberty Plaza, 20th Floor, New York, NY 10006, USA

477 Williamstown Road, Port Melbourne, VIC 3207, Australia

314–321, 3rd Floor, Plot 3, Splendor Forum, Jasola District Centre, New Delhi – 110025, India

103 Penang Road, #05-06/07, Visioncrest Commercial, Singapore 238467

Cambridge University Press is part of Cambridge University Press & Assessment, a department of the University of Cambridge.

We share the University's mission to contribute to society through the pursuit of education, learning and research at the highest international levels of excellence.

www.cambridge.org
Information on this title: www.cambridge.org/9781009372190

DOI: 10.1017/9781009372169

First published 2023

A catalogue record for this publication is available from the British Library.

Library of Congress Cataloging-in-Publication Data
Names: Buzan, Barry, author.
Title: Making global society : a study of humankind across three eras / Barry Buzan.
Description: Cambridge ; New York, NY : Cambridge University Press, 2023. | Series: Cambridge studies in international relations | Includes bibliographical references and index.
Identifiers: LCCN 2022062067 (print) | LCCN 2022062068 (ebook) | ISBN 9781009372190 (hardback) | ISBN 9781009372183 (paperback) | ISBN 9781009372169 (epub)
Subjects: LCSH: Social institutions. | Social structure. | Civilization. | World history. | Historical sociology. | International relations–Philosophy.
Classification: LCC HM826 .B88 2023 (print) | LCC HM826 (ebook) | DDC 306–dc23/eng/20230130
LC record available at https://lccn.loc.gov/2022062067
LC ebook record available at https://lccn.loc.gov/2022062068

ISBN 978-1-009-37219-0 Hardback
ISBN 978-1-009-37218-3 Paperback

To all the colleagues and friends with whom I have collaborated over the past five decades. Deep thanks for the stimulating and enjoyable education you gave me about so many things. This book would not exist without it.

Contents

Tables

x

Preface

How does this book relate to my earlier work, and why did I write it? This book grows out of the two main strands of my work over the last twenty years on International Relations (IR) theory and world history. Its aim is to synthesise these two strands, while adding some new research and new thinking. In a nutshell, I want to construct a novel type of world history, with the social structure of humankind as the main object of study, and using a global society perspective based on the English School (ES) as the analytical approach. In this sense, this book might be thought of as a follow-on to Buzan and Little (2000). Both books address the same scale of time and space, and the question of how to periodise history. But whereas the earlier one started from a (neo)realist question about international systems, and ended up knocking on the door of the English School, this one starts right from the beginning with the English School – or at least my conception of it as developed in Buzan (2004a). It ends up suggesting both a new angle on how we can understand the unfolding of modernity, and a new perspective on how the ES might re-base itself on more global foundations.

The main theoretical strand is the ES, and in particular, its idea of using primary institutions to define the structure of interstate, transnational and interhuman society. My earlier work on this has been partly about the general theory (Buzan, 1993, 2004a, 2014a, 2018a; Buzan and Schouenborg, 2018); partly about regional international society (Buzan and Gonzalez-Pelaez, 2009; Buzan and Zhang, 2014; Buzan and Schouenborg, 2018); and partly about developing a framework for the empirical study of specific primary institutions (Buzan, 2014a; Falkner and Buzan, 2019, 2022). This ES approach has been complemented by adding to it the differentiation theory from sociology (Buzan and Albert, 2010; Albert, Buzan and Zürn, 2013), and by attempting to understand the dynamics, and the strengths and weaknesses, of the resulting structure (Buzan and Schouenborg, 2018). The book could be seen as an attempt to justify the claims I have been making for more than twenty years that: 'the ES framework offers the best available basis on which to synthesise quite a few of the main lines of IR theory, and thus to revive a "grand theory" project' (Buzan, 2001: 481). The counterpoint to the theory side is the more empirical, historical strand of my work. One part of this has focused on world history and the evolution of the international system/society (Buzan and Little, 2000; Buzan, 2011, 2022; Buzan and Lawson, 2014a, b, 2015, forthcoming). Another part has focused on particular countries or regions: the US (Buzan, 2004b; Buzan and Cox, 2013, 2022) and Northeast Asia (Buzan, 2010b, 2014b, 2018b; Buzan and Koyama, 2019; Buzan and Zhang, 2019; Buzan and Goh, 2020).

Complementary to these two strands has been a parallel strand of work with Amitav Acharya on the history of IR as a discipline, and how to move it away from its Western foundations to more global ones (Acharya and Buzan, 2007, 2010, 2017, 2019, 2022). I see this book as a contribution towards the goal of developing a discipline of truly Global International Relations (GIR) as sketched out in Acharya and Buzan (2019: 285–320). It does so by setting out an approach to world history that works at the level of humankind as a whole, and is therefore able to transcend the parochial particularities that still burden IR as a discipline. To do this, it picks up an idea first floated in Buzan (2022) that if the ES wants to stay in tune with the shift towards GIR, it needs to think towards something like a *global society approach* as a way of understanding the structures, momentums and dialectics of the global whole (Albert and Buzan, 2013). By aggregating society, and making humankind the object of study, the global society approach provides a powerful way of developing GIR.

The empirical side of this book is partly drawn from these earlier works and their sources, though there are many new sources, and several expansions into previously unvisited topics such as religion, science and sport. The theoretical side is a bit more ambitious. It tries to draw together the various threads of ES work by combining the main existing disaggregations (e.g. the classical one between international and world society; and my idea of interstate/interpolity, transnational and interhuman societies) into the integrated and holistic vision of *global society*. The basic idea, first floated in Buzan (2018a), is that many of the primary institutions of interstate society are also rooted in the transnational and interhuman domains (i.e. 'world society'), and that institutions with their main root in the interhuman and transnational domains also reach into the interstate one. Think, for example, of how nationalism spans across from the interhuman domain, where it defines one form of collective identity, to the interstate one, where it defines a principle of political legitimacy for the state. In other words, the approach through primary institutions enables one to take a detailed and integrated view of the social structure of humankind as a whole, linking together its various layers, and at the dynamics of change and evolution within that structure. Having constructed global society as an analytical lens, the book then uses it to look at the entirety of human history as a story of periodisations and transitions defined by continuities and changes in both material conditions and the structure of primary institutions. What do you see when you look at global history through this specific social structural lens of the ES? Certainly not history in terms of who did what to whom, when, where and why, in some given period of time and space. The ES approach to global history tells the story in a more abstract way in terms of how and why human society as a whole has structured itself, and how, why and when that structure has undergone periodic transformations. There have been hints of this in my earlier works, but only in scattered and sporadic ways. This book attempts to pull everything together into a single vision, providing both some novel perspectives on the story of humankind and a demonstration case of how a global society approach generates a powerful and distinctive theoretical understanding that links together International Relations, Global Historical Sociology and Global/World History. In a sense, after the long and immensely fruitful excursion into a differentiation between interstate and world society triggered by Hedley Bull's (1977) seminal work, this book aims to return the ES to the more integrated world historical approach championed by Martin Wight and Adam Watson.

Why bother to do this? There are three reasons.

First, because, if people think it works, this exercise should strengthen the claims of the ES to mainstream analytical status in IR theory. It offers a way of using ES theory to bridge World/Global History, Global Historical Sociology and IR theory, hopefully getting the best out of all three. This book shares something in approach with Buzan and Little (2000) in tackling global history from a quite specific IR theoretical perspective. It differs from it in having a much stronger focus on society than system, and within that a detailed way of assessing social structure on the level of humankind as a whole. So this book is not like Global/ World History, because it approaches history in a more abstract social structural way rather than in terms of strings of causally related events. This makes it closer to Global Historical Sociology, but with the difference that it brings to bear the specifically ES toolkit of primary institutions. It is not like most IR because it privileges a historical narrative and an empirical approach. It is a way of seeing, rather than deductions from abstract first principles. I have some hope that this bridging approach might enable a more compact telling of a very big story that could be accessible not only to a wider, cross-disciplinary, audience within the social sciences and history, but also possibly to the informed public. This book, however, is addressed primarily to an academic audience. A book aimed at a wider readership will require a different language and a less abstract, theoretical, approach. I am working on it.

Second, this social structural approach offers a limited, but I think significant, ability to look into the future. This is not an obvious quality for an approach rooted in the English School. The ES does not generally aim at cause–effect explanations or predictions. A lot of its methodology is historical sociology, and it does not shy away from forward-looking normative issues. Since the social structure of global society is mainly quite durable, there is a perhaps under-appreciated element of prediction present in ES analysis about both continuity and change in the structure. A social structural approach that is sensitive to both what looks durable and what seems to be changing does allow a certain amount of looking ahead. That is the approach taken in Chapters 7 and 8. The ES, like most other IR theories, does not make possible reliable predictions about who will do what to whom. But it can tell us some significant things about the social structures within which such decisions will be taken, and how those social structures are evolving. So this book is not focused around history as an account of events and how they unfolded. Instead, it tells the simpler, more abstract, story of the material and ideational conditions that have shaped human societies, and the primary institutions that have structured them. In a sense, it picks up Marx's (1852) observation that people 'make their own history but not in the circumstances of their own choosing'. It is a book about the circumstances of humankind, both material and social. Some of these circumstances are made by people, and some of them stem from the natural world. This approach both reveals some large-scale patterns around which to organise the story of human history and provides handles for understanding the dynamics of change. It draws attention to periods of transition and points of crystallisation when one set of material and ideational conditions is replaced by another. As the elitist Western world order that has dominated humankind for two centuries gives way to a more equal planetary distribution of wealth, power and cultural and political authority amongst states and peoples, we are in particular need of ways of looking ahead at the moment. The global society approach offers one of those ways.

The third reason is because it is intrinsically interesting, and the Covid-19 lockdowns have provided me with a good stretch of time to read, think and write about it. Covid quarantines provided good conditions and good motivations for a prolonged concentration on a big topic.

This is an ambitious book covering a huge amount of ground and it is therefore bound to contain errors. I hope these are relatively minor and infrequent. More certainly, many readers will no doubt think there are omissions, where important things have been either left out or insufficiently explored. Such omissions are unavoidable in a synoptic and panoptic work like this. I hope that they will be more than offset by the ability of the framework to enable the very long and complex story of human history to be told in a relatively clear, compact and accessible form. Since this work rests heavily on my earlier writings, I have taken the liberty of referencing my own writings more liberally than would normally be the case. There are two reasons for doing this. First, to show how the different parts of my opus fit together in the context of this project; second, to lessen some of the burden of referencing on the book and the reader. Those wanting more sources on particular topics can find them in the relevant earlier works. Those with a more theoretical bent can read the book as an application of ES theory on a larger scale than has been done before. Those more interested in just getting an overview of global history can read it as a somewhat novel general history and forward look.

In the contemporary spirit of warning people when their intellectual comfort zone is about to be challenged, readers who hold a religious faith should take note. In what follows I treat religion as Geertz (1993 [1973]: 87–125) does, as an entirely sociological phenomenon which 'projects images of cosmic order onto the plane of human existence' (90). Harari (2016) is similarly secular, though taking a wider view of what counts as religion, including any superhuman system of laws, such as communism (207–31). I would add that in my view religions very much reflect the human societies that invent them. I like Geertz's analytical way of seeing religion as a catalogue of behavioural dispositions observable in individuals, but embedded and reproduced in cultures. People choose to believe unprovable stories that spiritual realms and divine beings not only exist but play causal and judgemental roles in the affairs of humankind. Importantly, they choose to share that faith, and its particular stories and rituals, with others, and thereby differentiate themselves from people both of different faiths and none. As Geertz (1993 [1973]: 87), nicely quoting Santayana, puts it, religions create 'another world to live in'. Such other worlds often involve one or more planes of existence beyond the earthly one, thus extending the social world both in time (via the immortal soul) and space (heavens, hells, purgatories and suchlike). To my mind, the very diversity of such beliefs renders them implausible, and exposes their origins as human social constructs. More combatively, I see religions and other forms of mysticism as tantamount to a kind of intellectual surrender to a fear of big unknowns (death, the meaning of life). I nonetheless accept religions as a powerful social fact, deeply rooted in human history and prehistory, and essential to understanding how humans see themselves, their collective identities, and their social and physical environments. They constitute a long-standing institution of human social structures, and are for many people still the most important one.

Acknowledgements

I give general thanks to all those on whose work I have built my own. The list starts with H. G. Wells, whose *Outline of History* opened my eyes when I was in secondary school. The pyramid of scholars on whose shoulders I stand is now so deep that I can no longer see the bottom of it, and so wide that I cannot see its edges. I can only hope that my own work will help to render the same service for those who follow me.

I would like to give particular heartfelt thanks to all those who have co-authored with me, for challenging and stimulating my thinking in myriad ways. It has been an education and a pleasure to work with you. This book was not a conscious long-term plan that informed the choices of subjects and co-authors in the making of some grand teleological design. Those choices were made on the basis of interests, opportunities, friendships and encounters as they occurred by chance along the way during the past decades. If there were connecting threads to all this, two stand out. The first is the addiction to world history that I acquired in the late 1990s working with Richard Little. Ever since the eureka moment of first thinking that I was able to tell some kind of coherent story of human history, I have been drawn to the bottomless, but by no means thankless, task of filling in the gaps, and deepening my knowledge. Writing together with George Lawson has been the main vehicle for that.

The second thread is my interest in the English School (ES), which got going during the 1990s. Since the ES is also interested in bringing history into IR theory, there is significant entanglement and reinforcement between these two threads. As I began to develop a structural approach towards international and world society during the noughties, and to focus on primary institutions as the key to this, the entanglement between these two threads thickened. Working with Amitav Acharya, Mathias Albert, Tarak Barkawi, Mick Cox, Dan Deudney, Thomas Diez, Robert Falkner, Evelyn Goh, Lene Hansen, Hitomi Koyama, Richard Little, Laust Schouenborg, Gerry Segal, Ole Wæver, Jaap de Wilde and Yongjin Zhang, and benefiting from their insights and expertise, stimulated my journey in many significant and useful ways. So too did my engagement with the rising IR community in China, which was interested both in the English School (as a non-American approach to IR theory) and in historical approaches to IR and what China could contribute to them. Particular thanks here to Liu Debin, Qin Yaqing, Yan Xuetong, Cui Shunji, Wang Jiangli, Ren Xiao and Zhang Feng for their help, intellectual engagement and friendship. Thanks also to the many other colleagues within the English School who have in various ways encouraged and stimulated my thinking, most prominently: Filippo Costa Buranelli, Ian Clark, Tim Dunne, Rosemary Foot, Ana Gonzalez-Pelaez, Kal Holsti, Andrew Hurrell, Charles Jones, Tonny Brems Knudsen, Jorge Lasmar, Andrew Linklater, Cornelia Navari, Chris Reus-Smit, Yannis Stivachtis, Adam Watson, Nick Wheeler, Peter Wilson and John Williams. Special thanks to H. O. Nazareth for both friendship and a lifelong conversation about how the world works.

Particular thanks to the following for reading and commenting on all or part of the manuscript at various stages: Amitav Acharya, Mathias Albert, Tarak Barkawi, Robert Falkner, Rita Floyd, Charlotta Friedner Parrat, Hitomi Koyama, George Lawson, Richard Little, Cornelia Navari, H. O. Nazareth, Frances Pinter, Chris Reus-Smit, Justin Rosenberg, Laust Schouenborg, Ann Towns and John Williams. And thanks to John Haslam for shepherding this project through the hoops, and to the three reviewers for Cambridge University Press, who took the time to understand what the book is trying to do and to point out how to improve it. Finally, a big appreciation to Filippo Costa Buranelli, Robert Falkner, George Lawson, Laust Schouenborg, John Williams and Yongjin Zhang for agreeing to act as my intellectual executors for this project should Covid-19 or some other intervention have finished me before I could finish it. I am happy to say that their services were not needed, but it was very reassuring to me during the dark and surreal days of writing through the pandemic to know that they were there.

1 Introduction

This chapter has four tasks. The first, following on from the general background set out in the Preface, is to explain the approach of the book. The second is to set out the concepts, terms and definitions that I use to conduct the discussion, and explain some of the underlying theoretical positions. I appreciate that this long section makes a dry and difficult start to the book. Those who prefer, can skip these definitional essays now, and go straight to the historical chapters. They can refer back to the conceptual discussions as and when needed, using this section as a glossary. The third task is to give an overview of how the empirical part of the book is structured, and to explain the logic that defines the subdivisions into parts and chapters. The fourth is to set out the aims of the book. I hope this will give readers as clear an idea of why they are reading it as I have of why I wrote it.

Approach

This book is aimed at an audience interested in the study of how humankind works on the largest scale as a system/society. Its 'big picture' approach has resonance with the more macro-style of work in International Relations (IR), Global Historical Sociology (GHS), International Political Economy (IPE) and Global/World History. It uses ideas from the English School (ES) to build bridges among these fields. It is more abstract and less detailed than historical approaches, focusing mainly on the broader narrative of how the social structure of humankind has evolved. By social structure, I mean what the ES calls *primary institutions*: ideas ranging from kinship, territoriality and trade; through dynasticism, empire, diplomacy, law, religion, human equality/inequality and sovereignty; to nationalism, the market, sport, science and environmental stewardship. These ideas, and others like them, are the key both to what kind of collective entities and identities humans form, and what kinds of behaviour among people and polities are judged appropriate and legitimate, or not. This is further discussed in the next subsection. The narrative in this book is structured around the story of these institutions. There are thus almost no personal stories in here, whether about great kings and queens; victorious generals or warlords; heroic workers, women, soldiers, or intellectuals; wealthy merchants, or brave explorers. While it addresses war as an institution of global society, it does not focus much either on specific wars, big or small, or on the rise and fall of particular empires or great powers. Conversely, the approach taken here is much less abstract than the grand sociological theories of Marx or Wallerstein, or the IR ones of Waltz, that seek big and simple driving forces such as class, capitalism or power to explain history. In classical English School style, this book offers a middle path, developing an alternative way of telling the human story on the largest scale.

It is not the first book to venture into the space between History, IR, IPE and GHS. Some historical sociologists such as Michael Mann (1986) have tried it, and so have some 'big' historians, such as David Christian (2004, 2019), both making path-breaking contributions. So while this territory is not exactly new, neither is it yet fully or convincingly occupied. Global historians venturing there have the problem that their narrative method, for all of its many merits, comes under increasing stress as the scale of space and time covered increases. Those coming from the social sciences usually try to solve this problem by seeking big simplifications that somehow embrace all the differences. This book aims to split the difference by finding a level of simplifying abstractions that, on the one hand, solves the problem of how to deal with large scale in time and space, while on the other hand offering an approach that is sufficiently fine-grained to sustain a global narrative across a timescale of over fifty millennia. In that sense, it has quite a lot of resonance with Mann's 'IEMP' scheme in which he looks for ideological, economic, military and political sources of power as they define 'the capacity to organize and control people, materials and territories' (1986: 1–3). The key difference is that Mann uses the IEMP framing to concentrate on comparative civilisations. He is not particularly concerned with defining eras, and uses his scheme to look in detail at the differences across many cases. As Mann acknowledges, his scheme produces a very complicated picture of human societies as a 'patterned mess' with innumerable different combinations of factors in different times and places (Mann, 1993: 4). My approach aims to expose more pattern with less mess.

This pattern-seeking approach brings into focus, and combines, three broad factors:

1. The state of the planet itself as it provides conditions for human life and civilisation. This includes the climate, sea levels and the

biosphere, as well as the ability of the planet to provide resources in relation to human wants and needs. This material factor is a fairly orthodox and well-understood story that is not controversial except for the remaining deniers of contemporary human effects on climate change.

2. The material conditions of humankind in terms of the technologies possessed by humans, and what kind of materials, energy sources, and means of transportation these make available to them and their societies. This factor is likewise not particularly controversial, and is well documented by archaeologists and historians.

3. The social resources possessed by humankind in terms of the *primary institutions* that give structure to human societies. This is the most novel part of the approach, both in itself, and in the combination with material and planetary conditions. It is the key to opening up an analysis of the whole human story that is both abstract and quite fine-grained.

These three factors play into each other as both causes and consequences.

In the more than 50,000 years under surveillance here, all three of these factors have undergone major changes. They are not independent from each other. Each feeds into the others in myriad and significant ways, creating a Gordian knot that makes it extremely difficult to give simple answers as to what drives the historical changes in the human condition. That sounds dauntingly complicated, and in some ways it is. But the payoff for placing one's perspective in the space in-between historical detail and general abstraction is that larger patterns, along the line of what Bayly (2004: 1) calls 'global uniformities', come into view, simplifying the complexity. These patterns define long and durable eras in terms of a distinct set of material conditions and primary institutions that structure their societies. I broadly accept the conventional view that there are three such eras – hunter-gatherers, conglomerate agrarian/pastoralist empires (CAPE), and modernity (e.g. Gellner, 1988). I depart from that view by emphasising that there are transitions between these eras, when material conditions and social structures, and sometimes the condition of the planet, undergo major conjunctural changes. At the time of writing, we are still in, or perhaps just emerging from, the transition from the CAPE era to modernity. These eras, and the transitions between them, are how the book tells the story of humankind. When looked at through the lens of this analytical scheme, eras come into a clear and detailed focus. So too do the forms of social glue that hold societies together. This allows a fine-grained assessment not only of continuities and changes, but also of the essential material and social characteristics of both the eras themselves, and the transitions between them. Up to a point it also allows modest assessments of the driving forces behind eras and the transitions between them.

On this scale, causality is multiple and complex, emerging from the crystallisation of a range of contingent processes. For example, a warming and stabilising global climate played a big role in the transition from mobile hunter-gatherers to sedentary and, eventually, agrarian CAPE societies with bigger populations and more differentiated and hierarchical social structures. Technologies sometimes play a big role, as in the discovery of hard metals (bronze and iron) during the CAPE era, and the development of steam power exploiting the vast reserves of fossil fuel that launched the transition to modernity. This book offers a characterisation of the CAPE era that is more homogenous and precise than other interpretations. It makes a feature of the neglected question of how to track and understand the transition from CAPE to modernity, and how we might assess when 'modernity proper' has arrived. The opening phases of the transition to modernity were both a complex social transformation involving old and new primary institutions, and an unrestrained, often rapacious, pursuit of wealth and power. The emerging third phase confronts environmental limits that seem to be forcing a choice between some degree of planetary catastrophe, and a wrenching turn towards a much more constrained pursuit of sustainable development.

Concepts, Terms and Definitions

This subsection sets out the main terms and concepts that will be deployed in subsequent chapters. Many of these are drawn from the English School, which has a well-established and distinctive analytical vocabulary and taxonomy for thinking about international relations. But framing a very large-scale study like this one also requires concepts drawn from elsewhere in IR theory, but which are interoperable with the ES approach. The ES concepts are:

> *International system, international society* and *world society*
> *Interpolity, transnational* and *interhuman domains*
> *Primary* and *secondary institutions*
> *Solidarism* and *pluralism*
> *Raison de système and raison de famille.*

The concepts from elsewhere in IR theory are:

> *Interaction capacity*
> *Evolution*

Dialectics
Differentiation theory and sectors
Uneven and Combined Development

There are three other non-ES concepts that I have reconstructed to serve the particular purposes of this book:

Era
Social glue
Globalisation and Global society.

Finally, to help orientate the discussion at the level of humankind, I have set up a simple model of *five possible pathways* that the species can take: regression, extinction, empowerment, suicide and self-replacement.

English School Concepts

The core of the English School's approach to the study of international relations is the idea that just as people live in societies, which both shape them and are shaped by them, so too do states (or more broadly, polities).[1] In my view, society is what frames Baldwin's (2017 [1958]: 166) observation: 'People are trapped in history and history is trapped in them.' The same is true for the durable collective polities that people construct, and the societies that those polities form. This looks like an idea that should be rooted in Sociology. But in practice sociologists have not taken much interest in developing this perspective, perhaps because of antagonism to the idea of second-order societies (i.e. societies whose members are other societies, rather than individuals) (Buzan and Albert, 2010). The idea of a society of states emerged first during the nineteenth century among positive international lawyers. Positive legal thinking assumed that such law required a society to make it. The clear existence of international law thus easily led to the idea of international society, because if there was positive international law, then that must reflect the existence of an international society. Positive law is made by states and cannot exist outside a society of states. The term international society thus became intrinsic to discussions of international law well back in the nineteenth century (Schwarzenberger, 1951). Knutsen (2016: 2) argues that the nineteenth-century international lawyer James Lorimer (1884) already largely sketched out the concept of international society, in form similar to that which would emerge out of the work of the English School during the 1960s and 1970s, but that his pioneering work has been

---

[1] The text in this section draws on that in Buzan (2014a: ch. 2) and Buzan and Schouenborg (2018).

forgotten. By the late nineteenth century, American legal and political thinking about IR had clearly identified the existence of an international society among 'civilised' states, and captured this in the term *internationalism* (Schmidt, 1998: 124). Elsewhere, the German historian Heeren's (1834) discussion of states-systems set up the idea of international society picked up later by thinkers in the English School tradition (Keene, 2002; Little, 2008).

The ES does not focus on material conditions, but it does not exclude them either. It accepts that material power plays a big role in international relations, but then focuses mainly on the social structures that arise to try to deal with that. As noted above, for analytical convenience and clarity, I discuss material factors separately from social structures, though taking into account the strong interplay between them. I also divide material factors into two categories: planetary conditions, and the more general material resources available to humankind in terms of resources, energy and technologies. Most ES work has focused on the period since the transition towards modernity began, with occasional, but growing, excursions to earlier times (e.g. Wight, 1977; Watson, 1992; Linklater, 2016; Neumann, 2020). Since material factors vary so much when looking at the history of humankind as a whole, it is necessary to take them into account in a systematic way. Putting material factors back into the ES in a structured way is part of the purpose of this book. As I will show, variations in material conditions are part of what motivate, shape and define not just the social structure but also large historical eras. As the later discussions in the book demonstrate, the rapid rise of environmental issues during the past few decades is a major case of the interplay of material conditions and social structure.

A key reason for choosing the ES is that its societal approach to international relations and international history generates a taxonomy of concepts and types that is rich and distinctive compared to other IR theories. Taxonomy constructs what one sees and chooses to analyse (or not), and is the foundation of theory. I concentrate in this book on the ES's taxonomy of primary institutions as what defines global society, trying both to extend this, and apply it in a new way to the large-scale analysis of world history. In building on the ES, I follow two theoretical positions set out in my earlier work.

First, as argued in Buzan (2004a: 169–71) my approach adopts the same micro-foundations as Bull's in the propensity of humans to form societies on functional grounds to limit violence, establish property rights and stabilise agreements. Like him, I see the imperative to form societies working at multiple levels from small to large groups of humans, and including 'second order' societies, like Bull's 'anarchical society' of states. My approach also draws on the functional argument from Buzan (1993: 340–3) about interstate societies being derivable from the logic of anarchy in giving advantages to the units that form them, which links to Waltz's (1979) arguments about socialisation and competition generating 'like units'. Some form of society is the default condition of human beings whether as groups, or as groups of groups.

Second, since this book emphasises social structure in the form of primary institutions, it requires a position on the agent-structure debate. I take the same position in this book as I have done in previous work (Buzan and Little, 2000; Buzan, 2004a), following the mainstream constructivist idea of structuration, in which agency and structure are co-constitutive. The mutual constitution of agents and structure was identified by Giddens (1979) and taken forward by (Wendt, 1999), and to my mind is the practical essence of the mainstream ES view: that the units of international society both constitute, and are constituted by, the social structure. As structure, primary institutions such as sovereignty, territoriality and nationalism constitute the state and shape its behaviour. As agents, states and other actors both reproduce those structures, or amend or even dismantle them, by their behaviour. Sovereignty is reproduced in uncountable daily statements and actions, but is also pressured and questioned by changing understandings of human rights and environmental stewardship. Imperialism and racism used to be reproduced daily, but became illegitimate after 1945. This process of reproduction and contestation goes on continuously across the interpolity, transnational and interhuman domains.

International System, International Society and World Society

Traditional English School thinking is built around this triad of key concepts: *international system*, *international society* and *world society* (Cutler, 1991; Little, 1995: 15–16). Broadly speaking, these terms are understood as follows:

- *International system* is about power politics amongst states/polities, and puts the structure and process of international anarchy at the centre of IR theory. This position is broadly parallel to mainstream Realism and Neorealism and is thus well developed and clearly understood outside the ES. It privileges the distribution of material power among states (polarity, balance of power) over all else as the main driver of international relations. If all international systems are also societies, it makes sense to downgrade this differentiation, and address the question as being about the relative weight of calculations about the distribution of power as against the influence of shared norms, rules and institutions. There are now different views within the ES about retaining system, with some thinking it should be kept, and others that it is redundant.[2]

- *International society* is about the institutionalisation of mutual interest and identity amongst states, and puts the creation and maintenance of shared norms, rules and institutions at the centre of IR theory. Wight (1991: 137) nicely captures it with the idea that international society is a social contract among societies themselves each constituted by their own social contract. But because states/polities are very different entities from individual human beings, this international society is <u>not</u> analogous to domestic society (Bull, 1966; Suganami, 1989), and has to be studied as a distinct form. When units are sentient, how they perceive each other is a major determinant of how they interact. If the units share a common identity (a religion, a system of governance, a language), or even just recognise each other as like-units sharing a basic set of rules or norms (about how to determine relative status, and how to conduct diplomacy), then these intersubjective understandings not only condition their behaviour and identity, but also define the boundaries of a social system.

- *World society* takes individuals, non-state organisations and ultimately the global population as a whole as the focus of global societal identities and arrangements, and puts transcendence of the state system at the centre of IR theory. It is mostly about forms of universalist cosmopolitanism, which could include communism, but as Wæver (1992: 98) notes during the heyday of US primacy, was usually taken to mean liberalism. This position has some parallels to transnationalism, but carries a much more foundational link to normative political theory. World society has for long been something of a conceptual dustbin, useful as a moral referent (representing the great society of humankind) for normative theorists, but being too vague to be of much use to social structural approaches.

Following earlier work of my own (Buzan, 2018a, where interested readers can find a more detailed discussion), I disaggregate world society into three meanings:

1. *Normative* world society reflects both Bull's 'great society of humankind', and Buzan's (2004a: 118–59) idea of 'interhuman societies' mainly expressed in patterns of shared identity, which can be partial, such as nations, civilisations, races, and religions, or holistic, generally as humankind.

---

[2] For a summary of this debate, see Buzan (2014a: 171–2).

2. *Political* world society comprises all the non-state social structures visible within humankind as a whole that have both significantly autonomous actor quality, and the capacity and interest to engage with the society of states to influence its normative values and institutions. It is therefore close to transnational perspectives. These non-state actors might be rooted in religion, or commerce, or civil society more broadly.

3. *Integrated* world society is an aggregating concept, representing the idea that the social structure of humankind can best be understood by linking together international and world society. It is what global governance, with its emphasis on the intermingling of states, inter-governmental organisations, non-state actors, and people, points towards as an eventual outcome of an ever-more densely integrated and interdependent human society on a global scale. This is one foundation for what I call *global society*, on which more below.

Interpolity, Transnational and Interhuman Domains The English School has so far mainly thought about integrated world society as something not yet achieved, but which might lie in the future as something to be aspired to (e.g. Vincent, 1986). In this book, I stand this assumption on its head by using the idea of *three domains*, defined by the type of actor and activity dominant with them (Buzan, 2004a: 118–28, 257–61; Buzan and Schouenborg, 2018: 27–8). The scheme of three domains is intended to replace the traditional ES triad, by clarifying and separating its essential components, and making them the component parts of *integrated world society*.

The *inter-polity/state domain* is about the second-order society of states/polities, which has been the main focus of the ES. Given that states are relatively recent, I use Ferguson and Mansbach's (1996) useful term 'polities' to cover the quite wide range of political entities, and the interactions among them, in play over the course of human history: chiefdoms, city-states, kingdoms, empires, states, etc. Generally, I will use the term *interpolity domain*, though in modern times I will also use *interstate* domain. The defining activity of the interpolity domain is politics, and the reason for treating it separately is that political actors usually claim primacy over all other types of organisation.[3]

---

[3] This might – justifiably – be thought a vulnerable basis for making such a big taxonomical differentiation. While it is true that politics, broadly understood as the process of legitimate government in human societies, has been the dominant sector since the beginning of civilisation, its primacy is not automatic. It can be, and has been, challenged by commerce and religion. Europe at the time of the Crusades was arguably led by the Roman Catholic Church. Venice and many other city states and Leagues were dominated by merchants. It is entirely possible to imagine the dethroning of politics (e.g. Pohl and Kornbluth, 1960; Vernon, 1971), and therefore giving primacy to politics has to

The *transnational domain* is about collective non-state/polity actors (e.g. guilds, firms, religious organisations, many kinds of interest groups from sport to stamp collecting), and how they relate both to polities, and to each other as transnational actors (TNAs) across polity boundaries. The transnational domain does not have a single defining activity. Many of the organisations within this domain will have advocacy as one of their purposes, both up to the interstate domain (e.g. lobbying government, participating in diplomacy), and down to the interhuman one (e.g. proselytising/recruiting, marketing). Some of the actors here will be uncivil, such as criminal and terrorist entities.[4]

The *interhuman domain* is about people, and its defining activity is collective identity formation, a rather subtle and amorphous process, but one with big consequences for the social structure of humankind. In the interhuman domain, only individuals have actor quality, and the main social structure is patterns of collective identity ranging from the universal one of humankind as a whole, through civilisational and religious identities, to racial, national, tribal, and kinship ones, all of which are subglobal in extent. These identities do not in themselves possess actor quality, but they do act powerfully as constraints and opportunities to enable or restrain various kinds of actors in the transnational and interpolity domains, for example, religious institutions and nation states.

When the analytical lens of the three domains is deployed instead of the classical ES triad, it quickly becomes apparent that integrated world society has been around for a very long time, and that the nature of primary institutions cannot be understood apart from it. Demonstrating and illustrating this is a key theme of the book. These three domains are, like functional differentiation and sectors (on which more below), another way of approaching the social whole. The interhuman domain is the closest to the traditional sociological understanding of society as being composed of individual human beings sharing an identity. As noted, the classical ES's discussions of 'the great society of humankind' suppose that no such society exists at the global level in practice, and its

be seen as a provisional categorisation based on empirical current conditions, and not something chiselled in stone. Given that both interstate and transnational are second-order societies (composed of collective actors), they could be merged into a single grouping differentiated from interhuman, and without primacy being given to any particular type of collective actor. Alternatively, religious, commercial, or even criminal actors could, in principle, or in fiction, or should empirical developments justify it, be elevated to prime position, and differentiated from the others. The tension between political and religious primacy is most evident in current global society in the Islamic world, and in the role of the Christian right in the US Republican Party. This is, therefore, only a provisional and contingent way of dividing up the social whole. For definitions, see under 'Differentiation Theory and Sectors' below.

[4] On the civil/uncivil distinction, see Buzan (2004c).

main function in the ES has been as a moral referent against which to judge interstate society. I think there is more to it than that. 'Humankind' is becoming a significant collective identity, and there are many powerful collective identities (e.g. religion, civilisation, race, nation) operating below the global level and across the political structures. Interpolity and transnational societies are both *second order* societies in which the members are not individual human beings but organised collectivities of people (polities of various kinds, and the various types of NSAs). In practice, as I will detail in the chapters that follow, there is a lot of crossover of both interaction and social structure, among these three domains. That crossover is the key to integrated world society, and eventually to global society. Seeing integrated global society as stretching across the three domains, rather than being largely located in the interpolity domain, brings into focus some primary institutions that have been obscured because they are not primarily located in the interpolity domain, religion, science and sport most obviously. The key to much of what follows is the idea that primary institutions are normally located across, and embedded within, not just one, but two or three domains.[5]

Primary and Secondary Institutions The English School's understanding of institutions differs from most of mainstream IR in focusing on the deeper rather than the shallower meaning of this concept. Its main concern is with *primary institutions*, which are deep and relatively durable social principles, and the practices associated with them. In ES work starting from Bull (1977), primary institutions have mainly been thought about as an artefact of the interpolity domain, and within that mostly the modern interstate one. A key aim of this book is to show how limiting a view this is: Primary institutions can and should be thought about across both the three domains and the history of humankind. This book emphasises that primary institutions are as much or more constitutive of the three domains, as constituted by them. In particular, I argue in the empirical chapters that for the interpolity domain, there is a useful

---

[5] This argument is a major modification to that in Buzan (2018a), which was trying to push away from the standard path in ES thinking that, mostly unthinkingly, locates primary institutions in the interpolity domain. I took two paths there: one to try to identify primary institutions that might be located principally in other domains; the second to show how most of the currently acknowledged primary institutions in fact work strongly across domains. In this book, I am scrapping the first approach. Advocacy is not a primary institution of the transnational domain, and collective identity is not a primary institution of the interhuman one. Rather, these are characteristic activities of those domains, as argued above. Apologies to anyone whose work is affected negatively by this change of mind. For me it was perhaps a necessary venture down a dead-end before I could break through into the second path. Thanks to Joseph Haddon for making me think hard about this.

approach to polity-formation through primary institutions in which ter-ritoriality, sovereignty, dynasticism and nationalism play central roles.

Traditional English School thinking has not devoted much attention to whether primary institutions could also be embedded in, or even stem from, the other two domains. Nothing stops actors and ideas from crossing between domains. State and non-state actors interact with each other all the time, and it is difficult to understand primary institutions like religion, trade, nationalism and sport without seeing them as operat-ing across the interpolity, transnational and interhuman domains. Both in theory and in practice, all sorts of mixtures are possible. Primary and secondary institutions stretch across domains, and that fact is the key to shifting the social structural perspective of the ES first towards an integrated world society framing, and then to a global society one.[6]

Primary institutions in ES thinking are deep in the sense of having evolved more than being designed. By evolved I mean that something like territoriality, or war, emerged out of practice, eventually becoming a recognised principle, in a way similar to the development of customary law. This is different from designed, where a secondary institution such as the League of Nations was negotiated into being at a specific point in time, and for a specific purpose, by a group of states. The distinction between evolved and designed might blur for latecomers to an inter-national society who accept, or have imposed on them, institutions that evolved earlier. The obvious example here is sovereignty, which became both a prize, and a condition, of decolonisation. Primary institutions must not only be substantially shared amongst the members of global society, possibly across all three domains, but also be seen amongst them as defining both membership and legitimate behaviour. They are the axioms that human societies agree to live by, and are thus about the shared identities of the members of integrated world society within all three domains, and how those identities are understood to relate to each other. They are durable, often lasting for centuries or even millennia, but as will become clear in the chapters that follow, they are also malleable, and may undergo significant changes in how their basic principles are interpreted, and what practices they do and don't legitimise. Mayall (1990), and Holsti (2004), pioneered the study of how primary institutions arise, evolve and sometimes fall into obsolescence. Primary institutions are the key to understanding the classical ES's social structural approach to

---

[6] The ES has given rather more thought to regional/subglobal international societies, largely within the interpolity domain: for a survey see Buzan and Schouenborg (2018: 96–122). In what follows, I do not specifically address the regional/subglobal level, and broadly assume that the main argument about global society and the three domains applies to it as well.

analysing interpolity society, but they also work across integrated world society, or global society, more broadly. I demonstrate in Chapters 2 and 3 how they work for the long span of human history preceding modernity. The classical 'Westphalian' interstate set includes sovereignty, territoriality, the balance of power, war, diplomacy, international law and great power management, to which can be added monarchy/dynasticism, nationalism, human (in)equality, science, sport, and more recently and controversially, the market and environmental stewardship. The featuring of primary institutions in what follows not only maps out the normative structure of global society, but also highlights those values and practices as they were understood and practised in the context of their own time.

It is important to flag up here what some might think of as my own perhaps idiosyncratic understanding of the question of how to define and classify institutions in general, and primary institutions in particular. In this book, I take the position argued at length in Buzan (2004a: 163–90), rejecting the differentiation in the literature between constitutive and regulatory institutions, and all similar constructions. I see this distinction as incoherent and unworkable because as regime theorists argue, and I concur, all social institutions have constitutive effects. My definition of primary institutions is therefore both fairly general, and more homogenous, than, for example, Holsti (2004: 9–10), and Reus-Smit (1997: 556–66), who prefer layered approaches to institutions in terms of their depth and function. I stick with the simpler distinction between primary and secondary institutions. As I have also argued earlier (Buzan, 2004a: 182–4), I accept the idea that primary institutions might well be arranged in hierarchies of master-derivative, and that there is important interplay between primary and secondary institutions (on which more below).

That said, how to identify whether something counts as a primary institution is still not straightforward (Buzan, 2004a: 161–204). After much thought on the question, my own conclusion is that primary institutions cannot be deduced from any prior set of principles or functions. Their potential number and variety are open to the infinity of human social inventiveness, and therefore identifying them has to be a matter of systematic empirical investigation. Societies will range across a broad spectrum, from relatively simple ones defined by a few institutions, to complex, elaborate ones with many institutions interwoven across the three domains. There is no basic, given, or minimal, set that can be put between bookends (Buzan, 2014: 173–8).[7] In this book, I am looking for

---

[7] On this point, my disagreement with Laust Schouenborg remains, although we share the aim of building a better foundation for cross-cultural and transhistorical analysis, and the view that institutions are the best way to do that. He has for long been developing a functional approach to primary institutions (Schouenborg, 2011, 2017), which he argues

all of the highest level of primary institutions that define integrated world societies, and global society, generally. In order to answer this question, Robert Falkner and I devised a four-tiered analytical framework to test empirically the status of any candidate to be a primary institution (Falkner and Buzan, 2019). We were looking specifically at environmental stewardship in the context of modern interstate society,[8] but with a bit of flexibility, the general idea of this framework can be applied to pre-modern integrated world societies as well. First, we expect to find the emergence of a clearly defined value or principle applicable as a norm across international society (whether global or regional). Second, we expect to see the creation of secondary institutions reflecting and embodying the underlying norm. Third, we expect to see observable and significant patterns of behaviour by states (or polities) in accordance with the core norm. Fourth, we expect to see the new norm, and its associated practices and secondary institutions, making an impact on the existing array of primary institutions, whether reinforcing them, amending them, disrupting them, or making them obsolete. Like Holsti's (2004) approach, this analytical scheme uses a set of empirical criteria, albeit different ones from Holsti's, to show both the rise and consolidation of new primary institutions, and the decline and decay of ones becoming obsolete. I see no obstacle to applying it generally across the three domains.

The scale of this book prevents me from applying this scheme in close detail to all of the primary institutions discussed. But it sets the standard for the selections I have made, and how I have told the various stories along the way. It also gives the reader a standard by which to hold me to

is a superior way to counter 'state and stage' approaches that impose a modern state teleology onto the past. I agree with him that this form of Eurocentrism needs to be tackled, and we both like the approach through 'polities'. But I still think that the best, perhaps only, way to capture primary institutions is empirically, and I want to retain the inside–outside distinction that he prefers to dissolve. For the purposes of this book, the distinction between societies composed of individuals, and societies composed of polities, is crucial to the argument. Rather than placing all of humankind into a single seamless society, I think that keeping the differentiation, and mapping the interplays across the three domains, pays bigger dividends in understanding what is going on. Schouenborg attempts only a limited range of functional institutions, thereby avoiding the problem of what I see as the inability of functional approaches to define a complete set. While he certainly demonstrates the flaws in the state and stage models, his limited selection of cases (all from the margins of what I describe below as the CAPE era) make him unable to provide either an alternative typology or an alternative sense of evolution. The empirical approach I use here both provides an alternative typology defined by eras, and a story of evolution that tackles the problem of imposing the present on the past. It does the latter by starting with the deep past, millennia before Schouenborg's cases, and working forward from them to the present.

[8] See Buzan and Falkner (forthcoming) for an application of this framework to the market.

account. By claiming to offer a complete list of primary institutions in human history, it also offers a foil against which others can either contest particular inclusions or exclusions, and/or contest the definitional criteria for identifying primary institutions generally. I would be very surprised indeed if mine were the last word on this issue!

Primary institutions in human history

This is the complete list of primary institutions and their derivatives (indented) used in this study, in order of their main introduction. Naturally, not all of these institutions apply to all times and all places, but keeping this complete set in mind, and in play where appropriate, is a useful way of both tracking the development of global social structure over time, and of comparing the different phases of the social development of humankind. It is also useful for tracking transitions, when some institutions go out of play, others are transformed in meaning and practice, and new ones arise.

> Kinship
> Human equality
> Trade
> Territoriality
> War
> Human inequality
>> Slavery
>> Patriarchy
>> Racism
> Monarchy/Dynasticism
> Imperialism
> Religion
> Sovereignty
> Diplomacy
> International Law
> Balance of power
> Great Power Management
> Nationalism
> Market versus economic nationalism
>> Multilateralism
> Science
> Sport
> Development
> Environmental Stewardship

Secondary institutions are usually thought of as those featured in regime theory and by liberal institutionalists, and relating to the shallower organisational usage of the term. In this view, they are consciously constructed, instrumental arrangements. Within a classical interstate perspective on modern international society, secondary institutions are mainly the product of liberal orders, and are for the most part intergovernmental arrangements consciously designed by states to serve specific functional purposes. They include the United Nations, the World Bank, the World Trade Organization, the Nuclear Non-proliferation regime, and myriad others. This type of secondary institution is a relatively recent invention, first appearing in the later decades of the nineteenth century. They link to interstate primary institutions in the sense both that they are reflections of underlying primary institutions (e.g. the UN reflecting sovereignty, diplomacy, multilateralism, international law) and that they serve as forums where primary institutions are produced, reproduced, renegotiated and sometimes made obsolete (e.g. the role of the UN in promoting human equality, development, and environmental stewardship, and in making colonialism and human inequality illegitimate). A key function of modern secondary institutions is to reflect and reproduce the primary institutions that make up the international normative structure. They both socialise states into the norms and practices of international society, and are sites of political contestation and conflict over those norms and practices. Secondary institutions thus play important roles in the embedding, reproduction, development and sometime decay of the primary institutions of global society (Spandler, 2015; Navari, 2016; Knudsen and Navari, 2019).

Although the ES has not explored it, secondary institutions can also be found through a much longer run of history, mainly associated with religion and trade, and more recently, sport. The transnational domain is not new, but as I show in Chapter 3, has been there since the dawn of civilisation, and historically has been a significant source of primary and secondary institutions. Even for the modern era, work towards widening the understanding of primary and secondary institutions within a global society context has barely begun, and I hope this book will contribute towards it. It seems unlikely that a single set of primary and secondary institutions operates equally across all three domains. It is true that individuals can and do accept things like nationalism, sovereignty, territoriality and human equality, and that TNAs can and do accept sovereignty, international law, diplomacy, and so on. Individuals and TNAs thereby become part of the social processes that reproduce and legitimise these institutions. Clark (2007) has made a useful start on making explicit the role of the transnational and interhuman domains in the institutional structures of interstate society.

It seems unlikely, however, that this happens evenly across the three domains, and this question is explored in the empirical chapters of this book. In what follows, I also make the radical move of including polities in the category of secondary institutions. The ES is mainly ambiguous about how to position the state within the scheme of primary and secondary institutions. Despite his huge contribution to developing the concept of primary institutions, Bull was party to this fudging. He does at one point say that 'it is states themselves that are the principal institutions of the society of states' (Bull, 1977: 71), but he does not develop the idea, and does not give either states or sovereignty (or, indeed, territoriality, monarchy/dynasticism and nationalism) a chapter alongside the other primary institutions he discusses, instead treating them as givens in his scheme (Buzan, 2004a: 52–6, 169–70). It strikes me that there is an unexplored opportunity here to formulate a distinctive ES approach to state, and more broadly polity, formation. Like other types of secondary institution, polities are consciously constructed for instrumental purposes. And also like other types of secondary institution, polities produce, reproduce, renegotiate and sometimes make obsolete, primary institutions. Thus, while primary and secondary institutions remain conceptually quite distinct, there is an eternal sense of practical co-constitution between them of which polities are an important part. If one counts polities as secondary institutions, then, as noted above, it becomes possible to analyse polity-formation in terms of the primary institutions that define and support different types of polity. In the empirical chapters that follow, the principal theme is how empires were generated by the primary institutions of sovereignty, territoriality and monarchy/dynasticism, while modern states were generated by sovereignty, territoriality and nationalism. This approach to polity-formation through primary institutions opens up a novel and quite powerful way of understanding not only both empires and modern states in their own terms, but also the nature and process of the transition from one to the other as the dominant form of polity during the first century-and-a-half of the transition towards modernity.

Solidarism and Pluralism Within the ES, and particularly related to the debates about order and justice, human rights and (non)intervention within modernity, two positions have emerged, which are labelled *pluralist* and *solidarist*. The terms were coined by Bull (1966), and have remained central structuring concepts for the core normative debates within the English School (Wheeler, 1992; Dunne and Wheeler, 1996; Bain, 2010).

- *Pluralism* represents the communitarian disposition towards a state-centric mode of association in which sovereignty and nonintervention serve to contain and sustain cultural and political diversity. It is in this general sense *status quo* orientated and concerned mainly about maintaining interstate order, and the cultural diversity that is the legacy of human history. As a rule, pluralists, following Bull, will argue that although a deeply unjust system cannot be stable, order is in important ways a prior condition for justice. Pluralists see the prospects for international society as limited to a fairly narrow logic of coexistence.
- *Solidarism* represents the disposition either to transcend the states-system with some closer mode of association based on humankind, or to develop the states-system beyond a logic of mere coexistence to one of cooperation on shared projects such as managing a global economy, pursuing human rights as a universal principle, and/or environmental stewardship for the planetary ecosystem. In principle, solidarism could represent a wide range of possibilities (Buzan, 2004a: 121, 190–200), but in practice within the English School it has been mainly linked to liberal cosmopolitan perspectives and to concerns about justice. Solidarists typically emphasise that order without justice is undesirable and ultimately unsustainable. Most of the debate about solidarism has linked it to the interhuman domain in the form of universalist cosmopolitan values, notably human rights. But solidarism can also be rooted in the interpolity domain, in such projects as managing a shared global economy (Buzan, 2014: 114–20).

In the English School context, it is important to see pluralism and solidarism not as opposed and mutually exclusive positions. Their proponents may sometimes think of themselves as opposed, and the language of the debate may sometimes take oppositional form. But in a detached perspective, their core function is to define the central, permanent tension in the English School's 'great conversation' about how to find the best balance between order and justice in international/global society.

Raison de système and raison de famille Raison de système was coined by Watson (1992: 14) and defined as 'the belief that it pays to make the system work'. This concept can be seen as a way of encapsulating the English School's core normative debate between pluralism and solidarism. It stands as the main counterpoint to the idea of *raison d'état*, which is central explicitly to realism and implicitly to much Western IR theory. *Raison de système* is fairly specific to modernity. When taking a longer historical perspective, one should add to this set *raison de famille*, as the logic of kinship systems generally, and in particular the dynastic imperial systems preceding *raison d'état* (Green, 2013). *Raison de système* is not yet widely used in the ES literature, but has a good claim for more general deployment. It neatly encapsulates the logic underlying international and global society, and therefore what differentiates ES thinking from most other lines of IR theory, particularly realist and rationalist ones.

Other Concepts from IR Theory

Interaction Capacity The concept of interaction capacity developed with work that I and others did that was aimed mainly at neorealism: Buzan, Jones and Little (1993: 66–80); Buzan and Little (2000: 80–4). Interaction capacity is a way of looking at international systems/societies in terms of their carrying capacity for information, goods and people, and the speed, range and cost with which these things can be done. Interaction capacity determines not only the size of such systems, but also how loosely or tightly they are integrated, and consequently how weakly or strongly the neorealist logics of socialisation and competition can work. This concept was not initially inspired or framed by ES thinking about international society but is compatible with it. Interaction capacity is a key aspect of the material conditions of international systems/societies, particularly in determining the limits and shape of trade, war, empire and cultural exchange. There is a huge difference between systems/societies in which information can be sent instantaneously from anywhere on the planet to anywhere else, and those in which it might take nine months to get a message from London to Australia, or from Beijing to Istanbul. Interaction capacity also has a social side in the extent to which primary and secondary institutions facilitate interaction. International law and diplomacy work this way as primary institutions, and secondary institutions such as banking systems and forum organisations like the UN respectively facilitate financial transactions and diplomatic interaction.

Evolution The concept of 'evolution' as used in this book is not strictly Darwinian in the sense of being driven by mutation and natural selection in a struggle for survival. As Tang (2013) and Neumann (2020:

23–5) point out, the social world evolves in ways different from, and not analogous to, the biological one.[9] Social collectivities evolve not only in themselves, from their internal dynamics, but also in interaction with both other social collectivities and the material environment. Social evolution is Darwinian in the sense that it is partly about how living things adapt (or not) to the environment they inhabit, and to changes in that environment, however such changes might be caused. Evolution in this sense is not teleological (Tang, 2013: 28–9, 35). The idea that evolution is a process with outcomes that are contingent, rather than predetermined, fits well with the ES tradition that international society is a contingent phenomenon whose fortunes wax and wane over time. Evolution exposes the logic of change without supposing any particular outcome. The idea that it is the fittest that survive is contingent rather than absolute. What might be fittest for one set of conditions might be a weakness when those conditions change. Ask any woolly mammoth, or any empire, about that. Evolution charts the successes, but also the failures and extinctions. A non-teleological view of evolution also leaves open the question of how to evaluate progress: evolution as a process can move towards lower levels of complexity and diversity as well as higher ones. A useful way of approaching social evolution is through the idea of dialectics as the mechanism of social change.

Dialectics Since biological analogies for social evolution are a bit limited, dialectics offers a useful complement for looking at how social structures evolve. It is not my intention here to get involved in any deep philosophical rumination on the complexities of dialectics. Nor do I want to accept, or get involved in the debates about, the peculiarities of Marxian dialectical materialism with its assumptions that social evolution is teleological.[10] I do not want to go much further than the idea that in the social world one can often see the primary institutions of integrated world societies falling into paired contradictions, or even antagonisms, that have somehow to be worked out because the tensions they generate cannot be left unaddressed. In the contemporary context, think, for example, of globalisation and territoriality, or human inequality and human equality, or human rights and state sovereignty, or monarchy/

---

[9] I broadly accept Tang's (2013: 3–40) theoretical case for a 'social evolutionary approach', though less so his rather Realist application of it.
[10] But see the useful contribution by Rosenberg (2013b).

dynasticism and popular sovereignty, and many more. These contradictions, and their dynamics, provide one of the engines, alongside changes in material conditions, that drives the evolution of societies at all levels.[11] The emphasis in what follows is on dialectics as process, not as teleology.

That leaves one complexity needing to be addressed. There are at least two ways of understanding the mechanism of dialectics, a situation that feels amusingly appropriate to the concept. The first is generally referred to as Hegelian, and reflects broadly how dialectics is understood in the West. The second is Chinese (*zhongyong* dialectics), and is probably not yet widely understood outside those familiar with Chinese culture.[12]

Hegelian dialectics is built around the resolution of contradictions, and starting the cycle over again from a new place. This is expressed in its concepts (not Hegel's terminology) of *thesis* and *antithesis* ending in *synthesis*, with the synthesis becoming the new thesis that restarts the cycle by generating an antithesis, and so on. This form of dialectics may or may not be progressive (a matter of normative judgment), but it is certainly a mechanism for continuous evolution. Its driving force is that contradictions are socially unsustainable and have to be resolved, and therefore its central mechanism is conflict. A potential problem with this form of dialectics is its assumption that each synthesis must start the cycle over again. This has an appealing dynamism and simplicity, but seems at odds with the fact that historically, many societies achieved sufficient stability and longevity to belie that kind of permanent turbulence. It seems possible that some syntheses will actually constitute islands of stability rather than springboards for a new contradiction. Constitutional monarchy, for example, might be seen as a durable synthesis from the contradiction between monarchy/dynasticism and nationalism/popular sovereignty. As I show in the empirical chapters, there can be mutually supportive clusters of primary institutions that form islands of stability. Hegelian dialectics are therefore sometimes resolvable by negotiation and compromise.

This idea of stabilised contradictions points to *zhongyong* dialectics. *Zhongyong* dialectics starts from the same idea that there are dyadic contradictions in society that need to be addressed if society is to be stable. From there, however, it takes a different route, based on the well-known *yin/yang* symbol in Chinese philosophy.

---

[11] The argument about contradictions amongst primary institutions as a driving force in the evolution of international society is foreshadowed in Mayall (1990), and Buzan (2004a: 250–1).
[12] I draw heavily on the work of Qin (2011, 2018) for this discussion.

In the perspective of *zhongyong* dialectics, the polarity in Chinese dialectics is contradictory, but not necessarily conflictual. There is a *yin/yang* complementarity and co-evolutionary process, whereby the 'thesis' and the 'antithesis' always contains an element of the other, and the balance between them shifts according to circumstance. The point of *zhongyong* dialectics is not to resolve contradictions that are seen as intolerably zero-sum, but to manage contradictions that are seen as a permanent feature of the social structure. Good management in the light of ever-changing circumstances is the path to achieving social harmony in the presence of contradiction. That, and not a new synthesis, is the essence of Chinese dialectics. In contrast to Hegelian thinking, Chinese *zhongyong* dialectics favour 'co-theses' (Qin, 2018: xvii). As Qin (2018: xvii) puts it, 'while the Hegelian tradition tries to diagnose the key contradiction, which is key to crumpling the old and creating a new synthesis', the '*zhongyong* dialectics always tries to find the appropriate middle where the common ground lies'. Conflict exists but does not have any ontological status (Qin, 2018: xvii).

One clear implication of *zhongyong* dialectics as a way of thinking is in the perspective it gives on social contradictions. In the Hegelian perspective, contradictions are basically unsustainable. But in the Chinese perspective, contradiction is the natural condition of being in society. Contradictions change in form and significance, and need to be handled in order to achieve harmony, but they do not disappear. The Chinese way of thinking is therefore much more comfortable with contradiction than the Western one, and this might go a long way to explaining what to a Western eye often looks like the incoherence of China's foreign policy.[13] But from a *zhongyong* perspective the pursuit of contradictory policies may not look like a problem at all, just the normal way of responding to complex situations in which policy needs to be continuously manoeuvred within standing contradictions.

In principle, both the Hegelian and *zhongyong* approaches look like viable understandings of dialectics. Yet in a dialectical perspective, each by itself, looks too narrow and extreme an interpretation. Not all contradictions have to be fought through to a new synthesis and a new cycle of conflict, and not all are endlessly manageable without needing some deeper resolution. The point here is not that all Western thinking is Hegelian and all Chinese thinking *Zhongyong*. Marxism, still influential in China, and especially in its ruling party, is strongly Hegelian in its view of dialectics. The point is that all contradictions and dialectics can and should be viewed in both of these perspectives. The example given above of constitutional monarchy as a stable synthesis, although a mainly Western one, might fit quite comfortably into a *zhongyong* perspective of managed contradiction. But the challenge of fascism in the 1940s had to be fought, and was a strong enough challenge to unite communists and liberals, albeit temporarily, to do so. I therefore keep in mind both understandings of dialectics, and apply them pragmatically. And since the evolutionary dynamics of societies are generally complex, and seldom reducible to simple dyadic contradictions, I add to this framework the idea that in either the Hegelian or *zhongyong* schemes, it is not uncommon for two or more dialectics to intersect in such a way as to entangle their dynamics. I will refer to such situations as *multilectic*.

Differentiation Theory and Sectors Differentiation theory and sectors are partly overlapping ideas, but with quite different origins and implications. Differentiation theory comes from Sociology, and is a deep idea aimed at defining the fundamental structure of societies. It offers three basic principles of differentiation applicable to all forms of society: *segmentary*, *stratificatory* and *functional* (Buzan and Albert, 2010; Albert, Buzan and Zürn, 2013):

- *Segmentary* (or *egalitarian*) differentiation is where every social subsystem is the equal of, and functionally similar to, every other social subsystem. This points to families, bands, clans and tribes. A segmentary form of differentiation is the one most prone to be

---

[13] On the various reasons for the incoherence of China's foreign policy see: Buzan (2010); Wang (2011); Odgaard (2012: 2–4); Shambaugh (2013: 61–71); Garver (2016); Ren (2016); Jones and Hameiri (2021).

organised in terms of territorial delimitations, although this is not necessarily so.

- *Stratificatory* differentiation is where some persons or groups raise themselves above others, creating a hierarchical social order. Stratificatory differentiation covers a wide range of possibilities and can be further subdivided into rank and class forms distinguished by whether or not there is significant inequality not just in status (rank), but in access to basic resources (class). This points to feudal or caste, or aristocratic or religious, or military social orders. As this suggests, stratification can occur in many dimensions: coercive capability, access to resources, authority, status, level of skill, etc. In IR it points to the many forms of hierarchy: conquest and empire, hegemony, a privileged position for great powers, and a division of the world into core and periphery, or First and Third Worlds.

- *Functional* differentiation is where the subsystems are defined by the coherence of particular types of activity and their differentiation from other types of activity, and these differences do not stem simply from rank. It is closely related to the idea of a division of labour in the sense understood by economists, but when applied to society as a whole it points to its increasing division into legal, political, military, economic, scientific, religious and suchlike distinct and specialised subsystems or sectors of activity, often with distinctive institutions and actors (Albert and Hilkermeier, 2004). The study of functional differentiation is closely, and as I will show wrongly, associated almost exclusively with modernity.

The sense of history in differentiation theory involves an idea of evolution in which more complex forms grow out of the simpler ones that precede them. The orthodox view is that segmentary hunter-gatherer bands precede the stratified city states and empires of ancient and classical times, which precede the functionally differentiated societies characteristic of modernity. In this view, segmentary, stratificatory and functional differentiation form a sequence in that the higher tiers depend for their existence on having developed out of, and overcome, the ones that came before. The sequence is thus both empirical (roughly corresponding to the general pattern of human history) and qualitative (from simpler forms of differentiation to more complex ones). Although such evolution is common, it is certainly not inevitable. Specific societies can end up in stasis, or can revert back to simpler types (Diamond, 2005). Evolution does not mean that higher forms of differentiation eliminate those below them. The logic is structural: social orders are characterised by the co-presence of different forms of differentiation, the key question being which form is dominant in shaping the social structure as a whole. Looked at the other way around, one can find elements of functional differentiation even in segmentary hunter-gatherer societies (shamans, tool-makers, pottery makers). As shown in Chapter 3, there was a lot of functional differentiation in the stratificatory societies of agrarian civilisation. Differentiation theory sets up a helpful context within which the social function of primary institutions can be understood.

The concept of sectors is more a practical taxonomy than a theory. Sectors differentiate on the basis of the type of relationship – military (coercion), political (power), economic (exchange), societal (identity), etc. – and therefore lean strongly towards a functional differentiation of society. Within IR, it was developed in the context of security studies to provide a functional parallel to the scale-based differentiations of levels of analysis that were widely used in IR (Buzan, 1991: 107–19; Buzan, Jones and Little, 1993: 30–3; Buzan and Little, 2000: 72–7).[14] Buzan and Little (2000) combined sectors and levels of analysis into a matrix in an attempt to capture the social whole. The practice of thinking in terms of functionally differentiated sectors is also not uncommon amongst historians and sociologists (e.g. Braudel, 1985: 17; Mann, 1986: ch. 1). In IR analyses of the social world, there are five commonly used sectors: military, political, economic, societal and environmental, with law as an arguable sixth. Similar to primary institutions, the concept of sectors neither specifies any particular set nor set limits to how many there might be, nor explains why we have this particular set. It merely observes empirically that modern society and academia operate in ways that reproduce this particular set, and so differentiate society functionally along those lines. Sectors provide a useful way of grouping primary institutions in functional terms.

- The *military sector* is about relationships of forceful coercion, and the ability of actors to fight wars with each other. It usually focuses on the interplay of the armed offensive and defensive capabilities of actors in the international system, and their perceptions of each other's intentions. Institutions are war, balance of power, and partly imperialism (because empires are mainly created and sustained by force).
- The *political sector* is about relationships of authority, governing status and recognition. It concerns the organisational stability of systems of

---

[14] Although levels of analysis has featured quite strongly in some of my earlier work, it is relatively in the background in this book. That is partly because most of the focus here is on the global level, although the regional one comes up here and there, and partly because I have shifted the main emphasis to the three domains, which do some of the same work, but in a different way.

government and the ideologies that give them legitimacy. Do polities accept other polities as equal in law and rank? Or are relations hierarchical, with superior and inferior status acknowledged by both sides? Or do polities deny each other recognition, in effect treating each other as unoccupied territory available for seizure (*terra nullius*)? The political sector can be interpreted in a more state-centric sense as being about government, or in a looser, more liberal, sense as being about governance, including norms, rules, and institutions above, or instead of, the state. Some might wish to differentiate a *legal sector* from the political one. Institutions are sovereignty, territoriality, monarchy/dynasticism, diplomacy, international law, great power management. Partly also imperialism (when it is a legitimate framing for rule), religion (where tied to the polity), nationalism, and human equality/inequality.

- The *societal sector* is about social and cultural relationships. It concerns the patterns of collective identity by which humans place themselves into groups, and how those groups relate to each other: that is, the various principles of differentiation and stratification in social orders. It involves the sustainability, within acceptable conditions for evolution, of traditional patterns of language, culture and religious and national identity and custom. Interactions in this sector are about the transmission of ideas between peoples and civilisations. They may involve ideas about knowledge, technology or about political and religious organisation. Institutions are kinship (family to tribe/clan), partly religion, nationalism, human equality/inequality, science, sport.

- The *economic sector,* is about relationships of trade, production and finance, and how actors gain access to the resources, finance and markets necessary to sustain acceptable levels of welfare and political power. For most of history, economic interactions have been about trade and the financing of trade. Only in very recent times have they also come to be about the far-flung organisation of production and finance. Institutions are trade, trade diasporas, market/mercantilism, development, and partly imperialism, human equality/inequality (wages versus slavery).

- The *environmental sector* is about the relationship between human activity and the planetary ecosphere as the essential support system on which all other human enterprises depend. The most traditional environmental interaction is disease transmission, but since the Chinese and European voyages of discovery in the fifteenth century, one must add the intercontinental movement of plants, animals and peoples, and local and global pollution. The environmental sector, and the debates about an *anthropocene* era (Dalby, 2020), become increasingly important in the later chapters on modernity. Institutions: environmental stewardship, sustainable development.

It is quickly apparent that sectors, despite their absence of theoretical grounding, fit quite comfortably within functional differentiation, even if as nothing more than convenient labels (Buzan and Albert, 2010: 316–18, 328; Albert and Buzan, 2011, 2013). Both are approaches to understanding the social whole by differentiating it in terms of types of functional relationships (Albert and Buzan, 2013). In this usage, they are close to being synonyms for sociological labels such as subsystems or function-systems. But sectors, like functional differentiation, also resonate widely within the social sciences, many of whose disciplines have set themselves up along functionally differentiated/sectoral lines: for example, Economics, Law, Politics, Sociology. Within IR, there is a long-standing division of opinion as to whether the discipline is a subfield of Politics (International Politics) or an amalgam of the macro-ends of most of the social sciences plus history. I am firmly of the latter view, and that will be reflected in this book. Neither IR as a discipline, nor the global society approach, can be confined to the political sector.

Uneven and Combined Development The concept of uneven and combined development (UCD) has been developed in several works by Rosenberg (2010, 2013a, b, 2016, 2020, see also Buzan and Lawson, 2016) to provide a framework for understanding modernity, and indeed the dynamics of international relations more generally. In terms of explaining the global historical dynamics of modernity, UCD stands as an alternative to Waltz (1979). Both Waltz and Rosenberg see 'socialisation and competition' as consequences of 'combination' (units unavoidably interacting with each other within the same system). But they disagree deeply about their effects: Waltz famously favours homogenisation into 'like units', while Rosenberg stresses that the particular timing and circumstances of socialisation and competition necessarily produce varied outcomes. The extreme conditions created by macro-historical transformations such as the one that took place during the long nineteenth century expose the logic of the latter with great clarity. Major transformations of this kind have a distinct point or points of origin in which a particular configuration emerges and is sustained. This configuration is produced and reproduced through inter-societal interactions across time and space, generating diverse outcomes. These interactions can be coercive, emulative and/or reactive, and each social order that encounters the new configuration has its own way of adapting to it. Some social orders resist the new configuration, and may be eliminated as a result. Others develop indigenous versions of it. 'Late' developers are not carbon copies of the original adopters, but develop their own distinctive characteristics.

Interactions between different social orders therefore produce not Waltzian convergence, but (sometimes unstable) amalgams of new and old. Modernity sometimes displaces, but just as often reconfigures, ideas, rituals and symbols associated with 'tradition': monarchies, religions, class hierarchies, and suchlike. Each society finds its own blend of new and old: for example, the British version of constitutional monarchy, the modern Japanese emperor, the contemporary reworking of Confucianism in China. During the nineteenth century, German, American and Japanese industrialisations were not replicas of British development, but distinct amalgams. Even as they borrowed both from the British experience and from each other, they adapted modernity to their own contexts and traditions, often trying to use the modern state to accelerate the process so as to 'catch-up' with the leading edge. Likewise, Soviet and, more recently, Chinese developments also maintained their own characteristics, combining new technologies and productive forces alongside inherited social formations. As ideas spread, they are adapted to local cultures and conditions (Acharya, 2004). Each society has to find its own way of coming to terms with the multiple challenges presented by modernity, and each encounter is shaped by local histories, cultures and institutional contexts, as well as by the timing and circumstances of its encounter. There is both convergence (most obviously in the common assuming of aspects of functional differentiation, nationalism and forms of rational statehood); and divergence (ideological, cultural and organisational, and understanding of class structure).

Through the analytic lens of UCD, it becomes clear that development is multilinear rather than linear; proceeds in fits and starts rather than through smooth gradations; and contains significant variations in terms of outcomes. One indicator of the ways in which polities adapted in diverse ways to the nineteenth-century global transformation is the variety of ideologies that have emerged to define different assemblages of economy, politics and culture in the modern world: liberalism, social democracy, conservatism, socialism, market socialism, communism, fascism, patrimonialism, and more. Another indicator is the literature on varieties of capitalism (Jackson and Deeg, 2006; McNally, 2013; Buzan and Lawson, 2014b; Milanovic, 2019). A third is the idea of 'multiple modernities' (Eisenstadt, 2000). UCD underlines how and why the deep pluralist world order (see Part III) now emerging from the ongoing spread and deepening of modernity, will be as much, or more, culturally, economically and politically differentiated than homogenised.

The perspective of UCD resolves the long-standing, and politically charged, equation of modernisation with Westernisation, which assumed that adopting modernity must mean becoming a clone of the Western model. It doesn't.

Although this book focuses on the similarities that come into view when human history is observed through the lens of primary institutions, it is essential not to lose sight of the fact that primary institutions operate at quite a high level of abstraction. Underneath that, one must not lose sight of the widespread diversities of culture and politics that differentiate civilisations even when all face the pressures of modernity.[15]

Three Repurposed Concepts

Era The term era is commonly used in IR in a flexible way to define longish periods marked by a particular dominant characteristic, such as the nuclear era. It works alongside other, usually vaguely defined periodising terms such as 'age' (e.g. Bronze Age), 'epoch' (as in geology), and 'period' (e.g. interwar period). As Guillaume (2021) points out, history can always be periodised in various and overlapping ways, with common themes being modes of government (type of dominant polity), modes of production (Marxism), modes of destruction (weapons, wars), and modes of social differentiation (classical Sociology). Any subdivision of history presupposes a pattern of continuities and ruptures or transitions, and it is up to the periodiser to specify 'the working hypothesis and the conceptual premises behind it' (Guillaume, 2021: 565–6). Epple (2021: 49) helpfully sums up the act of periodising as follows:

Anyone who applies such a concept is claiming that there are criteria according to which a time span can be described as a cohesive period. Instead of merely pointing to a break, the epoch concept prescribes at least a minimum of inner consistency over the length of time in question. It becomes meaningful when it links up with some interpretation that goes beyond mere chronology. There are three possible ways of doing this: the weakest is to define an epoch as lying between two caesurae (as, for example, with the 'interwar period' or the 'Middle Ages'). An epoch concept is stronger when it invokes common features (for example 'feudalism'). However, the concept is at its strongest when it claims that a specific epoch is characterized by a general, comprehensive trend and can be conceived in terms of a process (for example, the 'age of industrialization').

---

[15] The UCD debates accord with the mainstream view by generally assuming that what I called 'modernity proper' arrived during the nineteenth century. I hold this question open, seeing the nineteenth century as the beginning of the transition towards modernity.

Here I use the term era in a strong sense to identify long – often very long – time-spans. These are defined internally by a specific pattern of material conditions and social structures that remain dominant throughout an identifiable stretch of time; and externally by transition periods during which those defining variables change. My premise is that significant patterns of continuity and rupture/transition can be found even when one combines modes of government, production and destruction. In Epple's terms, I am less concerned with pinpoint dates, because I see eras as separated by transition periods. I am much more concerned to use my material and social-structural framing to find new patterns of common features and general trends. My working hypothesis is that the English School's concept of primary institutions can be used to open a detailed look at the social structure as a whole, and that patterns occurring there can be matched to developments in the material condition of humankind. The key to identifying such long eras is to differentiate between changes occurring <u>within</u> a relatively fixed set of material and social conditions, and changes that <u>transform</u> those conditions themselves. The dual framing of material conditions and primary institutions I use to shape the empirical analysis is designed to generate an analytical level of generality that brings these long eras clearly into view. An era is therefore defined by a specific form of socio-material order. The resultant level of analysis is higher than those used by most historians to identify continuities and ruptures.[16] My scheme also uses clusters of big changes that occur together not only in material conditions but also across a range of primary institutions, to identify the continuities and changes that define these long eras. The empirical material used in this exercise is not in itself new, though most readers will probably find things in it with which they were not familiar. It is the way that the material is organised that generates new insights about continuity, change and periodisation in the long view of history.

This usage makes eras the longest form of socio-historical periodisation for humankind. Each era may contain a variety of periods, phases, stages, etc. defined by narrower criteria. Eras are both separated and connected by transition periods in which one set of material conditions and social structures morphs into another. These transitions may themselves be quite long. In earlier eras, when humankind was scattered into separate civilisations with often very thin connections, they occurred at different times in different places, as for example with agriculture. The focus in what follows will be on the earliest transitions, and these were

---

[16] For example, Bentley (1996); Parzinger (2020: 290–304).

usually in Eurasia. As with functional differentiation, each era contains legacies from its predecessors as well as the new material conditions and social structures that define it. In this sense, eras are a bit like genomes: the genome of *Homo sapiens*, for example, still contains significant traces of the DNA of extinct hominin species such as Neanderthals and Denisovans.

Social Glue The second repurposed concept, *social glue*, is not used much if at all in IR, though the idea that the term represents – what is it that holds social orders together? – is strongly present in many IR discussions.[17] Although he does not use the term social glue, Wendt (1999: 247–50) provides a simple and very useful answer to the question: coercion, calculation and/or belief.[18] Close to pure forms of these three types of social glue are imaginable: for example, coercion in rule imposed by alien conquest; calculation in pure systems of market relations; and belief underpinning religions and secular ideologies. But blendings are the standard form. Religions and secular ideologies might well have a core of belief, but also be supported and promoted by force, or adhered to out of calculation. Market relations start from calculation, but can also involve an element of ideological belief, and for others might be influenced by elements of coercion from criminals or political leaders. Invaders might find support from a 'fifth column' on the basis of calculation or belief. There is a strong general sense that these forms of social glue stand in a hierarchy of efficiency. Social structures held together mainly by coercion, such as empires of conquest, will be costly to maintain, will inspire resistance, and will evaporate once the coercion weakens. The Assyrian and Qin Empires are often given as examples of coercion-heavy social structures (e.g. Lieven, 2022: 49, 94–100). Those held together by calculation, such as markets, are stable only so long as they deliver the desired goods. They are vulnerable to changes in circumstance, such as war, that alter the calculations negatively. Those held together by belief are the easiest to maintain, and because they have the deepest roots they are likely to be the most durable. Christianity outlasted the Roman Empire, Islam outlasted the Abbasid Caliphate, Buddhism outlasted the Mauryan Empire, and Orthodoxy outlasted the Soviet Union. It is important to note that belief does not have to be nice. Warrior cultures and fascist societies often believe that war promotes the health and progress of a society, cultivates masculine

---

[17] See Buzan (2004a: 98–138) for a more extensive discussion of this.
[18] For other formulations see Kratochwil (1989: 97); March and Olsen (1998: 948–54); Hurd (1999).

values, leads to the survival of the fittest, and is therefore a desirable activity.

This hierarchy of forms of social glue is about the degree to which a social order is internalised within its members. Coercive orders are shallow. They can generate the conformity of behaviour that marks a society, but not in an internalised, self-sustaining, way. Calculated orders are by definition dependent on the maintenance of particular conditions. They are partly internalised, but not in a deep way. They might or might not be durable. Orders held together by shared belief are deep because they are internalised. This is one explanation for the relative durability of religion in global society, and for the success of nationalism since the nineteenth century. It is what secular ideologies such as liberalism, socialism, fascism and communism hope to achieve. In IR, neorealists, neoliberals and other forms of rationalist focus mainly on the shallower orders of coercion and calculation. Constructivists and the ES focus mainly on deep order.

In Wendt's scheme, 'belief' is very close to what Anderson (1983; see also Harari, 2011: 361–4) famously labelled *imagined communities*: groups of people who identify themselves as a society or community on the basis of some agreed myth that binds them together. The reason why these communities are 'imagined' is that they are too big for all of their members to have any chance of meeting or knowing each other personally, as they might expect to do in a local kinship community. Despite this limitation, imagined communities can develop great depth and power, easily forming the basis on which people will treat other members of the group as if they were kin, and kill outsider, non-members if they are thought to be threatening. Whether the binding myth is true, partially true, or pure invention, does not matter. All that matters is that the relevant group of people accept it. This myth could be an extended version of kinship, like a common ancestor. It could be a religion whose stories and god(s) and rituals all adherents accept and bind themselves to. It could be a national myth, where the shared identity is constructed out of some mixture of language, ethnicity, culture and history. It could be an ideological myth, in which the community defines itself by adherence to some secular doctrine. Like many conspiracy theories, it could be complete and unsubstantiated nonsense, but nonsense that is packaged into a compelling story. Some imagined communities are fairly closed and difficult to join (e.g. ethno-national ones), while others are relatively easy (e.g. proselytising religions, conspiracy theories).

The blends and mixtures of these three forms or social glue change over time and place, and at all levels of society from family to global. They are one factor in what can be used to define eras.

Globalisation and Global Society In IR, globalisation has many layers of meaning, ranging from the spread of humans across the planet in Neolithic times, through the connecting up of the continents by the opening of oceanic shipping during the fifteenth and sixteenth centuries to the two modern views focusing on massive increases in the depth and intensity of global interactions of all kinds, one highlighting the nineteenth century, and the other the world since 1945 (Buzan and Lawson, 2015: 311–14). All but the first of these layers tends to privilege the economic sector, because that is generally the one in which humans connect on the largest scale, mainly through trade, in any given era (Buzan and Little, 2000; Acharya and Buzan, 2019: 181–2). In its economic meaning, globalisation allows space for the non-state actors who conducted trade, traditionally merchants, to be a significant part of the picture.

In what follows, I take a broad view of this concept embracing all of these meanings. I am basically interested in using globalisation to capture the increasing scale of how humankind organises itself across the inter-polity, transnational and interhuman domains eventually generating a global society. This encompasses much more than just trade. Global society enables an important differentiation to be made from the ES's *world society*. World society, and some other uses of 'world' in IR theory, suggests the encompassing of the whole of a social system without that necessarily requiring planetary scale. It is common to talk about the Roman or Sinic 'worlds' during classical times. Global society means planetary in scale. In what follows, therefore, globalisation in the sense of increasing scale works in tandem with the concept of *integrated world society* discussed above. Globalisation carries the factor of scale, and integrated world society captures the extent and intensity with which the organisation of humankind works in a connected way across all three domains. For much of human history these define mainly separate civilisational tracks that are lightly linked. At most there was progress towards planetary scale as the size of human societies increased. But once the scale of human society reached planetary extent, as it had by the early sixteenth century, these two tracks started to merge. By the nineteenth century, integrated world society had effectively become global society, turning the story from one mainly about expanding scale, to one almost wholly about intensification within global scale.

At this point many readers will be thinking about *global governance*, an idea that has been active in IR thinking for several decades. Such thinking emerged partly from IPE, where the role of non-state actors, particularly firms, was obvious; and partly from liberal cosmopolitans wishing to challenge the narrow state-centrism of realists (Gilpin, 1987;

Strange, 1988; Stopford and Strange, 1991; Rosenau, 1992; Held et al., 1999; Karns and Mingst, 2010; Zürn, 2010; Weiss, 2013). Global governance emphasised the deterritorialisation of world politics as states opened themselves to both economic flows and issues such as the environment that could not be dealt with effectively even by superpowers. It highlighted the significant roles played in contemporary international relations not just by some minor states as well as for great powers, but also by both intergovernmental organisations, and a wide range of non-state actors from multinational corporations to civil society actors acting not only as lobbyists, but also as providers of resources and expertise. The main drift of the global governance literature was to see great powers more as a problem than a solution to global troubles, and to emphasise that a much wider range of actors and networks were powerfully in play. It mostly wanted to see great powers as increasingly enmeshed in cobwebs of networks from which they could no longer escape. Great power management was seen as ineffective at best, and part of the problem at worst. The idea was of an emergent multi-layered form of global management that was more diverse, more democratic, and often more efficient, than great power interventions, and whose development should be supported.

The ES played little part in this. It was handicapped by its focus on the society of states, its failure to engage with IPE, and its relative disinterest in secondary institutions. Within the ES, Hurrell (2007) was notable for acknowledging and engaging with global governance. A few others within the ES noted the effective merging of global governance, on the one hand, and great power management, on the other hand, as the agenda of global governance issues grew ever wider (Bukovansky et al., 2012; Cui and Buzan, 2016). Global governance lost momentum within IR after the economic crisis starting in 2007–8 exposed the dependence of the global market on state management and rescue. It was further battered by the emergence and intensification of the second cold war after 2015.

The idea of global society that I am raising here has two resonances with global governance. Both focus on planetary scale. And both incorporate a wider range of actors than states/polities, bringing in corporations, intergovernmental organisations, and civil society organisations. But there are substantial differences too. I argue that the linked ideas of integrated world society/global society can and should be pushed back a lot further in time than the last few decades or centuries that preoccupy global governance. I also argue that the framing in English School terms as society, and the explicit analytical approach through the three domains (interpolity, transnational, interhuman), differentiates global society from global governance. The framing as society opens up for deployment

of the ES's concept of primary institutions, which, except for sovereignty
and territoriality, are not much present in global governance. The three
domains both transcend the narrowly political emphasis implied by
'governance', and bring in patterns of identity in a much bigger way.
Global society could thus be seen as a way of putting global governance
onto much firmer theoretical and historical foundations. Multi-layered
governance involving a range of actors other than polities stretches back a
very long way. In some respects, it is the norm of how humankind has
organised itself on the largest scale for several thousand years. Global
governance thus suffers badly from presentism. By focusing far too much
on contemporary developments, it occluded a long and highly relevant
prior history. It thereby set up as exceptional and unique, what was in
many ways normal and routine.

    Global society is thus aimed at re-founding global governance by put-
ting it into a much wider historical and theoretical perspective. The term
is not (yet) associated with the English School, though one purpose of
this book is to argue that it should be, and to demonstrate how and why.
Within an ES framing, global society means an integrated world society
on a planetary scale, bringing the interpolity, transnational and interhuman domains under a single heading, and ensuring that all of them are
given equal opportunity in analysis without any automatic privileging of
one over the others. In the manner of the English School's three traditions, let the historical record set the relative strengths in any given place
and time. Bull's differentiation between international society and world
society has been extremely useful and productive in shaping ES thinking
by creating space for normative concerns and dynamics. There was a
definite need to fill the space left by Sociology's disinterest in second-
order societies.[19] But as a result, the ES has tended strongly to privilege
the interpolity/state domain as the practical site of international society,
and to underplay both the non-state societal aspects in themselves, and
the extent to which primary and secondary institutions in fact often
operate together within and across the three domains in very significant
ways. Global society is not about rejecting the interpolity domain, but
about viewing the interplay of social structure – primary and secondary
institutions – across all three domains. The aim is to shift the vocabulary

---

[19] Shaw (1996) discussed global society in relation to the ES, but was essentially about
using a weaker definition of society in order to elevate the standing of people and non-
state actors against a declining state system (Buzan, 2004a: 68–70). A mainstream
textbook on so-called Global Sociology (Cohen and Kennedy, 2007) has no index
references to any aspect of international society.

of both the ES, and IR more generally, to talk about the three domains and institutions of global society within a single framework.

My purpose in this is to find a framework at a general enough level of analysis so that the similarities amongst the various polities, cultures and civilisations come into the foreground, putting their everyday differences into the background. It is these everyday differences – whether Rome and China, or Western and Confucian, or many others defined by polity, culture or civilisation – that normally structure historical analysis. This book is not about comparative civilisations, but about the history of humankind as a whole. Global society, and its history, is the book's contribution to making a more global discipline of IR. With an analytical level that foregrounds similarities, one can have more confidence that when discontinuities do appear, they are of major significance. My choice for the social element defining that transcendent analytical level is primary institutions. Alongside material conditions, primary institutions work nicely to highlight continuities and similarities, and to identify deep discontinuities and differences when they appear. Transcending the everyday differentiating approach in this way provides a firm grip on the kinds of changes that mark out eras.

A key idea here is that integrated world society, and eventually global society, is to be found in the way in which primary institutions integrate the three domains. Most primary institutions have their main roots in one of the domains (e.g. diplomacy, war, international law and great power management in the interpolity domain), but many of them stretch significantly into one or both of the other domains (e.g. trade, nationalism, religion, human (in)equality, sport). It is pretty obvious that some of the primary institutions rooted in interpolity society penetrate deeply into the transnational and interhuman domains. As noted, the obvious example of this is nationalism, which within the transition towards modernity, resonates powerfully between the interhuman and interstate domains. This has been a two-way street, with states promoting nationalism downward, and interhuman identity dynamics pushing it upward. Nationalism, like football, has almost everywhere now been deeply internalised and naturalised in both the interstate and interhuman domains. It meets more resistance in the economic and religious cosmopolitanism within the transnational domain. Similar, if less dramatic, cases could be made about several other interpolity institutions. The ideas of sovereignty and territoriality are pretty widely and deeply embedded in the public mind, and accepted as legitimising the organisation of political life within states. Think of the way Boris Johnson used sovereigntism to promote Brexit, and Donald Trump and Xi Jinping to promote their visions, respectively, of America and China. The values of human equality and development are also embedded across the three domains. Increasingly environmental stewardship, despite many ongoing breaches in practice, is also accepted across the three domains (Falkner and Buzan, 2019). The right to war under specified conditions (e.g. self-defence), and not others (e.g. imperialism), also probably has wide support. Most of these institutions are widely and popularly supported as matters of belief almost everywhere.

The market and international law probably have less resonance in the interhuman domain, but are hugely important to the transnational one because they legitimise and support the non-state organisational forms and activities within that domain. Whereas many of the institutions just discussed are held in place mainly by belief, the market almost certainly has a more mixed profile, being held in place partly by belief, partly by calculation, and partly by coercion, and with complex possibilities for the distribution of support and opposition between and among people and elites. Some of the other institutions of interstate society are mainly of interest to state elites, and only occasionally resonate strongly into the other two domains. This might be said of diplomacy, great power management, the balance of power, and war. There are times when peace movements and organisations mobilise around these institutions, for example in the peace movement of the interwar years that opposed secret diplomacy and 'the merchants of death', and the various anti-nuclear movements that accompanied the Cold War. But these more technical institutions generally don't play strongly into the identity and organisational rights of the transnational and interhuman domains.

Looking at this traffic across the three domains, it is clear that there is also much that goes from the interhuman and transnational domains towards the interpolity one. Some collective identities, most obviously nationalism and religion, but also in significant ways humankind as a whole, have substantial legitimacy as the basis for making claims in the proceedings of interstate society. Think, for example, of the Kurds, the Tibetans and the Palestinians; or of Russia's claims concerning ethnic Russians living in neighbouring countries; or of organisations such as the Islamic Conference, the Arab League and the Nordic Union. Think also of the interstate machinery around human equality and human rights, which, since the 1948 Universal Declaration of Human Rights (UDHR) are now embodied not only in the Charter of the UN (Clark, 2007: 131–51), but also in many UN Conventions and Committees, and in many regional bodies. The UN has a Human Rights Council, and there is a body of international humanitarian law. Nationalism, indeed, stands alongside sovereignty and territoriality as one of the key primary institutions that define the modern state.

Transnational diplomacy is now widely and deeply accepted in inter-state society. There is a very long history of political authorities negotiating not only with religious ones, but also with powerful guilds of transnational merchants. At times, indeed, such as in post-Roman Europe, the transnational authority of the Roman Church was the dominant social structure, and merchants controlled powerful polities such as the Hanseatic League, Venice and Malacca. For the two centuries of the transition towards modernity, states have welcomed, or at least allowed, non-state actors to participate in many of their diplomatic activities. From the Congress of Vienna, through The Hague Conferences and the League of Nations, to the UN system and the many specialised IGOs and international conferences, many INGOs and firms are now deeply and formally embedded in the processes of multilateral diplomacy. They are still there only by permission, making this fall short of a fully integrated world society. But they are now firmly part of the process, and play an important role in both strengthening its legitimacy and providing resources and expertise. It is on this basis that the term 'global governance' took on its meaning. When one thinks, for example, about environmental stewardship, it embodies a mix of state and non-state entities and activities: not just the United Nations Environment Program (UNEP), but also the Intergovernmental Panel on Climate Change (IPCC), the International Union for Conservation of Nature (IUCN), the 1972 Stockholm Conference, the Rio summit of 1992, conferences in Copenhagen (2009) and Paris (2015), Greenpeace, and the World Wide Fund for Nature (WWF), among others.

Global society in this integrated and open sense, with primary and secondary institutions stretching across and through the three domains on a planetary scale, is the guiding idea of this book.

Five Possible Pathways

Finally, to help navigate the story at the level of humankind, it is useful to step back a bit and consider the universe of possible pathways for our species. There are five such secular pathways for humankind:

• Species regression – in which humankind loses wealth, power and knowledge, and shrinks in numbers. This might have natural causes (e.g. environmental changes) or human ones (resource exhaustion). There are many specific examples of this in human history from the collapse of Western Mediterranean civilisation around 1200 BC, through the impact of the fall of Rome in Western Europe, to the downfall of the statues culture on Easter Island a few hundred years ago (see Diamond, 2005; Cline, 2014).

- Species extinction – in which natural disasters from which humankind is unable to escape or protect itself, destroy the living conditions for our species. Think of the dinosaurs – or the Neanderthals (Sykes, 2020).
- Species suicide – in which humankind destroys itself through its own actions such as nuclear war, unwise technological tinkering, or an inability to maintain a habitable planet (*Dr. Strangelove* [film, 1964]; *Battlestar Galactica* [TV series]; David Attenborough's 'witness testimony', *A Life on Our Planet* [Documentary]).[20]
- Species empowerment – in which humankind continues to increase in wealth, power and knowledge, and expands in numbers. Down this pathway lies both an extension of modernity and the possibility of transition to eras beyond modernity (*Star Trek* [TV series]; the 'Culture' novels of Iain M. Banks).
- Species self-replacement – in which species empowerment enables humankind to replace itself with some other form of dominant intelligence, whether an improved version of itself, or a machine intelligence or a 'cyborg' mix of the two. It would then be an open question about whether humankind was any longer in play, or the subject of history had become something else whose characteristics were so different as to open a gulf between its history and that of humankind (*The Terminator* [film, 1985]).

Regression, extinction and empowerment have been options throughout human history, and examples of all can be found. But species suicide and replacement are recent options, exclusive to the era of modernity.

Conclusions

In my mind, this toolkit of concepts, terms and definitions makes this book an English School project, albeit one that pushes beyond the normal boundaries of the ES in various ways. The aim is to build on ES theory and concepts in such a way as to enable the ES to engage more closely with World/Global History, IPE and Global Historical Sociology

---

[20] It might be objected that 'species suicide' is the wrong term because humankind is not an agent in itself, and the scenarios for it, such as nuclear war, are therefore about some parts of humankind taking actions that destroy the whole. This is true, but I need a term that differentiates from species extinction. To the extent that states, firms and any other entities that pull the trigger are legitimate within the framing of global society, the term suicide is justified. The species dies by its own hand in the sense that it created the social structures that destroy it. Thanks to Rita Floyd for raising this question.

(GHS). These four approaches each have distinctive and valuable characteristics of their own, yet they also overlap in significant ways. In particular, they all make historical processes and timelines a central part of their analyses, and are concerned with the broad question of international order. All could probably subscribe to the idea that history is 'what the present needs to know about the past' (Maza, 2017: 6). All four approaches have needed to shed legacies of state-centrism, methodological nationalism and Eurocentrism (Conrad, 2016: 1–5; Go and Lawson, 2017: 1–3; Maza, 2017: 45–82), and make what Conrad (2016: 4) nicely calls 'an assault on many forms of container-based paradigms, chief among them national history'. For GHS this also involved differentiating itself from the more abstract, ahistorical and state-centric forms of sociology (Go and Lawson, 2017: 6, 12).

The English School is unusual within the mainly presentist field of IR in privileging history. As set out above, its distinctive contribution to understanding international relations is to impose a societal perspective onto the system one, with a well-defined society of states constituted by a set of primary institutions, resting on a much vaguer 'world society' comprising all of humankind. The ES has applied this societal mode of analysis to both the modern and classical worlds, and this approach fits quite comfortably within the general definition of GHS as a specific form. Go and Lawson (2017: 2, 5) define GHS as meaning:

the study of two interrelated dynamics: first, the transnational and global dynamics that enable the emergence, reproduction, and breakdown of social orders whether these orders are situated at the subnational, national, or global scales; and second, the historical emergence, reproduction, and breakdown of transnational and global social forms. The first of these dynamics provides the 'global' in our enquiry; the second constitutes the 'historical sociology'.... We conceive global historical sociology as the study of the transnational and global features of these processes. Such features vary widely, ranging from the global dynamics of capitalist accumulation to the role of transnational ideologies and social movements in fostering change within and across state borders – to many things besides.... Rather than starting analyses from the assumptions of methodological nationalism, global historical sociology starts from the assumption of interconnectedness and spatially expansive social relations.

Both the ES and GHS are in turn compatible with World/Global History, whose core concerns

are with mobility and exchange, with processes that transcend borders and boundaries. It takes the interconnected world as its point of departure, and the circulation and exchange of things, people, ideas, and institutions are among its key subjects. A preliminary and rather broad definition of global history might describe it as a form of historical analysis in which phenomena, events, and processes are placed in global contexts. (Conrad, 2016: 5)

As the world has evolved more and more into a single political, economic, and cultural entity, causal links on the global level have grown stronger. And as a result of the proliferation and perpetuation of such links, local events are increasingly shaped by a global context that can be understood structurally or even systemically. (Conrad, 2016: 11)

Global historians thus see connectivity evolving into forms of integration (Conrad, 2016: 6).

In an argument that could also be applied to the ES, Go and Lawson (2017: 5–6) argue that the key difference between GHS and trans-national/global history is that while 'GHS is concerned with temporality and historicity, it differs from these enterprises in its explicit focus on social relations, overarching patterns or structures, social forms, and causal mechanisms'.... [It occupies] 'a register at one remove from such studies through the overt deployment of conceptual abstractions, analytic schemas, and theoretical frames.' Even this apparently large methodological gap may not be all that big. World/global historians already have to resort to big themes in order to keep their work to manageable length, and such themes are already a substantial step in the direction of the explicit abstractions preferred by social scientists.

If this bridge-building move works, it will enable the ES to offer a way of filling in the space that now separates the fields of World/Global History, GHS, IPE, and IR, and to expand and enrich the intellectual and empirical space that they share. These fields already overlap and interweave in various ways. The aim is to thicken their ties sufficiently to enable a coherent subject on a larger scale – global society – to come more clearly into view. This is not an invitation to dissolve or merge these approaches in any wholesale way. Each has many strengths of its own and a lot of institutional momentum. Rather the aim is to encourage a joint project among them that will both interest a section of the scholars within each of them, and provide a shared perspective that will benefit all of them.

This is not the first book to venture into this space. Some 'big' historians, such as David Christian (2004) have tried it, and so have some historical sociologists such as Michael Mann (1986), both making path-breaking contributions. Various authors have sought to bridge-build between historical sociology and IR (e.g. Phillips, 2011; Zarakol, 2011; Buzan and Lawson, 2015; Phillips and Sharman, 2015; Spruyt, 2020). World/global historians mostly adopt a comparative civilisations approach (e.g. Harvard University Press's six volume set on *A History of the World*;[21] Goody, 2010; Morris, 2010), as does the classical ES (Wight, 1977; Bull and Watson, 1984; Watson, 1992). Although a few manage to encompass all of human history, most retreat into narrower time frames (e.g. Kennedy, 1989; Bobbitt, 2002; Bayly, 2004; Osterhammel, 2014; Dunne and Reus-Smit, 2017). Those coming from the social sciences usually try to solve the problem of overwhelming detail by seeking big simplifications that somehow embrace all the differences (e.g. Wallerstein, 1979, 2004; Gellner, 1988; Frank, 1990; Frank and Gills, 1993). Mann (1986) is distinctive here in coming from Sociology, but attempting a comprehensive, comparative civilisations approach with all of its detail and complexity.

This book aims to split the difference between detailed historical narrative and over-simplifying grand theories by finding a level of abstraction that, on the one hand, solves the problem of large scale in time and space, while on the other hand offering an approach that is sufficiently fine-grained to sustain a subtle global narrative across a millennial timescale. This approach does not aim at comparative civilisations within eras, but at comparative eras in their own right. It does not offer a theory of global society, or indeed of history, in the sense that it identifies any single causal driver or predictable pattern of events. But I think it is a new way to write world/global history from a theoretical perspective. It provides an analytical framework and conceptual architecture for describing global society, tracking its material and social dynamics, and identifying criteria for differentiating periods of structural stability from times of change and transformation. Given that social dynamics are often sticky, and slow to change, it also offers a limited capability to look ahead.

I see this still very much as English School theory on the grounds that it is rooted in an ES understanding of society, and gives pride of place in its analytical framework to primary institutions. Even the three domains are essentially within the ES conceptual architecture, albeit here more clearly specified, and given a much more central place in the analysis of social structure and dynamics. But it is an enhanced and enriched ES, and I do appreciate that accepting all of this might be too big an ask for some within (and indeed outside) the ES. It is indisputable that while within the conceptual bounds of the ES, this global society approach also transforms it in quite radical ways.

<hr />

[21] www.hup.harvard.edu/collection.php?cpk=1493

The Structure of the Book

Part I contains two chapters, each structured around an era. Chapter 2 looks at the hunter-gatherer era, mainly since the last ice age, up to the onset of widespread settlement and agriculture after 10,000 BC. It also covers the seven millennia transition period to the conglomerate agrarian/pastoralist empire (CAPE) era. Chapter 3 looks at the CAPE era, running from the third millennium BC to 1800 AD. These two eras, and the transition between them, are discussed in terms of how they laid the foundations for the global society that has been the work of humankind since the nineteenth century. Part II contains four chapters that cover the opening of the transition towards the modern era from the late eighteenth century to the present, during which time an intense and highly penetrating global society was put into place. Chapter 4 covers the material transformation. Chapters 5a and 5b look at the changes in social structure. Chapter 6 assesses where we are now in the transition from CAPE to modernity. Part III contains two chapters. Chapter 7 looks at the material conditions going forward into a phase of *deep pluralism* over the next couple of decades. Chapter 8 does the same for social structure. Part IV contains the Conclusion chapter, which sums up the main contributions of the book. It sets out the case not just for the English School, but also for IR, to adopt a global society approach, and use it to build bridges towards GHS and Global/World History.

The general order is thus chronological, but within that, close attention is paid to how each new era incorporates, rejects or adapts the older institutions from the eras that preceded it. In the social realm, as in the material one, the arrival of the new builds on, as much as displaces, what was there before. To visualise this interpretation of eras, lay out a timeline 1 kilometre long, in which 1 metre represents a thousand years, the total therefore covering a million years. Modernity would occupy the last 20 centimetres of it, the CAPE era the next 5 metres, the transition to the CAPE era roughly 7 metres, and the hunter-gatherer era the remaining 987.8 metres.

The general story up to the present is one of rising human empowerment expressed in societies that get ever larger and more complex, albeit with a lot of ups and downs along the way. The overall trend is for the integration of world societies to become deeper and wider, until global scale is reached, at which point the intensification of integration becomes the main story. The general theme and question linking all this together, is how did these different eras contribute to, and build towards, the making of a global society that is planetary in scale, and integrated across all three domains? What material and social technologies did they develop to extend the reach, speed, cost, and depth of transportation and communication (*interaction capacity*). What forms of social glue did they invent that could support the organisation of humankind on an ever-larger scale? What, in other words, did they contribute to the making of globalisation in its fullest sense?

I am fully aware that such an approach seems to place the book firmly on the teleological side of how history is told, thus contradicting my remarks in the previous section about evolution and dialectics not being teleological. But I am also fully aware that global society in a deep sense has not yet been reached, and may not be. The whole story could have come off the rails at many points along the way, and the fact that it didn't, by no means guarantees that it might not still do so in the decades and centuries ahead. If chance and personality had played differently during the Cold War, humankind might have bombed itself into a regression back to the Stone Age, or even to species suicide. This book certainly views the past as leading to the present (Whig history), and has a broad sense of evolution in moving from smaller, less complex and less capable societies, to larger, more complex and more capable ones. But it is not Whig history in the sense of seeing this either as inevitable, or as progress towards some societal and political golden age. In normative terms, the picture is, as shown in the following chapters, highly mixed across the eras.

The dawn of the nuclear era was the first time that humankind possessed the means for rapid species suicide, but before that, natural events could have terminated us in other ways. An unlucky strike on the planet by a large enough space rock could at any time have devastated the human race. As we move forward into modernity, an obliterating war seems less of a threat than during the twentieth century, though it has by no means disappeared. But the extraordinary material and energy resources now at our command could disrupt the globalisation story in an increasingly long list of ways, from climate change and pollution, through mass extinctions within the biosphere, to pandemics and the collapse of political order. It may be that humankind comes off the rails before it achieves a deep form of planetary-scale global society. What I hope to show in the chapters that follow is that despite these risks, and whether by skill or luck, there has nonetheless so far been a powerful momentum towards global society in human history. The empirical observation here is the general proposition that the structure of human society has, with significant ups and downs, tended over the long run to get bigger and more complex. That observation is, of course, an almost unavoidable characteristic of any attempt to explain the present in terms of how the past got us to where we are now. It necessarily discounts the paths that might have been taken by humankind, but which for many contingent reasons were not. Whether or not, and how, humankind might yet achieve something deserving the name of a planetary-scale global society, is an open question, as is what it would look like. Along with the ES, I see global society as largely open and contingent in the longer run. In the shorter run, the social structural approach offered here does give some ability to anticipate whether the direction will be more pluralist or solidarist. Like any evolutionary process, this one can be thrown off course or terminated by events. But that does not mean that we should ignore it as a way of understanding human history.

There are some other obvious problems with this approach. One is about the temporal balance of the book. Part I covers more than twenty-two millennia of human history in two chapters, while Part II takes four chapters to cover less than three centuries. Part III uses two chapters to think about a few decades. Even allowing for the undeniable fact shown by the timeline given above that history has accelerated in an unprecedented way since the nineteenth century, this imbalance smacks of presentism. In my view, a degree of presentism is justified, because it is useful to focus on what the longer history means for where humankind is now. It is also justified, because analysing these last few centuries within the grand framework of eras, is a far from simple task. At this relatively close range in historical time, one has a lot more data and information but a lot less benefit from the wisdom of hindsight. Close range also means that it is harder to see the patterns, and tricky to tell whether the patterns one does see are stable, or ephemeral.

The era of modernity has barely begun. Compared to either of the previous eras, it is characterised by an extraordinary degree of dynamism and change. It is not at all clear how long modernity as an era will last. Using the definitional criteria for era set out above, modernity looks very much like a new era in terms of the changes in material conditions and social structure. But are the times we are in best characterised as modernity in some pure form, or as the transition period out of the CAPE era into modernity? In favour of modernity as an era is the extent and depth of the changes in material and social conditions that differentiate it from the CAPE era. In favour of our times being transitional are both the shortness of time since the change, and the extent to which institutional legacies from the CAPE era are still strongly in play in our 'modern' times. If we are now fully within the modern era, then the transition to it from the CAPE one was extraordinarily short and sharp. If we are not fully in the modern era, then we have to think hard about where the transition we are in is headed. The chapters in Parts II and III pay close attention to these issues.

My whole approach rests on the assumption that social structure matters to how international relations has been, is, or might be, theorised and practised. Those of a materialist disposition, whether simple like neorealists and neoliberals, or complex like Marxists, might well question this assumption. In their perspectives, the realm of international relations might be understood as having particular structural qualities that privilege material factors over social ones. Neorealists and classical economists, for example, treat international relations as a *system*, with all the mechanical implications that term carries. Even for those not ideologically wedded to materialism, the systemic approach has specific appeal for the realm of the international. As Martin Wight (1966: 26) memorably put it, the domestic realm is one where progress is possible, while 'International politics is the realm of recurrence and repetition'. If it is the case that the international realm is marked by extremely weak social and political structures, and consequently generates a high probability of conflict amongst whatever kinds of units compose it, then it might well display a relatively unchanging materialist and mechanical character, having some resemblance to a branch of physics.

My approach is neither mechanical in the simple 'system' sense of neorealists and classical economists, nor in the complex 'mode of production' sense of Marxists. I seek to keep the materialist dimension very much in play as a key part of the story, but without giving it any automatic priority over the social structure as the foundational line of explanation. Thus, the discussions of the three eras all share a similar framing. They open with a general discussion of the material and social conditions that define the era. They then focus more closely on the social structure defined in terms of primary institutions. This scheme takes inspiration from Tainter's (1988: loc. 1548) co-constitutive idea that:

From the simplest familial unit to the most complex regional hierarchy, the institutions and patterned interactions that comprise a human society are dependent on energy. At the same time, the mechanisms by which human groups acquire and distribute basic resources are conditioned by, and integrated within, sociopolitical institutions. Energy flow and sociopolitical organisation are opposite sides of an equation. Neither can exist, in a human group, without the other, nor can either undergo substantial change without altering both the opposite member and the balance of the equation. Energy flow and sociopolitical organisation must evolve in harmony.

My approach, thus, partly aligns with others who analyse history in terms of highly generalised framing assumptions that are assumed to have universal application. Examples include: Lasswell's (1935: 3) understanding of all politics as being about 'who gets what, when and how'; Bull's (1977: 67–71) understanding of all human society as requiring agreements about security against violence, observance of agreements, and rules about property rights; and Waltz's (1979) understanding of all international politics as being driven by the distribution of power. Where it differs from these understandings is in having a much more detailed and open approach to the possibilities of both social and material structures.

Within this broad scheme, each primary institution is examined not only in itself, but also in relation to the others with which it cohabits. Each is also examined as to how it is located within the interpolity, transnational and interhuman domains. In which domain does it have its main roots, and to what extent does it play, or not, into the other domains? This technique is an important tool in being able to see global society not just as primary institutions located in separate domains, but as social structures that connect, and often integrate, the domains into a deeper sense of integrated world/global society. This is a significant departure from ES practice, which has tended to focus mainly on primary institutions in the interstate domain (*international society*). The ES has rather neglected both how those institutions played in the other domains, and what if any primary institutions might have their main roots in the transnational or interhuman domains. Doing this is much facilitated by bringing the economic sector more into play when thinking about international society than the ES has done so far.

Aims

The aim of this book is primarily theoretical. Although there is a lot of empirical material in what follows, none of it is original. All of it will be familiar to those who are experts in the areas covered. The book's contribution lies in the theoretical framings that enable this empirical material to be seen in a new light, and to tell some familiar stories in an unfamiliar way. It fuses together a big empirical story (the history of humankind), and a set of theoretical perspectives mostly derived from the English School. The resulting synthesis generates insights relevant not just to the ES, but also to the wider discipline of IR, including IPE, and beyond that to nearby cognate disciplines, particularly Global Historical Sociology and Global/World History. The aim is to demonstrate both to the ES and these other disciplines, what the analytical apparatus of the English School can do when enhanced and expanded in the way shown here.

For the ES, the main theoretical offerings are:

• To tell the whole story of primary institutions in much more depth and detail than has been done before, and to show how primary institutions cannot be properly understood without seeing them as embedded across the three domains. Primary institutions are not just a phenomenon of the interpolity domain, but also of the transnational and interhuman ones. The three domains are thus a crucial part of the ES theoretical framework. Without them, one cannot see either the full extent or the full meaning of primary institutions.

• On this basis, to drive home the point that the rather stark differentiation between 'international' and 'world' society used by the classical ES has outlived most of its usefulness. It might still have some mileage in staging 'the great society of humankind' as a normative referent. But in structural terms, integrated world society has existed for a very long time. It is true that world society understood as global cosmopolitanism still has only a thin empirical existence. But if understood as including subglobal transnational and identity structures, its empirical existence is rich and long-standing. Understanding that integrated world society across the three domains has been around for a long time is crucial to understanding the shift to global society.

• To demonstrate how, after long neglect, the economic sector can and must be incorporated into the understanding of international and world society. It is crucial to understanding one of the main ways in which the interplay between the interpolity and transnational domains constructs integrated world society.

• To point out that the ES's conceptual framework contains a rather useful theory of the state, or more broadly, of polities, understanding them as secondary institutions that reflect particular combinations of primary ones. Changes in these combinations are an important marker of changes in eras.

For IR/IPE, the main theoretical offerings are:

• To show how the material and social worlds can be brought together in a complementary way that largely makes the distinction between system and society unnecessary. All social systems are societies and all societies are systems. The main question is about how the societal variables (primary institutions) and the systemic material ones (interaction capacity, distribution of wealth and power), interact.

• An additional theory of the state as described above.

• To reinforce the transition to a more Global IR by taking humankind as the object of study. That approach undermines many of the Eurocentric assumptions and perspectives that still blight the discipline. It also bypasses many of the pitfalls of methodological nationalism.

• To re-base the discussion of global governance. Governance, in the sense of extensive participation by non-state/polity actors is not recent, but stretches back a very long way in human history. It is a historical norm that has been hidden by the analytical state-centrism of IR. Global is not recent either. In the planetary sense it has been in operation for half a millennium. In the meaning of integrated world society, it has been in operation for much longer than that. Global society provides a framing that can revive the discussion of global governance on a much sounder and deeper basis.

And for GHS and Global/World History, the main theoretical offerings are:

• An approach to defining historical eras that combines material and social factors in a complementary rather than oppositional fashion.
• To set out a planetary dimension of the material and social worlds that is distinct from the usual understandings of material conditions, and plays a key role in defining eras.
• An additional theory of the state as described above.
• A different way of looking at eras by introducing the idea of transition periods between them that distinguish periods of relative stability in material and social conditions from periods of change and turbulence. This bears on two debates:
  o First, it helps to clarify some of the heated debates about the pre-history era. It does this by separating out as a transition period the several thousand years before the onset of civilisation, during which a warming and stabilising climate enabled settlement and then the development of agriculture.
  o Second, it sets out a quite radical departure in the understanding of both the CAPE era and modernity. The CAPE era is much more stable and uniform in material and social conditions than is usually thought. And modernity did not just jump into being fully fledged during the late eighteenth and early nineteenth centuries. There was, and might still be, a period of transition marked by changes in both material and social conditions. The old gives way to the new, and the new raises a host of contradictions that have to be worked out, both within itself, and in relation to what carries over from the previous era. The idea of transition periods between eras provides a novel perspective on how to interpret developments since the late eighteenth and early nineteenth centuries.

For all of these disciplines, this book aims to show one way of building bridges among them. It opens up the empirical and theoretical space between IR/IPE, Global Historical Sociology, and Global/World History, and offers a way of occupying it that is compatible with all of them. It does not threaten either their identities or their particular skills, methods and perspectives. But for those so inclined, it offers common ground on which they might stand in order better to pursue some of the big questions that they all share. Historians will, I hope, be attracted by the ability to continue to work in a narrative style even if at a higher level of abstraction. Global Historical Sociologists will, I hope, find interest in a more fine-grained level of abstraction that nonetheless retains coherence across eras. Those from IR/IPE who are interested in big picture approaches will, I hope, be attracted to the global society approach for two reasons: first, as a relatively clear way of dealing with the issue of states versus empires as the dominant form of polity; second, as a way of getting a holistic picture of their subject that spans across the three domains in an integrated way.

More grandly, the social sciences and History in particular, and humankind in general, are in pressing need of an Earth System Social Science to act as a companion to the emergence of Earth System Science in the natural sciences. Earth System Science reflects the understanding that the natural and social sciences need to develop an integrated, planetary perspective if they are to address issues like global warming and the sixth great extinction (Steffen et al., 2020). The social sciences and History need to do more to move in the same direction, joining hands with Earth System Science in pursuit of understanding the big picture. I hope this book might act as one further step in that direction.

Part I

Laying the Foundations for Global Society

Introduction to Part I

The two chapters in this section serve as the prelude to the discussion of the transition towards modernity that occupies the bulk of the book. In order to understand modernity, it is necessary to understand the cumulative building of global society over the two eras that preceded it: what each did and did not contribute to the one that followed it. Without understanding the material conditions and social structures of each era, it is not possible to get a clear view of the transitions between them, what got carried forward and what not, and what the changes were. These two eras are, of course, interesting in themselves when viewed in this perspective, but the immediate purpose of analysing them here is to set up the historical flows that led to, and into, the transition towards modernity. A second purpose is to lay the groundwork for the comparative study of eras, though that is only lightly followed-through in this book.

2   Pre-Prelude
The Hunter-Gatherer Era

Introduction

This chapter first surveys the hunter-gatherer era, mainly from the last ice age up to the onset of increasingly widespread settlement and agriculture after 10,000 BC, and then the roughly 7000-year transition from the hunter-gatherer era to the conglomerate agrarian/pastoralist empires (CAPE) one. In total, it therefore covers 994.8 metres of the one-kilometre timeline noted in Chapter 1. It provides a brief look at the deep background of global society, before humankind organised itself into cities and empires. Initially, it is the story of humans organised into small community groups of mostly mobile hunter-gatherers operating across a vast and mostly sparsely populated landscape that was itself subject to many big fluctuations of climate. By comparison with all of the historical human eras that followed it, this one was both unfathomably long, stretching back hundreds of millennia, and rather slow moving, with significant changes to its material and social conditions being few and infrequent. After 10,000 BC, it is a hugely complex and contested transition story in which climate change (warming and stabilisation) enabled settlement, and later agriculture, to play an increasing role in shaping human societies. A major problem for this chapter is the thinness and uncertainty of the evidence underpinning archaeological and anthropological research, and the often hotly contested and frankly ideological ways of interpreting it. As Neumann (2020: 27) nicely puts it: 'possible future finds, possibly false analogies and possible unknowns explain why the words "probably" and "perhaps" tend to litter archaeological texts'. With that in mind, the interpretation given here is necessarily tentative.

Perhaps the most distinctive feature of the hunter-gatherer era in relation to the framing of global society was the fact that its social structure was largely within the interhuman domain, and mainly shaped by kinship: *raison de famille*. At least until the transition period, the dominant mode of differentiation was mainly segmentary (i.e. the units

55

were all similar), with stratification being either low or nearly absent, or happening only in some places but not generally. Functional differentiation was fairly minimal. There was probably little or nothing that could be thought of as transnational or interpolity, though, as shown in Social Structure below, some interpretations speak of war. Neumann (2020: 32–9) defines diplomacy as 'the institutionalised communication between groups', and on that basis sees a kind of diplomacy in the contact and hospitality rituals among hunter-gatherer bands (HGBs). If uneven and combined development operated at all, it was very faint. Unevenness and level of development were both minimal and change was slow. There was some degree of combination inasmuch as technologies did diffuse widely, albeit slowly.

For most of this long era, biological evolution and Darwinian logic were in the driving seat, with improvements to the human species itself, most notably bigger brains, and the ability to talk. By around 30,000 years ago, *Homo sapiens* had replaced the previous variety of hominins that included Neanderthals, Denisovans and several others, though not before interbreeding with them. Along the way, *Homo sapiens* in different regions with different climate conditions, pathogens and food resources evolved different physical and genetic characteristics. During the transition to modernity, these differences, especially skin colour, became the basis for differentiation into races and the hierarchical discriminations of race theory. Overall human numbers remained low, no more than a few million even towards the end of this era. At some point before 50,000 years ago, and possibly much before that, *Homo sapiens* acquired complex language, a hugely significant development but one that is difficult to date accurately. A recent study argues for around 70,000 years ago (Manning, 2020: 36–68), but since almost everything about this remote period is contested, it is difficult to know for sure when and why this happened. Whenever it happened, complex language enabled more sophisticated forms of social evolution, and a greater distancing of humans from both the animal world and other hominins that either did not acquire complex language, or did so less fully. From the inception of language, social evolution became the lead dynamic, with *Homo sapiens* becoming the sole carrier of the human biological legacy.

This kind of social order is far from what the English School was originally designed to analyse.[1] But its toolkit can nevertheless give us both insights and ways of linking and comparing this social form with

---

[1] Indeed, the whole discipline of International Relations (IR) is based on the idea of political units being territorially fixed, and has few tools for dealing with units that are intrinsically mobile.

what came later. The following sections look at the material and social conditions that underpinned and defined the hunter-gatherer lifeway. Finally, this chapter looks at the many changes and developments in human society that took off as the climate warmed and stabilised after 10,000 BC. It concludes by assessing this era in terms of the three domains, and its contribution to the development of global society.

Material Conditions

This era extends far back into the time before *Homo sapiens* became the dominant, and eventually sole, form of human being. During this long era, there were huge fluctuations of climate between ice ages and warmer periods, with consequent dramatic variations in sea level that expanded and contracted the available land. These climatic variations did not really settle into the relatively stable form that has accompanied the rise of civilisations until around 7,000 years ago. The human population lived by hunting and gathering (foraging), and was mostly organised into generally mobile bands of a few dozen people. Land, food and the other material resources that people required (e.g. wood, tool stone, bone, hides), were relatively abundant in relation to the numbers of humans using them. However, although the HGBs themselves were generally small, they were usually connected by quite extensive networks of relations with neighbouring bands that provided trade, breeding opportunities[2] and the possibility of mutual support in hard times. This made them part of a much larger and more geographically extensive social structure (Graeber and Wengrow, 2021: 119–25, 281). Most HGBs were mobile, which is to say that they moved around within an 'estate' that provided them with different sorts of food and shelter according to the season, and with which they identified in significant ways. Such groups might also relocate to another estate in response to climate change, or as part of the various great migrations that peopled the continents.

Until the climate warmed, sites that were productive enough to support a sedentary hunter-gatherer lifeway were probably scarce. Humans had to adapt to the changing climatic conditions, moving to find productive landscapes where they could. Somewhere between 65,000 and 50,000 years ago, *Homo sapiens* made the migration out of Africa into Asia, and eventually Europe and the Americas, learning to adapt to different climates and ecologies as they went. From around 15,000 BC the ice sheets were beginning to melt, making some areas more habitable,

---

[2] Individual HGBs were too small to provide sufficient genetic diversity for sustainable breeding (Mithen, 2003: loc. 2888).

but submerging others under rising seas. From around 10,000 BC, the global climate moved into a relatively stable warming trend, generating richer flora and fauna, which made it possible for some hunter-gatherers to settle in locations that could provide ample quantities and varieties of food year-round. But the winding down of the ice age was a long process, and the climate and sea levels did not stabilise into their current forms until around 5000 BC. Between about 10,000 and 5000 BC, and starting in Mesopotamia (later in other places), this mainly mobile hunter-gatherer lifeway began to be challenged first by more settled communities, and then increasingly by agricultural ones.[3]

A mobile lifeway meant there was little or no attempt to accumulate a surplus. While this lifeway might be described as hand-to-mouth, hunter-gatherers ate what would by later agrarian and modern lifestyles be thought of as an astonishingly wide variety of foods. Mobile hunter-gatherers had an intimate relationship with the land, possessing empirical knowledge of, and holding spiritual ties with, the landscape they harvested: its flora, fauna and some mineral resources. They understood their landscapes well enough to know where foods could be found at all times of year. Periodically, they might meet with other HGBs to share foods that occurred in particular abundance at certain times of the year. Should they run into difficulties feeding themselves from their own estate, they could call on kinship ties with neighbouring HGBs to share resources. When a group outgrew the carrying capacity of its estate, or experienced too much internal friction, it fissioned, with some people splitting off to find a new estate elsewhere. Hunter-gathering was not an efficient way to exploit the potential of the land to support human populations, which, alongside fluctuating climate conditions, is one reason why human numbers never exceeded a few million worldwide during this era. Their small groups, and only occasional encounters with the animals they hunted, largely protected them from the epidemic diseases that would later take a high toll on farmers and city dwellers. Large clusters of humans and animals living together at close quarters provided ideal environments for disease.

However, the HGB relationship with the landscape should not be overly romanticised in environmental terms. The HGB lifeway was not focused around sustainability in the modern sense. For their own welfare and survival, HGBs wanted to sustain the productivity of their estate. Unlike farmers, they did not generally stress the ecosphere by exhausting

---

[3] For overviews of the early interplay of climate change and human societies, see Mithen (2003) and Fagan (1993, 2004).

soils, or polluting the landscape in any systematic way.[4] Yet despite their relatively primitive hunting tools and their small numbers relative to the scale and productivity of the landscape, HGBs were notoriously capable of driving megafauna to extinction, possibly helped by the stresses on such animals of climate change. While the land might have been sacred to them in some senses, HGBs did not simply accept passively what the land had to offer. They had no hesitation in using fire to reshape landscapes in ways that favoured some flora and fauna over others in order to suit their eating preferences. There was a kind of environmental stewardship here, but one that was very local in scope, and as much shaped by a lack of sufficient human numbers or technological capacity to do more damage than by any reverence for keeping nature pristine. Given the natural climate instability during most of this era, it was, indeed, more likely that the environment would put stress on HGBs, forcing them to adapt or relocate if climate change or sea-level rise disrupted their estate.[5] So while HGBs had a close relationship to the landscape, they could and did move on if need be.

As noted, towards the very end of the hunter-gatherer era, a warming climate enabled some HGBs to settle down, living off the productive riches of wetlands or coastal fisheries (Graeber and Wengrow, 2021: 157, 286). Settlement was a momentous move. A sedentary existence allowed both a higher birth rate,[6] and more opportunity to begin tending the local plant resources (i.e. by weeding them, or selecting them, a step towards, but short of, farming). With higher birth rates and fixed locations, sedentism generated not only a sense of territoriality, but also risks both of exhausting the carrying capacity of the local flora and fauna, and of conflict over resource-rich locations.

In more specific terms, the material conditions of hunter-gatherers were quite basic. But they were sufficient not only to give them huge advantages over other animals, but also to enable them to achieve the first globalisation by occupying all of the planet except Antarctica.

In terms of materials, they had wood, stone, animal and vegetable fibres, glue, horn, bone and clay. They also had good knowledge of the

[4] That said, the impressive rubbish heaps left by HGBs have been a major resource for archaeologists!
[5] For details of the more dramatic impacts of climate change on geography, see Mithen (2003).
[6] Mobile HGBs had to spread their children. When they moved, they had to carry everything with them, including children, which limited their capacity to support infants. Without that constraint, sedentary people could, and did, breed faster, which is one reason, along with the higher food productivity of agriculture, why farmers quickly outnumbered hunter-gatherers once the agrarian revolution took hold.

useful properties of many plants, whether for food, fuel, fibre or medicine. For energy, they had mainly their own muscles. They did not domesticate animals other than the dog (Outram, 2014). But they also possessed fire over 200,000 years before *Homo sapiens* came on the scene, and used it not only for warmth and cooking but also to preserve food (by smoking it), process clay, move to colder environments, and reshape local environments to favour the flora and fauna they preferred (Christian, 2004: 194–5, 199; Scott, 2017: 3, 37–42; Parzinger, 2020: 46, 52). In terms of interaction capacity on land, they had no wheels or pack animals, and were entirely reliant on their own two feet. But as evidenced by the migrations into Australia and the Pacific, and down the West coast of the Americas, feet could take you a long way. They also mastered basic water transportation in terms of rafts, canoes and small boats of various kinds, not just on lakes and rivers, but also for coastal navigation and island-hopping (Paine, 2014: ch. 1). In terms of technology, there was little differentiation between civil and military: tools for hunting could be used against other humans if need be. They had a range of efficient tools made from wood, stone, bone and horn, including spears, bows and arrows, digging sticks, axes, clubs and a variety of cutting implements. The making of stone blades and tools improved over the millennia, and the making of distance weapons such as the bow and arrow, the spear-throwing stick (*atlatl*) and the sling date back several tens of thousands of years. They could also make sophisticated sewn clothing to adapt to different environments.

Social Structure

How can we describe the social structure of this pre-transition HGB world in terms of primary institutions? There are three such institutions that look quite firm, and apply across very long periods of time (kinship, trade and human equality), two that are more questionable and with a more restricted application (territoriality and war) and one perhaps best described as a precursor (religion).

Perhaps the most obvious primary institution of this world is *kinship*. The day-to-day social scale was small, mainly constituted by family, household and possibly clan. *Raison de famille* covered most of the social order. As Gellner (1981: 34) nicely puts it, for nomads 'genealogy ... is their only address'.[7] As noted, there were larger networks of occasional contact for breeding, security and trade, and this created widespread and

---

[7] This remark was applied to much later nomadic pastoralists, but works for nomadic hunter-gatherers too.

complex kinship networks, and bonds of obligation, among the bands (Buzan and Little, 2000: 115–33). There were also sometimes extensive, kinship-like forms of clan based on shared animal totems, extending across bands (Graeber and Wengrow, 2021: 279–80). In sociological terms, this was more like a *community* (something natural, evolved, with strong bonds of identity and responsibility) than a *society* (something instrumental, contractual and constructed, with much looser bonds of identity and responsibility). The key point is that kinship defined both local and more extensive social networks.

The significant role of kinship raises interesting questions about social glue. It would be easy to say that kinship is just a form of belief, and in its more extended forms that might be true. Belief would also cover the social glue of shared animal totems. Neumann, Haugevik and Lie (2018: 1, 7–8) argue that in practice kinship is both 'blood and metaphorical', and that it is in some ways 'the default mode of social organization'. But there is room to wonder whether, on the small scale of immediate family, there is a form of social glue that is essentially biological, not dependent on the belief implied by metaphor. The undeniable bonds between parents and children formed by the long dependency of babies and children on their parents and extended families could provide a social glue for small-scale societies that did not need much, if any, coercion, calculation or belief.

The second primary institution was *trade*, which had a very long tradition in prehistoric times. The basic mechanism was not merchants carrying goods from one place to another, for that kind of functional differentiation into specialist jobs did not exist in the HGB world. There were two mechanisms, one local, one long distance. The local one was mainly between neighbouring bands whose estates produced different foodstuffs and materials. That might involve regular trips between the two by delegates to exchange wares.[8] The long-distance one was mainly a system of relay trade, where things were passed down the line between neighbouring peoples, gathering scarcity value and exotic quality as they moved further away from their source. The things traded included quality tool stone, amber, decorative materials and seashells. Such trade could eventually move materials hundreds, even thousands, of kilometres (Mithen, 2003; Coggan, 2020: loc. 351). It is important to note that there were many cultural motives for trade from gift-giving to vision-quests that had little or nothing to do with the market logic of profit (Graeber and Wengrow, 2021: 21–4).

---

[8] This was particularly so in places like the west coast of South America, where steep mountains meant that quite different ecological zones could be located close to each other.

While kinship and trade seem pretty firmly established, the third primary institution of the HGB world, *human equality*, is more difficult to prove. In principle, small, mobile groups with a low division of labour and a subsistence economy should have little room for social stratification and hierarchy, nor for functional differentiation into specialised roles. There was little or no surplus for any would-be elite to expropriate, and the mobile lifestyle did not favour encumbrances of material wealth that would have to be carried around by its possessor. Slavery was uncommon in HGBs (Lerner, 1986: 76) and was probably confined largely to settled HGBs, and almost unknown in mobile ones. The survival of such small groups favoured self-reliance, both individually and collectively, with each person knowing how to do most things. With everyone knowing everyone else well, there was probably little in the way of systematic or permanent leadership or political structure. Should disputes arise, the group could split and the factions each go their own way.

Within that general egalitarianism lies the specific issue of gender relations. That women and men contributed equally to the supply of food, clothing and shelter seems fairly clear. It thus seems plausible that gender relations were quite, if not totally, egalitarian, though the details remain hazy and disputed. Since women had to spend most of their (generally short) adult lives either being pregnant or breastfeeding and taking care of highly dependent children, there necessarily had to be some sexual division of labour. Whether or not this generated a degree of patriarchy is difficult to determine given the scarcity of evidence. It remains a matter of dispute (Manning, 2020: 118). Was fighting amongst males in hunter-gatherer communities about competition for females (Mithen, 2003: locs. 3913–74, 7266–308; Fry and Söderberg, 2013; LeBlanc, 2016: 39–42)? Even if so, HGBs were vastly more gender-egalitarian than either the male-dominated hierarchies of gorillas and chimpanzees in the animal kingdom that preceded them, or what followed in the highly stratified and patriarchal human societies of the CAPE era. There is considerable agreement that systematic male dominance over women probably did not crystallise until the onset of the general stratification of society associated with the formation of the first cities and states (Lerner, 1986; Christian, 2004: 257, 263; Engels, 2010 [1884]). If HGBs had fairly open sexual and extended family relations, that would necessitate matriarchal lineage, since only the mothers would know for sure which were their biological children.[9]

---

[9] Matriarchal lineage does not imply matriarchy, which in such egalitarian societies would be as unlikely as patriarchy. Lerner (1986: 26–35) argues that there is no evidence for prehistoric matriarchal societies. Graeber and Wengrow (2021: 432–40) argue for

Social hierarchy and differentiation seem to increase when mobile lifeways are replaced by sedentary ones, and there certainly was a minority of foragers for whom environmental conditions allowed settlement. How far back such settlement goes is disputed, but sedentary hunter-gathering certainly increased dramatically once the climate began to warm after the ice age. As Graeber and Wengrow (2021: 258) note, the global warming after 10,000 BC was first of all a 'golden age for foragers' within which farming developed later and slowly. Perhaps a reasonable summary of what we know is that up to 10,000 BC settled forager communities were relatively rare because there were few sites that could support year-round occupation with a foraging lifeway. Once the climate began to warm and stabilise, such sites became more plentiful, initiating a substantial increase in sedentary hunter-gatherer communities. It is also possible that foragers could be sedentary for part of the year, and mobile for another (Graeber and Wengrow, 2021: 102–11).

The two more problematic candidates for prehistoric primary institutions are closely linked, because *territoriality* only really arises in any strong sense of exclusive possession once settlement has occurred. It is generally agreed that conflict which might be thought of as *war*, did happen over possession of rich territories (Jones and Allen, 2016: 363–8; LeBlanc, 2016: 30). Since most forager settlement took place only after 10,000 BC, this is mainly a very late development during the transition between the HGB and CAPE eras. Under the conditions of socially connected networks of mobile HGBs in a low-density occupation of vast landscapes, competition over territory was probably not much, if at all, an issue. The meaning of territoriality for mobile HGBs was intimate in a local sense but relatively open in relation to others. Territoriality in an exclusive sense probably crystallised as more and more foragers adopted sedentary lifestyles in the rich territories opened up by global warming.

There is a question about whether 'war' is an appropriate term to describe conflicts between such small groups, and this issue has unfortunately become entangled in the contemporary political question as to whether war is intrinsic to human nature, or a consequence of certain forms of society. Foragers certainly possessed the tools to fight with, and sometimes kill, each other. There is evidence that they did so (Jones and Allen, 2016: 362). But Graeber and Wengrow (2021: 243) argue that

Minoan civilisation as a possible candidate for matriarchy, but if true that falls within the CAPE era.

even by the ninth millennium BC, 'so far, there is only limited evidence for interpersonal violence, let alone warfare'. Whether fighting was about personal feuds, homicides, men squabbling over women or whether there was also an element of organised group conflict between HGBs remains a contested question (Mithen, 2003: locs. 3193–974, 4052, 11195, and chs. 32, 34, 36, 46; Christian, 2004: 242; Fry and Söderberg, 2013; LeBlanc, 2016). Mithen (2003: locs. 3193–974, 4052, 11195, and chs. 32, 34, 36, 46) highlights only four major cases of violent dispute over territory, only one of which, in the Nile valley circa 14,000 BC, falls within this era. The other three are all within the transition period: northern Australia circa 6000 BC, southern Scandinavia circa 5000 BC, and the Pacific Northwest in North America (no earlier than 6000 BC because the salmon runs did not begin until then, but certainly by 500 BC).

The sixth institution is religion, though that is perhaps not quite the right term, which is why I call it a precursor. The spiritual dimension of the hunter-gatherer lifeway might best be thought of as a kind of proto-religion, a forerunner of the more formal religions that developed during the CAPE era. Such evidence as we have suggests strongly that hunter-gatherer societies developed the idea of a spiritual plane of existence in interaction with the day-to-day world. They therefore had religion in the sense of 'another world to live in'. From at least 40,000 years ago, *Homo sapiens* buried their dead accompanied with various kinds of grave goods (Parzinger, 2020: 51). This suggests notions of an afterlife, and continuity between the living and the dead in a spirit world. That world could be accessed by shamans using trances and/or herbal drugs (Mithen, 2003: locs. 419, 2916, 2933, 3049; Gehrke, 2020a: 34–5), and could also contain other spirits associated with the land and its flora and fauna. The spiritualist 'religions' of hunter-gatherers were individualistic, egalitarian and local, and lacking in gods and hierarchies (Christian, 2004: 189, 287). If it is true that the social structure of religion follows that of the society that invents it, then it is no surprise that like early hunter-gatherer societies themselves, their spirit world was quite egalitarian.

The Long Transition from Hunter-Gathering to Conglomerate Agrarian/Pastoralist Empires

As noted, from around 10,000 BC, a warming climate improved the productivity of the landscape. Some places – notably the extensive wetlands where the Tigris and Euphrates met the Persian Gulf, but also where there were rich coastal fisheries – allowed the proliferation of

settled HGBs that did not need mobility in order to find their living.[10]
The shift from nomadic to sedentary foraging lifeways was momentous.
It preceded agriculture, while at the same time facilitating its development. As agriculture developed, it reinforced sedentary lifeways, generating seven millennia during which a great variety of human societies
developed, some varying seasonally between sedentary and mobile living,
and many combining agriculture and/or pastoralism with foraging.

Graeber and Wengrow (2021) argue that settled communities
developed a wide variety of social and political forms, some more egalitarian, some more hierarchical. They deny any hard and fast linkage
between either size in general, or agriculture, and hierarchy, arguing that
farmers could and did develop communal forms of self-government on a
considerable scale to deal with issues such as the creation and maintenance of irrigation works. The functional link to hierarchy is perhaps
stronger for pastoral and warrior communities. Settled living increased
the birth rate, which both raised the density of population in a given area,
and put more strain on the sustainability of wild food resources in the
locality. Over many millennia, it facilitated a broad, but by no means
universal, shift from foraging to farming and herding. Some foragers
resisted the shift to farming even when they knew about it. Farming
meant planting and tending selected crops; herding meant corralling
and owning flocks and herds rather than chasing or ambushing them.
Although both were harder work than hunting and gathering, they
expanded the size (though also narrowing the variety) of the food supply.
Tending wild plants easily turned into selecting and sowing them, and
herding meant that animals could be domesticated and bred, and the
herd owned and protected.

Both settlement and farming strengthened the sense of territoriality
and property. Settled foragers had to defend the rich site that nourished
them. Farming meant investment in the land, and the accumulation of
riches. The vagaries of weather, pests and suchlike to which farming was
prone, meant that it was prudent to accumulate a food surplus in good
years to tide the population over during lean ones. This in turn provided
other opportunities. One was for warrior raiders to make a parasitic living
by stealing the accumulated food and wealth of farmers, creating a need
for defence. That scenario remained so durable that it was the subject of
Kurosawa's famous film *The Seven Samurai*, and its equally famous
Hollywood remake, *The Magnificent Seven*. Another opportunity was

---

[10] The general sources for this discussion of the transition period are Fagan (1993, 2004),
Christian (2004), Mithen (2003), Morris (2010), Scott (2017), Manning (2020),
Parzinger (2020: 58–148), Graeber and Wengrow (2021).

for social stratification, and the emergence of elites who controlled and appropriated the surplus production. Although farmers could also be herders, space opened up, particularly in Eurasia, for nomadic pastoralism to become a distinct lifeway adapted to the steppe lands. The mobile lifeway of the steppe supported superior warrior skills that increasingly made the steppe pastoralists the prime predatory threat to sedentary agrarian populations.

This transition was slow, stretching over the seven thousand years between 10,000 BC and the rise of empires in the third millennium BC. According to their local circumstances, people could combine degrees of farming and herding, with continued hunter-gathering, and many did so. As the agrarian revolution spread, hunting steadily shrank to being the vestigial sport of a small aristocratic elite, who set aside the land necessary to sustain it for themselves. Eventually, only farming could support the increased human numbers, and over time, farmers out-bred hunter-gatherers until they became the bulk of the human population. This process was not always smooth. Early farmers had to learn from scratch the art of conserving the productivity of the land. When they failed to do so, they exhausted the soil, or allowed it to become salinated, which could cause local collapse, and either emigration, or reversion to hunter-gathering by a reduced population. And although the climate during this transition was relatively stable compared to before 10,000 BC, it was not totally so. Variations could increase or decrease productivity as the climate in some place either warmed or cooled, or became drier or wetter.

This transition emerged first in Mesopotamia and Egypt, where by 5000 BC the ease of farming on rich, and annually replenished, alluvial soils, meant that farmers and pastoralists had become dominant. It then unfolded independently in many places at different times, and involving different flora (e.g. wheat, millet, barley, rice, maize) and fauna (e.g. cattle, sheep, goats, horses, camels, elephants, llamas). The main grain crops and animals that became the foundations for the CAPE era were domesticated between 8000 and 2500 BC. Unlike the basic self-sufficiency of hunter-gathering, farming and herding were quite specialised operations. This drift towards increasing functional differentiation was intensified by the manufacture of pottery, and by the development of a metals industry. Metals required a spread of specialised skills: prospecting, mining, smelting, producing charcoal, making end products, and distribution (Parzinger, 2020: 149, 205, 237). As farmers focused on producing larger quantities of fewer things, aiming for surplus rather than sufficiency, and as potters and metal-workers generated new goods, both the need and the capacity for trade increased, as did the opportunities for other kinds of functional specialisation (blacksmiths, merchants, artisans). This was particularly so in Mesopotamia and Egypt, where the productive alluvial farmland was far removed from the supplies of wood, stone, metals, and animals that were needed to create a balanced lifestyle. More trade, and rising populations, meant that villages, towns, and by the fourth millennium BC, cities, crystallised as nodes for wealth, trade, religion and defence. As these concentrations of population became bigger and wealthier, they also became more hierarchical, paving the way for the social structures and political formations of the CAPE era.[11] Nightingale (2022: 24) nicely characterises cities as 'energized crowding'. He goes on to argue that they were, and still are, central to the whole story of human empowerment, from being storehouses of knowledge and innovation, to being the central nodes for trade and empire. As Graeber and Wengrow (2021: 284) observe: 'Wherever cities emerged, they defined a new phase of world history.'

Conclusions

The forager pattern of material and social conditions and social institutions constituted the oldest, and by far the longest, human lifeway. Its key benchmarks are difficult to pin down to specific dates, because new evidence is arising all the time that teñds to push dates back. But whatever the actual dates are, benchmark developments would include the domestication of fire (perhaps 400,000 years ago), the emergence of *Homo sapiens* (perhaps 300,000 years ago), the emergence of complex language (perhaps 70,000 years ago), and the making of cave paintings perhaps (50,000 years ago). With the onset of agriculture, and the slow shift from what Gehrke (2020a: 21) calls an 'acquiring' to a 'production' lifestyle, starting around 10,000 BC, a radically different human lifeway, mainly sedentary, more territorial, more differentiated, more hierarchical, and with a much higher birth rate, took over. This new lifeway eventually pushed hunter-gathering to the margins of human existence, and is the subject of Chapter 3.

   In terms of the framing of global society within three domains, it is easy to see that during this very long era, human society operated almost entirely within the interhuman domain. Except for the last few millennia, when settlement had begun, the basic social glue of this era was kinship,

---

[11] Some early towns remained egalitarian, as shown by their buildings all being of the same type. Stratification and functional differentiation are revealed when the architecture begins to include temples, palaces, bastions, merchant and artisan quarters, and suchlike (Parzinger, 2020: 155–60).

which provided the main ordering principle and form of identity, and generated a sense of community sufficient to order relations within and between forager communities. These standout features are by themselves a useful way of showing how different it was from the era that followed it. Social relationships were generally egalitarian, and probably so also between men and women.

The interpolity domain was, compared with later eras, effectively empty until the last couple of millennia before the rise of empires. Given the small numbers of human beings, their mainly thin, and mostly mobile, occupation of a vast landscape, and their low levels of stratification and functional differentiation, there is almost nothing that belongs to it. Small scale and mobility made it much more amenable to social structuring around kinship and community in the interhuman domain, which were sufficient to give order and direction without formal politics. Kinship, as Gehrke (2020a: 25) notes, could do a lot, extending 'lineage communities' far beyond face-to-face contact. Christian (2004: 245. See also Scheidel, 2017: locs. 872–918, 1001–12) puts a lot of emphasis on this point, arguing that:

most of human history ... has taken place in communities quite innocent of state power. Even in the villages of the early agrarian era, for most people, most of the time, the important relationships were personal, local, and fairly egalitarian. Most households were self-sufficient, and people dealt with each other as people rather than as the representatives of institutions.

Relatedly, for most of this era there was little or no activity that could be described as military in the sense of an interplay between the organised, armed offensive and defensive capabilities of polities. Since for nomadic foragers, territory was plentiful, material possessions a burden and slavery rarely practised, there was little for communities to fight over in an organised way. Mobile HGBs were too small to support anything like an army, and there was insufficient differentiation within them into specialised roles such as warrior. This began to change during the transition period, when some foragers took advantage of the warming climate to settle down and occupy specific rich territories. When that happened, the taking of slaves, and fighting between bands over control of such territory, became more common practices, and the transition to the CAPE era, with its well-developed interpolity domain, was underway.

Neither did the hunter-gatherer era generate anything significant in the transnational domain. While one can usefully and plausibly identify primary institutions operating during this era, secondary institutions are absent. Neither religion, which was fairly local, nor long-distance trade, which was relay, generated the kinds of secondary institutions that developed during the CAPE era. The economics of the HGB lifeway were mainly about self-reliance and subsistence. Local trade was done face-to-face, swapping produce with neighbours whose estate produced different kinds of food or other materials. This lifeway had neither the capacity nor the need to develop secondary institutions.

What, then, does this long pre-prelude contribute to this book's core theme of the evolution of global society? Clearly there was nothing like a global-scale society at any point during this era. Human numbers were too few, the landscape too vast, and interaction capacity much too low to make anything of that sort possible. As noted above, we are looking here at a social structure located primarily in the interhuman domain. Prehistoric times were marked by small kinship communities loosely tied into local networks, but out of touch with distant human communities across the wider world, and possessing nothing like transnational or state/empire actors. Despite this, the hunter-gatherer era nevertheless made three, and possibly four, big contributions towards the later development of global society.

First, and most obviously, it was HGBs that took *Homo sapiens* out of Africa to populate all of the continents except Antarctica. This provided the necessary condition for global society: that humankind occupied the planet. In that process, *Homo sapiens* adapted to a range of environments from tropical, through temperate, to arctic, and differentiated into various cultures. It also became a single dominant species as *Homo sapiens* became the sole surviving variety of hominin.

Second, and perhaps less obviously, hunter-gatherers developed an elaborate understanding of kinship, and used it to construct communal social structures bigger than the immediate family or household. A certain amount of kinship recognition can be found in the animal world, and this makes eminent sense given the need to avoid the dangers of inbreeding. But this seems to be largely confined to the immediate group, and does not generate any wider social structure. Mobile HGBs, by contrast, generated wide-ranging systems of kinship, and interbreeding, that both avoided inbreeding and provided kinship ties capable of supporting mutual aid between HGBs related in this way. The acquisition of language was perhaps a necessary condition for this development. Although, from a contemporary perspective, the use of kinship ties might seem a very limited sort of social structure, it was a crucial first breakthrough towards the making of wider human societies. And as I will show, kinship remained a durable and influential feature of the bigger, more differentiated and more elaborate, human societies that followed on from foragers. It might also be argued that this era's contribution to the making of religion grew out of its development of a deep commitment to kinship, even beyond the grave.

Third, HGBs developed trade over both short and long distances as a regular and desirable feature of human existence. Right from the beginning, trade has always been the largest-scale human activity, out-distancing political and social structures. That said, trade was seldom necessary to the survival of HGBs. The hunter-gatherer lifeway was largely self-reliant in the staples of life. What long-distance trade mainly provided, was either exotic goods such as amber, shells, feathers and decorative materials such as ochre, or things superior to what was locally available, such as high-quality tool stone. Long-distance trade was mainly of the relay kind, but it laid down trading routes that later played a role in the founding of towns and cities.

A possible, but much more contested, fourth contribution is that mobile, and sometimes settled, foragers developed relatively egalitarian communities in which slavery, patriarchy, and hierarchy generally, were either unknown, or by later standards very marginal features. This practice was increasingly abandoned in the run-up to the CAPE era, as both sedentary, agrarian societies and nomadic pastoralist ones, became more hierarchical. Whether egalitarianism can only work on a small-scale community basis with strong kinship ties, remains contested. Social egalitarianism has nevertheless remained an enduring idea(l) in human society, and the idea that a formula for combining it with large social scale and complexity might yet be found is still active in global society.

3 Prelude
The Era of Conglomerate Agrarian/Pastoralist Empires
2310 BC to 1800 AD

Introduction

This chapter looks at the conglomerate agrarian/pastoralist empires (CAPE) era, from the third millennium BC to 1800 AD. It covers about 5 metres of the one-kilometre timeline proposed in Chapter 1. It sets out a longer look at the first emergence and development of human societies that were much more populous and complex, and much more stratified and unequal, than those that preceded them. Whereas hunter-gatherer society was almost entirely in the interhuman domain, the CAPE era fleshed out the full spectrum, adding in the transnational (merchants, religions) and interpolity (cities, kingdoms, warlords, empires) domains. The political economy of this era rested on a fundamental shift from hunter-gathering (both nomadic and sedentary) to agriculture (sedentary farms, towns and cities) and pastoralism (nomadic herding). These were much more productive uses of the land than foraging, and were able to support larger populations. That the timing of this shift is closely associated with the warming and stabilisation of the climate looks causal more than coincidental. As shown in the previous chapter, this benign climate change enabled both settlement, and the rise of agriculture and pastoralism. This in turn allowed the scale of political, social and economic structures to expand dramatically. Two forms of society emerged that were strongly differentiated from, and deeply intertwined with, each other: sedentary agrarianism (aka 'classical civilisation'[1]), and nomadic

[1] 'Civilisation' is a complicated concept. I use it in this book in two general senses. First, and most basically, civilisation differentiates centralised urban cultures, with their typically concentrated populations and complex social forms (stratification and functional differentiation), from non-urban ones (e.g. hunter-gatherers, nomadic pastoralists) with their generally smaller, more dispersed, populations and lower levels of stratification and functional differentiation. Second, I differentiate among civilisations in the conventional way exemplified by Toynbee (1972) where cultural variations, particularly religion, but sometimes also language and ethnicity, support a large-scale identity that does not have to be politically centralised. Thus, Western, Christian, Islamic, Hindu, Confucian, Inca civilisations and suchlike. This second usage can be quite loose,

pastoralism (widely identified by sedentary, agrarian peoples as 'barbarians'). Almost up to its end, this era was defined by the interplay between these two forms of society, which was both collaborative (trade) and conflictual (raiding, war, conquest). The sedentary societies were generally much more populous, wealthier and more sophisticated, and the nomadic ones militarily stronger, and highly mobile across the land. They shared some cultural attributes (luxury goods, slavery, monarchy/ dynasticism, sometimes religion) but often viewed each other with contempt, and kept some significant cultural differentiations (e.g. adoption or not of writing). Both types of society generated dynastic conglomerate empires, which became the characteristic political form of the era, often in fusions between the two in which nomad dynasties ruled agrarian peoples.

In terms of UCD, the CAPE era displayed more unevenness (agrarian, pastoral, hunter-gatherer) but nothing like that which leapt up at the beginning of the transition towards modernity. The range, speed and intensity of combination increased substantially in the form of trade, war, conquest, and transfer of technology between nomadic pastoralists and sedentary agrarians. But their different economic foundations limited the amount of convergence between them. Foragers might get drawn or pushed into either pastoral or agrarian lifeways, but for nearly all of this era, pastoralists and agrarians retained their distinct forms of political economy. The level of development was moderate and generally changed slowly, albeit with occasional big breakthroughs in the material side of things: wheels, sailing ships, hard metals, glass.

The era of HGBs was marked by 'extensification', the slow but steady spread of humankind around the planet in small and mostly mobile forager groups (Christian, 2004: 190–3, 207; Manning, 2020: 68–82, 92–105). This process was largely complete by 13,000 BC. The signature of the CAPE era was 'intensification', marked by increasing human numbers, larger and more complex social and political organisations, and a more marked impact on the planetary environment. Unlike the hunter-gatherers, the CAPE era population lived in a period of relatively stable climate and sea-level conditions that enabled humankind to extend and intensify its occupation of the planet. This growing population, organised itself into much larger, and more centralised and stratified polities, characteristically empires, which frequently resorted to war over the control of people, territory and resources. The shift to farming,

---

allowing, for example, Arab and Persian Civilisation within Islamic, and Chinese within Confucian. But it is convenient for indicating larger-scale cultural and identity patterns, such as the multiple centres of civilisation within Eurasia.

and the consequent rise to a much larger human population, made a much bigger impact on the environment than any previous human activity. Farming transformed huge swathes of the landscape from natural to artificial. It favoured the multiplication of a few selected species of plants and animals, and to the increasing extent that it involved deforestation, it increased the CO_2 content of the atmosphere, and supported global warming. Substantial deforestation occurred in pursuit of human activities such as iron-smelting (Parzinger, 2020: 237), and shipbuilding (notably in thirteenth-century AD China. Paine, 2014: locs. 7291–306). CAPE societies had the power to deplete and salinate soils on a significant scale, though they also eventually learned how to maintain soil fertility. But like foragers, CAPE societies had little or no awareness of their wider environmental impact, and saw environmental changes or catastrophes as mainly a matter of fate or the whims of their gods. The environment was seen as limitless, and there to be expropriated and exploited.

The CAPE era rested on a distinctive set of material and social conditions that endured for 5000 years, right up to the end of eighteenth century AD. This is not to imply that there was no development during this era. There was a general increase in human empowerment, some of it pretty impressive. The human population expanded from fewer than five million around 10,000 BC; to between 200 and 300 million in the year 0; and to one billion by the end of the eighteenth century AD. This expansion was supported by improving knowledge about the domestication and breeding of plants and animals, which made agriculture more efficient, and much more widespread. Shipbuilding and navigation technology improved hugely, enabling not only larger and deeper trading systems, but also the construction of maritime empires, both at the end reaching global scale. Military technology became increasingly differentiated from civil, although there was still some overlap: If you could make a metal scythe you could make a sword. Yet all of this was accomplished within a set of basic material and social conditions that once set, remained relatively stable, displaying incremental, but not transformational or transcendent improvements. The ships at the end of this era were still, like those at the beginning, built of wood and powered by human muscle and wind. Monarchical/dynastic agrarian/pastoralist empires were the dominant polity throughout. The rising population was welcome because it increased the supply of labour for civil and military purposes. While dramatic, and sufficiently large to create sometimes severe local pressures on land and resources, this increase in human numbers did not come close to filling up the planet or challenging its overall carrying capacity.

The rising population fed by agrarian production meant that there was a general increase in the scale of human societies and networks. Larger numbers of people clustered together in towns and cities. These became both more numerous and bigger, and were themselves enmeshed in wider and deeper networks of connection in the form of city-states, city-state systems, empires and long-distance trading networks. Not until near the end of this era did the scale of these networks and connections become global, so this was a world with several 'worlds' that were either thinly and loosely connected (China and Europe), or not connected in any direct and sustained way at all (both China and Europe in relation to the Americas and Australia). There was no global-scale society until the very end of the era. These physical processes of concentration and connection both underpinned and were supported by a shift from a predominantly small, local, egalitarian, community-based organisation of people mainly based on kinship and subsistence hunter-gathering, towards larger, and almost always steeply hierarchical, societies, based on agrarian and pastoralist economies, in which politics, power, violence and inequality were prominent features. These larger-scale polities were notable for both their high degree of status stratification (from emperors and kings, down through local governors and subjects, to slaves), and their significant degree of functional differentiation (warriors, priests, administrators, artisans, farmers, mariners, servants, merchants). The depth and sophistication of their functional differentiation is often hidden behind their extravagant stratification. It can be grasped by thinking about how many specialised skills, and their coordination, were necessary to realise typical CAPE projects from building monumental architecture, ports, cities, and large ships, to staging vast pageants. Such functional differentiation began to develop in the transition to the CAPE era, when peoples not yet defined by cities could nonetheless build monumental stone circles using material from distant sites.

Alongside, and sometimes integrated with these polities, new, powerful and larger-scale forms of identity and community also emerged, mainly in the form of religions. During this era, there was a close bundling of political and military actors and institutions, and often of both with religious and economic ones as well. Traders could also be raiders; warlords often became emperors; armies mostly had personal loyalties to their leaders; kings might well lead their armies directly into battle; kings could be gods; the state could have trade monopolies; and temples could serve as centres for both agricultural production and trade. War and organised violence were the norm in both domestic and international politics, though the ability to make a clear separation between domestic and international was much more problematic than it became in modern times. CAPE empires did not generally have hard borders. With some exceptions for piracy and slave revolts, the successful use of force generally gave legitimate right of ownership over people, property and territory. This was a world made by emperors, armies, merchants and monks pushing empires and trade networks ever wider, and administrators pushing trade and empire and taxation ever deeper. What the warriors won, administrators, record keepers and tax officials tried to consolidate.

The central political feature of this era was conglomerate empires, a highly flexible form. Such political constructs could be short- or long-lived. Their boundaries were more fuzzy frontiers than hard lines, and even these were in a more or less permanent state of flux. CAPE empires expanded and contracted both in response to internal developments (weakening or strengthening of the imperial core) and external ones (rival empires or sometimes migrating peoples). It was generally the degree of authority of the imperial core that weakened or strengthened, rather than a clear moving of a hard border. This loose, decentralised, structure enabled both quick enlargement and quick disintegration. There was usually a large separation of leaders from the peoples they ruled. Such polities were mainly interested in extracting taxes, and sometimes specific resources, and in maintaining the peace. From the Persians and Rome, through China and the Mughals, to the Spanish, French, British and other European empires before 1800, each part of an empire usually had its own deal with the imperial core, and those deals often left considerable power in the hands of local elites. A Lieven (2022: 168) puts it:

As in almost all empires, battles over the succession were the likeliest cause of implosion. If the centre weakened, then all the centrifugal tendencies inherent in pre-modern empire would be unleashed. Warlords would surface in every region. Provincial governors would use their household troops and provincial networks to set themselves up as hereditary monarchs.

Agrarian empires did not generally exercise strong cultural homogenising effects on the parts that composed them, being more concerned about extracting resources for the centre without incurring major administrative or repressive costs to do so. New provinces could be added by a mix of military conquest, dynastic marriage politics, and political co-option. But if the centre weakened, then the parts could easily spin off towards independence. Many of the political and historical commentaries written during this period are strongly focused on the problem of how to hold such loose, conglomerate, constructs together, particularly in the face of weak or contested leadership as generated by dynastic cycles (e.g. Mulk, 2002 [written late eleventh century AD]; Khaldun, 1969 [1370]). Tainter (1988) sets out a similar view of the rise and fall of premodern empires, albeit with the emphasis on the economic logic of diminishing returns to expansion eventually undermining the capability and legitimacy of imperial rule. He notes that collapse in the CAPE era was simply a reversion to a lower level of social complexity, and since most people in CAP empires could fairly easily revert to more local, or subsistence, forms of economy, such collapses might well not have been a bad thing for the bulk of the population concerned (Tainter, 1988: locs. 3060–80). Empires mainly enriched elites. The mass of the people saw little or no improvement in their standard of living during this era because expanding population quickly ate up any increase in production (Galor, 2022). Some cultures, such as the Greeks, made language part of their civilisational identity. But some did not. On the steppe, neither language differences nor their associated ethnicities (Aryan, Turkic, Mongol) played strongly in the formation of steppe empires: shared steppe culture generally overrode ethnicity (Neumann and Wigen, 2018; Parzinger, 2020: 354).

In Eurasia and parts of Africa, this form of empire divided into sedentary agrarian ones, which could be long-lasting, and nomadic pastoralist ones, which tended to be short-lived. But because of their warrior skills, better weapons technology, and toughness, nomad empires were generally militarily superior. Nomad elites were so successful militarily, that they often became the ruling elites of sedentary empires (e.g. Yuan and Qing dynasties in China; the Arab Umayyad and Abbasid dynasties in the Islamic world; and various mainly Turkic rulers – Mamluks in Egypt, Ottomans in the eastern Mediterranean, Mughals in India). In so doing, nomadic elites risked losing their nomadic edge, and themselves being overthrown. So while steppe and sedentary were rivals, they were also closely intertwined, and interdependent, and for most of this era neither could eliminate the other. There were certainly many military rivalries on the steppe amongst rival warlords. There were also many rivalries between sedentary empires (Athens and Sparta, Rome and Carthage, Rome and Parthia, Byzantium and Persia, Ottomans and Persia, etc.). But arguably the central military-political-economic dynamic of steppe and sedentary was the main defining feature of Eurasian and North African history for nearly all of this era in terms of war, trade, and the making and breaking of empires.[2]

---

[2] General sources on the political economy of the CAPE era include: Mann (1986); McNeill (1991); Braudel (1994 [1987]); Christian (2004), Findlay and O'Rourke

The next section examines the material conditions that underpinned and defined the agrarian/pastoralist lifeways. The third section looks at the primary institutions that defined these lifeways. What was carried over from the previous era, and what was new? How did this suite of social institutions support and/or contradict each other? The conclusions assess the nature and balance of the CAPE era in terms of the three domains.

Material Conditions

The CAPE era carried forward the material repertoire of the HGB era in terms of materials, energy and interaction capacity, both improving it, and making a number of important additions. It added a lot in the way of technology, both military and civilian.

Materials

In terms of materials, the peoples of the CAPE era continued to use the basic set of working materials employed by HGBs (wood, stone, horn, bone, clay, and natural fibres, both animal and plant), and did so in larger quantities and in more sophisticated ways. CAPE societies retained some of the HGB knowledge of foodstuffs, and probably most of the knowledge of herbal remedies. They probably lost some of the range of local knowledge about plants, but as trading networks stretched further out, they discovered a wider range of foreign foodstuffs and materials. Their main addition to working materials was a fairly small selection of minerals that could be processed by more sophisticated use of fire. Hunter-gatherers already used fired clay in a fairly crude way, and during the CAPE era, more sophisticated kilns and furnaces transformed this into mass-produced pottery and fine ceramics (Mithen, 2003: locs. 9237–413). These same kilns eventually reached temperatures of 1000 degrees centigrade that could be used to process some metals. Metals were the key material addition because they could be cast or beaten into hard and durable tools and weapons that could be mass produced. Metal replaced stone for blades of all kinds, hammers, axes, scrapers, spearpoints and arrowheads. They opened up new possibilities not

(2007); Burbank and Cooper (2010); Paine (2014); Kennedy (2016); Scheidel (2017); Scott (2017); Neumann and Wigen (2018); Gehrke (2020b). Sub-Saharan Africa, the Americas and Australia lacked the rideable animals that underpinned much of this Eurasian dynamic. In the Americas, the European introduction of the horse briefly created nomad warriors during the last few centuries of the era (Hamalainen, 2019).

available with stone such as armour, swords, nails, spikes, construction materials, bells and eventually guns. Copper came into use somewhat before the first empires, but was a bit soft for tools and weapons. So too did lead, which the Romans made extensive use of for waterproofing and plumbing. Gold and silver were likewise too soft for tools and weapons, but good for jewellery, decoration and coinage. Mixing copper with tin or arsenic to make bronze, produced a much harder metal, and that breakthrough coincided with the beginnings of empire in Eurasia.[3] Later, from circa 1200 BC, the use of iron and steel (iron plus carbon) became widespread once the temperature of fire could be raised to around 1500 degrees centigrade by intensifying the air flow. Higher temperatures also enabled the processing of glass on an industrial scale (Whitehouse, 2012: 10–40; Radner, 2020: 404–6). Since iron was more widespread than copper, and even more so tin, which was rare, its coming into use lowered the price of metal products, making them more available across society.

This CAPE suite of basic materials remained more or less unchanged until nineteenth century AD. As with ships, Song dynasty Chinese porcelain was hugely more refined than the primitive clay pots of earlier times, but it was still basically the same material made in the same way. Iron replaced bronze for most functions, but bronze was still favoured for some precision instruments, bells, and for guns and cannons. Slow, and generally incremental improvement in many technologies was the order of the day, with occasional breakthroughs like bronze, iron, and, much later, gunpowder. Not until the sixteenth century were the British able to make cast iron of good enough quality to safely replace bronze for cannons (McNeill, 1982: 86; Van Creveld, 1991: 125–36; Headrick, 2010: 92).

Energy

In terms of energy resources, the peoples of the CAPE era continued to exploit those of the HGB era – fire and human muscle power – and added to them wind, water and animal muscle power. They made much more sophisticated use of fire to process minerals, and heat living spaces, but did not improve much on the sources of fuel, which remained limited to what could be harvested (wood, plant fibres, dried dung). Use of fossil fuels (peat, coal) was small and not widespread. Human muscle power

[3] Hard metals were not a necessary condition for empire. None of the empires that emerged in the Americas possessed them, though as the famous title of Jared Diamond's (1997) book – *Guns, Germs and Steel* – suggests, it left those empires vulnerable when they encountered alien civilisations that did have hard metals.

remained what it was for the hunter-gatherers, but it was organised differently, most obviously by the use of large-scale patriarchy and slavery in most CAPE societies. More on this is discussed in the following text. The use of domesticated animals as a source of power was one of the two big changes in access to energy sources that marked the CAPE era. Domesticated animals could be used for various kinds of traction work (pulling ploughs, wagons, carriages and chariots; turning millstones and winches), as well as carrying both people and goods on their backs. Big animals were a lot stronger than humans, and domestication made them available to all Eurasian CAPE societies in large numbers.[4] Animal power was, however, limited to fairly basic tasks. Animals could not be trained to dig mines, row ships, harvest crops, or act as domestic servants. For more elaborate and skilled forms of work, only human muscle power was available. The increased use of animal power began early, during the transition from foraging to farming and pastoralism, and was therefore part of the process out of which empires emerged.

The other big change was the use of wind energy, and the main application was to sailing ships. Sailing ships perhaps developed first on the Nile, where south-blowing winds could be used to counter the north-flowing current of the river. Sailing ships were thus integral to the economic and political viability of the early empires in Egypt. They became the foundation for much of the bulk trade, and some of the military activity (mainly as troop transports), of the CAPE era. Wind provided free fuel capable of supporting voyages over long distances. The only other way of powering ships over open water was by rowing or paddling, but this required large crews and had limited range. Rowed ships were good for fighting, but less suitable for trade. There was little or no use of animal power to drive ships in open water.[5] About two millennia ago, wind was also used to power mills and pumps. Water-powered mills also came into use around the same time. Compared with the impact of animal power and sailing, however, these additional energy sources were relatively marginal for most of this era. Coggan (2020: loc. 669) suggests that perhaps only 1 per cent of mechanical power in

---

[4] Due to the dying off of the megafauna associated with human occupation of the Americas, there was nothing larger than the rather slight llama and alpaca to be domesticated. These had some use as light pack animals, but could not be ridden by adult humans.
[5] Both animal and human muscle power could be and were used to tow ships on rivers and canals. Animals could in principle be used to power paddle-wheel ships, and the Romans at least thought about doing so. The Chinese actually built a lot of paddle-wheel ships during the latter part of the first millennium AD. It is not clear whether these were driven by human or animal muscle power, though the latter would pose the problem of panic in combat conditions.

the Roman Empire came from watermills. They became more important in particular places towards the end of this era, as for example in the Dutch use of windmills to pump water from reclaimed land, and the British use of watermills to power factories in the eighteenth century.

Although the CAPE era was energy-rich when compared with hunter-gatherers, from a modern perspective it looks very energy-poor and constrained. Industrial production requiring heat was limited by dependence on harvestable fuel sources. And given the shortage of fungible energy sources, and therefore continued dependence on human muscle power, it is probably no accident that all of the high urban cultures, and many of the smaller and less elaborate tribal ones, depended on slavery or other forms of command labour to maintain themselves. Both Athenian democracy and Spartan militarism were based on slave labour, and perhaps one-third of the population of Rome were slaves. The Islamic world had a particularly elaborate system of slavery. As Risso (1995: 15–16) notes: 'A characteristic of the Abbasid era – and long after it as well – was slavery, notably military but also domestic, sexual and agricultural.' The Islamic world used African slaves mainly for agricultural and domestic labour, and Turkic, Caucasian and Eastern European ones as slave soldiers. The taking and usage of slaves is a significant topic within a noted eighth-century Islamic treatise on the law of nations (Khadduri, 1966). The US was a slave society until the end of the civil war in 1865. In CAPE societies, the slave trade could perhaps be seen as analogous to the contemporary energy markets in oil, gas, coal and uranium, which from this perspective in a sense replaced them.

Interaction Capacity

In terms of interaction capacity, the CAPE era did not outdo the hunter-gatherers in terms of range. The latter had already peopled the habitable world. The CAPE peoples did not so much 'discover' places that were already inhabited, as invent technologies that enabled them to discover and use oceanic routes, and thus to encounter peoples and places unfamiliar to them. They also developed better technologies for moving people and things across the land. There were three key breakthroughs that enabled this big leap in interaction capacity: sailing ships harnessing wind energy as already mentioned; wheeled vehicles of various kinds (carts, wagons, chariots) all powered by animals, but especially horses; and what might be called *carrier animals*, that could be used to carry either goods or people on their backs (particularly horses, camels, donkeys, mules, llamas). There were also breakthroughs that facilitated social interaction capacity (writing, money, trade diasporas).

From the beginning of civilisation, CAPE peoples took advantage of the carrying capacity of water to move bulk goods. From as early as 3200 BC, the Egyptians developed substantial sailing ships and rafts capable of carrying the heavy building stones used for the pyramids and other monumental architecture (Singer et al., 1954: 730–40; Paine, 2014: loc. 1136–283). By 2000 BC, sailing ships were carrying construction timber from Lebanon into Egypt, while in Mesopotamia, sophisticated rafts were used to bring wood and stone from upriver down to the cities (Mann, 1986: 131–7; Scott, 2012: 157, 192; Paine, 2014: locs. 1466–648). There was a maritime trading network via the Persian Gulf connecting the early Mesopotamian civilisations and the Harappan culture in the Indus valley during the third millennium BC. Athenians ate grain imported from the Black Sea coasts, and Rome fed itself by importing grain from Egypt. An average freighter in Roman times might carry a cargo of 120 tons, and a big grain-carrier up to 1000 tons. Trade was on a very substantial scale, with Rome importing between 150,000 and 300,000 tons of grain per year, and exporting 1.3–2.6 million gallons of wine per year just to Gaul (Paine, 2014: locs. 2889–3019). After its unification in 221 BC, China knitted itself together with an inland network of rivers and canals used to ship food and other goods inside the country.

Maritime trade over long distances became common, with the Phoenicians trading tin from Cornwall (Britain) during the first millennium BC. The maritime silk road connecting East Asia to the Mediterranean began to open up from the fourth century BC (Paine, 2014: chs. 6, 7, 10, 11). By the ninth century AD, direct round trips by Muslim traders from the Gulf to Canton (Guangzhou), taking around eighteen months, had become common, and there was an Indian Ocean-centred trading system linked to Africa, the Middle East and East Asia (Hobson, 2021). During the fifteenth and sixteenth centuries AD, and still using wooden sailing ships, Europeans opened up the sea routes across the Atlantic, around Africa to the Indian Ocean, and from the Americas across the Pacific to Asia. By the eighteenth century, the Europeans' maritime advantage had enabled them to capture and link together the trade of the widespread 'industrious revolutions' of that time (Bayly, 2004: 59–64). The biggest of the East Indiamen ships that opened up global trade could carry several thousand tons of cargo. The Chinese could also build big, technologically sophisticated, ocean-going ships, and did so briefly during the early fifteenth century AD. But they did not develop these ships for regular commerce, and soon wearied of their great expense. This left the Indian Ocean open to the Europeans who arrived a few decades later. Commerce was crucial to making regular and sustained long-distance travel cost-effective and sustainable. These ocean routes carried people as well as goods, and during the first millennium AD became sophisticated enough to support a steady flow of pilgrims: Muslims performing the Hajj, Buddhists between India and China.

In addition to better shipbuilding, various other developments supported the operation and expansion of commercial (and military) shipping. One was the building of maritime infrastructure such as ports and lighthouses, which was a common practice amongst sea-going empires.[6] Equally important was the development of navigational knowledge about winds and currents and seasonal weather that eventually enabled voyages to cross open water rather than stay in sight of the coast. From early in the first millennium AD, navigational instruments began to enable mariners to measure ever-more precisely where they actually were. The quadrant dates from early in the first millennium AD, the compass was invented in China by the twelfth century AD, and the chronometer was produced in Britain in the early eighteenth century AD (Van Creveld, 1991: 51–6, 125–8).

The second CAPE breakthrough in interaction capacity was wheeled vehicles, which existed before 3000 BC. Although it occurred at about the same time as the emergence of city-states and empires, this development originated among the steppe peoples, and was crucial to their nomadic, pastoralist, lifeway. With wheeled carts and wagons pulled by animals, they could occupy the whole of the steppe year-round. These early vehicles were designed and intended for cross-country use, and did not require roads (Singer et al., 1954: 203–12, 713–26). Roads, indeed, were a relatively minor feature of interaction capacity during the CAPE era. A few empires, most notably Rome, China and Inca, were big road-builders, but their roads were mainly used for speeding up communications and military movements, not primarily for commerce.[7] Roads did not really become associated with vehicles and commerce until the modern era. Animal traction power was crucial to such vehicles, and oxen, donkeys and especially horses, were the preferred source of power. As with sailing ships, the fuel was free and widely available, so there was

---

[6] Ports were more a feature of the Mediterranean, Atlantic and East Asian empires. They were less important in the Indian Ocean, where trading ships were mainly constructed so that they could be easily beached. In the Americas, none of the empires developed comparable sea-going activity.

[7] CAPE era societies generally preferred river or sea shipping for commercial transport, not least because it was much cheaper than land transport. One estimate suggesting shipping cost ratios of 1 by sea, 4.9 by river and 28 by land (Meijer and van Nijf, 1992: 1). See also Scott (2017: 54). On CAPE road-building see Singer et al. (1954: 713–14).

no limit on range other than the suitability of the terrain, and the endurance of the people, animals and vehicles themselves (with the latter being very repairable on the go). The other key development was of spoked wheels in Central Asia around 2000 BC (Radner, 2020: 395). Spoked wheels were much lighter than the original solid ones. They required more sophisticated construction, but allowed for higher speeds. They enabled the invention of the war chariot, also by the steppe peoples, on which more below. The carts, wagons and carriages of eighteenth-century Europe were easily recognisable descendants of these early vehicles.

The third breakthrough in interaction capacity was the domestication of *carrier animals*. In one sense, this is simply part of the story of animal power discussed above, but it is also a very specific story related to interaction capacity. By 3000 BC, various animals (horses, donkeys, camels and later llamas) were coming into use not just to pull wheeled vehicles, but as pack animals trained to carry loads on their backs (Singer et al., 1954: 203–12, 705–6). Such animals provided the foundations not only for the formidable cavalry (horse-mounted warriors) of the steppe nomads, but also for the long-distance caravan routes, most notably the overland Silk Roads, and the routes across and around the Sahara desert, that were a feature of Eurasian-African trade during this era (Curtin, 1984: 93, 106–8; Bentley, 1993; Dale, 2010: 106–34; Liu, 2010; Hansen, 2012). Empires were interested enough in supporting this trade, both for the goods and for the tax revenues it bought, that they often provided infrastructure (bridges, *caravanserais*) and security for them. Even as late as the sixteenth and seventeenth centuries AD, there was an important overland caravan system connecting the Mughal, Safavid and Ottoman Empires, which protected the traders from banditry, and provided an extensive network of *caravanserais* along the main routes.

At some point the breeding of pack animals produced beasts that were strong enough, and controllable enough, to be ridden. This was true for donkeys and camels, but the big breakthrough, again from the steppe peoples, was rideable horses by around 900 BC (Parzinger, 2020: 234–6). The main impact of this, however, was military, on which more below.

In addition to technologies enabling improved physical movement, there were also very significant developments in what might be called social interaction capacity. Writing came into use along with the first city-states and empires, greatly facilitating, both, communication across time and space, and complex record keeping and administration (Goody, 2010: 81–2, 88–91). Alphabetic scripts emerged by the first millennium BC, making writing easier to learn and use. Writing also enabled the symbolic representation of numbers and equations, which opened up the development of mathematics. Coinage became widespread during the first millennium BC making trade and commerce easier (Manning, 2020: 133). The provision of credit, and forms of banking and bills of exchange stretch well back into classical civilisation (De Ligt, 1993). Trade diasporas, on which more below, emerged during the second millennium BC. Paper spread from China during the eighth century AD, followed by wood-block printing, and in the fifteenth century by Gutenberg's sophisticated press, which made mass printing widely available.

The vast increase in interaction capacity generated by these technologies opened up trade, and made it a formal, organised activity with its own class of practitioners (merchants). The increase in the range and volume of trade opened up cultural exchange among remote civilisations in everything from art and religion to fashion and food. It hugely extended the sense of comparative advantage, and the possibilities for trade, between parts of the world whose climate and conditions enabled them to produce different kinds of goods not available elsewhere. This exchange was mediated by the almost universal use of gold and silver as currency. On the darker side, these wide-ranging trading networks also opened the way to disease transmissions between cultures, which from the second half of the first millennium BC began to have the consequence of periodic plagues. These could and did cause massive drops in population, and the weakening of empires (McNeill, 1976; Diamond, 1997; Christian, 2004: 330, 367–72; Findlay and O'Rourke, 2007: 110–20; Harrison, 2013; Scott, 2017: 96–112, 189–95; Manning, 2020: 145–57). Higher levels of interaction capacity also facilitated long-distance slave-trading, and war, though war usually only at shorter ranges than commerce.

Military Technology

Organised violence between political units was one of the central practices of the CAPE era. This meant that equipment designed and produced specifically for war became a major new industry. War equipment was a key part of the material conditions of this era.[8] As noted, the new materials, particularly bronze and iron/steel, not only provided better and more standardised spearpoints and arrowheads for existing weapons, but also new weapons such as swords, metal armour and later, guns. Of the

---

[8] Useful sources on this topic include: Brodie and Brodie (1973); McNeill (1982); Van Creveld (1991); Headrick (2010); Paine (2014); Andrade (2016).

new sources of energy, wind was probably the most important militarily because it enabled navies and therefore maritime empires (think of Athens, Rome, Chola, Portugal and Britain); and troop transport and military logistics (think of the Greeks at Troy, the Persian invasions of Greece, the Roman conquest of Carthage, Napoleon's invasion of Egypt). Animal power was also hugely important, partly because of overland military logistics,[9] but mainly because first chariots, and later cavalry, became the dominant forms of warfare. Sailing ships and horses raised the level of interaction capacity, but they did not expand the range of war anything like as much as that of trade, cultural exchange and disease. Alexander the Great could not get his army to go further than the borders of India. Rome and China, and Rome and India, traded goods (and diseases), but had no military contact. China, indeed remained militarily isolated from all of the other sedentary agrarian civilisations except for one brief encounter with the Abbasid armies at the Battle of Talas in Transoxania in 751 AD, which the Chinese lost. Despite being mainly land-bound, the Mongols, whose society was specialised for overland movement, provide the main exception to this rule. They used their huge supply of horses – several for each warrior – to great effect both as cavalry, and to extend their range of communications and operations. Their empire eventually, albeit briefly, linked most of the civilisations of Eurasia.

Several basic weapons from the hunter-gatherer repertoire were carried forward into the CAPE era, albeit with improvements. Clubs and spears acquired metal heads. The bow moved from a simple wooden construction to an elaborate and more powerful laminated ('compound') form made from wood, horn, sinew and glue, again developed by the steppe peoples. The bow was later elaborated into the crossbow, firing a heavy, armour-piercing bolt, and the *ballista*, an artillery-scale form of crossbow. Arrows also acquired metal heads, and slings acquired more standardized lead 'bullets'.

But more important than these upgrades to existing technology were both new forms and types of weapons, and the idea of the warrior as a functionally specialised role. There was a steady stream of new weapons and military equipment throughout the CAPE era and several of what today would be called 'revolutions in military affairs' (RMAs). The building of defensive walls goes back to the earliest city-states, and so too does the use of body armour which takes many forms, both metallic and non-metallic, and also chain mail, which was probably developed by

---

[9] Overland military logistics was much less efficient and more costly than supply by sea, and to some extent CAPE armies could and did live off the land as they moved.

Celtic peoples during the first millennium BC. Formation fighting infantry using shield walls and a coordinated hedge of spearpoints evolved very early on in the CAPE era, and was famously deployed by Greek hoplites and Roman legions from the mid-first millennium BC. Horse-drawn war chariots came into use from 2000 BC, first on the steppe. This was a revolutionary weapon, enabling archers to outpace and outmanoeuvre formations of foot soldiers. Also during the second millennium BC, the compound bow became a key weapon. It combined greater power and range, with a shorter bow. Around the middle of the second millennium BC, bronze swords came into play, and later iron/steel ones.

A military revolution even bigger than war chariots was the development of rideable horses from circa 900 BC again by the steppe peoples. Mounted warriors could move fast, and fire arrows from their short compound bows. This form of light cavalry again overwhelmed the foot soldiers of agrarian states, hugely empowering the steppe nomads. Continued breeding of horses eventually allowed for heavy cavalry with armoured riders wielding lances. At about the same time, the specialised warship (a rowed galley with a ram) was developed in Greece, opening up the development of navies and naval strategy. The first millennium BC saw several other military innovations including war elephants from India, and a variety of artillery and siege engines, such as battering rams, wheeled assault towers, various forms of catapult 'artillery' (*onager, mangonel, trebuchet*[10]), and heavy crossbows (*ballista*), all of which had been developed in the Middle East and India. Later developments included Greek fire (a sticky incendiary material) from the seventh century AD (Brodie and Brodie, 1973: 14–15); the stirrup, probably originating in China but developed by the steppe peoples, by the eighth century AD; and gunpowder and guns, originating in China from the tenth century, and spreading to all of Eurasia by the thirteenth century AD (Andrade, 2016).

The idea of warriors probably emerged during the transition period, but came to full fruition within the CAPE era. Hunter-gatherers could transfer their hunting skills and weapons to fighting, but we do not have a clear picture of this. The idea of citizen soldiers carried over into the CAPE era such as those of the Greek city-states. But even for the Greeks, citizens were already an elite part of the population, many others of whom were slaves or otherwise excluded from soldiering, as women mostly were. Perhaps the strongest carry-over of the citizen-soldier idea was amongst the steppe nomads, where the idea that every person was

---

[10] Variously powered by torsion or counterweights, to throw anything (stones, incendiaries, poisonous insects or snakes, diseased corpses) against cities and their defences.

also a warrior, and trained as such, remained largely intact. The CAPE concept of warriors was in general a masculine one, but this was by no means an absolute condition. Toler (2019) shows the many ways and forms in which women could, and often did, join in the fighting, albeit then getting written out of history because of the threat that the very idea of women warriors posed to patriarchy. Motherhood and warriorhood were constructed as opposites of creation/nurture, and destruction/violence.

Warriors were both individual skilled fighters (think of Achilles and Hector at Troy, David and Goliath, and the idea of fighting 'champions' generally), and/or soldiers trained as formation fighters (think of the Greek hoplites, the Roman legions, Song and Ming dynasty Chinese armies, and European armies of the eighteenth century). Formation fighting involved groups of soldiers drilled to coordinate their actions, whether by locking shields together; marching, or riding horses, in tight formation; or throwing/firing their weapons (slings, spears, arrows, muskets) at the same time on command. The new weapons and methods of fighting required considerable training, and created a pressure towards professionalisation of soldiering (and sailoring), especially in the larger empires. Many CAPE empires hired professional mercenaries, often steppe nomads, whose warrior skills were much admired, to defend them. Some even created slave armies, though this entertained the danger that the army would overthrow its commanders, as the Mamluks did in Egypt in 1250 AD. The Ottoman Empire was famous for its Janissary slave army, which conquered Constantinople in 1453, and struck fear into the hearts of Europeans for several centuries thereafter. Perhaps the apex of military professionalism in the CAPE era was the drilled armies capable of sustained volley firing that the Chinese developed as early as the twelfth century AD, and the Europeans in the eighteenth century (Andrade, 2016: 153–9).

Despite these many and often impressive, improvements and additions, however, the CAPE era remained defined and constrained by quite strict limitations on the available materials, sources of energy, and technologies. Most of its basic material conditions were largely in place by the middle of the first millennium BC, the time of warring states in China, the classical period in Greece and Persia, and the Mauryan Empire in India. The only really new addition to its material toolkit was the explosive chemical energy of gunpowder. The 'gunpowder age' lasted a millennium between 900 and 1900. Initially used as an incendiary material, and for fire-lances, in China, its military development accelerated during the Song dynasty (1127–1279) to include bombs, rockets and guns. Gun and gunpowder technology reached the Middle East and Europe during the fourteenth century, and were quickly adopted there. A steadily improving range of handguns and cannons displaced spears, bows, crossbows and catapult artillery, giving rise to gunpower empires across Eurasia (Brodie and Brodie, 1973; Van Creveld, 1991; Andrade, 2016).

Civil Technology

This is far too large a topic to explore in detail. But since most of the technologies are familiar to a wide range of people, the following list that were significant to the political economy of the CAPE era, and that have not been mentioned under other headings, will suffice to give the general picture. Within the limits of their material and energy resources, CAPE societies produced a remarkable range of technologies, albeit not necessarily all in the same time and place:

> Aqueducts
> Bridges
> Casting
> Cement
> Central heating
> Cranes
> Dams
> Dyeing
> Glassware
> Harness
> Hydraulic mining
> Lighthouse
> Loom
> Medicines
> Paint
> Plough
> Pottery wheel
> Precision instruments (e.g. astrolabes, quadrants, clocks)
> Roads
> Rope
> Sewers
> Surgery
> Tanning
> Water wheels
> Wind mills
> In addition, they took stone-working to a high art for both architecture and sculpture.

The material picture of the CAPE era is thus both impressive and limited. It is impressive because it empowered human society far beyond what was possible during hunter-gatherer times. Humankind not only occupied the world, as the hunter-gatherers had done, but did so at a much higher density, and increasingly tied it together economically, politically and militarily. The new resources and technologies provided the foundations for much larger, more differentiated, and more complex human societies, and enabled a big intensification of globalisation. The material limits of the CAPE era were most obvious in its limited sources of energy, which boxed-in its material and technological development. This defined the remarkable stability of its material conditions over many millennia, a pattern that underpinned a parallel stability in its social structure.

Social Structure

Recall that for the prehistoric era the social structure was constituted by six primary institutions: three that looked quite solid and important (kinship, trade, and human equality), two that were thinner and more questionable (territoriality and war), and one that was a precursor (religion). Kinship was carried over into the CAPE era in a strong, but more specialised, and less central way; human equality was abandoned and replaced by its opposite; trade carried forward in a vastly expanded way, and with different motivations and functions; territoriality was transformed and intensified; war became a central institution on a large scale rather than an occasional occurrence between small groups; and religion acquired gods, and became formalised, institutionalised and hierarchical. But the story of social structure in the CAPE era is much more complicated than that. The transition from foragers to CAPE was away from relations within and between small and usually scattered groups of people organised primarily as kinship *communities*; towards relations within and between large groups of people organised primarily as *societies* – cities, states, empires, and civilisations – and much more densely packed together.[11] As noted, the CAPE era expanded society beyond the interhuman domain and into the transnational and interpolity ones.

---

[11] Here I draw on classical Sociology's two ideal types: *Gemeinschaft* (community) and *Gesellschaft* (society) (Tönnies, 1887) though I push them further back in time than their original usage. Community is where the social formation is a traditional, evolved, affective, historical construct based on shared values and culture, and involving a sense of mutual responsibility. Society is where the social formation is something instrumental, contractual and purposively constructed. It involves a shared identity but is more

Under these conditions, the social structure of the CAPE era quickly generated both a large role for power and politics and violence at all levels of human society, and a wider range of primary institutions than those that defined the hunter-gatherer era. In both respects, the CAPE era begins to look more familiar to us. It stretches across the three domains, and some of its institutions, such as sovereignty, territoriality, war, diplomacy and imperialism, carry forward into our own time. It also begins to have a strongly layered political structure with a marked distinction between domestic and international spheres. Because a more complex, layered, social structure comes into being during this era, one can begin to ask how primary institutions worked within and across all three domains. In asking that, the emphasis has to be on 'begin'. While the CAPE era brought into play a wider range of primary and secondary institutions, it was still, in terms of social structure, a very different place from contemporary global society. Not the least difference was that politics in the CAPE era was centred around monarchy/dynasticism and empires. In terms of the English School contribution to the theory of polity formation, empires reflected different understandings of sovereignty and territoriality from modern states, a difference largely explained by the fact that monarchy/dynasticism, not nationalism, was their third constitutive primary institution. In what follows, I will look first at the six institutions carried forward from the hunter-gatherer era, and how they persisted or changed during the CAPE era, then at the new institutions that generated, and were generated by, the CAPE era itself.

Kinship

Kinship in the sense of family, household, clan, genetic and marital lineage – *raison de famille* – was pretty much the key primary institution of the hunter-gatherer lifeway. It was the principal social glue of that era. In this commanding sense, kinship ceased to function as a distinct primary institution structuring the CAPE era in its own right. That role was superseded both by religion, and by explicitly political institutions such as monarchy/dynasticism and imperialism. But kinship remained an important element of the social order as a shadow, or ghost, institution. As Neumann, Haugevik and Lie (2018) note, kinship, whether blood or metaphorical, implies relations of trust, and it was used in this way throughout the CAPE era as a basis for networks of trust in many walks of life from monarchs to merchants. Kinship certainly did not disappear

impersonal than community. In this perspective hunter-gatherer bands were certainly communities. Societies began with the crystallisation of cities and empires.

from the CAPE lifeway generally, remaining very active in the local life of villages and towns (the interhuman domain), where imperial political control often did not penetrate deeply, and the sense of immediate community remained strong. In addition to this, kinship took specific and powerful roles as a component of three other major primary institutions of the CAPE era: monarchy/dynasticism, trade, and religion. In what follows, the main discussions of kinship are within those institutions.

Human Inequality

One of the most striking features of the CAPE era is the very radical shift from the social structure of relative *human equality* that was the general norm of mobile hunter-gatherer communities, to the extreme forms of *human inequality* that marked most aspects and levels of CAPE society. Human inequality was indeed a master institution with several derivatives, including slavery, patriarchy and dynasticism. Inequality embodied the idea that there should be leadership elites that had different rights and responsibilities, more access to resources, and a higher social status, than those under their control. This was exemplified by monarchy/dynasticism, discussed separately below, but could also be applied to warlords, religions and merchants. Lerner (1986: 77, 209), makes a strong case that patriarchy was the foundational form of inequality from which the others (slavery, class) developed. Stratification, often interwoven with functional differentiation, permeated through the middle ranks of society, where intense status layering differentiated amongst nobility, warriors, priests, artisans, merchants and farmers. This differentiation was often in quite rigid forms of caste or class in which it was difficult, but usually not wholly impossible, for individuals to transcend the rights, obligations and identities of their birthright. Kinship was thus partly absorbed into CAPE societies as one mechanism for reproducing hierarchy and stratification. In such caste and class systems, it was difficult for most people to marry outside their birth-given rank. Slaves and women were at the bottom of the CAPE social hierarchy.

Most of you who are reading this book come from societies in which at least formally, and often to a large extent in practice, both slavery and discrimination against women are illegal. It is quite widely felt in most (though not all) contemporary societies that slavery is not just illegal, but also immoral, though that does not stop it being covertly practised in various ways from the sex trade to forms of domestic service and indentured labour that come close to slavery in their mix of coercion, restriction of movement, and disrespect. Discrimination against women can be done as modern slavery, but also carried on in a variety of other more subtle ways: systematic inequalities of opportunity, pay, health care, food allocation, legal rights, etc. Although there is moral and legal condemnation of this, it is probably not as strong or widespread as that against slavery. Since elements of the CAPE practices carry forward into our own time, it is worth looking more closely at slavery and patriarchy as derivative institutions of human inequality within CAPE society.

From a modern perspective, it can be difficult to grasp the depth and legitimacy of human inequality in classical times, and all too easy to condemn such practices using current moral and legal standards. There are extremely strong and clear grounds for condemning such practices when they occur today. But there is little point in projecting moral outrage anachronistically back to distant times and places without first trying to understand the social institutions of CAPE society in their own terms. In their own time and place, such practices were considered neither illegal nor immoral, but a part of everyday normal life. Slavery and patriarchy were not peculiarly nasty, aberrant, aspects of CAPE society. They were intrinsic to its whole socio-economic structure and practice. That is the point of trying to understand the primary institutions that underpinned earlier societies. On this theme, Risso (1995: 94) offers the insight that when nineteenth-century Britain imposed its anti-slavery campaign on the East African slave trade, this generated a cultural and legal clash with those Muslims who viewed slavery as sanctioned by the Qur'an, and therefore an unquestionable right. Another reason for featuring slavery and patriarchy is that they were pretty much a universal feature across the many civilisations of the CAPE era. Slavery was almost everywhere, not only amongst the big agrarian civilisations of Eurasia and the Americas, but also among the steppe nomads, and the chiefdoms and kingdoms and empires of Africa. Patriarchy was most evident amongst the high urban civilisations of Eurasia, and perhaps less so amongst the steppe nomads and other smaller-scale societies. This near universality across a wide range of cultures reinforces the idea that structural explanations intrinsic to CAPE societies were in play.

Patriarchy There is considerable agreement that patriarchy and the reduction of women to subordinate status within society, correlates with the emergence of bigger, sedentary, more functionally differentiated, more urban, and more hierarchical societies. The prevailing assumption is that the small, mobile hunter-gatherer communities were relatively egalitarian, including between the sexes, and that this situation was turned into a systematic subordination of women during the transition to agrarian/pastoralist society. Explanations for why this happened vary, but the general point is that the subordination of women is not a result of biology, in which case it would be a historical constant, but a result of social structures, which change and can be changed. The four explanations that follow – one Marxist, one feminist, and two from global historians – all agree that the turn towards patriarchy began towards the end of the transition to the CAPE era. While they agree on the timing, they put different emphases on the causes. They do not have to be read as mutually exclusive. They are all plausible part-hypotheses about a process that still lies mainly beyond the methodology of both archaeologists and historians.

In an influential work, Engels (2010 [1884]: 58–114) argues for a social explanation of the suppression of women in society. His idea hangs on the increase in male wealth associated with pastoralism (cattle falling within the men's domain), which created inheritance incentives for the establishment of male line succession. Men who wanted to pass on their newly acquired wealth to their children, needed to know who their children were, something that was not possible in the more open and communal sexual and family relations of earlier times. Where sexual relations were relatively open, only mothers knew for sure which their children were, and lines of succession necessarily tended to be matrilineal. For patrilineal succession to work, women's sexuality and reproductive rights (but not men's) had to be brought under the strict control of monogamy. As Engels (2010 [1884]: 87), puts it: 'The overthrow of mother right was the world historical defeat of the female sex' … 'the woman was degraded and reduced to servitude'. Coontz and Henderson (1986) also take this line. Having dismissed all other biological and functional explanations, they, like Engels, see the subordination of women as happening during the transition from hunter-gatherer societies to CAPE ones. Similar to Engels, they see the key mechanism as being the creation of tradeable surplus production, specifically cattle, which enriched and empowered men in the social hierarchy. Men might also have been empowered by the male warrior status that grew with war at the same time (31–4). The new accumulations of wealth, power and cultural authority were largely in the hands of men, which had a transformational effect on the importance of inheritance within the family. Male lineage was central to that process, and controlling knowledge of that required the displacement of matriarchal lineage. This line of reasoning suggests a marked shift in the understanding and role of kinship in society. It also plays strongly into dynasticism, where lineage was closely tied to knowledge and control of reproduction, which in turn required control over women's sexuality. More on this below.

A second line of explanation also stems from the domestication of animals, but in a different way. The key is the invention of the plough. Whether the plough was pulled by people or oxen, ploughing required strength, which meant that it fell mainly to men. This amplified the gender division of labour, and pushed women into more domestic roles (Galor, 2022: 190–2; Nightingale, 2022: 25).

Some feminist historians put a different emphasis on the cause. Lerner (1986) and Chevillard and Leconte (1986), focus on the idea that the subordination of women was the crucial first step away from a broadly egalitarian social structure towards a more stratified, hierarchical, one. As Lerner (1986: 209) puts it: '[S]ex dominance antedates class dominance and lies at its foundation.' Their explanation hinges on the discovery that women could be involuntarily traded between groups. Because of their maternal attachment to their children, women could be much more easily integrated into another group than was possible with men. By this mechanism, women could be moved into different groups where they had no independent social position, and were vulnerable to male control. They were reduced to being a form of property, whose labour, and sexual and reproductive services, and indeed right to life, were controlled by fathers and husbands. Lerner (1986) sets out in formidable detail how this process unfolded over two-and-a-half millennia from early Sumer down to classical Greece.[12] By the second millennium BC, free men at all levels of society had complete control over women's bodies and rights, whether wives, daughters, concubines or slaves. These customary rights became enshrined in the legal codes of the state. The strictly enforced monogamy for women generated prostitution, and the differentiation of women into 'respectable' and 'disreputable'. With some time lag, the position in the pantheon of the mother-goddess, and female gods generally, correspondingly declined to the periphery. The idea of a dominant male god eventually even expropriated the power of life-giving that was traditionally assigned to a mother-goddess, as in the Torah/Old Testament story of creation, and the Greek story of Athena being born from Zeus's head. Women (Eve) were reduced from being the source of life to being the cause of humankind's fall from grace. These authors see the reduction of women to the status of male property as a social template for the later development of male slavery, with both being owned and controlled by the male master of the house. In this view, slavery did not amount to all that much more than the inclusion of men into the system of inequality, oppression and exploitation of labour

---

[12] Given the mechanism, this subordination of women could have happened much earlier, even far back in the hunter-gatherer era. Whether it did so or not is unclear.

already imposed on the vast majority of women. Women, like slaves, and often as slaves, were routinely treated as part of the victor's booty during wartime.

By the mid-first millennium BC, Aristotle could argue for the intrinsic physical and moral inferiority of women, a view that was typical within CAPE societies. One indication of the extent of their fall, and the attitude of contempt it generated in the bigger and more urban CAPE societies, is provided by Nizam Al Mulk (2002: 176–84) who was vizier to the Seljuk sultans during the eleventh century AD. In his handbook of advice to the princes of the day, he devoted a whole chapter to the denigration of women in politics, arguing that they had an inferior intellect, and should at all costs be kept away from power and policy-making. He recommended that should a woman offer advice on matters of political policy, the recipient of that advice should do the opposite.[13] Until very recently, the West shared the hostility of all premodern high civilisations to women in politics. Towns (2009, 2010), for example, charts the systematic exclusion of women from politics in Western societies during the nineteenth century, justified as a marker of modernity.

Writing from the perspective of 'big history', Christian (2004: 263–4) likewise argues that the genesis of patriarchy arose in the run-up to the CAPE era, when the general egalitarianism of hunter-gatherer societies shifted towards the general hierarchy and stratification that attended the rise of towns and cities. His argument is broader than Engels' emphasis on property, and does not give much weight to the feminist idea that the subordination of women was the leading edge toward stratification. He sees stratification as a result of increasing social size and complexity. In rather functional terms, he argues simply that this shift favoured men, because they were less necessary to the functions of the household, and therefore had more opportunity to take advantage of the functional and stratificatory opportunities that were opening up. This argument describes the general outcome, but somewhat begs the question of how women became associated with household tasks in the first place.

Considering these four explanations together, one might imagine a story along the following lines. In forager societies, life was mainly local, with both men and women closely tied to the household and band, and sharing many domestic responsibilities for sustaining day-to-day living. One exception was that men were mainly responsible for hunting big game, an activity that detached them from the household, and gave them skills at operating at a distance from it. Given the child-bearing and

---

[13] This would, of course, be an easy rule for smart women to game, though only at the cost of reproducing their image as inferiors.

minding responsibilities of women, a certain division of labour made sense. Lerner could well be right that women's strong attachment to their children made them tradeable, and easy to disempower. Engels might be right that the shift from hunting big game, to herding it, put cattle and other big domesticated animals under the responsibility of men, giving them ownership of tradeable property. Galor and Nightingale might be right that ploughing amplified a gendered division of labour. But Christian's broader explanation also seems powerful. As societies became bigger, many of the new functional and stratificatory opportunities (e.g. warrior, priest, administrator, merchant, artisan, aristocrat, king) not only favoured distance skills, but came with access to wealth, power and political and cultural authority. With these expanding resources in the hands of men, and women left with the static resource base of the household, it did not take long in any urban CAPE society for women to fall into a subordinate position. That process opened up a widening gulf between men occupying an expanding public sphere of politics, commerce, religion and war, and women remaining largely confined to the household and family matters. Men became more detached from the household, and the welfare of the household became more dependent on external resources mainly provided by men.

Whatever the balance of truth among these competing explanations, they all agree both that patriarchy had kicked in as a major element of human inequality by the beginning of the CAPE era, and that patriarchy is a consequence of changes in the social structure. Whatever the variations in its implementation in different times and cultures, patriarchy was therefore an intrinsic general feature of social structure in the agrarian, urban civilisations of the CAPE era. It is difficult to know exactly how egalitarian relationships between men and women were in hunter-gatherer societies. But even if the position of women there was to some extent inferior, this was as nothing compared to the drop in their status in urban CAPE societies.

Slavery As far as we know, slavery was not a feature of mobile HGB lifeways, though it can certainly be found whenever people settled down, whether as hunter-gatherers or farmers (Lerner, 1986: 76). Two structural features, one material and one social, largely explain why slavery was universal to CAPE societies (Meltzer, 1993; Patterson, 2018). The material reason was discussed above, namely that CAPE societies had limited energy sources, and were heavily dependent on muscle power for many types of work. Animals could provide some of that, but there were many skilled tasks that could only be done by human muscle power with its more complex repertoire of behaviours. The social feature was the institution of human inequality itself. With society being organised in a highly stratified way, and resources of wealth, power and cultural authority concentrated in small elites, nothing stood in the way of slavery as a means of solving the energy shortage, certainly not any notion of human rights. Slavery relieved others from 'subsistence chores', enabling both functional specialisation and leisured elites to form (Graeber and Wengrow, 2021: 188). Within CAPE society, slavery was supported by the legitimacy of the use of extreme violence at all levels of society. Most CAPE religions did not, in practice, generally stand against the use of violence, and sometimes promoted it themselves (the Crusades, militant Jihadism, the Inquisition).

Violence was certainly intrinsic to the management of slavery by the slave-owning classes, just as it was to the management of society by the ruling elite's use of cruel and unusual public punishments. On a day-to-day basis, CAPE societies were relatively indifferent to human life and suffering. Occasionally, violence went the other way in the periodic occurrence of slave revolts – for example, the well-known ones in Rome (Spartacus 73–71 BC), and in the Caribbean (Haiti, 1791–1804, Jamaica, 1831–2), and the less well-known ones in the Islamic world (869–83 AD) (James, 2001 [1938]; Findlay and O'Rourke, 2007: 50; Nightingale, 2022: 90–1). But it was not its sole support. Slavery was also underpinned by its social legitimacy as an accepted institution. It was a not uncommon fate for people at any level of society to find themselves enslaved. In some cases, this meant hard labour, cruel treatment and a short life. But in others it could mean finding oneself in a comfortable and well-rewarded position. Systems of slavery varied, with some, like the Atlantic slave trade to the Caribbean and North America offering little chance for escape or improvement, and others, like Rome, being much more varied in possibilities across a wide spectrum. Given the intense stratification of CAPE societies, and the general subordination and oppression of the lower social classes, slavery was not such a noticeable difference in status as it became in the colonial Americas, where, towards the end of this era, it became unusually and starkly associated with race.

The generally violent and uncaring attitude of CAPE societies is captured in the history of Atlantic sea crossings. The suffering and brutality inflicted on Africans during the three centuries of the Atlantic slave trade are well known and rightly condemned (Williams, 1944). What is perhaps less well known is that, apart from the shackles and floggings, the coerced nature of the transportation of slaves, and their fate on arrival, conditions for paying passengers on transatlantic voyages at the same time were not dissimilar to those for slaves. Space allowances per passenger on late fifteenth-century pilgrim ships were about the same (1 square metre, i.e. the minimum possible) as on slave ships. Even as late as the mid-nineteenth century, conditions for paying passengers in terms of crowding, poor ventilation, and inadequate food and water, were appalling, and for indentured labourers, mainly from India and China, especially so. During the Irish famine, deaths amongst passengers on a few notorious North Atlantic voyages reached 20 per cent, and health and safety standards to protect passengers and reduce ship losses did not come into play until later in the nineteenth century (Paine, 2014: locs. 7133–53, 9836–909, 10819–911; McMahon, 2021: 146–55). While it is important not to minimise the horrors of slavery, if one wants to understand the normative structure of global society at this time, it is equally important to see it in its general context of extreme human inequality and a widespread indifference to the suffering of fellow human beings.

Slavery as an institution was rooted deeply in all three domains. In the interstate domain, war was often as much a method of acquiring slaves, as it was about extending territorial control. When cities were sacked, both citizens and slaves were part of the booty, to be distributed amongst the officers and soldiers as slaves, or sold into slave markets for profit. Another indicator of the deep normality of slavery in CAPE societies was, as mentioned above, that more than a few empires had slave soldiers, or even slave armies. To the modern mind (with the possible exception of fans of *Game of Thrones*), the idea of a slave soldier, let alone a whole army, sounds dangerously contradictory: If you give slaves weapons and military training, why would they not revolt against their owners? The fact that slave armies were both quite common, and militarily effective, particularly in the Islamic world, suggests just how deeply legitimate the idea of slavery was within the CAPE lifeway. The Mamluks were Turkic slave soldiers who became the rulers of Egypt. The Ottoman Janissaries, often recruited from among the Christian minorities, were both a bulwark of the Sultan at home, and a much-feared army abroad. The British practice of using press-gangs to forcibly abduct men into the Royal Navy continued as late as the early nineteenth century, and might be thought of as a late example close to the use of slave soldiers.

In the transnational domain, the main practice supporting this institution was the slave trade. Within these societies, slave raiding and trading were legitimate and widespread occupations. For merchants, slaves were simply another form of merchandise, bulk-shipped along with commodities such as wood, metal, fabric, olive oil, wine and grain. Like animals, slaves were a source of energy, and sometimes of skills, and were valued as such. They were used for a wide variety of purposes, from sexual services on one end of the spectrum; through domestic staff, soldiering, and administrative and professional services; to the hard, dangerous, unskilled labour of mining, rowing, and constructing city walls and public monuments, on the other end. When the Mongol Empire reigned supreme, the Mongols made sure to capture artisans and other skilled workers when they sacked a city, even when they massacred most others. Specialised slave markets served this trade, and were a common feature in most CAPE societies. The last one, in Zanzibar, was not closed until 1873. Being a slave trader was a legal and respectable profession seen as necessary to the functioning of society.

Interestingly, one of the key, and long-standing, trading interactions between steppe and sedentary societies was slaves, with the steppe people selling the captives of their raids into the slave markets of the sedentary civilisations. Swedish Vikings traded Slav captives to the Byzantine Empire. Between 1000 and 1500 AD, Europe, both East and West, supplied European slaves to the more advanced core of the Islamic world (Findlay and O'Rourke, 2007: 88). The Mongols used captured Persian military engineers to assist them in their conquest of China. Slave-trading from East Africa, and across the Sahara, to the Middle East long predated Islam. The Fatimid caliphs used Africans as soldiers, and Muslim slave traders took African slaves to India and Southeast Asia, with some of them being given as tribute to the Chinese emperor (Findlay and O'Rourke, 2007: 54). During the 1790s, British slave traders shipped some 400,000 slaves. A prime minister of the time reckoned that the slave trade and related businesses provided around three-quarters of the country's overseas earnings (Micklethwait and Wooldridge, 2003: 47). Between the seventh and the eighteenth centuries something like twelve-and-a-half million slaves were exported from East Africa, along with gold, ivory and tropical woods, to the Islamic world (Paine, 2014: locs. 5656–743; Brown, 2020). And something like twelve million slaves were shipped from Africa to the Americas between the sixteenth and the nineteenth centuries, of whom about ten-and-a-half million survived the journey (Walvin, 2007: locs. 110–13, 594–603).

In the interhuman domain, being a slave or a slave owner was a common, everyday experience. The exact nature of that experience varied a lot from place to place and culture to culture. In many CAPE societies (e.g. Rome, China, the Islamic world, the Mongol Empire), slaves could rise to quite high and powerful stations. But they could also be treated harshly as an expendable resource in occupations like mining and rowing, or as gladiators. Even those who rose to high station could be killed by their owners if they fell out of favour. Slaves might be closely integrated into family and business environments, or treated like animals as a source of primitive energy to be maintained at the lowest cost feasible. Slavery and slave-ownership was often personal, and had all of the variations that go with personal relations from affection to brutality. There were debates in CAPE societies about how slaves should be treated, but, with the possible exception of Athens (Lerner, 1986: 208–9), no widespread debate questioning the principle of slavery itself (Walvin, 2007: locs. 157–435). Given the material conditions, much of the economic and social structure of CAPE societies depended on slavery to make it work.

Religions, even when they promoted notions of all being equal in the sight of god(s), seldom took a stand against the principle of slavery. Both Christianity and Islam had self-serving doctrines against enslaving co-religionists. But such prohibitions were widely ignored in both the Christian and Islamic worlds, with each trading co-religionists to the other as slaves (Davis, 2003). Becoming Christian did not do much, if anything, to relieve the burdens of race discrimination and gross inequality suffered by Africans enslaved in the Americas even during the last few centuries of the CAPE era. But for all that hypocrisy, religion, in this case some British and American Protestant sects of Christianity, eventually played a prominent role in the eighteenth- and nineteenth-century campaigns to ban the slave trade and slavery. The success of this campaign, helped by the Haitian slave revolt, and the more general struggle for wider human and political rights, marks one of the transitions from the CAPE era towards the modern one. It was perhaps the beginning, though certainly not the end, of bringing down the principle and institution of human inequality.

As noted above, there is a feminist view that sees patriarchy as the precursor to slavery, and the model for the later enslavement of men (Lerner, 1986: 76–81). Whether that is correct or not, there is no doubt that women were a large part of the slave population, and that sexual use, whether as a hired-out prostitute or a concubine, was frequently part of the female experience of slavery in a way that was much less the case for male slaves, although probably more so for boys. Although the later practice in the CAPE era was to enslave both the male and female parts of defeated populations, the earlier practice was to kill all the adult males, and enslave only the women and children. One explanation for this is that men were more difficult and dangerous to keep as slaves, whereas women could, again, be more easily subdued and integrated by exploiting their strong attachment to their children (Lerner, 1986: 46–53, 78). Having learned the principle of slavery through the practice of capturing and exchanging women, later CAPE societies added the enslavement of men as a valuable source of muscle power and skills.

The enslavement of men, however, was not much more than a deferred execution. It was a common practice to mutilate male slaves in some way in order better to dominate and control them. This was done by blinding, amputation, branding and castration, the latter being a form of sexual control comparable to that exercised over women (Lerner, 1986: 78–87), and arguably more extreme. Castrated males (*eunuchs*) were a widespread feature of the CAPE era. They were a flourishing sector of the slave market, commanding a higher price than ordinary slaves (Scholz, 2001: 22–7), and were another example of the era's general cruelty.[14] Eunuchs were common, inter alia, in Byzantine, Chinese, the Ottoman, Mughal and Safavid Empires, and the Abbasid caliphate. They were used not only in imperial harems, where they could have no reproductive interest in the dynastic breeding stock, but also as high government and military officials, because they could have no personal dynastic political ambitions (Scholz, 2001). In various times and places, palace eunuchs had substantial control over the government – for example, the eunuch faction in the government of Ming China acting as intermediaries between the outside world and the insulated royal elites and harems. Eunuchs were used as tribute gifts to Chinese emperors from Korea (Swope, 2009: 42–3). The famous fifteenth-century Chinese admiral Zheng He was a eunuch. Castration was done on quite a large scale, and even eunuch armies are not just another fantasy of *Game of Thrones*. During the tenth century, Caliph 'Abd al-Rahmān III, ruler of al-Andalus, had a palace guard of 14,000 *Saqāliba* (European, often Slavic) eunuchs in Cordoba (Fadlan, 2012: loc. 179). The general concern of CAPE societies with male kinship lines, and the control of sexuality and reproduction necessary to keep them pure, thus had consequences for a substantial group of men, as well as for all women.

Perhaps surprisingly for many contemporary readers, race was not a notable feature of either inequality generally, or slavery in particular, during the CAPE era. As Bayly (2004: 46–7) notes, even as late as the eighteenth century, '[n]either race nor nationality, as understood at the end of the 19th century, was yet a dominant concept' as compared with rank, caste, status, culture or religion. Anyone could become a slave as a result of the (mis)fortunes of war, or the bad luck of being captured by slave raiders. Capturing slaves was economically more efficient

---

[14] Castration was also a punishment for some crimes, and was even practised voluntarily by some for aesthetic, sexual, or, where cults of chastity were prominent, religious reasons (Scholz, 2001).

than breeding them because it saved the costs of raising and educating children (Graeber and Wengrow, 2021: 188). Citizens who became impoverished for whatever reason had the option of selling their children or themselves into slavery as a matter of survival, and many did so. Our contemporary view of slavery tends to be highly skewed by its association with racism in the Atlantic trade of African slaves to the Americas. This tie between race and slavery was something that emerged only at the end of this era, in a specific location, but it did so in such a strong (and ongoing) form that it colours how those whose perception is ensconced in modernity now see the wider history of slavery. For Arab and European traders in the late CAPE era, the reasoning was more economic. African slaves were relatively easy to obtain, and had a good survival rate in tropical climates. Africans themselves did most of the work in capturing slaves and bringing them to the coasts to sell. European and Middle Eastern merchants had merely to buy them and ship them out. The Europeans tapped into this local trade on the west coast of Africa, as Middle Eastern merchants had done since before the eighth century AD on the east coast, albeit the Europeans destructively amplified local practice by feeding guns into the African equation.

But the association between racism and slavery was not a general feature of CAPE societies. The Atlantic slave trade was the exception rather than the rule. Greek cities enslaved their defeated compatriots in the many wars among them. The Romans captured slaves from all around the periphery of their empire. Vikings shipped Slavs, Finns and others to the slave markets of the Byzantine Empire and the Abassid Caliphate. Several Arab Islamic empires used mainly Turkic slave soldiers. Christians and Muslims enslaved each other in the long period of their struggle over the Mediterranean. Most CAPE societies made a parochial distinction between 'civilised' (themselves) and 'barbaric' (foreigners) peoples, but this was more on the basis of culture than race. Those who did not share one's own culture, language and religion were barbarians, and those who did were civilised. For the Greeks, the Persians were barbarians as much as the Scythian nomadic tribes of the steppe. Anyone could become civilised by mastering the relevant language, culture and religion. During this era, differentiation by culture, caste and class was the dominant form. Race as a form of social differentiation in itself, played much less of a role in most of CAPE society than it came to have under modernity, and had little or nothing to do with the practice of slavery generally. The link between race and slavery is a peculiarly Atlantic-American phenomenon whose legacy has spread worldwide. For the rest of time and space in the CAPE era, it was just normal for human beings to be a tradeable commodity.

Trade

As discussed in Chapter 2, trade was a long-standing feature of the HGB lifeway, partly for basics in local networks, and partly, over longer distances, in relay trade for exotic goods. During the CAPE era, more widespread settlement increased the necessity and desire for trade, and, as discussed above, new modes of transport made trade even in bulk goods such as wood, stone, metals and grain, possible over quite long distances. So a distinctive feature of the CAPE era was the replacement of thin, mostly relay trading networks by organised trading networks with massively increased range and depth. These networks were supported by the development of functionally specialised merchant, artisan, administrative and transportation professions to organise, finance and implement trade. Trade also generated a very substantial set of transnational secondary institutions: guilds, companies and trade diasporas.

Both settlement and the move to agricultural production increased the necessity for trade. The alluvial plains of Mesopotamia and elsewhere were excellent places to farm, but far removed from sources of wood, stone and metal. Cities could not be built there without trade, and agricultural and craft production (especially fabrics: cotton, linen, wool, silk) provided the exportable surplus to pay for imports. The move to agriculture was a shift away from self-sufficient subsistence, to a narrower, more specialised, form of production that both generated tradeable surpluses, and often required the importing of other foods and/or raw materials. The basic model of the CAP empire depended on trade not only for the exotic luxury goods from afar that supported the status differentiations among the highly stratified layers of CAPE society, but also for some basic requirements, including food and metal. The advent of the Bronze Age, for example, necessitated long-distance trade, because copper and tin were not found in the same place, and tin was found only in a few (Radner, 2020: 314). This logic applied to steppe nomad empires as well as to sedentary agrarian ones, and the two types were notably linked by the overland trade routes of the Silk Roads (Schouenborg, 2017: 108–13). The trading networks of the CAPE era expanded steadily, albeit with ups and downs during periods of plague, turbulence and war, eventually reaching global scale during the fifteenth to the eighteenth centuries AD. Hobson (2021) argues that the Indian Ocean trading system, and particularly its export of Indian cotton textiles, constituted the first global economy. The British tapped into this, were shaped by it, and eventually took it over. He sees this first, Asian, global economy as a major element in the late CAPE globalisation, alongside, and eventually integrated into, the European-centred one that developed with the opening up of the oceanic routes across the Atlantic and Pacific Oceans. Relay trade remained important in connecting distant regions such as Europe and Northeast Asia, but steadily gave way to the creation of organised trading networks on a regional scale. It was more or less eliminated by the creation of global oceanic trading networks.

The English School has been generally poor in taking the economic sector adequately into account as part of either international or world society (Falkner and Buzan, forthcoming). A few classical English School writers (Wight, 1977; Holsti, 2004) identified trade as an institution of international society – indeed, the institution in the economic sector – and up to the nineteenth century, they were correct to do so. But what these vanguard thinkers missed was that trade was the signature accomplishment of the CAPE era in terms of laying the foundations for global society. They missed this point partly because they focused only on a narrow range of historical examples, and partly because IR generally was (and although less so, still is) biased towards the military-political sectors, and neglectful (and mostly ignorant) of the economic one. This neglect of the economic sector was partly due to the difficulty of mastering the increasing technicalities within which the discipline of Economics wrapped itself. But it was perhaps, more subtly, also due to a preference for the state level in thinking about international systems/societies, and a downplaying of the transnational domain. Even IPE still focuses largely on the modern world economy from the nineteenth century. Buzan and Little (2000) made the case that trade was always the leading edge in the making of international systems, and was always the largest-scale human system when compared with political and societal spheres. But they too underplayed the point that because trade was the sector that first linked up different societies and civilisations, it was therefore foundational to the making of global society. Trade was usually the first point of direct contact between alien societies.[15] It was not, like monarchy/dynasticism and human inequality, a shared characteristic requiring mainly recognition, but something that required extensive and sustained physical and social interaction. It was therefore instrumental in promoting both the transmission of culture, especially religions, and the development of primary institutions between and among alien societies. Like much of the rest of IR, excluding Marxists of course, the ES has marginalised the role of the economic sector, and therefore the

---

[15] An interesting recent, and therefore relatively well-documented, example of this is the encounter between Europeans and indigenous peoples in what is now the US and Canada (Hamalainen, 2019).

transnational domain, and put too much emphasis on the political-military sectors, and therefore the interpolity domain.

Throughout the CAPE era, trade had a much greater range than either empires or war. Trade promoted cultural mixing in terms of facilitating the transmission not only of religion and styles of art and design, but also knowledge of technology, minerals and varieties of flora and fauna that could be used as food, drugs and manufacturing materials. It also added a large-scale slave trade to the more natural processes of migration in promoting both cultural and biological mixing. As the extent of trading networks grew, it gave the peoples enmeshed in them a wider sense of the world and all its variety. More specifically, it could be argued that trade laid the foundations for both positive international law (in terms of agreements about private contracts, shipping and piracy), and diplomacy between states and non-state actors (in terms of merchants having ambassadors, and negotiating with political authorities for terms of trade and extraterritorial rights to govern their own diaspora communities). During the CAPE era, trade stood largely by itself as the economic primary institution of global society. There was no real conceptualisation of the economy as a distinct sphere of activity that needed to be understood and managed in its own right. States and empires generally supported trade, as well as taxing and regulating it, but mostly did not interfere much in merchant activity. Merchants were allowed to organise themselves into business partnerships and professional guilds to promote their interests, and did not concern themselves with the larger economic and political consequences of such activities for state and society (Finley, 1973: 155–66; Bayly, 2004: 36–40). This remained true during the economic revolution in Europe led by the Italian city-states from the tenth to the sixteenth centuries, where there was no intellectual or abstract interest in 'the economy' or economics, as such (Goldthwaite, 2011: 555–8). Mercantilist thinking in early modern Europe began to build a crude understanding of the economy in terms of the need to serve the military purposes of the state, especially by encouraging a trade surplus, and thus the ability to accumulate specie. From the nineteenth century onwards, things got more complicated in the economic sector, as a more sophisticated understanding of the economy came into play around the concept of the market. More on that in Part II.

Trade as an institution of the CAPE era stretched across all three domains: interpolity, transnational and interhuman. What is a bit harder to call is whether its primary location was in the interpolity domain or the transnational one? There is a lot of blurry ground between merchants and trade on the one side, and the state, politics and military activities, on the other side. States and empires might provide protection for merchants within their territories by policing caravan routes and giving foreign merchants their own spaces in port cities (Darwin, 2020: 4–38). But merchants carrying valuable cargos outside the bounds of empires usually needed to protect themselves against bandits and pirates. It was therefore normal for merchant ships and caravans to travel armed. Armed merchants could easily turn to piracy themselves, or use their weapons to intimidate those with whom they traded. They could also provide military goods: Goldthwaite (2011: 70) notes a fifteenth-century Florentine syndicate formed, inter alia, 'to rent and arm galleys'.

There is no question that the states and empires of the CAPE era were heavily involved in trade. Capturing trade routes and trade resources was often a motive behind imperial expansion and war, and for long-distance trade, it was states that permitted merchants to trade or not. The Ottoman 'capitulations' from the sixteenth century, for example were a means of legitimising trade with Christian Venice and Genoa (Paine, 2014: loc. 8779). Most states and empires depended to some degree on tax revenues from trade, and this dependence could be very substantial (e.g. for the Southern Song in China and the Safavids in Persia). Some states and empires, notably Venice, Genoa, the various polities near the Malacca Strait, and Britain, were largely built around long-distance trade. States and empires could seek to control trade routes both for reasons of prosperity (tax revenue) and security (if they were dependent on resources outside their domain). Some port cities such as Malacca and Aden flourished because they were at the interface of the different regional monsoon weather systems that defined where and when trading ships could sail (Darwin, 2020: 19–23). State and imperial elites also wanted access to exotic goods, both for amusement, and to embellish their status differentiation. Polities played a direct role in trade, not just by regulation and taxation, but also by being participants themselves. It was not uncommon for states to award themselves monopolies on profitable essentials such as salt. The Mauryan Emperor Ashoka seems to have had a monopoly on shipbuilding, renting ships to merchants and fixing taxes and levels of profit (Paine, 2014: locs. 3067–199). In Roman times, between 15 and 30 per cent of imported grain was carried in government ships, the rest in private ones (Paine, 2014: loc. 3009). Findlay and O'Rourke (2007: 135) note that the Sultan of Melaka had his own trading fleet, trading 'on his own account as well as in partnership with private traders'. States were also crucial to the award of monopoly rights over particular economic sectors or trade destinations to merchants (more on this below).

This blurring of roles could also work the other way around, with merchants taking on polity-like qualities in terms of diplomacy and the use of force. It was common practice for merchant adventurers to mix trading and raiding. Merchants could also become auxiliaries in war if the state or some other military actor hired or commandeered their ships. In Song China, the government was: 'forced by the exigencies of war to frequently requisition merchant vessels to serve as warships or military transports' (Findlay and O'Rourke, 2007: 64). The Christian armies of the Crusades were largely carried in armed commercial shipping, and made good profits for Genoa, Pisa and Venice (Paine, 2014: locs. 6706–843). European privateers stood halfway between merchants and the state, being privately owned armed ships licensed by the state to attack the commerce of designated enemies. Some of these were not too scrupulous about who they attacked, blurring the boundary with piracy. In Europe, the distinction between armed merchant ships and naval vessels did not become clear until the brink of the modern era in the eighteenth century.

The culmination of the armed merchant tradition was probably in the European chartered companies of the seventeenth and eighteenth centuries, such as the Dutch *Vereenigde Oostindische Compagnie* (VoC), and the English East India Company (EIC) (Findlay and O'Rourke, 2007: 144–57, 167–87, 262–75; Phillips and Sharman, 2015, 2020). Both of these had polity-like properties of diplomacy, armed forces and powers of government despite being essentially trading companies. These companies were chartered as state monopolies (Micklethwait and Wooldridge, 2003: 25–36), but in fact constituted a temporary bridge between the interpolity and transnational domains that enabled the premodern European states to perform globally beyond their own capacities. At its height, the EIC conquered and governed India, and had a private army of 260,000 men, twice the size of the British army (Micklethwait and Wooldridge, 2003: 4). The Hanseatic League in the thirteenth and fourteenth centuries was likewise a cross-domain blending of political and commercial interests, both controlling trade and sometimes making war, in northeast Europe (Paine, 2014: loc. 6902–7043). Paine (2014: loc. 8052) indeed argues that: 'the evolving symbiosis between rulers and merchants so characteristic of the Italian city-states like Venice, Genoa and Florence, through whose influence this dynamic spread to Iberia and northern Europe', was a key innovation behind the rise of Europe from the fifteenth century.

Despite the significant role of states and empires in trade, there seems to be a stronger case for rooting this institution primarily in the transnational domain. As already suggested in relation to trade in prehistoric times, such activity did not fundamentally depend on political oversight or initiation. Like religion and other forms of identity creation and reproduction, trade has an autonomous quality. It has for long been a feature of interhuman relations occurring spontaneously in most forms of human society. In the more intense and complex social structure of the CAPE era, trade had necessarily to come to terms with the proliferation of other social structures around it, particularly the political ones. Political conditions affected the extent and profitability of trade in very substantial ways, both positively and negatively. Even where political authorities tried to suppress or limit foreign trade, as sometimes happened in China, it continued anyway, albeit in more circuitous ways. Perhaps the clearest illustration of this enduring relative autonomy of trade during the CAPE era are the significant secondary institutions associated with it: *companies*, *guilds* and *trade diasporas*. There is considerable overlap, indeed blurring, amongst these three, and the historical records of them are often thin and patchy, but the following account hopefully gives a sufficient sketch to justify placing trade primarily in the transnational domain. Given that my focus is on global society, I concentrate mainly on these three institutions as they played into long-distance trade.

Companies Companies are the foundational secondary institution for trade, for without them guilds and trade diasporas would not exist. That said, there is an immediate problem with using the term 'companies', which is loaded with baggage associated with the formation of modern limited companies in the nineteenth century. The 'companies' of the CAPE era are for the most part quite distant relatives of the modern company, though their functions in terms of production, trade, finance and labour are in many basic ways recognisably similar. On the production side, workshops for the mass manufacture of such things as fabrics and weapons existed in early Mesopotamian civilisations, and in Greece and Rome. China also had large-scale production facilities for such things as ceramics, often as monopolies (Micklethwait and Wooldridge, 2003: 14–16). These, however, were mainly domestic, local, affairs, even though their supplies of raw materials and their markets might depend on trade. The key to companies as a secondary institution of global society is trade, and the merchants who carried it out.

In part, this CAPE story is intended to put into perspective the often Eurocentric claims that the company is: 'the most important organisation in the world'. And 'one of the West's great competitive advantages' (Micklethwait and Wooldridge, 2003: 2, 8; see also Stavrianos, 1990: 95–6). To get at the meaning of 'companies' in the CAPE era one has to start with merchants. Recall that in the hunter-gatherer era, trade was mainly by relay along strings of adjacent human communities. It did not require a specialised class of merchants, and hunter-gatherer communities did not anyway support that degree of functional differentiation. As settlement occurred, agrarian production (both agricultural and artisanal) became locally specialised according to comparative advantage. Such production generated tradeable surpluses, and this in turn supported the development of a merchant class specialising in trade. Much of this trade was local, but some of it was long-distance. Expanding interaction capacity made such long-distance trade viable. At some point around the dawn of civilisation, merchants became part of an increasingly specialised and differentiated society. Some of them took up long-distance trade, where high profits were to be made from bringing in exotic goods from faraway places.

Given the technological limits on transportation during this era, much long-distance trade, especially for heavy bulk goods (e.g. grain, timber, stone, wine and metals) had to go by water. Although some of that could be done by river, increasingly it was done by sea. Shipping goods by sea was a risky and expensive business, though also potentially very profitable. Ships were costly things in themselves, and their cargos represented a big concentration of value. They might be overwhelmed by the sea or by pirates, and in the days of oar and sail, neither fate was uncommon. The origin of transnational 'companies' is to be found in the solution to this problem. Goldthwaite (2011: 27) sets out the idea of an evolution from individual merchant adventurers, sailing with their own cargos, to what he calls the 'sedentary mercantile firm', in which the merchants operated from a fixed central base using a variety of shippers and agents to carry and handle their goods. As trade increased, the whole business became more sophisticated and more differentiated. Shipowners, mariners, merchants and financiers separated into distinct professions. Individual merchant adventurers gave way to various forms of business partnership. Kinship certainly played a large role in this process, because it helped to solve the problem of trust in the taking of financial risks (Goldthwaite, 2011: 31). For this reason, family companies were common, though where the legal and political environment became stable and supportive enough, risk could be shared beyond families.

Although he was writing about Renaissance Florence, and allowing for lots of local variations, Goldthwaite's idea provides a useful framing for the larger picture of CAPE era 'companies'. A pattern generally along these lines evolved in many different places at different times. Forms of business partnership in premodern times go back to ancient Mesopotamia, where from the second millennium BC merchants would form business partnerships to finance, and spread the risk of, trading operations, in return for profit sharing. These tended to be short-term arrangements around specific voyages rather than standing organisations, though such partnerships could also be set up for longer periods (three to five years) and be renewable if the partners agreed to do so. Such practices existed in classical Greece, Rome and China (Micklethwait and Wooldridge, 2003: 14–16). From at least as early as Roman times, the practice of lending to cover the costs of commercial voyages was a common form of investment (Paine, 2014: loc. 3009). The Islamic world was particularly conducive to this kind of merchant activity. It had a form of commercial law within Islamic jurisprudence that covered market behaviour, business partnerships, financial arrangements and customs rates. Even though 'there was no provision in Islamic law for a corporate person', Islamic traders had the financial arrangements of merchant capitalism in which trading voyages were financed and insured by investors. Islam 'was a portable, legalistic faith, attractive to and suitable for merchants' (Risso, 1995: 19–20, 70–1, 104). Paine (2014: locs. 4729–868, 7153–202) also notes the significant development of commercial law in the Mediaeval Mediterranean blending Jewish, Muslim and Christian practices, and supporting the expansion of trade flowing among Europe, Asia and Africa. The use of investment and insurance to spread the risks and profits of shipping was a great lubricant to commerce given that the probability of ships being lost was quite high. The Byzantine Empire and the Islamic world both had administrative and legal systems that supported trade (Goldthwaite, 2011: loc. 374). Venice picked up both these practices from the ninth century, spreading it to other Italian city states and eventually to Europe (Micklethwait and Wooldridge, 2003: 17–20).

This general story covering most of the CAPE era blends into the better-known European story of companies. As a relative backwater in Eurasia, post-Roman Europe was amongst the last to pick up these practices which had been going on for millennia elsewhere in Eurasia. Italy was the front-line for this transfer of ideas, and within a few centuries after the fall of the Western Roman Empire, was unfolding its own version of the story of evolving from merchant adventurers, through flexible partnerships, to sedentary mercantile firms. Rising Italian city-states such as Venice, Genoa, Pisa and Florence increasingly captured both trade and manufacture from the Byzantine Empire and the Islamic world, learning to improve their business methods as they did so (Goldthwaite, 2011). An important part of this story is the evolution of banking out of the operation of mercantile companies. The logic is fairly simple. Mercantile traders will sometimes have surplus cash to invest, and sometimes will need to borrow in order to cover gaps. Investments by outsiders in shipping ventures easily morphed into deposits on which merchants would pay interest. Outsiders, from other companies, to princes and popes, might also want to borrow from merchants (or guilds) that had surplus cash. All of this easily generated 'merchants' who began to specialise in finance, and thereby to become bankers (Goldthwaite, 2011: locs. 433–511, pp. 1, 29–30, 167–210). Once commerce reached a certain scale and stability, banking in some form was a natural development. The rise of banking and finance in mediaeval and early-modern Europe is a well-documented story. Frequent references to 'moneylenders' throughout the CAPE era suggest that the structural logic that gave rise to banking and finance in Europe also worked elsewhere, though the documentary evidence for it is much thinner. It is clear that investing, lending, bills of exchange and other such financial practices did not originate in Europe but were a long-established practice throughout Eurasia.[16]

From the fifteenth century, the European story of companies shifts to the chartered company, whose distinctive story Davis (1971 [1905]) sets out in detail. Among other things, this development was enabled by improvements in interaction capacity by sea opened up by the development of sturdy ocean-going ships in Europe, and the navigational knowledge and skill to take them on transoceanic voyages. Trading companies such as the Company of Merchants of London, and the Company of Merchant Adventurers, emerged during the fifteenth century. They were licensed by the state to perform overseas functions that the state at that time lacked the administrative and financial capacity to perform itself, but wanted to have done. In effect, the state mobilised private capital to take the risks of opening up trade in new areas, and sometimes also new colonies, in return for the grant of political and commercial privileges, and monopoly rights to trade. The state, of course, was also interested in getting a share of the profits. During the sixteenth century, ventures such as the Muscovy Company (1554), the Levant Company (1581) and the Morocco Company (1588) were set up to this end. The golden age of these chartered companies began in the seventeenth century with the Dutch VoC and then the British EIC already mentioned above. The success of these two was encouraging, and by the end of the century, a hundred new companies had been formed (Kindleberger, 1984: 196). These were joint-stock companies, and were given not only exclusive rights to trade, but also substantial political, military and diplomatic

---

[16] Buzan and Little (2000: 212–13, 335). A bill of exchange works like a modern cheque, being an instruction written by one person to a second person in a different location, to pay a specified amount to a third person on presentation of the document.

rights to do whatever was necessary to their pursuit of trade. As noted, this famously led to the takeover of much of India by the British East India Company during the eighteenth century. These chartered companies were high-risk ventures, potentially durable (the Hudson's Bay Company is still going), had a degree of limited liability, and sold tradeable shares thus giving rise to stock markets (Ogilvie, 2011: 30–8). They saw out the CAPE era before being largely replaced during the nineteenth century by the modern firm.

This long history of companies, and its deep entanglement with polities and princes, makes the case that integrated world society, and forms of 'global governance' stretching across the three domains, are not new. They go back a very, very long way. No concept of international, or world, or global society makes sense without taking them into account.

Guilds Guilds were an institution common to many cultures, stretching far back in time almost to the beginning of the CAPE era, where societies and economies were first becoming more functionally differentiated into specialised occupations. They had social and religious functions for their members, and were described by Bain (1887: 4) as an organisational development to handle collective affairs that were beyond the scale of the individual family. Moll-Murata (2008: 217) defines guilds as: 'a common-interest group of merchants or artisans' possessing quarters, regulations and recognition by the local government. They can be differentiated into what might be broadly called *craft guilds*, those associated with artisans and production, and *merchant guilds*, associated with traders. According to Bain (1887: 7–12), at least in Europe, merchant guilds tended to be wealthier and better connected to government and the ruling classes, whereas trade/craft guilds were less wealthy, and needed to struggle, sometimes violently, for their interests and rights. Bain (1887: 2–14) makes a structural argument that guilds had a certain similarity across time and space because they 'all sprang from the one common instinct of men seeking strength by union or combination' (2).[17] They usually had origins in particular towns or localities, and craft guilds often stayed local. But merchant guilds in particular often developed overseas branches and became transnational networks. Guilds were clubs for merchants and their 'companies'.

---

[17] The reference to 'men' begs the question of whether women were allowed to play any role in these seemingly patriarchal organisations. Perhaps there is a story similar to that of women warriors to be excavated.

Ogilvie (2011: 1) describes their international history as follows:

Privileged associations of merchants have been widespread since ancient times. They existed not just in Europe but also in North Africa, the Near East, Central and South America, India and China. Merchant associations were active in Egyptian, Greek and Roman antiquity, and survived in European and Mediterranean trading centres during the five centuries after the fall of Rome. They became a salient institution in much of Europe during the medieval Commercial Revolution, between c. 1000 and c. 1500.

In India, guilds (*shreni*) go back to pre-Mauryan times and had some linkages to the development of the caste system, tending to have hereditary leaderships (Thaplyal, 2001). During Chola times (850–1279 AD), there were 'large, well-organized Tamil merchant guilds that hired their own mercenary troops' (Findlay and O'Rourke, 2007: 67). Guilds of self-managing artisans and merchants existed in classical Greece and Rome (*collegium, collegia, corpus*), and in Rome had a legal corporate identity distinct from that of their individual members (Micklethwait and Wooldridge, 2003: 14; Ogilvie, 2011: 20–1). Roman guilds reflected an elaborate division of labour into many specialised crafts, from dyeing, copper-smiths and nail makers, to shippers of wine, pottery, grain and slaves (Arnaoutoglou, 2016: 281–2; Rice, 2016: 99–100). In the Islamic world, the rise of Turkic military leadership from the eleventh century led to a hands-off, arms-length style of government that excluded other elites, and motivated merchants to organise themselves into guilds, Sufi brotherhoods and suchlike. Networks of Muslim merchants established themselves in settlements along the west coast of India, the east coast of Africa and in Southeast Asia (Risso, 1995: 31–2, 42–50, 100). In China, guilds date back at least to the Tang dynasty, by which time there was a class of very wealthy merchants and shipowners, many of them foreign Muslims (Findlay and O'Rourke, 2007: 39, 62–5). From the eighth to the fourteenth centuries, Chinese guilds were mainly instruments of the government to control the economy, but from the sixteenth century they became more independent, and functionally similar to European guilds. The *Cohongs* played a major role in managing trade with the Europeans in the eighteenth and nineteenth centuries (Moll-Murata, 2008).

The story of guilds in Europe is more recent, and so better documented than in most other places (e.g. Goldthwaite, 2011: 305–12). It seems probable that European guilds grew out of the remnants of Roman ones that survived in some towns after the fall of the Western Roman Empire (Ogilvie, 2011: 20–1), and to which they bore many similarities (Bain, 1887: 5). By the tenth century, guilds were an important institution in Europe's emerging economy. They declined from the sixteenth century, as Europe, led by the Netherlands and Britain, shifted towards a preference for more open markets with competition, and rules provided by the state. Guilds were predominantly local to particular towns and cities, but there were also what Ogilvie (2011: 94–159) calls 'alien merchant guilds'. These operated in much the same way as local ones, seeking deals with rulers for monopoly rights and other economic privileges in return for a share of the profits, but did so on the basis of extensive transnational networks. Alien guilds were key nodes for trade in the European and Mediterranean systems. The Hanseatic League was amongst the most conspicuous developments of this type.

Guilds seem to arise from two lines of functional logic common to all societies that were moving into the more complex and larger-scale forms associated with the shift to sedentism and agriculture. First, there were economic efficiencies to be gained by people in the same trade grouping together to pursue common interests. This covered such things as collective purchasing of raw materials, control of entry into the profession, making loans, training of apprentices, gathering information about market and political conditions, maintaining agreed standards for production, setting and administering rules for trading, including price-fixing and control of supply, and disciplining members who broke the rules or violated the norms of the guild. But the central purpose of guilds was to gain and enforce a monopoly over their particular trade, and that could only be done in league with the local political elites who alone could grant such rights (Ogilvie, 2011: 41–93).

This set up the second functional logic for guilds: that there was advantage to be gained for actors in the economic sector to combine together in order to deal with the political authorities that governed them. Guilds were in part about protecting trade from the local political authorities who could always wield coercive powers to extract resources in destructive ways. They thus became political actors in their own right. Their typical strategy was to enter into partnership with their political authorities to seek mutual advantage: an alliance of coercion and capital to use Tilly's (1990) terms. From the political authorities, guilds negotiated on behalf of their members such things as recognition, tax-exemptions, granting of monopoly or other licensing privileges, and port privileges. The political authorities might also provide a degree of security, and infrastructure such as ports. In return, guilds might undertake tax collection on behalf of the political authorities, provide them with loans on favourable terms, provide gifts or honoraria (aka bribes) to officials, and support wars with money, shipping or other goods and infrastructure. Guilds might also undertake charitable obligations and public works within society. From this perspective, guilds can be seen as the institutional form in which the holders of capital came to terms with the holders of coercive power by doing a deal in which they would in various ways share the profits to be extracted from monopoly rents (Ogilvie, 2011: 13–17, 170–9).

It is worth pausing for a minute here to consider this joint enthusiasm between political and economic elites for economic monopolies. In contemporary liberal economic theory, monopolies (unless they are 'natural') get a bad press. They are thought of as inefficient, both raising costs to consumers and stifling innovation, and a good case can be made for that interpretation. Yet during the CAPE era, the seeking of monopolies also made sense. Both polities and merchants sought to maximise their revenues from trade. Innovation was much less of an issue in people's minds at that time. There was little or no thinking about 'the economy' as a whole, and not much concern for the rights of consumers (CAPE societies were rarely democratic, and those that were mostly had a narrow franchise). Empires sought monopolies as a matter of course, both for security, and to increase their revenues from trade. Capturing trade routes was one of their rationales for expansion. 'Companies', then as now, sought to maximise profits for their owners (shareholders), managers and investors. In the high-risk environment of long-distance trade during the CAPE era, having a monopoly was a good way of pursuing all of these aims. Under the conditions of the day, it is not surprising that both merchants and political elites agreed on this.

Guilds often had more resources than local governments, and they 'increased the revenues rulers could extract from their subjects' (Ogilvie, 2011: 160, 168). Within dynastic systems, merchant guilds also provided for the crown a political counterweight to the nobility in a three-sided political game (Bain, 1887: 14; Ogilvie, 2011: 179–82). In addition, guilds usually had substantial social and religious functions for their members. They were often associated with a religious institution and religious observances, and they provided members with club facilities (guildhalls) and a variety of ceremonial and social occasions. Guilds created social as well as economic capital for their members (Ogilvie, 2011: 6–12). They typically set up a common fund, which they financed from fees for entry and continued membership, fines for rule-breaking, and suchlike (Arnaoutoglou, 2016).

The pervasiveness and durability of guilds in CAPE societies suggests that the force of these two logics was strong. When they acted together, there was strength to be had in both economic and social terms for artisans and merchants. And all in the economic sector had to come to terms with the local powers that be if they were to be able to operate successfully. Guilds were the institution through which the economic and political elites could pursue their mutual interests (Ogilvie, 2011). As Ogilvie (2011: 3, 79–81) argues, lobbying was a key activity for guilds. They fought (sometimes literally), and lobbied their local rulers (often expensively), to gain and preserve their privileges. Guilds were thus one of the key secondary institutions of the CAPE era. Underlining the argument that the distinction between companies and guilds can be blurry, Ogilvie (2011: 30–8) argues that the European chartered companies from the fifteenth to the eighteenth centuries were like guilds in some ways, most notably in being arrangements between merchants and rulers to create monopoly rents, and divide the benefits from them. Such organisations reflected the administrative weakness and limits of CAPE polities, which needed to make alliances with merchants in order to advance their economic interests.

Trade Diasporas Trade diasporas were communities of merchants supporting long-distance trade using networks of trust based on shared kinship, ethnicity or religion, and providing letters of credit, loans and other financial services. There is obviously a considerable degree of overlap between this concept and the activities of both long-distant merchant companies and alien guilds discussed above. Yet trade diasporas tend to be discussed as a distinct structure, though it is not entirely clear what additional element they contain after companies and guilds are brought into the picture. The two likely points are that trade diasporas created settlements along trade routes, and that there was possibly a more extended role for ethnicity and religion. Yet the role of kinship, ethnicity and religion was also strong in companies and guilds, which ran the logistics of long-distance trade, and negotiated terms with the local rulers and polities. The discussion of trade diasporas is heavily associated with shipping and maritime trade, though this did not exclude a major role in the overland caravan trades. They provided import and export opportunities, and tax revenue, for the state. Such trade diasporas operated since at least the second millennium BC, and throughout the CAPE era. A well-institutionalised system of trade diasporas developed alongside the evolution of cities, forming a kind of commercial world society within the CAPE world. The Roman economy had a sophisticated system of trade diasporas that provided information and networks of contacts to connect the Empire's trading ports (Rice, 2016: 102–8). Dynastic, warrior and religious elites tended to look down on merchants, trade and finance even though they depended on them.[18] They were thus

---

[18] This varied from culture to culture. Confucian, Græco-Roman and Christian cultures ranked merchants and trading low in status, whereas Buddhist and Islamic cultures were

happy to let foreigners, or in Rome slaves, or freed slaves (Rice, 2016: 108–9), play a major role in commerce. That created opportunities for minorities, who had low status anyway, to occupy a lucrative, although sometimes dangerous, economic niche.[19] This institution provided networks of trust, skill and logistics that helped to overcome obstacles to trade, including suspicion of foreigners (Curtin, 1984: 1–14, 112–15, 127–35).

Trade diasporas were usually based on shared ethnicity and religion as the basis of trust over long distances. McNeill (1963: 509), for example, notes how the Jews were well-placed to act as economic intermediaries between the Christian and Islamic worlds because their networks crossed the boundaries between them. Many other peoples from Assyrians, through Phoenicians and Greeks, to the Islamic merchants long settled in China's ports and along the East African coast, also played this role. By the thirteenth century, merchant communities in the Indian Ocean were well organised to deal with both predatory and supportive local states, and to adapt their trade to the fluctuating political situation (Paine, 2014: locs. 7527–635). Trade diasporas were a form of social infrastructure, partly self-regulating in terms of trade and finance, partly in collaboration with local political powers who often allowed their settlements and practices to be self-governing, although subject to local regulation and taxation (Curtin, 1984: 112–15, 127–35). Merchant communities were bound together by well-established conventions about contracts and trade. Loss of reputation because of cheating or setting harsh or unpredictable charges could mean exclusion from the system, and considerable loss of income, as trade moved to more congenial and reliable partners or ports (Chaudhuri, 1985: 12–13, 36). As an institution, trade diasporas successfully mediated among the political, social and economic sectors. The merchants got some degree of protection, the political rulers got goods and taxes, and religious and social differences were mediated by allowing the merchants to establish self-governing enclaves in foreign cities. Trade diasporas, along with alien guilds, thus also practised diplomacy across the transnational and interstate/empire domains. They were a comfortable fit with dynasticism, religion and empires.

These stories of companies, guilds and trade diasporas point towards the emergence of mercantilism in Europe from the sixteenth century.

---

much more supportive, and Hindu cultures somewhere in between (Kim and van Bergeijk, 2022).

[19] The Greek god Hermes was the patron of both thieves and merchants (Curtin, 1984: 76), suggesting that in CAPE civilisations, the two roles were not strongly differentiated.

As Europe emerged from being a barbarian backwater of Eurasia, mercantilism was the form it found to institutionalise the typical CAPE pattern of a deal between merchants and the local holders of political power to share the benefits of monopoly rents. This story might be told here, but I save it until Chapter 5b, because it also involves the emergence of 'the economy' as a modern concept that might be theorised and acted upon. In Chapter 5b, this works to clarify the extraordinary changes that occurred in the economic sector during the nineteenth century.

If the institution of trade was rooted in the transnational domain, and strong in the interpolity one, it was also influential in the interhuman domain. Trade depended on, and influenced, matters of collective identity. As noted, trade diasporas depended vitally on the shared identity of their membership as a source of trust. This could be as narrow as direct kinship, or extend to shared ethnic identities and religions. In the Mediaeval Mediterranean, for example, Christian and Muslim merchants had entirely separate enclaves in major ports like Alexandria (Findlay and O'Rourke, 2007: 55). The other way around, as also noted, trade routes played a major role in shaping both culture and identity. Shared religious identities such as Islamic, Christian and Buddhist, and often the missionaries that promoted them, travelled successfully along trade routes. The slave trade generated a lot of biological blending (Lerner, 1986: ch. 4), and all cultures engaged in long-distance trade were shaped by the ideas and products that it brought to them. In terms of human inequality during the CAPE era, the story of trade suggests that differentiations by function and by religion/culture, were much stronger than differentiation by race.

Territoriality

Territoriality is closely tied to settlement. For mobile HGBs there was an intimate connection to their estate, which they needed to know well in order to survive, but the general attitude towards territory for such mobile small groups was relatively open. Settled foragers developed more possessive attitudes towards territory. During the CAPE era, there were two distinct, but overlapping, dynamics of territoriality in play, one attached to sedentary, agrarian civilisations, and the other to steppe nomads.

For the sedentary, agrarian civilisations, territoriality followed the logic of settlement, increasing ties to the land, and investment in it (e.g. irrigation, terracing, forest-clearing), and the cultivation of a sense of ownership. Because fertile land was the principal source of food and wealth, control of it, and its produce, was sufficient cause to fight, more so as the density of human occupation increased. The question of who owned the land (the peasants or the lords) varied from place to place, but the point is that somebody, or sometimes competing claimants, asserted the right either to own it, or to control its use, and that right could legitimately be challenged by force. At this point, the shaping logics of monarchy/dynasticism and imperialism on territoriality come into play. Monarchy/dynasticism and empire were both essentially open-ended as regards to the extent of territorial ownership that could be claimed. In practice, this produced conglomerate empires loosely stitched together by the effective wielding of military power, and dynastic legitimacy and marriage. Such structures were in a more or less constant process of expansion and contraction, sometimes reaching huge extent, and some-times disintegrating down to many fragments. These fluctuations meant that while the ownership of territory was important in terms of claims for status, tax rights, and a degree of political control, it was by modern standards also relatively ephemeral and superficial. What one empire or sovereign owned today, might well be owned by another tomorrow (Holsti, 2004: 73–5). This might be styled as *flexible territoriality*, in which claims to ownership of territory and its inhabitants were a recognised and important part of both domestic and interpolity society, and often a motive for war. But the actual holding of territory was often transitory, and not deeply linked to identity other than at the local level. Flexible territoriality therefore supported many degrees of incorporation of terri-tories and peoples into empires. The Chinese tribute system, for example, while partly about rights to trade, was mainly about trying to validate the imperial claim to rule 'all under heaven'. It was often more symbolic than real, being content with leaving almost complete local autonomy in exchange for acknowledgement of suzerain status to the emperor. The British Empire likewise contained many degrees of auton-omy, from the near complete subordination of colonies, through the half subordination of protectorates, to the near-independence of the dominions. This kind of concentric circles construction, varying from strong central control, through dominion and suzerainty, to hegemony, was common to most CAP empires.

For the steppe nomads, the logic of settlement did not apply. While in some ways the nomadic lifeway of the steppe peoples was like that of mobile HGBs, it was not a direct descendent of it.[20] Steppe nomads also had 'estates' around which they moved themselves and their herds

---

[20] HGBs had no domesticated animals except dogs. The steppe could not be permanently occupied by humans until herd animals had been sufficiently domesticated to enable the nomadic pastoralist lifeway.

according to the seasons (Neumann and Wigen, 2018: 77–9). But they were part of a wider steppe society that was hierarchical, featured golden kinships of ruling elites, and had war as a regular feature. The nomad pastoralist lifeway was designed to be mobile, and the pressures of both climate change and wars amongst the steppe tribes could, and quite regularly did, push nomads off the steppe and into lands adjacent to, or within, the domains of sedentary civilisations. Sometimes the dynamics of the steppe produced steppe empires that mounted organised attacks, both raids and invasions, on sedentary societies. But equally often, climate change and/or warfare on the steppe expelled many steppe tribes in the form of decentralised, but well-armed, tribal mass migrations. Probably the best-known example of this is the Germanic peoples being pushed off the steppe and into eastern Europe during the first millennium BC. By the second century AD, they were being squeezed by the expansion of the Huns from the steppe behind them, and were regularly at war with Rome in front of them. They are often credited with being a main cause of the downfall of the Western Roman Empire, and similar cases can be found in Persia and China. Once having broken through, these tribes settled most of Western Europe, the Vandals even occupying as far afield as North Africa. The inherent mobility of the steppe nomad lifeway, when combined with military skills, made for a very thin sense of territoriality, a kind of *flexibility-plus*. Neumann and Wigen (2018: ch. 1), and in a different way Zarakol (2022), make the important point that the Western analytical tradition about the state is very strongly wedded to the sedentary/territorial model, and has largely ignored the nomadic state tradition. The steppe nomads, like the sedentary peoples, accepted the legitimacy of ownership of territory by force. When steppe nomads came to rule sedentary empires, they tended to take on the sedentary view of territoriality.

Towards the end of the CAPE era, a harder form of territoriality began to emerge in seventeenth-century Europe, moving towards the relatively firm and fixed boundaries characteristic of the transition towards modernity. This development reflected not only the improving administrative capacity of states in Europe, but also better technologies and techniques for surveying the land, and military interests in defensible borders. Flexibility remained in the many acceptable procedures for exchanging territories between states/empires, but the territories themselves were more precisely defined and demarcated (Holsti, 2004: 75–88).

An interesting twist to the hardening of the institution of territoriality developed during the CAPE era, its application to a second dimension: the sea. For those kingdoms or empires owning a coastline, defence against both enemies and pirates was a problem, as was the protection of fisheries. Coastal defence underpinned the process of extending territoriality to the sea. But the limited range of CAPE era 'artillery' before gunpowder did not lend itself to control of the sea directly from the land. To defend your coast, you needed ships. It is not clear when specific claims to own or control coastal waters began, though it seems likely that internal waters such as bays, inlets and estuaries, where land and sea intertwine, were the starting point. The Chinese claim to rule 'all under heaven' logically included the seas, but in practice China rarely controlled its maritime borders effectively. When Rome was at the height of its power, having eliminated Carthage, and controlling all of the coastal territories and enjoying naval supremacy, it claimed the Mediterranean as its *Mare Nostrum* ('our sea'). This was more a practical claim than a legal doctrine.

Perhaps the explicit territorialisation of the sea is best dated from the eleventh century, when Venice, having gained naval control over the Adriatic, conducted an annual ceremony proclaiming its 'marriage' to the Adriatic. Genoa likewise claimed its adjacent sea. Papal Bulls in the fifteenth century adjudicating between Portugal and Spain in the Atlantic put what were effectively territorial dividing lines across the sea (Paine, 2014: locs. 8044–94, 8222–70). Early modern states in Europe began to claim various widths of territorial sea, and by the early seventeenth century, the legal debate there had crystallised with Grotius' *Mare Liberum* (1609) and Selden's *Mare Clausum* (1619), setting out the opposing positions of open and closed seas (Paine, 2014: locs. 9179–223). At around the same time, the three-mile rule, representing the range of coastal defence cannon shot, emerged as an attempt to standardise claims to coastal waters, and to create a clear dividing line between territorial seas (owned by the coastal state) and high seas (a common space open to all). This extension of the institution of territoriality to the seas adjacent to states was not of great significance during the CAPE era itself, but it set the precedent for an imperative to territorialise additional dimensions (air, space, cyberspace) that became extremely important from the twentieth century onward.

In the interpolity domain, ownership of territory in some sense was the basic currency of inter-empire relations, being one key measure of their size, status and wealth. In the transnational domain, a continuously fluctuating territorial map was the context within which merchants had to trade. For the most part they were quick to adjust to changes that made some routes and destinations safer and/or more profitable than others. In the interhuman domain, territory often had a strong local importance, but was not much connected to wider patterns of identity.

War

During the CAPE era, *war* was almost the default condition of world politics, and one of its central political institutions. This is hardly surprising given both the general violence of the era, and the way that several other institutions of this social order (imperialism, monarchy/dynasticism, territoriality, human inequality and religion) all supported the functionality of war in synergistic ways. Imperialism encouraged war in three ways. First, empires had outward expansion built into their DNA, and war (along with dynastic marriages) was the main mechanism for that. Second, because conglomerate empires were quite loosely integrated structures, secessionism was a continuous threat, which often required the punishment or reconquest of insubordinate provinces. This meant that war was part of the domestic politics of empire. Third, it was not uncommon for there to be civil wars when ruling elites were divided over who should rule the empire, and reap its material and status rewards. Monarchy/dynasticism, on which more below, contributed to this last dynamic by generating its own internal succession disputes, the resolution of which was often pursued by war. Monarchy/dynasticism also had synergies with the expansion imperative of empires, which served the power, glory and status interests of kings and emperors: *raison de famille*. The CAPE era understanding of flexible territoriality, in which territory could be legitimately taken and owned by force, facilitated war. So too did human inequality, which legitimated the capture of slaves as a war aim.

Human inequality also underpinned a general indifference to high levels of violence in everyday life, and an absence of concern about human rights. There were few if any significant normative constraints against violent practices, however extreme, and violence was mostly up close and personal. Warriors fought and killed, and torturers and executioners did their work, face-to-face with their opponents or victims. Even amongst the supposedly civilised Greeks, sackings of other Greek cities by victorious armies often went on for days, with much rape, slaughter and enslavement to enliven the looting. Some Mongol conquerors celebrated their victories by building mountains of skulls, and while perhaps extreme, this practice was not out of line with the *Zeitgeist* of the CAPE era. Stories of extreme punishments and torture as a routine part of justice proceedings, often as a form of humiliation and public entertainment, are the everyday stuff of classical history. The Romans enjoyed crucifixions and forum games. The Chinese used ankle-crushing devices and death by a thousand cuts. European practices included flogging, impalement, witch-burning, and hanging, drawing and quartering. As noted above, it was a common practice in many CAPE societies to castrate men for certain kinds of public service. Religion could be complicit in this violence, as most notoriously in the Catholic Inquisition which in various forms ran from the thirteenth to the nineteenth centuries. Religion easily provided motive for war both against those of different religions, and heretics within one's own religion. Some religions, most notably Christianity and Islam, had traditions of proselytising at the point of a sword. Religion could also stand against war, as in Ashoka's famous conversion to Buddhist pacifism, but this was the exception rather than the rule.

The widespread use of violence in CAPE societies, when combined with the flexible sense of territoriality, the frequent lack of clarity in distinguishing between domestic and international, and the different types of polity in play, raises a definitional problem about war. In CAPE societies war easily blurred across the interhuman, transnational and interpolity domains. Wars to expand empires, or wars between empires, might be seen as interpolity. Wars to maintain empires, prevent secession, or settle dynastic succession disputes, might be seen as civil wars. A religious war like the Crusades feels mainly like a transnational war. Some long wars, like those between the Byzantine Empire and the Islamic Caliphates, those between Shi'as and Sunnis within Islam, and the Thirty-Years War in Europe, combine political and religious rivalries. Wars between sedentary and nomadic peoples are difficult to classify in this scheme. Where they are wars between nomad and sedentary empires, such as the Mongol takeovers of China and Persia, they might count as a form of interpolity war. But where they are wars against uncoordinated armed migrations, like those fought by Rome against the Germanic tribes, or Egypt against the sea peoples, they seem to mix polity, transnational and interhuman in a way perhaps similar to the contemporary global war on terror, and cyberwar.

War in the CAPE era was not just an upgrading from forager feuding and occasional conflict over particularly productive bits of territory. It is better seen as something more or less wholly new, and closely tied to the quite different material conditions and social structures of CAPE societies. The CAPE era generated much larger, explicitly political, entities with a firmer sense of territoriality, much more complex patterns of identity, increasingly professional armies, and strong links to empire, monarchy/dynasticism and human inequality. This was an era in which the general assumption of realists that power politics creates a continuous probability of war was largely true. Only universal empire could bring peace, and then only until it fell apart. War and the general resort to violence made coercion a major form of social glue for the CAPE era.

To say that most CAPE polities were essentially warrior societies might be an oversimplification, but it does not misrepresent the general condition. The warrior ethos and the CAPE social institutions were mutually reinforcing, and this was true regardless of whether soldiering became a skilled profession, or was done by male citizens as part of their regular civic obligation, or as for the steppe nomads, was an intrinsic part of the lifeway. To be a good general was one of the pathways to becoming king or emperor. And to be a good general under CAPE era conditions, one had to be a skilled fighter capable of leading troops on the ground, a good strategist, and a ruthless leader. Although monarchy was the norm, republics were not much different from monarchies in either their competence at, or their enthusiasm for, war (think of Athens, or republican Rome). For both types of polity, there were almost no restraints on either why they went to war, or how they fought. Similarly, there were almost no restraints on polities' right of conquest and seizure.

One of the very few constraints on the right to use force and seize goods, developed in response to pirates. Piracy was a common occupation throughout the CAPE era. It was parasitic on trade, an institution and practice on which most CAPE polities depended, often heavily. Rome, for example, developed the concept that pirates were not just enemies of the state, but enemies of all humankind, whose activities were set beyond the pale of legitimacy (Paine, 2014: loc. 2880). While this might be thought of as one of the first attempts to limit the use of force, the picture is quite complex. Merchants themselves could double as pirates when opportunity offered. They could also be in league with states, as was very evident in early modern Europe when states often gave licences to privateers to pillage the commerce of their enemies.

Interestingly, although settlement started out being a necessary condition for the development of war during the seven-millennium transition from the hunter-gatherer to the CAPE era, it did not entirely stay that way. The steppe nomads developed a distinctive mobile lifeway that was not only compatible with war, but gave them a considerable comparative advantage in the practice of it. War was part of their lifeway both on the steppe, and between the steppe and sedentary civilisations (Schouenborg, 2017: 87–93). The military advantage of the steppe nomads did not end until the seventeenth century, when the gunpowder empires of China and Russia expanded into the Asian steppelands. The Treaty of Nerchinsk in 1689 marked the meeting of these two empires, and the effective closure of the steppe (Neumann and Wigen, 2018: 259). This development removed the 'pastoralist' element from CAPE as an independent force, effectively reducing it to a warfare system of conglomerate agrarian empires.

During the CAPE era, war operated across, and was embedded within, all three domains. In the interpolity domain, and between sedentary and nomadic peoples, war was almost the default condition, as it also frequently was within empires as part of their domestic dynamic of expansion and contraction. In the transnational domain, war could be fought by non-state entities, most notably religions (early Islam, the Roman Catholic Church). For the most part, navies were not clearly delineated from commercial shipping, whether for combat or troop transport. Merchants generally went armed, and there was sometimes a blurry spectrum from state action, through various forms of privateering in which civilians fought in association with states, to outright criminal piracy. The European chartered companies of the seventeenth century were perhaps the apex of this fusion between commerce and war. In the interhuman domain, war was, if not an everyday experience, at least a common one. On the steppe in particular, and in the periodic mass outward migrations from the steppe, war spilled into the interhuman domain.

Religion

The institution of religion in the CAPE era built on the egalitarian spirit world of the hunter-gatherers in terms of belief in another plane of existence. But it reflected its own hierarchical social structure by adding to it layers of gods that stood in varying degrees above humankind. CAPE religion can be understood as a collective, organised belief in higher being(s) and higher, or 'other', worlds that control or affect human destiny. Religion in this form arose early in the CAPE era. It was in some ways, particularly in terms of hierarchy, closely connected to the CAPE package of political institutions (kinship, human inequality, monarchy/dynasticism, imperialism), but also separable from them. Religion could be a useful, if tricky, tool for monarchs and empires (Burbank and Cooper, 2010: 61). Or it could stand outside and apart from them. The early city-states developed local gods of their own. Temples may indeed have been the foundational cores for many early cities, with a form of theocracy preceding explicitly monarchical, political, rule (Nightingale, 2022: 46–56). As city-state systems and then empires developed, local gods were amalgamated into syncretic religions with systems of gods.

Big CAPE era religions – Hinduism, Buddhism, Zoroastrianism, Christianity and Islam; and social philosophies such as Confucianism[21] and Daoism – transcended kinship and local collective identities in

---

[21] Bayly (2004: 326, 332) notes that Confucianism embodied the ritual and identity aspects of religion, without depending on god(s).

important ways. They were perhaps the most distinctive and enduring characteristic of CAPE era societies, leading the way in constituting belief as a major social glue for human societies. The most successful of them created communities of collective identity that numbered tens, and occasionally hundreds of millions of people. These communities far outreached kinship bonds, and in the most successful manifestations stretched well beyond the scale of even the largest empires. They also differentiated Eurasia's civilisations: monotheistic ones with one god, mainly Mediterranean, polytheistic ones with many gods (India) and atheistic ones with no god(s) (China) (Wang, 2019: locs. 1944–2059). There is much that can be said against them. They created opportunities for corruption, exploitation, factionalism and repression. They played a significant role in the specific suppression of women (Lerner, 1986). And, as Marx famously put it, they were 'the opium of the people' generally. But despite all that, and underlining the power of belief as social glue, these forms of collective identity have been impressively durable. For better or worse, they have been one of the main carriers of CAPE civilisational identities into the modern era.

In relation to human society, the gods and their world were a higher order than humans, and usually a gateway to various forms of afterlife. Such access was commonly mediated by how individuals lived their earthly lives, thus empowering religion as a form of social control. This aspect inevitably attracted political interest, as did religion as a potentially rival form of hierarchical authority. But in a telling reflection of the limits of human social imagination, this higher world of gods was constructed in the same hierarchical, stratified, form as CAPE societies themselves. With some allowance given for the miraculous powers of the gods, they were even subject to the rules of kinship, which played in heaven much as it did on earth. It also mediated the relationship between the heavenly hosts and their representatives on earth. For Christians, Jesus is the son of God and Mary. In Islam, kinship linkages back to the Prophet, and his family and entourage still play a powerful role in both giving status and fuelling schisms among Muslims (Lieven, 2022: 158–69). Concepts such as 'lord' easily bridged between the secular and heavenly hierarchies. There was generally one god who was in some sense the king or emperor of heaven (god of gods), though this was sometimes fudged by enabling this god to take several forms. Under the top god were various layers of local gods, saints, etc. that could be tailored to specific groups within human societies. There might also be alternative hierarchies of devils, perhaps alienated from the gods, but engaged in a division of labour with them to reward and punish humans for the kinds of lives they led. Even monotheistic religions that focused on one supreme god, generally still retained some form of heavenly host as a supporting cast.

Early religions were often closely linked to agriculture, and sometimes directly involved in the process of agricultural production and management. Religions could be used as a way of explaining environmental issues such as droughts, earthquakes, floods and plagues whose natural causes were not understood by CAPE societies. Such phenomena could be construed as punishments by the gods for insufficient practices of good behaviour and worship. This gave religions an early interest in astronomy as a way of predicting the agricultural cycles.

Religions could also be used to support or strengthen dynastic legitimacy by association between rulers and gods. This could take many forms. Rulers could claim to have what the Chinese referred to as 'the mandate of heaven', a kind of performance legitimacy that linked good governance and prosperity to the approval by the gods of the ruling lineage. This, however, was a two-edged sword, because if they were seen as losing the mandate of heaven because of poor performance or natural disasters, their legitimacy could be swiftly undermined (Gehrke, 2020a: 32). Rulers could also claim some form of usually vague kinship with the gods, such as being the 'son of heaven', or having a long kinship lineage with the gods stretching back into deep antiquity. They could even claim to be gods, as some Egyptian and Roman rulers did. The expression 'God save the king/queen', is a good illustration of the enduring political linkage between secular rulers and religion. CAPE religions, like CAPE empires, increasingly pretended to be universal without ever actually getting there. CAPE empires saw themselves as universal polities, and CAPE religions saw themselves as representing universal truths. Linking the two together was a powerful move even though it never resulted in either becoming actually universal across humankind.

Empires could seek legitimacy by constructing themselves as representatives of a religion. Empires could be attractive as well as simply being coerced impositions, but they were not especially strong at providing the linkage of shared identity on a large scale. Religions, by contrast, were exceptionally good at doing this. The later Mauryan Empire in India under Ashoka adopted Buddhism, the later Roman Empire adopted Christianity under Constantine, and the Byzantine Empire represented Orthodox Christianity. Many empires claimed to represent Islam as a whole (Umayyad and Abbasid caliphates) or some subdivision of Islam (Saffavids, Ottomans, Fatimids). This could be a useful binding force, but it could also define lines of fragmentation. Different Chinese dynasties supported or opposed Buddhism. Many Islamic empires were torn between trying to convert their non-Islamic subjects, or tolerating them and using them as a source of tax revenue (Armstrong, 2002: 29; Kennedy, 2016). Religion by itself could not overcome the temptations to warfare in a politically divided world. It could become one of the sources of conflict by defining ideological enemies representing competing religions (e.g. the Crusades; the long war between the Byzantine Empire and various Islamic caliphates and empires; and those between Muslim and Hindu kingdoms in South Asia). When a civilisational area was politically fragmented, shared religion did not stop warfare amongst the different polities, especially so when different divisions within one faith aligned with different polities. This was true within Christendom, Islam, and the Hindu and Confucian worlds. Almost all religions fragmented into competing sects, and these schisms opened the way for the narcissism of small differences to operate among them. This fragmentation easily fuelled forms of civil war within the religious community that might look like an interstate war in the political sphere (e.g. the Thirty-Years war, and the long rivalry between the Sunni Ottoman and Shi'a Safavid Empires).

But while there were many ways to incorporate religion into the political institutions of CAPE society, there was also an important sense in which religions could and did stand independently outside the political sphere. Religion was the key CAPE era social innovation for creating larger-scale identities that were not just above household, family, clan, tribe, village, town and city, but that could also outreach kingdom and even empire. Nothing in the basic idea of religious faith required a link to the state or the political sphere. Religions could be linked to the state, and to the extent that religion could be made co-extensive with city-state, or kingdoms, or empires, it could reinforce their political structures. But religions could also be an independent organising force apart from the state. The phrase attributed to Jesus 'Render unto Caesar the things that are Caesar's, and unto God the things that are God's', captures this flexible character. Religion could ally with the state, or coexist with it, or stand apart from it or oppose it. Once a religion had fissioned, all of these relationships could be in operation simultaneously, as was the case with both Islam and Christianity during the second millennium AD.

During the CAPE era, there were important ways in which religions either transcended, or even in some senses replaced, the political sphere. Many religions developed organisations of their own – secondary institutions – although they differed markedly in how they did this. Some, like Christianity, set up institutions of central control and leadership, such as the Papacy and the Vatican for Catholic Christians. Others were more decentralised, like Hinduism, Islam and Buddhism, leading to a variety of quite independent but often networked institutions such as Buddhist monasteries, Christian orders, and Sufi sects within Islam. Some of these religions, most notably Hinduism, Islam and Buddhism, reached so deeply into society that they created wider communities of sufficient depth and structure so as to weaken the need for kingdoms or empires to organise society and economy (Mann, 1986: 327–40, 379–90; Hodgson, 1993: 121, 182, 194; Braudel, 1994 [1987]: 226, 228; Bayly, 2004: 252–4; Bennison, 2009: 47–53). The caste system of Hinduism structured so many economic and social roles as to render the state somewhat marginal to these purposes. India consequently had a rather ephemeral system of states, which became, like war, mainly the sport of kings. Much the same was true of Islam. This is illustrated by stories like that of the fourteenth-century Islamic traveller Ibn Battuta, who journeyed over many years from Morocco to China, finding work, and having his status recognised, in Islamic communities all along the way. Like India, the religious framework of Islamic civilisation, the *umma* (community of believers), gave it a durable underpinning of social structure that enabled society, and up to a point the economy, to continue functioning at scale regardless of whether the political structures around it were strong or weak. Empires and states could come and go in the Islamic and Indian worlds without completely disaggregating society. This fact, and the possibilities for social order that it represents, is largely missed by the Eurocentric and state-obsessed thinking of mainstream Western IR.

During the Middle Ages, the Orthodox Christian church remained associated with the Byzantine Empire, but the Roman Catholic church found itself operating more or less independently within a political system that was occasionally integrated loosely (the Carolingian Empire), but mostly highly fragmented (feudalism). From the eleventh to the thirteenth centuries, the Catholic Church motivated and mobilised a series of military crusades, mainly against Islam in the holy lands and Spain (the *Reconquista*), but also into northeast Europe, and on one occasion against the Byzantine Empire. By the standards of the day, these were quite massive events, almost amounting to a war of civilisations. The Roman church also established chains of monasteries throughout Europe, which helped to preserve literacy and civilisation in the post-Roman age. It played a reduced version of the 'king of kings' role by validating and crowning local kings. Sometimes it played a significant role in diplomacy, as in the series of Papal Bulls during the fifteenth century that tried to sort out the competing territorial claims of Spain and Portugal in the Atlantic. It also played a role in the process of empire-building, both seeking converts in Asia and the Americas, and trying to define rules for how native peoples should be treated by colonisers. The church did not become the state (except in the limited domain of the Papal States and the Vatican itself), but it did operate to considerable effect when the political order was weak in Europe during the feudal period, and when the new system of sovereign states was beginning to emerge.

Religion, then, was strongly rooted in all three domains. In the inter-polity domain, religion was sometimes closely identified with states and empires, shaping their enmities and alliances and diplomacy in signifi-cant ways. Given the strong social hierarchy of CAPE polities, converting the prince of a kingdom or empire could convert the whole polity. Even when empires were not defined by a religion, they had to have policies that dealt with religious differences. In this domain, religion could be a significant cause of wars, though it was certainly not the only one. In the transnational domain, religion also made a big impact, not least through its creation and networking of many secondary institutions. Many trade diasporas were defined by shared religion alongside kinship and ethni-city. Where religions were at war, trade was often restricted, though that did not stop smuggling. Religion became intertwined with trade routes, sometimes being spread along them by merchants, and sometimes becoming part of them, such as the Buddhist monasteries along the Silk Roads. Yet it was in the interhuman domain that religion was most deeply rooted and had the most significant impact. At the end of the day, religion is about personal belief, and it is thus individuals who have to become believers. During the CAPE era, religion became the first great mass patterning of human identity outside kinship and locality. It was generally much stronger than language or ethnicity, which did not account for as much in terms of identity as they do now. Religion decisively demonstrated the power of belief as a social glue.

The very radical changes in these six primary institutions carried over from the hunter-gatherer to the CAPE era were in part caused by their interplay with a host of new institutions that defined the larger and more complex CAPE social structure.

Monarchy/Dynasticism

Perhaps the most obvious of the new CAPE institutions was monarchy/ dynasticism. In principle, monarchy and dynasticism are separable. Monarchy is the idea that a single individual should be given the right and responsibility to lead a polity, and to have considerable power and authority to do so. *L'état, c'est moi* was not just an extreme boast usually attributed to Louis XIV, but a statement of the general political principle of monarchy: the state was the estate of the monarch. This idea emerged early in the history of civilisation, not reaching the Eurasian backwater of

Europe until much later. It is not all that difficult to understand in functional and social terms why monarchy became the political default of the CAPE era. Past a certain point, the much bigger and more complex societies of the CAPE era could not function without some clear form of leadership to handle both internal and external threats and conflicts.[22] The more obvious political distinction between inside (domestic) and outside (international) that came with greater size, complexity and territoriality, required a sovereign leader of some sort, and by implication some version of sovereignty. The key to understanding monarchy, and the kind of 'international relations' it generated is that while it contained the idea of sovereignty, this was substantially attached to the sovereign him- (and very occasionally her-) self. It was not, as now, strongly attached to the people or nation, though some polities, such as the Roman Empire, also had standing separate from that of their particular rulers.

Dynasticism addresses the process of succession once a monarchy is in place. It is not difficult to see why dynasticism became so closely associated with monarchy. CAPE-era leaders often needed to be, and were, warriors. Being a good general was a common pathway to becoming, and remaining, a monarch, most notably in Rome.[23] But if this meant a big succession fight each time a monarch died, then monarchy alone was so chronically unstable as to threaten the peace and stability of the polity. Given the ongoing vitality of kinship in CAPE societies, dynasticism was also attractive to those who had made it to the throne. As noted, dynasticism could be seen, along with slavery and patriarchy, as a derivative institution of the primary institution of human inequality. Yet it is worth highlighting it separately, because for most of the urban and steppe civilisations of the CAPE era, it was closely tied to monarchy as the default form of political legitimacy right through to the nineteenth century. It was not the only form, as shown by the much-celebrated republics in Athens, early Rome, some early Indian states in the first millennium BC, and later Venice and the Netherlands. Sometimes it was contested, but only at the end of the nineteenth century, with the American and French revolutions, did such challenges become strong enough to overthrow the principle. Its practice was very varied. In some times and places the principle was strictly applied, in others, more

---

[22] Graeber and Wengrow (2021) argue that communal self-government could handle quite complex governance tasks such as irrigation. The need for defence in a more densely populated and territorialised interpolity system, however, favoured hierarchical leadership.

[23] This was less true for post-Qin China (Lieven, 2022: 87–94).

loosely. Imperial Rome for example, was more committed to monarchy than to dynasticism (Lieven, 2022: 57–65). Although emperors might try to establish dynasticism, this often broke down quickly. Many Roman emperors were successful generals who seized power in the empire's frequent civil wars. Rome also diluted the blood-line principle of dynasticism by allowing adopted sons to succeed if there was no blood-line heir. Monarchs usually tried to establish dynastic succession, but they did not always succeed in doing so. Nevertheless, for over four millennia, dynasticism was one of the main keys to political legitimacy in CAPE society. Dynasticism took the ancient kinship idea of *raison de famille*, and elevated it to being a core principle, along with monarchy, sovereignty and territoriality, of the CAPE political order, both domestically and internationally. On this theme, Haldén (2020: 8) notes that 'kinship and political order were not only interdependent but co-constitutive'. Monarchy/dynasticism injected a strong element of family politics into interpolity relations, not the least part of which was the central role of dynastic marriages in diplomacy.

The danger posed by disputes over succession could be reduced if there were clear principles governing how it should be done. The advantages of dynasticism as a solution to this problem were two. First, it incorporated a principle of succession that rested on the familiar and comfortable ghost institution of kinship, which conferred legitimacy of a kind that could, and often did, muster deep social support. Everyone understood kinship from their own experience, and dynasticism simply required that a particular kinship line (or lines if there was an elaborate aristocracy behind the monarchy) be elevated above the rest – so-called golden kinship lines. Second, dynasticism offered some prospect of meritocracy on the assumption that the founder of a dynastic line had proved his worth in order to get to that position in the first place. That talent might be both passed down the lineage, and cultivated by privileged training for the job. The system was also open enough to allow for some talented leaders to rise to dynastic status on their merits: think of Chinggis Khan, Julius Cæsar and Napoleon. These advantages were strong enough to makes dynasticism the preferred choice of most CAPE societies.

Dynasticism, however, also had two disadvantages that were the mirror image of its strengths. First, while kinship lineage could provide clear principles of legitimate succession it could also generate conflicts in its own right, especially so when lineages got complicated. To start with, there are various principles of dynastic succession: Is it the eldest son who inherits, or the eldest brother, or is there some form of competition amongst a range of possible candidates within the golden lineage to determine who is the strongest (*tanistry*)? Tanistry was often favoured by the steppe nomads, and could make succession processes quite chaotic and destabilising (Neumann and Wigen, 2018). Are women excluded from the succession process or not? There could be mixtures of these principles. And what was to happen when nature, or assassins, intervened to eliminate the legitimate candidates (no male offspring, no brothers, or the eligible candidates die before inheriting)? Even dynasticism periodically opened the way to struggles for power amongst competing warlords. The exact rules of dynastic succession varied from place to place and time to time, but the historic record shows that dynastic successions could generate civil wars, and fracture empires (the Seljuk Empire, Alexander the Great's empire, the Mongol Empire). The Ottoman solution to this problem infamously allowed the killing off of all the losers in the power struggle, once a new ruler had emerged, a technique that, however ruthless, helps to explain the notable longevity of that empire.

The second disadvantage of dynasticism was that the luck of the draw on genetic heritage might produce weak leaders rather than strong ones. This problem was exacerbated by the common dynastic habit of encouraging inbreeding by marriage to close relatives. The Egyptian pharaohs and the Habsburgs were notable examples of this issue (Lieven, 2022: 44, 197). A solid empire might survive a weak leader, but a fragile one might not. One solution to this problem, used in some dynastic systems, was to allow the current ruler to adopt his heir, thus bypassing weaknesses in the blood line. And as Lieven (2022: 48) notes, during this era, when lives were mostly short, medical treatments fairly limited, and diseases rife, 'the fate of all hereditary monarchies depended greatly on medical chance'.

In general, dynasticism was closely associated with patriarchy. A frequent privilege of dynastic rulers was to be allowed multiple wives and concubines. But there were aspects of this arrangement that opened opportunities for women. One was that dynasticism necessarily gave women a central and irremovable role in the reproduction of 'golden kin' lineages. Women from within those lineages were of course privileged in this process, but through the widespread norms of polygyny and concubinage, others could get access as well. Mothers in this system, whether wives or concubines, had a certain entry into the power politics of dynasticism, and this generated the famously vicious politics of the harem as mothers vied to promote themselves and their sons. Very occasionally, the CAPE dynastic succession system allowed women to become not just the wives of kings and emperors, or regents for males who inherited rule too young, but rulers themselves: Hatshepsut and

Cleopatra in Egypt, Boudica in Roman Britain, Wu Zetian in Tang China, Catherine the Great in Russia, Elizabeth I in England.

Monarchy/dynasticism was mainly rooted in the interpolity domain, where it both defined the polity, and set its rank in relation to others (more on this under diplomacy below). The social glue supporting it was partly coercion, partly belief in kinship lineage. For the transnational realm, dynastic rulers were the authorities with whom merchants had to deal if they wanted to trade. Dynasticism also had deep, though variable, roots in the interhuman domain. Most dynastic leaders tried to cultivate the loyalty of their subjects, some by love and some by fear. But regardless of individual cases, monarchy/dynasticism as an institution had widespread legitimacy. People could be rallied to the call to fight for king and country, and for the rightful heir.

Within the overall repertoire of institutions of CAPE societies, monarchy/dynasticism was a very close, comfortable and compatible fit with the other key political institution, imperialism. Along with imperialism, it defined the meaning and practice of territoriality within and between CAPE societies. It was also compatible with the more broadly societal institution of religion, though there the relationship was more complicated. As Bayly (2004: 86–106) argues, by the late eighteenth century this whole political system of dynasticism, and the kinds of polities it generated, was coming under increasing pressure both because of its inability to sustain the rising costs of war, and because of the declining legitimacy and authority of the ruling elites, both dynastic and religious.

Imperialism

The key to understanding the close fit between dynasticism and imperialism lies in the point made above about sovereignty in dynasticism being embodied more in the sovereign, and not so much in the polity. Putting sovereignty in terms of the people or the nation generally points towards a fairly restricted (although far from always precise!) view of territoriality in terms of the homeland of the relevant people, though it can also support an imperial *lebensraum* policy. But putting sovereignty in terms of the sovereign leaves the question of how much territory entirely open. In CAPE societies, the sovereign normally had the right to control whatever territory he or she was able to conquer and rule, potentially without limit. The aspiration to universal empires was common in the CAPE era and linked closely to the institutions of war and territoriality. CAP empires could take territory from other empires, absorb lesser kingdoms, or, as the Phoenicians and Greeks famously did, establish colonies in 'empty' spaces (i.e. places where the inhabitants were at a lower level of development and could be pushed aside or absorbed). None ever achieved universal dominion, and the alleged peace that would accompany it, but the claim of Chinese emperors to rule 'all under heaven' (*Tianxia*) gives the general flavour of the aspiration. So too does the use of extravagant titles. Cyrus the Great (ruled 559–530 BC), the founder of the Achaemenid dynasty in Persia, styled himself: The Great King, King of Kings, King of Anshan, King of Media, King of Babylon, King of Sumer and Akkad, King of the Four Corners of the World. The Roman emperor Nero (ruled 54–68 AD) was no less modest with: Ruler of rulers, chosen by Ptah, beloved of Isis, the sturdy-armed one who struck the foreign lands, victorious for Egypt, chosen of Nun who loves him. The idea of emperors as being 'king of kings', or 'world conquerors', common in many civilisations, nicely captures the form of a conglomerate empire in which the local rulers retained considerable autonomy in return for bending the knee, or performing the kowtow – and paying the taxes – to the emperor. As a political form, the conglomerate empire was fairly quick and easy to put together if you had the military skill and resources, because it did not require deep penetration or management of the subordinated polities. They could just be added on while largely retaining their own rulers. But it was also fairly quick to fall apart if the central power weakened, and the subordinate kings saw their chance to take back their autonomy. CAP empires were essentially extractive, and with some exceptions not that much interested in undoing cultural diversity. Many of them might be thought of as older versions of today's kleptocracies.

This open-ended view of the scale of imperial dominion is the key to understanding empire in the CAPE era. CAP empires were almost always created by conquest, though dynastic marriage also played a significant part. They were held together by local garrisons and the threat of military action from the core. Once in place, empires could offer the positive inducements of public goods such as security, trade expansion and promotion, *lingua franca*, common currency, law and participation in a wider cosmopolitan society. Their social glue was calculation as well as coercion, and sometimes belief in the institution of empire itself. City-states could be seen as the basic building blocks for empires, and sometimes, as in the cases of Athens and Rome, as the cores around which empires were built. When empires collapsed, civilisation did not disappear, but dropped down a level to smaller scale. Only in exceptional circumstances of collapse, such as that in the eastern Mediterranean around 1200 BC, and parts of Western Europe after the fall of Rome, did civilisation itself degrade down to village level. Such building blocks could be assembled and reassembled in different ways, and it was not uncommon for specific places to be parts of many different empires at different times. The history of places like Sicily, Cyprus, the Levant, Sri Lanka and Taiwan tell this story clearly. Dynastic rule fits this bill perfectly, by providing a form of political legitimacy that could be acknowledged in a flexible way without much impinging on local identities. Monarchy/dynasticism was the ideal political form for imperialism, enabling diverse populations to be assembled and governed within a framework of political legitimacy.

Acceptance of monarchical/dynastic rule was also an important link between the empires of sedentary and nomadic societies. Steppe empires were conglomerates of tribes pulled together by particularly talented warlords, both by force and by charisma. They were mainly formed to support more effective raiding or invasion of sedentary societies, for the steppe warlords needed resources from the bigger and richer sedentary societies to sustain their own empires. Like sedentary societies, steppe ones also worked on the basis of golden kinship lineages, though they tended towards tanistry principles of succession that could easily result in chaotic succession conflicts (Schouenborg, 2017: 66–72). Tanistry worked to produce strong leaders when there was a clear winner, but sometimes just resulted in sustained civil wars with no clear winner, and the break-up of the empire. Nevertheless, when steppe warlords conquered sedentary empires, they could slot fairly easily into the monarchical/dynastic principles of leadership. Over time, steppe leaders learned from the bureaucrats of sedentary empires, often Persians, that ruling was a bigger and more durable source of revenue than raiding (Dale, 2010: 107–10). If one looked after the peasants and the merchants, and encouraged farming and trade, the tax revenue lasted forever. A raid often achieved only a one-time gain, while damaging or even destroying the source of wealth that produced it. Thus were successful nomad warriors seduced into sedentary lifeways when they became rulers over agrarian cultures.

In the interpolity domain, empire was the top-of-the-line form. International system/societies were to some extent inter-imperial systems (as often in the Mediterranean and the Middle East), though when they achieved something like universality within their region, they became almost a form of imperial international system/society in themselves, oscillating between periods of imperial unity and periods of fragmentation. China provides the clearest example of this, sometimes being effectively pulled together (Qin, Han, Tang, Yuan, Ming and Qing dynasties), and sometimes falling apart (as most notoriously during the famous 'warring states' period, and between the Han and Tang dynasties). In the transnational domain, empires provided frameworks for trade. They often encouraged both trade and production for trade, and contributed to the stabilisation and protection of trade routes. Then as now, most merchants preferred to operate within a stable political framework rather than a chaotic one in which they were vulnerable to bandits and pirates. Empires could of course be seen as merely a dressed-up form of banditry/piracy, and there is some truth in this. But empires generally (not always!) had a more reasonable, orderly and predictable view of the limits of extraction on trade if they wanted it to be sustained, and they negotiated with merchants about this. At the interhuman level, empires did not, with some religious exceptions, put much effort into trying to homogenise identities. But when they were long-lasting, they often succeeded in achieving this anyway, laying the foundations for wider civilisations, as Rome, China and the Abassids did. China, indeed, is still in the process of turning the Qing conglomerate empire into a nation state (Wang, 2019: ch. 5).

Sovereignty

Sovereignty is about the claim of a polity to the exclusive right of self-government that could be both effectively exercised within a claimed territory, and recognised by others as a valid claim. Jackson and Rosberg (1982) label these respectively *empirical* and *juridical* sovereignty. As discussed above, for most of the CAPE era, the idea of sovereignty was closely bound up with, and derivative of, monarchy/dynasticism, though it could also be attached to god(s). There was ample space within CAPE societies for clashes between spiritual and temporal claims to sovereignty. When it was a property of temporal sovereigns, it was what they exercised over their estates and dominions, often in the name of a divine right to rule. As such, it marched in close step with the flexible territoriality of the CAPE era that marked monarchical/dynastic polities. Zarakol (2022) notes the Chinggisid practice of the Mongol empires as an extreme example of concentrating sovereignty in the ruler. Only in the relatively rare cases of republics, such as some of the Greek city-states, and early Rome, was something like the modern link between the state as such and sovereignty possible. Wight (1977: 23–6) distinguishes between states-systems based on mutual recognition amongst equals, from suzerain systems where the members did not recognise each other as equals, but one member asserted primacy in some ways. He saw most international societies during the CAPE era as suzerain systems, but identified the classical Greek system as a states-system comparable to the modern European one, implying that some form of sovereign equality was in play at that early time (Wight, 1977: 23, 46–72).

Modern sovereignty emerged with and alongside territoriality in a long process of state consolidation and integration in Europe starting in Renaissance Italy during the fifteenth century (Wight, 1977: 129–73; Brewin, 1982; 1993: 161–4; Watson, 1992: 138–97; Keohane, 1995; Krasner, 1999; Sørensen, 1999; Onuf, 2002; Buzan, 2017). Sovereignty in this sense was corrosive of the idea of 'universal' conglomerate empires. It was a system fitted for giving an operational political form, within a defined territorial package, to the cultural and political diversity of peoples that was the historical legacy of humankind. It was also associated with an increasing separation between religious and secular power and authority going on in Europe at this time (Holsti, 2004: 118–28). The key to this move was the steady replacement of sovereignty as a property of dynastic sovereigns, mainly expressed in flexible conglomerate empires, towards sovereignty as something embedded in the polity itself, and before modernity mainly expressed in a more centrally controlled nation state with the harder sense of territoriality noted above. This was a long process, arguably not completed until the delegitimation of empire after 1945. Up until the nineteenth century, sovereigns, as noted, could rightly say '*L'état, c'est moi*'. Only a handful, mainly in the Arab world, can now plausibly make that claim.

Diplomacy

The modern system of diplomacy with its distinctive practices of resident ambassadors and multilateral conferences, and its foundations in sovereign equality, emerged towards the end of the CAPE era in fifteenth-century Italy. Before that, there was a clear, but somewhat simpler, form of diplomacy that was, with some differences in style, common to most CAPE civilisations in Eurasia. Neumann (2020: 42–6) argues that forms of diplomacy must have existed even during the transition period, as larger-scale polities, and monument-building societies emerged. Once the CAPE era consolidated during the third millennium BC, diplomacy was based primarily on dynastic and patriarchal hierarchical relationships within and between empires. Both blood and metaphorical kinship were very much in play in the diplomatic process. It was almost entirely about bilateral relations, and it was mostly done by the sending of envoys with specific one-off missions, carrying both gifts and written personal messages.[24] The practice of using envoys was old even at the dawn of civilisation, having been used among transitional polities such as chiefdoms (Watson, 1982: 83). Relations were not so much between empires/states as between their patrimonial rulers. Zarakol (2022: 25–6) nicely adopts the terms 'great house' and 'inter-house orders' to capture this family-based form of hierarchy. Envoys represented the rulers. Some kings and emperors would acknowledge others as equals ('brothers'), but most relations were between higher- and lower-ranked leaders on the dynastic scale (father–son). As noted in the section above on trade, there was also another strand of diplomacy in which guilds and trade-diasporas conducted their own negotiations with local princes to determine the terms and conditions on which they could pursue their interests (or not). Alexandrowicz (1967: 97–101) notes the Asian practice of 'capitulations', which allowed trading communities rights to trade, live and govern themselves, constituting 'a sort of miniature society with the larger community whose hospitality they enjoyed'. Merchants long ago pioneered the idea of resident 'consuls', which only later got incorporated into interpolity relations (Neumann, 2020: 56–85).

Holsti (2004: 178–9) argues that the practices of CAPE societies before fifteenth-century Italy were at best proto-diplomatic, not amounting to an institution of diplomacy. But others disagree. As Watson (1982: 84) observes, from the beginning, diplomacy 'was an alternative to mere reliance on force' in relations amongst states and empires. Cohen and Westbrook (2000: 234) identify a similar logic facing any 'great king' in the Amarna system, that diplomacy became a necessity when he had neighbours 'that he could neither ignore nor subjugate'. Then as now, throughout the CAPE era, states and empires needed to make agreements about alliances, cease-fires, status and trade. Sometimes they accepted arbitration of disputes, a practice that was in place by Hellenistic times (Watson, 1982: 89). And they also needed information on what was going on in the neighbourhood around their borders. Then as now, diplomacy was a mix of communication and intelligence-gathering. CAPE diplomacy lacked both a professional class of diplomats, and any sense that *raison de système* was or should be a goal (Watson, 1982: 87). Since the polities of the CAPE era were as a rule highly personalised, patriarchal, patrimonial, constructions, much of diplomacy was governed by aristocratic norms of etiquette and hospitality. As Reus-Smit (1999: 87–121) argues, right up to the nineteenth

---

[24] Perhaps the closest thing to a multilateral conference was a series of meetings between the Persian Empire and a set of Greek city-states from 392 to 367 BC, to negotiate a general agreement about relations between them (Watson, 1982: 86–8).

century, including in Europe, diplomacy was mainly about dynastic rather than national interests. There were no foreign ministries as such, but there were norms (not always observed) about safe-passage for envoys, and about allowing them to return home. There was also use of *lingua francas*: for example, Akkadian in the Amarna system, Greek between Rome and Parthia, French in early-modern Europe. This seems enough to count diplomacy as an institution of CAPE society.

Watson (1982: 89–93) notes the shared functional logic that, despite situational and cultural differences, produced a structural similarity of diplomatic practice in the Mediterranean, Indian, Chinese and premodern European international societies. The Amarna system during the second millennium BC, generated a diplomacy that had to work across several different cultures and religions. Its basic metaphor was the hierarchical patriarchal household with great kings using kinship metaphors. As Lerner (1986: 209) puts it: '[T]he patriarchal family is the form which the archaic state takes.' Cohen and Westbrook (2000) argue that with its need to deal with alliances, trade and status issues, this system was the first clear example of something analogous to modern international relations (IR). Rome made many treaties, and treated them as public documents. Given Rome's generally hegemonic position, only Parthia was treated as anything like an equal. The early modern European system of diplomacy was, more like the classical Greek one, set up within a culturally homogenous community (Christendom) (Watson, 1982: 95). China's diplomatic practice was more hierarchical. It tried to draw other cultures into its Tribute System, but where this was not possible, was flexible enough to deal with them more or less as equals in practice, even while striving to maintain the symbolic forms of hierarchy (Zhang, Y., 2001: 51–55; Zhang, F., 2009; Zhang and Buzan, 2012; Spruyt, 2020: 142, 153–68). The Tribute system's blend of gift exchange and trade was more of a CAPE norm than a novel Chinese practice.

From the earliest stages of CAPE civilisation, dynastic marriage was a key tool of diplomacy for rulers (Lerner, 1986: 67–8). This meant that having a plentiful supply of sons, and especially daughters, for this purpose was a dynastic asset for diplomacy, something that the polygamous sexual relations allowed to elite males in the harem was well-suited to produce. This usage of elite women allowed at least some women to acquire education, because when daughters were sent abroad in alliance marriages, they became in some respects a type of resident ambassador. This function was but one aspect of government by ruling family, in which offspring and other kin, including women, acted as deputies for their fathers/husbands, and served as a kind of 'patrimonial bureaucracy' for the rulers (Lerner, 1986: 54–75). Here, as elsewhere, kinship was a major key to trust in CAPE societies. Negotiations over marriage contracts were a key part of Amarna diplomacy, reflecting the acute sensitivity of the great kings to issues of status amongst them (Meier, 2000). If used deftly, dynastic marriage could be an alternative to war in expanding an empire, an art at which the Habsburgs were notably accomplished in early-modern Europe (Watson, 1982: 99–100). The modern European system of diplomacy emerged first in Renaissance Italy, which was more in contact with the civilised Mediterranean world, both Byzantine and Islamic, than the rest of Europe, and was at the cutting edge of Europe's transition from mediaeval to modern. It was in Italy that commercial city-states moved away from what Ruggie (1983, 1993) called the *heteronomous* structure of mediaeval relations, in which territoriality was disaggregated along functional lines, and towards the modern idea and practice of centralising sovereign territorial states. This model quickly spread to the rest of Europe. In some ways, that transition was unique, because the fragmentation of authority in mediaeval heteronomy (aka feudalism) was distinctive to Europe, and did not fit well with the general model of CAP empires. But in other ways, the transition to sovereignty simply meant that a previously backward Europe began to look more like the rest of the CAPE polities, albeit with a firmer sense of territoriality and more ambition about centralising state authority. During the period of monarchical absolutism in Europe, there was not so much difference between the emerging European states and the dynastic, patriarchal, imperial, polities of classical civilisations, in which sovereignty was embedded in the sovereign, whose estate was the state/empire. The eighteenth-century claim of *L'état, c'est moi* could be seen as Europe finally catching up with civilised practice in the rest of Eurasia. Not until the nineteenth century did sovereignty begin to be widely embedded in the people (nation) rather than the ruler.

The key Italian innovation in diplomacy even in this early stage was the practice of having resident ambassadors (citizens of one's own state) acting as the representative (and eyes and ears) of the monarch in neighbouring states.[25] Watson (1982: 96–8) and Neumann (2020: 56–85) suggest that the idea of resident ambassadors might have come from the commercial practices that were a long tradition of the Italian

---

[25] Perhaps the only political precursor to the idea of resident ambassadors was the classical Greek system of *proxenoi*, in which a citizen of another Greek city would look after their interests in that city. The *proxenoi* was resident, but he was not a citizen of the state he represented, so this did not amount to having resident ambassadors in the modern sense (Watson, 1982: 88–9).

city-states and of trade diasporas generally. For the merchant community, having their own people permanently on the ground in foreign ports was standard practice back to ancient times. As in CAP empires, the Italian diplomats were representatives of their prince, not of the state as such, though in the case of the Italian city-states, the dynastic legacy was relatively weak, putting more emphasis on raw power politics and balance of power (Watson, 1982: 96–9). As the new diplomatic system spread throughout Europe, diplomacy became more of a profession. The shift towards sovereignty underway in Europe at that time necessitated the invention of extraterritoriality: embassies acknowledged as a patch of foreign territory under its own jurisdiction within the host country (Ruggie, 1993: 164–5; Holsti, 2004: 178–98).[26]

From the seventeenth century, foreign ministries began to emerge as a distinct department of government (Watson, 1982: 100–8). After 1648, the practice that major multilateral diplomatic conferences should periodically address questions of *raison de système* became embedded (Holsti, 2004: 179–89). Such conferences periodically settled the rules and norms of the new international order after major wars (Holsti, 1991). It seems possible that because this new system of diplomacy evolved in parallel with mercantilism, it involved a shift away from the monarch-merchant aspect of diplomacy as mercantilism made trade a matter of *raison d'état*, and chartered companies were developed as national champions. From the sixteenth century to the nineteenth, mercantilism helped to raise war and territoriality to the top of the international political agenda, and marginalise the place of trade negotiations between monarchs and alien guilds. This would only have been true in Europe, though by the eighteenth century Europe was becoming more influential in the world. That legacy of European diplomacy being mainly focused on war and peace was one of the things that were challenged during the nineteenth century, when the market displaced mercantilism, and merchants were restored to a more independent diplomatic role.

Then as now, diplomacy was primarily an activity of the interstate domain, largely conducted by ruling elites, and often particularly concerned with their dynastic and economic interests. Some form of

---

[26] There is a good deal of discussion in the English School about diplomacy as one of the key practices of states-systems generally, but also the particular modern form of it that emerged in Europe from the fifteenth century onwards. With the notable exception of Reus-Smit (1999) and Neumann (2020), this discussion does not generally draw a strong distinction between the nineteenth century and what developed earlier in Europe (Armstrong, 1977; Bull, 1977: 162–83; Watson, 1982, 1992; Palliser, 1984; Wight, 1991: 141; Reus-Smit, 1999; Jackson, 2000; Neumann, 2001, 2003; Hall, 2002, 2006; Sharp, 2003).

diplomacy seemed necessary for all states/empires that had neighbours that they 'could neither ignore nor subjugate'. Diplomacy was also a regular feature of the transnational domain, where religious, merchant and political elites needed to deal with each other on a regular basis about the terms and conditions of trade, and the status and safety of merchants resident in foreign places. Merchant practices may indeed have been the inspiration for the emergence of modern interstate diplomacy, a key example of integrated world society during the CAPE era. It is difficult to see much position for diplomacy in the interhuman domain during the CAPE era. The people might be either victims or beneficiaries of diplomatic deals, but they were generally remote from the practice of diplomacy itself.

International Law

As Onuma (2000: 2–11) notes, it is difficult to talk about 'international law' in a premodern context. We live in an era in which one system of law became globally dominant during the nineteenth century, and that system has come to define what counts as 'international law'. The modern form of international law also depends on there being a system of states accepting the principle of sovereign equality, and that was rare in the CAPE era. Therefore, in comparison to modern international law, other systems can only be law-like, even if they were accepted in practice, and used in a way similar to international law in their own time and place. To avoid falling into this Eurocentric trap, one needs to keep an open mind about what counts as representing this primary institution in earlier times.

The CAPE era certainly had forms of law, both civil and religious. The two often mixed given that the gods had a role in enforcing even civil law. The oaths that made agreements binding were often made in the name of god(s). Since religion was generally taken seriously in CAPE societies, with the gods seen as having a real and close involvement in the day-to-day human world, such oaths were not superficial. The Greek, Roman, Chinese and Middle-Eastern civilisations all had codes of law and systems of legal justice to govern their civil affairs. Some of these were man-made, some supposedly given by the god(s). Whether they had international law in any sense is a more difficult question. At this point, the perennial question of 'What is "law"?' cannot be avoided. There are various ways of deriving or constructing 'law'. One is 'natural law', where social laws are seen as somehow inherent in nature/god, and therefore like the laws of the physical world need to be discovered by investigation and rational thinking. Natural law is inherently universal, and not subject to cultural relativism. It played a foundational role in the development of European law, not so much as a legal code, but as a set of norms of conduct that could underpin such a code (Neff, 2010: 6–7). As Bull (1979, 1990: 80–3) argues, whatever the weakness of its foundational claims, natural law is useful for putting the rights and duties of individuals upfront, and for providing a universal basis for those rights.

A second approach is positive law, where law is created by the political authorities, for example, the various civil codes of antiquity: Hammurabi's code, Justinian's code, the Tang code. Law laid down by the sovereign might be rule <u>by</u> law, if the sovereign remained above the law, or rule <u>of</u> law if all were equally bound by it. In the extremely hierarchical and dynastic world of the CAPE era, rule <u>by</u> law was much the more common approach. That system still prevails in some places, most notably China, where the Communist Party both makes the law, and requires the law to serve its purposes. A third approach is religious law as delivered by god(s): for example, the Ten Commandments, and Sharia law in Islam. Where religious and secular authority comingled, as they often did in CAPE societies, law, and indeed political authority itself, might be a mix of civil and religious. This was the case with Islamic caliphates, and with those kings and emperors elsewhere who declared themselves either as gods, or as closely linked to them. A fourth approach is customary law. In most cultures, practice generates a body of custom about obligations, rights and exchanges, and as those customs become formalised, they begin to look more like law (Holsti, 2004: 144–6).

For most of the CAPE era, law was mainly customary, positive or religious. All three forms could play in the interpolity and transnational domains. Except in the rare cases where empires encompassed their known world, customary and religious law easily extended beyond the bounds of any individual polity. Positive law could be found in the treaties made between sovereigns, though these might well be entangled with religion and custom. Cohen and Westbrook (2000: 230), for example, argue that there was something like international law in the Amarna period's 'system of rules regulating relations between kingly households'. More specifically, Westbrook (2000) argues that international law was customary, and, like Amarna diplomacy, rooted in the analogy of the patriarchal family hierarchy as a common frame of reference. The problem of thinking of this as 'international law' is that it was not about the state as such, of which at the time there was little or no concept. It was about the monarchs themselves, and relations between them. Again, as with diplomacy, this 'law' was highly sensitive to issues of status, with some treaties being between equals and some between vassals and suzerains. Because it was about agreements between sovereigns, or more broadly about norms of hospitality, this feels more like positive law, made by polities. Yet it had a closeness to religion in being witnessed (via oaths), and enforced (by divine punishment for transgressors), by the god(s). This worked because belief in the god(s) as an active presence in everyday life was strong (Westbrook, 2000: 36–8).

More in the transnational realm, or perhaps shared between it and the interpolity one, Paine (2014: locs. 2593–608; also Watson, 1982: 89) says that during the Hellenistic period, third century BC, Rhodes was such an influential maritime and trading power that it developed rules 'that later formed the basis of commercial maritime law in Rome, and the so-called Rhodian Sea Law of the Byzantine Empire'.

Onuma (2000: 11–18) argues that the Chinese Tribute System was the most alien of CAPE societies to any idea of international law. Because that system was conceptually so strongly Sino-centric, it made China's relations with others effectively expressions of China's domestic authority. Even treaties were constructed as imperial edicts, not as something negotiated between sovereign polities. Overweening hierarchy effectively trumped any form of openly dealing with others as independent entities. In contrast to China, Onuma (2000: 18–22) argues that the Islamic world, while also having universalist pretensions, was closer to having practices similar to international law. Having failed to achieve real universality, but being a major long-distance trading civilisation, the Islamic world had to learn how to deal with foreign polities, both Islamic and in the *Dar al Harb*. This created a permanent tension between the doctrinal imperative to convert infidels to Islam, and the practical need to trade and get along in a multi-power, ideologically plural, world. In addition, once it became permanently politically fragmented itself after the fall of the Abbasid caliphate in 1258, the different political components of the Islamic world also had to find ways of getting on with each other.

Onuma (2000: 22–7) sees Europe as having experienced a mix of ideological universalism (Christianity) without a strong commitment to political centralisation. Europe preferred political fragmentation, which both made war a constant problem, and set the conditions for dealing with others as equals. In his interpretation, modern international law had its genesis in Europe's need to constrain war with legal doctrines such as just war. As noted above, the distinctive form of European international law began to emerge towards the end of the CAPE era. As Holsti (2004: 146–52) observes, this starts mainly with natural law, which still had one foot in religion, but steadily acquired more positivist characteristics, moving the focus away from individuals and universalism, towards the state and particularism. The basic norms underpinning European international law were:

- The moral worth of individual political communities
- The legal equality of sovereigns
- The reciprocal obligation to observe agreements
- The validity of agreements depends on consent
- The right and duty of non-intervention

During the seventeenth and eighteenth centuries, this version of international law was increasingly codified and formalised by writers such as Grotius, Hobbes and Vattel (Bull, 1990; Neff, 2010: 3–12).

Alexandrowicz (1967) gives an interesting account of what happened when this emergent European system of international law encountered Asian practices after the Europeans joined the long-standing Indian Ocean trading system. He remarks that in relations with the polities within that system, the European powers 'often discovered a similarity of ideas ... as far as inter-State relations were concerned'. 'The idea of sovereignty (as vested in the Ruler) was deeply ingrained in Asian tradition' (28). He makes the point that it was natural law that enabled this cross-cultural encounter to function smoothly and pragmatically, and that this broke down as European international law became more positive (236–9). Prior to the nineteenth century, 'a confrontation of two worlds took place on a footing of equality and the ensuing commercial and political transaction, far from being in a legal vacuum, were governed by the law of nations as adjusted to local inter-State customs', which were 'in no way inferior to notions of European civilisation' (224).

Again, this seems a sufficient basis for allowing that a form of international law existed throughout the CAPE era across Eurasia, and not just at the end of the era in Europe. Like diplomacy, international law was primarily embedded in the interpolity domain and the practices of ruling elites, with significant roots in the transnational domain of merchants and religions. It was generally remote from the interhuman domain except, of course, that people were the objects of law, and that custom and religion were also rooted among the people. As European ideas about natural law began to develop, more space emerged for individuals to be subjects and not just objects of law.

Development

During the CAPE era, there was no particular sense of development as an institution, and I include it here mainly to set up the contrast with what began to unfold during the nineteenth century. New technologies did arise from time to time, and had a big impact (wheels, horses, bronze, iron, gunpowder). Some key technologies (shipping, metal-working, ceramics) improved steadily over long periods, and there was accumulation of knowledge, though not systematic in many areas: astronomy, medicine, engineering, mathematics, navigation, shipbuilding, metallurgy, chemistry, ceramics, animal and plant breeding, etc. Rulers might well have been interested in acquiring particular technologies, particularly those with military implications such as chariots, compound bows, siege engines and guns, but also those of economic interest, such as silk production. Such technologies were often stolen or captured or bought from those who possessed them. There was little or no sense that improvements in methods of production or technology should be pursued by the state either as a matter of expanding its own power, or as a way of improving the wealth and welfare of the people. Wealth was generally pursued by capture, trade, or bringing more land into production.

Conclusions

In terms of how it played into the three domains, the CAPE era was radically different from the hunter-gatherer one. Its greater complexity of primary and secondary institutions fleshed out the transnational and interpolity domains, generating integrated world societies balanced across the three domains for the first time. Coercion, calculation and belief all came into play as the glue holding the much larger and more complex forms of society in place, adding to, and modifying the role of kinship.

In the interhuman domain, kinship remained active both locally and in trade, and religion got added as a major new form of identity. Community was the dominant social structure in the localised world of HGBs, and it remained powerful in the CAPE one. Probably more so than for mobile HGBs, most people never travelled out of the locality in which they were born. But in the CAPE era, social structure became more varied and complex, and was consciously organised on a much larger scale, both building on and transcending the bonds of kinship. Larger-scale interhuman structures, especially religions, created institutions and practices that could both shape, and up to a point compete with, the new political forms. Hinduism and Islam were both notable for creating societal forms that could function and endure somewhat regardless of what happened in the interpolity domain. Within these new interhuman structures, CAPE societies were outstanding at creating a

variety of intense personal disciplines requiring high levels of commitment and training: martial arts and mind-sports of many kinds, physical
disciplines like yoga and tai chi, and mental ones like the many forms of
meditation and prayer.

Another striking feature of CAPE society was its skill at public
pageantry in all respects, and the weight of resources devoted to it.
Lavish rituals, ceremonies and public displays were common, as was
monumental architecture, both imperial and religious. Pageantry was
deployed extensively in support not only of monarchy/dynasticism and
empire (coronations, royal circuits around the empire), but also by
religions (festivals, pilgrimages, marriages, births, deaths), and sometimes they combined forces (coronations). The military also used this
technique (victory parades), which could draw in dynastic, religious and
imperial interests as well. One can still see echoes of this in royal coronations (Britain remains good at this), and religious events such as the
Hajj, Ramadan, Diwali and Kumbh Mela. During the CAPE era, these
were a deep part of everyday life for most people, and remain as a
significant interhuman carry-over from the CAPE era to the present
day. Extremely hierarchical modern societies – think of Nazi Germany,
the Soviet Union, North Korea and China – have retained the tradition of
grand political pageantry as part of their governing process.

In the transnational domain, religion and trade had a presence that was
both robust and often complementary. They generated networks of
secondary institutions and transnational networks from guilds and trade
diasporas, to monasteries, sects and pilgrimage operations. Trade routes
facilitated the spread of religion, and religious institutions often facilitated trade. The CAPE era developed a much more specialised, larger-
scale, and diversified approach to production, and a much deeper and
wider trading economy. This created a very substantial economic layer
above the subsistence one, in which large numbers of people, especially
those living in towns and cities, depended for their livelihoods and their
food on specialised work, and on the smooth functioning of the social
networks supporting production and trade. This trading system involved
elaborate, highly differentiated, networks of production, transportation,
finance and people that did not exist in the HGB era. Despite the much
higher level of functional differentiation, and the widespread interdependence it generated, there was little or no sense of either 'the economy' as a
distinct sector requiring management, or of development as a political goal.

The interpolity domain in the CAPE era was defined and dominated
by city-states and empires, along with monarchy/dynasticism and war.
Monarchical sovereignty and imperial politics became a central organising feature, absorbing and overriding kinship, and carrying with them a

stronger sense of territoriality, and early practices of diplomacy and international law. CAPE politics was founded on the idea of human inequality expressed in monarchy/dynasticism, empire, patriarchy and slavery, and it often used religion as a legitimising idea to reinforce dynastic privilege. But while politics was central to the social structure of the CAPE era, it was generally fragile. Empires and dynasties came and went, and although this process could be quick or slow, it underpinned a generally cyclical, Khaldunian, view of the political condition. With occasional exceptions, politics was a game reserved for elite classes. Even where republics popped up, as sometimes in classical Greece and pre-Mauryan India, a large percentage of the population (women, slaves) was excluded. Armies and wars were a central and virtually continuous feature, tightly linked to the expansion and contraction cycles of empire, the dynamics of dynastic succession and rivalry, and the back-and-forth of the rivalry and interdependence between steppe and sedentary peoples and polities. War both made, and unmade, empires. It drove some mass migrations, and sometimes obliterated whole peoples. Towards the end of this era, gunpowder empires closed the steppe, but while this was in one sense a major historical change, it did little or nothing to lessen the prominence of war and violence in human affairs.

Given the relative obsession of the discipline of IR with the interpolity domain, not only this distribution of the CAPE era social structures across all three domains, but also their operation and interlinkage across them, underline the relevance of an integrated world society perspective even in this prelude era. It is a striking feature of the CAPE set of primary institutions how well integrated they were with each other across the three domains. The central political package of the new CAPE social structure was a group of primary institutions that were not only compatible, but strongly mutually supportive. Imperialism, monarchical/dynastic sovereignty, flexible territoriality, human inequality, religion, trade and war all wove into each other, and defined supporting understandings of international law and diplomacy. Religion was mainly transnational, and could come into tension with empire and dynasticism, but it could also be, and often was, drawn into association with both the interpolity domain, and with transnational trade. Political and military structures depended on both the revenues and the materials supplied by trade, creating a complex system of political economy. And this dependence was reciprocal, with economic activity depending on both the muscle (and sometimes brain) power provided by slavery, and, up to a point, on the security that empires provided for traders and their goods. This level of harmony amongst its primary institutions may in part explain the longevity of the CAPE era. While hardly a time of peace and tranquillity for those living in it, the CAPE era did possess a remarkably durable, compatible, and coherent set of primary institutions.

In sum, the CAPE era was a master class in slavery, pageantry, hierarchy, empire, violence and patriarchy. It worked out viable accommodations between the holders of capital and coercion that worked to the advantage of both. Mainly in the form of religions, it learned how to build imagined communities on a large scale, but it made relatively little progress in applying this skill to the political sector. The peoples of this era did not have to confront planetary-scale environmental issues, and operated as if the environment was an unlimited resource there for them to exploit however they could. Interestingly, the CAPE era was not generally racist with the notable exception of later Western colonialism. Its extensive use of slavery, and its endemic violence, should not be confused with racism. Racism was to be one of the signature accomplishments of the transition towards modernity.

By looking at material conditions and social structures in some detail, the global society approach opens an opportunity to rethink the kinds of benchmark dates normally used to divide up the CAPE era. Bentley (1996) offers a fairly typical periodisation:

- 3500–2000 BC – early complex societies
- 2000–500 BC – ancient civilisations
- 500 BC–500 AD – classical civilisations
- 500–1000 AD – post-classical civilisations
- 1000–1500 AD – transregional nomadic empires
- 1500 AD – the modern age

The higher level of analysis of the global society approach, with its emphasis on continuity and similarity over change and everyday difference, disputes this kind of historical benchmarking in two ways. First, and most obviously, it bundles the whole lot into a single era that starts with the first CAP empires circa 2310 BC and stops not in 1500, but at the end of the eighteenth century. Second, the approach across the three domains suggests that internal benchmarking within the CAPE era should look quite different. For example, it does not confine the interplay between steppe nomads and sedentary civilisations to a particular time period, but sees it as continuous throughout the era up to 1689, when the Treaty of Nerchinsk closes the steppe. It gives more prominence to material factors amongst which the spread of the iron age after 1200 BC, the development of horse-riding and steppe cavalry a few hundred years later, and the gunpowder revolution of the fourteenth century AD, count as major turning points. It sees the form of monarchical/dynastic, imperial, political economy as more stable and continuous right through the era, and on that basis the development of universalist religions and philosophies from circa 500 BC deserves independent recognition. So too do key developments in the economic sector such as the opening of Eurasian trade routes (Silk Roads) from 200 BC, the opening of the Atlantic sea routes in late fifteenth century AD, and the creation of a global trading network in the sixteenth century. The year 1500 is not the beginning of modernity, but it is the beginning of a global trading system based on CAPE technology and practices. Around the same time (1453), the Ottomans took Constantinople opening a period in which 'The Turk' conquered large swathes of southeast Europe, and become Europe's military and cultural other. This period did not end until the defeat of the Ottomans at Vienna in 1683, which was the last time before the rise of Europe that a power from the Global South seriously threatened Europe's core.[27]

Similarities across the CAPE era notwithstanding, it is also true that by the seventeenth and eighteenth centuries, Europe was beginning to diverge from the general pattern in some key respects. There was not much change in the centrality and function of war, and violence generally; or the dominance of the political sector by monarchy/dynasticism; or the importance and practice of trade and finance; or the principle and practice of human inequality, including slavery and patriarchy. There were, however, the beginnings of changes that would in the nineteenth century sweep away the CAPE era. First was the increasing consolidation of sovereign states with a tighter sense of territoriality, and new departures in diplomacy and international law. These states were still monarchical/dynastic, but from 1648 they were loosening the links between politics and religion. With the rise of mercantilism, there was a growing sense of the economy as a distinct sector needing to be managed in the interests of state power. There was the beginnings of a systematic development of science and technology, with knowledge seen as separable from religion, subject to replicable methods, and to be pursued in its own right. By the eighteenth century, there was even questioning of human inequality, with a growing interest in both individual (at this stage largely male) rights, and a rejection of slavery. The people were beginning to emerge as a political force, as they did in the French, Haitian and American revolutions. The transition to modernity was beginning to dawn.

---

[27] Within the similarities and continuities of the CAPE era, there are, of course, many variations of theme. For those interested, the differences among CAPE civilisations are well-covered elsewhere (Toynbee, 1972; Braudel, 1985; Onuma, 2000; Hobson, 2004; Burbank and Cooper, 2010; Katzenstein, 2012).

Bayly (2004: 1–120) goes beyond this idea of a mere European divergence to argue that while Europe was in some respects at the leading edge, there was a global crisis of the CAPE model of which Europe was only one part. In his view, the CAPE model was being undermined by a variety of factors that could, in varying degrees, be found in all the leading civilisations. Despite worldwide improvements in production and trade from the 'industrious revolutions' of the eighteenth century, in which the efficiency of capital and labour both improved, state revenues could not keep pace with the rising costs of military technology and wars. All polities became vulnerable to financial crises that they could not solve by increasing taxation. Higher taxes would destabilise their internal politics by fomenting rebellions by peasants and/or landlords. Industrialism did not become widespread enough to solve this dilemma until the 1830s, and then only for those that mastered it quickly (Bayly, 2004: 49). At the same time, the growth of literacy and mass media created a more active civil society. This reinforced a rising propensity to challenge the dignity, sanctity and legitimacy of the ruling elites, both religious and political, in ways ranging from religious schisms to satire. This development was both expressed and mightily reinforced by the American and French revolutions, which expanded the political recourse to the idea of 'the people', and stimulated consolidation of national identities. Even before industrialism became influential in the global political economy, Bayly therefore sees a worldwide unravelling of some of the key socio-political foundations of the CAPE model: monarchy/ dynasticism, religion and conglomerate empire. When the transition to modernity exploded onto the scene in the early-middle decades of the nineteenth century, the traditional social structures facing it were already weakened by their own internal dynamics and limitations.

Since the CAPE era had many more structural similarities to our own time than the HGB era, what can be said about its contribution to the evolution of global society? I have labelled this era the 'Prelude' for three reasons. First, because it expanded society into the transnational and interpolity domains. Second, because it developed the full range of social glue. And third, because only at its very end did the dynamics and developments within it reach global scale, and then more in the sense of a thinly integrated world society than of a global society. The CAPE era made three major contributions to the evolution of global society.

First, while hunter-gatherers had populated the planet, it was the CAPE era that developed the social structures and the material capabilities to connect all of those populations into a global system and the beginnings of a global society. It began the cultural mingling, mixing and cross-fertilisation among societies and civilisations worldwide. It created a global economy, in the process moving flora and fauna between continents; mingling the peoples and cultures into which humankind had evolved; and opening pathways for both diseases and ideas to move across and between continents. By the end of the eighteenth century, there was a robust global trade in everything from slaves, spices, sugar, silk and silver, to firearms, furs, horses, metals, porcelain, coffee, tea and timber. There was also a growing flow of ideas, both technological and social, around the planet.

Second, CAPE societies not only developed ever-larger scales of society, but also the idea that social structures could be universal in scale. This idea came in two explicit forms, 'universal' empires and 'universal' religions. Both were legitimised by the idea that the achievement of universal society would bring peace. Neither empires nor religions actually achieved universal (global) scale during this era, but the more successful of them believed that they could do so, and should strive towards that end. Their efforts opened up two pathways towards the achievement of ever-larger scale: the use of force to bind more territories and peoples together, and the use of proselytising ideas to bind more souls and identities together. These efforts were subtly backed by ever-widening trading systems, always larger in scale than either political or identity social structures, which generated wealth, knowledge and motive for religious and imperial expansion. Trade was implicitly rather than explicitly universalist. It was without outer limits, and always pushing to find new sources of profit and exotic goods. It was traders who made the first global economy when the Spanish began shipping American silver across the Pacific during the late sixteenth century, so connecting all of the inhabited continents into a pattern of world trade.

Third, the CAPE era not only extended the range of trade, eventually up to global scale, but also changed its role in the aggregate life of humankind. For HGBs, trade was not generally necessary to survival, because their subsistence lifeway was largely self-reliant. A good deal of subsistence economy remained during the CAPE era, but, as indicated in the stories of Mesopotamia, Egypt, Athens, Rome and China above, for increasing numbers of people, trade involved the abandonment of local self-reliance, and acceptance of deep dependence on imported goods. When trade flourished, so did civilisation, and when it declined, so did cities and empires. In this sense, the CAPE era accepted, if it did not embrace, economic interdependence not just for optional luxury goods (although those too), but also for many of the basic necessities of both human life and the life of civilisation. Economic linkage, even interdependence, on an ever-larger scale, became a foundational condition of the CAPE lifeway.

The CAPE era set all this up, in the process laying the foundations for global society. But it had neither the energy resources nor the technologies of transportation and communication, to realise universal goals in more than a very thin and preliminary fashion. Perhaps more arguably, it did not have the necessary social ideas and forms of organisation either. Intensifying globalisation was to be the post-CAPE task of humankind.

Part II

The Transition to Modernity and the
Making of Global Society

Introduction to Part II

Chapter 3 has set out a sufficiently full sketch of CAPE society to provide a good sense of what the nineteenth-century turn towards modernity was a transition from. The questions to be answered in this second part of the book are two. First, what was that transition to? In other words, what is 'modernity'? And second, what was the nature of the transition itself? It is clear that the CAPE era ended. But it is less clear that modernity has properly or fully begun. Are we still within a transition period somehow parallel to that between the hunter-gatherer and CAPE eras? Or has history accelerated so much that the transition was very quick, perhaps only a few decades, and we are now fully into the modern era? What did the shift out of the CAPE era towards the modern one involve, both materially and in terms of social structure? How did this shift unfold over the last two-plus centuries, and where are we now? This sets up for Part III, which looks at where this unfolding seems to be heading.

Answering the first question about the origins and character of modernity could easily absorb one or more books by itself, and while we need a reasonably firm sense of it, I do not wish to derail this book with a long critical excursion into the vast literature on modernity.[1] As in recent work with George Lawson (Buzan and Lawson, 2015, 2020), I pretend neither to be able to resolve the debates in that literature, nor to come up with a grand causal theory of modernity. The causal nexus that drove the transition to modernity was a famously complex, interactive, blend of material and ideational breakthroughs. My main aim is to complement the mainstream understanding of modernity in two specific, and I think original, ways. First, I focus on the changes in social structure (primary institutions) that marked the transition from CAPE towards modernity. Second, I open the question of whether we are actually within modernity, as almost the entire literature about it assumes, or whether we are still in a transition period out of the CAPE era and into modernity.

---

[1] See, for example, Hobsbawm, 1962, 1975, 1987, 1990; Habermas, 1990; Giddens, 1991; Hall et al., 1996; Bayly, 2004; Wagner, 2012.

In approaching this task, I draw on, and elaborate, the understanding of modernity developed in Buzan and Lawson (2015). This does not try to explain modernity, but to observe how it manifests itself and with what consequences. This approach gives a clear starting point, and opens the way for further elaborations in the subsequent chapters.

I have a quite conventional, mainstream, understanding of how the unfolding of modernity differs from the characteristics of the CAPE era. Modernity is a historically contingent concatenation of material conditions and social forces that, during the nineteenth century, coalesced in a small group of states (initially Western plus Japan). From that core group both its effect (a revolutionary reconfiguration in the material and social foundations of power – what Buzan and Lawson (2015) call a new *mode of power*) and its challenge (how other polities responded to this configuration), became the principal dynamic through which international relations was conceived and practised. By intensifying the thin, integrated world society of the late CAPE era, transition towards modernity gave birth to global society. The crystallisation of the transition towards modernity consisted of multiple revolutions in technology, knowledge, politics, law, economics, society and psychology, which boiled down to five basic, but interlinked, types of change:

1. Mainly agrarian political economies based on land as wealth, and with cycles of prosperity and famine based on harvests, were superseded by mainly industrial political economies based on fossil fuels and capitalist accumulation and investment, and featuring boom-and-bust trade and financial cycles. Rapid and frequent technological transformations replaced slow and intermittent ones, and the market was extended to global scale with vastly greater depth and intensity than under late CAPE era merchant capitalism. This new structure for relations of production, exchange and value generated big changes in class structure, with the aristocracy losing influence, the peasantry shrinking, and both the bourgeoisie/middle-class and the proletariat expanding and diversifying, as well as gaining in influence.

2. Four new secular *ideologies of progress* rose to prominence during the nineteenth century: liberalism, nationalism, socialism and 'scientific' racism. These ideologies challenged both monarchy/dynasticism and religion, largely displacing the former and transforming the latter. They generated new entities, actors and institutions (e.g. civil society, limited companies, intergovernmental organisations) and reconstituted some old ones (e.g. the state, religion). Expectations of historical progress underpinned the emergence of industrial societies. The new ideologies challenged personalised, conglomerate polities and reshaped the territorial sovereign state by vesting sovereignty in the

people and linking territory to the nation. Liberalism, socialism, and up to a point nationalism, unleashed a normative assault on the principles of human inequality that had governed the CAPE world.

3. A small group of *rational states* formed, in which increasing administrative and infrastructural capacity extended state power both at home and abroad. Rational states were legitimised and empowered by both the new ideologies of progress, and the new scientific methods and technologies, and the expanding wealth they enabled. They both caged their societies within nation states, and extended power outwards, via imperialism and the market, into a core–periphery colonial interstate society. Both processes were importantly facilitated by the rise of market ideology, and the creation of a new form of actor, the modern limited company, operating domestically and internationally within the legal and political framing of the rational state.

4. This tripartite configuration of industrialisation, ideologies of progress and rational state-building changed the global configuration of wealth and power in two foundational ways. First, it opened a massive and durable economic and military power gap between those societies that successfully adopted the revolutions of modernity and took them forward, and those that did not or could not. This gap generated a core–periphery global order defined by notions of 'development' versus 'underdevelopment', 'advanced' versus 'backward', 'First World' versus 'Third World', etc. Those countries on the wrong side of the power gap, such as China, were left with the pressing problem of how to regenerate their wealth and power so as to restore their status and their independence (Schell and Delury, 2013). The small group of countries at the leading edge of the transition towards modernity added insult to injury by using the revolutions of modernity to define a 'standard of civilisation', whose contours changed continuously, and which they used to justify racism and imperial expansion. Second, industrialism destabilised great power relations by exposing the balance of power to the pressures of rapid technological and social change, with the consequence of making military balancing dynamics within the core much more volatile.

5. In a classical sociological perspective, modernity can best be understood as a shift in the balance of social differentiation from mainly *stratificatory* to one in which *functional differentiation*, and the division of activities into *sectors*, played a much more prominent role. Although stratification in particular, and hierarchy in general, remain central to how social orders are organised, the signature feature of emergent modernity is a significant rise in the relative importance of functional differentiation as a means of cohering complex societies (Buzan and Albert, 2010; Albert, Buzan and Zürn, 2013).

Put as simply and starkly as possible, emergent modernity is defined by a very direct and rapid transformation in the material conditions of humankind in terms of energy, resources and technology, which is ongoing. This material transition is generally clear and well understood. Alongside it, there was a considerably slower and more turbulent transition in the social structure of humankind, whose contradictions and dialectics are still being worked through. For most of the nineteenth and twentieth centuries, these transformations took place in a context of unrestrained pursuit of human wealth and power, and a seeming absence of environmental constraints. The four chapters in this part of the book put flesh onto this bare-bones picture of emergent modernity by setting out in some detail the nature and dynamics of the material conditions and social structures that define it. The key question is whether all this is best seen as modernity proper, or as a transition process out of the CAPE era and towards modernity?

This approach raises a vexed question about how to deal with what look clearly like degrees of modernity between different states and societies (think of the difference between South Korea or Denmark, on the one hand, and Afghanistan or Chad, on the other hand). At first glance, this might look simple: South Korea and Denmark are clearly more advanced in their relative levels of modernity, both material and social, than Afghanistan and Chad. Such a view is reinforced by the common usage of terms such as 'early' and 'late' developers, and 'developed' and 'developing' countries. It is also supported by the dozens of indexes that measure levels of development in terms ranging from the very basic, such as access to clean drinking water, through access to education for girls, to the high-tech, such as access to the Internet. How is one to understand programmes such as the UN's Millennium Development Goals, and its successor the Sustainable Development Goals,[2] as other than saying that development comes in degrees and levels? But the spoiler here is that all states and societies, with the exception of a few uncontacted tribes, have been deeply embedded in the revolutions of modernity for over two centuries, and are in that sense modern. The products of modernity have penetrated everywhere, from mobile phones and vaccinations, to AK-47s and SUVs, and so have its ways of thinking and mobilising (think of Islamic State online). In addition, as Buzan and Lawson (2014b, 2015, 2016) set out, there is no single standard of modernity to measure others against. Notwithstanding the teleological dreams of some liberals and some leftists, the reality is uneven and combined development, multiple modernities and varieties of capitalism.

[2] https://sdgs.un.org/goals (accessed 24 February 2021).

This embedding of all within modernity, and each people finding its own path, generates strange mixes: Think of Saudi Arabia and Iran as seemingly equal mixes of modern and traditional; or of Britain, Saudi Arabia and Thailand as variations on how to handle monarchy/dynasticism within modernity. But it also makes it impossibly complicated to answer questions about whether A is more modern than B, or whether C is modern at all? All are modern in their own distinctive ways.[3] My way of getting around this dilemma is to replace the question of 'How modern, or not?', with one about 'what degree of capacity have states/societies developed to maximise the amount of wealth and power they can extract from the material and ideational resource portfolios of modernity?' For those of a quantitative disposition, a very rough proxy for this capacity might be GDP/capita, though that might need to be modified to account for how evenly or unevenly wealth and power are distributed within a society/state. This approach enables reasonable differentiations about levels and types of development, and thus comparisons, to be made within an unfolding modernity that encompasses all. It is, however, a cold calculation, leaving open the question of whether being able to extract more wealth and power from modernity is a good, or even a sustainable, thing or not.

With this summary idea of modernity in place, there remains the second question about how to position the last two centuries within the large framework of eras? I am still firmly of the view, argued with George Lawson in our 2015 book, that the nineteenth century very clearly marked the transition out of the CAPE era, and towards modernity. One can of course find many precursors of modernity in preceding centuries, from philosophy, through state bureaucracy, to science and engineering. But the point is that these did not coalesce to produce deep and widespread global effects until the nineteenth century. By itself, however, that insight does not solve the problem of how to characterise the short, but extremely intense, period since the early nineteenth century. Do the huge material and social changes since then count as sufficient to define a post-CAPE era? Are we in modernity proper? The nineteenth-century changes did not open up new social domains in the way that the CAPE era had done by adding to the interhuman domain the trans-national and interpolity ones. Neither did it expand on the basic types of social glue, though it did give them new applications. But it did introduce major new institutions and actors across the domains, inter alia: human equality and nationalism into the interhuman domain; the market, the modern firm, science, sport, and a huge variety of non-state actors into the

---

[3] I am grateful to George Lawson for having the patience to help me understand this point.

transnational domain; and the replacement of empires by rational, sovereign, territorial states, as the dominant unit in the interpolity domain. The question is whether it makes more sense to treat the time since this turn as basically a period of transition from the CAPE structure towards modernity, or to see the transition as incredibly short and sharp by historical standards, and treat the last two centuries as being fully in and of the modern era? This question plays through and around the one about how to differentiate degrees of modernity. The lesson of the move from the HGB to CAPE eras is that transitions can be long before a new crystallisation of social and material structure takes place. But there is no doubt that the pace of history – how quickly and frequently there are major changes in material conditions and social structure – has accelerated sharply during the last few centuries. Since we are still very close to all of this in historical terms, and highly aware of the scale and depth of the changes wrought since the early nineteenth century, the dominant view leaps straight into an assumption that we are in modernity proper, not really thinking much about transition periods. What strikes observers first and hardest from our present position is the extent, and accelerating pace, of change, especially material change, since the early nineteenth century. Yet it is possible to argue, as Bayly (2004: 125–69) comes close to doing, that the period between the late eighteenth-century revolutions, and the upheavals of the mid-nineteenth century,[4] constitutes a transition between the decaying *ancien regimes* and modernity.

Alternatively, one could see the nineteenth century and the first part of the twentieth century, as transitional, with modernity proper not kicking in until the second half of the twentieth century, or perhaps not yet having arrived at all. It is clear that despite the huge transformations in the nineteenth century, there were also major institutional carry-overs from the CAPE era, most notably empire, human inequality (patriarchy, racism, class), monarchy/dynasticism, war, diplomacy and trade. The decisive turns against monarchy/dynasticism did not occur until after the First World War, and against human inequality, empire and war until after the Second World War. Has the acceleration of history reduced the transition period to almost nothing? Or was the first post-CAPE century, or even the second, a transition? Or is our view from within the process still so blinkered that we cannot see that everything so far is transition?

With all of this in mind, the four chapters that follow are therefore not organised around a definite prior decision in favour of transition, modernity proper, or some compromise. Instead, they centre around two key processes – globalisation and inequality – the links between them, and

[4] 1848 in Europe, the Taiping and other rebellions in China, the Indian Mutiny and the American Civil War.

how they play into the question of transition. I follow Reus-Smit and Dunne (2017: 28–40) in seeing the globalisation of international society as a more appropriate approach than the traditional English School idea of an expanding European one (Bull and Watson, 1984). The rapid and ongoing intensification of globalisation, massively pushed by technology and economy, has drawn humankind into a fully global society for the first time. Within that, and closely tied to it, has been the creation of deep inequality on a global scale: a core–periphery system in economic, political, military, social (particularly race), and legal terms defined by different levels of development and military power. This pattern of inequality was in many ways different from the inequality of the CAPE era. It came about quite abruptly towards the middle of the nineteenth century, creating a small core holding most of the wealth and power, and a large periphery relatively poor and disempowered. As Sassoon (2019: 509) puts it: '[T]he industrial world continued to grow, subduing much of the rest of the world.' One of the key dynamics within the last two centuries has been the dramatic opening of this gap during the nineteenth century, and the ongoing struggle to reduce, and eventually close, it that got underway during the second half of the twentieth century.

The making of a global society was in itself a remarkable turning point for humankind, something aspired to for millennia, but never previously achieved. What Bayly (2004: 41–4) calls 'archaic globalisation' was long pursued by empires and religions seeing themselves as 'universal', and merchants seeking ever-more distant points of trade. Yet the path to globalisation taken during the nineteenth century had inequality built into it. As Buzan and Schouenborg (2018: 39–56) set out, in principle, a global society could form in either of two ways, *monocentric* (in which one civilisation expanded to dominate all the others, as happened during the nineteenth century), or *polycentric* (in which several civilisations expanded until they all came into close contact with each other, rather as Europe and the Islamic world did in the Mediterranean, and the Hindu and Islamic worlds did in South and Southeast Asia). On the historical evidence, either process would almost certainly have involved considerable violence, and probably also durable suspicion and hostility. But driven by the new wealth and power provided by modernity, the monocentric one came much faster and more intensely than would have been the case if the centres of civilisation had expanded into contact with each other under CAPE conditions. A single global system was made in a historical instant, with inequality as a given. The polycentric process would have been slower, and might have produced more equal relations. The aim is to track developments in globalisation and inequality in order to generate some leverage on how to understand the transition question. Part of that is tracking the upheaval in the primary institutions of global society that marked the last two centuries. Which CAPE institutions became obsolete, or adapted, and what new institutions specific to modernity arose?

The approach in this part of the book is both similar to and different from that in Part I. It is different in that in Part I each era got its own chapter, whereas here, the discussion of the transition to modernity is divided into three chapters. The inverse rule applied to earlier eras also applies here, with three chapters needed to cover the last 20 centimetres on the one-kilometre timeline. These three chapters follow the internal structure of the earlier chapters. Chapter 4 covers the material conditions of modernity since the nineteenth century. Chapters 5a and 5b cover social structure (already partly familiar to most readers because they live in it, but hopefully providing a new perspective when looked at in both English School and historical perspective). The story of social structure is long and complicated, and I have split it into two chapters to avoid having a chapter over 40,000 words in length.

Chapter 6 departs from the earlier formula. Since the narrative has reached the present day, it addresses the question of where we now are in the unfolding towards modernity. It argues that, from a global society perspective, the transition process from CAPE to modernity displays three reasonably clear phases. The first phase, running from the early nineteenth century to roughly 1970, was constituted by a big material and social transformation from CAPE towards modern conditions. This phase was strongly shaped by extreme uneven and combined development in the form of a small Western core, plus Japan, dominating a large periphery. Almost everything, from population, through productivity, to wealth and power, grew seemingly without limit. The second phase ran from the 1970s through the second decade of the twenty-first century. During this phase, the material development towards modernity continued unabated, but its unevenness began to diminish. The core expanded as parts of the periphery found successful paths to development. The dominance of the old core of early modernisers diminished, and an overambitious attempt at economic globalisation led by the US, failed, triggering a general crisis of liberalism. In addition, environmental constraints on development began to kick in as the weight of human civilisation pressed ever-more heavily on the carrying capacity of the planet. The third phase begins from the early 2020s. It has two main characteristics. First, world politics becomes deeply pluralist. Superpowers fade away, leaving interstate society deeply divided among several culturally and politically differentiated great powers, and many regional ones. Second, climate change and all of its consequences loom ever-larger as a collective threat to humankind, challenging the norm of the first two phases that development can and should be unrestrained. This third phase is the subject of Part III. The Conclusions to Part II sum up the argument in the four chapters about the material and social elements of the transition towards modernity, and where we are now in that process.

4   Material Conditions

Introduction

There is a view of the human condition that rests on the idea of relatively steady progress, when taken in a perspective long enough to even-out the ups and downs of rising and falling civilisations. This is well-expressed by Tainter (1988: locs. 137–8):

> Human history as a whole has been characterized by a seemingly inexorable trend toward higher levels of complexity, specialisation, and socio-political control, processing of greater quantities of energy and information, formation of ever larger settlements, and development of more complex and capable technologies.

There is a sense in which this is true given that one can track such progress down through the millennia. But when viewed from a higher altitude, this process looks not steady, but distinctly uneven – uneven enough, I will argue, to help define clear historical eras. I have already hinted at this in Part I, by noting the relatively quick crystallisation of new material and social conditions at the point when humans first began to congregate in towns and cities, and the relatively long following period of incremental change within fairly narrow boundaries. The picture unfolded there was of the emergence of a profoundly new set of material and social conditions that then remained relatively stable for the next several millennia. This chapter confronts that discontinuity in a much starker form. As noted in Chapter 1, the key is to differentiate between change occurring <u>within</u> a relatively fixed set of conditions, and change that <u>transforms</u> those conditions themselves. The crystallisation of the conglomerate agrarian/pastoralist empires (CAPE) era was transformative, although only after a long period of transition from hunter-gatherer to agrarian/pastoralist production. Right from the beginning of the transition, the crystallisation of the modern era is unquestionably again transformative.

The key reason why the question of transition between the CAPE and modern eras is so difficult to answer, is the extreme rapidity and drama with which material and social conditions transformed from early in the nineteenth century. The rapidity and drama are so overwhelming, and so compressed in time, that it is easy to forget about the question of a transition period, and see something like a clean jump from CAPE to modernity proper in the historical flash of one or two human generations. Reinforcing this perspective is the extraordinary contrast between the two eras, with modernity seeming almost to stand the material condition of the CAPE era on its head. As shown in Chapter 3, the CAPE era was defined by a relatively fixed set of material and energy resources, and a largely cyclical pattern of empires and dynasties. Within those limits there was significant progress: sailing ships got bigger and better, trade become more widespread and sophisticated, some empires got big and lasted a long time, and some religions learned how to expand the range of shared identities beyond the local. But this progress was almost entirely within a fairly stable set of material and social conditions, and did not transcend them.

The revolutions of modernity very quickly blew the lid off all this. They opened seemingly permanent revolutions in both material and social conditions. They reversed the balance between agrarian and industrial production that had sustained the CAPE political economy, in the process making much that had always been scarce, abundant. They removed the material and knowledge constraints that had capped and limited CAPE lifeways. New sources of energy tore away the long-standing dependence of the CAPE era on human and animal muscle power and wind. Partly as a result of that, a cornucopia of new materials became available. The increase in resources transformed the fairly slow growth of the human population by feeding (literally) a nearly geometric expansion in human numbers, enabling the human population to grow faster than ever before, from around 1 billion in 1800 to over 8 billion today (Christian, 2004: 342; Bricker and Ibbitson, 2019: 23–9), with doubling times themselves accelerating. During the nineteenth and much of the twentieth century, this increase was broadly welcome for all of the traditional reasons that applied during the CAPE era: more workers, more soldiers, more consumers, more taxpayers. Malthusian concerns about being unable to feed the rising numbers were repeatedly pushed aside by rising productivity and the opening up of new land and resources.

By the end of the nineteenth century, there was growing awareness amongst the colonial powers that they had filled-up the planet politically and economically. There were no more territories or markets that could be expropriated from their indigenous inhabitants because everything that could be colonised, had been. The so-called frontiers between 'civilisation' and 'barbarism' were closing, leaving the colonial powers facing each other worldwide. A geopolitical struggle amongst them to re-divide the spoils seemed imminent (Lenin, 1975 [1916]; Mackinder, 1996 [1904]). But the planet did not yet seem overcrowded with people. That concern only became evident during the 1970s, when estimates of population growth seemed likely to outrun the carrying capacity of the planet (Meadows and Meadows, 1972). In 1979, the new government of Deng Xiaoping in China tightened its policy of population control to allow couples only one child. The unfolding of modernity threatened to fill the planet with human beings beyond its capacity to sustain them, generating unprecedented questions about population control, and the position and reproductive function, of women in society.

Technological innovation shifted from being slow, unexpected and episodic, to being rapid, systematic, expected and continuous. Up to a point, technological innovation could now be planned and steered by both corporations and governments. The process of innovation was driven not only by the systematisation of knowledge, but also by the incentive structure of industrial capitalism, which directed capital investment towards innovations that could produce profit. Systematic knowledge began to expand exponentially as scientific method became a universal standard. And a series of social revolutions displaced both monarchy/dynasticism and empire as the core of the political order, opening up a range of experiments about how human society should be organised. One of the social and political impacts of seemingly permanent technological innovation was to marginalise the mainly cyclical view that CAPE societies had of themselves, and replace it with the linear progressive view of the future that was a key element of modernity. The nineteenth century opened an era of seemingly endless change and progress that would be driven by rapid and continuous improvements in knowledge and technology.

New techniques of production, science and technology gave societies huge new resources of all kinds, raising standards of living for broad sections of some societies to unheard of levels, and providing powerful support for ideologies of progress. Alongside this, standards of inequality also found new forms and extremes, creating cores and peripheries both within and between states. This huge expansion in the production of everything, has been widely recounted and will be familiar to most readers (e.g. Landes, 1969; Pomeranz, 2000; Morris, 2010; Osterhammel, 2014; Buzan and Lawson, 2015). Its details are far too deep and wide to account for fully here, and the following discussion focuses instead on the main highlights. That said, there were, of course, many continuities. Potters continued to use clay; wooden sailing ships remained commercially significant until the late nineteenth century; tool- and weapon-makers continued to use iron and steel; and paper and printing presses remained central to those needing to keep records or communicate across space and time. But the main story is the way in which the transition towards modernity quickly left behind most of the material constraints of the CAPE era. To give thematic clarity, this story is subdivided into materials, energy, interaction capacity, military tech- nology and civil technology. Although there are some technologies that are clearly civil or military, there are many that are dual-use, from boots, batteries and cameras, to railways, rockets and radar. Even when technologies seem distinctly military (nuclear submarines) or civil (smartphones), the knowledge and technology in physics, chemistry, material science and engineering that lie just beneath the surface, are common to both.

Materials

The CAPE era made its way on the basis of a relatively narrow repertoire of materials, many of them natural, and already known to hunter- gatherers. A couple of hard metals, iron and bronze, plus glass, were its key additions. By contrast, transition towards modernity very quickly opened up the whole of the naturally existing periodic table, making its many elements, and an increasing number of their innumerable combin- ations, known and available. There were some carry-overs, albeit trans- formed in the process. Iron and steel continued to play a central role in industrial society, but in much larger quantities, qualities and varieties, and at much lower cost. A range of newly found elements additional to carbon and arsenic could be combined with iron to produce varieties of steel with different qualities: chromium, cobalt, manganese, nickel, tung- sten. Glass remained in widespread use for many applications, and like steel became much more diverse. Copper re-emerged with entirely dif- ferent uses in the electrical industry. Lead found new uses as an additive in paints and petrol, and in rechargeable batteries. Gold, silver and a variety of gemstones carried on in their traditional roles in currency and jewellery. Gunpowder carried on for a few decades before being replaced by more efficient explosives.

But a great deal was entirely new. A few examples will suffice to give the general picture. Aluminium opened up a universe of applications for a lightweight, but strong, metal, including aircraft bodies, engine parts, foil, pots and pans, and suchlike, with titanium also having some of these properties. Carbon, already the basis of wood, opened up an entire subfield of 'organic' chemistry, and became an essential material for making many things in common use, from a nearly infinite variety of plastics, through nylon and artificial rubber, to carbon fibre, nanotubes and graphene. A range of gases became available that could be applied in different ways, from lighter-than-air craft (hydrogen and helium), through fuel (hydrogen, methane), and refrigeration (nitrogen), to lighting (neon), cutting (acetylene), and medicine (oxygen, laughing gas [nitrous oxide]). Artificial nitrogen fertilisers enabled much larger crops to be grown more reliably, underpinning the geometrical expansion in the human population. A set of fissile materials (radium, thorium, uranium, plutonium) became available for a wide variety of applications from medicine, through power generation, to weapons of unprecedented explosive power. The discovery of antibiotic chemicals, starting with penicillin in 1928, opened the way to a whole armoury of drugs that, at a price, could be used to combat, ameliorate or potentially eliminate the diseases that had plagued humankind since the beginning of civilisation. Late in the twentieth century, nickel and then lithium found major uses in batteries, the latter in particular supporting a rapid diffusion of portable electronic devices. Rarer minerals such as cobalt, tantalum and palladium became crucial to the manufacture of smart mobile phones. The ability to work with materials at the molecular scale (nanotechnology) revealed new properties of familiar elements (Falkner and Jaspers, 2012: 35). In prospect at the time of writing were such things as superconducting materials that worked at manageable levels of temperature and pressure, and long fibres having the strength of molecular rather than just chemical bonds.

Underpinning many aspects of these developments in materials was a revolution in precision engineering and instrumentation. Precision engineering is about both how finely one can shape any given object, and how consistently one can achieve such tolerances. For an everyday example, think of how screw-top caps fit onto plastic water bottles perfectly enough both to make a reliable air- and watertight seal, and to be interchangeable across millions of the same type of bottle. Such precision is crucial not only to the efficiency of all kinds of devices from clocks to cannons, but also to the ability to manufacture in bulk, complex items with interchangeable parts. Think of the closeness or looseness of the fit of pistons into their cylinders in either steam or internal combustion engines. Or think about how closely or loosely a ball or a bullet fits into the barrel of a gun. Too tight, and the gun will explode when fired. Too loose, and the propellant gases will escape, reducing the force and accuracy of the shot. Skilled individual gunsmiths might be able to produce good quality weapons, but each would be unique. The increasing use of machine tools in the nineteenth century enabled guns such as the Colt 45 revolver to be made with interchangeable parts. Occasional uses of interchangeable parts can be found during the CAPE era, but the idea did not really become central to manufacturing until the late eighteenth to early nineteenth centuries, when the British navy famously standardised the manufacture of wooden blocks for the rigging of its sailing ships during the wars with France. During the nineteenth century, precision engineering improved rapidly, and was vital to the shift in manufacturing to mass production of identical items, and to the use of assembly lines to do so. By the later twentieth century, precision engineering had moved into electronics, and become crucial to miniaturisation. In the 1960s, a small portable radio might have a handful of individual transistors. These were quickly grouped together on circuit boards and then chips, which by the 1970s might contain a few thousand transistors. By the time of writing, chips were available with many billions, and even trillions, of transistors. This development enabled exponential improvements in computers, and powered the ongoing digital revolution.

A similar sort of exponential revolution took place in instrumentation, and the ability to look inside material things in ever-finer detail. Microscopes enabling people to see bacterial life in drops of water became available in the seventeenth century, and with the benefit of precision engineering and better materials, were much improved during the nineteenth century. X-rays, enabling people to look directly inside solid objects, came into use late in the nineteenth century. Electron microscopes, using wavelengths much shorter than those of visible light, were available by the 1930s. Ultrasound scanners came into use during the 1960s and 1970s, and magnetic resonance imaging (MRI) scanners by the 1970s and 1980s. Scanning tunnelling microscopes, which enabled people to see structure down to the atomic level were available by the 1980s. These technologies opened up the physical world in unprecedented depth and detail. Most readers will be familiar with their invaluable medical applications, but they also underpinned huge advances in the natural sciences generally, and in materials science in particular, creating a virtuous circle.

A further unfolding of the multidimensional expansion of human understanding and control of the material world was the revolution in biotechnology. This too benefited hugely from the advances in instrumentation just discussed. The principles of plant and animal breeding had been known and practised for millennia, and Mendel's insights into the genetic code date back to the middle of the nineteenth century, but it was not until the late twentieth century, that techniques had advanced sufficiently to enable humans to begin tinkering with the basic structures and mechanisms of life itself. By the early 1950s, Crick and Watson had crowned decades of earlier work by others to produce an accurate model of DNA. From the 1970s, genes were being transplanted from one type of organism to another, to create genetically modified organisms. Biology had begun to develop its own branch of engineering, a process land-marked by the successful cloning of Dolly the sheep in 1996. In 2012, Doudna and Charpentier offered the world CRISPR-Cas9, the first reliable tool for editing DNA. This opened up, for better or for worse, a whole new universe of biological engineering possibilities from growing meat without animals to making improvements to the mark-1 human being, enabling humans to seize control of both the biosphere and their own evolution as a species.

From the nineteenth century onwards, humankind therefore had access not only to a huge variety of new materials, but also to the tools and techniques enabling it to expand this access in seemingly unlimited ways. Particular materials might, for a time, appear to become limited in supply, but technology could often either find ways of extending their supply, or find substitutes for many of their uses. There seemed to be no stopping the improvements in precision engineering and instrumenta-tion, and a vast new domain of biological engineering was just opening up. Humankind not only had immediate access to a vast array of new material resources, but increasingly to the keys to complete command over the material world.

Energy

The cornucopia of new materials was partly dependent on breaking out of the energy constraints of the CAPE era, and learning how to harness electricity in myriad ways. But access to what seemed like unlimited sources of energy was a transformation in itself that was perhaps even greater in its consequences than new materials. The cornucopia of energy that was being unleashed by the nineteenth century quickly accelerated into top gear the formula of Tainter (1988: loc. 1548) noted above, that: 'Energy flow and sociopolitical organisation must evolve in harmony'. The sudden acquisition of huge energy resources largely blew away the CAPE era's dependence on wood, wind and muscle power. In the process, it greatly weakened the need for slavery, adding another strand to the moral and political campaigns against it in the core, and to the slave revolts in the periphery. It demoted the horse from its central position in production, transport and military power. It released vast amounts of land that had been needed for biofuel and fodder, and made it available to farming for human food. And it provided the power to fuel a massive expansion in the industrial manufacturing part of the economy, quickly enabling it to overtake agriculture. In the perspective of thousands of years of agrarian civilisation, the term industrial <u>revolution</u>, was no exaggeration. It played into the multiple revolutions of modernity, including changes in class structure, urbanisation and human mobility.

This transformation involved a series of new openings to sources of energy, and means of deploying them, that is still ongoing. The key breakthrough was shifting from wood to fossil fuels, initially coal, to provide heat. Coal was used as fuel in a fairly small way at various times and places during the CAPE era, but the shift to using it on a large scale did not begin until the seventeenth and eighteenth centuries, initially in Britain, and took off there in the nineteenth. The use of coal tapped into a finite, but huge, reserve of energy built up over millions of years, and buried under the planet's surface. It constituted a gigantic windfall from the past that provided a concentrated source of energy useable for a wide range of purposes. Coal was used for space heating, but much more important was its use to provide heat for industrial processes (e.g. smelting, kilns) and to power steam engines. The use of coal in Britain had been rising since the sixteenth century, driven by the shortage of local wood. By 1800, Britain was using around 11 million tons per year. This had doubled by 1830, doubled again by 1845, and passed 100 million tons per year by 1870 (Landes, 1969: 96–7). Britain was the leader in producing and consuming coal, and the global production take-off came a bit later rising sixteen-fold from around 80 million tons a year in 1850 to over 1.3 billion tons a year by 1914 (Osterhammel, 2014: 655). As Pomeranz (2000: 52–60) argues, the nineteenth century turn to coal was a necessary condition for much of the industrialisation of that time, for without it there would have been insufficient energy to support the expansion of iron and steel, steam power, glass-making, brewing and suchlike.

Steam engines co-evolved with coal-mining, initially providing the power to pump water out of the mines. They soon became efficient enough to replace water mills as the centralised source of power for factories, thereby freeing the location of production from proximity to suitable rivers. By the early-middle nineteenth century, steam engines had become small enough and efficient enough to power first ships, and then railway engines, and coal was a portable enough fuel to enable this development. From the 1870s, and particularly from the 1880s, by which time long-distance electricity transmission was possible, coal began playing what became a big role in the generation of commercial electricity using steam engines. Via the medium of steam engines, coal thus quite literally powered the industrial revolutions in production and transportation. It did so partly in a centralising way, providing power to run massive factories and electrical generating stations, and partly in a decentralised way, as the fuel for steamships and railway engines. Although a transformational technology, the closeness of steam engines to the CAPE era, and their place in the transition from CAPE to modernity, is perfectly illustrated by the poignant fact that the output of the new, fossil-fuel engines was measured in units of horse-power (Darwin, 2020: 80). The new engines quickly displaced horses from their long-standing roles as the main providers of traction for land transportation and farming, and as the key to military mobility on land. The social function of horses was largely reduced to sport and ceremony.

Coal was the earliest fossil fuel, but not the only one. Oil and natural gas were being extracted by the 1830s, initially mainly for use in lighting, for which kerosene was distilled from crude oil. The use of oil, or its derivatives, to power engines did not really take off until the late nineteenth century, but was well established by the outbreak of the First World War. Various technical problems in distilling, transporting and burning liquid hydrocarbons had to be solved first. One pathway was using oil instead of coal to make steam in external-combustion engines, and this was happening in navies from the 1890s with the transition largely done by 1914. Oil was more efficient than coal in terms of energy per unit of weight, and vastly so in terms of refuelling. 'Coaling ship', was a slow, dirty, labour-intensive and much disliked process. The other pathway was to use distillates of oil to fuel internal combustion engines (diesel, petrol). This technology was being developed throughout the nineteenth century, and was good enough by the 1880s to be used in motor vehicles, and by the first decade of the twentieth century (mainly diesels) in ships. Internal-combustion engines were an indispensable element in the take-off of the aircraft and motor-vehicle industries during the twentieth century. Oil and gas could also be used to power electricity generation, but did not seriously begin to displace coal for this function until after the Second World War. All of these fossil fuels were inherently limited in supply. The rapidly rising use of them created a still ongoing tension between worries that supplies would run out (often promoted by the industries concerned), and the pace at which new discoveries and new extraction technologies extended the expected lifetime of the resource. This was true for coal during the nineteenth century, and oil, and up to a point nuclear, during the twentieth.

As noted above, the mechanical energy of internal- and external combustion engines powered by fossil fuels could not only be used directly to do work, but also to generate electricity. Electricity could not be directly mined or harvested from the natural world in any significant way (e.g. by capturing lightning). Although not therefore a new source of energy in itself, electricity was a highly desirable form of energy, and an increasingly central part of the new energy portfolio of the transition towards modernity. Once adequate generators (dynamos) became available during the 1860s and 1870s, electricity generation became an increasingly important use of mechanical energy on a large scale. In addition to providing this mechanical energy using fossil fuels, the very old idea of taking energy from water was repurposed to generate hydroelectricity. Before the entry of coal and steam into the equation, mechanical water power was important in the consolidation of production into factories during the eighteenth century. From the 1880s onwards, hydroelectric dams began to become a major element in electricity generation. Once the tricky technical problems of generation and long-distance transmission were solved, electricity became the favoured form of energy. Because power grids could be used to deliver electricity almost anywhere, it enabled the use of energy to become highly decentralized. Factories no longer needed one giant central source of power, but could set up separate workstations each with its own power source. Energy could be delivered to individual homes and offices, and distributed to every room and desk within them. Electricity was a highly fungible form of energy, which could be used for lighting, heating, mechanical power, welding, communications, data processing and weapons. Increasingly, in the late twentieth and early twenty-first centuries, electricity began to break away from dependence on a centralised delivery grid. From the 1980s and 1990s, battery technology was enabling communication to roam free of the grid. By the time of writing, that revolution was well advanced towards replacing internal combustion engines in motor vehicles and other applications requiring stored energy. The centrality of electricity to the material revolutions of modernity was well put in the famous statement by Lenin in 1920 that: 'Communism is Soviet power plus the electrification of the whole country'.

Nuclear fission reactors began to be used during the 1950s as power sources for driving ships, especially icebreakers and military submarines, and for generating electricity. Nuclear power, however, failed to achieve the high expectations that it might quickly provide a cheap and clean source of electrical energy. Its costs were much higher than expected, and it suffered from enduring concerns about safety, and the dire consequences of big accidents. It became a component in the energy portfolios of many countries, and a dominant component in a few, such as France. But it did not displace other sources in the way its proponents had hoped. Nuclear energy was more successful in the military sphere, where its use as an explosive added a geometrical increase to the destructive capacity of chemical explosives. Fusion reactors as a potential source of unlimited energy still remain on the technological horizon.

Fossil fuels, and fission reactors and explosives, all depended on natural resources that were large, but finite. Dams might look like a renewable resource because of their place in an endlessly repeated water cycle, but they had limited lifespans and were subject to silting up. Only during the 1970s did interest turn to truly renewable resources when the widespread deployment of solar power and wind turbines began to unfold. The long-standing use of wind to power ships was largely eclipsed by steam, but from the 1970s, wind began to make a comeback as a means of electricity generation. By the time of writing, the price of electricity generated by solar panels and wind turbines was competitive with fossil fuels, and these technologies were spreading fast. On the horizon were plausible prospects of large-scale extraction of renewable energy from the movements of tides and waves in the oceans; launching huge solar collectors into space; and mining geothermal energy from the planet itself.

Within only a century and a half of its beginning, it was apparent that the transition towards modernity had tapped into essentially infinite and inexhaustible supplies of energy. Despite the ongoing worries about running out of energy that haunted this first phase, no such thing happened or even came close. Some of those worries were simply promoted by the fossil-fuel and nuclear industries for their own purposes. But the basic story is quite different. Humankind had tapped into not just one, but several new sources of energy. Some of these were indeed finite, but they were also vast. Even given the rapidly rising rates of use, new technologies kept extending existing reserves. New technologies also opened up new sources of energy, which just kept coming. Some of these tapped into inexhaustible reserves, such as wind, solar, wave, tidal and geothermal. At least for the leading-edge societies, the material revolutions of modernity seemed to have solved the shortage of energy that defined much of the CAPE era. Electricity was being widely and deeply diffused through society, right down to the level of individuals. It was even becoming possible for individuals to achieve a degree of independence both by converting some of their own energy into electricity to power portable devices, and by harvesting small amounts of electricity from the man-made energy environment around them.

The swift and remarkable transformation from the shortage of energy in the CAPE era, to the effectively unlimited supply of it achieved by early in the twenty-first century, seemed to mark out infinite energy, at least relative to human life on a planetary scale, as a key characteristic of modernity. This was underlined by the rapid movement now underway from dependence on the massive, but finite, windfall legacy of fossil fuels, to the inexhaustible supply from renewable sources. The energy shortage that had shaped and constrained human society since the beginning of urban life had quite suddenly evaporated, albeit energy poverty remained a key development issue for many less developed countries.

This remarkable breakthrough did not come without costs. The principal one was that the earlier and ongoing use of fossil fuels had injected into the atmosphere sufficiently large amounts of greenhouse gases, particularly CO_2, but also methane and others, to begin warming the planet and changing the environment. Initially, this was noticed only as severe local pollution: Blake's 'dark Satanic Mills'. But by the early twenty-first century, the global effects were becoming increasingly noticeable, and politically controversial. Concerns were rising that if not enough was done there would be climate change on a civilisation-threatening scale by or before the end of the century. This major externality had not been priced into the energy revolution, and doing so belatedly would have large economic and political consequences. Some of its effects were durable in the sense that existing CO_2 in the atmosphere stays there for a long time even if no new is added. Renewable, 'green' energy was a major part of any solution, but the timing of the move away from 'dirty' to 'clean' energy was crucial to how serious and how prolonged the environmental costs would be. The energy cornucopia itself was not threatened, but the civilisation that depended on it clearly was. The legacy question from the energy revolution was how quickly what Dalby (2020: 95–113) nicely calls 'carboniferious capitalism' could be phased out.

This specific climate consequence of the energy revolution was accompanied by an increasingly global problem of pollution created by the vast production and disposal of the new materials that infinite energy made possible. Many of these, like CO_2, were durable. Pollution by everything from heat, through nitrates and plastics, to heavy metals was having a seriously deleterious effect on the biosphere. Along with excessive hunting and fishing, and destruction of habitats by the expanding human population, the planetary biosphere was, by the twenty-first century, heading into a sixth great extinction of species. While the energy problem had been solved technologically, its environmental consequences raised new material problems that would themselves become a defining part of the transition to modernity. The hunter-gatherer era had put little or no pressure on the environment. The CAPE era generated local, and sometimes severe, pressures on the environment, but these did not much disturb the planetary climate or biosphere as a whole. The transition to modernity, however, raised questions about how long it could be compatible with the relatively stable planetary climate and biosphere that had so far sustained and nurtured human civilisation.

Interaction Capacity

For interaction capacity, as for materials and energy, the transition towards modernity gave humankind comprehensive access to all the dimensions of planetary space (land, sea, air and near-earth orbit), breaking out of the constraints that had limited the scale and intensity of CAPE era systems and societies. Right from the beginning, new energy sources, materials and technologies, created possibilities for moving around the planet with speeds, carrying capacities, reliabilities and low costs that could scarcely have been dreamed of by CAPE era people, even a century or two before. Globalisation by rapid improvements in transportation and communication arrived almost from the beginning of the transition. The cornucopia of new materials plus the wide availability of energy in transportable forms, underpinned the well-documented process that, during the nineteenth century, shrank the world into a single space.[1] Global communication became more or less instantaneous, and bulk goods and people could be transported cheaply, quickly and reliably from anywhere to anywhere else where people lived in significant numbers.

The CAPE era had, as its climax, achieved a thin and tenuous form of globalisation by opening up wind-powered sea routes across the Atlantic and Pacific Oceans, and connecting them to the long-established Indian Ocean/East Asian and Mediterranean/European regional trading systems. The first phase of the transition modernity rapidly deepened this into a dense network of transportation, communication, trade, finance, migration and information that penetrated quickly and deeply into all corners of the world. The industrial and scientific revolutions released interaction capacity from its long dependence on wood, sail and pack-animals. The horse, the camel, the cart and the wooden sailing ship were quickly left behind by iron- and steel-built steamships, railways, roads and motor vehicles. Inter-oceanic canals linked the Mediterranean to the Indian Ocean (Suez in 1869), and the Atlantic to the Pacific (Panama in 1914), dramatically cutting the length of ocean voyages. During the twentieth century, aircraft became an increasingly big part of the equation of modern interaction capacity, and by the 1970s, airlines could fly millions of people halfway around the world, in journeys lasting

---

[1] For details and sources on the development of both physical and social interaction capacity during this period, see: Buzan and Lawson (2015: 70–96).

less than a day. World trade as a percentage of GDP rose from 2 per cent in 1820 to 22 per cent by 1913 (Darwin, 2020: 296). A century into the transition, Osterhammel (2014: 726–7) reckons that the transportation costs of moving a given unit of mass from Britain to India in 1906 was just 2 per cent of the cost it had been in 1793 at the end of the CAPE era.

These developments relate interestingly to the unfolding portfolio of sources and forms of energy. Shipping started with coal, then moved to oil, and might end up back with wind, albeit in a high-tech form. Railways started with coal, moved to oil, and ended up with electricity. Motor vehicles skipped coal and went straight to distillates of oil. They too are now headed for electricity. Aircraft likewise started with distillates of oil, and a partial transition to electricity is just beginning. Rockets used various forms of chemical energy, and by the 1960s were capable of taking people into near earth orbit (NEO) and to the Moon. At the time of writing, a permanently inhabited multinational space station (with rotating crews) has been in NEO for more than two decades, and there is increasingly serious talk of, and more to the point action towards, establishing permanent bases on the Moon, and even on Mars within a decade or two.

In and of themselves these new transportation technologies, and the planetary networks they created, speeded up communication through the rapid movement of mail. But very quickly the new technologies separated communication from transportation and made the latter almost instant-aneous on a global scale. Alongside the spread of railway networks from the middle of the nineteenth century was the parallel spread of the telegraph and its cable networks. These not only followed the railways (and enabled them to keep time), but quickly spread to intercontinental links with the laying of underwater cables thousands of miles long. Towards the end of the century, radio allowed 'wire-less' communica-tion over ever-longer distances. Marconi had established reliable transat-lantic radio communication by 1902, and in 1912 the sinking liner *Titanic* was famously able to broadcast the first SOS, and its location, to rescue ships. After 1945, television was added in, followed by the development of communications satellites to facilitate global transmissions.

'Smart' mobile phones and the Internet generally took off from the early 1990s with the introduction of the World Wide Web format in 1993. The Internet rapidly exploded to global scale, with perhaps half of the world's population able to be online at the time of writing. It made global communications almost free, in the process connecting people with each other in unprecedented numbers and ways, opening up access to (and generating) huge amounts of information (and misinformation), and transforming social relations. The Covid-19 pandemic lockdowns from 2020 exposed just how much of business and social relations could (and couldn't) be moved online, in the process raising a major, and perhaps permanent, challenge to the global travel industry. All kinds of meetings, from bilateral negotiations, through seminars and workshops, to conferences with thousands of participants, could be done with varying degrees of effectiveness through video links on the Internet. From the two-dimensional, land and sea, world of the CAPE era, physical interaction capacity moved first into the air, and then into space, and then into cyberspace. People almost anywhere on the planet could have 'face-to-face' meetings in real time with people almost anywhere else, and at least for smaller-scale events, do so at very low cost. Cyberspace quickly became something like a new territorial dimension to add to land, sea, air and space. It became the venue not only for much economic and social interaction, and education and entertainment, but also increasingly for spying, cyberwar, political interference, criminality and other threatening activities.

In parallel with this huge ramping up of physical interaction capacity, and largely caused by it, was a parallel development of social interaction capacity. This came in three forms. First was the expansion of positive international law which increasingly displaced natural law. Positive law was needed to smooth the way for an increasingly interconnected and interdependent global economy. This required shared standards for a widening range of things from shipping safety and navigation rules; through the management of shared river and railway systems, and common standards for weights, measures and industrial products; to agreements on wavelength usage, orbital spaces and protocols for the Internet. Second, and closely tied to both the increasingly integrated global system/society, and the expansion of positive law, was the development of intergovernmental organisations (IGOs) and regimes. Most of the early IGOs were clearly functional in this way: the International Telecommunications Union (1865), the Universal Postal Union (UPU) (1874), the International Bureau of Weights and Measures (1875), and the International Conference for Promoting Technical Unification on the Railways (1882). IGOs underwent a big expansion after both the First World War (the League of Nations system), and the Second (the United Nations system). These expansions added to the ranks of functional agencies, but also provided general forum organisations for the conduct of international diplomacy. Less formal regimes also became notable. A famous early example of this was the gold standard, which during the later nineteenth century linked governments and the financial sector in a scheme of fixed exchange rates which created, in effect, a single currency amongst those who adopted it (Frieden, 2006: 32–9, 45–9; Eichengreen, 2019: 5–40). Another example is the Bank for International Settlements (BIS) which was initially set up to handle the reparations payments from Germany after the First World War, but which later coalesced around the more transnational function of promoting cooperation and coordination among banks. Its principal members were the main central banks, and it also became a provider of research and statistics to the banking community.[2]

Finally, there was the development of international non-governmental organisations (INGOs), representing a hugely varied range of interests from peace and anti-slavery, through worker's and women's rights, to science, sport and religion. In effect, these INGOs marked the first coalescing of global civil society. By 1913 there were 400 or so, paving the way for the steady expansion that took place during the twentieth century, and especially from the 1970s. By the end of the first decade of the twenty-first century, there were around 25,000 INGOs operating worldwide, most of them based in the West. One should perhaps add to this list, the massive social media companies exemplified by Facebook, Google, Amazon, Tencent, Alibaba and others. These both rode on the back of, and themselves provided, the expanding capacity of the Internet to store and transfer data. These companies emerged rapidly during the second decade of the twenty-first century. At the time of writing, they not only dominated the heights of the global corporate world, but also were becoming repositories of big data and information-processing powers that were changing social, political and economic relations in major, and not altogether well-understood, ways.

These material and social revolutions in interaction capacity could not much <u>expand</u> the integrated world society that the CAPE era had already made global in scale. But they could and did <u>intensify</u> it hugely, resulting in massive increases in the amount of goods, capital and information, and the number of people, transported around the planet. The scale of this is indicated by the explosion of migration during the nineteenth century, which dwarfed the 10 million or so Africans shipped to the Americas as slaves in the days of sail. Between 1800 and 1914 over 50 million Europeans emigrated, mostly to the Americas; and some 37 million people left India, China, Malaya and Java, mostly as indentured labourers (Buzan and Lawson, 2015: 31–2). By 2018, the global airline industry was moving over 4 billion passengers per year around the planet.[3] Quantitative changes of this scale and speed amounted to a

---

[2] www.bis.org/about/history_1foundation.htm (accessed 21 June 2019).
[3] https://data.worldbank.org/indicator/IS.AIR.PSGR (accessed 6 December 2020).

qualitative transformation of interaction capacity sufficient to make and support a global society stretching deeply and widely across all three domains.

Over the first two centuries following the CAPE era, the planet shrank into a single economic, military, social and environmental space. During most of the CAPE era, the very concept of global was almost without social meaning. People looking to their horizons saw only more land and sea stretching into the unknown. Only towards the very end of it did connectivity on a global scale begin to open up the idea of globalisation. Before that, almost everything in the social sphere was local, or at biggest regional, in scale. The revolutions of modernity overthrew this limitation with remarkable speed. By the end of the nineteenth century, it was already well understood that the international system had reached closure. What became clear only later was that this closure also applied to the global economy, and its relationship to the planetary environment (Boulding, 1966). Between the early nineteenth century and the early twenty-first, the social condition of humankind was transformed from a tyranny of distance to what some have labelled the 'death of distance' (Cairncross, 2001). In a space of two centuries, people were catapulted from a world in which it was slow, difficult, dangerous, expensive and uncommon to travel or communicate over long distances, to one in which a majority, could, if they wanted to, travel and communicate almost anywhere, and have up-to-date news and information (and disinformation) about everywhere, and in which that was a normal and everyday thing. From being unreachable and unknowable to the bulk of humankind locked into their own localities, the world itself became local and familiar in most people's lives.

Military Technology

The combination of new materials, new sources of energy and vastly improved technologies for interaction capacity, not surprisingly had an enormous impact on the military sector. As Buzan and Lawson (2015: 240–304) argue, this triggered a permanent revolution in military affairs (RMA), making the continuous and rapid improvement in weaponry (the *arms dynamic*) into a new variable especially in great power relations, but also in the whole military dimension of international relations. Continuous improvements in weaponry not only permanently destabilised relations amongst the great powers, but also, for most of the period covered in Part II, opened up a massive, and difficult to close, military power gap between a handful of industrialised states in the core, and the great mass of states in the periphery. That the French revolutionary and

Napoleonic wars were largely fought with the smooth-bore artillery, infantry weapons and wooden warships of the late CAPE era, underlines the argument that the big transition to modernity took place in the nineteenth century. The French revolutionary and Napoleonic military innovations were in tactics, strategy and the use of the *levée en masse* to raise huge armies with a strong motivation to fight (Giddens, 1985: 224–5). The *levée en masse* began to dissolve the distinction between civilian and military, with total war requiring the total mobilisation of the country.

Not until the 1830s were new and much improved weapons becoming available in a steady, and apparently unending, stream. Underlying these impacts was the stark fact that within little more than a century from the British defeat of China in the first Opium War, destructive capacity had gone from being something that was in short supply, and required the skilled marshalling of armies and artillery, to something of which there was so much that the surplus destructive capacity of nuclear weapons during the first cold war made it suicidal to use them. In this sense, military technology went through the same rapid trajectory as materials, energy and interaction capacity: from chronic shortage to superabundance. This is a well-known story that does not need detailed retelling here (see Brodie, 1941; McNeill, 1982; Pearton, 1982; Buzan and Herring, 1998; Headrick, 2010; Gray, 2012; Buzan and Lawson, 2015: 240–304).

In a nutshell, the continuous and rapid improvements in materials science, precision engineering and sources of energy, that took off from the early-middle nineteenth century, transformed all aspects of military function. The rates of fire of infantry weapons went from three rounds per minute for a well-trained musketeer to hundreds, and then thousands of rounds a minute for machine guns. The range of artillery went from a few hundred metres to several tens of kilometres, and with the introduction of rocket-delivery, quickly became global. At the same time, accuracy improved to the point where warheads could be delivered over long distances with precision sufficient to target individual buildings. The destructive power of what was delivered went from the smashing force of a heavy iron cannonball fired from a smoothbore cannon; through sophisticated artillery pieces such as 18-inch naval guns firing high explosive shells weighing 1.5 tons over distances up to 42 kilometres, to multi-megaton nuclear weapons deliverable halfway around the world in half an hour, and capable of incinerating big cities in a single strike. First aircraft, and then missiles, greatly extended the range over which payloads could be delivered.

The ability to protect also improved, first with armour, and later with more active forms of defence against incoming aircraft and missiles, but in general the advantage lay with improvements in striking power. Even the thousands of tons of thick steel armour plate, and the ranks of anti-aircraft guns, used to protect battleships during the 1940s were insufficient to stop many being sunk by bombs and torpedoes: think of *Arizona* and other US battleships at Pearl Harbor, and the fates of the *Prince of Wales, Repulse, Barham, Bismarck, Tirpitz,* and *Yamato.* The advantage of firepower was enhanced by improving means of detection, first optical, then electronic (radio triangulation and passive sonar by the First World War, radar and active sonar by the Second), that could be used for target acquisition. Surveillance from aircraft and later satellites meant that by the 1970s, the advanced powers could increasingly detect almost any big target of military interest almost anywhere. Unsurprisingly, these developments shifted the competition between firepower and armour, to one between detection capabilities versus the ability to make things less visible, or ideally invisible. Camouflage, of course, has a very long military history, and submarines learned early the value of keeping quiet. But so-called 'stealth' technologies began to come into play from the 1960s, by which time armour had lost much of its use against the combination of firepower and detection. Stealth used materials and designs that would weaken the signals returned to a wide range of detection equipment, whether by sound, heat, or radio waves.

The general speed of military movement was liberated from the constraints of foot, horse and sail, by the deployment first of steamships and railways during the nineteenth century, then by motor vehicles and aircraft during the twentieth. The physical domain of military activity, long confined to just land and the surface of water, expanded into the water column and onto the seabed, into the air, and into space. Near-earth orbit was particularly valuable for communications and surveillance, and space was also used by long-range ballistic missiles in the upper part of their trajectories. The military benefited from the revolutions in transportation and communication in the same way as civil and commercial activity. Both goods and information could be transported more quickly and more cheaply than before, bringing intelligence into real time, and enabling military goods, whether troops and equipment, or a rain of destruction, to be delivered almost anywhere in a highly coordinated fashion.

Amongst the great powers, this arms dynamic created an environment of continuous fear that they could suddenly be outclassed, surprised and defeated by an opponent wielding some new technology. During the nineteenth century, the British worried that the French might use steam warships and transports to move their superior army across the Channel before the Royal Navy could respond. The rise of air power during the

First World War extended the battle front to home territories, making populations and infrastructures vulnerable regardless of what was going on between armies at the battle fronts. During the Second World War, there was the question of who would solve the puzzle of nuclear explosives first. During the first cold war, the US and the Soviet Union worried that the other might get the capability to inflict a disarming first strike on it, and/or use defences against ballistic missiles to degrade its retaliatory strike. The US now worries that China and Russia might be able to blind it by rapidly degrading or destroying its space-based surveillance and communication satellites. Smart drones are emerging as a highly flexible form of weapon that can be used for everything from individual assassinations to swarm attacks on the scale of mass destruction. The technological revolution placed all of the great powers on this endless, nerve-wracking and dauntingly expensive treadmill of keeping up as best they could with the ever-expanding frontiers of new weaponry. Falling behind to any significant degree carried the dual risk of both possible defeat, and of loss of status if perceived by others not to be keeping up. Under the discipline of modernity, there was no room for decisions such as that taken by the Mamluks in the fifteenth century, to limit their acquisition and use of gunpowder weapons because that technology clashed with the honour and traditions of their horse soldiers (Findlay and O'Rourke, 2007: 132). The Mamluks paid the price for this when they were overthrown in 1517 by the Ottomans, who had embraced gunpowder weapons, and were for a time the leading user of heavy artillery.

Between the core powers and the periphery, the military imbalance that opened up during the nineteenth century was nicely captured in Hilaire Belloc's famous lines about the colonial wars of the time:

> Whatever happens
> we have got
> the Maxim gun,
> and they have not.[4]

During the nineteenth century, and the first half of the twentieth, the peoples and polities in the periphery could occasionally win battles against the colonial powers, but almost never a whole war.[5] There were some successes in adopting elements of the new technologies. Native

---

[4] The Maxim was an early type of machine gun.
[5] Among the more famous battles won were the Mahdi's taking of Khartoum (1885) and the Plains' Indians victory over Custer at the Little Big Horn (1876). The most famous exception in war being the Ethiopian defeat of an Italian invasion at Adwa in 1896.

Americans, for example, made effective use of rifles to fight against white colonial encroachment in both North and South America (Headrick, 2010). Some periphery powers such as the Ottoman Empire and China made attempts to modernise their armed forces, but they often had difficulty integrating new weapons into their armies and navies, which, reminiscent of the Mamluks, still retained strong elements of conservative traditionalism. The Qing dynasty in China, for example, was able to buy, and up to a point even build, modern warships, and by the late nineteenth century had acquired an outwardly impressive looking steam navy. But the Chinese did not maintain or supply their fleet properly, or fight it to advantage. They were easily defeated by a technically less powerful, but much better integrated, trained and led, Japanese navy during the Sino-Japanese war of 1894–5. By then, Japan had become part of the modern core, and China had not. The military gap that opened up between core and periphery during the early nineteenth century lasted for nearly a century and a half, not ending decisively until the 1970s.

Civil Technology

This vast topic requires no detailed elaboration here. It is again a story of moving very rapidly from a long-standing condition of scarcity, and a slow-moving pace of innovation with only occasional breakthroughs, to abundance, and a fast-moving pace of innovation with continuous breakthroughs across a broad front. Some of this has been covered substantially in the discussions above, and is anyway familiar ground to most readers because it is our everyday environment. The availability of safe, rapid and affordable transport by steamship, train, bicycle, motor vehicle and later aircraft, quickly became a normal part of life for most people for both short distances and long ones. Tourism into space has now become possible for those with deep enough pockets. A mind-boggling array of new materials became part of everyday life, ranging from medicines and pesticides; through plastics and carbon fibres, composite material, and gels; to paints and adhesives. Electronic devices penetrated everywhere: first electric motors and control mechanisms, the telegraph, electric lights and the telephone; then radio, sonar, radar and TV; and towards the end of this period computers, and scanning equipment of many kinds from making copies, through observing space, to looking deep inside bodies and solid materials. In biology, this period saw the introduction of vaccines, anaesthetics, antibiotics and birth control. Newspapers emerged with the printing press in the seventeenth century, but mass media, and with it public opinion as a political and social force, took off in the nineteenth century as the population became more literate. During the twentieth century, mass media spread to radio and television, and in the twenty-first century to the Internet, along the way transforming the economy (advertising), politics (opinion-forming), and society (fashion-setting in its widest sense). By the twenty-first century, advances in robotics meant that rovers were exploring the Moon and Mars, and that the gap between prosthetic limbs for humans and parts for robots was beginning to close. During this first century-and-a-half, an almost unbelievable range of new technologies became available. Remarkably, it did so without the nagging worry of impending shortage that accompanied the mass use of coal, oil and nuclear fission. The innovation driving this cornucopia looked bottomless, which by itself was sufficient to make believable the promises of open-ended progress that accompanied the transition towards modernity. But like energy use, and related to it, in the later twentieth century, this abundance of disposable consumables also began bumping up against environmental limits.

5a   Social Structure I
CAPE Institutions Carried Forward into the Transition

Introduction

The transformation in material conditions during the opening century of the transition towards modernity was so fast, wide-ranging and deep that it smashed through the material constraints of the conglomerate agrarian/pastoralist empires (CAPE) era, and transformed the circumstances of humankind. Like a dam breaking under the force of a rampaging torrent, the drama, and in a sense straightforwardness, of this material development go a long way towards explaining why it is so easy to see the transition from CAPE to modernity as a direct jump.

The situation regarding social conditions, however, is considerably more complicated. In some ways, the changes were almost as stark and quick as in material conditions. But in other ways, there were many carry-overs, blendings and adaptations that unfolded over a long time, some still unfinished. The case for a transition period between the two eras, is thus mainly to be found in the social structure. Basically, one subset of humankind, a handful of Western powers plus Japan, underwent the revolutions of modernity during the nineteenth century, and on the basis of the big advantages in wealth, power and cultural and political authority that gave them, established a colonial global economy and international society on their own terms. It was a classic, and very dramatic, case of uneven and combined development. This vanguard generated a new set of secular ideologies of progress – nationalism, liberalism, socialism and 'scientific' racism – to challenge not only kinship and religion in the dynamics of interhuman identity, but also monarchy/dynasticism and empire in the interpolity domain (Buzan and Lawson, 2015: 97–126). They proceeded in various ways, intentional and unintentional, to spread both these ideas, and the breakthroughs in materials, energy and technology, all around the planet. The CAPE system of fairly dispersed agrarian empires and civilisations, thinly connected by trade and religious networks, was swiftly replaced by a core–periphery global industrial economy and colonial international society in which a small core group of modern states had most of the wealth and power, and a very strong hand in cultural and political authority. Yet despite the magnitude of the changes, imperialism, human inequality, religion and even monarchy/dynasticism, adapted and held firm for more than a century into the transition. As Bayly (2004: 430–1) argues, a good case can be made that during the nineteenth century both powerful new transformational forces, and successful adaptations by old institutions, were in play.

Since the post-CAPE transition period is still so short, it is impossible to say whether it will, like the CAPE era, settle into a fairly stable, and mutually supporting, set of primary institutions. At first sight, it does not look like that. In big contrast to the relatively slow-moving technical innovations of the CAPE era, the transition is powerfully driven by the seemingly open-ended revolutions in material conditions. In addition, from what we can see so far, there are more contradictions and tensions amongst the primary institutions defining modernity than there were in the set that defined the CAPE era. This story is best unfolded by looking in detail at the sometimes dramatic changes in social structure that occurred during this period, and linking that to divergences from, and accommodations with, the social structure of the CAPE era. Readers should keep in mind that compared with the preceding two eras we are looking at a very short space of time into which an enormous amount of deep change has been compressed. In its short history, the transition towards modernity has thus been, and continues to be, profoundly and continuously revolutionary. Whether such compression and intensity of change can continue into a kind of permanent revolution without being overwhelmed by its own contradictions remains to be seen. This period has been one of wrenching transition from the material and social structures of one era to those of another. One can see the nature of this transition in the way in which some institutions became obsolete, some new institutions arose, and the meaning and practices of many existing institutions underwent significant adaptation in response to the dialectics of the emergent new social configuration. The transition towards modernity weakened or dissolved many elements of the social glue that had held the CAPE era together for so long. Emerging modernity needs to find a new formula for its social glue, and that experiment is still ongoing.

One key to thinking about the transition is the unevenness with which the revolutions of modernity took hold. Initially, they occurred deeply only in a small number of states/societies, mostly parts of Europe plus the United States (US), Russia and Japan. That vanguard became the core and leading edge of the transition towards modernity throughout the nineteenth and for most of the twentieth centuries. Its members used their advantage to shape the material and social conditions of the world to fit their own interests. Much of the rest of the world had these conditions imposed on them by core imperial powers wielding both new ideas and superior force. Think of the way in which China and Japan were battered open by both gunships and revolutionary social thinking during the mid-nineteenth century. As Buzan and Lawson (2015) argue, the rest of the world had to confront not only the power and colonialism of the vanguard states, but also the secular ideas of modernity itself, from science and technology to the ideologies of progress. This idea-set was a profound challenge to their traditional ways of doing and organising things. Even when it was not coercively imposed, it was a powerfully known and pervasive alternative to traditional thinking and practice. Things that had been unquestioned and without rival for hundreds, even thousands, of years were abruptly under interrogation. The problem for those outside the first round of modernisers in the nineteenth century was to find ways of integrating the idea-set of modernity with their own cultural conditions in ways that would unleash the wealth and power of modernity without destroying their own societies. With the exception of Japan, modernity had crystallised strongly only within Western civilisation. Its nineteenth- and early twentieth-century form was therefore associated by the rest of the world with the particular social forms that emerged from the disruptive interplay between late-CAPE European societies and the revolutions of modernity. It was not initially clear that the two could be separated. If modernity required more or less complete Westernisation, then it faced peoples and states with the dramatic devaluing and loss of their own traditions and culture, a trade-off that many found difficult or impossible to make. So the key question was whether and how modernity could be synthesised with non-Western cultures.

This was no simple matter. China wasted the nineteenth century trying to figure out how to keep its own ideas and traditions in the driving seat, while taking on board just enough Western technique, especially military modernisation, to enable it to maintain its independence (Sassoon, 2019: 89–108). This approach did not work. Gray (2002: vii) rightly observes that Japan and China were initially very similarly placed in relation to Western intervention and modernity. Yet they experienced such different outcomes, that Western imperialism cannot be seen as the key factor in China's failure. China's attempt at selective modernisation was so ineffective that it even exposed the country to defeat by a newly rising Japan in 1894–5. Unlike China, Japan found a way of blending modernity with significant elements of its own culture, and doing so as quickly as some of the European states (e.g. Italy, Russia) that were also late runners in the first round of modernisation (Sassoon, 2019: 108–17; Buzan and Goh, 2020: 81–3). The Japanese soon understood that transition to modernity was very recent in the West, and that the gap was therefore not all that big and insurmountable if they worked hard enough to close it (Jansen, 2000: locs. 5364–438). Modernisers elsewhere in the periphery, such as the Ottoman Empire, Egypt and Ethiopia, had the same thought, but were far less successful than the Japanese in implementing it (Sassoon, 2019: 118–33).

There are reasons additional to unevenness for keeping open the idea of a transition period separating CAPE from modernity. One is that the transition to modernity has so far come in two stages: the first in which a small core of societies made the transition and imposed it on others in a colonial global society; and the second in which modernity is spreading successfully to a wider circle of states and societies. Another reason is that although much was new, and indeed revolutionary, right from the beginning of the transition, there was also a very substantial sense in which major elements of the CAPE era social structure carried forward into the nineteenth century and beyond. Sometimes this carrying forward was transitional, substantially fading away after a century or two, as with monarchy/dynasticism, imperialism and extreme human inequality. Sometimes it seemed more permanent, albeit transformed by its encounter with modernity, such as territoriality, sovereignty, war, diplomacy and religion. Surprisingly, few CAPE social structures were entirely snuffed out. This interleaving and interweaving of the two eras in terms of social structures, becomes in itself a way of understanding the transition between them. This is the purpose of this chapter and the next.

The question of causality between material conditions and social structure is extremely complex, and will not be explored in any great depth here. That would require a different approach and a separate book. It is clear that for the transition to modernity, there is no clear and simple driver, such as the climate warming and stabilisation that drove the transition to the CAPE era. Many writers on this topic focus on the unique assemblage of supportive factors in Britain that enabled it to become the breakthrough case that then seeded the rest of the world (e.g. Landes, 1969; Pomeranz, 2000; Sassoon, 2019: 169–96). Galor (2022) offers a recent entry into the competition to find a general explanation for the turn to modernity. He sees a critical mass of human population, knowledge and social scale as explaining the onset of modernity. Humankind escaped the Malthusian trap of any rises in productivity quickly being followed by population growth and a return to subsistence. Investment in education caused a virtuous circle between falling fertility rates and rising productivity.

My aim in these two chapters is simpler, but not lacking in ambition. I take a close look at the continuities and changes in the social structure; make links between the social and material when these are relevant; and try to tease out what features of the new social structure differentiate emergent modernity from the CAPE era. The approach in Chapters 5a and 5b is therefore to revisit the primary institutions discussed in Chapter 3 as defining the social structure of the CAPE era, and to add to that list some new primary institutions that were distinctive to modernity. Some of the CAPE institutions were eventually made obsolete, but most survived, albeit with adaptations to fit them to the new conditions. All of the CAPE primary institutions were carried forward at least into the nineteenth century, and many into the twentieth and twenty-first. This chapter looks first at those CAPE institutions that survived for a time into the modern era, but then became obsolete (monarchy/dynasticism, imperialism, human inequality) and then at those that survived, albeit sometimes with significant modifications: religion, war, territoriality, sovereignty, diplomacy, international law, trade/mercantilism. Chapter 5b examines those institutions that emerged from the nineteenth century onwards: balance of power, great power management, nationalism, the market, science, sport, human equality, development, environmental stewardship. As I have argued elsewhere (Buzan, 2014: 158–61; Buzan and Schouenborg, 2018: 200–2), I do not consider either democracy or human rights to have yet succeeded in becoming institutions of global international society. While they have certainly been vigorously promoted as such, mainly by the West, they remain either rejected or contested by many states and peoples. The undulations of democracy indexes are witness to this failure to achieve the global level of acceptance necessary to count as a primary institution.[1] Human rights is a more complex issue, whose standing as an institution depends very much on how it is defined (Zhang and Buzan, 2019).

But I begin with the idea of kinship, which fits none of these categories. As discussed in Chapter 3, kinship had already during the CAPE era become what I called a 'ghost primary institution', one that had lost its standing as a general social organising principle, but still continued to be widely recognised and practised at some levels of society.

---

[1] For example, the Global State of Democracy Indices www.idea.int/data-tools/tools/global-state-democracy-indices and the Democracy Index https://statisticstimes.com/ranking/democracy-index.php

Kinship

Kinship was the foundational social structure for humankind. It continued to play very significant roles in the CAPE era, mainly by taking residence as a principle and practice in other institutions such as dynasticism, religion and trade. This CAPE pattern of kinship being not a primary institution in itself, but remaining below the horizon as a ghost within other primary institutions, continued into modernity, albeit with some notable adaptations. Although eroded in some ways by the cultivation of individualism that went along with the Western, and particularly the Anglosphere, model of liberal modernity, kinship was not displaced from some of its key CAPE roles. For example, those religions that made the transition beyond the CAPE era generally did so with their basic stories intact. To the extent that those stories contained kinship elements, such as those in Islam to the associates and family of the prophet, these carried forward intact. This was also true of Confucianism, with its deep embodiment of family hierarchy, which has made a powerful, if partial, comeback in China since the 1990s. Likewise, some forms of dynasticism clung on, and nationalism picked up and transformed some of the logic and emotion of kinship, on which more below.

Within the transition, kinship also continued to play a substantial role in the economic sector. During the CAPE era, kinship was one way of providing the necessary trust to sustain commercial and financial transactions over long distances when interaction capacity was relatively limited. Modernity quickly solved much of this problem not only by hugely increasing the reliability and speed of transport and communication, but also by putting into place rules, laws and organisations that supported trust by impersonal, institutional, means. The new form of modern limited company that developed during the nineteenth century was designed to facilitate commercial relations on an impersonal, law-governed basis. Yet throughout the nineteenth century and beyond, family firms from giants such as Cadbury, the Sassoons, BMW, Walmart, Tata and Samsung, to corner convenience stores, were, and still are, a major part of the economic landscape. Kinship continues to provide a competitive foundation for trust in the commercial world, and this remains true even amongst the oldest modern societies in the West and Japan. It is an interesting question as to whether this role of kinship in business is stronger in Asia, where the family generally retains a more central role in people's lives, than in the West, where, as families have shrunk, many of their former functions, such as welfare, and care in old age, have been taken over by the state. As the fertility rate drops, families everywhere are shrinking, becoming too small to achieve many of their traditional functions in society. While no longer an institution of Global International Society (GIS), kinship nonetheless continues to play a significant role across the three domains, albeit somewhat diminished. It remained noticeable in the dynastic domestic politics of many states. But it largely lost its status as a recognised principle of political legitimacy in the interstate domain, simply being tolerated within the scope of national sovereignty. In the transnational domain, kinship continued to play in religion as before and in commerce somewhat differently. In the interhuman domain, kinship lost some of its force as the operation of modernity both loosened and shrank families in the richer countries, and promoted individualism and meritocracy as alternatives.

Next are those CAPE institutions that survived into modernity for a time, but have by the time of writing become obsolete: monarchy/dynasticism, imperialism, human inequality.

Monarchy/Dynasticism

From the American and French revolutions onwards, monarchy/dynasticism as the main foundation of political legitimacy in global society was severely challenged, and in many additional places toppled, by nationalism and popular sovereignty (e.g. Mexico, Brazil, China, Russia, Austria-Hungary, Germany, Turkey, Egypt, Iran). Nationalism was a global phenomenon, and across Eurasia, wars and revolutions sharpened identities from vague local patriotism towards nationalism (Bayly, 2004: 112–14, 199). As Reus-Smit (1999; see also Navari, 2007) puts it, there was a shift in the moral purpose of the state from dynastic interests to popular sovereignty. Some monarchs were killed, as in the French and Russian revolutions. Some were shunted aside or disowned, as in the Chinese and American revolutions. Yet many monarchs remained in place until at least the First World War, and some well beyond that, by adapting to the national/popular sovereignty framing. As Darwin (2020: 332) observed, even by 1914: 'Europe was the most industrial of continents, but more than half its area was ruled by dynastic empires, not by governments answerable to representative assemblies.' Monarchical/dynastic rulers still helped to provide political stability and legitimacy in many states and empires, and retained a good deal of public support into the twentieth century (Bayly, 2004: 395–9). In a related way, the landed gentry also often succeeded in maintaining their social and economic positions, taking leading roles in the new administrative structures of the modern state, identifying themselves with nationalism, and investing in the new industrial economy (Bayly, 2004: 418–26).

Where monarchies survived, they had to become national monarchies rather than vehicles for building conglomerate empires. Britain's monarchs were exceptional in clinging onto the shadow of imperial role in the Commonwealth. Traditional forms of royal dynasticism, in which the monarch had real political power, survived in Saudi Arabia and the Gulf Arab states, Jordan, Morocco, Brunei, Thailand and Lesotho. Elsewhere, monarchy was consigned to a largely symbolic role as head of state but not of government (Britain, Sweden, Denmark, Spain, Japan), still observing dynastic principles, maintaining pomp and ceremony, and holding some of the wealth and status, but mainly without the political power. There was still some room for occasional female monarchs: Victoria and Elizabeth II in Britain, and Cixi (as regent) in late Qing China. There were some curious hybrids as in Japan up to 1945, where the god-emperor was both detached from government, and immensely influential in symbolic terms for mobilising the nation. This odd duality perhaps provides a good explanation for why, during the period from the 1930s to 1945, Japanese fascism produced only relatively faceless leaders, not charismatic figures like Mussolini, Franco or Hitler.

Even when de-linked from monarchy, as in modern republics, a kind of political dynasticism continued to be in play that did carry some legitimacy, if far short of entitlement to rule. Perhaps most notably in the US, political dynasties such as the Roosevelts, Kennedys and Bushes have been influential. This is despite the fact that US, which has a good claim to being the first major country that was born after the CAPE era, had a revolution explicitly rejecting royal dynasticism. The Gandhis were likewise influential in Indian politics, the Bhuttos in Pakistan, the Trudeaus in Canada, the Sukarnos in Indonesia, the Rajapaksas in Sri Lanka, the Bongos in Gabon, the Obiangs in Equatorial Guinea, and the Gnassingbés in Togo. In authoritarian China, kinship links to the founding revolutionaries of the Communist Party still play a significant role. Under three generations of Kims, North Korea has even developed the oxymoronic political form of dynastic communism.

Although monarchy/dynasticism remains an active feature of political life during the transition, it has lost its status as a primary institution. While it remains an acceptable political form under the rules of sovereignty and self-determination, it no longer carries recognition as the gold-standard of political legitimacy. Where it has survived, it has mostly done so by conspicuously accommodating to nationalism and popular sovereignty. A few monarchs, such as those in the Gulf Arab states, still have clout in the economic sphere, but the link there that was strong in the CAPE era is now marginal rather than general, and confined to a few places. The remaining dynasties, both those with real political power and those with mainly symbolic roles as head of state, try to cultivate the loyalty and affection of their subjects, rather than imposing it by fear. Few are now in a position to coerce support, though the exceptions, such as Thailand's oppressive use of laws against *lèse-majesté*, are a reminder of how things were during the CAPE era. The ongoing links with religion make cultivating loyalty to symbolic monarchs easier to do. With a few local exceptions, dynastic monarchs have become part of the machinery of nationalism and sovereignty, rather than being an institution in their own right.

Imperialism/Colonialism

The main switch from the legitimacy of imperialism/colonialism to the legitimacy of sovereign equality, popular sovereignty and national self-determination did not take place until after the Second World War. The mandate system after the First World War hinted at what was to come, as did the anti-imperialism of Wilson and Lenin.[2] But the mandate system did not deeply question the legitimacy of imperialism in itself, mainly focusing on the conditions of it.[3] The wave of decolonisation that began after 1945, had, by 1975, almost completely dismantled both the empires and the imperial pretentions of the core powers, making colonialism illegitimate, and the institution of imperialism obsolete (Bain, 2003: 134–9; Holsti, 2004: 262–74).

Yet the legitimacy of imperialism was not questioned right from the beginning of the transition, but actually reinforced for the first century and a half. As noted in Chapter 3, the pastoralist form of empire had been extinguished by the seventeenth century. But the agrarian form was initially strengthened and intensified by industrial capitalism, undergoing a burst of expansion in the late nineteenth century, and remaining actively legitimate until the middle of the twentieth (Bayly, 2004: 227–33, 242–3). As several ES scholars have argued, imperialism and colonialism created a system of divided sovereignty (Keene, 2002; Suzuki, 2005, 2009. See also Holsti, 2004: 239–74). The core practised sovereign equality among its members, but expropriated some or all of the sovereignty of the periphery, where many subject polities retained

---

[2] Lenin was of course only opposed to capitalist imperialism. He almost certainly did not understand the reabsorption of the Russian empire into the Soviet Union as imperialism, although that is what it looked like to many of those on the receiving end of it.
[3] For a contrary interpretation, see Mayall (2000a: 17–25).

some rights and ceded others to the metropole. Should any reminder be needed of the centrality of colonialism, it is clear that competitive empire-building was the main dynamic of international relations up until 1945. Wars both global (the First and Second World Wars) and regional (e.g. Crimea, Franco-Prussian, Sino-Japanese, Russo-Japanese) were fought between empires, and were about contestation over spheres of imperial power. Even the first cold war, which ran in parallel with the process of decolonisation, had strong echoes of inter-imperial competition over spheres of influence and power, albeit in ideological disguise. Despite both the US and the Soviet Union definitely not identifying themselves as empires, rejecting dynasticism, and supporting decolonisation, they competed for 'neocolonial' spheres of influence and power in Europe, Asia and the Third World.

During the nineteenth century, the conglomerate agrarian empire morphed into the industrial one centred on a core nation state. It was within this imperial framework that the modern core–periphery structure of the global political economy was laid out. The story that empires were somehow just replaced by modern, national, rational states is far too simple. Realist claims for some kind of ontological primacy for the state as a defining principle of IR are simply wrong. For a long time, empires were an integral part of early modernity, and international relations was as much or more inter-imperial as interstate. Certainly some empires did eventually fragment into states (e.g. Austria-Hungary, Ottoman, British, French, Russian/Soviet). But for the nineteenth century and the first half of the twentieth, modern nation states both consolidated themselves, and became or remained the cores of empires. After decolonisation, former metropoles retained the upper hand in economic and political relations with former colonies in many places. Even now, more than two centuries into the transition, the influence of empire continues to influence international relations, albeit in camouflaged form, not daring to speak its name. One can, without much distortion, think of Russia and China as empires that have converted themselves into more tightly integrated states. Both have empire-like attitudes towards maintaining themselves, and possessing a sphere of influence in their surrounding regions. Many have thought of the US as a kind of empire, although one that operates more by demanding open access than by wanting direct territorial control (Bacevich, 2002; Prestowitz, 2003: 19–49). That, however, was a late switch. For most of the nineteenth century, the US was clearly an empire, albeit one also constructing itself as a federal state. Although the core–periphery structure of the global political economy set up during the nineteenth century has weakened very substantially, it has not gone away. The legacies of imperialism in the contemporary world are enduring, and constitute an important part of the case for thinking of the last two centuries as a transitional period between the CAPE and modern eras.

In its CAPE heyday, this institution stretched across the three domains. It more or less continued to do so in the same way during the nineteenth and twentieth centuries, though it was increasingly contested, both by those subject to it, and by those within the core making arguments questioning its morality and economic efficiency. Market ideology posed a powerful challenge to empire. In the interstate domain, imperialism remained legally and politically strong up to 1945, and lost legitimacy and legality quickly thereafter. Advocacy within the transnational domain became increasingly opposed to imperialism and colonialism, but in the economic sector, firms divided between those who benefited from empire, and those wanting to eliminate imperial preferences and tariffs. In the interhuman domain, imperial identity was substantial, more so within the metropolitan states, but up to a point even among the colonised peoples. The project to build a 'Greater Britain' was based on that shared imperial identity, albeit mainly restricted to white people (Bell, 2007). After 1945, the legitimacy of imperialism and colonialism in the three domains collapsed quickly, though vestiges of it remain in the domestic politics of some countries. In Russia, Vladimir Putin has exploited a desire to recover some of the territories lost when the Soviet Union imploded. In China, nationalists are strongly behind the idea of a 'return to normality' in the form of China reasserting its primacy in Asia, though this is not declared in imperial terms, but in expansive claims to 'lost' territories.

Human Inequality

As with the institution of empire, and related to it, the story of human inequality is likewise one in which the switch from CAPE practices to modern ones – the legitimacy of human inequality to the legitimacy of human equality – did not take place until after the Second World War. I have put human inequality in the group of CAPE primary institutions that, after carrying over into modernity for a time, became obsolete. But this institution is not quite the same as monarchy/dynasticism and imperialism in this regard. Human inequality did not exactly disappear so much as get replaced by its opposite: human equality. A good case could be made for thinking of human equality as a new institution, distinctive to modernity, but the break between the two is far from clean. For the sake of clarity, I therefore keep the discussion of this all in one place here, making a brief reminder in Chapter 5b about human equality in the discussion of post-CAPE institutions.

As argued in Chapter 2, the move from a fairly high degree of human equality, to a very high degree of human inequality, was one of the key markers for the shift from the hunter-gatherer to the CAPE era. The CAPE era featured slavery as a major source of energy, developed patriarchy to extreme forms, and concentrated wealth into small aristocratic, religious and commercial elites. Yet while the transition from the hunter-gatherer era to the CAPE one was clear and quite stark in respect of human equality/inequality, the transition from CAPE to modernity in this regard was rather complicated and unclear.[4] Some things got more equal, while others became less so. A strong argument can be made that the package of social and material revolutions that comprised the first phase of the transition towards modernity contained a powerful imperative to swing the balance back towards a principle of human equality. Partly, as argued below, this imperative stemmed from the logic of nationalism. Various well-known early foundational statements of modernity embody the equality principle in unequivocal terms. The American Declaration of Independence in 1776, for example, famously claims that: 'We hold these truths to be self-evident, that all men are created equal, that they are endowed by their Creator with certain unalienable Rights, that among these are Life, Liberty and the pursuit of Happiness.' The French Declaration of the Rights of Man and of the Citizen in 1789 opens similarly with the idea that: 'Men are born and remain free and equal in rights.' It went on to assert freedom of political association, and claimed against traditional dynasticism that the principle of sovereignty arises from the nation. These sweeping assertions were grand openers to the post-CAPE era, and as Bayly (2004: 86, 107) argues both threatened the CAPE regimes, and paved the way towards the modern state. But the practices to back them up did not come quickly, smoothly, completely, or without sustained opposition.[5]

In practical terms, this opening phase of the transition towards modernity saw big strides towards equality in both the delegitimation of slavery by a successful campaign from civil society, and the steady erosion of the dynastic right to rule. By the early nineteenth century, Britain, despite being internally divided on the matter, was moving to lead the abolition of the slave trade. This was no small matter. The sixty-year campaign to end the slave trade cost Britain more than 5,000 lives,

---

[4] This observation has to be tempered by the fact that the transition from hunter-gatherer to CAPE took a few thousand years, and was long in the past, while the transition from CAPE to modern is still all around us, and we are talking within a time frame of two centuries.

[5] For the ES sources on human equality/inequality see Buzan (2014a: 107–8, 158–60).

as well as an average of nearly 2 per cent of national income per year (Kaufmann and Pape, 1999: 631).[6] Yet this campaign was not wholly successful in suppressing the slave trade, and despite it, the practice of slavery, and similar practices such as bonded and indentured labour, and transportation, continued even into the twentieth century (Bayly, 2004: 402–10). Darwin (2020: 168, 177–8) notes the 'strange experiment in slave-based modernity' in the American South that flourished for the first half of the nineteenth century. This was not brought to a formal end until the 1860s, when the US fought a massive and costly civil war over the issue, in which well over half-a-million people died, and which resulted in the ending there of slavery as a legal practice. British divisions on the question were manifest in the substantial support within the country for the Confederacy, on whose cotton the British textile industry depended. Britain built some of the Confederacy's steam warships. By the end of the nineteenth century, legal slavery was almost universally abolished, though the practice, and ones not far removed from it such as indentured labour, continued, as most notably in the US and South Africa did racism and measures of apartheid.

Even with their limits, these changes constituted real and substantial movements away from some of the extremes of human inequality that marked the CAPE era. But against this picture of a swing towards human equality stands the altogether less impressive movement away from patriarchy, and, for the best part of a century, the strong and widespread support for 'scientific' racism that powerfully reinforced the norm of human inequality. While anti-slavery could be seen as an early version of human rights, its logic did not necessarily extend to a general principle of human equality. One could be against slavery on moral or economic grounds, without necessarily supporting a comprehensive picture of human equality and universal human rights.

As regards patriarchy, it is revealing that the foundational modern statements of human rights tended to refer to 'men', and that such expression was not just the privileged use of the masculine to cover both sexes. As Towns (2009, 2010, 2017, 2021. See also Bayly, 2004: 15, 399–402) argues, until very recently the West shared the hostility of all premodern urban civilisations to women in politics. She charts the systematic exclusion of women from politics in Western societies during the nineteenth century. This was often done by using the 'standard of

---

[6] For comparison, 2 per cent is roughly the percentage of GDP spent annually on defence by many developed states. This cost, has, of course, to be seen in the light of the very substantial economic benefit that Britain had reaped from the slave trade, noted in Chapter 3.

civilisation' argument that it was only in 'primitive' tribal societies that women had a significant role in political life. 'Civilised' societies should therefore mark their status as such by excluding them. Even in the core countries, wives were legally little more than the chattels of their husbands and in colonial practice women were even more blatantly treated as property. As Bayly (2018: 3) puts it, even by 1850, 'women were effectively bonded servants within extended families'. Although modern calls for equal rights for women date back to the late eighteenth century (e.g. Olympe de Gouges, Mary Wollstonecraft), little came of them in practice. Despite the founding of advocacy INGOs such as the International Council of Women (ICW) in 1888, women did not even begin to be granted the vote in core states until the early part of the twentieth century. That significant, but limited, breakthrough was only achieved by relentless campaigning, much assisted by the important role that women played in war mobilisation during the First World War. While 'men and citizens' might have the right of political participation, women were excluded from this right throughout the nineteenth century, and widely kept as second-class citizens well past the middle of the twentieth. Broader feminist and women's rights movements took off at different points during the twentieth century around the world, but the roots of patriarchy remained deep.

The story of 'scientific' racism marks a second counter-current to any general drive towards human equality for the first century and a half of the transition towards modernity (Buzan and Lawson, 2015: 118–25; Klotz, 2017). Driven by the move to industrial capitalism, increased migration and competition for jobs, the period between the middle of the nineteenth and the middle of the twentieth centuries saw a great flourishing of racism (Sassoon, 2019: 288–309). Ironically, nationalism helped legitimise 'scientific' racism at the same time as it supported human equality. This arose from a combination of the nineteenth-century mania for scientific classification (taxonomy) plus the highly unequal encounters that were going on between Europeans and people across the rest of the planet. Both of these were blended with a dose of the social Darwinism (survival of the fittest) that also infected nationalism. Slavery might have been made illegitimate, but race hierarchy nonetheless became a dominant mode of thought about global society. Yao (2021: 193) notes that: '[R]ace and racism as powerful global ideas acquired their modern meaning during the 19th century.' And Bell (2013: 1) argues that: 'for the opening few decades of the [20th] century, race was widely and explicitly considered a fundamental ontological unit of politics, perhaps the most fundamental unit of all'. One result of this was the rapid demotion in status of indigenous peoples from diplomatic interlocutors and sometime military allies, to 'savages' standing in the way of the deluge of land-hungry white settlers and railway builders unleashed by steam globalisation. Where such people could not be assimilated or herded into reservations, they were treated as vermin to be exterminated (Bayly, 2004: 432–50; Hamalainen, 2019).

'Scientific' racism underpinned the new imperialism in Africa and Asia, supporting a widely held taxonomy that people could be classified partly, or in some eyes wholly, on racial grounds as 'civilised' (i.e. white, modern), 'barbarian' (mainly yellow and brown, with an urban 'high culture' as in India, China and the Islamic world), and 'savage' (i.e. mainly black, or in North America, red, and understood as peoples without an urban 'high culture' living in societies understood as 'tribal'). In this perspective, progress could be understood as improving the racial stock by culling and careful breeding. The promise of progress was linked closely to a 'standard of civilisation' that, along with 'scientific' racism, served as the legitimating currency for coercive practices against 'barbarians' and 'savages' (Gong, 1984; Keene, 2002; Anghie, 2004; Suzuki, 2009; Hobson, 2012). 'Scientific' racism reached its awful apotheosis as one of the ontological foundations of fascism, culminating in the Nazi and Japanese programmes to eliminate or subordinate 'inferior' peoples. The horror and backlash at that goes a long way towards explaining the turnaround to human equality, and to a lesser extent against imperialism, after the Second World War. That turnaround, of course, was contingent on the Axis powers losing the war, which was not a foregone conclusion until 1942–3.

In terms of economic inequality, the first round of the transition towards modernity did more to change the form rather than the fact of the CAPE condition. Industrial capitalism shifted the concentration of wealth away from aristocrats and towards industrialists. Merchants and financiers remained rich in both eras. But the new imperialism imposed the economic inequality of a core–periphery structure onto the periphery. Within the core states, the advance of functional differentiation opened the way to prosperous professional classes. But the inequalities of capitalism were stark enough to fuel the Marxian reaction, and substantial redistribution towards the working classes in the core did not really take off until the twentieth century.

The ongoing strength of patriarchy during the nineteenth century, combined with the surge in 'scientific' racism that occurred in its later decades, and the continuation of economic inequality suggest that at least up until 1945, the move towards human equality was narrow and selective, and in racial, sexual and economic terms, still strongly contested. This partial and uneven outcome can be read in at least two ways.

First, if human equality was to be understood as a core principle of modernity, then a comprehensive transition out of the inequality norms of the CAPE era was going to take a very long time, and the journey would be along a path strewn with obstacles. Second, it might be that modernity was not going to be marked by a full transition in all respects from human inequality to human equality, but by a compromise in which some elements of CAPE inequality (most notably slavery and monarchy/dynasticism) would be delegitimised, but some would continue alongside aspects of modern equality. The obvious points of contestation here were sex, race and wealth. There was almost certainly no going back to mass slavery, which had anyway largely lost its economic purpose as a major source of energy, though niches such as sex slavery remained economically viable. There was probably no going back to ruling monarchical/dynasticism either, given the power of popular sovereignty. But while modernity countered some forms of CAPE inequality, it constructed others of its own. Both racism and concerns about non-heterosexual, non-binary sexuality seem much stronger in most modern societies than they were in most CAPE ones.

The progress, or not, towards more human equality, can be tracked through its representation in IGOs. The League of Nations did not make much impact on the issue of inequality. Since it was mainly a club of imperial and patriarchal and capitalist states, it is hardly surprising that it did little to undo the legitimacy of imperialism (other than by increasing the responsibilities of the colonisers to the colonised), or racism, or sexism, or economic inequality. The Charter of the League of Nations is a scrupulously sovereigntist document, tightly focused on issues of peace, war, territoriality, the management of colonialism, conflict resolution and international law.[7] It was hardly concerned with human rights and the creation of greater human equality, except to reaffirm opposition to slavery (Article 22), oppose 'the traffic in women' (lumped together with drugs), and commit to 'endeavour to secure and maintain fair and humane conditions of labour for men, women, and children' (Article 23). Notoriously, in the negotiations at Versailles in 1919, the Anglosphere powers rejected a Japanese attempt to be accepted as racial equals (Shimazu, 1998; Clark, 2007: 83–106). As Shimazu (1998) argues, the issue of racial inequality threatened Japan's hard-won standing as a great power by casting it as biologically inferior to white powers and placing it alongside the non-white subjects of the colonies. This humiliation was rubbed in by explicitly anti-Japanese and anti-Asian

---

[7] https://avalon.law.yale.edu/20th_century/leagcov.asp (accessed 29 November 2020).

immigration policies in the US, Canada and Australia. Without recognition of their equality as people, how could Japan avoid being seen as a second-class great power? It seemed that the apparently open and meritocratic 'standard of civilisation' was in fact a hypocrisy trumped by racism. This victory for white supremacism resulted in an anti-Western turn in Japanese policy that laid the basis for geopolitical contestation during the interwar years (Zarakol, 2011: 166–73). The Pacific war between Japan and the US between 1941 and 1945 was fought and propagandised with unrestrained racism on both sides (Dower, 1986), forcing the US to address its domestic racism in order to lower its vulnerability to Axis, and later communist, propaganda.

For racial and sexual inequality, the big turning point did not come until after the Second World War. Whereas the League of Nations had done relatively little in this regard, the United Nations (UN) did quite a lot. The extreme horrors of the racism and imperialism of the Axis powers during that war, paved the way for a substantial shift towards norms of human equality. So too did the fact that the main victors were a combination of liberal democracies and socialist great powers. Although hardly untainted by racism themselves, the US and the Soviet Union were both anti-imperialist in principle (considerably less so in practice), and in their different liberal and socialist ways committed to a principle of human equality. Britain was still clinging to empire even though its position was unravelling, and like the US, was torn between liberal principles on human rights, and a continuing legitimacy and practice of racism in its society and empire. Despite both differing views of anti-imperialism between the liberal-democratic and socialist powers, and ongoing social contradictions around racism, the post-1945 world nevertheless managed major shifts towards human equality as a primary institution of global society. This shift was all the more notable for the fact that it took place in a global society still dominated by the white West, before decolonisation trebled the membership, and the ethnic and cultural diversity, of the UN.

The 1945 Charter of the United Nations made the normative shift towards human equality very clear.[8] The preamble reaffirms 'faith in fundamental human rights, in the dignity and worth of the human person, in the equal rights of men and women'. Among the purposes of the UN stated in Article 1 is: 'promoting and encouraging respect for human rights and for fundamental freedoms for all without distinction as to race, sex, language, or religion'. Among the purposes of the Economic

[8] www.un.org/en/charter-united-nations/ (accessed 29 November 2020).

and Social Council (ECOSOC) (Article 62) is that it: 'may make recommendations for the purpose of promoting respect for, and observance of, human rights and fundamental freedoms for all'. In 1946, the United Nations established a Commission on the Status of Women as part of ECOSOC, which subsequently held several conferences on women's rights. The 1948 Universal Declaration of Human Rights asserts 'the equal rights of men and women' (Preamble), and rejects slavery (Article 4) and discrimination on many grounds including race, sex and religion.[9] These documents explicitly took women into account, and unlike the foundational statements of the late eighteenth century, with their focus on 'men' and 'citizens', were careful to use inclusive terms such as 'all human beings', 'everyone', 'no one', 'men and women'. In 1965, the UN General Assembly adopted the International Convention on the Elimination of All Forms of Racial Discrimination (ICERD) and in 1979 the Convention on the Elimination of all Forms of Discrimination Against Women (CEDAW). CEDAW has been widely ratified, but with the conspicuous absence of the US.

These measures did not, of course, eliminate the practices of racism and patriarchy. Far from it. Both racism and patriarchy were generationally embedded attitudes, often backed-up by laws, customs and practices that would take a long time to erode. In some places, racism still remained domestically legitimate as policy, although no longer internationally legitimate. These measures did, however, make domestic discrimination on grounds of race much more difficult to sustain for countries such as South Africa, the US and Israel. They were also a necessary underpinning for the narrower, but more dramatic, international political move towards decolonisation that was getting underway in the late 1940s. With echoes of Japan's 1919 complaint that racial discrimination against it undermined its position as a great power, so too it would be difficult to grant sovereign equality to former colonies without recognising the human equality of their citizens. The UN became the central international forum for the pursuit of greater human equality in practice. Notwithstanding many remaining shortcomings, all this stood in sharp contrast to the prevailing norms, attitudes, practices and institutions in global society up to 1945. It added up to an extremely important shift in principle towards a more comprehensive acceptance of human equality in the social and political normative structures of global society after the Second World War.

---

[9] www.un.org/en/universal-declaration-human-rights/index.html (accessed 29 November 2020).

Economic inequality was, however, a trickier question. The winding down of empire after 1945, and the shift towards development as a new primary institution (on which more in Chapter 5b) pointed toward the lifting of economic inequality imposed militarily by the core onto the periphery. There was also considerable recognition in the core, exemplified by the acceptance of Keynesianism, that economic inequality within the core states needed to be lessened in order to preserve political stability. Against this was the fact that the question of economic equality, and how best to achieve it, sat at the heart of the first cold war's ideological contest between the socialist and capitalist blocs. Meritocracy was at the centre of liberal capitalism, which in principle necessarily accepted that there would be economic inequality, and held that the pursuit of economic equality (aka socialism) was pernicious to the pursuit of prosperity.

The question of economic (in)equality ties into the complex and difficult place of functional differentiation within modernity. A much-increased role for functional differentiation was one of the markers distinguishing the transition towards modernity from the CAPE era. Certainly there was a marked shift towards thinking about human activities, and organising them, in terms of separable sectors. This was most notable in liberalism's attempt to separate politics and economics. This shift, however, absolutely did not mean that functional differentiation and sectors replaced stratification. Stratification and hierarchy remained powerful social forces albeit with functional differentiation woven throughout. There was, as discussed in Chapter 3, functional differentiation in CAPE societies, but often this was determined by birthright, most obviously in dynasticism, but also in caste systems, and other forms in which either by tradition or by law, sons inherited the work of their fathers (which might be quite functionally differentiated), and daughters that of their mothers (generally domestic work). Merit usually played second fiddle to birthright in determining the hierarchy within any given functional differentiation. There were obvious exceptions to this. Champion warriors or sportsmen could win high status, and so too could particularly skilled artisans and craftsmen who would obtain royal approval. But birthright nevertheless remained the dominant principle of the CAPE era, and meritocratic reaction against this type of stratificatory privilege/subordination was one of the social drivers towards modernity in both its liberal and socialist forms.

Liberals and socialists wanted a much bigger role for merit as a qualification for both functional differentiation and status, though they differed on the resultant status issues. The socialist formula was 'from each according to his ability, to each according to his need' (note again, the nineteenth-century sexism of 'his'). Liberals were happy to let indi-viduals reap whatever rewards their merit could bring them. Both, how-ever, thought that unleashing meritocracy would bring much more benefit to society than staying with a strong system of birthright privilege or obligation. Merit was a fundamentally different principle of hierarchy and stratification from birthright. In a meritocracy, in principle, hierarch-ical status was open to anyone with the talent to achieve it. Merit made hierarchy more acceptable and legitimate, and took a lot of the unfairness and inefficiency out of it.[10] On an oceanic voyage, one would logically prefer a ship's captain who had mastered, and been rigorously tested for, the mathematical skills of navigation, than either an aristocrat whose main qualification was good breeding and a privileged social and political network, or someone chosen mainly on grounds of race or gender rather than skill.

The key point here is that modernity was never about eliminating hierarchy and stratification from society, but only about changing its basis. This was true even in the debates about class structure. Modernity and industrial capitalism changed the class structure by ele-vating the proletariat and the bourgeoisie, and demoting the aristocracy. But it opened up a struggle to reshape the class hierarchy rather than to make it egalitarian. Liberals wanted to elevate the position of the mer-chants and capitalists, while Marxists fought to put the proletariat on top. Anyone who thinks that Marxists were about class equality needs to take a close look at Chinese domestic politics under Mao, where the 'right' class origins (peasants and workers) were privileged, and the wrong ones (landlords, bourgeoisie) could get you discriminated against or killed (Dikötter, 2011, 2016). The large infusion of functional differentiation under modernity made major modifications to social structures. Modernity in all of its forms certainly generated mass societies with much more complex social differentiations, but these were not anywhere close to being egalitarian. In capitalist societies there was a specific ideological commitment against economic equality. Socialist societies aimed for economic equality, but mostly failed to achieve it.

As argued in Chapter 3, the strong shift to patriarchy from the outset of the CAPE era mostly excluded women from the functional differenti-ation that opened up in the early towns and cities. In general, and with

---

[10] Another view would be that it merely substituted the unfairness of differences in talent, for that of the unfairness of rigid social hierarchy, both, in a sense, forms of birthright. Then the argument for meritocracy is only about its great social efficiency and benefit for all. There are also bottomless questions about why different types of merit are rewarded differently. Why are nurses and many other 'key workers' paid little, and footballers and financiers a lot?

some exceptions and local variations, women were largely confined to the domestic sphere, or the new social role of prostitute, and mostly excluded from politics (except as associates of male rulers), trade, the military, the artisan guilds, education and suchlike. They, and the female gods, were also reduced to subordinate positions in most high religions. Industrialisation and professionalism expanded hugely under modernity, and along with capitalism, opened up myriad functionally differentiated pathways around the stratificatory birthright constraints of class and caste. For men, meritocracy got more play in everything from sport to science, during the nineteenth century. But women were largely barred from meritocratic competition, still being valued mainly for their looks, their reproductive capability, and their expropriated labour. Other than at the bottom of the labour hierarchy as factory workers, women did not initially get much of a look-in at the burgeoning restructuring of both hierarchy/stratification and society that was opened up by the transition towards modernity. As with the right to vote, to have equal standing before the law, and to have a living wage, this situation did not begin to change substantially until after the First World War, when women entered into white-collar employment, and thereby a degree of economic empowerment, in jobs as receptionists, typists, telephone operators and suchlike. It has been a long and slow climb. There were continuing restrictions on women's participation in education, the professions, the military, politics and business, and only a slow and often reluctant opening up in the decades following the Second World War. Even where access to higher ranking jobs and professions was opened up, glass ceilings to promotion and unequal pay to men for the same work remained.

Even with those gains, there have been setbacks, such as the failure of the equal rights amendment (ERA) to the US Constitution in the 1970s–1980s, which was intended, in line with the UN Charter, to remove all legal differentiation between men and women. As shown by the ERA campaign, women themselves are divided on this issue, and it remains unclear and contested as to in what form sexual equality might eventually be achieved. This suggests an interesting but difficult difference in the dynamics of the human equality principle as applied to race and sex. Racial equality has a clear and simple meaning that is shared by both those who advocate it and those who oppose it. This is that 'races', however imagined, should have equal rights in all respects, including equal access to the logic of meritocracy in structuring social stratification. In its full realisation, racial equality should mean an absence of differentiation between races in the statistics for education, health, wealth and welfare and suchlike. Sexual equality is more problematic. Some of its advocates, like those backing the ERA read it in the same way as racial equality, meaning absolute equality across the board. But differences in the reproductive functions and obligations associated with sex, intervenes in this in a way that has no parallel for racial equality. As the reaction to the ERA showed, considerable numbers of women wanted some differences to remain in the rights of men and women, particularly around reproductive issues and children. This vision of justice entails a view of men and women as 'different but equal'. This is an ongoing debate, now expanded into a widening array of genders and sexualities, which muddies the waters around sexual equality in a way that does not occur with racial equality. More on this in Chapter 8.

To sum up this complicated story, the transition out of the CAPE era involved an epochal shift from a primary institution, in both principle and practice, of human inequality in almost all respects; to one of human equality in principle, in some social and political respects, with economic equality remaining more contested. Even where mainly agreed, equality in practice was only partial, still with a long way to go. However you look at it, this was a massive change in the social structure of humankind, reversing substantially in principle, if somewhat less so in practice, an institution that had been central in extreme form to CAPE societies for several thousand years. But this was hardly a clean, quick, clear or absolute shift. It took a century to end the legal practice of slavery, and to topple monarchy/dynasticism from its position of being the core legitimising principle for government. It took a century and a half to elevate the principle of human equality regarding racism and patriarchy to the level of a primary institution of global society. In practical terms, there is still a long way to go in the elimination of both racism and sexual inequality. Slavery remains a substantial, if illegal, practice, as does the selective abortion of female foetuses. Discrimination against sexualities other than heterosexual ones remains a contested public issue. Race discrimination as a practice continues still, widely in structural forms, as for example in the US, where the *Black Lives Matter* movement has drawn attention to it. It is also visible on a personal level in the form of various right-wing white-supremacist organisations and movements that are now a feature of political life in most Western countries. The practice of gender discrimination, both structural and personal, continues still, ranging from second-class citizenship and legal rights in some countries; through glass ceilings and pay gaps in others; to face-to-face macho attitudes almost anywhere.

Human equality has perhaps made its most obvious gains in the interstate domain, where the various declarations and agreements cited above have changed the norms, and sometimes the laws, in its favour.

That change has rippled down into the laws and constitutions of many states. In the transnational domain, both advocacy of, and opposition to, human equality are represented in many INGOs, with the former still dominant, and as with the foundational civil society campaign against slavery, active in promoting human equality into the interstate domain. This issue is perhaps less noticeable in the commercial sector where firms tend to follow state law, but their practice cuts both ways. Some firms are content to turn a blind eye to slave-like working conditions and gender discrimination, while others promote the opposite, and are happy to benefit from meritocracy. The interhuman domain also cuts both ways. In some societies, racial and sexual equality have substantial support, and have become part of 'rainbow' and 'multicultural' group identity. It is easier to marry across race, class and caste lines. In other societies, racist and patriarchal attitudes remain dominant, and are also part of the collective identity. Most societies are in varying degrees, still split on this matter.

The next group of primary institutions is those that have so far survived within modernity, albeit almost always with significant changes in how they are understood, and what practices are legitimised by them: religion, war, territoriality, sovereignty, diplomacy, international law and trade.

Religion

During the CAPE era, religion was a huge success at creating large-scale patterns of collective identity based mainly on belief. There can be no doubt that it was a core primary institution of the CAPE era, recognised as legitimate in principle and practice.[11]

I argued in Chapter 3 that religion was one of the more successful carry-overs from the CAPE era to the modern one. This is obviously true in the sense that most of the major Eurasian universal religions and philosophies from the CAPE era are still very much alive and operational in the modern one: Hinduism, Confucianism, Judaism, Buddhism, Christianity and Islam. Amongst the more widespread CAPE religions only Zoroastrianism has shrunk. These religions have carried not just their beliefs and stories, but also most of their secondary transnational institutions, across the divide between the CAPE and modern eras. As Bayly (2004: 235–65, 322–4) argues, religions quickly adapted themselves to the new conditions of modernity, and the opportunities

[11] Religion and its observances were legitimate in a general sense, but specific religious practices, such as human sacrifice, might well not be seen as legitimate between one religion and another.

(e.g. new forms of communication and organisation) and constraints (e.g. competing secular ideologies, the challenge of science to belief in the supernatural), that those conditions offered. There was a World Parliament of Religions held in Chicago in 1893 (Bayly, 2004: 20). Liberal thinking about human equality had roots in Christian ideas about equality before god, and science could be constructed as revealing god's work. He goes so far as to say that religions 'did more to shape the mental life of the period' than secular ideas (Bayly, 2004: 284).

Religions survived some stiff tests in the transition to modernity. They were disestablished in the US, France and elsewhere, sometimes with extensive confiscations of religious properties. Ruthless, communist-led, revolutionary secularising projects in the Soviet Union and China broadly failed to purge religion. Orthodoxy bounced back after seven decades of repression in Russia. Confucianism was brought back by a Chinese Communist Party (CCP) that initially tried to eradicate everything old from Chinese culture, but by the 1990s was eagerly looking for new sources of legitimacy in traditional Chinese culture. The CCP is still working hard to persuade itself and the Chinese people that a Leninist party/state is in legitimate continuity with China's Confucian political legacy (Pines, 2012; Buzan and Lawson, 2020). The nineteenth and much of the twentieth centuries provided a huge opportunity for Christianity to proselytise in Africa and Asia on the back of Western power. Islam picked up a lot of social and political strength on the back of poor results by some secular modernisers in the Arab world. Sometimes Islam is still closely linked to the state, as in Iran, Pakistan and Saudi Arabia. But often it operates at one remove, whether politically, as in Al Qaeda and Islamic State, or in more specialised ways, such as the Red Crescent, and forms of Islamic finance.

But while CAPE religions have survived the transition remarkably well, their place in the social structure has changed considerably. Perhaps most striking in this respect is the altered relationship of religion to politics, particularly, but not only, in the West. Religion lost out in the transition to the extent that it was de-linked from monarchy/dynasticism, and therefore from government. As argued above, monarchy/dynasticism itself lost legitimacy, becoming a residual political form. Religion also lost its links to imperialism as that institution became obsolete. Whereas religion had played a central role in the core political package of the CAPE era, it was initially shunted to the margins of politics by the transition to modernity although that did not prevent it from expanding into the social sphere (Bayly, 2004: 336–40). As early as 1648, the Treaties of Westphalia removed religion as a legitimate reason for war (Mayall, 2000a: 11), thus beginning a secularisation of European politics, a separation of church and state, and a personalisation of religion, in Europe and North America. This marginalisation of religion from politics, was not, however, true everywhere, and at the time of writing is beginning to look like part of the Eurocentric perspective of world history.

The connection between religion and politics remained stronger in Asia. The Islamic world never lost its deep link between religion and politics. Some of the major rebellions against the Qing dynasty, such as the Taiping (1851–62), had strong religious elements, and so too did the Indian Rebellion of 1857–9 (Bayly, 2004: 148–55). Religion played important roles in the mobilisation of anti-colonial campaigns, and successfully entangled itself with nationalism, most notably in Russia, Poland, the Balkans, Ireland and Israel. Even within Europe, the Vatican managed to hang on to its status as an independent state, and some political parties identified themselves as Christian. In recent decades, the so-called Christian right within the US has played a powerful role in domestic politics, mobilising around socially polarising issues such as abortion and same-sex marriage. Within the modernising core during the nineteenth century, Japan's Meiji reformers constructed a revitalised Shintoism to support the legitimacy of the restored emperor (Totman, 2005: locs. 8038, 8198). In the Islamic world, religion became a prime node of resistance to colonialism and Westernisation from the nineteenth century onwards, and remains so today (Acharya and Buzan, 2019: 62–3, 106–7). It also plays a key role in the legitimacy claims of many states and governments. Significantly, Islam supports a large IGO, the Organisation of Islamic Cooperation set up in 1969.[12] Islam has been particularly successful in maintaining its link to politics, not least because as a religion it always combined, rather than separating, faith and politics (Buzan and Acharya, 2022: ch. 5). Khadduri (1966: 10) makes this clear by defining the *umma* not just as the community of believers, but as 'a political community ... endowed with a central authority'. This fusion of religion and politics has proved particularly effective in creating highly mobilised militant groups capable of challenging states and empires.

Religion played a major role in the break-up of the British Raj into India, Pakistan, Sri Lanka and Burma in 1947, and the establishment of Israel in 1948. It plays an important role in either defining the government and legitimacy of quite a few states – for example, Iran, Israel, Pakistan, Saudi Arabia – or of some of the major political parties within states – for example, India, Iraq, Poland, Turkey. It continues to be a

---

[12] Initially, the Islamic Conference (1969), then the Organisation of the Islamic Conference (1972), and in 2011, the Organisation of Islamic Cooperation.

significant factor in many disputes and conflicts such as those between Sunni and Shi'ia states in the Middle East; between Buddhists and other religions in both Sri Lanka and Myanmar; between Serbs and Albanians; between both Tibetans and Uighurs and the CCP in China; between Armenia and Azerbaijan; and so forth. At the time of writing the ruling party in India is having some success in promoting *Hindutva*, as a closer association between Hinduism and the Indian state. Since religion is about firmness and rectitude of belief, and modern politics, especially within democracies, and between sovereign states, is about compromise and deals, there is considerable tension between the two.

But while religion remained a political force in the modern era, and seemingly at the time of writing an increasing one, it had much more competition both in the political arena and in identity politics more broadly than was the case during the CAPE era. With a few exceptions, the CAPE politics of monarchy/dynasticism and imperialism was more about submission and consent, than about shared identity. This meant that religions, and related social philosophies such as Confucianism, pretty much had the field to themselves when it came to the construction of broader identities. Right from the opening up of modernity in the late eighteenth century, a variety of powerful secular ideologies arose to contest the political and social space earlier occupied almost exclusively by monarchy/dynasticism and religion. These included nationalism, with its corollary of popular sovereignty; liberalism; humanism; socialism and communism; and 'scientific' racism (Buzan and Lawson, 2015: 97–126). Many of these, of course, competed with each other, as well as with religion and monarchy/dynasticism. Some of them challenged religion directly, most notably humanism and communism; while others could either live alongside personalised forms of religion (liberalism and social-ism), or align themselves, as dynasties and empires did, with a religion (nationalism and 'scientific' racism).

The idea of 'imagined communities' nicely captures all of these ideolo-gies, both religious and secular, and how they create 'a deep horizontal comradeship' across a large scale (Anderson, 1983: 15–16). Anderson linked the emergence of nationalism to religion and monarchy/dynasti-cism. He saw it as building not only on religious concepts of community, but also on monarchical/dynastic concepts of realm. He saw nationalism as another way of breaking religion's monopoly on resolving the fear of death in the secular world: the nation provided 'a secular transformation of fatality into continuity'. And he saw popular sovereignty as breaking the long-standing monopoly of monarchy/dynasticism as the legitimating principle for political order (Anderson, 1983: 17–28). People 'saw the nation as a guarantor of rights, privileges, and claims on resources', and thought that government should be not just for the ruling elites, but for the good of the people, thereby galvanizing civil society (Bayly, 2004: 243, 295–6).

For the nineteenth and much of the twentieth centuries, and particularly within the core, it looked as if these secular ideologies might drive religion permanently to the margins of politics, and perhaps even of society. The twentieth century in particular was largely about global-scale clashes amongst secular ideologies – communism, socialism, nationalism, liberalism, fascism, racism – about which of them would provide the dominant framing to take modernity forward. These struggles are by no means over, though perhaps most or all of their major wars have been fought. Yet by the twenty-first century, religious politics was making its way back onto the agenda of global society. Increasing numbers of great powers were incorporating religion or a classical philosophy into their own political and social identity: China, India, Russia, the US. Islam had no great power (Lustick, 1997), but was generating a strong political dimension that ranged from IGOs, through Islamic states, to a variety of militant transnational groups and franchises. After being eclipsed for more than a century, religion and its philosophical associates appear to have resisted the assault of secularism quite well. They have retained a great deal of their power as mobilising ideas, and increasingly worked their way back into politics, both local and global.

On this basis it seems reasonable still to think of religion as an institution of global society, albeit one that is less important and more contested than was the case during the CAPE era. Religion remains a right widely recognised in the interstate domain, both as a private right, and as a basis for political organisation. In the transnational domain, it is less important in trade and commerce, but perhaps rather more important in terms of its presence in many INGOs in both civil and uncivil global society. In the interhuman domain, it is still, despite all the secular competition, a major factor in patterns of human identity: the most important for many people. Despite the challenges of science, globalisation, and an array of powerful secular ideologies, religion has successfully adapted and endured. It is, indeed, to the puzzlement of many rationalists, perhaps the great survivor of the CAPE era, making it, apparently permanently, into modern society and politics despite all of the challenges to it inherent within the transition towards modernity.

War

Recall that during the CAPE era, war was almost the default activity. It was driven by monarchical/dynastic and imperial motivations; the desire/

need for plunder and slaves; the imperative to control trade routes, resources and taxes; and the honour and status imperatives of warrior societies. This general picture of war was broadly true also of the European empires that spread across the world from the sixteenth to the eighteenth centuries towards the end of the CAPE era. Bowden (2009: loc. 1933) cites the sixteenth-century international lawyer Vitoria as saying: '[I]t is a universal rule of the law of nations that whatever is captured in war becomes the property of the conqueror'.

Like religion, war was a major carry-over from the CAPE era, but one that was even more changed in the process of transition than was religion. Both, the material means of warfighting and the social motivations for war, were transformed. Most obviously, war was made more expensive and destructive by the enormous and rapid improvement in weapons. This material change tends to attract the most attention. From China, through South Asia and the Middle East, to Europe, the gunpowder revolution had made war more technically demanding and expensive since the fourteenth century, but given the limits of the technology, not hugely more destructive. It had also spread fairly quickly and evenly across CAPE civilisations in Eurasia, not generating big disparities of military strength except in the initial encounters of Europeans with people in the Americas and the Pacific islands (Diamond, 1997). The revolutions in firepower, mobility and organisation that took off in the nineteenth century, however, had much more consequential and uneven effects. Unlike early gunpowder weapons, they were ever-more difficult to copy, maintain and use effectively. As a consequence, modern weapons opened up a fast-widening military gap between the small group of core countries capable of making, maintaining and deploying them, and the large group of periphery ones for whom they were beyond independent reach. The continuous revolution in military affairs (RMA) that kicked off in the nineteenth century was announced by Britain's quick and easy defeat of China in the First Opium War. This opened up not just a century-and-a-half of military dominance of the periphery by the core, but also a destabilisation of great power relations within the core that is still ongoing.

It also, as noted in Chapter 4, opened up the *defence dilemma*, in which fear of war, because of its increased costs and destructiveness, began to rival fear of defeat. Fear of war on these material grounds was a distinctive feature of the transition towards modernity. This fear was qualitatively different from the war-weariness that sometimes followed extensive periods of fighting during the CAPE era. The often exuberant enthusiasm for new developments in weapons technology that marked the opening centuries of modernity began, by the late nineteenth century, to be accompanied by calls and campaigns for limitations on the types and numbers of weapons that could legally be used in war. This is the well-known story of arms control and disarmament (ACD) (Buzan and Herring, 1998), seeking to control weaponry; and of peace movements, both of which were in evidence by the late nineteenth century. ACD was about constraining the means of war. Peace movements were not only against particular wars, but, for some, against the legitimacy of war generally in global society. The defence dilemma was thus mainly a response to the awesome changes in the material conditions of war. By the early-middle decades of the twentieth century, changes such as air power, poison gases and nuclear weapons were raising plausible fears about both a threat to the future of Western civilisation (after the First World War), and a threat to the existence of humankind (with the deployment of increasing numbers of nuclear weapons during the first cold war). To growing numbers of people, both commoners and elites, the defence dilemma was making war look at best irrational, and at worst, insane. Even to those who remained committed to the right of states to use force, the emphasis shifted to strategies of deterrence and war avoidance.

But material conditions were not the only transformation to impact on war in the transition to modernity. The social conditions that defined the uses and meanings of war also changed radically. Modernity was as much about transformations in the ideas defining society, as it was about new ideas and technologies for controlling the material world, and these two strands of transformation were linked in myriad complex ways. The key here was the rise of various secular ideologies to challenge the monar-chical/dynastic, religious, economic and imperial motives that had underpinned the practice of war during the CAPE era. During the nineteenth and twentieth centuries, nationalism, liberalism, socialism, communism and fascism increasingly replaced dynasticism and religion as the driving motivations for war. Fascism even revived elements of warrior culture, seeing war as a way of selecting the fittest nations. In contrast, imperialism remained robust for the first century-and-a-half of modernity, with not a lot to distinguish the motives for imperial wars – control of trade, resources, loot, settlement and taxes – from CAPE era practices. In some ways, modern ideologies contributed to the older rationales for colonialism. Some liberal and 'standard of civilisation' thinking, for example, held that superior races had the right to rule or displace 'inferior' peoples, and, in a twist on the theme of meritocracy, that land and resources that were not being 'properly' exploited by the indigenous people were fair game to be expropriated and brought into the global economy (Bowden, 2009: locs. 1558–633, 1791–2081).

This attitude was not all that far removed from the contempt with which steppe nomads – the 'barbarians' of classical history – viewed sedentary agrarian civilisations. Forms of imperialism could also be supported by ideological claims made in universal terms that justified the creation and maintenance of 'camps' or 'blocs', competing with each other to achieve their universal truth. Much of the first cold war worked that way.

Where the new ideologies kicked-in earliest and most noticeably was in wars within the core. From this perspective, the American War of Independence, and even more so the French revolutionary and Napoleonic Wars, appear more important than their rather marginal role in the orthodox benchmarking and periodisation practices of IR, which often skip from 1648 to 1919, would suggest (Buzan and Lawson, 2014a). One reason for their marginalisation is that both were fought with late CAPE era technologies, which makes them look old-fashioned. But from a social structural perspective on the transition from CAPE to modernity, these count as modern wars because they very explicitly opened the campaign against monarchy/dynasticism as the ruling principle of legitimacy for government. The American War of Independence was motivated by taxes and popular sovereignty more than by identity, but the French revolution also brought nationalism to the table, and both promoted republicanism against monarchy.[13] On social structural grounds, these two wars thus stand as ideational markers for the start of the transition towards modernity, despite their use of CAPE era military technology and tactics.

As the transition unfolded, the displacement of monarchy/dynastic and religious drivers for war by ones deriving from modern secular ideologies became increasingly apparent, especially so within the modernising core. The mid-nineteenth-century wars of German and Italian unification were strongly motivated by nationalism. For the reasons just noted, the American civil war (1861–5) was not driven by nationalism, but it was a struggle between an industrial society and a principle of human equality, on one side, and an agrarian society supporting racism and slavery, on the other side. The Chinese civil war, which in one form or another carried on through most of the years between 1911 and 1949, was a struggle between nationalist authoritarianism and communism in a context of the need to leave dynasticism behind, recover national sovereignty

---

[13] The Americans initially had difficulty with nationalism because of the closeness of their culture and history to that of Britain (Hobsbawm, 1990: 18–20). Even though France lapsed back into dynasticism under Napoleon and various Capetian restorations, nationalism and republicanism were firmly out of the bag. The Haitian revolution registered more against slavery and colonialism than against monarchy/dynasticism.

and modernise as quickly as possible. The Balkan wars preceding the First World War were about nationalism and self-determination. The First World War began mainly out of balance of power motives rather than ideological ones, but by its conclusion had turned into a rout for dynasticism, and a boost for self-determination, communism, fascism and liberal democracy. The Second World War and the first cold war were explicitly driven by secular ideological rivalries from the beginning, though they were also infused with modern material concerns about the arms dynamic and the balance of power. The Second World War pitted a coalition of democracies and communists against one of fascists. The first cold war was a kind of second round in which the victors against fascism turned on themselves, and competed in proxy wars (Korea, the Middle East, Vietnam, Afghanistan, Africa) over ideology and spheres of influence in the periphery. The Crimean war (1853–6) stands as the exception to this rule. While fought with modern weapons, it was not about modern ideologies, having originated in disputes about religious jurisdiction, and otherwise being mainly motivated by balance of power considerations, and geopolitical rivalry over access to the Mediterranean Sea. So too do the Russian wars on Ukraine in 2014 and 2022, which were mainly about territory and power, albeit with nationalism also in play.

These ideological wars were focused in the core but often fought worldwide as part of imperial competition. Such wars need to be differentiated from colonial wars by core powers against the periphery. As noted above, up until 1945, these largely continued in the CAPE imperialism mould. Think of the American-Mexican war (1845–8), Britain's suppression of the Indian mutiny (1857–9), the French occupation of Indochina from the 1860s, the scramble for Africa from the 1880s, the British occupation of Egypt (1882), Japan's wars against China and Korea (1894–5), and against China (1931–45), Italy's invasions of Ethiopia (1895–6, 1935–7), and suchlike. After 1945, such directly colonial wars became illegitimate, but the ideological competitions within the core were increasingly imposed on, and transplanted into, the periphery. Think of the Korean War (1950–3), the war in Vietnam (1955–75), various interventions in Latin America, and the many post-colonial liberation struggles in Africa and Southeast Asia during the 1950s, 1960s and 1970s. These latter were generally fought in the name of modern ideas – popular sovereignty, racial equality, nationalism, socialism, communism – as were the interventions from the core that frequently accompanied them.

Although there had been 'South-South' wars in areas not colonised, or colonised late, by the West and Japan, such as China and Southeast Asia, decolonisation reopened this option much more widely. There were quite a few takers, some of the highlights being the Paraguayan war (1864–70), the war of the Pacific (1879–84), various India–Pakistan wars (1947, 1965, 1971, 1999), the India–China war (1962), various Israel-Arab wars (1948, 1956, 1967, 1973), the China–Vietnam war (1979), the Iran–Iraq war (1980–8), Iraq's occupation of Kuwait (1990), and the wars between Armenia and Azerbaijan (1918–20, 1988–94, 2020). Nearly all of these were about borders/territory, and/or resources, with relatively little ideological element other than the old one of religion, which played a role in some of them. Wars and clashes of this type remain active in many parts of the Global South, as do diplomatic and peace-keeping efforts to prevent or contain them by the UN and various regional organisations.

From early in the twenty-first century, two developments, terrorism and cyberwar, began to widen the institution of war away from the Westphalian understanding that it was a practice confined to states (or would-be states), and defined largely by military conflict. Terrorism has been around for a long time as a fringe practice, but its status changed dramatically after the Al Qaeda attacks on the US in 2001. When George Bush declared a global war on terrorism (GWoT) in response, he ele-vated militant non-state actors to the status of opponents in war, thus marking a significant, and largely uncontested, departure from the norm that war was between states. The attacks of 9/11 could be seen as the opening shots in a kind of fourth world war between radical non-state elements in the Global South, and the leading powers of the West.[14] The declaration of the GWoT significantly moved war from the interstate domain into the transnational and interhuman ones, rooting it in global society. This war involved asymmetric counterattacks on the core from the periphery to balance the core's ability to inflict damage and punish-ment on the periphery using sea and air power (more on this in Chapter 8). This new form of world war was quickly accepted by most of America's allies. It was also taken up by Russia and China, which saw it as usefully legitimising their repressive domestic policies. Since then, state wars against non-state actors have dominated the military agenda, albeit that some terrorism is state sponsored, either directly or through non-state intermediaries. Islamic State has become a global franchise that has to be fought from the streets of London and Paris, through the Sahel, to Libya, Syria, Iraq, Afghanistan and other places in Africa and Southeast Asia. To the extent that the terrorists were mainly radical,

---

[14] I am grateful to Tarak Barkawi for this idea. Fourth world war takes the first cold war as being the third world war.

political, Islamists, there was an element of religion versus modernity, albeit the Islamists had picked up a lot of tricks from the modern toolkit, both ideational and material. There were perhaps also echoes of the independent CAPE era religious players in war. To the extent that terrorists did not have easily identified fixed bases or territories, it was difficult to apply normal military strategies of deterrence to them other than targeted assassination programmes.

Terrorism retains the traditional military component of war, but blurs the issue of who the actors are. Terrorists might be independent non-state actors, or they might be the arm's-length tools of states. Cyberwar moves even further away from traditional understandings of war. Cyberspace did not open up until the 1990s, adding an unexpected new 'territorial' dimension to the traditional ones of land, sea, air and space. It is occupied by both state and non-state actors, and its peculiar characteristics make it difficult to identify who the players within it are, and what counts as territory. There is, indeed, significant overlap between cyberwar and terrorism, because cyberspace is also used by terrorists. Cyberwar mostly does not involve traditional military capabilities and forms of combat, but nonetheless retains some important similarities with traditional warfare. Cyberspace can very profitably be used for spying, and in that sense is just a new tool in the traditional business of espionage. The *Sunburst* attack on the US in 2020, is an example of this, and might be seen as a modern form of the traditional activity of raiding for plunder, now in the form of information, ransoms and property rights. In this sense, hackers are analogous to pirates: parasitic actors who, if they are too successful, can bring down the system on which they feed. But cyberspace can also be used to inflict damage on a wide variety of electronically controlled systems from power grids and water supplies to transportation and communication networks. This capability is increasing as automation spreads. The famous example here is the *Stuxnet* attack on Iran's nuclear programme in 2009–10, allegedly by Israel and the US. In this mode, cyberwar takes on weapon-like characteristics that can be used to punish or disable opponents. Both terrorism and cyberwar all but dissolve the distinction between 'military' and 'civil' technology, and both can also be seen as forms of response to the defence dilemma. Compared to armed conflict amongst great powers, with its huge costs, and its risk of escalation to nuclear exchanges, terrorism and cyberwar are relatively cheap, difficult to deter, and have a lower risk of escalating to Armageddon.[15]

---

[15] For a good overview of cyberwar, see Azhar (2021: 189–203).

The question of interstate war has, of course, hardly disappeared since 2001. The US, on the one hand, and North Korea and Iran, on the other hand, threaten war against each other; US–China relations increasingly have an element of classical great power military rivalry and threat of war between them; and India and Pakistan, and India and China, continue their interconnected local game of military push and shove along their borders. Russia is trying to occupy more of Ukraine, and in the Middle East there is a peculiar and lethal fusion of interstate military rivalry and conflict, civil war and armed transnational actors. My argument is therefore not about a jump-shift from one form of military rivalry to another, but about a process of transformation. Great power war is not impossible, but remains highly constrained by the fear of enormous costs and the possible use of nuclear weapons. The acquisition of territory by force (Russia in the Ukraine, and China in the South China Sea notwithstanding) remains illegitimate. But there can also be no doubt that 2001 marks the beginning of a substantial transformation in the global military relations and practices that are understood as 'war'.

Within this complex narrative, there is an interesting story about the evolution of war. Prior to the nineteenth century, wars among Europeans, wars between Europeans and others, and wars among others, did not require much differentiation. Indeed, they were often entangled with each other. From the nineteenth century to the middle of the twentieth, the major wars were mainly among core imperial powers, and were strongly differentiated from colonial wars between core and periphery. The first and second world wars were all-out affairs within the core. The periphery was seen mainly as an arena, and as spoils, but ironically these core wars did much to open the way to decolonisation, not least by involving substantial numbers of colonial troops and workers. The first cold war retained the core, great power focus, but nuclear weapons pushed active all-out fighting into the background. Instead, a mixture of proxy wars and people's wars became prominent in the periphery. If seen as the opening of the fourth world war, both 2001 and the rising concerns with cyberwar, opened the way to deterritorialised forms of long war between and among mixtures of states and non-state actors. It is not yet clear how the development of war as a phenomenon of global society will square with the ongoing potential for traditional, interstate, cold-war-like relationships among rival great powers such as the US, China, India and Russia.

With all of this in mind, we need to consider the peculiar nature of war as an institution of GIS. What is particular about war as a primary institution of 'modern' European international society is what kind of restraints were put on both the ways in which it could be fought, and the reasons that were considered legitimate to justify resort to it (Williams, 2010; see also Howard, 1966, 1976; Bull, 1977: 184–99; Holsti, 2004: 275–99; Navari, 2007; Pejcinovic, 2013). The treaties of Westphalia, for example, made an early move by largely taking religion off the list of legitimate reasons for war <u>within</u> the realm of Christendom. In principle, war can remain legitimate as a primary institution across a wide spectrum of conditions, ranging from almost no constraints at all, as during the CAPE era, and up to 1945, on the one end; to, on the other end, tight restrictions in which war can only be used legitimately either for self-defence, or in response to a UN Security Council resolution calling for a specific armed intervention against a designated criminal regime. Only a reduction to zero of the permissible reasons for war would actually eliminate it as an institution. War therefore does not rise and decline in quite the same way as most other primary institutions. Although increasing restraints could be seen as a pathway to decline and elimination, that is not necessarily the case. So long as war is legitimate for some purposes, it is still in full force as a primary institution of global society.

The interesting question then becomes not so much about whether war is becoming obsolete, but where it stands on the spectrum of unregulated/unconstrained to highly regulated/highly constrained. Regulated here means diplomatic agreements or international laws that limit the means and/or the ends of war. Constrained means that the high costs and risks of war reduce the rationality of resorting to it. From this perspective, the picture moves from relatively unregulated and unconstrained up to 1945, to increasingly regulated and constrained from 1945 to the 1990s, to a complex and incoherent mix thereafter, in which regulation and constraint differ from place to place.

Up to 1945, notwithstanding natural law arguments about *jus ad bellum* (the right to war) and *jus in bello* (the law in waging war), war in practice was more or less unconstrained, and only lightly regulated. The revisionist great powers going into the two world wars could reasonably calculate that if they won they might make big territorial gains, even become superpowers. If they lost the costs would not be unrecoverable within a generation or two. Mayall (2000a: 17–19) argues that after the first world war, war was discredited as an institution and became seen more as 'the breakdown of international society'. There were a few arms control agreements such as the Hague Conventions (1899, 1907), Geneva Conventions and Washington Naval Treaties (interwar years), that restricted some types of weapons. The Kellogg–Briand Pact of 1928 – a General Treaty for Renunciation of War as an Instrument of National Policy – was famously ambitious in principle, but amounted to little in practice. The wars fought up to 1945 generally used nearly all the kinds of weapons that were available, and had little regard for civilian casualties.

From 1945 into the 1990s, war was both constrained and increasingly regulated. At the level of the major powers, it was constrained by fear of escalation to nuclear wars. The means of destruction had outgrown both the states that deployed them and the institution of war that justified them, creating new levels of 'violence interdependence'.[16] Under the UN system, imperialism and racism became obsolete, and the Security Council had an important role in authorising war. The delegitimation of occupation and seizure of territory by force, took away one of the main traditional functions of war. The move towards freer trade reinforced this by de-linking prosperity and direct control over territory, resources and markets (Bull, 1977: 195). The functions of war were legally pared down to self-defence, and actions authorized by the UN Security Council, although Pejcinovic (2013: ch. 6) argues that for a time the shift to decolonisation after 1945 legitimised wars for independence against colonial powers such as France and Portugal. As discussed above, this did not stop there being quite a number of wars at various levels of global society, and neither did it stop the superpowers from preparing for a vast nuclear showdown. But there nonetheless did seem to be a significant trend towards war being both more constrained and more regulated.

From the 1990s, there has been some rollback of this trend. The constraints of the defence dilemma generally, and the fear of nuclear weapons specifically, continue to operate. But the reasons for going to war, and the means used, have both expanded. The rise of Western-driven humanitarian intervention interests, manifested in the 'right to protect' (R2P), began to expand the legitimate uses of war during the 1990s and early 2000s, when the West was unconstrained by great power rivals. These were controversial because they clashed with the right of non-intervention associated with sovereignty (Mayall, 2000a: 95–6, 102–4; Hurrell, 2007: 63–5). Then, after 2001, the GWoT dramatically eroded restraints on the use of force. The US reacted to this attack by declaring open season on terrorists and their supporters, and claiming a much wider right to resort to war in its self-defence against the new type of threat, explicitly allowing torture and assassinations in response to the ruthlessness of their opponents (Holsti, 2004: 146–50; Jones, 2006; Ralph, 2010). Vicious civil wars in Afghanistan, Colombia, Iraq, Libya, Mali, Nigeria, Sri Lanka, Sudan, Syria and elsewhere seemed to erode

---

[16] Deudney (2007: chs. 7–9) makes the interesting argument that rising violence interdependence might support moves towards a loose form of world federal government.

almost any idea of restraints on the use of force. This generated a patchwork world, in which constraints and regulations operated strongly in some places, and hardly at all in others.

The picture is now very mixed (Holsti, 2004: 283–99; see also Hurrell, 2007: 165–93). War is pretty much obsolete within the West, where the EU is close to being a security community. If there had been a trend towards war becoming more or less obsolete amongst the great powers as a whole, the current second cold war between Russia and NATO, and China and the US, suggests that Pejcinovic (2013) was right to argue that it is still an important institution of international society. In many other parts of the world, war is returning to CAPE era practices and norms with modern weapons, whereby any sense of restraint on violence or limits to its use have eroded away. Between the West and the rest is a murky zone of actual interventions (Iraq, former Yugoslavia, Afghanistan, Libya, Syria) and potential ones (North Korea, Iran). Low-level military interactions remain widespread: border incidents; harassment at sea by quasi-military forces (especially coastguards); military probing and shadowing and threatening exercises. There is increasing pushback by coastal states against threats from offshore naval forces (China, North Korea and Iran against the US; Southeast Asia and Japan against China).

War as an institution and practice thus remains strongly embedded in the interstate domain, but there are also signs, especially since the 1990s, that it is expanding beyond the strictly Westphalian framing that dominated the transition towards modernity up to 2001. Closest to the Westphalian model of war are many insurgencies and counter-insurgencies that are wars between states, and would-be states, often with foreign allies on both sides. The dynamics of propaganda mean that insurgencies are often branded as terrorists by their opponents, with both sides using some terrorist methods. Indeed, the blurring of what counts as 'war' also extends to warriors. Women have increasingly been allowed into combat roles not just by the armed forces of some states, but also by some non-state military players. And although there is still some face-to-face combat, both of traditional kinds, and such as suicide bombing, there are questions as to whether remote drone pilots should be counted as warriors for purposes of awarding combat medals. The war-linkage between merchants and the state in the CAPE era has not reappeared, but there are transnational firms that are closely involved in the business of war. Most obvious amongst these are weapons manufacturers, but they also include what are politely called 'private military companies' (PMCs – aka mercenaries), which are well-equipped to take part in both logistics and military operations either alongside states, or independently from them (Buzan and Hansen, 2009: 233). The linkage of terrorism to religion also extends war as an institution into the transnational, and indeed interhuman domains, as do the opportunities opened up by cyberwar. War is no longer primarily in the interstate domain, but has become a feature of global society as a whole.

Territoriality

During the CAPE era, the sedentary agrarian lifeway made territoriality the framing within which most politics was done. When the great majority of people spent their entire lives close to where they were born, territoriality also acquired a deep social and cultural meaning. Towards the end of the era, European states began to develop a somewhat harder sense of territorial polities, though less so towards their imperial attachments. They also began to territorialise the seas and oceans.

The impact of the transition towards modernity on territoriality has been extremely mixed. While territoriality carries on as a key institution of global society, it does not yet seem to have settled into any stable form. In some important ways, territoriality has carried over from the CAPE era. In a general sense, it remains the basic framing for politics, and as discussed above, even the imperial form of flexible territoriality continued on into modernity until after the Second World War. The tendency to territorialise other dimensions, not just the sea, but air and cyberspace has continued. That said, territoriality has been heavily pressured by some of the core developments of modernity. On the material side of things, territoriality has been hugely impacted by the vast increase in interaction capacity that took off from the nineteenth century. The shrinking of the planet has undermined what might be thought of as the naturally local territoriality of sedentary peoples during the CAPE era. In contrast to the CAPE era, long-distance travel has become easy, and a familiar experience to a majority of humankind, whether by migrating from countryside to cities, or by journeying to foreign countries for a wide variety of purposes, or by being visited by many foreign travellers, again for a wide variety of purposes. The global mingling of flora, fauna, people and ideas has not yet come close to homogenising the world, but it has made the foreign familiar, and the local less distinctive. The global Internet, with its instantaneous and cheap access to worldwide communications, organisation and information is only the latest iteration of this assault on the local.

Alongside material change, and enabled by it, the ideational impact of market ideology has become a powerful force pressing for a deep deterritorialisation of economic life in the name of globalisation. The fate of territoriality is closely entangled with the dialectic between the market and economic nationalism, on which more in Chapter 5b. Economic nationalists have wanted to impose territoriality onto the economic sector, while economic liberals have wanted to open borders to flows of goods, ideas, capital, and up to a point labour (i.e. people). Market ideology requires that polities of whatever sort open themselves substantially to global flows of goods, capital and labour, punching major holes into the territorial boundaries that define states, and up to a point, cultures. The result of all this has been the emergence of contradictory trends – perhaps another dialectic – between the intensification and the erosion of territoriality. Both trends have been in play since the beginning of the transition towards modernity, and at the time of writing there does not seem to be an obvious synthesis, or even point of stability, in sight.

On one side of this equation lies an array of developments tending to intensify territoriality. This side of the story is skewed by the very specific European history of moving from the heteronomy of the mediaeval period, with its many overlapping jurisdictions, to the anarchic system of territorial, sovereign states identified with the Westphalian order, in which territoriality, sovereignty and dynasticism constituted the state (Wight, 1977: 129–73; Ruggie, 1993: 161–4; Watson, 1992: 138–97; Buzan, 2017). This story is justified inasmuch as it was the resultant European political form that was eventually imposed on the rest of the world during the colonial era. Acceptance of this form was the key to decolonisation and political independence. But it is a Eurocentric take on world history given that the rest of the world did not experience feudalism. Europe was a latecomer to the top table of Eurasian civilisations, and its transition from the unique peculiarities of mediaeval heteronomy to a Westphalian order were indeed a dramatic transformation towards a much harder form of territoriality. The rest of the world experienced a direct, and often coerced, transition from the CAPE era imperial arrangements of flexible territoriality, to the colonial order of hard boundaries and divided sovereignty imposed during the ascendency of the West and Japan. The transition from the flexible territoriality of the CAPE empires was thus less dramatic because, unlike in European feudalism, they already had the idea and practice that territoriality plus sovereignty (in its monarchical/dynastic form) constituted the political order. But it was still a very considerable jolt, causing much trauma and difficulty, to make the transition from suzerain systems to Westphalian ones (Neumann, 2011; Zarakol, 2011).

With that story in mind, several developments led to a hardening of territoriality. First, was simply the increasing technical capability to demarcate borders and populations, which was partly to do with improved instrumentation, and partly to do with the expanding administrative capability of the state (Holsti, 2004: 75–88). This capacity was applied not only in Europe, but as a colonial practice to deal with the 'empty' spaces of the Americas (Branch, 2012). It harmonised well with the growing sense of national economy engendered by mercantilism. This process was already underway in Europe and its colonies during the eighteenth century, but was not sufficient in itself to undermine the principle of flexible territoriality. The dynastic states of late-CAPE Europe were defined by territoriality and sovereignty, but remained comfortable with the CAPE monarchical/dynastic and imperial practice of acquiring and losing territories through marriage and war.

The decisive change towards a harder form of territoriality came with the adoption of nationalism in Europe after the French revolution. This was one of the key markers of the transition towards modernity, for it added nationalism to sovereignty and territoriality, displacing monarchy/dynasticism as the third constitutive primary institution for the modern state. In sharp contrast to monarchy/dynasticism's flexible territoriality, nationalism reinforced territoriality by linking territory to people in an emotional way and transforming the idea of the dynastic state/empire to that of the nation state. So effective has this reconceptualisation of the state been, that the term 'nation' has become a synonym for 'state', and we talk without thinking about it of 'international relations' and 'international society', rather than 'interstate' ones. It was this modern form of nation state, not the dynastic one, that the Europeans transplanted around the world (more on this below). In this modern reformulation of the state, nationalism sacralised territory (Mayall, 1990: 84, 2000a: 84; Holsti, 2004: 83–8) by linking it to the people. This move undermined the flexible territoriality of the CAPE era.[17] The sacralisation of territoriality in this way made it much more difficult to legitimise either the seizure of territory by war, or its transfer by dynastic marriage, unless it could be linked to national principles (Holsti, 2004: 103–11). As Zacher (2001: 246) argues, this move consolidated a new norm of territorial integrity in which 'mutually recognized and respected boundaries are not what separate peoples but what binds them together'. Williams (2002) sees territoriality as an institution of modern international society whose ethical justification is that it supports a desirable social pluralism that to

---

[17] China was perhaps an exception to this general political indifference to culture and ethnicity in Eurasian CAPE practice. The Chinese differentiated amongst those peoples who were culturally similar enough to be assimilated, those close enough to be subject to loose rule, and those to be excluded from the Sinosphere (Zhang, F., 2015: 210–12. See also Zhang, F., 2009; Zhang and Buzan, 2012).

some extent defends people against oppression. Jackson (2000: 23) sees the system/society of nation states as being about the preservation and/or cultivation of the political and cultural difference and distinctness that are the legacy of human history. This is also the line taken by the CCP in defence of 'Chinese characteristics'. The shift from empires to modern, rational, national states made borders harder, more precise, and in principle more permanent than they had been in the days of empire. Transfers of territory are now only legitimate by consent, and after the major round of decolonisation following the end of the Second World War, the political map of the world has taken on an increasingly fixed character.

Other factors tending to strengthen territoriality were wars, economic crises, migration crises and pandemics. The wars and economic crises of 1914–45, were accompanied by much hardening of borders and attempts at achieving greater autarchy. The economic crises from 2008, the recent migration crises in Europe and the US,[18] and the pandemic in 2020–2 have all hardened borders and strengthened territoriality in their various ways. The extension of territoriality over the seas and oceans has continued with the international legalisation of coastal state jurisdiction over territorial seas, exclusive economic zones and the continental shelf. Many states have extended their jurisdiction into the airspace above them. Because of the inescapable physics of orbital dynamics, near earth space has so far escaped being territorialised. But as technology increases ease of access to the Moon, the asteroids, and Mars, this hiatus might soon come to look obsolete as a general rule. Even the newest dimension of cyberspace is, after a period of libertarianism, steadily being subjected to territorialisation, most notably, but far from only, by China's great internet firewall. Cyberspace is becoming a new realm for rivalry and a new type of war. Within this framing, as noted above, hackers might be seen as the new pirates/privateers of this dimension, as in the CAPE era, sometimes an enemy of all, sometimes in alliance with states for political purposes.

In parallel with all this territorialising have been equally powerful factors tending to erode territoriality. The key link here is the impact of market ideology and globalisation, on which more in Chapter 5b. Both the golden age of the market in the last decades of the nineteenth century, and the period of neoliberalism from the 1980s to 2008, involved major erosions of territoriality in terms of trade, finance and migration. The latter period was accompanied by an influential literature on

---

[18] For a more general assessment of migration in relation to an earlier European crisis, see Wæver et al. (1993).

globalisation, whose core argument explicitly framed it in terms of deter-ritorialisation, and the dissolving of the inside/outside framing of IR (Clark, 1999: 111–18; Held et al., 1999: 7–9; Scholte, 2000: 2–3, 8–9; Woods, 2000: 3–5).[19] Globalisation and deterritorialisation were seen as rapidly emerging processes that were transcending territorial states by entangling them in interdependence, and embedding them in networks and flows. This entanglement was not just economic, but also in terms of migration, the environment, patterns of identity and suchlike. New non-state actors of various kinds were becoming more influential: transnational corporations, and a wide variety of civil (and uncivil) international non-governmental organisations (INGOs). IGOs were becoming increasingly important to the management of world affairs. Economic linkages, when added to shared fates, such as the environment and global disease issues, and to a growing array of transnational INGOs linking people together across state borders for a wide variety of pur-poses, pointed towards a deterritorialising world order in which states were becoming less relevant to the scale of policy issues, and world politics would drift towards the emergence of global governance (Held et al., 1999; Weiss, 2013).

There is a permanent contradiction between the assertion of territori-ality by states in order to define and consolidate themselves, and the globalising tendency of markets on which states depend for prosperity and growth. In the short term, the operation of this dialectic for and against territoriality seems to be swinging back towards territoriality. There is significant retreat from globalisation in those areas where borders can be reasserted to some effect: trade, production, finance, migration, communication. But in the longer term, the big question is how this will evolve? How sustainable are territorialising restraints on trade, finance, migration and communication? There is a long history of smuggling and other forms of avoidance of restraint, but the new dia-lectic here will be between such behaviours and the ever-rising capacities for mass surveillance. There is also the bigger, and ever-more pressing, difficulty over globalisation in the form of shared-fates against which territorialisation by individual states is of limited or no use (disease, climate change, maybe space rocks). Yet if intensifying globalisation is the task of modernity, then territoriality might face a long-term decline in salience. More on this contradiction in Chapter 8.

---

[19] More generally, see: Hirst and Thompson, 1996; Sassen, 1996; Clark, 1999; Held et al., 1999; Keohane and Nye, 2000; Scholte, 2000; Woods, 2000; Ripsman and Paul, 2010; Buzan and Lawson, 2015: 311–14.

As in the CAPE era, territoriality is central to the interstate domain because it continues to play the key role as the framing for state and interstate politics. In this sense, the dialectic between territoriality and deterritorialisation is an existential matter for the state. It is far from clear how politics would be conducted in a deterritorialised global society. At the very least, government divorced from territoriality would be a radical change in how politics is performed. The transnational domain has become the most powerful driver of deterritorialisation through the activities of both transnational firms and a great variety of INGOs, both civil and uncivil. These actors still have to operate within the rules and jurisdictions of the interstate domain, but there is a significant sense in which they are also the antithesis to the society of states. So far, there is no stable equivalent to the accommodation made between capital and coercion in the CAPE era, though the arrangements in Putin's Russia for the state and the oligarchs to share monopoly rents has strong echoes of CAPE practices. The proliferation of transnational non-state actors additional to economic and religious ones, is a major development that had no real parallel in the CAPE era. In the interhuman domain, the big change is that territoriality has scaled up from the local, with nationalism providing a larger pattern of identity that often comes with strong territorial attachments. Other forms of collective identity such as religion, and even more so ideology, remain loosely, or not at all, connected to territoriality.

Sovereignty

During the CAPE era right up to the end of the eighteenth century, sovereignty was mostly a property of sovereigns, and therefore a derivative quality of monarchy/dynasticism. Modern sovereignty is the claim that a given collectivity of people have the right to self-government, and cannot be bound by rules or laws to which they have not given explicit consent. In practice, sovereignty has co-evolved with a harder territoriality in constituting the state (James, 1984: 12–13, 17; 1986; 1999: 468). As Wight (1977: 135) argues, 'It would be impossible to have a society of sovereign states unless each state, while claiming sovereignty for itself, recognised that every other state had the right to claim its own sovereignty as well'. By this logic, the combination of sovereignty and territoriality co-constitute the state and the anarchic structure of international society, making them opposite sides of the same coin. By itself, sovereignty does not specify how the relevant collectivity of people is to be legitimately determined, and various possibilities for this are in play:

monarchical/dynastic rights, ethno-nationalism, religion and popular sovereignty (civic nationalism).

The claim to sovereignty is about political autonomy, and the process of mutual recognition therefore strongly implies an accompanying right of non-intervention. As Holsti (2004: 112–18) argues, the linkage of sovereignty and non-intervention is a form of protection within the club of the states-system. Mayall (2000a: 11) points out that the removal by Westphalia of religion as a legitimate reason for war was the 'ancestor of the modern practice of non-intervention'. Holsti (2004: 131–4) also notes how the right of conquest began to be eroded from 1815. Modern sovereignty is strongly tied to the idea of sovereign and legal equality among states, which contrasts with the unequal sovereignty under monarchy/dynasticism in which princes, kings and emperors had different degrees of royal status. Under modernity, there was a matching link between the idea that people(s) were equal, and the sovereign equality of their states (Bain, 2003: 173–92; Hjorth, 2011: 2590). This link formed a powerful tie across the interstate and interhuman domains.

Until the nineteenth century, the emergence of modern sovereignty was mostly conducted by autocratic dynastic states, which themselves rested on the CAPE package of three primary institutions: sovereignty (defining the claim to political autonomy, and legal equality with others doing likewise), territoriality (defining the container of the state) and monarchy/dynasticism (defining the legitimate holders of sovereignty). It was this predominantly autocratic Westphalian process that was thrust into the revolutions of modernity, subjecting sovereignty to the same set of forces that were simultaneously strengthening and eroding territoriality. From the American, French and Haitian revolutions onward, nationalism and popular sovereignty steadily displaced monarchy/dynasticism in this institutional package, shifting the holders of sovereignty from the rulers to the citizens. This process did not displace territoriality and sovereignty, but instead changed aspects of their meaning, and the practices associated with them. Sovereignty became popular, meaning that the people became citizens of the state rather than subjects of the crown. Under popular sovereignty, the people or nation became the repository of this institution rather than the monarch. It was this move towards popular sovereignty that sacralised territory by associating it with the people and their culture and history. This made boundaries more rigid, and transfers of territory only legitimate within a narrow range of conditions. It also weakened the hierarchy of sovereignty amongst princes, kings and emperors (Reus-Smit, 1999: 101–2) and facilitated the move towards a norm of sovereign equality that picked up speed during the nineteenth century (Hjorth, 2011: 2588–95).

Nationalism and popular sovereignty generated and supported mass societies in various forms: democratic, fascist, communist. They pushed states into taking on increasing responsibility for the welfare and security of their citizens, with the material resources of modernity giving them the means to do so.

The replacement of monarchy/dynasticism with nationalism as the defining principle of political legitimacy for the state, constituted a fundamental change in the nature and meaning of the state. This change might be comparable in significance to the emergence of the monarchical/dynastic state itself. It is mainly defined by the shift from monarchy/dynastic principles to nationalism, which made the modern state a very different form of polity indeed from the monarchical/dynastic one. These changes in the underlying institutional package that constituted the state, thus amount to a step-level change up to the modern state despite the deceptive continuity of territoriality and sovereignty from the earlier, dynastic, Westphalian form.[20] In this sense, the styling of the modern state as 'Westphalian' is profoundly misleading. Failure to give full recognition to this nineteenth-century transformation of the political units explains why IR, against the grain of the other social sciences, eccentrically clings to 1648 as its benchmark date for modernity. This is simply wrong. By the argument in this book, the whole idea of 'early-modern', especially as applied to political developments, should be thrown out as Eurocentric at best, and deeply misleading at worst. The monarchical/dynastic Westphalian state fell well within the general political, social and material parameters of the CAPE era. Its main novelty lay in its transition out of feudalism, which was itself a condition unique to Europe. It was the modern, rational state, reconstituted around nationalism, and not the monarchical/dynastic Westphalian one, that Europeans eventually imposed on the rest of the world as the new standard of political legitimacy and effectiveness. Nationalism not only made the modern state, but, as discussed above and below, was also instrumental in undoing the legitimacy of empire.

This process, however, was neither smooth nor quick. We have already seen how monarchy/dynasticism and empire remained active as mainstream institutions of global society up until 1945, and this had big consequences for how the story of sovereignty unfolded. The essence of this story is very well known, although not necessarily from this angle. The consolidation of a small group of modern states from the end of the eighteenth century went along with the creation of a core–periphery,

---

[20] For more detailed looks at the nature of the modern state, see: Bayly (2004: 247–83) and Buzan and Lawson (2015: 127–79).

colonial, global society (Buzan and Lawson, 2015: 171–96). The successful first round modernisers in Europe, the US and Japan, built on the overwhelming material and ideational resources that modernity provided to them to become the metropolitan states of empires. Even quite small modern powers could do this: Belgium, the Netherlands, Denmark. This meant that for the first century and a half, modernity was structured around divided sovereignty as two worlds: core and periphery. In the core, modern states worked out both their new domestic structures of popular sovereignty, and, amongst themselves, a form of interstate society based on sovereign equality, territoriality and nationalism. The domestic side of this was not easy, generating some serious revolutions (American, French, Russian, Iranian) and big civil wars (American, Turkish, Chinese). The international side went relatively smoothly during the nineteenth century, when this small group of powers divided up most of the rest of the world amongst themselves. Within the core group, sovereignty pushed against the monarchical/dynastic principle of hierarchy. It pushed towards the idea of sovereign equality amongst those states prepared to give recognition to each other as equally 'civilised', and equal in legal standing, even if not equal in wealth and power. But once the system became geopolitically closed, as it did around the end of the nineteenth century, the so-called long peace within the core broke down. That 'long peace' was so called because it was mostly peaceful for the core states, disturbed only by a handful of relatively contained wars amongst core powers (Crimea, Franco-Prussian, Russo-Japanese). It was far from peaceful for the periphery, which was subjected to the new imperialism powered by material modernity.

In the periphery, states and peoples had to submit to divided sovereignty, in which their political autonomy was restricted in varying degrees, and particularly so in relation to foreign policy and defence. While modern sovereignty was being advanced in the core, it was being retarded in the periphery. The core Western states set up a 'standard of civilisation' based on their own evolution into modernity. This standard was used both to justify colonialism, and to subject outsiders such as Japan and China, to challenging entry criteria for membership in global society. These criteria involved conditionality on such issues as law, property rights, human rights and good governance. Speaking about Japan, Murphy (2014: 63) brilliantly summarises the depth and intensity of the social and material challenge across the three domains, posed by modernity's 'standard of civilisation' to non-Western states and peoples:

The Meiji leaders faced three urgent and intertwined tasks. They had to build a military strong enough to act as a deterrent to Western imperialism. They had to assemble the capital and technology needed to turn their country into an industrial power sufficiently advanced to equip that military. And they had to create the institutions necessary not only to accomplish these other tasks but to convince the West that Japan had accumulated the prerequisites for membership in the club of countries that were to be taken seriously. That meant not only a credible military – preferably evidenced by victories in imperialist wars waged on weaker lands – but also such institutions as parliaments, courts, banks, monogamy, elections, and ideally, Christian churches, not to mention familiarity with Western ways and appearances in such matters as architecture, dress, sexual mores, and table manners. It was only by governing as leaders of a convincing imitation of a modern imperialist nation that these men could persuade the West to revise the Unequal Treaties and thereby wrest back control over their country's tariff regime and security apparatus from the Europeans.

Colonised peoples were notionally under tutelage on such things. Non-colonised peoples such as in China, Japan and the Ottoman Empire were not given full recognition as sovereign equals until they could meet the standard. As Bain (2003: 92) argues, this was a system in which a 'superior' West decided on the readiness for self-government of less developed peoples: 'self-determination implied granting powers of self-government and autonomy in proportion to the capacity of a people to make good use of them'. Their unequal status was inscribed in the humiliating extraterritorial rights demanded by Westerners in treaties with them, which put Europeans above the local law. Although a handful of non-Western countries made it into global society, this system of divided sovereignty, and the racism that most often accompanied it, largely stayed in place until the breakdown of imperialism/colonialism as an institution after the Second World War.

The system of formally divided sovereignty shrank rapidly after 1945 with the delegitimation of imperialism and racial hierarchy. The Second World War, with its catalogue of barbaric behaviour by Westerners to each other, delegitimised rule by 'superior' over 'inferior' on grounds of the 'standard of civilisation'. It opened the way to mass decolonisation on the basis of a transcendent right of self-determination that trumped all arguments about unreadiness for self-government in the modern world (Bain, 2003: 134–5). Holsti (2004: 128–30) charts the consequent shift in criteria for recognition from the strict rules of the 'standard of civilisation' during the nineteenth century, through to the 'almost anything goes' attitude during the post-1945 decolonisation. Decolonisation massively and quickly expanded the membership of global society beyond a small group of modern, mainly Western states and Japan, plus the Latin American countries decolonised earlier in the nineteenth century. Global society quickly came to include almost all polities and peoples at whatever level of development they might be, and however ready, or not, they were for self-government under the demanding and intrusive conditions of an intensifying modern globalisation. In many cases these new states were arbitrarily packaged into the territorial boundaries drawn by the colonial powers for their own purposes. This was done mostly without regard to local patterns of culture, ethnicity and geography, which stored up serious problems for these new states in making nationalism the foundation of their political legitimacy. Decolonisation meant recognition as a sovereign equal, and thus entry into global society. It shifted the cultural foundations of global society away from the West, leading to the worry for the first generation of English School scholars about whether international society was sustainable without a shared cultural core to underpin its values (Buzan, 2014: 67–70; Hall, 2017).

The association of modern sovereignty with the principle of non-intervention in the domestic affairs of other states recognised as sovereign, was much strengthened after 1945 by the political dynamics of decolonisation and anti-colonialism (Holsti, 2004: 131–4). The countries of what was then called the Third World were keen to defend their new status, and to make the most of the political opportunities it offered. Sovereign equality was a powerful weapon against both (neo)colonialism and racism. But the rapid collapse of divided sovereignty generated its own legacy of problems. While the norm and practice of juridical sovereignty remained very strong after decolonisation, some of the new states were too weak and fragile to exercise empirical sovereignty effectively, making them vulnerable to intervention. Like Italy a century before, they had a state, but had to make a nation, or at least a coherent civic demos, to fit with it. While the right of non-intervention was much observed in rhetoric, it was less observed in practice. During the Cold War, the superpower ideological competition provided the initial justifications for interventions into the Third World. Later, after 1989, neoliberalism and human rights formed a new 'standard of civilisation' (Gong, 1984: 90–3; Donnelly, 1998; Fidler, 2000; Jackson, 2000: 287–93; Gong, 2002; Keene, 2002: 122–3, 147–8; Clark, 2007: 183; Bowden, 2009: locs. 2289–322, 2398–448). These new standards could be used to justify interventions, for example on humanitarian grounds, or conditionalities, for example about property rights and financial practices, in terms of the right of entry into various international clubs. Although divided sovereignty was formally gone, a long shadow of it remained in practice.

After the Cold War was over, a seemingly even bigger threat to sovereignty emerged during the 1990s. Globalisation was not just about some having more sovereignty than others, but about whether sovereignty was sustainable at all as an institution of global society. As already discussed above, globalisation was a threat to territoriality (deterritorialisation), and much the same argument applies here. Globalisation, with its combination of ever-rising interaction capacity moving ever-more people, goods, money and information around the planet, and backed by market ideology, appeared to threaten the entire trilogy of institutions that underpinned the modern state. Territoriality was threatened by the global market and the power of transnational firms. Nationalism and other localised patterns of collective identity were threatened by migration and cosmopolitanism. And sovereignty was threatened by the apparent movement of effective decision-making power upward to various international regimes and IGOs, and downward to a host of transnational actors from terrorists, through lobbyists, to corporations (Zürn, 2010).

But whether globalisation was actually the threat to sovereignty it seemed to be is a difficult question. Manning (1962: 167–8), though writing well before globalisation became a fashionable topic, was emphatic on this point: 'What is essentially a system of law *for* sovereigns, being premised on their very sovereignty, does not, by the fact of being strengthened, put in jeopardy the sovereignties which are the dogmatic basis for its very existence. Not, at any rate, in logic.' In other words, states could decide whether they wanted to constrain their freedom of action by entering into legal agreements about trade, the environment, arms control, etc., and that itself would be an exercise of their sovereignty. The catch, however, lies in Manning's final two words: 'in logic'. Anti-globalisation politics did not stem so much from the logic of sovereignty, as from the consequences of globalisation for jobs, the ability of governments to shape the destinies of their states and peoples, the environment and the maintenance of national identities. It was these dialectics that from the 1990s onwards, and particularly after the 2008 crisis and the votes for Brexit and Trump in 2016, led even in the heartlands of liberalism to a surge in economic and social nationalism, and sovereigntism. At the time of writing, such trends seemed to point towards a future of *deep pluralism* (on which more in Part III) in global society. Everyone began to use variations of the long-standing American sovereigntist arguments that the integrity and legitimacy of national democratic politics must not be compromised by ceding control over policy areas to international bodies or binding treaties. This ambivalence has been visible in the US since its decisions to stand aside from the Concert of Europe, and reject membership of the League of Nations. It resurfaced most recently with Trump's multiple attacks on regimes and IGOs (Buzan and Cox, 2022).

Although at first glance, sovereignty might appear to be another primary institution in flux within the transition to modernity, in fact its core meaning has remained pretty constant. Recall the definition given at the opening of this subsection: Modern sovereignty is the claim that a given collectivity of people has the right to self-government, and cannot be bound by rules or laws to which they have not given explicit consent. Up until 1945, this principle was applied only among the 'civilised' group of powers within the core, with divided sovereignty for the rest. After 1945, it was opened up to all states. But this move created a disjuncture for many between being awarded, or winning, juridical sovereignty, yet not having the requisite capacity to exercise empirical sovereignty to anything like the extent of the core states. Many of the new states were weak both in having low socio-political cohesion (Buzan, 2007 [1991]: 92–100), and in being unable to extract much wealth and power from modernity. Sassoon (2019: 158–68) tellingly uses (in)ability to tax as a metric for the strength/weakness of states. That, plus a degree of hypocrisy and cynicism among the core states, led to erosion of both the non-intervention corollary, and the notion of equality. Both of these derogations were supported by the idea of great power management, which gave great powers special rights and responsibilities within global society, on which more in Chapter 5b.

Yet at the time of writing, sovereignty was looking more robust. The seemingly existential challenge from economic globalisation had been driven back, and the spread of development was reducing the problem of weak empirical sovereignty, albeit far from everywhere. The key challenge was those other aspects of globalisation, such as global pandemics and climate change, which posed planetary-scale shared fates unsolvable on the scale of states, even of superpowers. The story of modern sovereignty still seemed to be in transition. On the one hand, it was consolidating more evenly around the planet from its very lopsided start during the nineteenth century. On the other hand, it still faced existential questions about its viability as a political framing for a modernity whose underlying thrust has been towards intensification of globalisation across a wide spectrum.

In terms of how it is positioned within the three domains, sovereignty necessarily has its main roots in the interstate domain because of its close association with the constitution of the political sector. In many ways, modern sovereignty is, as discussed further below, the key to some other primary institutions. Sovereignty defined not only a new form of international politics, different from that generated by empire and monarchy/ dynasticism, but also the modern forms of diplomacy and international law. IGOs do not threaten sovereignty, but in contrast are mainly structured around it, and enact and reproduce the institution in their daily work. As Holsti (2004: 135–42) argues, the basic constitutive functions of sovereignty that underpin the state, international law and international society have remained robust despite changes in the relative autonomy or autarchy of states. Sovereignty would not be compromised unless states eliminated themselves as the dominant political unit. So far this has not happened, and it does not look like happening any time soon.

Yet although clear in principle, the standing of sovereignty is still under question within the interstate domain. The market does not, as often thought, undermine sovereignty, because in line with Manning's argument above, it is an exercise of it. Indeed, as will be made clear in Chapter 5b, a global market requires strong global governance by states. Within the trilogy of state-constituting primary institutions, the market mainly undermines territoriality, and in some ways (e.g. migration) nationalism. But human rights does pose a complex challenge to sovereignty, and particularly to its corollary of non-intervention, by a supposedly 'universal' value. If sovereignty is mainly understood as juridical, then it is largely given by international society in the form of diplomatic recognition and acceptance as a rightful member. In that case, juridical sovereignty is in its essence a conditional right. To the extent that international society embraces human rights as a form of state-centric solidarism,[21] there can thus be legitimate erosion of the right of non-intervention on those grounds, without such erosion affecting the institution of sovereignty itself, at least in its juridical aspects. But there are sharp differences of opinion within global society as to whether intervention on human rights grounds is legitimate or not. Ralph (2005), for example, uses the case of US opposition to the International Criminal Court to explore the ongoing tension between sovereignty in the context of international society, and individual rights rooted more in world society.

In the transnational domain, commercial actors, as in the CAPE era, partly operate within the interstate domain, and in that sense accept the framework of state sovereignty and help to reproduce the institution. But as discussed above, more so than in the CAPE era, modern commercial forms of organisation also challenge sovereignty, and at least in theory, could be an alternative form of global order. Many transnational firms now have the wealth and power to negotiate with states from a position of considerable strength (Stopford and Strange, 1991). The same is true for the many INGOs that have tailored themselves to an advocacy role that

---

[21] See Buzan (2014: 114–20) on this concept.

makes them supporting actors in the politics of sovereignty. Some, however, and most notoriously amongst uncivil global society actors such as Al Qaeda and Islamic State, put themselves outside the society of sovereign states, and act in opposition to it. There are perhaps echoes here of that aspect of Islam noted in Chapter 3, that the religion covered many aspects of governance, and therefore had less commitment to political structures than was the case in Europe and China (Buzan and Acharya, 2022: ch. 5). Sovereignty's position in the transnational domain is thus mixed, partly accepting and conforming, and partly oppositional.

In the interhuman domain, sovereignty has put down roots as part of the package of institutions that define the state. Just as dynastic sovereigns sometimes sought legitimacy amongst their subjects, so the modern package of sovereignty territoriality and nationalism has come to play a substantial role in the patterns of collective identity. Identity as a nation is partly a historical legacy, a natural outcome of human diversity. But partly it is also a social construction pushed into society by the modern state using education, common language and conscription, to support its own legitimacy (Weber, 1976). Nationalism is the main mover here, but nobody who listened to the years of debate around Brexit could be in any doubt that sovereignty and territoriality were a strong part of the mix of identity issues seen to be at stake. When sovereignty becomes popular, it becomes part of the identity of the citizens. In addition, as argued above, there is a strong link between the principle of human equality and that of sovereign equality.

The robustness of the package of sovereignty, territoriality and nationalism that comprise the modern state, is indicated by the central role it plays as a facilitating condition for what can and cannot easily be securitised (Buzan, Wæver and de Wilde, 1998). When dynasticism was in play as the legitimate form of government, as was the case in Europe and elsewhere until the nineteenth century, then, as the many 'wars of succession' suggest, it was easy to securitise royal genealogy. When dynasticism is not the gold standard for good government, as now, securitising genealogy in global society is difficult. But for the modern state, as the very term 'national security' suggests, it is pretty obvious that its trilogy of constitutive institutions has an enormous influence on what can be easily securitised. References to sovereignty, the right of non-intervention, territorial integrity, and the right to distinctive cultural and political practices are the everyday staple of securitisation rhetoric. This is very obvious in places like China and Russia that do not conform to the liberal values of the West. But democracies such as the US and India are also sovereigntist to a fault, as are many weaker states and powers that seek to use sovereign equality and non-intervention as a way of defending themselves against cultural, political and economic intrusions. As noted above, one significant consequence of the shift from dynasticism to nationalism was the sacralisation of territory. The continued force of this in the processes of securitisation can be seen in East Asia where China, Japan, Vietnam and the Philippines are currently replaying this game in their ongoing disputes over a variety of small reefs and islands in the East and South China Seas.

Diplomacy

The transition towards modernity challenged and changed the institution of diplomacy in several important ways, but there were also some carry-overs from the late CAPE era developments in Europe. The practices of resident ambassadors and extraterritoriality, for example, were continued, as were the trends towards more professionalism (much enhanced in the nineteenth century; Holsti, 2004: 179–98), and formalised foreign ministries as part of government. A general shift towards focusing on the priorities of great powers, and the balance of power as defining *raison de système*, also continued (more on these in Chapter 5b) (Holsti, 1991: 25–113).

But beyond these continuities there were many substantial changes. The replacement of monarchy/dynasticism by nationalism in the package of primary institutions defining the state was largely completed by the First World War, though only for the core states. It had big implications for the aims and purposes of diplomacy. Reus-Smit (1999: 87–121) charts the nineteenth-century shift from a diplomacy based primarily on monarchical/dynastic interests and concerns, to a modern form of multilateralism reflecting the interests and concerns of the rational, national, bureaucratic state where sovereignty was vested in the people rather than the prince. Right from the beginning, with the republican challenge to monarchy/dynasticism in the US and France, one consequence of this shift was to infect diplomacy with the pressures of ideological competition that had not been present when monarchy/dynasticism was the ruling principle. Der Derian (1992) labels the twentieth-century version of this 'antidiplomacy', the propagandist, coercive and self-promoting behaviours designed to '*dis*order international society' (Hall, 2006: 160). 'Antidiplomacy' might be seen either as a weakening, or as a shift of emphasis, in the functions of diplomacy. The characteristics and consequences of modernity impacted on diplomacy in several other quite complicated and often interlinked basic ways.

First, increases in the speed and safety of transportation and communication steadily reduced the isolation of diplomats in time and space from their governments. It made foreign ministries better informed about world affairs independently of their diplomats, and increased the possibilities for greater central control over, and erosion of, the discretionary powers of diplomats. Whereas Lord McCartney's delegation was on its own when negotiating with the Qing emperor in 1793–4, by the middle of the nineteenth century the telegraph network was spreading worldwide, followed in the twentieth by telephone and radio, and in the twenty-first century by the Internet. Improving physical interaction capacity made it easier and quicker for government ministers and heads of state to talk or meet directly, not just centralising diplomacy, but also in some ways bypassing diplomats. State leaders could talk directly to each other, and so could representatives of lower tiers of government from different states. This kind of development has gone furthest within the EU, where diplomacy in its traditional sense no longer really describes the process of governance within the grouping, and embassies and ambassadors are of decreasing relevance (Holsti, 2004: 206–10). That said, the EU itself has become a diplomatic player. The centralising of diplomacy, and the bypassing of diplomats, were underlined recently by the Trump administration in the US, which put Trump himself at the centre of negotiations, and ran down the State Department.

Second, and substantially as a result of the dramatic increase in physical interaction capacity, the range of issues to be dealt with by diplomacy also widened. Although the traditional central focus on war and peace remained robust throughout the nineteenth and twentieth centuries, on top of it was added an ever-wider agenda of economic management (trade and finance), interoperability of communication and transportation systems (rivers, canals, railways, sea lanes, telegraph lines, air routes, broadcast wavelengths, satellite orbits, etc.), development (aid, loans, conditionality), environmental concerns (greenhouse gases, pollution control, biosphere management), migration (asylum seekers, economic migrants), cultural issues (human rights, common heritage of humankind), etc. Many of these issues were intrinsically ill-suited to resolution by force, so this widening agenda expanded diplomacy's function beyond being 'an alternative to mere reliance on force', towards being a wider set of more managerial functions.

Third, alongside, and associated with, this widening agenda, was an expanding number and type of actors involved in diplomacy, and a consequent increase in the volume of diplomatic interactions throughout global society. The transition towards modernity steadily brought an increasing proportion of the population into political life whether as trade unionists, voters, members of political parties, lobbyists, activists, etc. Engagement of the masses in political life necessarily had spill-overs into diplomacy, as such movements connected themselves transnationally and internationally in order to further their interests, in part by lobbying the states-system. The anti-slavery movement was an early example, and by the later nineteenth century, trade unionists, women, peace movements, sports bodies, corporate interests and many other INGOs were in play within global society (Buzan and Lawson, 2015: 89–91, 93–5). Although states remained the dominant players, and sovereignty and territoriality the framing institutions, diplomacy was incorporating an ever-wider circle of actors.

During the interwar years, public opinion in the West became a significant factor when 'secret diplomacy' was identified as one of the causes of the First World War, and states were pressured to make diplomacy a more open practice (which traditionalists thought would destroy much of its effectiveness). Popular sovereignty, especially where expressed as democracy, gave rise to an increasingly expressive and well-organised global civil society. This, in turn, generated INGOs, both as advocacy groups and as participants in diplomatic conferences and IGOs (Clark, 1995: 508–9; 2007; Holsti, 2004: 198–205; Hurrell, 2007: 99–104). After the First World War, INGOs were admitted to a variety of IGOs (most obviously the International Labour Organisation). As noted, firms have increasingly become players in diplomacy, in some ways marking a post-mercantilist return to CAPE practices of diplomacy between monarchs and merchants. The contemporary world has around 25,000 INGOs, the vast majority of which have been formed since 1970 (Mazower, 2012: 417; Davies, 2013: 6, 19).

Fourth, diplomacy added a growing layer of multilateralism to its largely bilateral tradition, and multilateralism can be considered as the distinctively modern feature of diplomacy (Neumann, 2020: 46–8). There were already some harbingers for this in the CAPE era, most notably the European practice of convening major international conferences after big wars in pursuit of *raison de système*. This specific tradition of post-conflict conferences carried on after 1648 at Utrecht (1714), Vienna (1815), Versailles (1919) and San Francisco (1945), but seems to have been broken at the end of the first cold war in 1989. In the absence of great power world wars, and the presence of standing IGOs, it seems probable that this specific tradition has ended as a way of handling power transitions in GIS, though multilateralism itself has become an ever-more central feature of diplomacy. From the early nineteenth century, the great powers added to this tradition the practice of meeting periodically to consider the management of international order, the so-called Concert of Europe. Having no permanent structure, this was not an IGO in the modern sense, but something more like an ad hoc committee of great powers. One example of its operation was the Berlin Conference of 1884, which met to consider and resolve the problem of how to divide up Africa amongst the colonial powers without disturbing the balance of power among them. The Hague Conferences of 1899 and 1907 to discuss arms control might also be counted under great power management. They were notable for allowing the participation of civil society interest groups, founding the Permanent Court of Arbitration as a dispute settlement mechanism, and paving the way for the Permanent Court of International Justice (PCIJ) that was part of the Versailles Treaties in 1919.

By the last quarter of the nineteenth century, another layer was added to the practices of multilateral diplomacy in the form of standing IGOs (Buzan and Lawson, 2015: 88–9, 92–3). As discussed in the section on interaction capacity in Chapter 4, these were initially formed in response to the widening agenda of issues generated by modernity, and the need to coordinate the increasingly dense and complex functions arising from the expansion of interaction capacity. It could also be linked to the rise of the market and the undoing of mercantilism during the nineteenth century, and the quantity of goods, money, information and people moving around the planet ever-more quickly. Specific functionalism was the character of most of the early IGOs discussed above. By 1913, there were forty-five IGOs (Wallace and Singer, 1970: 250–1), a modest start, but establishing the foundations for the more ambitious developments that followed the First World War. The founding of the League of Nations in 1919 was thus not the start of something new, but the culmination of IGOs as a development in multilateral diplomacy that had been underway for more than half a century (Reus-Smit, 1999: 145–9). What was distinctive about the League was its standing as a general forum, aiming at universal membership, to manage the political and economic affairs of global society. The practice of having a universal political forum IGO with a family of specialist functional agencies around it has continued ever since, being embodied in the United Nations system after 1945. Decolonisation, and the expansion of sovereign equality, gave a boost to IGOs. Many Third World states were unable to afford individual diplomatic representation in 200 countries, and needed a centralised forum in which to conduct most of their diplomacy (Buzan and Little, 2000: 316–18). Perhaps one of the signature accomplishments of the period of US primacy in global society was the embedding of IGOs, INGOs, and multilateralism generally, as the main way of doing diplomatic business. As Hurrell (2007: 96–9) argues, the huge proliferation of functional IGOs and international conferences has not only created new actors and new nodes of communication, but has also created a structure of global governance that has taken on a life of its own alongside interstate diplomacy. Quite how to assess where these developments leave diplomacy as a primary institution now, is a matter of controversy. For those who see diplomacy as a strictly state-to-state affair, it might be seen as weakening because of what Hall (2006: 160–1) calls 'the erosion of "diplomatic culture"'. For those who take a broader view, the practice of diplomacy is flourishing, albeit not in its traditional forms. Indeed, to see diplomacy as strictly the business of states might itself misrepresent its history, putting too much emphasis on the mercantilist period in Europe. In a long view, diplomacy has always involved non-state actors such as merchants and religious officials. Diplomacy in this wider sense does not seem under threat: Davos culture and its imitators are flourishing. But within that, multilateralism as the normal practice does seem to be in some difficulty. From the late 1990s, it came under hard questioning as Washington adopted more unilateralist attitudes and practices. This turn became much more extreme under Trump, who turned the US directly against many of the regimes and IGOs, and indeed the principle of multilateralism itself, that the US had been the prime mover in creating for much of the twentieth century. The evening-out of wealth, power and cultural authority that became visible early in the twenty-first century could well force multilateralism into a more pluralist form as the old Western order gives way to deep pluralism. So too could a rollback of economic globalisation if economic nationalism continues its current comeback.

Jackson's (2000) defence of 'statecraft' as having a central role in preserving order might be true as global society swings back to a more pluralist form. But diplomacy more broadly may not depend on states being the dominant unit. Something very like diplomacy would be necessary even for what Buzan and Little (2000: 349–68) called 'a postmodern international system' composed of states, non-state actors of various kinds, and people as independent holders of rights. The development of diplomacy during the first two centuries of modernity feels very much as if it is broadly headed in this direction. It is less about negotiating order amongst states, though that still remains important, and increasingly about negotiating the social order across the three domains of global society.

In the CAPE era, diplomacy had its main roots in the interpolity domain, a significant secondary root in the transnational domain, and not much play in the interhuman domain. Under modernity, the roots in the interstate domain remain strong, albeit altered in character. In the transnational domain, they have become both relatively and absolutely more significant, and there are now at least some connections to the interhuman domain. The interstate domain remains the main base for diplomacy, and sovereignty and territoriality are still the key institutional framings for it. The rise of IGOs under modernity provides both a new forum, and an extended cast of characters, for diplomacy. But even to the extent that some IGOs gain a degree of autonomy, they remain tightly bound to the interstate domain (Buzan and Little, 2000: 266–7, 290–1). But the practice of diplomacy is growing away from just state-to-state. The tradition of negotiating with merchants has revived and expanded, and the involvement of a whole swathe of non-state actors from global civil society is a new development.

This involvement not just of firms, but of many INGOs bringing advocacy, expertise, conflict resolution and resources into diplomacy has changed its meaning and practice. Diplomacy does not now have to involve states at all, though it often still does, both between and among states, and between states and non-state actors. But it might also be among multinational non-state actors of various kinds from firms to sporting bodies to terrorist and criminal organisations. In the interhuman domain, the shift to popular sovereignty opened up more room for play. During the CAPE era, the people were largely excluded from diplomacy, and it had little or no impact on collective identity. It still continues to be true that most people remain remote from the concerns of diplomacy, which has little direct relevance to patterns of collective identity. But with the shift to popular sovereignty, public opinion became a factor in the conduct of diplomacy, putting constant pressure on secrecy, and changing how states related to each through diplomacy. There was also scope within the framework of modern diplomacy for private individuals to play a role. Recent examples would include: Greta Thunberg, Klaus Schwab, David Attenborough, Fethullah Gülen, Bob Geldof, Bill Gates and Carl Sagan. Older ones include: Mahatma Gandhi, Rabindranath Tagore and W. E. B. Du Bois.

International Law

As discussed in Chapter 3, the CAPE era had law-like practices and institutions throughout, but these did not fit the modern understanding of international law. Only towards the end of the CAPE era, in Europe, did a system of international law for sovereign equals develop. As noted in Chapter 1, this late-CAPE legal thinking has been an important influence on the English School's development of the concept of international society, especially through the work of Grotius (Bull et al., 1990; Keene, 2002). The transition towards the modern era built on this late-CAPE legacy, the main departure being an increasing move towards giving positive law among sovereign and legal equals pride of place (Holsti, 2004: 118–28, 146–50). Modern international law is overwhelmingly of the positive type framed by sovereign equality. It is this form that under- lies the link between international law and international society, as for example in Wight's (1979: 107) statement that: 'The most essential evidence for the existence of an international society is the existence of international law.' If positive international law existed, as it palpably did by the later nineteenth century, then there must be an international society to have made it (Schmidt, 1998: 124).

The expansion of positive international law was driven, among other things, by the increasing global influence of market ideology combined with the explosive growth of interaction flows of all kinds across inter- national society consequent on the nineteenth-century material revolu- tions of modernity. Darwin (2020) nicely labels this 'steam globalisation', though as with earlier breakthroughs such as rideable horses, from the point of view of many agrarian civilisations it came with barbarians in the saddle. Intrinsic to all this was a major expansion in functional regimes to regulate and coordinate the new global infrastruc- tures of rail, steamship, post, telegraph and radio, as well as the expanding activities of international trade, investment and finance, and the rights of European citizens abroad (Armstrong, 2006: 129–33). If states still wanted to go to war, they certainly could. But if they wanted to pursue commerce and peace, then an ever-denser sphere of positive international laws governing commerce, transportation, communica- tions, and even up to a point, armaments, helped to coordinate interstate behaviour (Davies, 2013; Koskenniemi, 2001). The rise of positive inter- national law during the nineteenth century was also an expression of divided sovereignty and colonialism. It reflected the increasing domin- ance of Europe, for positive law was initially European law. The inclin- ation within the natural law tradition to treat (most) non-Europeans as equals was replaced by an association of positive law with the hierarchy provided by the 'standard of civilisation' (Gong, 1984: 5–32). This made the acquisition of international law a priority for powers that were weak at the time, such as the US, Japan and China, and explains the popularity in those places of Wheaton's (1866) famous text on the subject. It was only 'civilised' states that made and practised international law. Only when decolonisation made sovereignty more or less universal, did international law become subject to the logic of sovereign equality and the right of consent.

The widening and deepening of positive international law continued apace during the twentieth and twenty-first centuries, covering a range of issues from law of the sea and space law, through human rights, to the environment. Yet even while international law became a properly universal, and expanding, primary institution of global society, it continued to attract criticism for still being the law made by the old colonial core. This criticism was strengthened by what might be thought of as a partial return to natural law when, particularly after the end of the first cold war, leading Western powers began to push the idea of human rights as a universal principle into international law (Zhang and Buzan, 2019). When viewed as universal, human rights quickly generated claims for universal jurisdiction that overrode the sovereign rights of states both to the principle of non-intervention, and to consent, or not, to be bound by such laws (Holsti, 2004: 156–61). Concepts such as the 'right to protect' could be used to justify intervention into states seen as violating human rights even if those states did not consent, a development long ago foreseen, and opposed, by Hedley Bull (1977: 127–61).

The extension of international law in a cosmopolitan direction to take in non-state actors and individuals would be a marker for a development beyond interstate society towards global society. Armstrong (1999) reviews the case for and against seeing international law as still predominantly state-based or moving towards being a world law for a world society of people. He concludes that international law is still state-based rather than cosmopolitan, but its content has been driven into a more solidarist direction by the changing nature of the leading powers, and their commercial and moral interests. Since Armstrong wrote, the heyday of unilateral liberal universalism that marked the 1990s is long past, and the rise of China, along with the durability of other authoritarian regimes, has curtailed the cosmopolitan project on human rights. This is not, however, the end of the matter. The growing concern about the sustainability or not of a habitable environment on the planet involves a different route towards overriding the principle of non-intervention. Partly this is about the right to intervene in cases of gross threats to the ecosystem, and partly it is about the rights of future generations of humans to inherit a liveable planet. But for the time being, positive international law with a right of consent remains the core of the primary institution. The extent to which the coverage of that law shrinks or grows will depend on the extent to which a politically and culturally diverse set of great powers will wish to coordinate their responses to shared threats or not (Acharya and Buzan, 2019: 261–84).

In terms of its placement in the three domains, international law remains predominantly interstate, but also important as a framing for many of the players in the transnational domain. Its extension to the interhuman domain remains controversial because it cannot avoid contradicting the rights associated with state sovereignty, which is still the key ordering principle for the interstate domain. There are nevertheless significant and durable pressures to find ways of moving it in that direction, not least the right to a liveable environment, and it is not impossible that at some point this might be done by consent.

Trade

Like human equality/inequality, trade is a somewhat awkward institution to place cleanly in this sequence. I flag it here under CAPE institutions that carried forward into modernity albeit with changes and adaptations. This is clearly the case for trade as such. The main discussion, however, is located in the next chapter under the heading of market versus economic nationalism. During the transition towards modernity, trade gets transformed into a fully blown global economy, and the character of the primary institution defining the economy gets transformed beyond recognition as mere trade among polities, also involving investment, production, finance and labour organised on a global scale. Under these circumstances, the institution shifts from a single activity, to the principles that define the structure of the new global economy.

5b   Social Structure II
Institutions New with the Transition

This chapter examines the group of primary institutions that had no standing during the conglomerate agrarian/pastoralist empires (CAPE) era, but which came into being during the transition to modernity. These coalesced from the nineteenth century onwards, though a few of them were already emergent in Europe during the eighteenth century, right at the end of the CAPE era. Most of them crystallised during the nineteenth century (balance of power, great power management, nationalism, market versus economic nationalism, science and sport). Two crystallised after the Second World War (human equality and development), and one only late in the twentieth century (environmental stewardship).

Balance of Power

Like modern international law and modern diplomacy, and alongside sovereign equality, the balance of power as a primary institution of global society emerged first in Europe right at the end of the CAPE era. Otherwise, there was no institution of this kind elsewhere before modernity. Almost all empires, especially those with universal aspirations, sought hegemony, although they might agree to temporary truces. The aspiration to universal empire was therefore the opposite of the balance of power, aiming to achieve peace and stability by imposing and maintaining a universal hierarchical order. This way of thinking still echoes in the recurrent idea in the US (e.g. Reagan and the 'Star Wars' project), that if only it could recapture the absolute military superiority it held fleetingly after 1945, that would be the path to world peace. Many in the US and Asia now fear that China is thinking along the same lines about resurrecting the Middle Kingdom. That said, of course, there can be no doubt that during the CAPE era, many polities saw threats rising around them, and took 'balancing' measures to strengthen themselves by finding allies and/or building up their own forces. There is plenty of evidence for that in the well-known stories of the Peloponnesian Wars told by Thucydides, and of the Punic Wars told by Polybius. But individual balancing behaviour by polities, whatever its mechanical predictability might be (or might not, see: Kaufman, Little and Wohlforth, 2007), does not constitute balance of power as an institution of interpolity society. It is just a predictive hypothesis about individual state behaviour set up by realists. Little (2007: 66–7; see also Bull, 1977: 104–6) usefully calls this form of individual balancing *adversarial*, contrasting it with balance as a principle of international order agreed by states, which he labels *associational*.

Associational balancing might be seen as an attempt to systematise and make more efficient, the individual adversarial balancing practices of states. Once established, fear of falling back into the costs and risks of adversarial balancing helps to sustain associational balancing as an institution. A more cynical view would be that associational balancing is no more than a temporary response to war fatigue, as after 1815, with it being just a matter of time before adversarial balancing reasserts itself. The underlying motive for both forms of balance of power is anti-hegemonic, and a preference to maintain an international society of political multiplicity and sovereign equality. As the eighteenth-century jurist Vattel put it, no one power should be in a position to lay down the law to the others (Bull, 1977: 101). Anti-hegemonism/balance of power as an institution in this sense fits closely with sovereign equality, modern international law and modern diplomacy. It might even be thought of as a necessary condition for the development of an interstate society of sovereign equals that wishes to pursue a degree of international order without submitting to the hegemony of any one great power (Bull, 1977: 106–7; Hurrell, 2007: 32, 51; Clark, 2009a: 203–5, 220–3).

Watson (1992: 181) argues that balance of power was preceded in premodern Europe by the idea of anti-hegemonism, especially against the Habsburgs. Somewhat later, after the Treaty of Utrecht (1713), the balance of power as an agreed ordering principle amongst the great powers began conspicuously to challenge dynastic principles as a key institution for regulating relations among states (Bull, 1977: 101–6; Holsti, 1991: 71–89; Watson, 1992: 198–213; Clark, 2005: 71–84; Keene, 2013). The balance of power principle was then enshrined in the Treaty of Vienna (1815) (Reus-Smit, 1999: 134–40; Simpson, 2004: 96–7). The Concert of Europe, mentioned above as a development towards multilateral diplomacy, became the archetypal embodiment of associational balance of power. As Little (2006: 113–15) observes, by the nineteenth century, colonial acquisitions were feeding back into the European balance of power, which explains the Concert's 1884 Berlin Conference to divide up Africa in such a way as to maintain the balance of power among the core European states.

Associational balancing constituted a strong primary institution during most of the nineteenth century in Europe. In 1902, Japan joined in, but the US stayed aloof until 1917. By the late nineteenth century, the institution of associational balancing was weakening, while adversarial balancing, reinforced by strong nationalism and social Darwinism, paved the way towards the First World War. The idea of associational balancing was embodied in the League of Nations' aspiration to provide collective security. But the US once again stayed aloof, and associational balancing had only a weak and short-lived revival before crashing into the harsh adversarial balancing of the 1930s. Hope for reconstruction of an associational balance after the Second World War through the UN was quickly dashed by the onset of the first cold war, and a prolonged round of adversarial balancing between the two superpowers. A dialectic between hegemonic aspirations and anti-hegemonic responses, remained the driving motive throughout, and there was not much sense of associational balancing except in relation to the pursuit of arms control agreements to reduce the risk of war between the US and the Soviet Union. There were perhaps elements of associational balancing within the West in such secondary institutions as the EU and NATO, but adversarial balancing against the Soviet bloc was the main game, becoming three-sided after the Sino–Soviet split.

After 1945, the appearance of nuclear weapons made a substantial difference to the operation of the balance of power by adding to it the balance of terror (Bull, 1977: 117–26). In the numbers that were being accumulated during the 1960s and 1970s, nuclear weapons raised the possibility of species suicide for the first time. This existential threat amplified the *defence dilemma* which was succinctly captured in the opposed Western slogans: 'better red than dead' versus 'better dead than red'. Adversarial balancing was about keeping strong enough to avoid defeat. Associational balancing in the nuclear age was about managing both the distribution of power, and the technological characteristics of the means of destruction (arms control), in a fair enough way to adjust to changes without creating opportunities for hegemony or incentives to strike first. To the extent that the threat of going to war was an important element in the balance of power, the need to avoid war by maintaining deterrence was a problem. Deterrence required credible threats of war. Also problematic was the ability that nuclear weapons gave to even quite small states to deter much more powerful ones if they had nuclear weapons (Smith, 2006). All of this, however, was mainly relevant to adversarial balancing, which dominated the first cold war. Associational balancing was at best weakly in the background. It was implicit in détente and arms control if the superpowers were serious about learning to coexist. But it was little more than a cover if they were really engaged in a zero-sum game to purge the other out of the system.

With the end of the first cold war there were two decades of what some thought of as being unipolarity, in which the US was the last remaining superpower.[1] During this period, both adversarial and associational balancing moved into the background. The frenzied adversarial great power balancing predicted by polarity theory under such circumstances did not occur. Indeed, initially the sole superpower hardly attracted any adversarial balancing, and there was not much call for associational balancing. To the extent that balancing was visible at all, it was adversarial, and largely confined to the regional level in the Middle East and South Asia. Global society briefly settled into a hiatus in which American 'unipolarity' did not threaten other powers sufficiently to trigger adversarial balancing. The US lead in military and economic power was too big to challenge easily, and the nature of the US-led order was acceptable enough not to foment major rebellion against it, and not to require associational balancing. For a time, economic globalisation carried enough benefits to lubricate this arrangement. It could thus reasonably be thought during the 1990s and the noughties that perhaps the balance of power had reached the end of its relevance in international relations, apparently succumbing to the onrush of economic globalisation and interdependence that marked these two decades. Nau (2001: 585), for example, argued that 'when national identities converge, as they have recently among the democratic great powers, they may temper and even eliminate the struggle for power'.

But during the second decade of the twenty-first century, this hiatus drew to a close. US power and legitimacy were weakened in several ways: by expensive and largely fruitless foreign wars; by the US-led global financial crisis from 2008; and by the election of Trump in 2016, who pursued a nationalist, populist agenda that quickly burned through much of America's global social capital, and alienated most of its allies. China made rapid strides in wealth and power, and especially from 2012 under Xi Jinping, began openly to challenge the US position in Asia both militarily and economically. Russia re-emerged as a resentful power, and after its first invasion of Ukraine in 2014, challenged the West in various ways, and moved into a strategic partnership with China. Japan, and to a lesser extent Europe, had to start thinking about how to position

[1] In fact, the system was not unipolar in the sense of one superpower and no other powers of consequence. It fell outside the simplicities of polarity theory, being composed of one superpower, several great powers and a variety of regional powers (Buzan, 2004b).

themselves between a rising and increasingly assertive China, and a declining, and increasingly introverted and unreliable US.

Adversarial balancing continued to burn brightly in some regions, most notably the Middle East, but also began to return to the level of the great powers. In Asia particularly, the regional and global levels intersected. China's neighbours were initially inclined to hedge rather than balance, hoping to find a sustainable position between ongoing security reliance on the US and increasing economic ties to China. But as China became more aggressive about asserting its claim to primacy in Asia, not only in the South and East China Seas, but also on the border with India, hedging began to ease towards adversarial balancing. One indicator of this movement was the strengthening of the 'Quad' grouping of democracies: India, Japan, Australia, US. Although at the time of writing it is too early to say for sure, China's ruthless suppression of the democracy movement in Hong Kong during 2020, with its powerful symbolism of a showdown between authoritarianism and democracy, looks like a good candidate as the benchmark date to mark the opening of the second cold war between China (and Russia), on the one hand, and the West, Japan, India and others feeling threatened by China, on the other hand. In Europe, Russia's second invasion of Ukraine in 2022 seems, at the time of writing, to have triggered adversarial balancing between Russia and EU/NATO. Sweden and Finland, both long-standing neutrals, have moved to join NATO. The military budgets of Europe's major powers are rising. NATO is reinforcing its eastern frontier, and has supplied quantities of aid and advanced weapons to Ukraine to strengthen its resistance to Russia's invasion. In late 2022, it was becoming difficult to tell whether all this was still best seen as a form of robust adversarial balancing, or had tipped over the line into a form of limited war.

By the early 2020s, balancing was back, but only in adversarial form. There was no sign that associational balancing might return as an institution of global society. For that to happen, there would need to be some fairly clear agreement amongst the major powers about their status and their spheres of influence. In the longer-term context of the relative decline of the West, Japan and Russia, and the rise of China, India and others, no such agreement is in obvious prospect. More on that in Chapter 8.

Associational balance of power is almost by definition principally an institution located in the interstate domain. In its adversarial form, in which it is not an institution of global society, as currently between the US and China, and NATO/EU and Russia, it might well engage nationalism in the interhuman domain. But in its associational form, in which it is an institution, it does not put down much in the way of roots into other domains. It might have consequences there, for example, in facilitating or constraining commerce, but it is similar to international law in being a relatively technical institution largely confined to interstate relations. It might be thought that the elevation of non-state actors to a kind of parity with states by the declaration of the global war on terrorism (GWoT) would open up a strong link to the transnational domain. But in practice, there is little or no scope for either adversarial balancing between states and terrorists (because the warfare between them is asymmetric), or associational balancing (because they share no interest in global order). Indeed, taking a long view of balance of power using Little's distinction between adversarial and associational suggests that balance of power as an institution is a relatively rare, and perhaps so far mainly European, phenomenon. This may bring into question its quite prominent role in classical English School (ES) thinking. At the time of writing, the balance of power as an institution of global society was at the very least dormant, and possibly dead. Its brief, if intense, run during the nineteenth and the twentieth centuries begins to look like an exception rather than a rule.

Great Power Management

There are close links between associational balance of power and great power management (GPM). At their foundations, they overlap, because associational balancing is by definition a form of GPM in which the great powers seek to manage their relations in order to reduce the risk of war. In Bull's (1977: 200–29) formulation, great powers not only assume themselves, but are also recognised by others, to have managerial rights and responsibilities for international order (see also: Waltz, 1979: 198; Brown, 2004; Little, 2006). The key to GPM as an institution of global society is that the powers concerned attract legitimacy to support their unequal status as leaders by accepting special responsibilities as well as claiming special rights (Clark, 2009a: 207–20; Bukovansky et al., 2012: 26–7). GPM thus requires some derogations from sovereign equality in order to establish the special rights and responsibilities of great powers (Simpson, 2004).

But within modernity, not only has GPM spread much more widely than mere associational balancing, it has also existed in the absence of associational balancing. This suggests that GPM is the key institution, with associational balancing being one form within it. It might even suggest that elements of GPM existed during the CAPE era. The general aspiration of empires to become universal stood in the way of the more pluralist conceptions of international order required for associational balancing. But agreements over access to religious sites for pilgrimage might not only confirm the status of religion as an institution of global society, but also count as a form of GPM.

Because of these close historical and conceptual links, it is a common-sense hypothesis that when balancing is adversarial, expectations of GPM must be low; and when balancing is associational, the prospects for GPM should be better. Once associational balancing is in place, it provides the foundations for cooperation on other issues, but without it, the rivalries of adversarial balancing would foreclose most or all prospects for any wider cooperation. But does this hypothesis stand up? A case can be made that while this foundational link between associational balancing and GPM can sometimes be the case, we need also to consider whether a functionally based GPM could work in a context of adversarial balancing. For this to happen, two conditions would have to be met: first, global shared threats would have to be big enough to require common action; and second, those threats would have to be sufficiently differentiated from issues that could be mobilised into the adversarial power struggle. Climate change and pandemics are difficult to weaponise for adversarial balancing, but migration (Greenhill, 2010) and nuclear proliferation and cybersecurity are easier to use in that way. In my view, this understanding of GPM working alongside adversarial balancing is becoming increasingly relevant to the contemporary world order.

Up until the Second World War, associational balancing and GPM co-evolved, but after that their paths diverged. Like the balance of power, the logic and legitimacy of great power interests strengthened during the nineteenth century as the dynastic principle weakened. Holsti (1991: 71–82, 114–37) shows how the institution of GPM emerged along with the balance of power during the eighteenth and nineteenth centuries as replacements for a declining dynastic principle. He argues that this practice became much more evident and formalised from the Treaty of Vienna (1815) and the Congress of Europe (see also Wight, 1977: 42, 136–41). Simpson (2004) sees this shift as moving away from the relatively pure and undifferentiated practice of sovereign equality set up at Westphalia, to a quite strong form of 'legalised hegemony' in which great powers saw themselves, and were recognised by others to have, managerial responsibility for international order (see also Watson, 1992: 138–262; Hjorth, 2011: 2591–8). That practice continued into the first half of the twentieth century in the League of Nations after 1919 and the UN Security Council after 1945. Both of these global forums embodied a hybrid structure with sovereign equality recognised in the general assembly of all members, and the legalised hegemony of the great powers in the smaller council. Both tried, but failed, to elevate associational balancing up to the level of collective security. With somewhat more success, both also made some beginnings towards extending GPM into sectors other than military security, such as the economy and public health, and in the case of the UN, human rights.

After 1945, associational balancing and GPM follow increasingly separate paths. As discussed in the previous section, the first cold war was almost entirely about adversarial balancing, with only a smidgeon of associational balancing in relation to arms control. This was when Bull (1980) rightly castigated the two superpowers as 'great irresponsibles' in relation to GPM. Yet within this period, there were rather substantial subglobal developments of GPM amongst the West, Japan and some sections of what was then called the Third World. These took place under quasi-hegemonic, but quite widely accepted, US leadership, particularly in the economic sector. During the 1980s and 1990s, this subsystem of GPM became a progressively more global 'rules-based international order', as China joined in from the late 1970s, and the successor states of the former Soviet Union during the 1990s. As argued in the previous subsection, during the 1990s and the noughties, in the heyday of globalisation, it could be thought that the balance of power was largely irrelevant at the level of great powers, though still active, adversarially, in some regions. It seemed that GPM could nonetheless flourish in a consensually backed hegemonic order led by the US (Clark, 2009a, 2009b, 2011). Post-Cold War, the US was perfectly willing to see itself as the 'indispensable' leader, and to claim privileges for itself on that basis. After 2001 under the Bush administration, it did not seem to care much whether anyone followed its lead or not, and its legitimacy as leader consequently declined (Hurrell, 2002a: 202; 2002c: xxii; 2007b: 262–83; Dunne, 2003; Morris, 2005; Buzan, 2008). After the economic crisis of 2008, US leadership came under increasing question, and the rise of China began to put adversarial balancing back on the table. The Trumpian turn in US politics largely took US GPM leadership out of play, leaving a legacy that at the time of writing remained unclear, except that for others to trust the stability of US leadership over the long term is now considerably more difficult and risky.

The question on the table at the time of writing (2022) is whether or not the US and China are heading for a replay of the Cold War as 'great irresponsibles', or whether they and others can conjure up a version of GPM within a system of adversarial balancing. With the rise of China, India and other non-Western powers, there has been growing interest in the great powers and their roles and responsibilities in international society (Suzuki, 2008; Jones, 2014; Gaskarth, 2015; Lasmar, 2015). I will return to that conjecture in Chapter 8.

At this point, it is helpful to look more closely at the institution of GPM, and how its meaning and practices have expanded during the period of modernity. Cui and Buzan (2016) argue that GPM is not linked to polarity in either material or ideological terms, but can and has taken place in systems that are unipolar, bipolar and multipolar materially and/or ideologically. Their key point, however, is to show how the agenda of GPM has steadily widened, adding more sectors to the foundational one of military security (aka associational balancing), and in so doing, looking more similar to global governance. In other words, under modernity, the *raison de système* confronting the great powers, and therefore the legitimate scope of their special rights and responsibilities, has expanded into additional sectors. One good way to explain and track this is to see international security as the foundational justification for GPM, and then follow how the agenda of international security has itself widened, with many non-military issues coming under the ambit of international security (Buzan, Wæver and de Wilde, 1998; Buzan and Hansen, 2009: 187–225).

Cui and Buzan (2016: 195–203) observe that Bull's (1977: 205–29) original discussion of GPM was firmly rooted in the traditional, military-political security agenda, broadly representative of the Concert of Europe during the nineteenth century, and in weaker form in the League of Nations and UN up to the middle of the twentieth. This strategic aspect of GPM has not gone away. Great powers still need to manage their own rivalries, as well as collective problems within the scope of traditional security such as nuclear proliferation, terrorism, regional conflicts and failed states. Alongside it, however, has grown an agenda of non-traditional security (NTS) that is about a range of functional issues not necessarily, or even usually, linked to political violence. Economic management by great powers goes back to the later decades of the nineteenth century, when Britain promoted the gold standard and free trade. It was also prominent in the decades before Bull wrote in the form of the US-led Bretton Woods system (Buzan and Falkner, 2022, forthcoming). After the experience of the 1930s and 1940s, it was widely accepted that there was a major link between the global economy and the risk of war, summed up in the expression that 'if goods can't cross borders, soldiers will' (Gardner, 1969: 7–10). It might even be argued that from the end of the first cold war through to the noughties, managing the global economy displaced the traditional military/political concerns as the first priority for GPM. Indeed, hegemonic stability theory essentially argued that management of the global economy was best done by a single hegemonic great power, and that such economic management should be part of great power responsibilities (Kindleberger, 1973; Krasner, 1976; Gilpin, 1981, 1987: 72–80; Keohane, 1984). That theory might, of course, also be seen as self-serving propaganda on the part of the only two states to have played the hegemonic role, Britain and the US. In addition, environmental stewardship has come onto the GPM agenda (Reus-Smit, 1996; Falkner and Buzan, 2019), as have human rights/human security, migration, global health and cybersecurity. In parallel with this, the idea of managerial responsibility has widened beyond the great powers to include other actors – smaller powers, IGOs, INGOs – in possession of relevant capabilities (Bukovansky et al., 2012). The question for the future is how GPM will unfold when a return to adversarial balancing is accompanied by the intensification of shared-fate threats? More on this in Chapter 8.

Like balance of power, GPM is almost by definition largely in the interstate domain. To the extent that GPM is merging with global governance because of its widening agenda, there is a growing link to the transnational domain. This development is set out by Bukovansky et al. (2012) in the diffusion of responsibility both to lesser powers and non-state actors. GPM is generally remote from the interhuman domain, though it could be envisaged that a strengthening of the macro-identity of humankind might create such links by supporting a wider understanding of both security and responsibility. That would be a quite radical development in deepening global society.

Nationalism

Like balance of power and GPM, nationalism is a primary institution that emerged right from the beginning as a key element of the transition towards modernity. It was not present during the CAPE era as an institution, though many of its elements such as patriotism, and a sense of national solidarity and sentiment, were emerging in Europe and elsewhere during the last few centuries of the era. Bayly (2004: 64–83, 199–227) argues that nationalism was not just a European development exported from there to the rest of the world, but part of a more widespread economic and political integration taking place throughout Eurasia. The French Revolution is a key landmark in the development of nationalism as an institution, after which it spread quickly throughout Europe and the world. Partly it accompanied unifying, nation-state projects (Germany, Italy, the settler colonies). Partly it was a lever against colonialism (Greece, Hungary, Poland, much of the Afro-Asian periphery), and/or monarchy/dynasticism (the US, the European 'Springtime of Nations' in 1848).

As Buzan and Lawson (2015: 114) define it:

The central idea of nationalism is that the nation should be the basis of the state. The definition of 'nation', and the precise criteria for a group of people to be counted as a nation, are contested. But the basic idea is simple: 'nations', being self-identifying groups sharing some combination of culture, language, ethnicity and history sufficient to produce a strong sense of 'we', should have the right to claim their own polity. Within this logic, ideally all states should be nation-states, with the state becoming the container and protector of its particular national identity.

Nationalism transformed people from being subjects or slaves of their rulers to being citizens of their state, in the process relocating sovereignty from the ruler (*l'état, c'est moi*) to the people (popular sovereignty). It thus shifted the foundations of political legitimacy from the monarchical/ dynastic claims of aristocratic genealogies to the people constituted as a nation (Mayall, 1990: 26–8). There is a significant sense in which nationalism can be seen as a kind of macro-kinship idea, especially where it is based on shared ethnicity and language. This makes it a jump up from explicitly shared, even if mythical, bloodlines such as clan and tribe (Haldén, 2020: 16). This elemental quality of seeming to stretch far back in time is one of the things that give nationalism its potency as an 'imagined community' (Gellner, 1992: 289).[2] The use of kinship metaphors in modern politics applies not only to nationalism, but also to rallying cries to 'brothers' and 'sisters', as in the Muslim Brotherhood. The left's preference for 'comrades' is a noteworthy departure from kinship metaphors.

As already shown in the discussions above, nationalism was hugely influential in shaping the social structure of modernity in how it impacted on other primary institutions. It de-linked monarchy/dynasticism from empire by forcing it to tie its banners to the nation, and quite quickly displaced it as the gold standard of legitimacy for real, as opposed to symbolic, political power in global society. Nationalism itself became perhaps the major factor in differentiating the modern state from its dynastic forebears, with the shift to the people underpinning a rational state that was supposed to be responsible to, and in the service of, its

---

[2] For more debates around the emergence and development of nationalism, see: Anderson, 1983; Gellner, 1983; Hobsbawm, 1990; Smith, 1991, 1998; Breuilly, 1993; Özkirimli, 2010; Buzan and Lawson, 2015: 114–18. There is also the curiosity of 'religious nationalism'. This is not quite the oxymoron it might appear to be at first sight, because religion can also supply the necessary 'we' feeling to back this claim. As discussed in the section on religion above, contemporary religions have entangled themselves with politics in many ways. One of these is by transposing the logic of nationalism – a cultural referent group claiming the right to a state – to religion. The Hindu nationalism of the BJP has some of this quality, as does thinking about an 'Islamic state'.

citizens. It strongly challenged the political role of religion, though it did not displace religion either in politics or in humankind's patterns of collective identity. It strengthened territoriality by sacralising it, but also challenged territoriality by raising the question as to whether the social referent for sovereignty was the nation as a group of people, or a specific territory, or necessarily both in some kind of package. By elevating a certain ethno-historical pattern of identity as the legitimate foundation for the state, nationalism hugely strengthened the ties between the inter-state and interhuman domains. It made nations, and their distinctive languages, ethnicities and cultures, the premier product, and legacy, of human history. It glorified bio-cultural diversity over more homogenis-ing, cosmopolitan, views of a world society of humankind. Jackson (2000: 23) cast this normatively as the desire to preserve and/or cultivate the political and cultural differences and distinctivenesses that are the legacy of human history, seeing cultural diversity, like biodiversity, as desirable in itself. This ideal type (nation state), however, was a poor fit with global reality, which, especially after decolonisation, was much more about states trying to make nations within themselves (state nations) (Buzan, 2007 [1991]: 76–7). The famous remark by the Italian politician Massimo d'Azeglio that '[w]e have made Italy. Now we must make Italians' (Horn, 2013), could also apply to many of the new states that gained sovereignty after 1945.

By either path, nationalism smoothed the way towards human equal-ity, because if nations had equal cultural, legal and political standing, it was easier, and perhaps even necessary, to think that their peoples did too. Somewhat paradoxically therefore, nationalism also smoothed the path towards a shared identity of all humankind, though this cosmopol-itan opening was not nearly as strong as the fragmenting one. By delegi-timising imperialism, and dismantling empires and political dynasticism, nationalism took away the CAPE era's principal tools for achieving political scale (Osterhammel, 2014: 463), and replaced it with an idea almost guaranteed to lead to political and social fragmentation. Replacing monarchy/dynasticism with nationalism was the key to recon-figuring the institutional package of nationalism, sovereignty and terri-toriality that defined the modern state. It thus set up a powerful and ongoing dialectic with a logic of socio-political fragmentation, with a tinge of collective identity as humankind, on the one side, up against the rampant material and economic globalisation that was a signature feature of the transition towards modernity, on the other side.

Although mainly fragmenting on the global scale, nationalism was often integrative on the scale of states themselves. It provided an effective counter to both class and localism, which was crucial in the building of the modern rational state. In relation to class, Hobsbawm (1990: 101–30) argues that nationalism was one of several new forms of social and political consciousness being acquired during the nineteenth century as shared language was consolidated. This development pitched nationalism, which aimed to consolidate the identity of ethno-cultural groups, into contradiction with class, particularly in its socialist internationalism form, which aimed to mobilise a stratified identity on a global scale in pursuit of control over the process of modernity. In this dialectical perspective, nationalism could be seen as the bourgeois answer to class struggle, providing, successfully, a social glue to offset the new and potent class conflicts opened up by industrialism, and identified by Marx and Engels (1969 [1848]). Nationalism was strong enough to contain the cosmopolitan impulses of revolutionary internationalism (Halliday, 1999: 146), most notably in 1914 when appeals to it trumped rival appeals to proletarian solidarity. Nationalism's imagined community bound people together and facilitated the internal mobility required by industrial economies (Gellner, 1983: 137–43). Through national-scale schemes of education, public and military service, and welfare, nationalism facilitated the overcoming of local identities, so increasing the social cohesion of the state through the cultivation of distinctly national cultures. As nationalism took root, people who would not formerly have thought of themselves primarily, or at all, as French, Italian, Spanish, British or German, increasingly began to do so (e.g. Weber, 1976).

Nationalism (a French invention), like football (an English one) quickly conquered Europe, and eventually most of the world, naturalising itself as it went. But along the way, it encountered turbulence and resistance. The US and other Anglo-settler states had difficulty coming to terms with it because during the nineteenth century it was not yet obvious how to distinguish American, Australian or (Anglo-)Canadian identity from British on ethnic, cultural or linguistic grounds (Hobsbawm, 1990: 18–20). Racism played into this too, with most Anglosphere countries being hostile to non-white immigrants even if as part of the empire/Commonwealth they were British subjects. Japan picked up nationalism quickly, and applied it to overcoming the domestic tensions of modernisation much as the European states had done (Jansen, 2000: esp. locs. 5077–185, 5883–6073). It had its own distinctive take: as Murphy (2014: 71–8) puts it, the political aims of the Meiji leadership were to break down feudal loyalties 'replacing them with nationalism and emperor-worship'. It also had articulate and influential thinkers such as Yukichi Fukuzawa (2008 [1875]) advocating nationalism as the key to modernisation. For China, however, this was not initially possible, because its Manchu rulers feared, probably rightly, that Chinese nationalism would become Han nationalism and be directed first against them as alien rulers (Paine, 2003: 32, 205; Cooper, 2015: 490). This blockage was not overcome until the overthrow of the Qing dynasty in 1911 (Hsu, 2012: 506). It contributed significantly to China's 'century of humiliation', and general slowness in coming to terms with modernity (Buzan and Lawson, 2020). Under Mao, China temporarily reverted to class identity, but since then has naturalised nationalism in its own self-understanding. In India, the influential writer and activist Rabindranath Tagore (1918) saw 'race' as India's eternal historic prob-lem, by which he meant how a diversity of peoples and cultures could coexist peacefully together within the Indian subcontinent. In his view, India had addressed this quite successfully with a mixture of cultural and spiritual ideas, including the overarching caste system. This success was, he thought, existentially threatened by materialist Western modernity and its promotion of a homogenous national state. He thus saw nation-alism in its European and Japanese forms as profoundly threatening to India, and indeed the whole of Asia, with its more spiritual civilisations, and advocated Pan-Asian resistance to it. The Islamic world also resisted nationalism, privileging religion over ethnicity in defining its demos.

Although nationalism was part of the trinity of primary institutions defining the modern state, it was not necessarily always a comfortable fit with the other two, particularly territoriality. While, as noted, it sacralised territoriality, it also created numerous well-studied problems where nations and territories did not line up. There was a large disparity between the number of ethnic nations, conceivably several thousand, and the number of states, currently around 200. Some countries such as Russia, Nigeria, India and Indonesia contained dozens or hundreds of ethnic groups. This caused major problems of secessionism and irreden-tism if nationalism was interpreted in an ethnic way. It was a huge problem for many post-colonial states whose boundaries had often been drawn with little or no regard for the cultural geographies they contained or divided. Civic nationalism was a way of trying to address this problem by creating overarching 'national' identities such as British, American, Nigerian and Indian to allow a variety of ethnicities/cultures to coexist as a nation within a given territory. China has tried to go down this road by expanding the concept of 'Chinese' to include the minority peoples as well as the (big) majority Han population. From early on, Chinese reformers were divided about whether to promote a narrow, ethnic, essentially Han version of nationalism, or a wider, more culturalist version that would include Manchus, Tibetans, Mongols, Uighers and other minority peoples within the Qing Empire. This divided view of nationalism had implications for the territorial definition of the country with which it still struggles today (Duara, 1995: locs. 444–656, 866–1092). The CCP promotes an inclusive, multi-ethnic, view of Chinese nationalism (Hsu, 2012: 510), but at the same time it has a homogenising project to turn the Qing empire into a unified and integrated 'Chinese' nation state (Pieke, 2016: locs. 304–23, 2598–762).

Nationalism was enormously destructive and enormously creative at the same time. For better or for worse, from the early nineteenth century it was the great disrupter of the CAPE political order, and the great shaper of the new political order. It tore down empires and built up modern states, while littering the landscape with resultant problems of secession, civil conflict, irredentism and economic inefficiency. Sometimes it either broke up states, when these could not find adequate overarching identities – Czechoslovakia, Yugoslavia, India, Pakistan, Ethiopia, Sudan – or triggered destructive civil wars – Nigeria, Myanmar, Turkey, Philippines, Sri Lanka. Nationalism is part of the problem in the tense and dangerous stand-offs between Taiwan and China, and between the two Koreas. As Chong (2014: 948–9) points out, historically, nationalism in China has been as much or more a dividing force as a unifying one. China has a long record of provincial and local 'nationalist' separatism of which the reunification problem with Taiwan, and the resistance to Chinese rule in Tibet and Xinjiang, are simply the latest instances. It may yet unravel the UK if Northern Ireland rejoins the republic, and/or Scotland achieves independence. At its best, nationalism is potentially an ordering principle that could facilitate peaceful coexistence amongst the disparate parts of humankind: what John Herz (1969) called 'self-limiting nationalism'. At its worst, it is a pathological ally of racist extremism, underpinning apartheid, ethnic cleansing and genocide. Practices of apartheid, ethnic cleansing and genocide can easily be found in the CAPE era, but nationalism was part of the ideational machinery that transported them into modernity.

In terms of how it was placed, and operated in the three domains, the most striking thing about nationalism is how it enabled a huge drawing together of the interpolity and interhuman domains that had been largely separate during the CAPE era. Unlike agrarian/pastoralist empires, which mostly did little to promote linkages amongst their constituent communities, modern industrial states had to find ways of integrating their citizens into a coherent whole (Gellner, 1983: 8–38). This could be done either by building on existing cultural identities (ethno-nationalism), and/or building new ones (civic nationalism) (Smith, 1991). Nationalism thus drew on identity resources already present in the interhuman domain. The modern state focused these resources, and brought them into the domestic and interstate domain as the legitimating political principle to replace monarchy/dynasticism. In the interhuman domain, nationalism was thus a major addition to the kinship, civilisational and religious patterns of identity carried over from the CAPE era, partly combining with them but not displacing them. As already noted, nationalism was not the only addition to collective identities made under modernity. There were secular ideologies such as communist, liberal, race, gender, and globalised class structures to choose from. The transnational domain did not have too much of a role here, because the advocacy groups and intellectuals who promoted nationalism tended to operate mainly within the domestic sphere. However, as I will discuss in the next subsection, nationalism did change significantly the operating environment for the commercial sector.

Market versus Economic Nationalism

As noted above, economic nationalism had been prevalent as mercantilism in Europe for over two centuries before modernity. The market (aka economic liberalism) was a new idea from the late eighteenth century that grew up alongside nationalism during the nineteenth century (Mayall, 1990). Nationalism became a central factor in the contest between the market and economic nationalism that has been playing out ever since. Market liberals try to square the circle between them by embedding a globalised system of trade, production and finance within an international political system/society of sovereign territorial states. They aim to build a global economy without a matching global government, relying instead on an array of agreements and secondary institutions among states. Economic nationalists try to bring the territorial state into closer alignment with the economy, lining it up with the political fragmentation of the international anarchy. Before that, as Allan (2018: 2) observes about the sixteenth century: 'Not only was there no idea of "the economy" as an entity distinct from "society," there was no discourse that divided society into a series of objects that could be understood and manipulated by the government.' The idea of progress, often rendered as the nexus between technological advances and economic growth, did not take off until the nineteenth century. As just discussed, nationalism was one of the key factors defining the political structure of emergent modernity, and as such it pointed towards economic nationalism. The market, however, was also one of the foundational ideas defining emergent modernity, thus setting off an intense and ongoing dialectic between them.[3] Within the framework I am using here, economic nationalism is a successful carry-over from the CAPE era into modernity, albeit extensively adapted to take account of the new context of industrialism, the understanding of a separate economic sector, and the vast increase in interaction capacity. The market is a new primary institution, strongly driven by both material and ideational changes, which is why this discussion is located here.

Somewhat like human inequality/equality, this is a particularly compli-cated story, because unlike with most other primary institutions, it is not clearly a decline or obsolescence, nor a linear carry-over or a new start. Trade does carry on, much amplified and reshaped by the material revolutions of modernity. But the transition to modernity also opens up a revolution in the whole conceptual framing in which trade is embed-ded. A wider understanding of 'the economy' develops in which trade is only one element, and this transforms the institution and its place in global society. It opens up a dialectic between market and economic nationalist ways of conceptualising and practising political economy, both domestically and internationally. As promised in Chapter 3, this section starts with the story of late-CAPE European mercantilism. It then looks at the contributions of modernity, both material and ideational, and at the dialectic between the market and economic nationalism from the nineteenth century to the present. Finally, it surveys briefly the rich legacy of secondary institutions that pursuit of the market has bequeathed to global society.

The CAPE Era Legacy

The CAPE era accomplished the intensification, elaboration and formal-isation of trade, and its extension to global scale as the leading edge in the formation of a global society. CAPE era trade carried religions, foods, fabrics, styles, flora, fauna, people and diseases, far and wide (Hobson, 2004, 2021), and developed sophisticated trading, banking and political mechanisms. But the CAPE era never developed much sense of 'the

---

[3] Mayall dances around this dialectic, but never quite crystallises it in these terms. His main concern was nationalism and in earlier work (Mayall, 1984) he excluded the market as an institution of international society, seeing it as having been subordinated to economic nationalism. In later work, Mayall (1990: 70, 150–1ff.) explores the complementarities between nationalism and market liberalism, leaving room for the idea that nationalism could play in both sides of the dialectic between the market and economic nationalism. His general view, however, contra the argument made here, was that economic nationalism had won.

economy' overall, or any interest in understanding or managing it. That wider sense of 'the economy' as something beyond the immediate details of specific acts of production, trade and finance, began to develop with the emergence of mercantilism in Europe. Mercantilism was an 'agent of unification' in the making of the sovereign, territorial state from the fifteenth century, and its target was the mediaeval combination of universalism (church, Holy Roman Empire) and political fragmentation (feudalism) (Heckscher, 1955 [1935]: 22). As a latecomer to development, Europe picked up the CAPE era trading and financing traditions and practices from the Byzantine Empire and the Islamic world, and began to develop them in its own way, from Italian banking houses, through merchant and artisanal guilds, to northern European chartered companies. Mercantilists saw economic transactions as embedded in, and governed by, systems of political control. They asserted the primacy of the state and national power over economic efficiency in the governance of commerce, and saw trade and wealth as zero-sum games. In trade, the aim was to achieve a surplus in order to accumulate specie, and in wealth, the idea was to grab the largest share of a fixed stock (Buck, 1974 [1942]; Bayly, 2004: 300; Findlay and O'Rourke, 2007: 143–310). Mercantilism was about 'a planned economy for the nation', 'the fundamental assumption ... was that the state was justified in exercising its powers in any department of the national economy in order to secure the power and welfare of the nation' (Buck, 1974 [1942]: 120). The mercantilists 'faced with equanimity, and even enthusiasm, the hard consequence that domestic order must be won at the price of international anarchy', and that national security and cohesion necessitated a conflictual international system (Buck, 1974 [1942]: 121, 113). In one sense, mercantilism reflected the weakness of late CAPE era European states, and their inability to organise and finance overseas ventures without the support of the commercial sector. Yet on the other hand, it reflected the growing power of the European state, and its ability to bend the commercial sector to its own purposes. Mercantilism was nevertheless very much in the CAPE era tradition of alliances between 'coercion and capital' in search of monopolies, whose high rents could be divided between them. The strong position of the merchants in these alliances underlines the long-standing nature of integrated world society stretching across the interpolity and transnational domains.

The Contributions of the Transition towards Modernity

The transition towards modernity thus inherited a rich, and in some ways quite sophisticated, tradition of international political economy. This had already been developed up to global scale, and had a long experience of finding ways in which economic and political elites could come to terms with each other in order to reap mutual benefits from trade and finance. The most obvious new factor was the enormous increase in interaction capacity discussed in Chapter 4. That development opened with the railways, steamships and telegraphs of the nineteenth century, and is still unfolding today with air transport, shipping containers, and the Internet. These material developments allowed modernity to deepen and intensify massively the thin global trading and financial systems of the CAPE era. People, goods, money, information and ideas circulated around global society with unprecedented speed, reliability, volume and cheapness. This intensified global political economy ensnared all whether they liked or wanted it or not, and took them on a roller-coaster ride driven by continuous inputs of new technology in production, free trade rules, transportation, communication and finance. Free trade benefited those at the leading edge of modernity, particularly Britain, but created serious problems for late-industrialisers (Bayly, 2004: 134–8, 177–83, 300), a problem that remains today. The deepening and intensification of globalisation got off to a fast start in the nineteenth century. As Findlay and O'Rourke (2007: 425) put it: '[T]he century that followed the final defeat of Napoleon saw the world's economic structure transformed in so radical a manner that it would have been virtually unrecognizable to a late-eighteenth-century observer.'

In addition to its spectacular material transformations of trade, production, migration and information flows, the nineteenth century also brought to the table a new way of understanding political economy, both local and global: *the market*. The traditional mercantilist system of political economy that supported the monarchical/dynastic politics of the Westphalian system of states was steadily challenged during the nineteenth century by the thinking and practice of economic liberalism (Frieden, 2006: 1). Something much bigger than mere trade was afoot, despite the campaign for 'free trade' being a leading feature of early economic liberalism. The market was one of the core features of the specifically liberal modernist project to separate politics from economics both intellectually and practically, and to give the market a considerable degree of autonomy from the state both conceptually and in practice (Ruggie, 1982: 385; Rosenberg, 1994). This opening up of separate sectors was a radical departure from the previous practice of European mercantilism, which tied the economy closely to the state in pursuit of monopolies (Holsti, 2004: 211–18). By the middle of the nineteenth century, the market principle was being applied much more widely than just trade, and was challenging European mercantilism as the primary economic institution.[4] The market refers to the idea and practice of an economic system of exchange in which independent economic agents interact on the basis of the principles of supply and demand, in a largely self-regulating way.[5] It is the opposite of a command or planned economy, which is based on the authoritative allocation of goods and services laid down within a hierarchical political system. The market is thus the opponent of both mercantilism, and the longer-standing CAPE practice of merchants seeking monopolies on production and trade. The market reversed mercantilist logic by assuming that putting economic efficiency first would better serve the interests of both the state (in obtaining wealth and power), and the people (in maximising individual opportunity and social mobility). Britain, as the leading industrial power of the opening century of the transition towards modernity, was the demonstration case, whose spectacular success at generating wealth and power put pressure on all others to follow (Landes, 1969; Pomeranz, 2000; Sassoon, 2019: 169–96). The market thus offered a new, and profoundly radical, solution to the age-old question of how best to harmonise the interests of political elites, who commanded coercive power and governing legitimacy, and economic elites, who commanded capital, and the skills of trade, production and finance.

In what follows, the understanding of 'the market' is what others have called 'market ideology' (Watson, 2018: 96–118) or 'market fundamentalism' (Oreskes and Conway, 2014: 38–49). For those promoting and accepting it, the market was a political ideology: using the supposed efficiency of the market, not only as a coordination system for the transactions of buyers and sellers, and as a guiding logic for innovation and investment, but also for the promotion and protection of individual liberty, as a system of governance that regulated human interactions in society (Lindblom, 2001: 4). Market ideology increasingly drew on the legitimacy of modern economics as 'science' to insulate politicians,

[4] In a Marxian perspective, industrial capitalism became the key institution, defining a political-economic system with free enterprise, private property and free markets at its core. There is thus considerable overlap between the market economy and capitalism, and both terms are often used interchangeably. However, I side with Gilpin (1987: 15–24), who argues that the market is more basic than capitalism, and Strange (1988: 63), who privileges the market as the concept that best differentiates from the state. Capitalism is already an aggregative concept, and I am trying to get down to the basic building blocks of social structure.
[5] Which is not to say that markets can operate in a completely free-standing way. Although opinion is divided on the necessary level of political support, markets generally require the backup of law and security in order to function smoothly – or possibly at all.

bankers and businesses from responsibility for making decisions that affected the distribution of wealth and welfare.[6] It was, and is, used 'in an attempt to naturalise market institutions and therefore close off the space for discussing non-market distributional settlements' (Watson, 2018: 96). In its extreme form, as put by Robinson (2020: 88), it means that people 'can't think in anything but economic terms, our ethics must be quantified and rated for the effects that our actions have on GDP'. This ideology could even have religious overtones. In a statement almost suggesting that the market was part of natural law, Bayly (2004: 136) notes that 'some statesmen and theorists believed that the laws of the free market were virtually the cornerstones of God's plan for mankind'. Market ideology amounted to a shift in the social purpose of the state away from the embedding of the economy within its political and social structures, and towards using the state, now itself a much stronger and more capable institution, to 'institute and safeguard the self-regulatory market' (Ruggie, 1982: 386; see also Holsti, 2004: 211–38). Under market logic, mass consumerism became something like the economic analogue of citizenship and popular sovereignty. It is in this political and ideational form that the market fits most closely with other primary institutions of global society.

The Dialectic of Market versus Economic Nationalism

The story of the market as a primary institution of global society is not, however, a straightforward one like that of sovereignty, diplomacy, international law or nationalism, in which the new institution emerges, consolidates and evolves in a relatively smooth and linear way. Instead, over the past two centuries the standing of the market has fluctuated, sometimes dramatically, in a kind of dialectic with various forms of economic nationalism. In brief, the story goes like this.[7]

The nineteenth century up to 1914, when the market, promoted and led by Britain, first became an institution of global society, is often referred to as the 'golden age'. It was defined by the linked rise of free trade and the gold standard as both norms and practices; by highly globalised foreign investment; and by the relatively open regime for mass migration that amounted in practice to free movement of labour in which

---

[6] Economics was just one of the social science disciplines that emerged during the nineteenth century based on dividing the social world into sectors for the purpose of analysis and theorising. In so doing, they could not help but reinforce the idea that such sectors were real and separable also in practice.

[7] For the story in more depth and detail, see Buzan and Falkner (2022, forthcoming), from which this section is drawn.

tens of millions of people changed continents. Market ideology became hugely influential in thinking and practice among the core states, although much less so between the imperial core and the colonial periphery, where all manner of market distortion was the norm. But as industrial trade competition increased among the core states, some other industrialising countries started to protect their 'infant industries' from British competition. This golden age came to an abrupt end with the outbreak of the First World War. From 1914 to 1945, the institution of the market suffered major reversals and breakdowns. War quickly shut down almost all aspects of the first golden age liberal world economy. There was a brief attempt during the 1920s to revive the golden age economic order, but Britain was too weak to lead it, while the US was strong enough economically, but unable/unwilling to do so because of its domestic politics. The financial collapse in the US in 1929, led to the dominance of not just protectionism (high tariffs, economic nationalism, imperial preference), but also the spread of command economy thinking and practice in the forms of communism (as embedded in the Soviet Union and its followers), and state capitalism (the fascist states, and periphery countries pursuing import substitution industrialisation once they were cut off from world trade and investment). Even Britain and the US resorted to high tariffs and forms of imperial preference, though market ideology clung on as an aspiration within them.

From 1945 to 1973, market ideology made a partial comeback led by the US. The Bretton Woods system revived world trade, albeit not including the communist bloc states and much of the Third World. It put the US dollar, still linked to gold, at the core of a financial system of fixed exchange rates and quite strict financial controls. For a time, Bretton Woods provided a compromise between the market desire for global trade and investment, and stable currencies, on the one hand, and the desire to protect domestic economies from the unacceptable pain of the recessions and unemployment required to defend currencies pegged to the gold standard, on the other hand. It broke down in the early 1970s, when the trade imbalances it generated for the US undermined the value of the dollar. Rather than raise taxes or curtail spending on welfare or the war in Vietnam, the US government preferred to go off the gold standard and leave currencies to float. The first attempt to find a balance between the market principle, on the one hand, and domestic political stability and economic welfare, on the other hand, had failed. That failure morphed into the period from 1973 to 2007, which was marked by a resurgence of both market ideology (neoliberalism) and market practice (globalisation). After a period of economic uncertainty and turbulence during the 1970s, an unrestrained form of market ideology found state support in Britain and the US. In the West, it rolled back the welfare state, deregulated the financial sector, and promoted economic efficiency (aka profits) through the globalisation of production. The collapse of the Soviet Union; the defection of China from Marxist economics under Deng; the 1990s economic reforms in India; the recurrent debt crises of the periphery states that had been pursuing import substitution industrialisation; and the conspicuous success of the Asian Tigers that had taken the path of export-led industrialisation, paved the way for a second golden age of the market as an institution of global society, albeit one punctuated by frequent and severe debt crises. Not until the end of the first cold war did the market once again achieve something like the fully global status as an institution of global society it had had during the nineteenth century.

In 2007–8, a massive financial crisis once again exposed the hazards and risks of financial liberalisation. Despite the undoubted gain of the neoliberal/globalisation decades, most notably the lifting of hundreds of millions of people from agrarian poverty to something like a middle-class standard of education and living, letting the market rip proved to be unsustainable. Excessive financial liberalisation made vast amounts of capital available for development, but in the process, the financial sector came to dwarf the 'real economy' of production, labour and trade. This unbalanced structure amplified intrinsic instabilities that threatened the whole system with debt crises and inequality. In practice, much of the surplus capital was consumed or invested wastefully, rather than put into productive investments. Since 2008, the system has been in turmoil, with rising tensions over trade, investment, financial liberalisation, and migration, and consequent hard questioning of the market ideology in both theory (Skidelsky, 2009: 28, 2018: 347–90; Wolf, 2014) and practice. At the time of writing, this turbulence remains ongoing and unresolved. Market ideology has been deeply wounded in principle. Yet there seems to be no alternative but to try to keep it going in practice, despite the obvious dangers exposed by both market golden ages. There is no desire to go back to the bloc protectionism of the interwar years and the Soviet Union during the first cold war. But neither is there an obvious new 'Bretton Woods' compromise on offer. The drift is towards unpicking globalisation, delinking the US and Chinese economies, and pursuing various forms of economic nationalism, not just by the usual suspects such as Russia, China and India, but also within the West.

These five rounds do not seem to have exhausted the market's dialectic with command economy of 'flourish, collapse, compromise, flourish, collapse, ??'. Nationalism remains very much a strong mediating factor between the two economic options. Indeed, it is worth noting that this story could almost be told the other way around, with command/planned economy as the primary institution, and the market as a repeating challenger. Sylvan (1981: 381–2), for example, sees three waves of mercantilist thinking: the traditional one of the seventeenth and eighteenth centuries; the developmental state one of the nineteenth century (Hamilton, List); and the reaction against the failure of the liberal global economy in the interwar years (Polanyi, Keynes). This line of thinking could be extended to include the Soviet bloc, various developmental states, some aspects (most notably financial) of China's 'market socialism' (which looks increasingly like state capitalism), and the post-2016 retreat into 'America first' of the US under Trump. A fourth round of command economy ideology could well be in the making. From this perspective, the periodic triumphs of market ideology would be viewed as temporary failures or breakdowns of a mainstream baseline of command economy. It is not impossible that the unfolding of events in the future might at some point make that seem the right idea. More on where this dialectic might go in Chapter 8.

Thus, over a period of some two centuries, the market has moved from being an elite idea held by few to being, periodically, the mainstream economic institution of global society (Bowden and Seabrooke, 2006). Many support it normatively as being good in itself, and linked to freedom and democracy. But many go along with it either on the instrumental grounds that it has proved to be the most efficient way to generate wealth and power (China), or because they are coerced into it by stronger powers. It remains contested, and the dialectic between economic nationalism and economic liberalism is far from finished. Very few states are completely open to the global market, and many cultivate forms of state capitalism in which economic nationalism is prominent. But led by China's defection from Marxist economics in the late 1970s, the twentieth-century struggle over whether to have the market or not, is over. Now the main game is about how to relate to the market, and how to make it work best both nationally and globally. In that sense, market ideology has won a major place in the thinking and practice of economics, but in a form far from the purity that its most ardent liberal advocates hoped for. If there is any lesson from the experiments with applying market ideology over the past two centuries, it is that while the market is an exceptionally powerful tool, any attempt to give it autonomy, detached from the political sector, will fail. Econometrics alone cannot capture how the dynamics of the triangle amongst market, command economy and nationalism work. The appropriate social science has to be political economy (or perhaps behavioural economics).

The Secondary Institutions of the Market

Recall that the during the CAPE era, the institution of trade, along with religion, generated significant secondary institutions – 'companies', guilds and trade diasporas – albeit these were mainly in the transnational domain. From the nineteenth century onwards, the primary institution of the market has been remarkably prolific in this respect, extending the array of secondary institutions that express, legitimise and reproduce it, also extensively into the interstate domain. The obvious explanation for this is that markets require a supporting framework of governance. In the absence of any global government, a web of secondary institutions was the next best option. Because it had a strong conceptual and practical orientation towards the economy on a global scale, the market has carried the economic sector's long-standing leading-edge role in extending glob-alisation, into the task of intensifying global society. It is beyond the scope of this book to recount this story in any detail, and it is well covered in the IPE literature.[8] But a brief review is worthwhile to show the depth and extent of it, and its central role in the global society of modernity.

In the nineteenth century, the story of secondary institutions in the economic sector splits between the interstate and transnational domains. The development of secondary economic institutions in the interstate domain was one of the signature features of the transition towards modernity, albeit during this first phase it was mainly about regimes rather than IGOs. The key regimes were the nineteenth-century free trade system backed up by bilateral treaties that promoted the most-favoured-nation (MFN) principle; and the gold standard, a fixed exchange-rate regime of parallel national policies that states could uni-laterally join or leave. The last quarter of the nineteenth century did see the creation of some permanent IGOs such as the International Bureau of Weights and Measures (1875), the Universal Postal Union (1874), and the International Telecommunications Union (1865). But these were specific responses to the material transformations wrought by the revolutions of modernity, and not aimed at general management of the global economy. The rise of positive international law at this time was closely related to the market, because of the associated need for agreed legal arrangements for commerce both among states and between states and firms (Buzan and Lawson, 2015: 87).

The other big development in this period was in the transnational domain: the founding of the modern limited company, which began to

---

[8] Again, for more depth and detail on this topic, see Buzan and Falkner (2022, forthcoming).

appear in numbers after 1830, and expanded rapidly from 1850 onwards (Jones, 2005). Although initially a domestic development, this quickly became a transnational one as, from 1870 onwards, firms and banks extended their operations abroad (Jones, 2005: 3–6). As noted in Chapter 3, big claims are made for the modern firm, some putting its importance as rivalling the modern state itself (Stavrianos, 1990: 95–6; Micklethwait and Wooldridge, 2003: 2, 8). Given the rich legacy of company development from the CAPE era, how valid are these claims? Business partnerships, corporations, forms of shareholding, and limited liability were all familiar in the CAPE era. The first key point about the modern firm is that it was easy to set up as a legal entity, not requiring a royal charter. This, along with its intrinsic flexibility as an organisational form, enabled it to spread rapidly within civil society. Firms could, and did, get big enough to rival states in wealth, and in some respects, power – though that could also be claimed for the British East India Company before the end of the CAPE era. The second key point is that the modern firm was specifically designed to operate, and either flourish or die, within the framework of a market economy (Jones, 2005: 16–24). Just as the chartered companies were closely linked to mercantilism, and the traditional practices of seeking monopolies, so the modern firm expressed and reproduced the idea that the market should operate independently from politics, giving maximum reign to innovation, entrepreneurship and the profit motive. That idea did not rule out states taking a close interest in 'their' firms, seeing them as intrinsic to their own wealth and power, and trying to help them in various ways. The principle of separation did not overrule the much older ideas and practices of political and economic elites coming to terms about wealth and power. But it was a radically different arrangement of this bargain. These points justify the claim that the modern firm was indeed an institutional turning point.

Even during the period 1914–45, when the market was in retreat, the development of secondary institutions continued. In the interstate domain, the League of Nations was central to the 1920s attempt to revive the golden age. It had an Economic and Financial Organisation (EFO) that in some ways anticipated the IMF; held several economic conferences, which mostly failed; and set up the International Labour Organisation (ILO), which still exists. In the transnational domain, the Bank for International Settlements (BIS), which also still exists, was set up to promote cooperation and coordination among banks.

The Bretton Woods period is strongly associated with the rise of global economic IGOs aimed at institutionalising the market norm: the International Monetary Fund (IMF), the World Bank and the General

Agreement on Trade and Tariffs (GATT).[9] The IMF and the World Bank set standards for accountancy, banking, fiscal and monetary policy, trade and corporate governance (Best, 2006: 135). In the absence of an International Trade Organisation, plans for which failed, GATT aimed to sustain tariff reductions and institutionalise free trade. At the same time, Europe embarked on the sequence of regional economic institutional developments that would eventually lead to the European Union (EU), and the Soviet Union set up the Council for Mutual Economic Assistance (COMECON), though that was more to oppose the market than implement it. The UN set up the United Nations Development Program (UNDP); and within the UN framework, Third World countries set up the UN Conference on Trade and Development (UNCTAD). Even the advocacy for development (on which more below), which often went against market logic in its demands for aid and preferential treatment, was often aimed at creating a level playing field for the less developed states. They argued, as the newly industrialising US, Germany and Japan had done during the nineteenth century, that unmediated market logic worked strongly and unfairly against them.

During the neoliberal period from 1973 to 2007, this market-friendly suite of IGOs was expanded, upgraded and repurposed. The IMF and the World Bank played a big role both in the many debt crises, and in promoting the neoliberal Washington Consensus. The BIS was revived during the 1970s to coordinate responses to financial crises (Helleiner, 1994: 171–2); and the GATT morphed into the World Trade Organization (WTO) creating a stronger and more formal institutionalisation of free trade. New and less formal IGOs also emerged to handle the political negotiations over the global market economy, the Group of 7 (G7) among the leading capitalist core; and the Group of 20 (G20), which responded to the global financial crises by broadening the global economic management committee. On the regional level, free trade agreements were institutionalised for North America and parts of South America, and the European Economic Community morphed into an enlarging EU.

From 2008, these institutions, both interstate (G20) and transnational (BIS) played a significant role in managing the economic crisis (Drezner, 2012; Frieden et al., 2012: 23–31; Pauley, 2017: 187–93). But by 2009, the role of secondary institutions was weakening, with national responses becoming dominant, as both creditors and debtors attempted to shift the pain away from their domestic economies (Frieden et al., 2012: 23–31,

---

[9] These organisations were global in principle, but at this time mainly Western in practice.

49–51). From 2016, the US itself, under the nationalist, populist, leadership of President Trump, began to attack and undermine much of this economic institutional framework, both primary (the market as applied to trade, production and investment) and secondary (various trade agreements, the WTO). At the same time, the existing framework of secondary economic institutions came under pressure from rising powers, most conspicuously China, who wanted more status and influence than the US and the West were prepared to allow. The BRICS set up the BRICS Development Bank (now New Development Bank) in 2014, and China followed with its Asia Infrastructure Investment Bank (AIIB) in 2016, which was part of its larger Belt and Road Initiative (BRI) (O'Brian and Williams, 2016: 307–10). These new IGOs could be seen both as competitors to the Bretton Woods institutions and as bargaining chips in the opening rounds of a long struggle to reconfigure the distribution of status and power in the management of the global economy. It was significant that the US under Obama refused to join AIIB, but could not persuade most of its European allies to follow its lead. What was clear in all this was that apart from Trump, there was no general abandonment of the idea that secondary institutions were a necessary part of managing global trade and finance. The dispute was more about how such IGOs should be structured and run, and what the distribution of power and status within them should be, than about whether they should exist or not.

This complex and fluctuating story of the dialectic between economic nationalism and the market is difficult to locate clearly within the three domains. Recall that for the CAPE era, I located trade mainly within the transnational domain though with some substantial penetration into the interpolity and interhuman ones. The picture for the last two centuries suggests that the dialectic between economic nationalism and the market is pervasive through all three domains, with none being obviously dominant.

There can be little doubt that the interstate domain now plays a much bigger and stronger role than it did during the CAPE era. One of the signatures of modernity is the rational, national state, which is hugely more capable both administratively and financially than its CAPE forebears. This modern state has expanded its responsibilities much more deeply and widely into society, including the economy, than was ever the case during the CAPE era. This strongly political element in the economy was obvious during late-CAPE mercantilism, and remains so whenever economic nationalism is in the ascendant. But right from the middle of the nineteenth century, the proliferation of regimes and IGOs around the market underlined the necessity of active state involvement. The modern state understood its deal with the market, and it was clear early on that globalising the market required at the very least coordination amongst states, as under the gold standard, and preferably a framework of rules and secondary institutions, as with the WTO. It remains a contested question as to whether, or to what degree, it is possible to have a global market economy without some form of global government, or governance, to stabilise it (Skidelsky, 2018: 347–90).

But while the interstate domain now undoubtedly plays a much larger role, the transnational one still remains a major site for this institution. Most obvious here is the role of the modern firm, which has proliferated beyond all expectation, and morphed into transnational and multinational forms. As noted above, the modern firm was designed for the market, and embodies it in many ways. During the nineteenth century, financiers such as the Rothschilds were major beneficiaries of the gold standard, and politically active in supporting it. Sometimes, they were prepared to put up their own money to bail out countries in danger of defaulting on loans because of adverse movements in the prices of their exports. Lying somewhere between the interstate and transnational domains, central banks were also active in mutual support during financial crises, and the Bank of England emerged as the main coordinator for managing the financial system and acting as lender of last resort (Frieden, 2006: 32–9, 45–9; Eichengreen, 2019: 5–40). By the 1960s, there were significant worries, both fictional and empirical, that big corporations would overawe the state and take over the world (Pohl and Kornbluth, 1960; Vernon, 1971). Such worries continue still as a small number of giant corporations come to dominate the US economy, using a 'winner takes all' digital economy to amass huge fortunes, and open up socially divisive levels of economic inequality.

This institution also had deep roots and deep repercussions in the interhuman domain. During the nineteenth century, changes in the class structure pushed by industrialisation and the market, created new patterns of identity that could be, and were, mobilised for political purposes. As noted in the previous section, for much of the nineteenth century, class identities competed with nationalism for primacy, though they lost ground during the twentieth. The market became embedded in people's identities as consumers, and in the extent to which market ideology became accepted as a legitimate form of governance. And while the classical class identities highlighted by Marxism had lost much of their political force by the twenty-first century, something perhaps analogous was opening up in the popular movements against 'globalisation' (aka the global operation of the market). The popular movements opposed market ideology both because of its consequences in a widening economic inequality between elites and masses, and because its environmental effects were seen as beginning to threaten not just the conditions for human civilisation, but possibly also for human survival.

Science

As far as I am aware, science has not been discussed as an institution of international society, but I now think it should be, especially in the context of thinking about global society. I certainly failed to pay attention to it in my earlier work on primary institutions (Buzan, 2004a, 2014, 2018a). Because of the move in this book to look at institutions as stretching across the three domains, science comes more easily and clearly into view as an institution of global society. In putting this idea forward, I am conscious of Peter Wilson (2012) looking over my shoulder and shaking his head at this further example of the arrogant theorist imposing schemes on reality. But I think science meets the criteria that Falkner and Buzan (2019) set out for empirically validating primary institutions. Science, I understand as the rational, methodologically systematic study of the physical and social worlds through observation, classification, theorisation and (where economically, ethically and technologically possible) experimentation. It requires not just transparent and coherent chains of causal logic, but accurately documented and preferably replicable evidence to support that logic. The availability of data became much more widespread during the nineteenth century not just through the activities of scientists, but also because the modern state quickly moved to understand and manage itself through the collection of statistics about the material and social worlds. Science requires measurement by agreed criteria of as much as possible, and measurement promotes practices of global comparison for everything from military capability and sporting prowess, to levels of development and environmental impacts (Epple, Erhart and Grave, 2020). If this can be done in quantitative terms amenable to mathematical methods, so much the better. That said, especially in the social world, quantification is not always possible, and carries higher risks of misrepresentation and error than in the physical world. The case for science counting as a primary institution is its widespread acceptance across cultures and ideologies as a new common standard of knowledge, and its embodiment into a wide range of global social and political practices, and secondary institutions.[10] Science is the social foundation for much of the material

[10] The claim that science is, or should be, the only standard of knowledge is much more controversial.

transformation surveyed in Chapter 4, and some of the social transformation discussed in this and the previous chapter.

The practice of science of course has deep roots that long predate the
take-off of the transition towards modernity. Science-like practices can
be found far back in the CAPE era, whether in relation to astronomy/
astrology, or the properties of chemicals used in manufactures, or the
development of mathematics in many places, or the methodological
ruminations of such natural philosophers as Socrates and Aristotle. All
premodern civilisations had ways of making empirical observations, and
organising knowledge (Bayly, 2004: 312–20). But while there was certainly accumulation of knowledge, there was little or no systematic and
general understanding of knowledge as such, either within or across
societies. There was no clear separation between religious or mystical
explanations for observed phenomena, and secular ones. Although religion and science would become cast as rival forms of knowledge by
some, religious institutions also played a significant role in the promotion
of science as a way of understanding the work of god.

Yet before the nineteenth century, there was not much sense of science
as either a human project or a shared mode of understanding. A small
elite of scientists had begun to take this view towards the end of the
CAPE era, but mainly there was just some common methodological
ground amongst merchants and taxmen in the use of numbers and basic
arithmetic, and a higher level of mathematical understanding shared
amongst a small intellectual elite. For most of the CAPE era, supernatural explanations dominated understanding of the natural and social
worlds. Think of the role of astrology and other mystical forms of
prediction right up to the end of the CAPE era, and to a significant
extent still, at all levels of society. Even as late as 1879, Darwin was vexed
by religious explanations for the rapid spread of flowering plants, a
phenomenon that he could not account for with his scientific theory of
natural selection.[11]

From the sixteenth and especially the seventeenth centuries, a social
movement towards a systematic and general understanding of knowledge
began to emerge in Europe. This movement challenged and drove back,
though by no means eliminated, explanations based on the supernatural,
whether religion, witchcraft, astrology, alchemy, etc. This efflorescence is
associated with great names such as Copernicus, Galileo, Descartes,
Francis Bacon and Newton. From the eighteenth, and more so the
nineteenth centuries, science quickly took root, and became both a

---

[11] www.bbc.co.uk/news/science-environment-55769269 (accessed 23 January 2021).

hallmark of Western civilisation, and the engine room driving forward the rising wealth and power of Europe. Enlightenment thinking promoted the idea that the order of the physical world (aka 'god's creation') could be uncovered by reason, and that reason could also be used to promote progress in the social world. Although science eventually won its place, its struggle was not easy and its victory far from complete. It encountered formidable resistance from religion, which, as the well-known story of the persecution of Galileo by the Catholic Church attests, was fought not only by argument, but by deploying directly coercive methods such as the Inquisition. The growth of scientific knowledge about astronomy, geology, archaeology and biology could not help but challenge religious (in this case Christian) views about creation: the place of the earth in the cosmos, the nature and age of its origin, and the nature and evolution of humankind, including questions of life and death.

Some modernisers anticipated that science would eventually sweep religion away as being mere unprovable myth and superstition. That did not happen. Even now, when considered in relation to humankind as a whole, the struggle between science and religion perhaps stands at not much more than a draw. Religion and mysticism retain the advantage of being able to provide definitive answers, and can adapt to changed circumstances by spinning off new variants (e.g. Protestants, Ismailis). Science, by its nature, is open to challenge, and revision, especially so when the questions are at the frontiers of knowledge. This process of contestation is essential to its strength. But it can be a weakness in the arena of public discourse, where scientists have always to hedge and qualify the limits of their current understanding. Religion has mostly accepted the legitimacy of science, and come to terms with its challenges to some religious myths. Christianity no longer tries to suppress science, though some Islamic extremists, such as Boko Haram, still oppose Western (i.e. scientific) education. Many scientists remain comfortable with holding personal religious beliefs, and seeing their work as understanding god's creation. Science has made huge gains in terms of what counts as knowledge, and how public and commercial policies are formulated and justified. But religion and mysticism still hold considerable ground in the public mind, providing fertile soil for endless conspiracy theories such as QAnon.

Science only became influential enough worldwide to become an institution of global society during the nineteenth century. One of its key advantages was that it offered a universally valid framework of knowledge to set against the fissiparous views of contending religions. During the nineteenth century, it became organised into the specialised disciplines that still shape its structure (Buzan and Lawson, 2015: 97–8). It also benefited from the host of new precision instruments generated by the industrial revolution, which greatly increased powers of observation and measurement. Science became part of the 'standard of civilisation' by which Europeans differentiated themselves from others, and thought themselves superior. Indeed, in its mania for classification and comparison, science bears a burden of responsibility for the 'scientific' racism that degraded global society between the middle of the nineteenth and the middle of the twentieth centuries. Science was thus carried worldwide by Western imperialism as a, perhaps the, core element of modernity. It was the essence of what might be called 'the Western way of thinking'. The message that science works was carried worldwide not only by the power of argument, but by the demonstration effects of its products: the global display of its fruits by European and American merchants, doctors and soldiers. Those who encountered steamships, machine guns, heavy artillery, aircraft, cheap but quality manufactures, and medical miracles, for the first time could hardly not get the message that they had to acquire science if they were to regain their wealth, power and cultural authority. The story of market ideology set out above was in part linked to the relative success, when compared to other social sciences, of the academic discipline of Economics in establishing its methodological, particularly quantitative, credentials as a science comparable to the sciences covering the physical world. Some other social sciences, most notoriously Politics presenting itself as 'Political Science', have attempted, with less success, to claim this mantle.

From the second half of the nineteenth century, the acquisition of science became a core part of the pursuit of modernity across all cultures. This was not without opposition, not just on religious grounds as noted above, but also from cultural conservatives. Chinese traditionalists successfully resisted 'Westernisation' for the best part of the nineteenth century (Buzan and Goh, 2020: 89–92). Mahatma Gandhi's preference for simple and self-reliant village economies contained more than a hint of traditionalism. Within the West, some sects such as the 'Shakers' tried to drop out of modernity. But during the twentieth century, science was embraced as an essential element of modernisation by all of the major secular ideologies in play, not just liberal-democratic, but nationalist, socialist, communist and fascist. In the political realm, science was understood to be essential to the acquisition of wealth and power. Individuals and some institutions might still resist it on religious, moral, traditional or mystical grounds, but almost every society found a way of accommodating it. It was elevated to being a global standard of knowledge and aspiration, embodying the seeming triumph of modernity, and humankind, over the material world. To call something science, or to validate an argument by calling it 'scientific', became a kind of cross-cultural global gold standard for knowledge. As noted, this still leaves plenty of room for dispute and disagreement, because challenge and response are intrinsic to how science evolves. But there is a world of difference, both epistemological and ontological, between setting one scientific argument against another, and opposing science with religion, mysticism or conspiracy theory. To what extent this standing is now under threat in a post-truth world where the power of rhetoric peddles big lies effectively enough to trump scientific reasoning and evidence, remains to be seen. Science has clouded its own credentials by opening up questionable policy practices from eugenics to nuclear weapons, and by occluding forms of social wisdom from societies seen as primitive and pre-scientific.

The embedding of science as a primary institution is evident not just from its widespread acceptance as the key to a vast store of useful knowledge, but also from the extent to which it has become incorporated into many intergovernmental and transnational organisations. The International Sanitary Conferences from 1851 applied medical science to the problem of containing pandemics. By 1875, the International Bureau of Weights and Measures reflected the standardising and quantifying practices of science as applied to manufacture and commerce. The League of Nations had an International Commission on Intellectual Cooperation (the predecessor to the United Nations Educational, Scientific and Cultural Organization: UNESCO), which included scientific cooperation in its remit. It also had a Health Organisation (the predecessor to the World Health Organisation: WHO), building on the International Sanitary Conferences, much of whose remit was defined in scientific terms. UNESCO has science in its name. Many other specialised agencies of the UN promote scientific practices and/or collect and use data in a scientific way: for example, the Food and Agriculture Organisation (FAO), the International Monetary Fund (IMF), the International Bank for Reconstruction and Development (aka World Bank), the World Health Organisation (WHO) and the World Meteorological Organisation (WMO). This embedding of science is mirrored in the secondary institutions in the transnational domain. Local scientific associations go back to the seventeenth century, with landmarks such as the French *Académie des Sciences* (1660) and the British *Royal Society* (1662). The spread of similar scientific societies in the eighteenth and nineteenth centuries, and the nineteenth-century specialisation into modern academic disciplines, created transnational epistemic communities of scientists linked by organisations, travel, publications and prizes. The American Association for the Advancement of

Science dates from 1847. At the time of writing, the International Science Council (ISC), a federative INGO, has over 200 national and international member associations.[12] Political responses to the major collective crises of the day, pandemics and climate change, are substantially shaped by scientific analysis, and debated in scientific terms.

As a primary institution, science is embedded, shared and contested across all three domains, with none having obvious claim to being its main base. In the interstate domain, from an early point some states encouraged the development of science. Now almost all do, and science is a standard of knowledge accepted by many IGOs. That said, it would be hard to make the case that science somehow originated in the interstate domain, however much it has been promoted and accepted there. That honour belongs more to the transnational and interhuman domains. Science is widely accepted and institutionalised in the transnational domain, though opposition to it is also located there. Except amongst scientists, science has not constructed major patterns of shared identity in the interhuman domain. Prestigious individuals are able to act across the three domains on the basis of their credibility and status as scientists. Think of Albert Einstein and nuclear weapons, Marie Curie and radiology, Charles Darwin and both biology and society, Carl Sagan and space science, Louis Pasteur and medical practice, James Watt and engineering, and many others.

Sport

Like science, sport is another modern primary institution that only comes into clear and obvious focus when one is looking at primary institutions across the interstate, transnational and interhuman domains. By sport I mean games involving mental and physical (strength, coordination) skills, that are played for entertainment, exercise, status and/or money. The money element underpins the distinction between amateur sport, mainly pursued for the first three motives, and professional sport, in which the activity becomes, in addition, a way of earning a living. Some sports are physically demanding, even violent, such as boxing, mixed martial arts and rugby; others require mainly good coordination, such as snooker and e-sports, while others are more sedentary 'mind sports', such as chess, go/*weiqi* and bridge. Some sports are one-against-one and some are team games, but all involve both mental and physical skill.

---

[12] https://council.science (accessed 24 January 2021).

Most are competitive and involve a will to win, but sports can also be cooperative and/or aesthetic. The institutionalisation of sport can be seen as part of a wider 'civilising' process of modernity that attempts to reduce the role of what Galtung (1969) calls 'personal' (as opposed to 'structural') violence in society (also see Linklater, 2016). Sports where the death of the opponent, or an animal, is the aim, such as gladiatorial combat, were popular in the CAPE era, but have been generally outlawed during the transition towards modernity, along with duelling and gruesome public punishments. Those such as boxing, where the violence is intentional and personal, and where there are some deaths, are on the borderline of acceptability. Those such as motor racing, rugby, horse-racing and free-climbing, where the nature of the sport involves significant risk of death or serious injury, fall within an acceptable level of structural violence and personal voluntary risk. These boundaries are subject to drift as society becomes more, or less, tolerant of death and injury. A better understanding of brain damage, for example, puts moral pressure on boxing, American football, rugby and football (soccer). Sport, in some ways like the market, is a way of civilising competition in global society, opening up alternatives to war.

Sport in this sense clearly meets the criteria for empirically identifying primary institutions set out in Chapter 1. It is a massive generator of secondary institutions across the transnational domain, and has implanted global standards of behaviour backed by rules and enforcements (albeit far from perfectly). Through its links to nationalism and human equality it penetrates up into the interstate domain, and down into the interhuman one. The concept of sport in its modern, functionally differentiated, sense was probably irrelevant to the hunter-gatherer era, though there is some evidence for wrestling and running. Sport is much more relevant to the CAPE era, when many civilisations invented distinctive games of many kinds, and turned them into sports. These were often closely tied to the mainly male activities of military training or hunting – running, javelin throwing, wrestling, archery, athletics, swimming, polo, jousting, chariot racing. Sport as a large-scale spectator activity reached a particular peak in the gladiatorial and chariot racing events of the Roman Empire, and the ball games of Mesoamerican civilisations, both of which had connections to politics. There were some hints of sport being organised and played across political boundaries, most obviously Greece and the Olympic Games, but this was more the exception than the rule.[13] For that reason, while the concept of sport was

---

[13] On sports in various CAPE societies see Vamplew (2021: 39–64).

clearly present in most CAPE societies, it was not an institution of relations among them except within rather tight cultural spheres. Sports had many local variations and customs, and attempts to standardise rules and practices did not begin in Europe until the last century or two of the era.

Sport did not become an institution of global society until the twentieth century, a process that is still ongoing. Attempts at standardising sports across wider communities predate modernity, but really got rolling during the nineteenth century. The nineteenth century saw much inventiveness in, and popularisation and standardisation of, sports such as football, golf, tennis and cricket. The process of federating national bodies into global ones, and of organising systematic international rules and competitions was mainly the work of the twentieth century. Governing bodies for sport at both national and international levels are non-state actors concerned with making and enforcing standardised rules of the game, organising competitions, prizes and championships, promoting the development of the sport, and advocating for it politically when necessary. With a few exceptions for Asia (go/*weiqi*, some martial arts), most of the sports that went global were European in origin, though many cultures can claim that they had similar games (e.g. forms of football) in earlier times. But European globalisation of sport set a broad pattern in which mainly white/Western/male national bodies formed during the nineteenth century, and these started to form international federations during the twentieth. The general pattern of this development, especially early on, was also partly shaped by the overt racism, patriarchy and imperialism of the day.

Perhaps the lead example of this globalising process is the modern Olympics, started in 1896, when fourteen nations, all European plus the US, held the first modern Olympics in Athens. This revived the classical Greek tradition that ran for a millennium between 776 BC and 393 AD. The 1900 Olympics added Russia, India, Iran and several Latin American countries, signalling openness to global participation. Before the First World War, Japan, Turkey and Egypt were included, but the total of participating countries was still only twenty-eight. The big expansion came after 1945, with African states joining in from the 1960s, and by 1972 a pretty global membership of 121 nations.[14] By aiming early for universal participation, and by establishing rules of competition that applied to everyone, the Olympics played strongly into both globalisation and human equality. But it also played to nationalism and the north–

---

[14] See: www.olympics.mu and www.olympic-museum.de (accessed 15 June 2021).

south divide, both in the identity of the teams and by becoming a prize for nations eager to show off their prowess by lavish hosting of the event. Another example is football. The English Football Association was founded in 1863, and the global one, FIFA (Fédération Internationale de Football Association), in 1904. FIFA was initially set up by seven European countries, but even before the First World War had expanded to include some Latin American states (Argentina, Chile), the US and Russia. During the interwar years, more Latin Americans came in (e.g. Brazil, Colombia), and the first FIFA world cup was held in 1930 in Uruguay. Membership also opened out into the Middle East and Asia (e.g. Egypt, Japan, Lebanon, Thailand and Turkey). Global expansion continued after the Second World War, partly fuelled by decolonisation, with Algeria, Ethiopia, India, Iraq, Liberia, Morocco, Venezuela and others joining during the 1940s, 1950s and 1960s.[15] Football developed a global market fed by global-scale leagues such as the Premier League, though the world cup has so far only been won by European and South American teams.

For chess, the International Chess Federation (FIDE) was founded in 1924. It had a weak start, with contested authority and poor control over rules and championships. Initially, it was a European affair, with the US and some Latin American countries joining during the 1920s, and more Latin Americans during the 1930s, when the eighth chess Olympiad was held in Buenos Aires. Palestine joined in 1935, but without a single Arab name amongst its players. An interesting imperial quirk in this story was that an Indian player, Sultan Khan, was a leading member of the English team at the third, fourth and fifth chess Olympiads during the early 1930s.[16] The Soviet Union joined in the early 1950s, and by the later 1950s Asian countries (Mongolia, India, Iran, the Philippines) and African ones (Tunisia, South Africa) opened the way to continued globalisation of membership.[17] Chess also became politicised when the Soviet Union dominated it during most of the first cold war, and used it as evidence for the supposed superiority of its social system.

Many more such stories could be told. The International Lawn Tennis Association was founded in 1913 by twelve national associations, mostly European, but also Australia, Russia and South Africa. By 1939, it had fifty-nine members, and now it has over 200 organised into six regional

---

[15] See: www.fifa.com (accessed 15 June 2021).
[16] See: www.thearticle.com/the-man-who-beat-them-all-and-then-vanished (accessed 14 June 2021).
[17] www.fide.com (accessed 14 June 2021), Fôldeâk (1979).

associations spanning the globe.[18] The International Cricket Council (ICC) was founded in 1909 among England, Australia and South Africa, though test cricket had been played amongst these since 1877. Internationalisation in this case tended to follow imperial lines. India, New Zealand and the West Indies were admitted in 1926 and Pakistan in 1952.[19] India first played test cricket in England in 1932, when racism was still the order of the day in much of society, and by that time a few West Indians were also playing in British cricket teams. By the time of writing, India, with its outstanding Premier League, had become the world centre of cricket, while Dubai hosted the headquarters.

International sports organisations founded after 1945 tended to begin life already partly or fully globalised. The International Go Federation was set up in 1982. Although go/*weiqi* is a Northeast Asian game, and the Federation was initiated by, and headquartered in, Japan, of its twenty-nine founding members, only six were from East Asia, with twenty-one from the West, and two from Latin America. By 2017, there were seventy-seven members, still largely from Asia, Europe and the Americas.[20] The World Bridge Federation was established in 1958, with delegates from Europe, the US and Latin America. It now has more than 120 national associations divided into eight regional zones.[21]

These cases suffice to illustrate the general point about the global institutionalisation of sport during the twentieth century. Further levels of global organisation into higher-level federations are now well established. The General Association of International Sports Federations was founded in 1967 and the International Mind Sport Association in 2005.[22] Sport initially followed a core–periphery pattern, with Latin America in a privileged position for rights of admission. Since 1945, sport has been a leading sector in the wider winding-down of the global core–periphery structure.

Sport is almost a poster-child for the positioning of primary institutions across the three domains in global society. It has become a major addition to commerce and religion in the transnational domain, greatly enriching the retinue of activities and secondary institutions found there. In the interstate domain it is represented by the considerable presence of competition among teams defined in nation state, or sometimes (e.g. Wales, Scotland) in purely national terms. Sporting organisations and

[18] www.itftennis.com/en/ (accessed 14 June 2021).
[19] www.icc-cricket.com (accessed 14 June 2021).
[20] www.intergofed.org (accessed 14 June 2021).
[21] www.worldbridge.org (accessed 14 June 2021).
[22] https://gaisf.sport; www.imsaworld.com/wp/ (accessed 14 June 2021).

activities have legitimacy in interstate society comparable to that of science and religion. In the interhuman domain, it has noticeable influence on identity, both in itself (fandoms), and linking to national identity. Football has become so successfully global that one can travel almost anywhere in the world and easily pick up a conversation about it. That fact, plus the strong tie of sport to the principle of human equality, arguably helps to underpin the identity of humankind.

The nature of sport, and its central positioning in the transnational domain, gives it considerable leverage on other primary institutions. As can be seen even from these few brief overviews, sport has been part of the process of winding back the legitimacy of racism, empire and in some ways human inequality generally, in global society. This was visible even before 1945, but much stronger thereafter. The spread of participation in sport had huge implications for racial equality. It meant shared rules and ethical boundaries for all participants, and it necessarily required acceptance of racial equality in competition, and the openness of sporting status hierarchies to performance, across all of humankind. As Vamplew (2021: 67) notes: '[T]heoretically everyone should have an opportunity to compete, and conditions of competition should be the same for all contestants.' Even though racism is still a problem in some sports (notably football) the institution of sport stands against it. Sport has had less of an impact on patriarchy because women mainly compete separately from men, and often get paid less for their work. This separation makes sense for the more physical sports, where size and strength matter. It makes less sense for mind sports and e-sports. Sport is thus a major area in which gender differentiation is widely accepted. Women have nevertheless achieved access to a significant status hierarchy of their own based on performance criteria. The same might be said for disabled people, where there is now a well-developed Paralympics, and some sports such as tennis have set up versions of themselves (wheelchair tennis) that allow disabled people to play in international competitions. The essential meritocracy of sport (drug cheating notwithstanding) might also be thought to complement the market by reinforcing ideas of competition within rules. In the other direction, sport clearly picks up the practice from science of measuring everything in agreed ways, and using that to construct global comparisons.

Human Equality

Human equality was discussed above, along with human inequality, under institutions that became obsolete after carrying over for a while from the CAPE era into modernity. The entry here is simply to remind readers that human equality in itself counts as a new institution arising within modernity. As sketched in Chapter 5a, the main turning point away from human inequality happened only after 1945. Despite many ongoing practices of human inequality, the norms, and in many cases the laws, both nationally and internationally, now support the principle of human equality, which does make this one of the distinctive institutional markers of the transition towards modernity.

Development

Development can be understood generally as the right of states and peoples to acquire the revolutions of modernity, particularly its material aspects, and the duty of global society to facilitate that process. This definition makes development explicitly an artefact of the transition to modernity itself, and even then, a late one. It was not until after 1945, with the process of decolonisation that the concept of development as an obligation and a right crystallised within the UN system. It did so as a means of addressing a post-colonial global international society in which sovereign equality had become universal, and racism illegitimate, but much of the global economy remained structured in core–periphery terms, with huge disparities in wealth and welfare. Development was both a demand of the Third World, and an accepted obligation of the rich core states. It focused on the material conditions, generally under-stood in the simple terms of GDP/capita and rates of economic growth. There is an implicit social side to development as well, but this is both less clear and more controversial. As the failure of attempts to modernise only the military (e.g. China, Ottoman Empire), without doing the same for society more widely, demonstrated, material modernity almost certainly cannot be had without some social basics such as scientific education, popular sovereignty and greater functional differentiation of society.

The logic behind development can be grasped clearly from the concept of uneven and combined development (UCD) introduced in Chapter 1. For modernity in UCD, 'development' means the acquisition of indus-trial modernity; 'uneven' means that this happens at different times in different places; and 'combined' means that all are linked together in a shared global process of political economy whether they like it or not. As argued in Chapter 4, modernity crystallised first in Britain, giving it an advantage in wealth and power that was both admired and feared. Both motives drove its spread, as others tried to catch up with this new mode of power. That, in turn, generated a small core of successfully modernis-ing states that was quite easily able to dominate and subordinate a large periphery of what had become 'underdeveloped' states. The periphery were either still largely in a CAPE era mode of power, or were much slower in adapting themselves to modernity, whether because of domestic resistance to it, or core interference, or both. As noted above, especially for the non-Western countries of the periphery, the powerful, but false, dilemma opened up of whether modernisation inevitably meant Westernisation and loss of their own cultural distinctiveness and identity. As UCD shows, each society modernises in its own way.

Nevertheless, from very early on, the transition towards modernity opened up a distinction between 'developed', or 'advanced', or 'civilised', or 'rich' countries, on the one hand, and 'underdeveloped', or 'developing', or 'backward', or 'barbarian', or 'poor', or 'disadvantaged' countries, on the other hand.[23] This distinction was historically novel because it was based on how much or how little states and peoples had absorbed and adjusted to the multiple revolutions of modernity, not just in technology and science, but in government, economy, society and psychology (Buzan and Lawson, 2015). Because all of the first-round modernisers except Japan were white, this distinction reinforced the 'scientific' racism and social Darwinism that held sway in global society between the middle of the nineteenth and the middle of the twentieth centuries. During the nineteenth and early twentieth centuries, the logic of UCD opened up two tracks leading towards development becoming an institution of global society, one largely within the core, and the other largely between core and periphery in the context of empire.

The first track was driven from early in the nineteenth century when awareness of a development gap emerged strongly within a core group of European countries, plus the US and Japan, where Germany, France, Russia, Japan and others were trying to catch up to Britain's imposing lead in industrialisation, finance and trade, and consequently in wealth and power (Sassoon, 2019). From the mid-nineteenth century, this generated what was later labelled *developmental states*, in which governments used strong state direction of the economy to push rapid industrialisation. Britain's path to modernity had unfolded slowly and without any specific direction, but those seeking to emulate it had a model to follow, and wanted government leadership to accelerate the

---

[23] It is worth noting that the standard for what constitutes being 'developed' is in continuous motion relative to a leading edge that has itself been continuously advancing since the early nineteenth century. In the 1850s, Britain was the most developed society of its day, but by current standards, 1850s Britain would be considered very backward. In this sense, all countries are 'developing', but some are further ahead, and some further behind in that process, and some are gaining ground quickly, and others slowly or hardly at all.

process. This required a close linkage between states and markets, thereby offering a challenge to the more liberal market, *laissez-faire* model of development pioneered by Britain. All 'late' developers required considerable capital if they were to catch up with early movers, and providing this was often beyond the capacities of the private sector (Blyth, 2013). Germany and Japan were the pioneer developmental states (McNeill, 1963: 730–44; Jansen, 2000: locs. 5604–96; Beeson, 2009; Blyth, 2013: 134). The US was partly so in its use of high tariffs to protect its infant industries. After 1917, the Soviet Union became an alternative model of developmental state that initially inspired many, but turned out eventually to be a dead end. A pure command economy did not deliver balanced development. Japan served as a particular source of developmental state inspiration for other peripheral, non-white, modernisers (Osterhammel, 2014: 560, 563). Japanese and German models of state-led development were pioneers of the 'catch-up' policies implemented, not always successfully, by a range of states since then. These early developmental states became in many ways the model for the Asian Tigers during the Cold War and contemporary China since the late 1970s. As Rai (2008: 10) notes, right from the beginning there were strong links between the parallel emergence of nationalism and nation-state building, which she correctly sees as 'the starting point of … the developmental state'. Development is thus not a derivative institution of the market, but was from the beginning, and still is, closely bound up with the dialectic between the market and economic nationalism, and was/is one of the crucial arenas for that struggle.

The second track towards development as an institution emerged in relations between the core and periphery. Ironically, this track grew during the nineteenth century within the institution of imperialism that carried over from the CAPE era, but became obsolete as a primary institution after the Second World War. It has the same roots in UCD as the story within the core, and also picks up the link to nationalism. A relatively small group of Western states plus Japan, embarked on a headlong process of transformation that rapidly, and seemingly open-endedly, increased their wealth and power, both absolutely and relatively, enabling them to form a global core. Those outside that core found themselves left behind, getting relatively poorer and weaker, and falling vulnerable to a colonialism reinvigorated by the immense wealth and power of modernity. The consequence of this gap was the construction of a global-scale core–periphery structure of international political economy, and a colonial international society (Buzan and Lawson, 2015: 185–90, 220–7). To the extent that this gap was understood in the core during the colonial era, it was mainly in terms of the 'standard of civilisation', and a frequently racist discourse about 'advanced' and 'backward' peoples. Some in the grip of race theory thought that the 'backward', 'inferior' peoples would simply fade into extinction as they lost the Darwinian battle of 'survival of the fittest', and were replaced by the mostly white peoples then at the vanguard of modernity. The rise of Japan within the first round of modernising states was a potent spoiler to this image of white supremacy, especially in the periphery. Others saw a moral requirement on the part of the 'advanced' peoples to bring the 'backward' ones up to the 'standard of civilisation'. This obligation was captured in both Kipling's jingoistic phrase 'the white man's burden', and in the idea of the 'civilising mission' for those in the vanguard of both modernity and imperialism.

Interestingly, the main discussions about international relations in the periphery at this time were mostly focused on the struggles against colonialism and racism, and seeking to regain political and social equality (Acharya and Buzan, 2019: 55–64, 96–110). There was a desire to industrialise, but with a few exceptions (Ganguli, 1965; Sun, 2017 [1922]), not so much discussion of the economic and welfare inequalities that are now central to the understanding of development.

Ironically, then, this second track towards development as an institution initially came mainly from within the imperial core, as a moral issue shaped by the self-understanding of the core states and societies of themselves as being 'civilised'. To assist with development was a paternalistic obligation on the part of the 'civilised' towards those less favoured. There was a lot of variation amongst the metropolitan powers in how much or little they acted on this obligation, and it did not override the essentially extractive and exploitative nature of nineteenth- and early twentieth-century empires. Colonialism both forwarded and retarded the transmission of modernity to the periphery, in myriad ways and complex mixes. For example, the grand colonial cities such as Hong Kong, Shanghai, Singapore, Calcutta, Madras and Bombay, and their associated railways and ports, built by the imperial powers were essentially to serve their own extractive needs (Darwin, 2020). Yet they also left a rich legacy for the countries in which they were built. Japan did considerably more to industrialise and modernise its colonies in Korea, Taiwan and Manchuria, than the Western empires did in their colonies, albeit the Japanese were motivated in this by their own strategic concern to create a viable imperial sphere (Buzan and Goh, 2020: 85–8). Britain brought India into the 'steam globalisation' mentioned above, unified the country, and educated a modern elite; but at the same time undermined its steel and textile industries, drained its finances, and sharpened some of its internal divisions.

The colonial construction of non-Europeans as being at a lower stage within a single model of development carried over into trusteeship and the post-colonial discourse of development (Bain, 2003: 13–21). The League of Nations mandate system took a step towards formalising development as an obligation of the mandate powers to bring their wards to readiness for self-government, which most had had for a long time before they were colonised. Readiness for self-government under the conditions of the transition towards modernity, however, was a much more demanding proposition. It implied a considerable degree of modernisation across the board so that the state could hold its own within a global society that was highly penetrative, both internally and externally, and in terms of government, trade, diplomacy, defence, law, human rights, etc.

From the First World War through the Second, the colonial obligation of the metropolitan powers to bring their charges up to a European 'standard of civilisation', morphed into an obligation on the part of the rich world to assist in the development of the 'Third World' or 'less developed countries'. From 1945 onwards, a rapidly expanding group of Third World countries began to press for a 'New International Economic Order' (NIEO), and to form their own IGOs such as the UN Conference on Trade and Development (UNCTAD). Development appears as a goal in countless UN documents, and IGO constitutions and charters. As with science, development's status as a primary institution is flagged in the names of many IGOs from the UN Development Program (UNDP), to the International Bank for Reconstruction and Development (IBRD, aka World Bank), the International Development Association (IDA) both part of the World Bank Group, and the UN Industrial Development Organization (UNIDO). There are many transnational charities such as Voluntary Service Overseas (VSO) and many others that define themselves primarily or partly in terms of international development, and university degrees, departments and institutes ditto. There are also government departments, such as the Department for International Development (DFID) in the UK (now replaced by the Foreign, Commonwealth & Development Office: FCDO).

Development draws legitimacy from both a sense of obligation by the former colonial powers (aka 'developed states') and a sense of entitlement by the post-colonial states that they are owed payback for their earlier exploitation and humiliation. Now that it has won political and racial equality, the Global South is free to focus on developmental inequality mainly cast in economic terms. Development also draws legitimacy from its synergies with the welfare and basic needs end of the human rights and human security discourses. These emphasise rights to adequate nutrition, clean water, shelter, education and suchlike, all of which are associated with better developed societies (Clark, 2013). Whether this right to development is about resources transfers from rich to poor, or about the necessity for the 'underdeveloped' to undergo their own revolutions of modernity, is of course hotly contested. Is aid to be understood mainly as reparations, or mainly as assistance for self-help? Development was thus not the successor institution to imperialism in any general sense. Imperialism was obsolete. But it was a successor, leaving as its legacy to the post-colonial world the discourse of aid and development (Holsti, 2004: 250; Bowden, 2009: locs. 1000–84, 2173–220).[24]

From 1945 onwards, the two tracks that led towards development blended into one. Many Third World states took up the developmental state approach, sometimes very successfully (e.g. Singapore, South Korea, Taiwan), sometimes with partial success (e.g. Brazil, India, Turkey), and sometimes with little success (e.g. Iraq, Egypt, North Korea, Tanzania). A few of them, most obviously China, followed Japan's path in attempting to both catch up and assert claims to great power status (Buzan and Goh, 2020: 18–34). Interestingly, and apparently without embarrassment, China still clings on to its UN status as a developing country despite being widely acknowledged as number two in world power rankings. Merger also took place in the sense that the new primary institution of development after 1945 continued to be embroiled in the contestation between the market and economic nationalism. This was particularly obvious during the first cold war, which was a contest not just over the future shape of the political economy of modernity, but also over the best pathway to development for the countries of the Third World. As noted in the discussion of war above, during the first cold war there was a transposition of core ideological struggles to wars in the periphery. The West, the Soviet Union and China competed amongst themselves both to win allies in the Third World, and to promote and validate their rival models of political economy as the best path to development (Frieden, 2006: 322–39; Westad, 2007: 27–32, 158–69). Development thus became a political football, with the various camps promoting different strategies that were as much informed by the self-interest of the promoters as by the belief that their strategy would be the most beneficial for developing countries.

The first cold war was won by the market, but not by liberalism or democracy. Consequently, at the time of writing there are growing

[24] Those wanting to get a more intimate sense of what this 'development' discourse looked and felt like during the colonial era, albeit only from the perspective of the core, should read Kerr (1916).

indications that a new round of this struggle for the soul of development might be underway between Chinese authoritarian market socialism, and Western models of democratic market political economy. This is becoming part of the second cold war. A dialectic of a different sort is how to bring the aspirations of development into harmony with the rapidly rising imperatives for environmental sustainability. Countries such as India and China struggle openly with this tension, often still privileging their right to development by giving priority to the energy poverty of their peoples, over their great power responsibilities towards climate change (Prys-Hansen, 2022; Yeophanton and Goh, 2022). More on that in the next section.

In terms of its positioning across the three domains, development is principally in the interstate domain. It was formulated in that domain right from the beginning, and has largely remained there both as state-to-state relations, and as the politics of quite a number of IGOs. The commitment to development can be understood as part of the social glue for a rules-based international order. It has penetrated into the transnational domain in terms of the quite numerous INGOs that make development part of their image, advocacy and remit. Its impact on commerce has probably been superficial. Firms invest and trade mainly on the basis of calculation of profit. It is difficult to see much impact on the patterns of identity in the interhuman domain. 'Third World', 'Global South' and suchlike do have elements of collective identity about them, but this operates largely within the interstate domain. At the level of people, it operates mainly as an expression of the unity of humankind, with some citizens of rich countries feeling an obligation to help out with development and disaster relief.

Environmental Stewardship

During the CAPE era, humankind began to have a considerable impact on the environment, both locally and globally, but this was accompanied neither by any coherent awareness of the environment as a system, nor by any sense of collective human responsibility for looking after it. In various creation myths, the environment was a gift of the god(s) to humankind, to be exploited by them, sometimes with respect and custodial responsibility, sometimes regardless. CAPE era societies could learn about bits and pieces of the environmental system, such as winds and currents and soil salination, but they had neither the means to see the environment as a global system, nor the tools to do much about it even if they could see it. In this sense, the environment was taken as a given, and changes in it, for better or for worse, attributed to rewards or punishments from the god(s). For the peoples of the CAPE era, the environment was thus somewhat like the economy: a wider system that people were unaware of as such, and did not try to manage other than very locally, but within which they operated in substantial and significant ways, from trade and finance, to farming, hunting, mining and deforestation.

Environmental stewardship requires not only awareness of the environment as a system, and some understanding of its causal mechanisms, but also possession of the knowledge and capacity for action to do something about it. In that sense, it cannot really happen in the absence of science. Environmental stewardship is thus another primary institution unique to the transition towards modernity. At the time of writing, it is the most recent such institution to emerge. The industrial revolution began to make accelerating impacts on the global environment from early in the nineteenth century, as can be seen from the familiar graphs that chart exponential curves for CO_2 emissions and human population growth. But not until the late nineteenth century had science reached either the necessary level of knowledge, or the planetary reach of operation, to enable understanding of the global environmental system to begin. The globe-spanning empires of Britain and France were important carriers of global science. By 1876, for example, the British Empire 'had the operational rudiments of a world climate observation system linked by telegraph and undersea cables' (Davis, 2002: 217). This 'observational revolution' combined scientific advances with global economic motivations (the linking of climate to agricultural production, famine and trade) and empire (giving the requisite scale of interest and placement of observers), enabling the observation of the planet as a single system (Davis, 2002: 227). Even so, not until the later twentieth century did consciousness of the growing environmental cost of industrialism, mass consumption and population growth begin to emerge as a social and political force. From the 1960s onwards, awareness grew in global society that the consequences of everyday modernity were becoming big enough to threaten its very foundations. Added to this from the 1980s was the warning that a major nuclear war could trigger a 'nuclear winter' long enough and severe enough to threaten not just civilisation, but the existence of humankind itself (Sagan, 1983/4; Nye, 1986).

The story of how environmental stewardship emerged as a principle, then became a norm, and finally by 2015, a primary institution of global society, albeit still a weak one, has been told in some depth by Falkner and Buzan (2019) and Falkner (2021), and there is no need to repeat that detail here. The highlights begin with the 1972 Stockholm Conference on the Human Environment (UNCHE), which was the breakthrough of the norm of environmental stewardship into interstate society, following a long gestation within both individual states, and non-state actors. Next was the 1992 UN Conference on Environment and Development (UNCED) in Rio, which moved developing country concerns to centre stage, enabling environmental stewardship to shed its Western origins and become global in scale as a norm. The key to this was linking it both to sustainable development, and to the idea of 'common but differentiated responsibilities', which put more responsibility onto the core powers whose wealth derived in part from their backlog of historic CO_2 emissions during the nineteenth and twentieth centuries. Finally, it was the Paris climate agreement in 2015 that marked the arrival of environmental stewardship as an institution of global society, with a majority of states of all types acknowledging both the problem of global warming, and their responsibility to act. It was a weak institution in that the regulatory obligations were softened for developed states, with voluntary rather than mandatory emission targets applying to all (Falkner, 2016).

Even though environmental stewardship is still a weak institution, there is evidence for its global standing in the impact it has already had on other primary institutions in various ways. It has added to the remit of great power management, pushing it towards global governance (Falkner and Buzan, 2022). It has also added to the constraints on war; and pushed development towards sustainable development. It is beginning to have potentially big implications for the market, both pressuring it to price in environmental consequences, and favouring green industrial policies such as those that promote renewable energy sources over fossil fuels. And it might impinge on territoriality and sovereignty/non-intervention by fragmenting the ability to act globally, and offering refuge to violators.

In terms of its placement across the three domains, environmental stewardship very much operates in all three. Its origins come from an interplay between campaigning by non-state actors both within states and in the transnational domain, and initiatives taken by states themselves. Environmental stewardship is well embedded in interstate secondary institutions and treaties, including: the 1973 UN Environment Programme (UNEP); the 1985 Vienna Convention on Ozone Layer Depletion and its 1987 Montreal Protocol; the Intergovernmental Panel on Climate Change (IPCC) created in 1988; the 1992 UN Commission on Sustainable Development; the 1992 Global Environment Facility; the 1992 UN Framework Convention on Climate Change (UNFCCC); the 1992 Convention on Biological Diversity; and the 1997 Kyoto Protocol. Following the creation of the US Environmental Protection Agency in 1970, many other states established their own national environmental agencies. Transnational, non-state actors such as the World Wide Fund for Nature (1961), Friends of the Earth (1969), Earthwatch (1971), Greenpeace (1971), Extinction Rebellion (2018), and many others both national and transnational, have been instrumental in mobilising public opinion, and lobbying governments and corporations. Individuals such as Greta Thunberg and David Attenborough have also been influential in this way, though it is not yet clear that environmentalism has come to define a strong shared identity in the interhuman domain.

6   Where Are We Within the Transition from CAPE to Modernity?

Introduction

The aim of this chapter is to focus in on the question that has driven the discussion so far, of whether there was a quick jump, or some kind of long transition, between the conglomerate agrarian/pastoralist empires (CAPE) and modern eras. If a quick jump, how do we identify when modernity began? If a transition, where are we in it? I make the case that while there are some good reasons, particularly on the material side, for seeing a quick jump, the case for understanding the last two centuries mainly as a transition between CAPE and modern is stronger, especially when the social structure is taken fully into account. As is apparent from the discussions above, the material side of modernity tends to be relatively simple. It has a fairly linear, or sometimes geometric, character, tending towards continuous improvement in knowledge and capability. There is a steady drive towards globalisation, particularly in terms of interaction capacity, but also in terms of knowledge. This contrasts with the ideational, social side, where the picture is also full of fragmentations, contradictions and their resultant dialectics. There are social movements and pressures both for and against globalisation. As hinted at in the preceding chapters, if one were looking for a single word to describe the condition of humankind and global society over the last two centuries, *turbulence* would be a strong choice. Both sides of the equation are turbulent, but in very different ways. The turbulence of the material side is like a fast-flowing river: rapid, relentless and transformative advances in knowledge and techniques. The social structural side is more like a slower-flowing river, with complex currents and back-eddies. It is full of contradictions and dialectics both within the social structure and between it and the material world. This dual turbulence is deep. It has not been like the CAPE era, just the occasional material innovation, and the comings and goings of empires, all largely contained in a fairly stable portfolio of material conditions and social structures. As the previous three chapters have laid out, over the last two centuries there have been both profound and frequent transformations in material conditions, and ongoing changes in the foundational primary institutions that compose the social structure.

It is tempting to postulate that social structures often lag behind material ones, playing a continuous game of catch-up. A recent example of this would be the Internet, which was put in place as a technical accomplishment, with little understanding of how deep or profound its economic, social and political consequences would be, or in which directions they would flow. Two decades on, these consequences are still unfolding, often in powerful and unexpected ways such as the socially polarising spread of misinformation via social media, the opportunities for cyberwar, and the networking potential for extremists of all stripes. An earlier example would be the industrial revolution, which upended the whole class structure, and reconfigured the foundations of political legitimacy. At the time of writing these contradictions and their dialectics are still being worked out in both authoritarian and democratic states. The answers are not yet fully clear, but already looking pretty dramatic, from the panopticon surveillance state to the empowerment of extremist views. Of course, it does not always work this way around. It might easily be argued that the idea of science had to be in place before the material take-off of modernity could occur. But if there is broadly a lag, with most social structures scrambling to keep up with changes in material conditions, then it makes sense to take a longer view of the transition process between CAPE and modernity, taking both the material conditions and the social structure, and the interplay between them, into account.

Taking this longer view opens up a deeper and more difficult question: If we are in a transition period, then what will modernity proper look like if and when we eventually get to it? By what criteria can one assess whether a period of transition has ended, and a new era has in some strong sense arrived in its own right? The hunter-gatherer to CAPE transition offers two possible clues. The first is that its turbulent combination of material conditions and social structures eventually settled down into a relatively stable portfolio of the CAPE era. That portfolio then pretty much defined the operating limits of humankind for a long period. There were of course changes within the CAPE era, both material and social, some like iron and new religions significant. But these changes were neither big enough nor frequent enough to breach the general pattern of multiple, hierarchical, religious and imperial social orders. The second, and possibly related, clue is that what today we would call the level of development in the CAPE era was relatively even. Innovations were few and far between, and those that proved effective spread fairly quickly and smoothly amongst those human societies that were in contact with each other across Eurasia. Stone tools improved during the hunter-gatherer era, and those innovations diffused. Weapons improved during the CAPE era, and those innovations likewise diffused.

These conspicuous features of the CAPE era may or may not be relevant to the modern one. There have not yet been enough eras in human history to give solid guidance about their general characteristics. Both the CAPE and hunter-gatherer eras were defined by relative material and social-structural stability. The problem with applying these criteria to modernity is that the main characteristic of the post-CAPE period so far are turbulence and unevenness. Neither the material conditions nor the social structures of modernity are showing any clear sign of settling down. The question then becomes: Is this turbulence mainly a characteristic of the transition period, or is it a deep and durable feature of modernity itself? In other words, should we expect that the turbulence will at some point settle down into a CAPE-like form of stability in which there are changes mainly within the material conditions and social structure, but not frequently of them? Or should we expect deep and frequent changes of the material conditions and social structure to carry on for however long modernity lasts? Is turbulence in this sense the defining characteristic of modernity?

Even if material progress and social innovation continue to feed turbulence, one might take a slightly more optimistic view about the possibility that levels of development could even out. The story of the transition towards modernity in Part II highlighted UCD. It noted how modernity was extraordinarily uneven and combined at the beginning, with a mere handful of first-round modernisers opening up a huge gap between themselves and a large periphery in terms of wealth, power and cultural and political authority. This core group was in more or less complete control of global society until the mid-1970s, and its membership did not change much, though the rank order among them did. Thereafter, however, a second phase of modernisation got underway, with many countries improving their position, and the core expanding relative to the periphery as some of these caught up with the leading-edge societies in their ability to generate wealth and power. It was notable that not only Japan in the first phase, but also many of the later developers in the second, such as the Asian Tigers and China, developed very fast once they had found a viable pathway into accessing the full resources of wealth and power from the revolutions of modernity. It is possible to imagine that process continuing to unfold so that more and more of humankind ends up within the core, and the periphery shrinks to a minority. If this is the way forward, then it will take a long time to realise a condition of relatively even development worldwide. All have been impacted by modernity, but their ability to extract wealth and power from it still differs a lot. There is not yet anything like equal access to wealth, power and knowledge, and the gap is not closing fast everywhere. There is thus quite a long way to go – decades at least, possibly centuries – before one can think of the global playing field being as even as it was during the CAPE era in terms of the widespread sharing across Eurasia of a set of similar material conditions and social structures.

At this point within the transition towards modernity, it is also possible to imagine that UCD is a more durable, or even permanent, condition. There are two ways in which this could happen. In the first way, a faster pace of innovation within the core would continue to regenerate the gap between core and periphery. The periphery would then be condemned to run in order to stand still, with no end in sight. The hunter-gatherer and CAPE eras achieved their stability in part because their rate of innovation was slow. Modernity may never have that option. A second way is the possibility that if constant innovation and turbulence are the defining characteristics of modernity, there could be another vanguard breakout, opening up a new development gap. This could not only reproduce the core–periphery relationship, but also reconfigure the core. Some of the Western panic about China has this flavour – that the Chinese party/state might have discovered a way of unleashing the wealth and power of capitalism, without having to link it to democracy or even loosen the degree of CCP control over society.

To locate ourselves in these questions, it helps to review and consolidate the material in Part II concerning the chronology and periodisation of the transition to modernity so far in terms of material conditions and social structures. Since humankind is facing some stark existential choices, I will also bring in the five pathways for the human species set out in Chapter 1: regression, extinction, suicide, empowerment and replacement.

Material Conditions

The breakout from the constraints of limited supplies and sources of energy and materials of the CAPE era happened from early in the nineteenth century, and thereafter has been a continuous development that appears to be ongoing. This has been supported by, and supports, a similarly rapid and ongoing deepening and diversification of scientific knowledge and technology. During the past two centuries, all of this has added a *technosphere* to the geosphere and biosphere that shape the planet (Dalby, 2020: 8–11). These developments in turn have supported, and been supported by, a geometric rise in the size of humankind from around one billion in 1800, to approaching eight billion at the time of writing. The general shape of material conditions thus looks to be relatively simple and coherent. A crystallisation of various strands early in the nineteenth century enabled rapid and seemingly open-ended expansion in both humankind and its material conditions. For the first two centuries of modernity, the human and material constraints of the CAPE era fell away almost completely, putting the species firmly on the path of empowerment. Recurrent worries about finite supplies of coal, oil, gas and uranium proved ephemeral. This pattern provides one firm foundation for the case that the transition from the CAPE era to modernity was quick and decisive, and that we have been fully in modernity since coal-powered industrialism took off in the early nineteenth century.

Within this overall picture of an ongoing material progression, one could pick out innumerable specific developments from tinned food and shipping containers, through antibiotics and transistors, to refrigerators and bicycles, that changed and advanced the material conditions of humankind in significant ways. But it is worth focusing on identifying the much smaller number of significant points of transformation in the chronology, where innovations in the material conditions had big and widespread impacts on the social order. These are interesting in themselves, but more to the point suggest a pattern of repeated challenges to the social structures that at the time of writing shows no sign of ending. Even those who argue that modernity has picked all the easy, low-hanging, fruit, and will therefore encounter more difficulty in maintaining the rapid progress in science and technology of the last two centuries, do not see the process as coming to an end (e.g. Cowen, 2011). Indeed, as more countries approach the leading edge of the transition towards modernity in terms of their ability to extract wealth and power, and join the core, the resources and people devoted to science and technology worldwide, increases. China's propagandists like to point out that China's own development helps all of humankind in this way, and they are not wrong to say so. This has been a characteristic of the transition to modernity so far as newly modernised powers such as Germany, the US, Russia, Japan, South Korea, Singapore, Taiwan and China have joined the core, and added their weight to the drive to expand human knowledge and empowerment. The US led the way in standardised mass production. Postwar Japan revolutionised design and production techniques, which then spread around the world.

During the nineteenth century, there were two specific technological transformation points that count as outstanding in their impact on global society. First, during the 1830s and 1840s, steam engines became efficient enough to become the dominant form of power for industry and transportation. This revolutionised industry by allowing factories to be located in cities, or indeed anywhere that coal could be delivered by rail or ship, in any numbers required. Steam engines revolutionised inter-action capacity by opening the world to steamships and railways for the mass transportation of goods and people. And they helped to remake the class structure in modern form. Second, from the mid- to late nineteenth century, electricity powered two revolutions. One was the telegraph, and later the radio, which transformed global communications. The other was the spread of electricity as a highly fungible form of power that made energy universally available down to the household level to run machines, lighting, heating and communications. Electricity brought the benefits of modernity to the mass of the people. There was also a general movement from the middle of the nineteenth century to improve public health with measures such as the provision of sewers, refuse disposal, clean water, disease control, better public medical services and suchlike. These are difficult to pin to a specific date, but spread widely once their effective-ness was proven.

During the twentieth century, there were five such material transform-ation points. First, was the liquid fuels that enabled internal combustion engines to revolutionise transportation on the ground (cars, trucks, roads), but more dramatically gave humankind controlled access to the air. More broadly, the shift from coal to oil and gas early in the twentieth century does not look particularly important in the larger picture. It merely replaced one fossil fuel with another to power ships, trains, factories and electricity generation, and was therefore about marginal improvements in efficiency rather than social transformations. But oil revolutionised transportation worldwide, personalising it on land, and opening a new dimension in the air that hugely speeded up the ability to move people and light goods around the planet, whether for peaceful purposes or for war. Second, during the 1930s and 1940s, the invention of antibiotics such as sulfonamides and penicillin transformed medicine, made surgery much safer, and opened the way to a flood of subsequent drugs and mass vaccinations, changing humankind's relationship to the age-old scourge of disease.[1] Third, during the 1940s, nuclear technology opened up a new source of energy for power, transport and weapons. So far, the main impact of this has been in weapons, where the technology potentially provided greater destructive powers than even military

---

[1] The history of vaccines goes back at least a millennium, and has nineteenth-century landmarks, but widespread use against many diseases occurred during the mid-twentieth century.

establishments could find a use for. It enabled humankind to commit species suicide for the first time. Nuclear technology has had a modest role in generating electricity, but it would require breakthroughs in contained nuclear fusion to expand this. It has had only marginal impacts on power for transportation. Fourth, access to earth orbital space, and then the moon and the planets, during the 1950s and 1960s, was a landmark technological accomplishment that will stand for all time in human history. As yet, however, it has not had a transformational effect on everyday life with the exceptions of enhanced global communications and surveillance; and a subtle, and possibly deep, change in how humankind perceives itself in the cosmos. The view of earth from the moon was, as widely observed at the time, perhaps a watershed moment in the psychology of globalisation. The big impacts of access to space other than for science lie in the decades and centuries ahead (Deudney, 2020). Fifth, computing perhaps also belongs here. It likewise started in the mid-twentieth century, and made some impact on data processing and storage, but its big impacts on global society came much more in the twenty-first century.

During the twenty-first century, there have so far been two material breakthroughs that have already begun to have major impacts on humankind and global society. The first was that by the time of writing, computing had begun to deliver big social impacts in two major ways. Perhaps the most obvious was the Internet, which began in the 1990s, but became transformational with the launch of widely used, internet-enabled, smartphones in the first decade of the twenty-first century. The impact of this on global society through cheap access to communication and information (and disinformation) is already huge, and expanding fast. The second way was the march towards machine artificial intelligence (AI). The obvious impact here was the rapidly expanding use of ever-more sophisticated algorithms, married to burgeoning pools of big data, on automation, surveillance, medicine, research, and capitalism and government generally. As symbolised by machine victories in chess and go/*weiqi*, specialised 'narrow' AI could outcompete humans at an increasingly long list of things. This development was pushed by both commercial and defence/security interests, neither of which could afford to be left behind, and the pressure from which made restriction of this technological development difficult or impossible (Stevens and Newman, 2019). The less obvious impact was down the line, where there was growing awareness that possibly within a few decades, all of this might coalesce into forms of artificial general intelligence (AGI) able to compete with the general intelligence of humans. That would certainly reshape global society in very significant ways, opening a pathway to species replacement that would challenge the position, or even the existence, of humankind (Kurzweil, 2005; Bostrum, 2014; Ord, 2020: locs. 2316–550).

The second twenty-first-century breakthrough is the advances in biotechnology that took off late in the twentieth century, with genetic engineering producing huge advances in both medicine (the mass production of insulin), and, more controversially, agriculture (improved crop species with a lower environmental impact) (Brand, 2010: 117–68). Perhaps the key benchmark date for this will come to be seen as 2012, when Jennifer Doudna and Emmanuelle Charpentier published their Nobel-prize-winning study on the use of CRISPR-Cas9 as a kind of genetic scissors that could be used to edit DNA. This capability opened up vast new possibilities for using biological resources for manufacturing, information processing and storage, medicine, food and fuel production and suchlike, a breakthrough that could perhaps be compared to the opening up of the periodic table of the elements to human use that took off in the nineteenth century. It also opened up a worrying link between science and capitalism that threatened to make the development of this technology difficult or impossible to control regardless of the dangers it might pose to humankind (Stevens and Newman, 2019). Ironically, this resource arrived just as the sixth great extinction was beginning to make a serious impact on the planetary biosphere by reducing genetic diversity. As well as revolutionising the material condition of humankind, biotechnology also offered the prospect – still distant given the current state of knowledge, but like AI, plausibly within this century – of species replacement: challenging the primacy of the mark-1 human being, *Homo sapiens*, by remaking ourselves as an improved, or new, species (Greely, 2021). By the time of writing, biotechnology was not only allowing the repair and redesign of existing organisms, but the design and production of entirely new ones (synthetic biology), thus dangling the prospect of controlling its own evolution/replacement before the eyes of humankind. It was also dangling the possibility of regression or extinction by the use, or unintentional escape, of militarised engineered pathogens (Ord, 2020: locs. 2048–305).

The increasingly plausible idea of humans engineering their own replacement species puts us in the position of god(s), albeit in an amusingly inverse way compared to mainstream religions. We are as god(s) to the extent that we can control our own evolution and create new forms of life/intelligence. But unlike the traditional life-creating, superior, god(s) imagined into being by most major religions, we will be gods inferior to the beings we create. What are the implications of this for creation myths? Who then, should worship whom? As Brand (2010: 20) puts it: 'We are as gods and have to get good at it', which will not be easy.

For a mere two centuries, this is not only an impressively long list of major material transformations having big impacts on social conditions, but also a compellingly regular, cumulative sequence that does not yet show signs of coming to an end. Quibbles about the particular changes chosen above would be unlikely to change the basic argument that material changes have thrown regular and frequent transformational challenges to the social structure, and that these look likely to continue. The CAPE era experienced nothing like it in pace and intensity. There may be some grounds for comparison in terms of expanded human access to energy and materials early on, when farming, animal power, wind power, and hard metals transformed the material conditions of human society, and remade its social structure, but these took place over a much more extended period of time.

Most obviously, this list and sequence point powerfully to a trajectory of species empowerment continuing to unfold into the future. This path points towards an ever-more knowledgeable and materially capable humankind whose society is regularly enabled and transformed by new technologies. In principle this could last a long time, and much of science fiction makes this assumption. Think of *Star Trek*, *The Expanse*, and suchlike fictional scenarios. This empowerment is beginning to give humankind some significant options to defend itself against natural threats of species extinction, such as those from space rocks or disease. Within this trajectory, however, lie distinct possibilities for both species suicide and species replacement. Species suicide has been an option ever since nuclear weapons became numerous during the 1950s and 1960s. Our species has, by a mixture of luck and skill, so far survived that particular test. It has, however, continued to develop other instruments that might bring about the same end by different means, ranging from genetically engineered viruses, through experiments with basic physics, to unrestrained pollution of the planetary ecosphere (Rees, 2003; Bostrum and Ćirković, 2008; Ord, 2020). If humankind survives, species replacement is a rapidly emerging possibility, whether by machine intelligence and/or bioengineering. Extinction or replacement would both bring the specifically human story to some kind of end, either by terminating the species altogether leaving no replacement, or by spawning a superior intelligence that replaces it and begins its own history. Species empowerment and species suicide are easy stories to tell in science fiction. Species replacement is much more difficult to tell even as science fiction. How does one imagine the mind of a superior species?

Yet these three pathways are not the whole story. Species regression also looms as a fourth pathway, ironically due to the environmental consequences of the material and energy bounty that the transition towards modernity has provided. The material consequences of modernity are throwing up ever-more formidable obstacles to just carrying on down the empowerment path to wherever it might lead. After a mere two centuries of operation, material modernity is hitting some serious limits. It is widely projected that human numbers will peak during this century, and then decline, and such projections are given credibility by the beginnings of accelerating demographic shrinkage in specific countries such as Japan, Korea, Russia, Germany, China and others (Bricker, and Ibbitson, 2019). More alarmingly, there are increasingly solid projections that the natural planetary systems are no longer able to support the technosphere, creating a rising risk of a phase change in environmental conditions, such as 'hothouse earth', that will bring the sustainability of the human story into doubt. Sea level rises, accelerating extinctions of species, retreating glaciers and ice sheets, melting permafrost, and increasing instances of extreme weather, are already on record. On the near horizon are changes in basic climatic conditions that have been stable for over ten millennia, and on which the story of human civilisation has rested. Well-established patterns of life conditions from bird and fish migrations, through the geography of disease distribution, to ocean currents and patterns of monsoon are beginning to change (Dalby, 2020: 32–3; Ord, 2020).

All of this points towards a distinct possibility that, in material terms, the relatively continuous trajectory of species empowerment is entering a passage of extremely rough, and possibly impassable, road. The social response to this has already begun with the rise of environmental stewardship as an institution of global society, though this might be seen as still fatally lagging behind material events. Some see the environmental challenge to ongoing species empowerment as a route to a slow form of species suicide in which global society does not adapt quickly enough to prevent environmental catastrophe. Others look to species transformation to get humankind out of the problem it has created, with superior minds able to solve the problems that mark-1 humankind has created but cannot solve (Mills, 2013). It might also be seen as just another twist in the story of emergent modernity, and its turbulent interplay between material conditions and social structures. H. G. Wells was not wrong when he wrote a century ago in his path-breaking *Outline of History*, that 'Human history becomes more and more a race between education and catastrophe' (Wagar, 1964: 402).

From a purely material perspective on the question of where are we now within the modern era, the answers might be as follows. There is a strong case for arguing that in material terms, there was a pretty short and sharp transition from the CAPE to the modern eras, which opened up a highly unequal core–periphery global society. This was a double jump, combining a rapid increase in immediately useable resources of wealth and power for the leading-edge core states and peoples, with a deeper command of the knowledge and social practices necessary to generate, reproduce and improve those resources. This was the dual challenge of modernity for those not at its leading edge: how to deal not only with the immediate threat of Western and Japanese power, but also how to respond to the deeper ideational and cultural challenge of modernity itself (Buzan and Goh, 2020: 8). The main character of modernity from a material perspective is the rapid and apparently open-ended accumulation of knowledge that enables access to an ever-widening pool of material, energy and technological resources. This puts continuous pressure on social structures to adapt, making turbulence the normal condition of modernity.

For most of the transition towards modernity so far, the distribution of access to its resources has been highly uneven. The global core–periphery structure among states gives a rough measure of this unevenness, and by that measure there are clear signs that the gap is narrowing: modernity is diffusing more widely, and the core is expanding relative to the periphery as more countries and peoples climb the ladder of development. But modernity remains a long way from the kind of material evenness across societies that characterised the hunter-gatherer and CAPE eras. To that extent, we might still see ourselves as being in the transition from CAPE to modern. Furthermore, leaving aside the state structures, there is a strong sense that a wealthy global elite is opening a widening gap between itself and everyone else. The stupendous material success of the last two centuries has empowered humankind with unprecedented depth and rapidity, but this success itself has raised three transformational possibilities that would interrupt the existing trajectory: species suicide, species replacement and species regression. Species suicide would stop the story of modernity. Species replacement might well continue the story, but probably not with humankind in the starring role. Species regression could take many forms, from being knocked back into the Stone Age in terms of human numbers and levels of development; to engaging in a long struggle to remake material modernity so that it is compatible with, and sustainable on, planet earth. It is significant here that after millennia of increasing human numbers, it is a near certainty that during this century those numbers will peak, and go into decline even if humankind otherwise stays on the path of empowerment.

Social Structure

What then, does the chronology of the transition to modernity look like, in consolidated form, for social structure, and what does it tell us about where we are in the transition from the CAPE era to modernity? As noted, there is a striking disjuncture between the cumulative, relatively simple and coherent developments in material conditions since the nineteenth century, no matter how dramatic and alarming they currently look, and the much messier, more complicated, and more contradictory developments in the social structure. There is clearly a strong interplay between changes in material conditions and changes in social structure. But that interplay is not just all one-way from material to social. Neither is it the only dynamic in play: There are contradictions and dialectics within and among the primary institutions of the social structure that have independent force. As with the material side of the picture, there have been innumerable points of change in the social structure during the past two centuries. The question is: How do we best consolidate these to identify the critical turning points along the way in both the transition from CAPE to modern, and the unfolding of modernity itself? In particular: How do we do so in a more balanced, global society, perspective, that avoids Eurocentrism, and challenges the orthodoxy of great war periodisations that is still so influential in thinking about international relations, both academically and in the public mind?

Since the social world is a messier and more complicated place than the material one, it is not always so easy to pin down precise dates. This is especially so for dates within the last few decades, where the consequences of social developments may well not yet be clear. With these caveats, it is worth thinking about the following global social transformation points on the journey from the CAPE era into modernity.

There are several social structural events clustered around the end of the eighteenth and early nineteenth centuries, which might be seen as marking the opening of the transition from the CAPE to the modern eras. The French, American and Haitian revolutions opened the challenge of popular sovereignty to dynasticism. Nationalism was injected into the social structure of global society by the French revolution. With the Treaty of Vienna in 1815, the balance of power and great power management began to displace dynastic order. The seizing of independence by the white settler colonies of the Americas led to both the rapid emergence of a new great power, and the expansion of 'Europe' to being 'the West'. It is important to note that this first big round of decolonisation did not bring the principle of empire into question, and was facilitated by the fact that the settler elites were of mostly European stock and culture, which by the racist standards of the day greatly moderated any questions about meeting a standard of civilisation for gaining independence and recognition.

During the nineteenth century, centred around 1840, there was another substantial cluster, which might be seen as marking the point at which modernity becomes the dominant trend over the CAPE era social structures. One element of this cluster was the initial opening up of a big military and economic power gap between a small, mainly European/Western core and a large, mainly Afro-Asian periphery. This brought to an abrupt end a long period during which Asia was the core of the global economy, and military power was relatively evenly distributed across the major civilisations. From the 1840s onwards, the core could increasingly occupy and/or punish the periphery more or less at will. A second was the beginnings of a permanent RMA amongst the core great powers that both destabilised relations among them, and pushed older great powers such as China and the Ottoman Empire out of the leading group of powers. A third was the initiation of the still ongoing dialectic between market and economic nationalism as the organising principle for world trade, production and finance. A fourth was the beginning of a general shift towards popular sovereignty in the countries of the core. This co-evolved with the consolidation of nationalism as a key to the political legitimacy of states, and together they sacralised territoriality by linking it to the nation state. A fifth was the opening of the multilectic amongst the new ideologies of progress that defined the politics of modernity: liberal democracy, socialism, nationalism and 'scientific' racism. And the final element of this mid-nineteenth-century cluster was the rising importance of science as the standard of knowledge defining modernity. This cluster was coterminous with the impact of steam engines on the material conditions and its various workings out, which dominated the social structure of modernity for more than a century.

The next fifteen decades can be seen as the working out of the dynamics unleashed during the 1840s and earlier. This working out was often done by war, but there was no big new turning-point cluster until the mid-1970s. Three of these wars stand out in the transition from CAPE to modernity. First, the defeat of Russia in 1905 marked the arrival of Japan as a modern great power showing that a non-Western, non-white people could match the West in its ability to extract wealth and power from modernity. This signature accomplishment, did not, however, open the way to any quick rectification of the imbalance between core and periphery. No other countries followed Japan on the path to full modernity until the 1970s. Second, and despite its prominence in orthodox IR benchmarking, the First World War did relatively little to change the social structure of global society. It resulted in only marginal shifts in the distribution of power within the core, and made hardly any difference to the balance between core and periphery. At best, 1918 might be taken as a benchmark date for the end of monarchy/dynasticism as the mainstream ideology underpinning political legitimacy; and as the start point for the rise of the defence dilemma, and the fear of war beginning to challenge the fear of defeat in politics within and among the great powers. It also marked the rise of socialism and fascism to government in great powers which, like the earlier embedding of liberal democracy in the US and Britain, was a significant way station in the working out of the multilectic amongst the ideologies of progress. It was coterminous with the widening impact of the internal combustion engine.

Third was the Second World War, which, while it deserves more of the benchmark prominence it enjoys in mainstream IR, still did not match the significance of the clusters around 1840 and the 1970s. The main social structural significance of 1945 is that it marks the delegitimation of imperialism and racism as primary institutions of global society, and the reversal of the age-old principle of human inequality to be replaced by the principle of human equality. These are unquestionably major way stations on the path from CAPE to modernity. It might also be argued that the acceptance of decolonisation should add to the credentials of 1945 as an important benchmark. But although political independence was a clear advance for the periphery states and peoples, it was in some important senses a hollow victory. The core powers still retained the whip hand militarily and economically, with what had been a Western-colonial, core–periphery, global society simply being taken down a notch to become a Western-global one. The year 1945 also coincided with the advent of nuclear weapons that massively reinforced the defence dilemma, and fear of all-out great power wars.

The second big transformational cluster in the social structure of GIS took place from the mid-to-late 1970s. This cluster is transformational because it started to draw to a close the first phase of the transition to modernity, in which a mainly Western core dominated a large, mainly Afro-Asian and Latin American periphery. This cluster opened up a second phase in which there was significant evening-out of military and economic capabilities between core and periphery; and the core began to expand to take in some leading non-Western states and peoples. The defeat of the US in Vietnam, and the winding up of the Portuguese Empire in 1975, marked the end of imperial-style colonialism. Guerrilla war and limited nuclear proliferation meant that the core lost its ability to easily and cheaply occupy and hold territory in the periphery.

This was a limited restoration of the military balance, because the core could still use its military superiority to punish the periphery. But it was highly significant politically, because, after a century-and-a-half of vulnerability, it re-established the empirical territorial sovereignty of the periphery. In addition, by the mid- to late 1970s, the Asian Tigers had made apparent the emergence of a second round of successful, full modernisations, and China had signalled its intention to join this club with Deng's reform and opening up. China's turn to capitalism, perhaps more than the demise of the Soviet Union, should be the benchmark for the victory of the market over socialist command economy.

The Islamic revolution in Iran in 1979 marked the resurfacing of religious politics in global society as a whole, adding a radical Islamic state to the global picture in addition to the Organisation of the Islamic Conference, already established in 1972. At the same time, the religious right began to become a force in American politics. The CAPE linkage between religion and politics was back in the mainstream, albeit in the modernised form for which the oxymoronic label 'religious nationalism' might be appropriate. This development reversed more than a century of religion having been pushed to the political margins, or just used as an excuse for colonial interventions. The late 1970s saw the Western turn to globalised neoliberal economics. This might now be seen as opening the last gasp of both Western dominance over the global economy and the first, West-centred, round of modernity. And the Stockholm Conference in 1972 marked the beginnings of global environmental consciousness as a potential obstacle to the unrestrained species empowerment model of the first round of modernity.

Since this big turning-point cluster in the 1970s, humankind has, as after the 1840s one, entered into a period of working out its dynamics and dialectics. Again, this big cluster has been followed by several significant, but not decisive events, not all of which were wars. The broad theme of these events has been the continued erosion of Western dominance, and therefore of the core–periphery structure established during the nineteenth century. The year 1989 features prominently in the benchmark dates of mainstream IR. At first, it looks like an enhancement of Western power, mainly on the basis of a declared shift from a bipolar to a unipolar power structure. It seemed to announce a resolution of the first multilectic around the ideologies of modernity with victory for liberal democracy. Some of this claim for 1989 stood, but only briefly. With the rise of China, the claim for unipolarity proved very short-lived. The claim for liberal democracy was largely hollow. Although the twentieth century did look like an elimination game, with monarchy/dynasticism, fascism and communism successively being knocked out in three world wars, the apparent victory of liberal democracy was not durable. After the massive economic crisis following 2007–8, and the votes for Trump and Brexit in 2016, neoliberal globalisation, and liberal democracy along with it, was in clear crisis even in its heartland. The crisis signalled the de-throning of the Western hegemony of ideas about how to run capitalism, and the 2016 votes signalled the effective abandonment of the will to sustain the pretension of global leadership by the Anglosphere. The real victory in 1989 was for capitalism, and that had already been announced by China a decade previously. By the beginning of the twenty-first century, capitalist authoritarianism was back in China and Russia, and a new competition was underway for the political soul of modernity. The year 2001 also features prominently in the benchmark dates of mainstream IR, because of the terrorist attacks of 9/11 and the consequent declaration of the global war on terror. The significance of 2001 is amplified by its linkage of terrorism as punishment power, to the return of religion into world politics, and by the elevation of religion-based non-state actors to the status of opponents in war. Another CAPE pattern, political religion, had resurfaced in modern form. This event takes on deeper significance if seen as a way of giving the periphery asymmetric means of balancing the core's remaining power to inflict military punishment. In that light, it is another major step, albeit still an asymmetric one, in the restoration of a military balance between core and periphery. The rise of China as a full-spectrum military power was also a telling marker of Western decline. Not since Japan had any non-Western country achieved that kind of equality.

The opening two decades of the twenty-first century thus saw not only a retreat of Western authority and leadership, but also the opening of a second round of the ideological multilectic. This new multilectic hinged on political varieties of capitalism and their interplay both with each other, and with the rising constraint of environmental limits. Could ongoing human empowerment be sustained in the political and economic form of the first two phases of the transition to modernity, which went for growth and expansion without pricing in environmental externalities? By 2015, the arrival of environmental stewardship as a new institution of global society had been announced by the adoption of both the Sustainable Development Goals and the Paris Agreement on Climate Change. The year 2020 might well come to be seen as the benchmark date for the opening of the second cold war, with China and Russia on the one side, and the West and many of China's neighbours, on the other side. China's ruthless scrapping of the 'one country/two systems' formula between itself and Hong Kong, along with its aggressive behaviour towards India, Japan, Taiwan and Southeast Asia, began to reconfigure the global order. The Quad grouping among the US, Japan, India and Australia, previously shallow, deepened towards something more like an alliance, and even Europe began to see China as a broad-spectrum threat. There were growing concerns around Taiwan in 2021–2, and when and how China might enforce its claim; about how the US capability to deter China is waning; and about Xi Jinping's desire to claim the mantle of finishing the civil war by reincorporating Taiwan (*The Economist*, 20 February 2021: 49). Russia's second invasion of Ukraine in 2022, and China's support for its 'strategic partner', underlined that a second cold war was setting in, probably for quite some time, as the new geopolitical and geoeconomic reality.

Conclusions to Part II

In the Conclusions to Chapter 3, working with the advantage of hindsight, I focused on the end of the CAPE era, its successful, if tenuous, connecting up of the whole planet by trade, and the precursors of its transition towards a new era of modernity. I looked in particular at the leading role of merchants and commerce in realising dreams of universality beyond the reach of any empire or religion, albeit mainly in the economic sector and not in the political and societal ones. I posited that the great achievement of the CAPE era was to achieve the first conscious globalisation, but that given the limits of technology and energy resources, this could only be done thinly. That pointed forward to the intensification of globalisation as the likely next step for humankind after the CAPE era. The four chapters in Part II could easily be read as fulfilling that expectation. Especially in material terms, globalisation was hugely intensified. The social picture is much more mixed, but can also be read as intensifying globalisation. It is absolutely clear that by the late eighteenth, early nineteenth century, the CAPE era was over. The question is how to read what followed it: as the opening of a third era, modernity, or as the opening of a period of transition between the CAPE era and an emergent modernity?

The mainstream view is that a new era of modernity began during the nineteenth century. That view is very obviously and visibly defined by the utter transformation of humankind's relationship to the material sphere since then. Within two centuries of the CAPE era ending, the material condition of humankind had changed beyond recognition. The materials available for human use had expanded from a fairly limited repertoire to a seemingly infinite variety. The sources of energy moved from few, and very limited, to many, and seemingly unlimited. Interaction capacity moved from being so low that most people's entire lives were local, to so high that the world itself became local for a majority of its inhabitants, including those from less-developed countries. Military technology moved from a scarcity of destructive power so stringent that marshalling it was a crucial skill defining great generals, to an overabundance so great as to make all-out war amongst advanced powers an irrational act that threatened the survival of the species. Civil technology burgeoned in quantity and quality sufficient to give billions of people lifestyles in some ways comparable, and in some ways superior, to those of the tiny CAPE era elites.

A transformation of the material conditions of humankind on such a scale, and carried out with such speed and intensity, could hardly fail to have huge consequences, both material and social. Two material costs stand out. The first of these became obvious by the 1950s and 1960s, when the possibility of species suicide by direct action first manifested itself in the form of nuclear arsenals big enough to be able to bomb humankind back to the Stone Age, or possibly even into extinction under some scenarios such as 'nuclear winter'. There were precursors to this after the First World War, when fears of air power in the form of bombers armed with poison gas, incendiary weapons and high explosives generated images of the end of civilisation not dissimilar to those of nuclear war. But these were influential mainly in the Anglosphere. It took nuclear arsenals comprising thousands of warheads in a context of hair-trigger rivalry between the US and the Soviet Union, to bring the possibility of species suicide to mass attention, and to make the *defence dilemma* a permanent feature of the human condition. The species was living on a knife edge in a way that it had never done before, and might have to do for the foreseeable future. Acquiring the option of species suicide opened the door for the first time to the question of what responsibility humankind had for ensuring the life and possibilities of future generations (Boulding, 1966: 10).

The second material cost came into general awareness during the 1970s. This was the rising concern that the material, energy and technological cornucopias of modernity were beginning to overburden the planet in various ways. Unlike the threat of nuclear species suicide, which was clear and simple, concerns about the environment were multiple, complex and contestable. Would key resources like oil run out? Was the expanding human population, and its accompanying industrial pollution, threatening the biosphere? Were specific forms of that pollution affecting the atmosphere in such a way as to promote global warming and climate change? Were any or all of these things happening in such a way, and on such a scale, as to undermine the foundations of humankind's achieved levels of prosperity and civilisation? Could they open an indirect path to species suicide if the derangement of the ecosphere and climate became so severe as to undermine the conditions for human and other forms of life? The catchword here was *sustainability* and the problem was captured in the title of a 1970s tract on the issue: *The Limits to Growth*

(Meadows and Meadows, 1972). The argument was that the model of modernity that had transformed the material and social conditions of humankind for the first century and a half of the new era was rapidly becoming unsustainable. This would become an increasingly pressing question confronting not only scientists, technologists, and business people, but also the political and social structure of humankind. As Tainter (1988: loc. 3268) makes crystal clear, in contrast to CAPE era societies, contemporary ones cannot collapse back into lower levels of complexity without there being widespread chaos. Modern populations are not only much bigger than CAPE ones, but also far more functionally specialised. Much higher percentages are urbanised, with a relatively tiny proportion of the population still engaged in food production. There is no route back to subsistence that would not involve a substantial portion of the human population starving to death, or being killed in struggles to acquire the diminishing supplies of resources necessary to sustain life.

These material changes and their consequences had big impacts on social relations, where the material and social transformations co-constituted each other in myriad and complex ways. Disentangling that Gordian Knot is the problem facing those seeking to explain the causes of modernity. Such unprecedented increases in wealth, knowledge, capability and human numbers could hardly leave the social structure unchanged. Whatever the intricate nexus of causality, the changes in the social structure of humankind during the last two centuries were almost as momentous and dramatic as those in its material condition. When one looks at the social structure of emergent modernity in terms of primary institutions, as was done in Chapters 5a and 5b, three questions arise. First, how coherent is the current set of primary institutions? Second, how do these institutions distribute themselves across the three domains in terms of where they are primarily rooted? Third, what do we learn about eras and transitions from viewing social structure in terms of the continuities and changes in primary institutions?

Coherence

In terms of coherence, does the current set of primary institutions mainly reinforce each other, or is there a lot of tension and contradiction among them? The primary institutions of the CAPE era, whether one approves of the values they represented or not, provided a set that was remarkably stable, mostly mutually supporting, and in harmony with the material conditions. Although many civilisations and empires came and went, the social structure defining and containing them all remained firmly in place for several thousand years. Transitions are by definition about turbulence in both material and social conditions, and that has certainly been true of the one out of the CAPE era so far. For the last two centuries, the material conditions of humankind have gone through, and are still going through, a dramatic, relentless and seemingly endless transformation. Those material changes have had huge impacts on the social structure in terms of both class, and the balance between stratificatory and functional differentiation. At the same time, the entire set of primary institutions has been in transition. Some CAPE institutions have sunk into obsolescence. Some have adapted to the new circumstances, and survived. Many new primary institutions have formed, and had to work out both their operational forms, and how they would relate to other primary institutions. According to the analysis in Chapters 5a and 5b, the transition towards modernity has made two CAPE era primary institutions obsolete (dynasticism and empire); partly, but by no means totally, reversed a third (human inequality); allowed six to continue, albeit often with substantial changes of meaning and practice (religion, war, territoriality, sovereignty, diplomacy and international law); and added eight new ones that did not have substantial precursors in earlier times (balance of power, great power management, nationalism, market/economic nationalism, science, sport, development and environmental stewardship).

At this point, the condition of humankind looks as if it will remain turbulent for the foreseeable future, with no island of stability comparable to the CAPE era anywhere in immediate prospect. It would be some kind of miracle if material and social transformations on this scale had produced a quick transition to the kind of stable, mutually supportive, set of primary institutions that characterised both the CAPE era as a whole, and the much briefer and more local Westphalian period in seventeenth and eighteenth century Europe. Are we to understand this as an inherent quality of a new era of modernity that will endure for the whole of it? Or should it be seen as a property of the transition from CAPE to modernity that will at some point beyond our present horizon settle down?

Mayall (1990, 2000b) pioneered the idea that the nineteenth century rise of the market and nationalism were disruptive of the older set of European primary institutions dating from the seventeenth and eighteenth centuries. He was absolutely correct to see them in that way, and to link that disturbance to the transition towards modernity. With the perspective developed in the preceding four chapters, we can now take a more comprehensive view of this theme. The disruption amongst primary institutions in the transition towards modernity is considerably deeper and wider than that charted by Mayall, and it feeds the deep questions about modernity just asked: Is this modernity proper, or is the transitional period from CAPE to modern eras still unfolding? Or, given the short time frame versus the long one of CAPE, can we sensibly answer this question from where we stand now, without the benefit of hindsight? I think we can attempt a preliminary answer. That answer favours seeing the period from the end of the CAPE era to roughly 2020, as definitely transitional. Whether the third phase now opening is more transition or modernity proper, I leave for Chapters 7 and 8. Here I confine myself to summarising the main tensions and contradictions within the current set of primary institutions, both in themselves, and in how they interrelate with changing material conditions.

The rapid advances in science and technology of the last two centuries have largely broken the twin constraints on the CAPE era of limited supplies and sources of energy, and a narrow suite of material resources. They have done so, however, at the price of raising an increasingly urgent question about the sustainability of modern global society in relation to the carrying capacity of the planet. This puts a number of dynamics between the material and social structures into play. Rising capacities for destruction make the traditional style of all-out war among states/ empires a threat to the survival of human civilisation, and possibly much of the biosphere. The uneven and combined development of the first two post-CAPE centuries has created a tension with the move towards greater human equality, and empowered development as a new institution. The threat to the planetary ecosystems and biosphere posed by modernity's unleashing of energy and material abundance, not only creates tensions around the dialectic of market versus economic nationalism, but also drives the emergence of environmental stewardship as an increasingly important new institution of global society. While the prevailing material conditions enable and encourage a global economy, this comes into a seemingly cyclical tension with the fragmenting effects of the political settlement around the package of sovereignty, territoriality and nationalism. Great power management could be a focal point for this contradiction. The positive feedback effects of science in raising wealth and power, work to reinforce the standing of GPM, but the rising costs of science, its sometimes negative results, and its seeming willingness to put humans at risk, also reinforce the ongoing challenge from religion, mysticism and conspiracy theories. The rise of machine-based societies no longer much dependent on muscle power has almost certainly facilitated the drift towards human equality generally, whether in terms of class or gender. Yet within this, there was a major back-eddy on race up to 1945. There remains both an ongoing gap between those more and less advanced along the road to extracting wealth and power from the revolutions of modernity, and between men and women. All of this has to be seen as detail against the possibility that the meta-dialectic between humankind and the planetary ecosystems might yet generate a level of environmental destruction sufficient to terminate the great game of human empowerment after a run of five millennia.

In addition to this material background and its effects, there are other, more or less independent, tensions and contradictions within the set of primary institutions that constitute the contemporary social structure. This is hardly big news in itself. Buzan and Lawson's (2015) discussion of the ideologies of progress (liberalism, socialism, nationalism and 'scientific' racism) that arose during the nineteenth century, shows how they have been working out their contradictions for the last two centuries, by both peaceful and violent means. The central intellectual edifice of Marxism is precisely about the global dialectics of class conflict between liberalism and socialism in industrial society. The point is not the contradictions themselves, but seeing them collectively as defining a process and a period of transition between eras. With a more comprehensive list of the primary institutions of modernity to hand, it still pays to take a closer look at the many tensions and contradictions using this more holistic perspective. There is tension between meritocracy, and the still significant residuals of kinship and birthright, and also between the residuals of dynasticism and imperialism, and nationalism and popular sovereignty. This includes a very substantial overhang of post-colonial resentment in the Global South, and lingering colonial arrogance and denial in the former imperial states of the North, that continues to poison relations between them. More on this in Chapter 8. The contradiction between human inequality and human equality is still unfolding, particularly in terms of sex, race and wealth/welfare, and potentially in terms of bio-engineered challengers to the mark-1 human being. The contradiction between religion and science, or more broadly between rationality and mysticism/faith, as valid ways of thinking, is ongoing. So is the related tension between religious and secular ideologies, including nationalism, in defining political legitimacy. Also ongoing is the contradiction between the practices of war and the market, on the one hand, and war and environmental stewardship, on the other hand. The contradiction between territoriality and, up to a point, nationalism, on the one hand, and the market and environmental stewardship, on the other hand, is growing. So too are the contradictions between sovereignty, and human rights (human equality), and the more solidarist aspects of international law, and environmental stewardship. The contradiction between great power management and sovereign equality/non-intervention remains long-standing, and could be intensified if environmental stewardship strengthens. There are tensions between development, and both the ongoing dialectic of the market versus economic nationalism, and environmental stewardship.

The length and complexity of these lists of material and social contradictions, and their potential to play into each other, points strongly towards a process of transition between eras. If this is modernity proper, then it is intrinsically incoherent. The relentless unfolding of the meta-dialectic between human civilisation and the planetary ecosphere suggests that this question might be answered more quickly than its complexity would suggest. It will either be made irrelevant by a collapse in the material conditions that support industrial civilisation, or resolutions will be found that prevent that outcome. More on this in Part III.

Distribution across the Three Domains

In Chapters 5a and 5b I looked at how each of the primary institutions discussed was positioned across the three domains: interpolity, transnational and interhuman. The purpose was to destabilise the English School's tendency to talk about primary institutions only in relation to the interstate domain, and to lay the foundations for a global society approach to IR by getting some idea of how much primary institutions operate across the three domains. In most cases, the answer was that primary institutions clearly and normally operate across domains, often deeply. Table 1 attempts a crude summary of this discussion. As the table shows, many of these primary institutions have strong roots not only in the interstate domain, but also in the transnational and interhuman ones as well. The table is necessarily oversimplified and impressionistic, but in principle it should be possible to undertake empirical studies that would refine or contest these results. Even if my estimates are only half correct, they would still support the case for repositioning our perspective from the global interstate society one, which has dominated most English School work, towards the global society one outlined in Chapter 1. On this evidence, global society is in many ways already here, and integrated world society has been around for a long time. This is not just a matter of the interstate domain projecting its institutions down into the other two. The traffic goes both ways, with the interhuman and transnational domains projecting institutions such as religion and environmental stewardship upwards. Institutions such as nationalism, the market (and earlier, trade), diplomacy, science and sport work in complex ways across the three domains.

I have argued that the post-CAPE task of global society was to intensify the thin globalisation that was the culminating achievement of the CAPE era. Even within the historically short period of little more than two centuries, this task has been accomplished. In material terms, the planet has been shrunk to local in terms of human access. Global consequences

Table 1 *Contemporary distribution and intensity of primary institutions across the three domains*

Primary Institutions	Interstate			Transnational			Interhuman		
	High	Med.	Low	High	Med.	Low	High	Med.	Low
(Kinship)									
Dynasticism to 1945		✓			✓✓		✓	✓	✓
Dynasticism since 1945			✓		✓	✓			
Empire up to 1945	✓				✓			✓	
Empire since 1945			✓✓			✓✓			✓✓
Human equality up to 1945	✓				✓				
Human equality since 1945	✓				✓✓			✓	
Religion	✓				✓✓			✓✓	
War	✓				✓		✓	✓✓	
Territoriality	✓				✓			✓✓	
Sovereignty	✓				✓				
Diplomacy	✓			✓		✓			
International Law	✓				✓				
Balance of Power	✓				✓	✓			
Great Power Man.	✓			✓	✓✓		✓✓		✓
Nationalism	✓			✓	✓				
Market/Econ. Nat.	✓			✓	✓		✓		
Science	✓							✓✓✓	
Sport		✓		✓				✓✓	
Development	✓				✓			✓	
Environ. Steward.	✓							✓	✓✓

Domains

322

are sufficient already to threaten the stability of the planetary ecosphere. In terms of social structure, some elements of it strengthen globalisation (most obviously the market, international law, science, sport, environmental stewardship), while some lean towards fragmentation (most obviously territoriality, nationalism, sovereignty, and the loss of dynasticism and universal empire). Some cut both ways (religion), and as argued above, there are many ongoing tensions, contradictions and dialectics within the social structure, and between it and the material one, that make the overall picture turbulent. This rapid and deep intensification of globalisation has been in many ways astonishing.

Yet while it has been planetary in scale, its implementation has for most of this period been extremely uneven. Initially, and for the best part of two centuries, only a handful of societies successfully maximised the wealth and power potential of the multiple revolutions of modernity. This enabled them to create, and dominate, a core–periphery global political economy. Even now, this skewed distribution remains, although the rise of China, India and others, signals that an evening-out of modernisation is well underway. An ever-widening circle of human societies is coming to terms with modernity sufficiently well to match, or possibly surpass, the success of the first-round modernisers in accumulating wealth and power. In the process, they are also recovering their cultural and political authority in modernised form. The extreme inequalities of uneven and combined development that marked the nineteenth and twentieth centuries have begun to fall away. As more societies come to terms with modernity, especially in Asia, the core is expanding, and the periphery is shrinking. Along with the crisis of planetary carrying capacity, this is the second major factor suggesting that humankind has reached a significant turning point in the evolution away from the CAPE era. The question still remains open about whether we are in the transition from the CAPE era, and the full character of modernity has yet to settle down; or whether we are within modernity proper, and this is what it looks like.

Implications for Understanding Eras and Transitions

It becomes clear from the discussion in these four chapters, that the last two centuries can and should be seen as a transition from the CAPE era to modernity, and not as modernity proper. This transition has so far displayed two clear phases. The first, from the 1840s up to the 1970s, was not just about the material and social breakouts from the CAPE era, but also that this breakout, and the unprecedented wealth and power it generated, was for a century and a half commanded by just a handful of countries and peoples. The consequence of that was a first phase defined by the imposition of a core–periphery global society dominated politically, economically and militarily by a few leading Western powers and Japan. This was the transitional phase of Western breakout and domination. The second phase runs from the 1970s through the second decade of the twenty-first century. With some ups and downs, its defining features have been the winding-down of Western dominance, economically, politically and militarily; and the expansion of the core by the entry of successful second-round modernisers, most notably China. This phase was about the spread of modernity beyond the first round modernisers to the beginnings of a more global distribution. This second phase also looks clearly transitional.

At the time of writing, global society is still a long way from any kind of general equality in wealth, power, and cultural and political authority. But by the third decade of the twenty-first century, it looked to be entering a third phase. By 2020, there was a significant, but far from total, equalisation gaining pace. There was an established reconfiguration of patterns of power and threat in a second cold war that was distinctively different from those in the period of Western domination. There was no sign that the overall material turbulence of the transition to modernity was slowing down. A new ideological dialectic was underway between democratic and authoritarian capitalism. And a new meta-dialectic was taking root between carrying on with the project of species empowerment at the maximum possible pace, on the one hand, and avoiding species regression and/or suicide, on the other hand. This third phase I call *deep pluralism*. It might be seen as a further stage of the transition out of the CAPE era, or it could be interpreted as the opening of modernity proper. More on that in Part III.

If this assessment is accurate, then we have a reasonably clear answer to the question about where we are in modernity, and what the transition from CAPE to modern looks like. The enlargement and intensification of globalisation hypothesis about the transition towards modernity has also certainly been vindicated. We are entering a third phase of the transition between CAPE and modernity, in which the following characteristics are emergent:

- The stark inequalities of the first phase are being eroded by the diffusion of wealth, power, and cultural and political authority.
- Consequently, the core of global society is expanding and the periphery shrinking.
- The dominant energy source is moving away from fossil fuels.
- The dominant technologies are becoming biological and digital.

Decades	Material Conditions	Social Structure	Phases of the Transition towards Modernity
1770s		Transition to modernity begins: American and French revolutions challenge dynasticism with popular sovereignty. Industrial revolution in Britain. Decolonisations in the Americas. Rise of nationalism, balance of power, great power management.	The first phase of the transition period between CAPE and Modernity. Dominated by the West and Japan, and unrestrained in pursuit of wealth and power.
1780s			
1790s			
1800s			
1810s			
1820s			
1830s	Commercial electrical telegraph.		
1840s	Steam becomes the dominant source of industrial power. Fossil fuel economy takes off. Permanent RMA.	The modern core imposes an imperial core–periphery structure on Asia and Africa. Permanent RMA disempowers the periphery and destabilises the core. Opening of the dialectic between the market and economic nationalism; and the multilectic amongst the ideologies of progress. Rise of science as a global institution.	
1850s			
1860s			
1870s			
1880s	Electricity generation and transmission.		
1890s	Radio transmission.	Rise of sport as a global institution.	
1900s	Internal combustion engines power motor vehicles and aircraft. Rise of oil alongside coal as key fossil fuel.	Japan's defeat of Russia breaks the white monopoly on acquiring modernity.	
1910s		First World War makes dynasticism obsolete; gives socialism a great power; and introduces fear of war (the defence dilemma) within the core.	
1920s		Failure to restore global market. Rise of fascism in three great powers.	
1930s	Antibiotics.		

325

Table 2 (*cont.*)

Decades	Material Conditions	Social Structure	Phases of the Transition towards Modernity
1940s	Nuclear technology. Early computers.	Second World War delegitimises racism and imperialism, and advances human equality. US becomes the leading power.	
1950s	Access to near-earth orbital space.		
1960s	Spread of nuclear weapons gives the first option for species suicide for humankind.		
1970s	Personal computers	Beginning of the end of Western-global order. Defeat of US in Vietnam. Break-up of Portuguese empire concludes decolonisation. China turns to capitalism. Resurfacing of religion in politics.	The second phase of the transition between the CAPE era and Modernity. Dominated by the expansion of the core beyond the first-round modernisers.
1980s		Rise of global neoliberalism. Rise of global environmental awareness.	
1990s	Internet. AI wins world chess championship.	Ending of Cold War gives a brief period of US primacy, and neoliberal market globalisation. Sustainable development as a new norm reflecting rising environmental awareness.	
2000s	Smartphones	Global economic crisis begins the return of economic nationalism and the dethroning of liberal teleology. GWoT completes the asymmetric military balancing of the Global South.	
2010s	CRISPR-Cas9 opens up gene editing. Possibility of humans controlling their own evolution/ replacement. Environmental constraints begin to limit the unrestrained pursuit of wealth and power.	Deep pluralism begins to emerge. Resurgence of authoritarianism. China follows Japan's model in seeking full developmental equality as a great power. New multilectic around varieties of capitalism/multiple modernities emerges. Environmental stewardship as a new institution.	
2020s	Covid-19 pandemic. Rising awareness of climate change as its consequences intensify. Uneven shrinkage of human numbers becomes apparent.	Second cold war consolidates between China and Russia, on one side, and the West and various allies, on the other side.	The third phase (deep pluralism) begins.

• The principal problem of this third phase is becoming how to deal with the rapidly mounting environmental constraints that are the legacy of the first round's hugely successful, but also hugely damaging, intensification of globalisation.
• There is mounting pressure on development to become sustainable.
• A new ideological multilectic centred on democratic and authoritarian versions of capitalism, and how they deal with a strengthening imperative for environmental stewardship, will have to be worked through.
• At this point, the next phase looks like being defined by a deepening second cold war.
• The human population is visibly approaching its peak in numbers, but the process of shrinkage is very uneven, with some parts of humankind already having peaked, and others still expanding.

The transition to modernity did indeed move fast, break things, and speed up history. But it is nevertheless wrong to think of the CAPE to modern transition as a quick jump happening early in the nineteenth century. It looks a bit like that from a purely material perspective, but not when the slower moving and messier perspectives of social structure are taken into account. From here on in, modernity will unfold increasingly on its own terms, albeit with the next phases having to cope with the enormous environmental problems that are a legacy of the first. Although it is too close in time to be absolutely sure, 2020 feels like a promising choice for benchmarking the shift into the third phase. The material and social highlights of these three phases are summarised in Table 2.

Part III

Deep Pluralism
More Transition or Modernity Proper?

Introduction to Part III

How will the third phase of the transition to modernity unfold? One way of approaching this question is through the five possible pathways for the human species set up in Chapter 1. From that perspective, there is an emerging dialectic between the ongoing push for species empowerment that has defined humankind's path for thousands of years, and the danger that path raises of species suicide, replacement or regression. There is not much point in dwelling on the options and scenarios for species suicide, extinction or replacement. The first two simply end the story. The third might well divide opinion on whether species replacement is part of the problem or part of the solution. Replacement could come in various forms, with no way of predicting which. It is anyway beyond my capacities to work out what the material capabilities and social sensibilities of a superior intelligence to ours might be. That leaves the option of exploring how humankind might try to stay on the path of empowerment, while adapting to the mounting environmental constraints it now faces. What will be the fate of modernity's project to intensify globalisation? Is some regression, such as a shrinking human population, necessary at least for a while? How will the third phase of modernity deal not only with the ongoing uneven distribution of wealth, power and knowledge, but also the failure so far to come up with any ideological equivalent to the socio-political homogeneity of the hunter-gatherer era around kinship, and of the CAPE era around imperialism, monarchy/dynasticism and religion? There has been some consolidation around capitalism, albeit with ongoing oscillations globally between the market and economic nationalism. Yet the contestation between democracy and authoritarianism – both compatible with versions of capitalism – as the appropriate political form for this phase, is ongoing. The outlook for the social structure of global society in the third phase of the transition to modernity still looks turbulent.

The two chapters in this part of the book follow the same scheme used for eras 1 and 2 of looking at material conditions and social structures. But they shift the perspective from looking backwards, as was done in

Parts I and II, to looking ahead into the rest of the 2020s and a bit beyond. The advantages of hindsight are therefore gone, replaced by the hazards of anticipating the future. The argument is not based on historical evidence of what happened, but on a structural logic of continuities and changes, and projections of how the dialectics and multilectics currently in play seem likely to unfold. In other words, the structural framework set out in Chapter 1 that I have been using as a lens to make sense of humankind's past, is here turned forward to see what leverage it provides in anticipating how the next phase of the transition to modernity will unfold. The framing concept for these two chapters is *deep pluralism*: the idea that wealth, power, and cultural and political authority will become increasingly diffuse, within a system that has high interaction capacity and is strongly interdependent. Since the present historical context for deep pluralism is the decline of Western dominance, it carries the additional twist that in the face of cultural and political differentiation, liberal teleology will decline as the supposed model for the future.

I conduct this exercise within the window of the assumption that humankind will be able to continue on the path of species empowerment, or at worst suffer some fairly mild regression. I do not do more than glance at options for species suicide, replacement, extinction or major regression. Within that assumption, I try to follow the likely dialectics of the established and emerging contradictions both within the social structure, and between it and the material conditions. I also entertain the question of whether deep pluralism is best seen as a third phase of the transition towards modernity from the CAPE era, or as the opening of modernity proper. The main focus of these chapters is to sketch out the likely characteristics of global society characterised by deep pluralism. But an additional key argument is that in this third phase, humankind faces a rapidly rising environmental constraint on the fossil-fuel driven, human empowerment imperative of the first two phases. This constraint raises major questions around how, or even if, the transition from CAPE to modernity will continue to unfold. It will, at the very least, have considerable impacts on the social and material conditions of humankind, and conceivably could derail the whole story of human empowerment. It also raises questions about how we should think about the material and social conditions that might constitute a stable third era of modernity.

Deep pluralism is not a new concept. I have been writing about it all through the last decade (Buzan, 2011; Buzan and Lawson, 2015: 273–304; Buzan and Schouenborg, 2018: 192–3; Acharya and Buzan, 2019: 261–84). In one sense, deep pluralism is a theoretical concept about structure, and in another it is an empirical projection of global trends in the current phase of transition from the CAPE era towards modernity. In a structural theoretical sense, deep pluralism can be compared and contrasted to both the CAPE structure and the first two phases of the transition towards modernity. The CAPE era also had diffuse wealth, power and cultural and political authority, but not within a system that had high interaction capacity and was strongly interdependent. The first phase of the transition had wealth, power and cultural and political authority concentrated in a small group of mainly Western states plus Japan and Russia, but within a system that had high interaction capacity and was strongly interdependent. This concentration peaked with the recognition of the US and the Soviet Union as not just great powers, but superpowers, after the Second World War. Deep pluralism follows from the logic of UCD once wealth and power and cultural and political authority have become less unevenly distributed than they were during the first phase. It is historically novel. In the terms discussed in the Introduction to Part II, it marks a kind of return to the polycentric model of globalisation, with several civilisations empowered, but only via the unequal path of the monocentric model in which the West, during the first phases of the transition to modernity, dominated all others and imposed an intensely interdependent system of modernity on them.

Both 'deep' and 'pluralism' carry specific meanings. Recall from the definitions in Chapter 1 that pluralism privileges the units of the interstate system/society over global society, valuing sovereign states as a way of preserving the cultural diversity that is the legacy of human history. It favours sovereignty and *raison d'état* (or *raison d'empire*) over *raison de système*, and operates by a logic of coexistence within a fairly thin interstate society. In this context, 'deep' means not just a diffuse distribution of wealth and power, but also of cultural and political authority. These criteria contrast sharply with the two centuries of Western domination and globalisation in which wealth and power, and cultural and political authority, were relatively concentrated. But while pluralism usually privileges interstate society, readers should keep in mind the arguments from Part II about how the first two phases of the transition towards modernity have created a global society, whose primary institutions operate across, and are embedded in, all three domains.

In the last few decades, much thought has gone into how to conceptualise what was agreed to be an important shift in the nature and structure of global society once Western dominance began to decline. Various labels have been put forward to capture the novelty and complexity of this emergent construction: *plurilateralism* (Cerny, 1993), *postmodern international system* (Buzan and Little, 2000: 363–7), *heteropolarity* (der Derian, 2003), *no one's world* (Kupchan, 2012), *multinodal* (Womack, 2014), *multiplex* (Acharya, 2014), *decentred globalism* (Buzan, 2011), *polymorphic globalism* (Katzenstein, 2012) and *multi-order world* (Flockhart, 2016). This array of concepts offered different emphases in their interpretations of the shift that was underway. Some assumed globalisation to be the main trend, and so emphasised the relative disempowerment of states and the rise of non-state actors of various kinds. Others emphasised the diffusion of wealth and power and the relative decline of the West. Most saw a more complex, multifaceted type of world order than a simple realist vision of a system of states jockeying for wealth and power. A reversion to the old realist idea of multipolarity could not capture the main architecture of what was happening even though there was a diffusion of power. Acharya and Buzan (2019: ch. 9) offered the concept of *deep pluralism*, in an attempt to aggregate the vocabulary. With the demise of the Soviet Union, and the relative decline of the US, deep pluralism pointed towards a world with no superpowers, but several great powers and many regional ones. More on this in Chapter 7. Acharya and Buzan noted that deep pluralism could unfold in two ways. *Contested pluralism* means that there is substantial resistance to the material and ideational reality of deep pluralism. This might take various forms: former superpowers (most obviously the US) refusing to give up their special rights and privileges; great powers refusing to recognise each other's standing, and playing against each other as rivals or enemies. *Consensual pluralism* means that the main players in global society not only tolerate the material, cultural, ideological and actor-type differences of deep pluralism, but also respect and even value them both as expressions of diversity, which like biodiversity is to be valued in itself, and as the foundation for coexistence.[1] Consensual pluralism might also be supported by a degree of intersubjective realisation of common interest in dealing with the set of inescapable shared fate issues that increasingly confront humankind as a whole.

Whether we like it or not, we are now entering into deep pluralism. It occurs as a third phase in the transition towards modernity, in which Western domination has given way to a wider diffusion of wealth, power and cultural and political authority. This diffusion is by no means yet anywhere near globally even. But substantial non-Western great powers

---

[1] Acharya and Buzan (2019) labelled this 'embedded' pluralism, but 'consensual' seems simpler and clearer.

such as China and India, and regional powers, such as Turkey, South
Korea and Mexico, have risen into the core. This means that for most
practical purposes, world politics increasingly functions within deep
pluralism. The period of Western domination of both the transition to
modernity and global society is over. The specific historical circumstances of this shift from Western dominance to deep pluralism matter.
One of these circumstances is that the shift occurs in part as a reaction
to the collapse of the short-lived heyday of neoliberalism, economic
globalisation and supposed unipolarity, during which the US-led liberal
order overextended itself. Under the imperative of neoliberalism, it
pushed for a global economy that incorporated too many illiberal
regimes, and whose governance mechanisms were inadequate
(Mearsheimer, 2019). The supposedly unstoppable rise of the market
state (Bobbitt, 2002) turned out to be short-lived, running into the
dialectic of rising anti-globalisation and resurgent economic nationalism. There were some big gains from this experiment in terms of
lowering production costs and spreading development. But there were
some big costs too, both in destabilising the societies and polities within
the liberal core, and empowering authoritarians in China and Russia.
The idea that liberalism and democracy would be transplanted everywhere by the spread of capitalism proved totally wrong. Now populists
both inside and outside the West want to pull down economic and
cultural globalisation, and reinstate the domestic/international divide
in a more robust form. Hardening the separation between inside and
outside is also the aim of the Chinese Communist Party, which seeks
homogenisation of thought and culture – and loyalty to the Party –
internally, and sharper differentiation ('Chinese characteristics') externally. Xi Jinping's China is in the vanguard of creating deep pluralism,
currently with a more contested than consensual drift (Zhang and
Buzan, 2022).

The much-used term 'emerging economies' captures the wider array
of states and societies now finding success in increasing the wealth and
power they can extract from modernity. As they do so, pluralism gets
both wider as more countries shift from periphery to core; and deeper, as
more varieties of capitalism and modernity unfold. This is where the full
picture of the third phase of the transition towards modernity begins to
crystallise, because it has now spread well beyond the founding elite, and
established itself effectively in a range of societies outside the West.
Multiple modernities and varieties of capitalism come into clearer meaning, as do the sustainable forms of global political economy. Now that we
are actually beginning to experience deep pluralism as it is emerging, one
can see some of its specific features more clearly. These are generally

driven by a mix of structural logic (i.e. they could be expected in any instance of deep pluralism) and historical circumstances (i.e. arising from the particularities of the recent history that led here). Turning the lens of material conditions and primary institutions to look forward tells us quite a lot about what deep pluralism will look like, and how it will function.

7   Material Conditions

I am not going to attempt an array of specific predictions about materials, energy, interaction capacity or technology. Rather, I will take a general look at the trends established under these headings in Chapter 4, to see whether they seem likely to continue with, or break from, those underway in the first two phases of the transition from conglomerate agrarian/pastoralist empires (CAPE) to modernity. From this perspective, the argument is that in terms of materials and energy, the pattern will remain much the same as during the first round. In terms of interaction capacity there will, with one big exception (space), probably be a slower pace of change. And in terms of technology there are some prospects of transformational breakthroughs. But before getting to that, we need to look first at the distribution of power as a key material element of deep pluralism.

The Distribution of Power

Deep pluralism carries a strong view that in the decade or two ahead, and maybe longer, there will be no superpowers, only great and regional ones. This is a dramatic claim, going against the widespread conventional wisdom that China is a rising, or even a risen, superpower, which carries the implication that we are moving once again into a world of two superpowers (*bipolarity* in the neorealist jargon). Supporting such claims either way requires clear definitions. In much day-to-day public discourse about world politics, and even in some academic literature on current affairs, the term *superpower* is used in a very loose way. At its most ridiculous, one even hears talk of 'regional superpowers', which amounts to an entirely unnecessary and unhelpful corruption of meaning.

To establish the baselines, I build on the definitions given by Buzan and Wæver (2003: 34–7), albeit with some modifications:

Superpowers – To be a superpower requires broad spectrum capabilities exercised across the whole of the international system/society. Superpowers must possess first class military-political capabilities (as measured by the standards of the day), and the economies to support such capabilities. They must be capable of, and also exercise, global military and political reach. They need to see themselves, and be accepted by others in rhetoric and behaviour, as having this rank. Superpowers must be active players in processes of securitisation and desecuritisation in all, or nearly all, of the regions in the system, whether as threats, guarantors, allies or interveners. Generally, superpowers will also be fountainheads of 'universal' values of the type necessary to underpin a particular form of world order in global society. Their legitimacy as superpowers will depend substantially on their success in establishing the legitimacy of such claims. Taking all of these factors into account, during the 19th century only Britain clearly had this rank. After the first world war, it was held by Britain, the US and the Soviet Union. After the second world war it was held by the US and the Soviet Union. After the first cold war it was held only by the US. The US is just about still the sole superpower, though its leadership legitimacy and ideological credibility are fraying fast, and could be finished off by a second Trumpian presidency. China is not yet in a position to treat the world as its region, nor to be accepted as a superpower. Though it certainly wants parity of power and status, its emphasis on 'Chinese characteristics' suggests that it might well not aspire to superpower status (Cui and Buzan, 2016: 192–4).

Great Powers – To be a great power does not necessarily require having big capabilities in all sectors. Neither do great powers need to be actively present in the securitisation processes of all regions of the international system, though they do need to be a significant factor beyond their own region. Great power status rests mainly on a single key: that they are responded to by others on the basis of system-level calculations about the present and near future global distribution of power. This might imply that a great power is treated in the calculations of other major powers as if it has the clear economic, military and political potential to bid for superpower status in the short or medium term. But great powers are sufficient in themselves to affect global calculations, and they may of course be declining superpowers. This single key is observable in the foreign policy processes and discourses of other powers. It means that actual possession of material and legal attributes is less crucial for great powers than for superpowers. Great powers will usually have appropriate levels of capability, though even before China could meet that standard it demonstrated an impressive ability over nearly a century to trade on future capabilities that it had yet to fully deliver (Segal, 1999). Great powers will generally think of themselves as more than regional powers, and possibly as prospective superpowers, and they will be capable of operating in more than one region. But while these characteristics will be typical of great powers they are not strictly speaking necessary. Occasionally, a declining power will be given honorary great power status.

Regional Powers – To be a regional power means to be a weighty actor mainly within a particular region or security complex. Where no superpowers or great powers are present in a region, this means being part of the count in defining the polarity of any given regional security complex: unipolar, as in Southern Africa; multipolar as in the Middle East, South America and Southeast Asia. Their capabilities loom large in their regions, but do not register much in a broad-spectrum way at the global level. Higher level powers respond to them as if their influence and capability were mainly relevant to the securitisation processes of a particular region. They are thus excluded from the higher level calculations of system polarity whether or not they think of themselves as deserving a higher ranking.

In a general sense, the very definition of deep pluralism, with its emphasis on the diffusion of wealth, power and political and cultural authority, leans against the idea of there being one or more super-powers within it. Superpower status depends on one or more states being able to acquire disproportionate weight within the system as a whole. That is a very demanding criterion. The concept of superpower itself leans against the idea that there could be more than two, or at most three, superpowers in any system. The direction of argument in this book has been that we are now in the third phase of the transition to modernity, a phase specifically marked by the wider diffusion of wealth, power and political and cultural authority. Since many are rising as the revolutions of modernity take root more widely, and since the first-round modernisers are not going away (they are mainly in relative, not absolute, decline), it will necessarily be difficult, if not impossible, for the US to retain superpower status, or China, or anyone else, to obtain it. Indeed, the US seems to be losing the political will, and the support of its electorate, to play the superpower role, and a reasonable case can be made that China does not want the role. The US still just about projects 'universal' liberal values, and thinks everyone should become like America, though its domestic political divisions are rapidly undermining this practice. China's exceptionalism is so far much more inward looking. The prospect is of a world of several great powers and many regional ones. The US and China might well be *primus inter pares* amongst the great powers, but they will not be superpowers.

In a technical sense, this system might look multipolar, and that will be the context in which any cooperation on great power management of global society has to be approached. But what is emerging will be novel in a number of respects. Increasingly, power, wealth and cultural and ideological authority will be wielded by non-Western as well as Western actors (Buzan and Lawson, 2015: ch. 9; Acharya and Buzan, 2019: ch. 9). As the last superpower wanes, and emerging powers rise, what is unfolding does not look like classical multipolarity. The emerging interstate society will not be multipolar as classically understood by realists, because, lacking any superpowers or any aspiring to be superpowers, it will not feature a realist type struggle for domination of the whole system. Most great powers are currently looking to avoid taking responsibility for managing global order, on which more in Chapter 8. Although they are all embedded in a highly interdependent global economy, and a single planetary environment, none wants to, or can, lead or dominate global society. The US is losing both the will and the legitimacy to do so, and among the old first-round great powers, neither Europe nor Japan can fill its shoes. The rising great powers China and India are still developing countries and have neither the capacity and the will, nor the legitimacy to play the hegemon. They still prioritise their own development over their global responsibilities. Russia is not a rising power, and is too weak, too unpopular, too self-centred, and too stuck in an imperial mindset, to take a consensual global leadership role even if one was on offer. Indeed, the idea of anyone being a superpower is further stymied by the fact that hegemony itself is illegitimate in deep pluralism (more on this in Chapter 8).

Since the global financial crisis that broke in 2007–8, the relative wealth, power and cultural and ideological authority of the West, and of the US in particular, have been in relative decline. The leadership of the US and the UK has been further undermined by the votes for Trump and Brexit in 2016 (Buzan and Cox, 2022). At the same time, the relative wealth, power and cultural and ideological authority of what were previously classed as developing countries, particularly China, but also India and others, have been on the rise. Trump burned the global social capital of the US at a prodigious rate, caring little or nothing for the effects of his policies on the alliances, intergovernmental organisations (IGOs), and trading arrangements that underpinned US leadership. Some of this damage will be unrecoverable given the uncertainty that now hangs over the polarised character of US domestic politics. In China, Xi Jinping has been pushing the country in a more authoritarian and aggressive direction that scares both its neighbours and many of the other great and regional powers. It seems likely that while the US and China will be *primus inter pares*, they will not be in an entirely different class from India, the EU, and possibly Russia, Brazil and Japan. They will be great powers in the sense that their influence extends beyond their own regions, and that they have to be taken into account at the global level. But the world will not be their region in the sense of the definition given above, and therefore neither will be a superpower. Their contest seems to be more about adjusting spheres of influence in Asia, and about bringing the US down a peg or two in its pretensions to global primacy and leadership. It does not look, at least in the short and medium term, or possibly the long term, like a contest for global primacy. Since many are acquiring the wealth, power and authority that go with modernisation, the very possibility of global hegemony is fading into history.

This will be a novel system/society, and not only because we have got used to living in an interstate society with a high concentration of power dominated by superpowers. As noted above, there has never been a system like the one now emerging in which the density and interdependence of the system is high and rising, but the distribution of power is relatively diffuse. Deep pluralism will also be deep because it is embedded across the three domains, making it a feature of global society as well as just the interstate domain.

Materials, Energy, Interaction Capacity, Technology

In terms of materials, until we work out what dark matter is, there is little prospect in the immediate future of finding new elements that are stable enough to be useable, but the scope for new combinations of known elements remains vast. This suggests a pattern not unlike that of the past two centuries, where there will be regular material breakthroughs that have substantial impacts on the social world, and these changes take place *within* the systematic framing of science opened up by the revolutions of modernity. An example might be the increasing industrialisation of food, which is already a long-standing trend. That trend may well continue to the point where food production becomes divorced from the cultivation of plants or animals on the land. Moves towards artificially grown meat, and hydroponically farmed vegetables, should be seen as the unfolding of the material conditions of modernity. Ongoing changes in material repertoires thus look to be a continuing pattern going forward. Possible examples include room-temperature superconductors (enabling big efficiency gains in the use of electricity), and superstrong molecular fibres (enabling, inter alia, space elevators).

The outlook for energy is not dissimilar. Energy supply is currently shifting more towards renewable sources, especially improved technologies for extracting electrical power directly from wind, water and the sun. There is a lot of scope for maintaining the existing pattern of effectively unlimited sources of energy. Geothermal power also has scope for major extension. In principle, the extraction of solar power could be vastly extended, both in the sunnier parts of the planet, and also by building big solar collectors in space. If efficient technologies can be developed, which looks possible in the medium term, tidal and wave power also offer considerable scope for clean, renewable energy collection. Nuclear fission plants seem likely to retain a niche as part of a green energy portfolio. The place of fusion power in this mix is difficult to pin down. In principle, fusion power offers a potentially unlimited supply of energy with much lower environmental costs than the long-lived radioactive waste products from fission power. In practice, developing the technology has proved daunting, and it remains a long way from practical application despite decades of substantial research and investment. Overall, it is reasonable to argue that developments within the existing energy repertoire of modernity keep open the promise of almost unlimited supplies of clean and renewable energy. If the technological progress of modernity remains in play, there should be no constraining ceiling to the energy that is available to humankind. Further down the line, probably much further is the 'known-unknown' of dark energy, thought to compose 68 per cent of the universe, which might open up new sources. But the full working out of the existing modern energy repertoire still has a long way to go. Notwithstanding the immediate problem of how to deal with the environmental consequences of past and present burning of fossil fuels, going forward, it will remain a characteristic feature of the transition to modernity in the third phase that it can supply as much renewable energy as humankind wants, and do so at a sustainable price, both economically and environmentally.

In terms of interaction capacity, the third phase of the transition to modernity does not offer much obvious scope for shrinking the planet further. In terms of transportation, the main prospect is of marginal improvements in speed (e.g. hyperloops, second-generation supersonic transport aircraft), and expansion of access to more people. In terms of communication, the technologies supporting the Internet will continue to improve speed, range of access and depth of experience. But there are also possibilities for regression. The environmental and health complications of mass travel might well inspire restrictions as they did during the Covid-19 pandemic. The political and cultural fragmentation under deep pluralism, caused by the political and cultural defensiveness of states and cultures, could well intensify the splintering of the

Internet. This process is already underway, being led by China. So in terms of planet earth going forward, there is mainly room for what will probably be relatively marginal improvements in intensification of interaction capacity. The planet will continue to shrink, but much more slowly than during the first two centuries of the transition. Even though shrinking, its fragmentation might well intensify as a consequence of deep pluralism.

That said, however, the third phase of the transition does offer a renewed opportunity to expand the scale of interaction capacity, something that has not happened since the international system became closed in the late nineteenth century. This opportunity lies in humankind reaching into space on a larger scale than hitherto. The rockets used to get access to space until recently were single-use only, which made them expensive. The first attempt to solve this cost problem with a reuseable launcher, the American Space Shuttle, did not reduce costs by anything like as much as hoped. But the recent development of successfully reuseable rockets by Elon Musk's SpaceX suggests that launch costs might be on the brink of a reduction significant enough to revolutionise access to space.[1] If more efficient rockets make access to space cheaper, then all kinds of commercial activities, as well as a very significant increase in the number and type of military assets that can be put into space, become possible. Cheap launchers mean that all kinds of space assets can be provided with sufficient fuel to increase both their manoeuvrability and their lifespan (Becker, 2021). Space could thus become much more important to both the global economy and international security than it has been thus far.

---

[1] Calculating launch cost is as much an art as a science, but it is possible to get a reasonable general picture. Since the beginning of the space age, launch costs have been high with some downward drift. In terms of US$ (FY2021) per kilogram, a 1960s Delta E rocket cost around 178k. The American Space Shuttle was around 65k. An Atlas 5 was around 8k. A Chinese Long March 3B was around 6k. During recent years, this largely government-led market has been seriously and increasingly disrupted by private rocket companies, particularly SpaceX, which have pushed the technology for reuseable launch systems, opening up huge cost-savings compared with single-use launchers. SpaceX's Falcon 9 cut the cost to 2.6k, and its Falcon Heavy cut it to 1.5k. SpaceX's Starship system, close to operational status at the time of writing, might cut it by another order of magnitude or more. If so, fuel could be economically transported to orbit, extending the lives of satellites, and enabling ships already in orbit to be refuelled for longer missions. Since miniaturisation enables small satellites to be quite powerful, there is a double impact on what kind of space activities are becoming affordable. Some useful sources on all this are:
  https://aerospace.csis.org/data/space-launch-to-low-earth-orbit-how-much-does-it-cost/
  https://wccftech.com/elon-musk-starship-launch-cost-reiterate/
  https://en.wikipedia.org/wiki/Space_launch_market_competition (all accessed 9 June 2021).

In thinking about space technology, it is important to note the social forces that support and oppose what Deudney (2020) calls 'space expansionism'. On the support side, it is notable that even now, nearly every state that has any kind of great power aspiration also has a significant space programme: the US, China, Russia, Japan, the EU, India, Brazil. Even some regional powers do: Iran, South Korea and the UAE. Partly this is because a space programme serves as a useful front for the development of military missiles, in the same way as nuclear power can serve as a front for the development of nuclear weapons. But partly it is driven by the military, commercial, scientific and status opportunities of space itself. There is also significant interest in the corporate sector, some of it aligned with state interests, but some of it interested in opening up commercial opportunities from tourism to mining. SpaceX, Blue Origin and Virgin Galactic are only the best known of a flock of new companies specialising in space technology. Space expansionism also has support in sections of the scientific community, and inspires enthusiasm in a section of the public. There is opposition to it on the grounds of costs, and up to a point, risks, from those who think that such substantial funds could be better spent closer to home. Probably a large body of public opinion is indifferent, and amenable to being swayed by the balance between risks/costs, and rewards/excitement. This division of opinion seems likely to be durable unless some substantial event shifts opinion decisively one way or another (e.g. an asteroid threat to earth or a major space accident that endangers earth). The firm interest of great power governments in having a position in space seems unlikely to change, on security grounds alone, and scientific and 'space cadet' interest is also likely to be durable. Corporate interest will vary according to calculations of profitability, and is likely to be somewhat up and down. Corporate interest will be partly attached to state commitment to space, but enthusiasm for other activities will depend on available technology, and assessments of profitability. The idea of asteroid mining, for example, recently fell out of fashion in the corporate sector when Planetary Resources Inc. wound itself up. Space expansionism will thrive, or not, depending on how successfully it associates itself with the pursuit of wealth, power and security. A key variable in whether it is successful or not could be how significant it becomes in humankind's attempts to address climate change, on which more below.

All of this suggests a good possibility that a move into space will at some point reconnect humankind to the expansion imperative of the CAPE era, which largely disappeared once the whole planet became accessible to humankind. Deudney (2020) counts near-earth orbital (NEO) space as part of earth for these purposes, and in the longer run he is almost certainly right. But for now, even a move into NEO space is an expansion beyond the planetary limits that defined the reach of interaction capacity during the CAPE era and for most of the last two centuries. It adds a fifth spatial dimension to land, sea, air and cyber-space. At the moment, the cost of getting into space is high even for machinery, and very high for humans, but it is coming down dramatic-ally, and commercial uses of space are already expanding. We might be within a decade of the first permanent human settlements on the Moon, and perhaps shortly thereafter even Mars, and that would open the door to humankind becoming an interplanetary species. Such an extension of scale raises several political possibilities, including extended conflict and a new imperialism (Duvall and Havercroft, 2008; Deudney, 2020). A serious extension of interaction capacity into NEO space and beyond would make current developments in space exploration, such as rocketry and space-propulsion systems, sustainable space habi-tation and the biology of humans in space count as precursors compar-able to the development of ocean-going shipping towards the end of the CAPE era.

In one sense, this extension into space can be seen as just an extension of the general processes driving the transition to modernity. In another sense, the permanent movement of humankind into space might count as era-defining in itself. One key to this would be the point at which off-planet human settlement reached sufficient critical mass to create a new and different type of 'solar society' incorporating an expanding human-kind. Looking ahead to that might suggest that such a project would require a considerable degree of planetary cooperation by humankind as a whole. For the deep pluralist phase immediately in front of us, that will not happen. The early phases of expansion into space will be competitive, even conflictual, reflecting the fragmented world politics of deep pluralism.

This discussion of space spills over into the last category of material conditions: technology. Because technology is an almost infinitely open-ended category, it is the trickiest of the four aspects of material conditions to deal with. There is a strong sense of continuity with the first two phases of the transition to modernity in the ongoing pattern of 'industrial revolutions' in which new technologies become dominant. That pattern was already evident in the discussions in Part II of mater-ials, energy and interaction capacity, all of which rest on continuing progress in technology. Even with the limited powers of hindsight from our present position, it is clear that earlier such 'revolutions' from coal and steam, through oil, chemicals, internal combustion engines, and electricity, to nuclear, were transformations *within*, and not *of*, the material conditions of the transition towards modernity. It is important to note that while technological progress is in some ways linear and incremental, it is also marked by jumps that open up entirely new areas (e.g. aircraft, satellites, cyberspace). Such jumps then peak as technologies mature. There are now only marginal gains from making cars, trains or aircraft faster, or building nuclear weapons with ever-higher explosive yields. That said, there is still a lot to be gained from faster computer chips, faster Internet connections and more efficient space rockets. The development of technologies to access space might be thought of as analogous to the development of aircraft in the early twentieth century. Both open up access to a previously inaccessible dimension, although space is incomparably larger and more significant than the planetary atmosphere. Indeed, the fact that the first flight on Mars took place a mere twelve decades after the Wright brothers' first flight on earth is striking evidence for the technological prodigality of modern humankind. In almost any average 120-year period within the CAPE era, there would have been no noticeable technological changes. But the bigger potential for progress lies in opening up entirely new technologies, like the telegraph and radio during the nineteenth century, and aircraft, nuclear energy and computers in the twentieth. Continuous and rapid advances in science and technology, both linear and leaps, are a key defining material feature of modernity, and as such that pattern is likely to continue. Looking ahead, it is easy to see the potential for transformations of the human condition inherent in the rapid advances of biotechnology and machine intelligence. These technological developments are already deeply rooted in the sense of being driven by the military, economic and societal structures that humankind has created for itself.

It is already commonplace to think of the rise of computers and digital technologies as the fourth industrial revolution. Azhar (2021: 2–11, 36–65) argues that we need to reconceptualise this in terms of 'exponential' technological growth, in which rapidly rising capabilities combine with rapidly falling costs, to empower new general-purpose technologies (e.g. computers, the Internet), that quickly become widely used. Such technologies transform society and outpace the ability of social institutions to keep up. Think of the possibly destabilising, or restabilising, effects of blockchains and cryptocurrencies on not only the financial industry, but also the foundation of money itself. New developments in computing turn data into an unprecedented master resource, raising the prospect that emerging forms of artificial intelligence will impact hugely on employment, privacy, knowledge, marketing and government. The term 'computer science' might at some not too distant point cease to be about the computers themselves, and begin to refer to what they do.

The digital revolution is already rapidly blurring the distinction between military and civilian technology. The surveillance capabilities available with computers and sensors now look like a much more effective form of control over people than simply intimidating or coercing them by shows or applications of force. And the rising concern with 'cyberwar' and 'cybersecurity' opens up the prospect of an entirely different kind of 'war' fought with an entirely different suite of 'weapons'. Cyberwar plays to the rising importance of data and computer networks in all walks of modern life, and the possibility of disrupting everything from elections to power grids that is latent in this configuration. As Azhar (2021: 11, 189–215) argues, exponential technologies are making a wide variety of effective and low-cost forms of attack available to an increasing range of actors, raising the probability that conflict could become more widespread (more on this in the subsection on war in Chapter 8). As discussed in Chapter 6, biotechnology might also be emerging as a fifth industrial revolution enabling humankind to remake not only many areas of manufacturing, but more broadly both nature and itself.

This pattern of continuous technological change is clearly an intrinsic material characteristic of the transition towards modernity, and there is no reason to think that it will not continue into the third phase. Since that phase will be defined by deep pluralism, it seems safe to predict that technological change will continue to feed the permanent RMA amongst the great powers that has been ongoing since the 1840s. Developments in the technologies for space, bioengineering, AI and suchlike all have military as well as civil applications. These will continue to have the destabilising effects on great power relations that have been their hallmark for the last two centuries. As discussed in Chapter 6, forseeable, and perhaps quite close, developments in AI and biotechnology have transformative potentials that could put humankind on the path towards species suicide or replacement. And failure to deal with the damage that the technosphere is doing to the natural systems of the planet, could, and perhaps already has, put us on the path to regression. But technology also gives humankind some protection from the natural forces that might generate extinction. Technology is thus the key material condition going forward. How it unfolds will not only continue to disrupt and reshape the social structure of humankind, but also substantially determine whether humankind continues on the pathway of increasing species empowerment, or diverts into one of the other four.

8   Social Structure

The argument so far has been that although the two-century transition from conglomerate agrarian/pastoralist empires (CAPE) to modern is now entering its third phase, turbulence will continue to be a feature of modernity. This is because the driver of ongoing and rapid changes in material conditions is still operating at full throttle; and because there are still strong contradictions and ongoing dialectics and multilectics within the social structure. The two combined make a meta-dialectic between unrestrained human species empowerment so ruthlessly pursued during the first two centuries of the transition, and the limits of planetary carrying capacity. Over half a century ago, Boulding (1966: 11) presciently observed: 'The shadow of the future spaceship [by which he meant the self-contained global economy], indeed, is already falling over our spendthrift merriment'. This combination makes it unlikely that global society will settle down any time soon so long as humankind remains broadly on the species empowerment track. This chapter therefore re-examines the array of primary institutions discussed in earlier chapters with two aims in mind. The first is to see how these institutions might fare under the environmentally constrained conditions of the third phase of the transition to modernity. The second is to elaborate on how the particular circumstances of deep pluralism will play into the social structure of global society. There will be some impact from deep pluralism on most primary institutions, but several, most notably diplomacy, sovereignty, territoriality, nationalism and the market and environmental stewardship, are likely to be impacted heavily.

This exploration opens with a brief look at those primary institutions that have faded away or been declared obsolete: kinship, dynasticism and empire. Human inequality I will consider in tandem with human equality later in this chapter. Will the dead stay dead?

Kinship

Kinship seems likely to continue as a pervasive ghost institution into the third phase of the transition to modernity. Partly, this is simply because it is deeply rooted in human practices. But significantly also, kinship remains highly valued in many of the societies now rising into the core of modernity. Deep pluralism will therefore reinforce this practice. It will do so partly by bringing societies that support it more prominently into global society, and partly by pushing back the dominance of the liberal teleology that was a powerful ideological force against it. Despite that boost, there are two new threats, possibly severe, to it going forward. First, the strong correlation between rising urbanisation and falling birth rates (Bricker and Ibbitson, 2019) is shrinking families all around the world, and thereby reducing the utility of kinship networks. And within modernity, meritocracy offers a powerful alternative to kinship that is not exclusive to liberalism. Second, and perhaps a bit further down the line, genetic engineering threatens to undo the biological foundations of family. If one's genome is open to tinkering, and this becomes standard practice, the whole idea of 'blood' linkages and lineages comes into question. Kinship might survive the intervention of biotech, but if so it will have to redefine its meaning.

Monarchy/Dynasticism

As an offshoot of kinship, the ghost of monarchy/dynasticism is vulnerable to the same two general threats affecting that. Although some dynastic families might be able to buck the trend of shrinking numbers of offspring, none can escape the competing logics of meritocracy and popular sovereignty. Neither can they escape the logic of genetic engineering, which potentially weakens the meaning of bloodlines, and provides alternative routes to the manufacture of elite leaderships. The possibilities for cloning and extended lifespans would eventually make any return of dynastic political principles extremely controversial. Existing practices of monarchy/dynasticism are likely to continue on as accepted practice in politics and business. Deep pluralism, with its cultivation of political and cultural distinctiveness, might even extend slightly the political space for monarchy. But the odds are strongly against it getting anywhere close to recovering its status either as a primary institution of global society, or as the mainstream foundation for political legitimacy.

Imperialism/Colonialism

Notwithstanding its radical defeat in the real world, imperialism nonetheless remains surprisingly attractive to science fiction writers depicting more advanced worlds. These visions often come with imperialism's equally defeated partner, monarchy/dynasticism, still firmly attached.

Despite the heavy rejection of imperialism after the Second World War, significant residues of what look like imperial thinking (territorial expansion, repression and/or assimilation of minorities, settlers) can nonetheless easily be observed in the behaviour and rhetoric of some states, such as China, Russia, Turkey, Indonesia and Israel. More broadly, it can be argued that many post-colonial states such as Brazil, Pakistan, Peru, India and Indonesia, and indeed the US, Canada and Australia, have political structures that are somewhat empire-like in that they seal indigenous peoples into them whether they like it or not, and put them at the mercy of 'imperial' state governments (Keal, 2003). Some might also find echoes of imperialism in contemporary practices such as the buying of land by one country in another for purposes such as farming or carbon offset. But while such practices may well endure, there seems no possibility that the general idea and legitimacy of imperialism as practised up until the end of decolonisation in 1975 will return. Russia and China might look somewhat like empires both in their internal behaviour towards minorities, and their external concerns to win back 'lost' territories on their margins. At the time of writing, Russia's rhetoric and practices against Ukraine look distinctly imperial to Ukrainians and the West. Should China carry out its threat to reacquire Taiwan by force, it too would raise fears of further imperialism. But neither country seems interested in constructing more than a sphere of influence beyond their 'reunification' claims, and under deep pluralism, both would meet fierce opposition if they tried. Their imperial-like behaviours look more aimed at trying to consolidate formerly imperial territories into modern states, rather than seeking the open-ended quest for territorial expansion that marked imperialism up to 1945. That kind of imperialism is almost certainly dead, and likely to remain so. Deep pluralism is essentially a defensive outlook, not a competition to build global empires. Economic practices that might look imperial ('neocolonialism') are generally better understood as part of the tension between sovereignty and territoriality, on the one hand, and the global market, on the other hand. Deep pluralism's swing to economic nationalism should reduce this issue of economic imperialism as compared with the period of neoliberal globalisation.

Next come the six primary institutions that carried over from the CAPE era to modernity, and adapted themselves to it: religion, war, territoriality, sovereignty, diplomacy and international law.

Religion

As argued in Chapter 5a, religion survived the formidable assaults against it during the first two phases of the transition towards modernity. It

carried over its essential beliefs and institutions from deep in the conglomerate agrarian/pastoralist empires (CAPE) era more or less intact,
and adapted to the new resources, particularly interaction capacity and
corporate forms of organisation, made available by modernity. It successfully worked its way back into politics and international relations
along many strands: anti-slavery, support for colonialism, resistance to
colonialism, providing values and identities to political parties, creating
voting blocs, establishing its rights in IGOs, and suchlike. Indicative of
the range and depth of its grip was that during the Covid-19 pandemic of
2020–2, it was not uncommon for political leaders in both developed and
developing states to call for prayer rather than the vaccines offered by
science as the first line of defence against the virus.

There is no obvious reason to expect the position of religion within
global society to change much during deep pluralism. Many secular
ideologies have come to terms with religion, and even those that still
try to suppress it, such as the Chinese Communist Party, seem to be
having no more luck than the Communist Party of the Soviet Union did
during its seven-decade reign. Religious differences define many of the
principal political divides, both domestic and international, in West, South
and Southeast Asia, and West Africa and the Sahel. Islamist movements
and transnational actors have established themselves as principal protag-
onists in the global war on terror (GWoT). There is nothing else emergent
within the social structure of global society that looks likely to challenge
either the faith foundations, or the restored political legitimacy, of religion.
To the extent that it plays into cultural differentiation, it will be a good fit
with deep pluralism. Although universalist religions might lean in principle
towards global cosmopolitanism, in practice most of them can make
themselves comfortable with the kind of identity blocs that deep pluralism
will encourage. Religion will therefore continue to play as a considerable,
perhaps even expanding, force across all three domains during the coming
phase of deep pluralism. A gathering climate apocalypse could benefit
religion as much as, or more than, it does science.

War

In thinking about war as part of the social structure, it is important to
keep in mind the English School's distinction between the practice
of war as such, and the social norms and rules around it in terms of
methods and motives that comprise the institution of war. The picture
remains messy in both respects. After the end of the first cold war, the
practice of war diversified in various ways, calling into question the
institutional constraints on it. The GWoT made war between state and

non-state actors a main practice, and in many places, most obviously Afghanistan, the Horn of Africa and the Democratic Republic of Congo, weak and failed states opened the way for rather Hobbesian wars amongst a variety of state and non-state armed entities. These were restrained mainly by the limits to the capabilities of the combatants rather than by any social norms or rules. These 'new wars' (Kaldor, 2001) often disregarded constraints on both means and ends, leaving the institution of war muddled and ambiguous. In addition, with the intensification of the Internet, 'cyberwar' of various kinds became increasingly possible and practised. This varied from interference in the public discourse via social media, which questioned where the boundary of 'war' was, to more obviously war-like attacks on infrastructure, such as the *Stuxnet* one on Iran in 2009–10, which aimed at physical destruction, and the ransomware attack on the Colonial Pipeline in 2021. Some aspects of cyberwar seemed to fit with traditional ideas of attack, but others stretched the concept of war far beyond its traditional military meaning.

This messy picture is likely to remain during the coming phase of deep pluralism. There will be some significant continuities. In the interstate domain, the constraint on all-out great power war provided by nuclear weapons and the defence dilemma will continue. So too will the permanent revolution in military affairs (RMA) that began early in the nineteenth century. So long as new technologies continue to come into play, they will drive this RMA just as nuclear and digital developments have done. The destabilising effects of this, particularly on great power relations, will therefore continue. This will be especially so if, as seems highly likely at the time of writing, deep pluralism is contested, and dominated by the second cold war. The particulars will, of course, be different: New technologies are increasingly opening up two new dimensions – space and cyberspace – as arenas for conflict. Clever hypersonic delivery systems are changing the game between stealth and detection, and AI-controlled drone swarms are emerging as a new form of weapon. AIs are replacing humans in functions requiring either or both of high physical stress (e.g. fighter pilots) or very quick response times (defensive systems like Israel's Iron Dome). Despite the destabilising effects of the RMA, the imperative to avoid nuclear war amongst the major powers will likely remain robust during deep pluralism. That imperative might well increase if the current trends towards greater concentration of population in cities continues. Such concentration, long evident in Japan and Latin America, and becoming more so in China and many parts of the Global South, makes populations easier targets both for nuclear attack and for terrorism and cyberwar.

The military imbalance between core and periphery will continue to even-out. As the third phase of the transition towards modernity unfolds, more powers will follow South Korea and China in picking up Japan's original symmetric strategy of seeking full developmental parity as a way of closing the power gap with the first-round modernisers. If China is indicative, this will result in broad-spectrum military competition even though the risk of great power war will remain low because of both high costs and risks, and low chances of meaningful victory. At the same time, the asymmetric strategies of guerrilla war, nuclear proliferation, terror-ism and cyberwar, will remain in play both for those less successful in pursuing development, and for militant non-state actors. It is quite easy to imagine that deep pluralism will see additional states becoming nuclear-armed, though for reasons perhaps as much or more to do with fear of neighbouring rivals than as a way of deterring intervention from the core. Indeed, the logic of deep pluralism suggests that it will increasingly be regional and local level concerns, and decreasingly ones about intervention from the core to the periphery, that shape the military sector.

The move towards deterritorialisation so diversifies what counts as 'war', and the means and purposes of war, as to make any single regime of control increasingly difficult to imagine. Forms of cold war look likely to dominate great power rivalries, while hot wars will be more common lower down the power ranks, and between state and militant non-state actors. Mishra (2020: 112) notes: 'the incendiary appeal of victimhood in societies built around the pursuit of wealth and power'. If he is right about the deep and militant resentment in the Global South unleashed by modernity, then elements of war crossing the interstate and trans-national domains will remain a durable and significant feature for a long time. More on this resentment in the discussion of diplomacy below.

The link between war and territoriality seems likely to come under a further pressure from the link between climate change and political breakdown, on the one hand, and migration, on the other, that could either break it, or deepen it. As Dalby (2020: 55–69) argues, migration is the classical, and sometimes the only available, human response to climate change. In today's warming world, this is opening up a deepening contradiction with the territorial political organisation of global society. Migration arising from economic motives, or the desire to escape political chaos or collapse, is already causing political divisions in destinations like Europe and America, and some of this is already partly driven by environmental stresses. One might, for example, want to leave parts of Central America as much to escape regular hurricanes as to leave behind poverty, criminality and misgovernment. If the need to escape areas that have become uninhabitable because of climate change increases, then something will have to give. Either wars to defend or take territory will come back into legitimacy, or the hard territoriality that has characterised the transition towards modernity will have to change.

Increasingly, wars look dangerous, expensive and unwinnable. Nuclear wars are unwinnable because the damage all round blurs the distinction between winners and losers. The GWoT and cyberwar look like 'forever wars' in which clear and decisive wins are almost impossible, and everyone loses. The US is trying to extract itself from forever wars, and China does not look at all keen to pick up this burden. The constraints on resorting to war, not just amongst the great powers, but also between great powers and lesser states with effective means of asymmetric response, raises questions about whether or how war, even if sanctioned by the UN Security Council, can be used in support of interstate order. Great powers can no longer lord it over smaller states if the latter have asymmetric capacities to strike back.

It has been argued quite convincingly that war has been a, perhaps the, principal shaper of the modern state (Howard, 1976; Tilly, 1990; Bobbitt, 2002). That argument raised the question of what would replace war in that role if, as seemed briefly possible after the end of the first cold war, and in the heyday of globalisation, it, and especially great power war, became obsolete? For a time, it looked as if the market might take the place of war as the key shaper of states, but with the winding down of economic globalisation that too now looks less convincing. Perhaps 'war' in its new forms will make a comeback in this role. Cyberwar pushes towards a security and surveillance, panopticon state of the kind being pioneered by China, but also available in democratic states. This new technology of big data and advanced algorithms appears to be profoundly enabling for authoritarian and totalitarian forms of government that were previously held back by the inability of human bureaucracies to deliver the necessary control and management efficiently enough. At the time of writing, it appears to be much more challenging for democracies, which, despite initial hopes of the Internet liberating individualism and creativity, have so far been unable to control the degrading effects of social media on standards of truth, integrity and civility. Cyberwar may become a principal maker of the state during deep pluralism.

Territoriality

As we move into deep pluralism, the seemingly big threat to territoriality from globalisation has undergone a significant shift. Territoriality remains a strong institution with deep roots in both the interstate and interhuman domains. The challenge to it is fast shifting from the economic sector and the Internet, both of which have been substantially re-territorialised, to the environmental one, which cannot be territorialised easily, or possibly at all. The global economic crisis from 2008, and the move towards contested deep pluralism that followed, have re-empowered economic nationalism, and put economic globalisation into a substantial, though not total, reverse. China has shown how the supposedly universal space of the Internet can be effectively divided up and territorialised. New technologies are making it easier to re-localise production, not only to states, but down to the level of cities (Azhar, 2021: 165–89). Yet while these two aspects of globalisation have been weakened, the environmental threat to the stability of human civilisation has grown stronger, not just with rising concerns about climate change and global pandemics, but also with worries about the sixth great extinction on both land and sea.

Although often hidden within the rhetoric of sovereigntism, territoriality is the main key for the appeal for the populist, authoritarian and neo-fascist politicians who are a hallmark of deep pluralism. China and Russia, and even the EU and the US, are obsessed with territorial issues. The building of border walls against migrants by leaders such as Trump and Orban is as clear a reassertion of territoriality as one could imagine. So too, in a more indirect way, are the trade blockades and reshoring of production promoted by economic nationalists: Think of the territorialising implications of the fracas over 5G internet technology and the supply of personal protective equipment (PPE) during the Covid-19 pandemic. So-called vaccine nationalism sprang up during the pandemic, showing the resurgent force of territoriality even on a globally shared-fate threat such as disease control. Climate change has also triggered responses from denier leaders that blend sovereignty and territoriality. Bolsonaro promoted deforestation in the Amazon, and Trump tried to revive the fortunes of the fossil fuel industry. Territorialising logic riding on securitisation has even spilled over into what is perhaps the most deterritorialised area of human activity, science. There are increasing rivalries and concerns about thefts of intellectual property around AI and quantum computing.

So, after a few decades seemingly in the wilderness, territoriality is back with a vengeance, and seems likely to remain dominant so long as contested deep pluralism and economic nationalism define the condition of global society. So far, even though climate change and global pandemics make a powerful case for a revamped form of globalisation to deal with them, this has not happened. Approaches to both climate change and pandemics remain largely structured by territorial principles, even though the science and production aspects of the response to the pandemic retain significant elements of globalisation.[1] Despite its current retreat, market globalisation is unlikely to disappear, though it is unlikely to make much of a comeback under contested deep pluralism. If the historical pattern holds, it will eventually re-emerge again in some newly styled form based on sustainable development, and better able to avoid the financial turbulence and inequality generated by the neoliberal experiment.

The dialectic between political territoriality, on the one hand, and the global character of economic and environmental systems, on the other hand, looks to be a defining one for the third phase of the transition to modernity, and indeed beyond that. The planetary infrastructure of interaction capacity created during the nineteenth and twentieth centuries continues to be improved. Deep pluralism starts from this legacy, and is quickly being thrown into dealing with the global consequences, especially the environmental ones, of the unrestrained pursuit of wealth and power that characterised the first two phases of the transition to modernity. Deep pluralism, however, especially in its current contested form, is exceptionally poorly suited to dealing with a shared threat on a planetary scale like climate change. This contradiction will be the focal point of globalisation during deep pluralism and whatever follows it. The outcome of this dialectic between unrestrained development and planetary carrying capacity will be instrumental in whether humankind can stay on the path of species empowerment, or takes one of the other paths.

Sovereignty

Sovereignty, like territoriality, is a close fit with deep pluralism, and therefore likely to remain in robust form. This is not surprising given that the two are closely tied together in the package of primary institutions that underpins the modern state. Sovereignty's corollary of the right of non-intervention is an important key to defending territorial integrity and control. Sovereign equality underpins the whole structure of diplomatic and legal relations among states, backing claims to equal shares, equal rights, and up to a point compensation for past humiliations and exploitations. Sovereignty shows no signs of weakening or fading away as an institution of global society, and deep pluralism encourages robust forms of sovereigntism. Sovereignty is still powerfully carried by the momentum from decolonisation and the overthrow/abandonment of divided sovereignty after 1945. This attachment is being reinforced by

---

[1] On the enduring territoriality of environmental great powers to climate change, see Falkner and Buzan (2022).

the rising number of former periphery states and peoples now able to extract more wealth and power from modernity, not only making them better able to assert their sovereign rights, but also expanding the core in the process. Post-colonial resentment remains strong in much of the Global South and China, and this keeps fresh the importance of sovereignty equality and the right of non-intervention that were the great prizes of decolonisation. Strong sovereigntism and territoriality are also a hallmark of populist, authoritarian and neo-fascist politics, from Brexit and Trump, through Orban and Putin, to the CCP. The US has always been strongly sovereigntist because of its particular brand of republican popular sovereignty, and that shows no sign of weakening. The UN, and even the EU, are tightly bound to the principle of sovereignty. The character of deep pluralism is likely to be strongly anti-hegemonic, perhaps even weakening the fudging of sovereign equality caused by the allowances made for great power management (GPM).

That said, again as with territoriality, the dialectic between sovereignty and globalisation is likely to be ongoing. Perhaps this will be more in the style of *zhongyong* dialectics, an ongoing contradiction fluctuating, and needing to be managed, according to circumstances, rather than a Hegelian style dialectic getting resolved in some new formulation, such as the loose styles of global government discussed by Deudney (2007) and Wendt (2004). As argued above, empire in its classical sense of divided sovereignty, is unlikely to be the source of major challenges to sovereignty. Non-intervention can be a tricky right to the extent that all interaction is, in a way, a kind of intervention. If states agree to global market rules and practices, then they exercise their sovereign right to allow certain kinds of intervention. The same logic applies to human rights and environmental stewardship. For both of these, the key is the extent to which global society collectively can claim a right to intervene if a state is in violation of rules or principles. Will environmental stewardship increasingly open new grounds for intervention as the climate crisis worsens? One difficulty with that scenario is that most of the big polluters are great powers well able to defend themselves both politically and militarily (Falkner and Buzan, 2022). In the decades ahead, the climate crisis is likely to generate the biggest challenge to sovereignty/territoriality. Since deep pluralism strengthens sovereigntism and territoriality, this could become the major contradiction in deep pluralism as the climate crisis continues to worsen.

Diplomacy

As the discussion of sovereignty and territoriality above shows, deep pluralism, by its very nature favours *raison d'état* over *raison de système*.

On that basis, we can expect quite marked changes in the practices and attitudes around this institution for the duration of deep pluralism. Indeed, many of these changes are already visible. As argued in Chapter 5a, the trend from the first two phases of the transition towards modernity was away from strictly interstate diplomacy, and towards a diplomacy for a global society. Neumann (2020: 171–6), for example, postulated a possible drift towards diplomacy as global governance. But as deep pluralism sets in, the supporting framing for a more cosmopolitan diplomacy for a global society gets weakened, and the move towards contested deep pluralism suggests a reassertion of interstate diplomacy. Firms still remain diplomatic players, as indicated by the current role of the social media giants, but their scope looks likely to be more constrained as the swing towards economic nationalism plays out. Firms are still now in regular negotiation with the EU, the US, China and others. In February 2021, for example, there was a dispute between Facebook and Australia over payments to media sources, and Facebook used withdrawal of services to Australia as a bargaining lever. Yet at the time of writing, China is reining in the independence of some of its big firms and their leaders. Overall, it is still unclear to what extent the blowback from the global crisis of overextended neoliberal globalisation will weaken the position of firms as the subjects of diplomacy. The signs are that firms will be most subjected to state control in China, and probably also in other authoritarian states. In the West it remains unclear whether big firms will face tighter controls or not.

That said, the Internet and social media are opening up new possibilities for so-called digital diplomacy, defined as 'the use of social media for diplomatic purposes' (Bjola and Holmes, 2015: 4; Roumate, 2021). The exact shape and consequence of this development is difficult to predict. On the one hand, both states and non-state actors, whether separately or in alliance, can use social media to communicate to foreign populations. They can do so in the form of traditional propaganda, or by using targeted misinformation campaigns to influence elections or more generally to try to destabilise politics and society in countries they see as rivals or enemies. Digital diplomacy to some extent depends on the global openness of the Internet and social media, and one line of response, most thoroughly implemented by China, is to territorialise the Internet and wall-off one's national domain.

There are at least four big ways in which deep pluralism will alter the face of diplomacy: the nature of the prevailing great powers and the relations among them; the substantial hangover of resentment from colonialism in a newly empowered periphery; a shrinking role for transnational actors as the liberal condition supporting them weaken; and a turn towards more diplomacy at the regional level, and perhaps less at the global one.

Introverted Great Powers and Anti-Hegemonism

As argued in Chapter 7, the material condition for deep pluralism is the existence of multiple centres of wealth, power, and political and cultural authority. Probably this will take the form of a system with no super-powers, several great powers and a lot of regional powers. The key social condition for deep pluralism, which is mainly historical, is strong anti-hegemonism. This stems partly from reaction against the two-century hegemony of the first-round modernisers (and in particular fuelled by post-colonial resentment against them, on which more below); and partly from the fact that rising powers generally cultivate strong sovereigntist, anti-hegemonic attitudes. Indeed, under emerging deep pluralism, the very idea of global hegemonic leadership, which has been closely associated with Western hegemony for more than two centuries, seems likely to be delegitimised. Such a world will feature diverse cultures, and economic and political ideologies and systems, including the remnants of the liberal order. Any attempt at hegemonic leadership would thus have an uphill struggle against both the principle itself, and the lack of any universally accepted ideology that might legitimate it, as liberalism did for the US until quite recently.

In a material sense, deep pluralism will look like a multipolar system. But because there is no hegemonic drive to dominate or lead global society, it will not behave as realist theories expect. This expectation is reinforced by the fact that the particular historical conditions of this point in the transition to modernity, suggest that all of the likely great powers will be introverted in their outlook and behaviour. Nothing in the theory says that deep pluralist systems are necessarily populated by introverted great powers, though the diffusion of wealth, power and authority perhaps makes that more likely than not. The concept of 'autistic' great powers has been used to capture this, and has been around in the IR literature for a long time. As argued in Acharya and Buzan (2019: 270–1):

The group of great powers that will dominate [global society] in the decades ahead will be inward-looking to the point of being *autistic* ... understood as where reaction to external inputs is based much more on the internal processes of the state – its domestic political bargains, party rivalries, pandering to public opinion (whether it be nationalist or isolationist), and suchlike – than on rational, fact-based, assessment of and engagement with the other states and societies that constitute international society (Senghaas, 1974; Buzan, 2007 [1991]: 277–81; Luttwak, 2012: 13–22). To some extent autism in this sense is a normal feature of states. It is built into their political structure that domestic factors generally take first priority, whether because that is necessary for regime survival, or because the government is designed in such a way as to represent its citizens' interests.

Autism will be strong in the current and near future set of great powers for two reasons. First, the old, advanced industrial great powers (the US, the EU, Japan) are not going to go away, but they are exhausted, weakened both materially and in terms of legitimacy, and are increasingly unable or unwilling to take the lead. ... The rising great powers (China and India, possibly Brazil) are very keen to claim great power status, and might provide new blood to the great power camp. But they are equally keen not to let go of their status as developing countries. They want to assert their own cultures against the long dominance of the West, and some, notably China, are cultivating a nationalism based on historical grievance. ... They argue, not unreasonably, that their own development is a big and difficult job for them, and that developing their own big populations is a sufficient contribution to GIS in itself. On that basis, they resist being given wider global managerial responsibilities.

'Autism', however, is a complex phenomenon, and its use as an analogy may not be the ideal way to capture the fairly simple quality of introversion and self-referenced behaviour in states.

In English School theory, great powers are partly defined by their wider responsibilities to *raison de système*. To the extent that states and especially great powers have introverted and mainly self-referenced foreign policies, they not only fail to uphold *raison de système,* but also lose touch with their social environment, and are blind to how their policies and behaviours affect the way that others see and react to them. In such conditions, a cycle of prickly action–overreaction – already visible in US–China, Russia–EU, US–Russia, and China–Japan relations – is likely to prevail. Building trust becomes difficult or impossible. Everyone emphasises their sovereignty and right to non-intervention. They see only their own interests, concerns and 'rightness', and are blind to the interests, concerns and 'rightness' of others. Often, they hold quite different views about the sources of, and responsibilities for, the current disorder (Hurrell, 2020: 133–6). If this diagnosis turns out to be correct, then we are unlikely to see responsible great powers. The absence of responsible great powers in conditions of deep pluralism points to a contested deep pluralist global society that is weak, and possibly quite fractious. Russia is the most extreme exemplar of a great power putting *raison d'état* first, and caring little about *raison de système.* China seems to be abandoning its earlier position of peaceful rise/development, and following the Russian playbook of bullying neighbours and cultivating a prickly victimhood nationalism. China and Japan, with their unresolved history problem, make a classic case of introverted, self-referenced relations (Buzan and Goh, 2020), and China's relations with India seem headed in the same direction. The US and China are pushed more towards contested deep pluralism by domestic political imperatives. The US seeks domestic unity in the face of a challenger to US primacy. China wants to seal itself off so as to reduce outside influence and consolidate CCP control.

Post-Colonial Resentment and Former Colonial Forgetting

The second predictable quality of emerging deep pluralism is that it will sit on top of a very tricky and corrosive history problem composed, on the one hand, of a large reservoir of post-colonial resentment in those still seeing themselves as victims of colonialism, and on the other hand, of a mixture of forgetting, ignorance and denial among the former metropoles.[2] The existence of this history problem is a particular effect of the monocentric route to globalisation set out in the Introduction to Part II. The uneven but combined development that took over with such force during the first two phases of the transition towards modernity came in a colonial, core–periphery, form in which one civilisation, itself fragmented into competing states, but undergoing a very rapid increase in wealth and power, subjugated all the others. With much ruthlessness and coercion, this new global core imposed many of its social and material forms on the many cultures that became its periphery, destabilising their social, political and economic structures in the process (Mishra, 2020). Colonialism came along with political subjugation, economic exploitation, cultural disrespect, scientific superiority, and racial inequality and discrimination. It also came along with elements of development, but these were generally pitched towards the needs and concerns of the individual metropolitan powers.

The experience of colonialism unsurprisingly left a deep and powerful resentment within almost all countries that experienced it, and that resentment is now a major part of what the Global South brings to the table as inputs from the non-West into thinking about, and practising, international relations (Zarakol, 2011; Acharya and Buzan, 2019; Buzan and Acharya, 2022). There is perhaps no better illustration of this than the hostility and contempt that Turkey's president Erdogan brings to his relationship with the West, denying it any right to set and enforce liberal standards on the rest of the world. Hodgson (1993: 224) nicely captures the humiliation in the 'sense of radical spiritual defeat' that the encounter with the power and ideas of the modernising West inflicted on the

---

[2] On history problems as a concept, see Buzan and Goh (2020: 1–14).

Islamic world and China. It was a blow to their inner prestige to have their sense of being the dominant world civilisation so rudely and abruptly displaced. Quite suddenly, what had been seen as barbarians were imposing a powerful new standard of civilisation on the leading lights of the CAPE era.

Post-colonial resentment against the racism, coercion and cultural contempt of the colonial West and Japan is not going to disappear any time soon. Indeed, as deep pluralism unfolds, the new wealth and power, and recovered cultural and political authority, of the Global South are increasingly linked to this still strongly felt grievance. The highly uneven onset, development and spread of modernity initially divided the world into core and periphery. As modernity now becomes more widespread and more culturally differentiated, the huge gaps in wealth, power, and cultural and political authority opened during the nineteenth century are beginning to close (Findlay and O'Rourke, 2007: 512–15; Buzan and Lawson, 2015). To get a measure of this resentment, one has only to look at the importance China still attaches not only to reproducing the memory of its 'century of humiliation', but also to making it an active factor in its day-to-day foreign and domestic policy. Victimhood politics comes up everywhere in the post-colonial Global South, from demands for aid as a form of reparations; through insistence on unequal responsibilities for the legacy polluters of the first round of modernisation in taking on the burdens of controlling climate change; to claims for the return of cultural objects looted or appropriated by the former colonial powers. Such claims certainly need to be addressed, but inept leaders in the Global South still can, and do, make good political use of blaming colonisation for their own ongoing shortcomings in achieving development.

By contrast, while public opinion in the liberal West remains sensitive to racism and slavery in its domestic spheres and histories, it has largely forgotten about, marginalised, or denied the racism and coercion it exercised against other peoples during the imperial era. The 'Black Lives Matter' movement going strong at the time of writing not only exemplifies this selective sensitivity, but the distinctive American version of it, which associated slavery and race much more strongly than was generally the case everywhere else during the CAPE era. So while there are, to be sure, ongoing campaigns against historical racism and slavery within the West, there are at the same time white nationalists and neo-fascists re-legitimising racism in relation to contemporary migration. Many in the West and Japan have forgotten, or are ignorant, about the colonial history of their countries. Some, not entirely without historical foundation, promote counter-narratives of the colonial period as a mainly successful civilising mission. The particular forms and patterns of this history problem vary from country to country, but overall there remains a huge and politically volatile gap between former colonised and colonisers about how to understand their shared history.[3]

When Hedley Bull (1984) worried about the Third World's 'revolt against the West' nearly forty years ago, that revolt could still be, and largely was, ignored by the West, because the newly decolonised states and peoples behind it were mostly poor, weak and culturally emasculated. Modernisation theory assumed that modernisation effectively meant Westernisation (Spruyt, 2020: 344–6). The West largely satisfied itself with some commitment to give foreign aid to the Third World in the hope that development along liberal lines would somehow be easy and automatic. But despite some significant progress, development did not even out globally. Instead, the revolt against the West has unfolded down two tracks. The first track is in the interstate domain, where substantial parts of the former periphery are growing strong, and some are knocking on the door of the core. They are finding, or in some cases such as China, South Korea, Taiwan and Singapore, have already found, their own paths to the wealth and power of modernity. They are not clones of the West, but distinctive syntheses between their traditional cultures and modernity. This means that the natural cultural diversity of humankind is now backed by globally significant wealth and power, and motivated by post-colonial resentment (Hurrell, 2020: 116–19). The second track is set out by Mishra (2020) who argues that the deep social turbulence unleashed by modernity has now gone global. This track is mainly in the transnational and interhuman domains where the carriers of resentment are individuals and groups, some fully prepared to use violence. Mishra draws a straight line between the philosophical and political reactions that arose in opposition to modernity in nineteenth-century Europe, and that gave rise to terrorism and fascism there, on the one hand, and the *jihadis* and anti-state and anti-globalisation terrorists of today, on the other hand. From his perspective, the West has failed to understand the deep social impact of both the enduring inequalities of modernity, and its violence against the Global South during the colonial-era and since then. Down either of these tracks, the historical grievance of the Global South against the West and Japan is growing. It is feeding contested deep pluralism, and can no longer be sidelined.

Coming to terms with the legacy of colonialism is necessary to the eventual construction of a consensual, deeply pluralist, global society

---

[3] For a detailed case study of the history problems between Japan and China, and in less detail Japan and Korea, see Buzan and Goh (2020).

capable of dealing with the rising tide of shared threats. Reconciling this colonial past will not be easy for either side, though the widespread acceptance of human and racial equality should help. The West and Japan need to acknowledge their role, and accommodate the sense of grievance and humiliation in the former colonial world. But the former colonial world also needs to acknowledge its own responsibilities and complicities. Colonialism was certainly a story of ruthlessly exploited inequality, but it was not a simple dyad between colonisers and colonised, exploiters and exploited. Collaboration was a big part of the story from Korea to Africa; and as the contrast between Japan's and China's responses to the Western challenge shows, colonised and/or exploited countries bear some responsibility for their own weakness and vulnerability (Gray, 2002: vii). China resisted modernity so successfully during the nineteenth century that it made itself weak and vulnerable to outside powers (Wang, 2019: esp. ch. 3). The Islamic world likewise proved unable to adapt itself to modernity quickly enough to prevent widespread colonisation by the West, and fragmentation into Western-style states (Piscatori, 1986).

If reconciliation occurs, it will have to be a two-way street in which both sides will need to examine their own faults as well as those of the other side. As wealth, power and cultural and political authority become more widely diffused in global society, the legacy of colonialism could easily poison diplomacy, push deep pluralism more towards conflictual mode, and impede functional cooperation on shared-threat issues such as climate change and disease control, and the process of reforming IGOs. How this history problem is handled by both sides, will be one key determinant of whether contested deep pluralism is brief or durable.

Declining Influence of Some Non-State Actors

Many of the discussions that tried to capture the nature of the emerging new world order, noted at the beginning of this chapter, took the view that non-state actors would play an expanding diplomatic and functional role alongside states. Non-state actors ranging across the spectrum from civil (e.g. Red Cross/Crescent, *Médecins Sans Frontières,* some transnational firms), to uncivil (e.g. Islamic State, organised crime), with many in between (e.g. Facebook, mercenary companies, proselytising religions, other transnational firms) would become prominent players in global society. States would probably remain the dominant form of actor, but much more entangled in webs of global governance than is implied in the term multipolarity. There would be many non-state actors in play in global society, some of which would wield significant amounts of wealth, power and authority. In other words, the transnational domain would become more equal to the interstate one in the composition of global society. That view reflected the strength of arguments about globalisation and global governance in the discussion of IR during the two decades following the end of the Cold War.

Until 2015 or so, I accepted that assumption. But with deep pluralism and the second cold war now unfolding in front of us, it is necessary to question it. The idea rests on the calculation that both firms and INGOs will continue on the upward track of diplomatic prominence that they have been building since the nineteenth century. Firms are now ubiquitous across the global capitalist system in both democracies and authoritarian states. Several of them already have valuations of more than a trillion dollars, a number exceeded by only sixteen states in terms of their GDP at the time of writing. They will probably be able to maintain, if not improve, their position.

INGOs, however, are more precariously placed, and might be set to decline for the duration of deep pluralism. Unlike the relatively even distribution of firms, global civil society (GCC) was always heavily associated with the INGOs of the West, and served to enhance Western dominance by projecting Western values (Armstrong, 1998; Clark, 2007; Hurrell, 2007: 111–14). Western INGOs both rode on the back of Western power, and the universalising thrust of liberal teleology, and reinforced them. As the West becomes just one core of wealth, power and cultural and political authority among several, and the liberal teleology loses its force, it seems a fair bet that the influence of GCC actors will decline. In a sense, democracy and the liberal teleology are back in the 1930s, facing both an internal crisis of legitimacy (inequality, financial crisis, unemployment) and being surrounded by an array of powerful populist, authoritarian, and even neo-fascist regimes that are in competition with them. The key difference is that the threat from outside is not now mainly of military invasion, because the risks of great power war are too high. Neither does capitalism itself seem much threatened by alternative ideologies. Now the challenge is more about the direct and indirect subversion of open societies, which is difficult to counter without the necessary measures themselves undermining open societies and the non-state actors that flourish within them.

China as a rising power does not look at all likely to generate its own stable of independent INGOs to throw into the ring. Authoritarian regimes in general do not provide fertile ground for independent non-state actors. Like the Soviet Union, they may cynically try to put forward their own front organisations, but these are hardly likely to be accepted widely as genuine representatives from the transnational domain.

The influence of INGOs will not disappear, but it might well be more confined to the sphere of liberal democratic states. During the later decades of the first round of modernity, there looked to be a movement towards the diversification of the actors engaged in diplomacy across the board, and therefore towards a kind of diplomacy for global society, rather than for global interstate society. This may well slow down or stall for the duration of deep pluralism. In principle, deep pluralism should not be a friendly environment for INGOs, and in practice there is both a weakening of their support base in the West, and a hostile environment of post-colonial resentment against Western liberal values. In addition to firms, another exception to this will probably be militant non-state actors, which are already mainstream participants in war, and up to a point, diplomacy.

Regionalisation

A more regional focus for diplomacy is a probable feature of deep pluralism. Regionalisation is a relatively recent development in international relations. As Buzan and Wæver (2003) argue, during the CAPE era, there were no regions in the modern sense, because there was no global international system/society for them to be part of. A global-scale system/society was created during the colonial period, but then regions, with Northeast Asia as the only partial holdout, were largely submerged in Western colonial spheres and had little or no autonomous international political life. The regional level thus did not really come into its own worldwide until decolonisation created autonomous subsystems of states, first in the Americas, and after the Second World War in South and Southeast Asia, the Middle East and Africa. Even then it was constrained by superpower overlay during the first cold war and up to a point thereafter by US primacy and globalisation. The relative decline of the US, the ending of Western dominance during the second decade of the twenty-first century, and the move into deep pluralism would seem to offer good prospects for a more regionalised global society.

The diffusion of wealth, power, and cultural and political authority, on the one hand, and the absence of superpowers treating the world as their region, on the other hand, both open up space for regional dynamics to gain more autonomy and prominence. But is that the way things will unfold? In relation to this question, a lot hangs on how the relationship between China and the US works out. If mainstream opinion is right, and global society becomes dominated by a globe-spanning superpower rivalry between the US and China, then, as during the first cold war, the autonomy of regional dynamics will be compromised by degrees of overlay, in which the global-level rivalry of two superpowers penetrates and dominates more local dynamics. The main question marks hanging over this scenario arise from the domestic politics in the US and China. In the US, the rise of Trumpism left the legitimacy of US claims to global leadership deeply in doubt, and damaged many of the secondary institutions that supported it. If, as seems likely at the time of writing, Trumpism remains a powerful force in US domestic politics, the stability of the US's will and capability to play a superpower role are in serious question. In the case of China, one has to reflect on the long-standing self-centredness of Chinese politics, in which concerns about its domestic order far outweigh concerns about foreign relations. Luttwak (2012) argues that China is the most 'autistic' of the great powers, not least because it is the biggest. Recall that during the 1930s and 1940s, the main political actors in China were, for most of the time, far more concerned about the civil war amongst them than about resisting Japanese invaders. China seems more likely to remain relatively inward looking in this way, than to want to be running the world.

If I am right, and the US and China will be merely big great powers with some global economic interests, then there is considerable scope for a more regionalised global society. In that case, the US–China rivalry would be mainly about spheres of influence, and zones of military dominance, in Asia, and not, as the US–Soviet rivalry was, a contest both to promote a universal ideology and to dominate the planet. In a no-superpower scenario of deep pluralism, many of the emerging powers would have as much or more focus on their own regions, and their position within them, as they would on the global level. When superpowers dominated the system, global level concerns generally trumped regional level ones. But in a world of several great and many regional powers, the regional level could well become a lot more autonomous. China has some global aspirations, but its main immediate concern is to gain primacy in Asia. Russia, India and Brazil want recognition as great powers, but are mainly interested in their own regions and those immediately adjacent. The observation of Buzan and Wæver (2003) about the relationship between regions and great powers remains salient here. Regions vary hugely in how they relate to great powers. Some are heavily dominated by a single great power within them (North America, South Asia, the former Soviet Union, and possibly South America). Some have created substantial institutional frameworks to mediate their affairs (Europe). Some have more than one great power within them (East Asia). And some have no great powers within them (Africa, the Middle East). Great powers can and do intervene in adjacent regions (China in

South and Southeast Asia; Europe and Russia in the Middle East; Europe in Africa; the US in Latin America). For the most part, great powers can no longer simply exploit their local preponderance to maintain regional order. They need to negotiate with their neighbours and regional powers. As the transition towards a post-Western deep pluralism progresses, the waning of superpowers should raise the relative autonomy of the regional level, and the regional dynamics with internal and adjacent great powers.

On this basis, one might anticipate that under deep pluralism, great powers will operate on two levels, global and regional. On the global level, the extent and character of cooperation/conflict will depend on whether deep pluralism is more contested or more consensual. That, in turn, depends on how a complex conjuncture of factors plays out. How will the great powers respond to the various shared-fate threats, such as climate change and pandemics, that affect them all? How deeply will post-colonial resentment poison relations between first- and second-round modernisers? Will great power rivalries over spheres of influence disrupt their ability to cooperate? The key danger here is that the global level will remain undermanaged because a more regionalised global society will draw interest and attention away from the global level. On the regional level, there is likely to be quite considerable diversity in how great powers operate. That diversity will be partly generated by different structures, and partly by different foundations of cultural authority. On one end of the spectrum will be Europe, with its relatively strong and consensual regional institutional framework, which is still in a class of its own even after Brexit. On the other end will be the spheres around Russia and China, both of which seem to be seeking primacy over their regions, and tending to think a bit like empires in relation to their neighbours.[4] Southeast Asia has elements of both regional institutionalisation and local great power dominance. Regions with no internal great powers – the Middle East and Africa – will either be left more to their own affairs, or intervened in by neighbouring great powers if they become securitised by them. The issue of migration from Africa and the Middle East to Europe is a current example of that securitising dynamic. In my reading, the odds favour a durable deep pluralism with a strong regional level. The global level of diplomacy will be generally weakened as a result. Part of that will be a long contestation over the reshaping of secondary institutions to accommodate the new realities of wealth, power, and cultural and political authority in a global society with

---

[4] In a smaller way, Serbia and Israel are also still thinking like empires.

no superpowers and no guiding ideology. The key question is whether the pressure of shared-fate threats will be enough to sustain specific functional forms of global GPM adequate to deal with them. More on that below.

International Law

Nothing in this analysis suggests that the basic structure of international law is going to change under deep pluralism. As with diplomacy, the immediate future of international law will be dominated by contested deep pluralism. That points to an increased role for state sovereignty, and a decreasing one for the moves towards a more cosmopolitan law for global society that animated the movement for human rights. Under deep pluralism, the liberal teleology as a guiding standard of civilisation will weaken and shrink. Calls for 'universal' rights will increasingly be challenged by the various newly empowered cultural and political exceptionalisms of which the leading current form is 'Chinese characteristics'. These communitarian exceptionalisms are likely themselves to feed off the substantial reservoir of post-colonial resentment that lies beneath global society. Within that, although there will probably be less in the way of shared values and visions among states and societies, there will remain plenty of room for states to make positive international laws in whatever functional areas they require them. Even a quite durable period of contested deep pluralism might still generate international law to regulate new technologies. The accelerating competitive moves into space will also require updates to the legal regime currently in place for that dimension.

Perhaps the big question in this regard is how global society will react to the gathering crisis over climate change and environmental management. Although climate change is clearly underway already, it still remains uncertain exactly how and when this crisis will unfold. Our knowledge of the climate system is not perfect, and there may well be surprises along the way that make things better, or more probably, worse. We have, for example, learned a lot in recent years about how glacial ice melts, which is considerably faster than what was anticipated earlier (Dalby, 2020: 39). It is not entirely clear how and when potential methane and CO_2 emissions from thawing arctic permafrosts and oceanic clathrates (ice-bound methane deposits) will be released. Least predictable of all is how global society will respond to such developments. It is easy to imagine responses right across the spectrum, from rising territoriality and conflict over migration, to the successful global securitisation of climate change, and the collective enforcement of action against those clinging to carbon-fuelled economies. International law might be either weakened or strengthened depending on whether the response is more fragmented and conflictual or more collective and consensual.

Finally, come the nine primary institutions that were born into the first two phases of the transition towards modernity: the balance of power, great power management, nationalism, the market/economic nationalism, science, sport, human equality, development and environmental stewardship.

Balance of Power

Consensual deep pluralism could support an associational balance of power, but contested deep pluralism points towards adversarial balancing. By the second and third decades of the twenty-first century, adversarial balancing was clearly on its way back as the second cold war got underway. This was most obvious in Asia, where by the second decade, military rivalry between China and the US was explicit, particularly in terms of China's attempts to push US military influence out of the East and South China Seas. Highlights were China's illegal building and militarisation of several islands in the South China Sea from 2014 to 2015; its bullying of Southeast Asian states over fishing, drilling and boundaries; its increasing pressure on Taiwan; and its ruthless violation of the 'two systems' agreement in Hong Kong in 2020. An independent, but also linked, adversarial balancing dynamic was emerging between China and India, pushed by ongoing clashes on their border, China's commercial and strategic push into the Indian Ocean, and its long-standing alliance with Pakistan. China's increasingly domineering policy in its region began to shift hedging arrangements such as the Quad amongst the US, India, Japan and Australia, more towards adversarial balancing ones. As argued above, the shock of China's repression in Hong Kong in 2020 might have been sufficient to count it as the benchmark date for the opening of the second cold war.

Less obviously than in Asia, adversarial balancing was also beginning to show itself in other places. The rift between the West and Russia that opened up when the latter made itself a major player in the Syrian crisis in 2012–2013, and then in 2014 seized Crimea and parts of eastern Ukraine, gave rise to military probings, frontier tripwires, and provocative deployments of troops and weapons reminiscent of the first cold war. Russia's second invasion of Ukraine in 2022 hugely deepened this process. Sweden and Finland applied to join NATO, and the alliance ramped up both its military expenditure and its border defences. Most

NATO members gave extensive support to Ukraine in terms of aid, training and a copious supply of weapons, some of which were game-changing in their sophistication. At the time of writing, this situation was starting to look more like proxy war than just adversarial balancing. In the Middle East, a complex, multi-layered game of rivalries was showing elements of adversarial balancing both among the local states, particularly Iran, Saudi Arabia and Israel, and among the various intervening outside powers. There was discussion of rising possibilities of increased proliferation of nuclear weapons in Asia and elsewhere (*The Economist*, 30 January 2021).

There does not seem to be much scope for a return of associational balancing under deep pluralism. Only if some sort of consensual accommodation about spheres of influence could be reached between China and Russia, on the one hand, and the West and its allies, on the other hand, could associational balancing make a comeback. Such an agreement might be possible as a way of ending the second cold war, but with the current momentum of events, that does not look likely until into the 2030s. So long as China's leaders see the West as in decline, and themselves as on the rise; while the US and the West try to maintain a status quo that advantages their past power, the grounds for associational balancing are unlikely to materialise. If China thinks it should have more power and influence in proportion to its rise, and the West and its associates should have less, or the West drags its feet on recognising the status of the emerging powers, then there will be no stable foundation on which to build associational balancing. The outlook therefore seems to be that the balance of power will remain dormant as an institution of global society so long as adversarial balancing dominates, and associational balancing has no foundation.

Great Power Management

There is a growing interest in the new great powers and their roles and responsibilities in international society (Gaskarth, 2015; Falkner and Buzan, 2022). This raises the question of whether countries still classified as 'developing' can also be classified as great powers? Since the nineteenth century, being at or near the leading edge of industrialisation and modernity have been necessary conditions for great power status (Buzan and Lawson, 2015: 240–70). If this condition is breaking down, what are the implications for deep pluralism about how we understand both the qualifications for great power status and the rights and responsibilities associated with it? As noted, big developing countries such as China and India, give their own development first priority, and argue that they should not be obliged to burden themselves with global managerial responsibilities. There has been a particular focus on rising China, which is pressured from without to become a more responsible great power, and from within to balance the domestic political needs of the CCP with the necessity to engage in a still, if decreasingly, Western-defined global economic order (Jones, 2014). More broadly, there has been interest in how rising powers gain the 'legitimate' great power status in 'recognition games' (Suzuki, 2008), and some discussions on the legitimacy of power (Reus-Smit, 2014). If, as seems already accepted, developing countries can now rank as great powers, then the general consequence will be a granting of great power rights to more states, alongside a reduction in great power responsibilities. The main hope for GPM will then be that developing-country great powers will at least mobilise themselves to take responsibility for pressing shared fate issues such as global pandemics and climate change.

Introverted great powers means that the exercise of GPM responsibility under deep pluralism will be more diffuse and more complicated than under the relatively concentrated domination of the US during the 1990s and the noughties, or the relative simplicity of the bipolar first cold war. One factor is the wider diversity of great powers created by the rise of China, India and others. Developed/developing is one element of this, but there are other ways of parsing this issue. Cui and Buzan (2016: 189–94), for example, explore an ideological spectrum ranging from universal, open and inclusive polities (e.g. pre-Trump US, Canada, Brazil), to parochial, closed and exclusive ones (e.g. China, Japan, Israel, a Trumpian US). Such ideological differentiations mattered during both the interwar and first cold war years. They may well matter again under deep pluralism and the second cold war, where there will not only be a divide between authoritarians and democracies, but also one between the different civilisational values represented by the US, Europe, Russia, China, India and the Islamic World. Both the likely rise in prominence of the regional level as compared with the global one, and the impact of empowered post-colonial resentment, could also play strongly into great power differentiation.

As per the discussion in Chapter 5b, this likely dominance of adversarial balancing narrows the question of GPM to whether it can be done in the absence of a supportive scaffolding of associational balancing. In principle, as already shown, a degree of GPM can be done even when adversarial balancing is dominant. In practice, whether or not it is done going forward into deep pluralism will depend on how the great powers and the rest of global society respond to the challenge from a rising array of shared threats. With its greater diffusion of wealth, power, and

political and cultural authority, and its reservoir of post-colonial resentment, deep pluralism will be notably anti-hegemonic and pro-sovereign
equality in sentiment. Out of practical necessity, it will probably retain
some of the long-standing fudge against sovereign equality of special
rights and responsibilities, but this will be an interstate society more
inclined to resist leadership than to look for it. It is highly likely that a
feature of the next decades will be a long-term renegotiation and reformulation of the structure of IGOs within global society (Acharya and
Buzan, 2019: 283–4). The shift from the G7/8 to the G20 was a harbinger of this reconstruction (Drezner, 2012: 9–12; Temin and Vines, 2013:
248–50). The prospects for GPM depend on whether the great powers,
and global society more broadly, respond to shared threats with some
form of functional consensus on the need for collective action, or by
seeking to exploit different levels of vulnerability in the pursuit of rivalry
(Cui and Buzan, 2016: 207). Will functional logic create significant
possibilities for GPM, or will adversarial balancing cause many such
issues to be weaponised?

As already noted in the discussions of territoriality, sovereignty and
International Law, climate change and pandemics look to be at the head
of the list in the array of shared-fate threats facing global society, though
the global economy, nuclear proliferation, cybersecurity, migration and
space rocks are also in the running. I will pick up the question of GPM
and the global economy in the section on the market below. Aside from
that, although it is early days in deep pluralism, the experience so far in
relation to both the Covid-19 pandemic and climate change is a mix of
contested and cooperative responses. In relation to the Covid-19 pandemic, there have been zero-sum responses to the production and distribution of both personal protective equipment and vaccines, and mainly
national level action in terms of controlling travel and territoriality. At the
same time, there has been quite a lot of cooperation around the science of
inventing the vaccines, and up to a point in pushing for global distribution of them. Similarly, on climate change, there has been notable
progress towards accepting collective responsibility to address the problem, but strongly sovereigntist defence against mandatory quotas.
Emerging powers have clung to the principle of 'common but differentiated responsibilities', in an attempt to lighten the burden on heavy
current carbon emitters such as India and China, while increasing it on
the legacy polluters from the nineteenth and twentieth centuries.

This mixed record perhaps suggests what the prospect for GPM will be
going forward into deep pluralism: not zero, but relatively constrained
and modest. Whether that pattern will change depends on whether the
pressure from shared-fate threats rises high enough to turn perceptions

and behaviours towards more coordinated collective responses. It is impossible at this point to say where such a tipping point might lie, though the lack of impact of events such as the flooding of New Orleans, wildfires in the US and Australia, more severe and erratic storm and monsoon seasons in Asia, droughts in Europe, China and the Middle East, the rapid melting of glaciers worldwide, and the thawing and burning of arctic tundra, suggest that the threshold event will need to be quite big and dramatic. Perhaps the simultaneous flooding of several major coastal cities would do the trick.[5]

Nationalism

As argued in Chapter 5b, nationalism was, for better or for worse, one of the great success stories of the primary institutions that grew up during the first two phases of the transition towards modernity. Nationalism, like the other two parts of the triad of primary institutions that constitute the modern state, territoriality and sovereignty, quite easily weathered the storm of economic globalisation. It looks well-placed to remain in robust form during the period of deep pluralism. In the coming decade or two, perhaps longer, this triad will be strengthened by deep pluralism. Nationalism will feed off both post-colonial resentment and the ongoing reactions against neoliberal globalisation. It will be claimed and promoted by populist politicians of all ideological stripes. Even where religion is being successfully remobilised for political purposes, this will be dressed up in clothing similar to nationalism: Hindu 'nationalism', Islamic 'nationalism', Christian 'nationalism', and suchlike. Nationalism will be reinforced by the swinging of the pendulum away from the global market, and towards economic nationalism (see next section). How long this state of affairs will last is difficult to say, and dependent on the impact of intrinsically unpredictable events. It will certainly be as durable as the second cold war. Eventually, barring some transformational event, the dialectic will turn back towards some form of globalisation. A new round of economic globalisation is one possibility: another turn in a familiar dialectic. Perhaps more likely is a globalisation pushed by environmental threats on a planetary scale. Nationalism might

[5] In terms of the overall cost of damage, the cities at the greatest risk are: (1) Guangzhou, (2) Miami, (3) New York, (4) New Orleans, (5) Mumbai, (6) Nagoya, (7) Tampa, (8) Boston, (9) Shenzen, and (10) Osaka. The ten most vulnerable cities when measured as percentage of GDP are: (1) Guangzhou; (2) New Orleans; (3) Guayaquil, Ecuador; (4) Ho Chi Minh City; (5) Abidjan; (6) Zhanjing; (7) Mumbai; (8) Khulna, Bangladesh; (9) Palembang, Indonesia; and (10) Shenzen. www.worldbank.org/en/news/feature/2013/08/19/coastal-cities-at-highest-risk-floods (accessed 9 January 2022).

then find itself challenged by identities that are either larger in scale (humankind), or smaller (local) if renewed globalisation was riding on the back of an environmental crisis that had become severe enough to undo politics on the national scale.

Market versus Economic Nationalism

During the first round of modernity, the market co-evolved with nationalism and entered into a kind of cyclical dialectic with it, in which the market and economic nationalism competed to be the dominant framing of, and primary institution for, the global economy. So long as this contestation continues, the economic primary institution will be in an unstable relationship with the powerful institutional trilogy that defines the modern state (sovereignty, territoriality, nationalism). As argued above, the current swing to economic nationalism was a response to the costs and failures of an over-extended and under-governed, neoliberal project of economic globalisation. That crisis is one of the major drivers of the turn to deep pluralism. It is far from clear how this dialectic will unfold. On the one hand, economic nationalism is gaining ground. The global market is under attack not only for generating frequent and damaging financial crises, but also for promoting increasing inequality. The Covid-19 pandemic also exposed the fragility of global supply chains in a crisis, raising demands for the repatriation of production. This crisis exposed the vulnerabilities of high dependence on economic efficiency criteria for medical supplies, with neither home production capacity nor adequate stockpiling being adequate to compensate for breakdowns in global supply chains.

Yet, regardless of the neoliberal crisis, the unwinding of global production chains was being pushed by automation technology, which threatened to end the comparative advantage of cheap labour and allow production to be returned to homelands. There seemed to be plenty of scope for the pursuit of technological alternatives to dependence on overseas suppliers for everything from minerals (ocean and space mining), through energy (diversification of sources, localisation, e.g. by solar, wind, wave and geothermal), to foods (vertical farming in controlled environments, industrially produced proteins). In addition, the global market seemed to threaten rising unemployment by replacing labour with capital in an ever-wider range of jobs. It was not clear how severe this effect would be, but the prospect that cuts would be deep and permanent was worrying. The same technologies that were enabling states to back away from dependence on global production chains were also threatening the employment model as a way of distributing wealth and sustaining consumption (Lee, 2018). That model, in which the industrial economy depends on a synergy between capital and labour, has been at the heart of political economy since the nineteenth century. All governments, from China to the US were becoming acutely aware that the economy needs to serve the people, not just enrich the elites. They were also becoming aware that market logic cannot any longer ignore the environmental externalities of economic activity. It has both to price them in, and take active measures to confront environmental issues.

Yet many aspects of economic globalisation in trade, production and finance remain in place, and the principle of the market remains strong at the domestic level. Even China stayed wedded to 'market socialism', though at the time of writing this commitment looked threatened by the CCP's increasing intervention into the operations of major Chinese firms. What was in retreat was the market as a global institution. The market's victory as a way of organising national economies was not threatened in the same way. And with its detachment from liberalism by China, what counted as 'market' became more open to interpretation. China seemed close to abstracting the market principle down to little more than the maintenance of strong competition (Kroeber, 2016: 101–7; Lee, 2018: 22–5). Even at the global level, despite Trump's attacks on both the primary and secondary institutions of trade, and the rising political opposition to further trade agreements, there were still firm signs of willingness to keep an institutional architecture for the global market economy in place. Early signs of it were the creation of new economic IGOs by both China and the BRICS. These new IGOs could be seen both as competitors to the Bretton Woods institutions, and as bargaining chips in what will be a long struggle to reconfigure the distribution of status and power in the management of the global political economy. Japan's taking up leadership of TTP – now re-labelled the Comprehensive and Progressive Agreement for Trans-Pacific Partnership (CPTPP) – in the absence of the US might be seen as part of this process of decentring global economic management away from the West. So might the rise of regional trade arrangements (RTAs) (O'Brian and Williams, 2016: 120–4). Deep pluralism might also be expressed in a move away from the US dollar as the *de facto* global currency, and towards a system more like that before 1939, with several leading currencies (*The Economist*, 26 June 2021: 72). This would reflect both the relative weakening of the US in the global economy, and resentment against its effective weaponisation of the dollar's global role, by using it as an instrument of sanctions in pursuit of its own policy aims. All of this suggests that even under contested deep pluralism, and with a second cold war well underway, economic management will remain on the agenda of GPM, albeit with more of an emphasis on 'management' and less on letting the market rip, than during the heyday of neoliberalism.

At the time of writing, the situation looked more like entering into another round of the dialectic between the market and economic nationalism than as if either were headed for any permanent victory. The immediate trend, reinforced by the consolidation of the second cold war, favoured economic nationalism as a major element of deep pluralism. But taking a longer view, one has to be impressed by the persistence of long-distance trade in human history, motivated by profit, status and curiosity, and marked by its ability to thrive whether encouraged or discouraged by the prevailing political structures. The extension of trade and finance over ever-longer distances has been the leading edge of globalisation since far back within the history of the CAPE era, and remained so, with the exception of the two world wars, in the form of intensification almost throughout the first two phases of the transition towards modernity. It would be more than a little surprising if this story had come to a permanent end now. As most recently demonstrated by China, it has been foundational to the extraordinary ability of the transition towards modernity to generate, and to distribute, unprecedented levels of wealth and power to billions of people. More likely, therefore, is that this dialectic will be ongoing into the next phases of the transition towards modernity.

Exactly what form further rounds of the dialectic between the market and economic nationalism might take is difficult to see. The efficiencies and wealth-generating possibilities of a global market will always exert a strong allure despite the inability so far of such arrangements to last more than a few decades without falling into crisis. And as most recently demonstrated by the Soviet Union, autarchy does not seem an attractive alternative at the other end of the spectrum. But the strong counter-pull from the need for the economy both to serve the needs of the people, and find a sustainable relationship with the planetary ecosphere, is not going away either. Neither extreme seems to work well, but what is still unclear is how these contradictory imperatives can be combined. The Bretton Woods attempt at combination had intrinsic flaws that made it unsustainable. While the precise shape of the dialectic, and how it will unfold, remain unclear, this dialectic is likely to remain active during deep pluralism despite the prominence of economic nationalism.

How this dialectic will work out remains unclear, but some of the issues that will play into the process even during deep pluralism are in plain sight. Consider the following three.

First, the rising availability of ever more sophisticated algorithms and AIs, combined with ever bigger datasets, raise interesting challenges to the market. Throughout the first two phases of modernity, supporters of market ideology could plausibly claim that command economies were doomed to inefficiency because of the physical inability of human bureaucracies to process the huge amounts of data required to run a modern economy. History largely supported this argument, culminating in China's defection from Marxian economics in the late 1970s, and the collapse of the Soviet system during the 1980s. Now, however, the claim that the market is the only mechanism that can do this efficiently is under challenge. AIs and big data are in a different league from filing-cabinet bureaucracies and idiosyncratic political leaders, and might be able to make forms of command economy work. China, which is striving to fulfil Xi's dreams of 'socialism with Chinese characteristics', is the most likely place for this experiment to be seriously tried. Using powerful new tools to overcome the disastrous weakness of earlier experiments in command economy in the Soviet Union and Mao's China, might perhaps offer Xi Jinping the ideological prize of vindicating the Marxian economics that Deng was forced to abandon in the late 1970s. That would make him a hero in China equal to Mao and Deng, and more broadly might make him a hero of the authoritarian left. An efficient cyber-command economy would be the biggest challenge ever faced by the market, and if attached to authoritarian surveillance states, also the biggest challenge to democracy.

Second, and staying with the theme of algorithms, AI and big data, if automation (AI plus robotics) destroys more jobs than it creates, then stable employment weakens as the means of distributing income to the people. In that case, various forms of Universal Basic Income (UBI) might have to become a feature of all advanced economies. Lee (2018: 197–32), for example, argues that if the employment system of distributing wealth breaks down because of high job losses and insufficient new forms of employment, then deep restructuring alternatives for finance will have to be considered. These might range from UBI, to reconfiguring the type of work that gets paid by giving income to socially productive activities (such as care, teaching, parenting) that are currently unpaid or poorly paid (for a critique, see Milanovic, 2019: 201–5). Such reforming routes would set up a new type of social contract that might well pose profound challenges to market ideology and capitalism, though it is not necessarily incompatible with them.

Thirdly, there are also big, and still open, social questions about the impact on market economies of ever-more sophisticated AIs combining clever algorithms, huge data processing capacity, and vast pools of big data. Will they concentrate ever-more wealth and information in the hands of a small number of private firms, exacerbating the inequality problem in various big ways? Could this necessitate and facilitate a shift to a political economy based on UBI as just discussed? Under the current system, the rich get much richer, while the rest stay the same or get poorer (Piketty, 2014). Extreme projections of this trend would have the rich eventually detaching themselves from the rest of society to pursue their own utopian visions of progress. There are signs of this already in the form of wealthy elites able to buy multiple residences, multiple passports, and their own private transportation and security. In return for investing, they also get substantial exemption from tax, and protection for their financial assets. Automation means that the traditional dependence of the rich on the masses for labour and soldiering, both big factors in the politics of the first two phases of modernity, is decreasing fast. If the rich can also find a way of no longer needing the masses as consumers, then they will have no need other than a tenuous moral bond of shared humanity, to stay linked to them at all. The often-extreme cruelty and inequality of the CAPE era, not to mention many ongoing contemporary practices of coercive exploitation and repression, show just how tenuous that moral bond can be. Some libertarian extremists advocate elite exit from the state and society in order to maximise technological progress without being held back by the in-built egalitarianism and redistribution of democratic welfare states (Land, 2013; Frase, 2016: ch. 4). If realised, this utopian/dystopian scenario would open up a starkly two-tier stratification of society. Stratification would return as the dominant form of differentiation, albeit in a very different way from that of the CAPE era and the first two phases of modernity, in which elites depended on the masses for labour, soldiering and consumption. That scenario, however, requires a linear projection of an existing trend of growing inequality. Along that path it will encounter dialectics of resistance and reform that might easily change the trajectory.

These three issues are not mutually exclusive, and there is obvious scope for their dynamics to play into each other in various ways. Their dynamics will almost certainly continue to unfold beyond the duration of deep pluralism.

Science

During the nineteenth and twentieth centuries, science was enormously influential both as an accepted standard of knowledge and rational discourse, and as the engine room for the material cornucopia of modernity. It pushed religion out of many areas of knowledge, and established its own grand narrative of progress, but it failed comprehensively to push religion into obsolescence. Faith, it turned out, did not require scientific validation. Revealed 'knowledge', conspiracy theories, and downright mysticism, remained socially potent in the absence of supporting evidence. Indeed, their social potency seems recently to have been amplified by the Internet, social media, and the resurgent power of the big lie. Science also generated its own antithesis in the form of postmodern philosophy, which rejects grand narratives, challenges the validity of positivist methods in the social world, and enquires deeply into the relationship between knowledge and power. Postmodernists deny the objectivity of science and its separation from the social dynamics of power. They look at competing 'regimes of truth', and the political effects they generate in terms of inclusion and exclusion, and validation or rejection of different forms of knowledge (Devetak, 1996a, b). On the positive side, postmodernism has been a powerful influence in academic and intellectual circles, validating criticism of claims about truth and progress, highlighting who benefits and who loses from different regimes of truth, and focusing relentlessly on the politics of knowledge. On the negative side, it has helped to create a rhetoric-driven 'post-truth' world in which the big lie increasingly rules the social and political landscape. Postmodernism has been a powerful facilitator of deep pluralism. Like realism, it is both a theory and a self-fulfilling prophecy.

Despite the huge success of science as an institution of global society, in Chapter 5b I described the contest between science and religion/mysticism, and more recently postmodernism, as something like a draw. Some version of that draw seems the likely prospect going forward into deep pluralism. It seems almost inconceivable that science will go down to defeat, because it is so central both to generating the material wealth and power that are the hallmark of development, and to solving the problems that a massively expanded and industrialised humankind has created for the planet and for itself. The mullahs who rule Iran are keenly interested in nuclear physics and rocketry. The centrality of science in this respect is evidenced by the securitisation of it discussed under territoriality above. For all of their disagreements, China and the West do not disagree about this aspect of science. All the secular ideologies of progress embrace it, and it is deeply embedded in all three domains of global society. Despite that seemingly robust position, there are serious grounds for concern. In many places there are significant-enough constituencies prepared to ignore or oppose science to make big political and social impacts. Such attitudes have long been on display in the opposition of the tobacco industry to evidence that its products caused cancer, and the opposition of the fossil fuels industry to the evidence that the

CO_2 emitted by use of their products is importantly connected to climate change. Most recently, a number of political leaders – Trump in the US, Bolsonaro in Brazil and Magufuli in Tanzania – either denied the Covid-19 pandemic, calling it a hoax, or downplayed the severity of the disease, despite the scientific evidence. The popularity and intensity of feeling in substantial sections of the Republican Party around the QAnon conspiracy theory in the US suggests that significant sections of the population, even in rich and relatively well-educated countries, do not require either evidence or logic to underpin strong political views on which they are prepared to take action.

More broadly, there is the alarming rise of the 'post-truth world' in which the assumption that everything is constructed reduces the social world to a mere competition for dominance amongst discourses. In such a world, the drama of rhetoric, conspiracy theory and faith override the dry methods and evidence of science as a gold standard for shared knowledge. All that matters is defending and promoting one's normative view, and winning the fight for the public mind. There is, of course, a deep sense in which it is true that everything is constructed. Even the discourse of science undergoes paradigm shifts in which newer understandings replace older ones, and therefore 'reality', or what we take to be reality, changes. Science is but a pathway towards truth, not the truth itself, and not the only pathway to understanding. Science as an institution attempted to anchor truth with method, and during the first two phases of modernity, this was quite successful, albeit much more so in the natural than in the social sciences. Going forward, the scientific mentality looks to be weakening, not amongst scientists themselves, but in the wider society. Governments, of course, are old hands at spinning the narrative to suit their purposes. Communists and fascists in particular have always tried to manufacture the social world and history according to their own 'big lie' version of the truth, albeit while retaining a firm grip on science for exploiting the material world, and reinforcing their own wealth and power. China remains in this tradition. It has been much more worrying to see leading democracies such as the US (during the Trump administration) and Britain (over Brexit), where debate and evidence are supposed to be at the heart of society, normalise the post-truth world in their everyday politics. Science and government bear considerable responsibility for this situation. Goldenberg (2016) argues that vaccine hesitancy has less to do with misunderstanding the science and more to do with general mistrust of scientific institutions and government.

For the foreseeable future, the contradiction between science, on the one hand, and forms of belief not requiring evidence, on the other hand, seems headed for a *zhongyong*-style dialectic in which science will hold its ground in the material realm because it is a vital key to wealth and power, but might well lose ground in the social realm, where it was anyway less strongly established and more difficult to apply. To the extent that large numbers of people plausibly think that science threatens their health, wealth and status, and treats them arrogantly as experimental subjects, science is in trouble. The big lie is back in mainstream politics everywhere, and, amplified by the echo-chamber effect of the Internet and social media, it works. Whatever one might think of Trump, he was a genius at this game, and opened the door for others to play.

This dialectic has played into the onset of deep pluralism. But the issues at stake are much larger and more durable than either deep pluralism or the second cold war, and will remain in play long after both have become old history.

Sport

Although sport has important links to nationalism, it seems likely that under deep pluralism sport as a primary institution will mostly be about more of the same. There will be continued widening of membership, global standardisation of rules and competitions, and sport will remain strongly placed across, and linking, all three domains. The Internet and global communications have greatly supported the globalisation of institutionalised sport. There will also be continuity in the ongoing struggle against the influence of drugs (undermining the principle of human equality) and money (from betting and media fees) as sources of corruption to the rules and practices of fair competition. The idea that sport represents human equality has been moderated to allow separate strands of competition for men and women, and able-bodied and disabled people. This seems likely to continue for most types of sporting competition, marking one of the many compromises in the dialectic between human equality and inequality. Pressure to widen the definition of sport to include e-sports seems likely to grow as they become ever-more popular and attract ever-larger audiences and more money. The arrival of new technologies will also open new possibilities for sport, that, like e-sports now, will have to be confronted and addressed, and brought into (or not) the institution of sport. The general definition of sport is flexible enough to incorporate a wide range of competitive activities.

But there are also some significant possibilities for transformation, particularly in who – or what – is allowed to compete. Computers have already been allowed into mind-sports, and quickly rose to being the top players. Robots are not yet in contention in the more physical sports, but seem likely to be in the coming decades. Robot football is already being talked about, and will be major benchmark for the progress of robotics when it happens. As these developments mature, rules and ethics will need to be reinvented to take account of the new variables in play. It is also not difficult to imagine computers, AI and robots soon being joined by biotechnology aimed at enhanced performance without the use of drugs. Such developments, and their various combinations and permutations, could easily influence the link between sporting competition and human equality, with mark-1 humans becoming equal only in their collective inferiority to machines and enhanced human beings.

The impact of all this on the willingness and interest of audiences to watch such contests remains unclear. Chess or go matches between AIs might appeal to those expert enough in the game to appreciate high strategy and aesthetics, but perhaps not to a mass audience. A drift in that direction might also reverse the trend towards reducing violence in sport. It is clear that at least for some, the attraction of seeing injury or death in sport has not disappeared, and could be revived as legitimate. Games that embody gladiatorial-style injury and death are a staple of contemporary science fiction writing (e.g. *Hunger Games, Star Wars*). In contrast to the endless 'lives' of e-game players, the staking of real human lives could become the trumping thrill over machines.

These are issues and questions that will endure beyond deep pluralism. They will not be much affected by deep pluralism unless the intensification of the second cold war starts to break up the globality of sporting competition. The boycotts of Russia by various sports because of its war against Ukraine could be either an exception, or a harbinger of a larger, although almost certainly temporary, disruption and fragmentation of the sporting world.

Human Equality/Inequality

Like dynasticism and imperialism, practices of human inequality continue, albeit quite unevenly and with much more contested legitimacy. At one end of the spectrum, some of these practices such as slavery and racism, continue despite being generally and strongly outlawed. Others, most notably patriarchy and class/caste, occupy a middle ground, partly opposed both legally and socially, but also partly sanctioned both socially and politically, and overtly and covertly. At the other end of the spectrum, economic inequality, while openly opposed by some, is widely sanctioned, and even celebrated, by others as a key feature of capitalism and the market. The dialectic between human equality and inequality has never been fully settled despite the general shift in principle after 1945.

That shift was most clearly against racism, and less clearly against both patriarchy and inequality of wealth, and that pattern remains and looks durable. The dialectic of human equality/inequality remains open and ongoing across the whole spectrum of inequalities. In absolute numbers, there may well be more people in slave-like conditions now, than there ever were during the CAPE era.[6] Extremist outfits such as Islamic State openly advocate a return to CAPE standards of patriarchy and slavery. In many countries, there is a masculinist, and sometimes religious, backlash against gender equality that favours 'traditional family values', and opposes the feminisation of popular culture and the military. The Black Lives Matter movement demonstrated again how widespread institutional racism remains. The anti-globalisation movement campaigned against extreme wealth differentiation and the resulting highly skewed access to life chances. And there is a growing possibility on the horizon that bioengineering might open up an entirely new dimension of the old aristocratic claim to 'superior breeding', leading either to biological stratification, or the replacement of humankind with a successor species.

This is another institution whose issues and dynamics transcend the immediate concerns and impacts of deep pluralism and the second cold war. Perhaps the key point of connection is that a broad concern with racial and cultural (in)equality is part of what underpins the dynamics of deep pluralism. The demand for more cultural differentiation, more respect for difference, and more political and economic autonomy, can be seen as part of the reaction against the two-century cultural, political and economic dominance of the white West plus Japan. Deep pluralism itself depends heavily on general acceptance of human equality, especially in racial terms. It will therefore not open the way for anything like a return to the general inequality of the CAPE era. Yet ironically, deep pluralism, with its claims for cultural distinctiveness, and its rejection of the liberal teleology and its universal values of human rights, will almost certainly provide more cover and legitimacy for many of these ongoing practices of inequality. Many types and forms of human inequality can be justified as defining the norms of different cultures.

Under deep pluralism, the dialectic between human equality and inequality will remain open and ongoing across a wide spectrum of inequalities. Even without the legitimation of cultural difference, there is still a lot of variability in attitudes towards different types of inequality. Some are condemned more strongly and/or widely than others, and many are tolerated in some degree. Solutions that seem acceptable in

---

[6] Depending on conditions, perhaps as high as 50 million. www.bbc.co.uk/news/world-62877388?at_medium=RSS&at_campaign=KARANGA (accessed 13 September 2022).

some areas, such as sexually differentiated strands in sport, would be much less acceptable in other areas such as business and politics. There is nothing in the dialectics currently in play to suggest that this highly differentiated pattern of equality/inequality is going to change quickly. Indeed, as the discussion of sport above suggests, it might gain additional dimensions as technology offers biological, mechanical and digital ways of enhancing the mark-1 human being. It is an interesting, difficult and fraught question as to what exactly is the overall direction of the shift towards greater human equality that has been going on for over two centuries. It is far from clear whether the dialectic between human equality and inequality is more Hegelian, in which case the transition to human equality will be full, but slow to manifest; or more *zhongyong*, being only partial, with some forms of inequality, and the contestation around them, remaining acceptable within global society for the forseeable future.

How are the various forms of inequality likely to fare under deep pluralism? There are few signs that slavery, or practices akin to it, will disappear totally any time soon, no matter how illegal they are made. The sex industry alone will see to that. To the extent that the sex industry dominates modern slavery, it might help to break the link between slavery and racism that came into being with the Atlantic slave trade. The market for sex slaves, just like the general market for slaves during the CAPE era, seeks all colours and races. Modern slavery is strongly linked to economic inequality and patriarchy, and neither looks like disappearing any time soon. And while it continues as a practice, modern slavery hides itself, and obfuscates its identity by avoiding the term slavery.

One of the key things about the practice of racial inequality, is that it inevitably plays strongly into relations across the three domains of global society. This will continue to be the case under deep pluralism. Between states, think of Japan in 1919, and the widespread racism in both colonialism and the Second World War. In the transnational domain, think of racism in sport. In the interhuman domain, racism makes a difference between seeing other identity groups as equally part of humankind, or as unequal, or in extremis as not human. The swiftness and intensity with which the Black Lives Matter movement went global during the second decade of the twenty-first century is a testament to the ongoing success of anti-racism since 1945. Yet despite having become both illegal and socially unacceptable in many places, racism remains strong as both belief and practice. While there has been a lot of progress towards racial equality internationally, this is often less so in the domestic realm. In this respect, racism has a curious dual relationship with sovereignty. On the one hand, the right of sovereignty and non-intervention enables states to defend themselves if their norms and rules on racism are out of line with international standards. Apartheid South Africa was the exemplary case here, but there are many others. On the other hand, as argued earlier, there is a strong link between the norm of sovereign equality which came in after 1945, and acknowledgement of racial equality amongst sovereign peoples. Deep pluralism will therefore cut both ways on the question of racial equality/inequality. To the extent that racial inequality plays internationally, deep pluralism will probably support equality. But to the extent that what is deepened is sovereignty/non-intervention and cultural rights, then it could simultaneously defend various practices of inequality justified on cultural grounds.

The strength of prejudice on grounds of race or culture is also subject to complex intervening variables. One is migration, which can quickly ramp up concerns in destination countries (Wæver et al., 1993), and which might intensify if climate change is not stopped. It is also easy to imagine that strongly differential birth rates might revive racist and 'standard of civilisation' attitudes. If, as projected, Africa remains the last place to have high birth rates when all others have fallen to replacement level or below, and if Africa remains relatively poor, this could revive fear and resentment, more so if climate change leads to mass migration out of Africa (Bricker and Ibbitson, 2019: 105–24; United Nations Department of Economic and Social Affairs, 2019).

As with racism, equality of the sexes has made huge progress both domestically and internationally, but still has a long way to go. As some feminist writers point out, for many women it remains the case that marriage, like the state, can all too easily be understood as a form of protection racket (Peterson, 1992: 49–58). But – and contrary to the view that 'gender and racial hierarchies were – and remain – intricately linked' (Klotz, 2017: 363) – unlike racism, sexual inequality never spilled over strongly into the interstate domain because it did not reflect a major differentiation at that level. This is absolutely not to deny either that men have hugely dominated politics, diplomacy, war, and the global economy, or that feminising/masculinising language and metaphor has played a major role in war, imperialism, nationalism and religion. But unlike racism, which strongly and provocatively differentiated states and peoples as players in global society, gender differentiations were broadly and similarly shared across global society in all three domains. As argued in earlier chapters, all high cultures during the CAPE era were strongly patriarchal, and that attitude and practice carried over significantly into all three phases of the transition towards modernity.

On that basis, deep pluralism should not make much difference to this issue. However, since the main imperative for sex and gender equality has come from liberalism's logics of meritocracy and human rights, even the slow trend towards greater equality may be about to encounter troubled times. As the West declines in relative wealth, power and cultural authority, the force of the liberal teleology of equal rights may well decline with it. In a world order defined by deep pluralism, CAPE era religions and philosophies such as Christianity, Islam, Hinduism and Confucianism, none of them notable for encouraging sexual equality, are, as argued above, becoming more politically influential. The widening of this issue to a complex array of gender differentiations between and beyond male and female seems likely to come under the same logic, with a retreating liberal universalism being challenged by the sovereignty of cultures with different views. Varieties of capitalism and modernity empowered by sovereign equality and deep pluralism might well generate different forms and practices of gender hierarchy and inequality. A further consideration in all this is what the impact on women in modern societies will be as they have fewer children. In societies where the fertility rate is below 1.5, a lot of people are choosing to have no children. Could this help to close the sex gap by limiting the traditional responsibilities of women for childbirth/childraising, and freeing them to take other roles in society? Will falling birthrates exacerbate or diminish the preference for sons that has led to skewed ratios of male to female in some societies? Will a relative shortage of women in society raise their status?

Economic equality/inequality remains hotly contested, with powerful forces on both sides. That does not look likely to change under deep pluralism. Some, perhaps many, will think that this question does not even belong under the general heading of human (in)equality because its main referents are in political economy: the market, freedom and meritocracy. Yet it is nonetheless the case that economic (in)equality has made it into the contemporary debates around human rights, which is the nodal point for the politics of equality/inequality. My position on human rights is that it is not a primary institution of global society in its own right, but part of the ongoing and hotly contested dialectic of human equality/inequality. This is reflected in the disagreements around human rights. The US and the West generally saw human rights primarily in terms of civil and political rights, seeing these as a key way of putting limits on freedom becoming dictatorship or some other form of social and political hierarchy. They have advocated these as universal rights that under some circumstances can and should override sovereignty/nonintervention. Their problem has been that economic inequality can lead to the same adverse outcome by giving wealthy elites too much control over politics. By contrast, China and many states of the Global South have put the emphasis on economic, social and cultural rights, and the right to subsistence/survival and development. As liberalism loses both its universalism and the force of its teleology under deep pluralism, the view of the Global South seems likely to gain in strength (Zhang and Buzan, 2019). Yet China is already confronting the problem of how to balance economic inequality with authoritarian socialism, and many contemporary Northeast Asian societies are noted for their hierarchical social relations. The contradictions with human rights seem likely to carry on affecting not just the West, but emerging economies too. Human rights seem likely to remain contested, though there is a possibility that some consensus might coalesce around a lowest-common-denominator approach focusing on the values of survival and development. That, however, is more likely to come about only after the second cold war and the phase of deep pluralism.

Development

At the time of writing, the standing of development as an obligation of the core to the periphery remains reasonably strong. Development is therefore still a primary institution of global society. But this situation looks increasingly fragile. Development was always supposed to be a transitional institution, and this means that the brutal question of how many generations can reasonably claim to be victims of colonial exploitation cannot be avoided. At some point, the logic behind development shifts away from compensation (a fairly strong claim to a right) towards humanitarian support to mitigate the effects of being underdeveloped (a more tenuous one). Underdevelopment then shifts from being a temporary condition with a clear cause, to a potentially enduring one with many possible causes.

In this sense, development can be compared with the balance of power. Recall that associational balancing counted as an institution of global society because it embodied agreement about the principle and how to make it work. Adversarial balancing was simply a set of individual choices, and was therefore not an institution. Development is a strong goal for all countries within the core, but like balancing, it can be competitive. Each core state wants to maximise its own development in order to keep up with the others. Development aid from the post-colonial core to the periphery was more like associational balancing in recognising a shared set of rights and responsibilities. As countries formerly in the periphery, such as China and India, move into the core, the core expands and the periphery shrinks. Fewer countries remain 'less developed', but the new countries in the core do not share the compensation logic that originally underpinned the idea that the former core of ex-colonial powers should assist the periphery. For those newly developed countries there is only the moral and humanitarian logic that the rich should help the poor. That logic might be strong enough to sustain development as an institution, but it might not.

This historical pressure on development as an institution is both separable from deep pluralism, and linked to it. It is separable inasmuch as the questions around historical distance and compensatory rights and responsibilities would have arisen anyway, just with the passage of time. But the expansion of the core by the entry of non-Western states is a key feature of deep pluralism. Within that, the former colonial powers cease to be the dominant element of the core, and command a smaller share of the global resources of wealth, power and political and cultural authority. As argued above under diplomacy, they are becoming more inward-looking, and are both less inclined, and less able, to take responsibility for managing global society. Yet with the embedding of the second cold war, deep pluralism is turning in an increasingly competitive, contested direction, and this could actually help keep the institution of development in play. During the first cold war, there were competing models of development in play, and this served the then 'Third World' by enabling it to play the ideological camps off against each other in order to increase aid. The second cold war might work in the same way for what is now called the 'Global South'. Despite the convergence on capitalism after the first cold war, development still remains caught in ideological disputes about which model to follow. The choice is now among varieties of capitalism ranging across the political spectrum from liberal democratic (US), through social democratic (EU, Japan) to authoritarian (China). Rising competition between China and the West might well serve the global south by stimulating flows of development aid and investment.

Because development is a long-term structural issue, we can even look a bit further ahead through the phase of deep pluralism. In principle, levels of development could become globally even. In practice, that seems highly unlikely. There may be considerable evening-out, as there already has been. But significant differences are likely to remain even within the core, and therefore the competitive, 'adversarial' element of development will remain durable. That is probably as close as modernity will get to the condition of the hunter-gatherer and CAPE eras, when levels of technology and modes of social organisation were relatively even across humankind. Countries not at the leading edge of development will try to make absolute and relative gains in their ability to extract wealth and power from modernity, and at least to avoid sliding backward in relation to the core. At the moment, we are in the middle of a second round of modernisation that started in the 1970s. If this round, like the first, promotes only a few countries into the leading ranks of development, then the process of achieving even a roughly even distribution of modernity will be long, possibly with third and fourth rounds. Development as a process, and possibly as an institution, could thus have a durable run in global society so long as the core continue to accept an obligation, on whatever grounds, to help less-developed countries catch up.

That said, there is room for the thought that the intrinsic material turbulence of modernity might differentiate it fundamentally from earlier eras in this respect. If materials, energy and technology continue to improve at anything like the pace of the last two centuries, then the era-analogy with hunter-gatherers and CAPE might be inappropriate. Although the core of countries at the leading edge of modernity is continuing to expand, it is doing so quite slowly. And it is vital not to lose sight of the fact that development remains a priority even for those already at the leading edge of modernity. Development is partly about those behind catching up, and being aided to do so. But it is also about those at the leading edge continuing to pursue their own progress and empowerment in competition with others in the core. It can be argued that continuous economic growth and progress is essential to the internal political stability of capitalism, as a counterweight to the otherwise unacceptable levels of inequality that capitalism generates. It is therefore possible that those left behind in the periphery will never catch up if the leading edge continues to unfold into new forms of modernity faster than those trailing can either acquire the older forms, or skip stages and jump to the frontiers. How easy, for example, will it be for those still at the bottom of the scale of development to pick up on the shift towards cyber-economies increasingly shaped, and possibly run, by advanced AI and huge banks of metadata? Leapfrogging over older forms may be possible, but this cannot be guaranteed. If uneven and combined development under modernity is a permanent condition rather than just a transitional one, then the issue of (under)development will not disappear any time in the forseeable future. If there were to be another breakthrough like that from CAPE to modernity, in which a small core tapped into a radically new source of wealth, power and authority, then the whole cycle of UCD, creating a new core–periphery structure, would be reset and the process start again.

The further spread of development, however it unfolds, should quickly lay to rest the long-standing, and pernicious, but fundamentally mis-guided, tension within development between modernisation and Westernisation. This was especially an issue for non-Western countries, starting with Japan, as they acquired the full spectrum of modernity. Since modernity was first framed and practised in the West, it initially seemed to mean that in order to modernise, countries had essentially to abandon their own cultures and identities, and become clones of Western societies. Many in the West flattered themselves that that was how it had to (and should!) go. Many traditionalists and nativists in the non-West understandably feared this was true and resisted modernisation for that reason. Japan was widely seen in Asia as being in the vanguard of modernity, and heralding Asia's reassertion against Western domination. But it was also seen as a threat to Asia if it became too Western and lost its Asian foundations (e.g. Tagore, 1918; Sun Yat-sen, 1924[7]). As argued earlier, the theory of UCD points strongly towards the opposite conclusion: that all modernisations will be different according to when and where they emerge. Japan's case should have made this clear early on, despite the views of its Asian critics. While Japan modernised, it certainly did not lose its own culture and identity, and the Western powers saw this and discriminated against it on that basis. But for a long time, Japan was an isolated case, leaving the idea of homogenising Westernisation inadequately challenged. By now, however, other big non-Western countries have made it into the core of modernity, most obviously China. China's mantra of 'Chinese characteristics' makes abundantly clear that its successful embrace of modernity will embody as little as possible of Westernisation. In the context of deep pluralism, China can, and does, celebrate its difference in a way that was much more difficult for Japan to do in the era of Western colonial dominance. Others, such as India, will certainly follow this path to multiple modernities, diluting the association between modernisation and Westernisation as they do so. The ability of capitalism over the last century to cohabit with both democratic and authoritarian governments is the demonstration case for multiple modernities. That process is part of the toppling of a Western-dominated world order, and its replacement by deep pluralism.

Development is already deeply entangled with two other institutions: environmental stewardship and human (in)equality. The contradictions between open-ended development and environmental stewardship have been emergent for several decades, and the dialectic between them is likely to be one of the key dynamics shaping global society during deep

---

[7] Sun Yat-sen's speech on Pan-Asianism, Kobe, 1924. https://en.wikisource.org/wiki/Sun_Yat-sen%27s_speech_on_Pan-Asianism (accessed 25 June 2021).

pluralism and beyond. For the first two phases of the transition towards modernity, development was the key imperative pushing, and being pushed by, the desire for species empowerment. Yet as has become evident over recent decades, as the climate and biosphere crises deepen, unrestrained development becomes the enemy of environmental stewardship. Only if development can be put into sustainable form, either by technological fixes or by reducing humankind's aggregate demand on the planetary ecosystems, or a combination of the two (Dalby, 2020), does this contradiction get resolved. Sustainable development requires no less than pricing into the economy all those environmental services that for the last two centuries have been treated as an infinite supply, and therefore free, and outside the market logics of supply, demand and cost. For development to be sustainable, the human economy and technosphere – and the discipline of Economics – have to be made compatible with the natural systems of the planet that sustain human life and civilisation.

The struggle to redefine development in sustainable terms has only just begun. India, for example, leads other developing countries in stoutly defending their right to develop by burning fossil fuels, just as all those before them from Britain to China have done. This stance prioritises development, both absolute and relative, over environmental stewardship, making them a zero-sum game. If unrestrained development wins this game, it will be a pyrrhic victory as the environmental support systems that underpin human civilisation degrade or even collapse. If draconian environmental stewardship wins, then it might well both perpetuate economic and developmental inequality, and push humankind into species regression. A key task for the third and no doubt fourth phases of the transition to modernity will thus be to redefine development as 'sustainable development'. The race to find ways of doing this is already underway, and the question is whether the pathways to sustainability can be found and followed quickly enough to outrun threatening environmental changes such as ocean acidification and global warming (with its accompaniment of sea-level rise) that would be difficult to reverse. A key problem here is that while we know such tipping points are out there, we do not yet know precisely how and when they will happen.

There are also entanglements between development and human (in)equality. Development can be cast as a human right, and doing so changes the basis of rights and responsibilities from temporary to durable. More deeply, development plays strongly into the material conditions that shape the politics of human (in)equality. Perhaps most obvious in this regard is that development is hugely effective as a contraceptive. Higher levels of development, especially in the context of increasing urbanisation, increase both the direct and opportunity costs of having children. Urbanisation is itself a major independent factor here given that it reduces fertility rates independently of whether people also get richer or not. The significance of this is amplified by the fact that humankind as a whole passed the 50 per cent mark for urbanisation in 2007. In 1800, at the end of the CAPE era, that figure was just 3 per cent; by 1900 it was 14 per cent, and on some projections, it is headed for 80 per cent by the 2050s (Brand, 2010: 25).[8] Whereas the CAPE era, despite its many famous cities, was overwhelmingly rural, modern humankind will soon be overwhelmingly urban. Urbanisation is now a characteristic of the whole species both rich and poor, and core and periphery.

As a consequence, many of the countries that modernised early now have static or declining populations with fertility rates below, and some-times well below, the replacement rate of 2.1: for example, Italy, Germany, Russia, Japan. Those leading the second round of modernisa-tion, are either already in the same boat (South Korea) or getting there quickly (China). Even India and Africa, are heading in this direction (Bricker and Ibbitson, 2019). Bricker and Ibbitson (2019) argue that countries whose fertility rates are below 2.1 face a choice: they can accept migrants to keep up the numbers, as Canada and the US (except under Trump) have done, or reject them and accept steep shrinkage of their populations (as seems mainly to be the case with Japan, China, South Korea and Eastern Europe). As urbanisation pushes down fertility rates everywhere, the availability of migrants as 'surplus population' will shrink. But this seems likely to occur in a world in which development remains uneven, leaving both push and pull incentives to migrate from poor, ill-governed and crisis-prone places to wealthy, better-governed places that are more able to deal with crises and need to keep up their population numbers. Given the tensions already manifest over migration from the Global South in Europe and the US, and the willingness of populist politicians to exploit them ruthlessly, it is, as noted, all too easy

---

[8] There is some difference of opinion about the numbers. Bayly (2004: 185) argues that urbanisation was 9 per cent by 1600, and 12 per cent by 1800, but even these higher numbers do not alter the general point that modernity greatly increased urbanisation. The OECD (2015: 20) reckons that the global proportion of humanity living in cities will be 66 per cent by 2050 and 85 per cent by 2100; and that the number of megacities (over 10 million people) will have risen from 2 in 1950 to 41 in 2030. It can be argued that there is an elite group of highly interconnected 'global cities' that increasingly dominate the economic and cultural life of humankind (Curtis, 2016).

to imagine how migration mixed with climate crises and concerns about the control of pandemics could revive not only human inequality logics of racism and 'standard of civilisation' but also intensified territorialisation and possibly war. That prospect by itself creates a powerful logic for deepening the institution of development so as to take the steam out of this potential engine of fear, contempt and conflict.

Environmental Stewardship

Environmental stewardship is so far the last of the primary institutions distinctive to the transition to modernity to emerge. It might usefully be thought of as marking the transition from unrestrained pursuit of human empowerment to having to confront the limits of the planetary ecosystem. It could easily become the principal feature of globalisation as the economy retreats in that role. The direction of argument so far points powerfully to the environmental sector becoming the main shaper of the transition to modernity even under deep pluralism. It might also be either the main shaper of subsequent phases, or the factor that brings the transition to modernity to a halt. This rise in priority in the place of the environmental sector within global society has been remarkably swift. It is hardly surprising that humankind is still fumbling over how to respond to it. Only during the second phase of modernity did both knowledge, and awareness of the extent and implications of human impacts on the planetary systems, begin to move climate, pollution, mass extinctions, pandemics and suchlike out of the natural background of humankind's existence, and into the context of the *Anthropocene*, a geological era identified by human impacts on the natural systems and processes of the planet (Dalby, 2020). Humankind is no longer the passive victim or beneficiary of changes in Earth's systems, but a major agent in generating them. Its impacts can be both positive (e.g. countering natural cycles that would head towards another ice age, as we have been doing since the beginning of agriculture) and negative (e.g. raising the planetary temperature to produce a phase change to 'hothouse earth' that would be difficult to reverse). Humankind is now in the position of either taking on the task of planetary management, or suffering the consequences from not doing so. The race for a sustainable modernity, and staying on the path of human empowerment, will probably be won or lost during the 2020s and 2030s.

Environmental stewardship is still a weak institution. It seems a reasonable bet that this situation will change if, as the mainstream scientific consensus expects, average global temperatures continue to rise, extreme weather becomes more frequent and widespread, ocean productivity drops due to warming and acidification, and sea levels rise. Increasing environmental pressure on the social and material structures of human civilisation might push towards collective securitisation and common action. Or it might push towards everyone for themselves, and conflict over the remaining habitable and productive spaces. It might also strengthen the inspiration of some to speed up developing the capability to get people off-planet so that the species does not have all its eggs in one basket. Dalby (2020) foresees a merger of climate politics and geopolitics. So far, all of these possibilities are in play, and that could easily remain the case throughout the period of deep pluralism.

Serious acceptance of the obligation to protect the planet would mark a fundamental modification to the ground-rules of global society. It would mean either questioning, or making major changes in the practices associated with the market, development, sovereignty, territoriality, nationalism, war and great power management. Development would have to become sustainable development both for those already at the leading edge, and those trying to catch up. By creating a collective purpose across humankind, sustainable development would redefine the nature and standing of development as an institution of global society. There would be strong global pressure to move towards renewable sources of energy and away from fossil fuels to make more efficient use of material resources, and to reduce the burdens of pollution on the planetary ecosystems. Achieving this would put major pressure on those primary institutions that segment humankind and support autonomous subsystems. It would require very substantial upgrading of global society so that it could operate effectively on behalf of humankind. Both of those have profound implications for human identity. At least there is no obvious reason to be concerned about general shortages of either energy or material resources, both of which look to be available in abundance, and in this sense the material foundations of modernity look stable. But to keep them so in relation to environmental constraints will require considerable changes in practice towards sustainability. Rapid technological innovation and deployment will therefore continue to be a feature of the transition towards modernity.

It is imaginable that environmental stewardship becomes the dominant institution defining the global order, though that would almost certainly have to mean the ending of deep pluralism and the second cold war. Yet it is equally easy to imagine a failure to do this. Deep pluralism and the second cold war could deepen and lengthen, with a consequent erosion of global society and possibly a descent towards systemic conflict.

Environmental stewardship is already interacting with many other institutions of global society. It reshapes the market by adding both new costs for externalities once treated as free, and new green opportunities for sustainable energy and recyclable products. There are growing signs of a shift by leading states and firms towards 'green industrial policy' rather than just pricing mechanisms for pollution. There is a case to be made that increasing urbanisation is a highly positive development in relation to reducing the pressure humankind puts on the planetary systems, because cities are, or can be made, ecologically efficient (Brand, 2010: 25–73; Robinson, 2020). Environmental stewardship potentially adds a major new issue area onto great power management, in the process generating tensions with sovereignty/non-intervention and territoriality. It could well affect the nature and legitimacy of war if mass migration becomes a major consequence of climate change. It plays into the standing of both science (as the framing for understanding and responding to climate change) and religion (reverting to CAPE-style apocalyptic visions of the end of times). It shifts the focus of globalisation from the economy to the physical and biological systems of the planet. It could potentially either strengthen nationalism, if it becomes a struggle for survival in a deteriorating world; or weaken it, if it becomes a collective enterprise for humankind as a whole.

Environmental stewardship might change the general understanding of the interhuman domain by strengthening not only the identity of humankind as a whole, but also expanding that identity to include an explicit and significant element of intergenerational responsibility. As many have pointed out (Boulding, 1966: 10; Schell, 1982: 109–78; Brand, 2010; Dalby, 2020; Ord, 2020; Robinson, 2020), until the middle of the twentieth century, humankind did not have to worry much or at all about succeeding generations. Religion might take care of their fate in some form of millennarian cycle or rebirth. Or given the ever-unfolding progress they would inherit, future generations could be left to look after themselves as all previous generations had been. Either way, the standard practice was to discount the future. But late during the first phase of the transition towards modernity, humankind developed the capacity to destroy itself and the planet, first with nuclear weapons, and later in a variety of ways, including climate change. These options generated a palpable risk of obliterating the existence and potentiality of uncounted future generations and the civilisations they might have developed. Preventing species extinction is therefore an unavoidable moral burden for humankind from here on in. If this is not accomplished, then the future of modernity could well be short. A new norm embracing the responsibility of each generation of humans to ensure that they do not destroy the prospects of future generations would be a very powerful amplifier of both environmental stewardship and the collective identity of humankind. It might well be the key to the realisation of modernity proper.

Conclusions to Part III

There is a considerable amount of historical momentum behind the move into deep pluralism. Structural shifts such as the wider distribution of wealth, power, and cultural and political authority, the fading out of superpowers, and the rise of regionalism are hard to stop. Points of historical baggage such as introverted great powers, post-colonial resentment, and the normative crisis of liberalism and its teleology also run deep. The power-shift currently underway is much deeper that just between the US and China. It is about the ending of two centuries of Western-dominated, core–periphery, world order, and the opening of a multi-civilisational one. Although deep pluralism could in principle take a consensual form, under these circumstances it is not all that surprising that at least for now it is taking the contested one. This will happen regardless of whether the US–China rivalry turns out to be global or inter-regional. The intensifying second cold war underlines and consolidates that the unfolding phase of deep pluralism will be contested. At the very least, the prospect is one of a more decentred international order. The spread of modernity will deliver more states into the core, displacing Western and Japanese dominance, but not eliminating the West or Japan as major centres of wealth, power and influence. Liberalism will become just one of a number of forms of modernity in play, and no longer provide the dominant teleology. Deep pluralism is emerging in contested form, at a major historical turning point in the transition towards modernity. As a result, some interesting political questions arise as the West-dominated, highly unequal, first two phases of modernity give way to an enlarged and diverse core, and greater regionalisation. How will this affect identity alignments? Will Japan, for example, continue to identify with the old first-round core, or will it return to Asia after a long detour (Buzan and Goh, 2020: ch. 7)? Will Russia stay aligned with China as the West loses dominance, or drift back towards Europe, or try to go it alone as a distinct Eurasian civilisation? How will a rising India play into the alignments game of the second cold war?

The move towards contested deep pluralism is in some ways a natural reaction to the winding down of Western dominance in general, and the failures of an over-ambitious and under-governed neoliberal attempt at economic globalisation in particular. It is in part a successful move to reassert sovereignty, territoriality and economic nationalism against the ideational and practical primacy of economic globalisation. Yet there will be limits to this reaction. Even with the pressures from the second cold war, there will not be a wholesale unravelling of the global economy, but a rebalancing between the global market and economic nationalism. The need and desire to trade is an age-old feature of the human condition. Despite the current swing of the pendulum towards economic nationalism, the market has not gone away. Even China, perhaps the most autarkically inclined of the great powers, recognises that orderly global trading is necessary, and that this requires cooperation on rules for trade, investment and finance. A modernity drifting into deep pluralism will not want, or be able to abandon global trade. This old dialectic will therefore remain in play.

It will not, however, any longer be the central issue defining globalisation. As the many financial crises of the transition towards modernity have demonstrated, global economic interdependence is a kind of shared fate. But the emphasis of shared fate is now shifting quickly from the economic to the environmental sector. The Covid-19 pandemic illustrated the mounting threat from environmental issues interplaying with the *Anthropocene*. The problem of climate change is already asserting itself in myriad increasingly obvious ways from melting ice to extreme and abnormal weather patterns. There is a powerful meta-dialectic emerging in parallel with deep pluralism between environmental integration/interdependence, on the one hand, and fragmentation (sovereignty, identity, territoriality), on the other hand. Environmental issues, probably led by climate change, look set to be the main challenger and counterforce to contested deep pluralism. Such shared fate issues require global management, just as economic globalisation did. But deep pluralism is a recipe for collective under-management of shared fates. Something will have to give.

Ominously, Bayly (2004: 464–7) notes the outcome of an earlier dialectic in the late nineteenth century between liberal and socialist cosmopolitanism/globalism, and fragmenting ideologies, as 'the decisive victory of ethnicity, religion, and nationalism over the left'. The current dialectic is inherently unpredictable inasmuch as it cannot be known precisely which shared-fate issue(s) will generate global crises, when this will happen, and in what form. Neither can it be known how the availability, or not, of new technologies, especially digital and biological ones, will play into these developments, and whether their impact will be positive or negative. The general nature of the problems and threats posed by pandemics, coastal flooding, extreme weather, mass migrations, capitalist crises, etc. are reasonably knowable, but the details, timings and placings are not. Will such issues deepen divisions and become weaponised as part of the armouries of rivalry in the second cold war? Or will they inspire, or necessitate, global cooperation and a change of mind-set about the priorities of global society, moving deep pluralism towards a more consensual form?

The first two phases of the transition towards modernity were hugely successful in intensifying globalisation by improving both physical and social interaction capacity. But unconstrained human empowerment has crashed into the limits of the planetary environment, and overreaching economic globalisation has once more crashed into the fragmenting logics of sovereignty, territoriality and nationalism, again failing to overcome them. Unlike the first two phases, deep pluralism will not take place under conditions dominated by market globalisation and unconstrained human empowerment. Its framing conditions will be dominated by economic nationalism and environmental limits. Economic and environmental globalisation are of course related, with the former being one of the dynamics giving rise to the latter. Either kind of globalisation challenges the fragmenting logics of global society. The big question is therefore whether environmental globalisation will hit the same buffers as the economic kind, failing to break through to a more integrated form of global society? Economic globalisation was to a considerable extent a choice. Some, of course, had it rammed down their throats by colonial- and Western-global society during the first phase of the transition towards modernity. But others, most notably China under Deng, chose it on the grounds that its developmental benefits outweighed its costs even for a government determined to retain a Leninist state. Environmental globalisation, by contrast, will not be a choice in the sense that one can opt in or opt out. Whether in terms of a shift to more intense forms of planetary management, or as a shared experience of environmental deterioration, all will confront environmental globalisation whether they want to or not. The rising constraints and conditionings of the environmental crisis will increasingly shape how the transition to modernity will move forward. This will be true regardless of whether in the form of trying to move towards more sustainable forms of development and economy, and finding the necessary forms of global cooperation; or in the form of coping with deteriorating conditions, and the conflicts they generate.

Within this broad picture, what comes into view for the third phase of the transition towards modernity if one shifts to looking ahead in terms of the three domains? Is global society becoming more integrated across the three domains or more fragmented? The potency of the trilogy of primary institutions underpinning the modern state – sovereignty, territoriality and nationalism – remains formidable going forward. Each of these institutions remains strong in itself, and even stronger in combination with the others. That is the formula that populist and authoritarian politicians of all stripes have used so effectively against economic globalisation and human rights. In the economic sector, they were able to do so because the economics of market globalisation fell victim to its own internal contradictions, delivering high benefits only to some, and high costs to too many others. The dialectic between sovereigntism and territoriality, on the one hand, and planetary-scale environmental threats, on the other hand, will not, in the medium and long term, provide such an easy target as market globalisation. Economic globalisation largely defeated itself by proving excessively crisis prone, and despite its impressive accomplishments, being unable to deliver on its promises to a wide-enough spectrum of humankind. Environmental globalisation will not be like that. It will simply, and relentlessly, deliver more cost and pain until humankind reduces its pressure on the planetary ecosystems sufficiently to restabilise them. If it does not, then the earth will provide an environment that is increasingly less supportive of human civilisation, and humankind itself. That is the big dialectic for the phase of the transition that we are now in.

The idea that social structure increasingly works across all three domains, and has up to a point always done so, gives a whole new way of understanding Wight's (1977: 33) much-cited (Buzan, 2010a) idea that: '[w]e must assume that a states-system will not come into being without a degree of cultural unity among its members'. The idea of 'a degree of cultural unity' then becomes not only a matter of prior condition, but also of co-constitution. This development towards global society is built on a major contradiction between fragmenting and unifying dynamics. On the one hand, the particularities of modernity are often fragmenting along lines of nation, class, race, wealth, gender, culture and ideology. As Williams (2005, 2015) points out, 'world' society is just as pluralistic and anarchic, as interstate society, possibly more so. Indeed, that character of world society was one of the justifications for the political and academic emphasis on states and an interstate world order. On the other hand, many of these fragmentations, most notably state, nation and religion, are incorporated into the institutions of global society, so becoming a legitimate part of a collective social structure. It is a societal paradox that fragmentation, when its rights and reasons are understood and accepted, becomes constitutive of a social whole. In addition, the transition towards modernity has promoted, and up to a point empowered, the direct identity of humankind as a whole in its own right. The crucial variable likely to shape the interplay among the three domains is the environmental pressure on development, within both the core and the periphery.

The Interstate Domain

The onset of deep pluralism suggests that the interstate domain will stay strong, even resurgent. In terms of social structure, there looks to be a major island of stability comprising the mutually reinforcing cluster of primary institutions around the modern state: sovereignty, territoriality, nationalism, diplomacy and international law. This cluster is strong not only because the institutions are mutually supporting, but also because the principal ones – sovereignty, territoriality, nationalism – have deep roots across the three domains. It is currently being reinforced by the swinging of the pendulum between the market and economic national-ism back to the latter. These institutions legitimise how global society is internally differentiated and fragmented. The bedrock of the anarchical society is that all of these institutions look robust in themselves, and their mutual support makes them stronger. Development might also count as part of this package because it is often embodied in the form of develop-mental states in both core and periphery. On current trends, the modern state and the anarchical interstate society will therefore remain durable going forward into deep pluralism, and possibly beyond. China, India and other post-colonial states now rising in wealth and power are strongly committed to it.

There are some challengers to the anarchical society, but nothing in prospect that is about to sweep it away. Transnational politico-military movements such as those in the Islamic world are an existential threat in principle because they deny the legitimacy of secular sovereignty and territoriality. In practice, however, such movements, like the cosmopol-itan leftists before them, might well be happy to enter interstate society by capturing a state. The idea that big corporations would sideline the state has retreated along with the crash of economic globalisation, although there are rising concerns about both state capture by big money, and the implications for the state and its citizens of corporate control over big data. On the ideological side, the spell of the liberal teleology of modern-ity has been broken, and it is clear that capitalism and the market can flourish under authoritarian as well as democratic governments.

Gellner (1988: 332–47) was prescient on this, noting the possibility that liberalism, having been necessary for the birth of modernity, might not be able to take it forward, and that fascism was not driven out of the picture by its defeat in 1945. Democracies have not yet solved the problems either of economic inequality giving the super-rich strong political influence or of big-data and sophisticated algorithms providing enhanced mechanisms of social control, but this is more a threat to liberal democracy than to the modern state as such. This island of stability in the interstate domain gains support from the strength of nationalism in the interhuman domain.

Despite this sturdy framework of support around the anarchical society of states, there are a lot of questions and uncertainties around the institution and practice of war, and how it will playout in the unfolding third phase of the transition towards modernity. As discussed above, during recent decades, war and the military sector have undergone substantial changes. There are some continuities, most notably the ongoing RMA and its destabilising effects on relations amongst the powers, and the constraints imposed on military action by nuclear deterrence and the prospect of 'forever' wars. But the very definition of what constitutes war is being transformed by cyberwar, migration and terrorism, and this is undermining the system of legal restraints on war that built up after 1945. There is also the question of how the anarchical society will deal with climate change, whether by strengthening global society to mount a collective response, or by allowing the stresses of climate change to push states further into contested deep pluralism. That poses a classical problem of collective action and free-riding (Olson, 1965). But it is also where the scope for agency lies in deep pluralism. It is important to remember that even contested deep pluralism does not exclude a degree of GPM on specific functional issues such as shared-fate threats. Down that path one can make a firm prediction that there will be a long struggle to reform the global architecture of IGOs to make a better fit with the new realities of deep pluralism's redistribution of wealth, power, cultural and political authority, and sense of shared threat.

The Transnational Domain

During the last half of the twentieth century, many, especially on the liberal side of IR, thought that the transnational domain was gaining ground on the interstate one. This thought was captured in concepts like 'globalisation', 'world society', and 'global governance', which painted a picture of states increasingly entangled in, and dependent on, flows and networks created by TNCs and INGOs, and mediated by IGOs.

The economic crisis opening in 2008, the rise of a powerful and increasingly authoritarian China, and the impact of the Covid-19 pandemic from 2020 have shredded this expectation. The state, nationalism and anti-globalisation are all resurgent, and the once dominant liberal teleology for the future is under severe attack even in its Western heartlands.

How, then, will the transnational domain fare, when the interstate one is resurgent? The likely prospect seems to be that while the transnational domain will remain robust, the types and mix of non-state actors within it will be considerably influenced by the relative decline of the West, the strength of anti-globalisation, and the dethroning of the liberal teleology. This change can be highlighted in relation to three types of actors: transnational firms (TNCs), the INGOs representing global civil society, and a variety of non-state actors constituting global uncivil society.

The prospects for TNCs are currently in flux. On the one hand, during the heyday of neoliberal globalisation, some firms became extraordinarily large and powerful. When the market capitalisation of Apple, for example, recently exceeded $2 trillion, that put it above the current GDP of Italy.[1] Concentrations of capital on that scale raise several troubling questions for both democratic and authoritarian governments, especially under the light regulation of capital that prevailed during the neoliberal period. Part of the crisis of capitalism is that it needs to rediscover the idea that the economy has to serve the people in a significant way if capitalism is to enjoy political stability (Sassoon, 2019). Democratic governments are under pressure to curb the ways in which big TNCs can exploit the tax rules to minimise their payments, while paying little in the countries where they do most of their business. They are worried by the prospect of state capture inherent in having such powerful and wealthy players on the loose in their political systems. And they have to deal with the political consequences of deindustrialisation and job losses, whether real or perceived, arising from big TNC's pursuit of economic efficiency without regard for social consequences. All of these problems feed a powerful societal reaction against the neoliberal project of economic globalisation, as expressed most strikingly in 2016 by the election of Trump as US president. China's authoritarian party/state has recently begun cracking down on its big companies in ways that reduce their independence, make them contribute more to society, and curb the possible challenge that their leaders pose to the authority of the CCP (*The Economist*, 14 August 2021: 51–3). Both democracies and authoritarian states are worried by the stark inequalities

---

[1] https://databank.worldbank.org/data/download/GDP.pdf (accessed 1 September 2021).

of income marked by high Gini coefficients: 41.4 for the US and 38.5 for China.[2] These have become extreme enough to threaten the political acceptability of capitalism, especially if economic growth is slow. It seems unlikely that big TNCs will be driven to extinction, but entirely possible that their position will become more constrained in both democracies and authoritarian states under a more stringent regime of economic nationalism.

The prospects for the transnational INGOs representing global civil society look mixed. The waning of both Western power and the liberal teleology is likely to lead to more constrained operation for those many INGOs that are based in the West but pursue liberal causes globally. They may well have fewer resources, less political backing, and a cooler reception abroad, though there may be exceptions for politically neutral, functional actors that focus on emergency aid. The global networks of scientific non-state actors will no doubt survive, but if national security concerns are driven up by the second cold war, as seems likely, their operations could easily become more constrained in areas with military, biotech or cyberwar implications. Authoritarian states are unlikely to project genuine INGOs of their own, so this component of the trans-national domain may well weaken considerably in the coming decades. It is possible that a cooperative approach to climate change might strengthen transnational environmental actors, but that could just as easily not be the case.

The strengthening political role of religion in many places could increase the number and scale of religious INGOs in this domain. If so, this could easily create a blurring into the interhuman domain in terms of religious networks, franchises and patterns of identity. Religion works in the interhuman domain as an identity that does not necessarily require non-state actors to give it agency. It is not easy to place, for example, lone-wolf individuals inspired and motivated by IS or Al Qaeda, in one domain or the other. That thought opens the way to the prospects for the transnational non-state actors representing global uncivil (i.e. violent) society: mafias and militant groups, sometimes with links to states. This ties in to the discussion of the diversification and de-institutionalisation of war above. Such uncivil actors can be linked to both religions, and/or the aspiration to be a state. Criminal ones may, or may not, be in various ways attached to, or in league with, particular states, such as hackers involved in cyberwar. Such actors get room to operate either by the tacit permission of a host state, or by taking

---

[2] https://data.worldbank.org/indicator/si.pov.gini?most_recent_value_desc=false (accessed 5 September 2021).

advantage of the many weak/failed states that do not have the capacity to police their own territories sufficiently to control them. On current trends, these types of actors look likely to play an increasing role in the transnational domain.

The transnational domain is thus unlikely to follow the track expected for it during the heyday of neoliberal globalisation. But its prospect is not so much to weaken overall, as to change character towards a more illiberal profile. Its economic element will almost certainly be weakened by economic nationalism, though it will by no means disappear. Its liberal INGO component seems also likely to weaken. But its religious and uncivil components look to be in a better position to increase their standing and activity in this domain, drawing strength from identities in the interhuman one. Environmental INGOs might or might not strengthen their position within the transnational domain, depending on whether the interstate response to climate change is cooperative or conflictual.

The Interhuman Domain

Patterns of identity tend to be deeply rooted and slow to change. The argument given within this framework suggests no grounds either for expecting wholly new forms of identity to emerge any time soon (though that of course does not rule them out), or for the established ones to disappear. What can be seen more clearly is the possibility that existing forms of identity might change in their relative strength, salience and influence. Long-standing patterns of identity such as gender, religion and civilisation remain robust, and so too do more recently established ones such as nationalism, political ideology, race, humankind as a whole, and sport. Class identities have perhaps weakened somewhat as Marxism has lost much of its political force. Gender differentiation shows signs of becoming more diverse as the gap between the male/female binary becomes increasingly differentiated and politicised, though this development is far from universally accepted. Something similar might be said about race, as people of mixed-race heritage become more common. These identities often help to underpin the entities in the interstate and transnational domains.

The transition towards modernity has provided a more complex and diverse menu of identities, and therefore opens the question of how they relate to each other. Most individuals now have layered identities, and the question this raises is: When conditions demand choices and priorities, is there a hierarchy amongst them? I, for example, am white, male, Western, Anglosphere, British (and Canadian), atheist, heterosexual (straight) and have little by way of strong sporting or class affiliations. In general, I have cosmopolitan leanings, and pragmatic, middle-of-the-road political views. I have been lucky enough never to have been confronted with crisis circumstances that forced me to prioritise amongst these layers. But during the First World War, for example, nationalism famously trumped class as the dominant identity for most people when extreme circumstances did force them to choose. Since decolonisation, the turbulent politics of the Middle East have often confronted people with choices between nationalism (e.g. Arab nationalism) and religion, or else pressured elites to find ways of making these two line up. The Bharatiya Janata Party (BJP) in India is posing choices between religion (*Hindutva*) and an all-embracing Indian nationalism. Do people with a strong gender or race identity rank that higher than, say, their religious or national ones? A current test of identity politics arises for people in those countries favoured as destinations by migrants, especially those who are refugees. The receiving population faces increasingly difficult choices between a broad humanitarian outlook, and fears of having their culture, ethnicity, religion and/or class structure significantly altered. Such choices can generate populist and fascist politics that thrive on anti-immigration platforms, and lead to border walls and other policies that put the lives of migrants at risk. The migrants themselves face difficult choices about what balance to strike between maintaining their existing identities and assimilating to their host societies. Such situations are complex and diverse, and there is no obvious global pattern to them.

Above the question of how people rank the various differentiating identities they hold, is the issue of whether the cosmopolitan identity of humankind, or the various fragmenting identities (religion, nationalism, race, gender, etc.) will be the more strengthened or weakened by the collective encounter of humankind with shared fates such as climate change and pandemics? The recent experience with the Covid-19 pandemic points in both directions, with some global scientific cooperation and some agreement to distribute vaccines globally, on the one hand, and quite a bit of vaccine nationalism, border closures and national scientific rivalry, on the other hand. At the time of writing, rich countries and rich people have far more access to vaccines than poor ones. The Covid crisis thus suggests that even in the face of a palpably global shared threat, national identity still ranks higher than human solidarity. It does so despite the evidence that such a policy creates a breeding ground for new variants that will threaten everyone. The next big test of this kind, is whether the rising crisis of climate change will favour the fragmenting identities or strengthen the identity of humankind?

How this question of identities plays out will be strongly influenced by how the process of securitisation of shared-fate threats is constructed. At the moment, the second cold war and contested deep pluralism are ramping up traditional forms of mutually exclusive *national security* (security against). Shared fate threats such as pandemics and climate change, could support a turn towards the principle of *common security* (security with) (Buzan and Hansen, 2009: 136–8). Shared-fate threats open up the long-standing contradiction between national security and common security more powerfully than before. This contradiction is not new, but it looks set to become particularly intense in the coming decades. Although the imperatives of 'security against' are still in robust play in world politics, the imperatives of 'security with' might gain ground as shared threats from pandemics and global warming to terrorism, mass migration and proliferation of weapons of mass destruction, increasingly impinge on global society.

During the first two phases of the transition towards modernity, the dynamics of fragmentation in all their diversity were unquestionably dominant across the board. While there was some consolidation of smaller entities into larger ones (e.g. Germany, Italy, US), and a significant development of global secondary institutions, the general dynamic was for the break-up of empires and the intensification of logics of fragmentation. Barring the brief foray of homogenising liberal universalism from the 1980s to 2008, the dividing dynamics of nation state, class, religious and secular ideology, race, gender and culture were what mainly drove global society. Going forward into deep pluralism, it would be easy to think that it was going to be more of the same in this respect. On the other hand, a form of globalisation based on shared fates/threats, particularly around the immediate pressures from climate change and pandemics, is also growing stronger. This is a new factor in modern global society, and however it plays out, whether in the form of collective response or the degrading of the conditions for sustaining human civilisation, its impact will be large and pervasive.

To control these shared global threats effectively will require collective action of a depth and scale that humankind has never attempted before. Such action is hardly imaginable without some quite fundamental changes in the social mind-set of the species. Ord (2020: loc. 3107) captures the magnitude of the required mental shift with his idea that:

I find it useful to consider our predicament from humanity's point of view: casting humanity as a coherent agent, and considering the strategic choices it would make were it sufficiently rational and wise. Or in other words, what all humans would do if we were sufficiently coordinated and had humanity's longterm interests at heart.

Humankind has never before consciously been all in the same boat with a growing awareness that their boat is leaking badly and in danger of foundering if all do not help with the bailing, and the leak is not fixed. This shared predicament might strengthen the identity of humankind as a whole simply on the basis of a short-term logic of collective survival. One key signpost for that would be a securitisation of environmental stewardship implemented by the UN Security Council across the three domains of global society, but so far this has not happened (Falkner and Buzan, 2022). A deeper institutionalisation would occur if this sense of collective survival got attached to an ethic of intergenerational responsibility that expanded the sense of humankind from those now existing, to all of those generations yet to come whose existence will be snuffed out if we get things badly wrong here and now (Schell, 1982; Ord, 2020: ch. 2; Caney, 2022). As Walker (1990: 13) pointed out long ago: '[T]he demand for world security is, in effect, a demand for a radically new understanding of political identity.' Such a development would amount to major changes in the social glue that holds global society together.

There is nothing inevitable about such a development. Environmental globalisation might as easily reinforce deep pluralism as counterbalance it, leading to squabbling and fighting as different groups seek survival advantages for themselves on a deteriorating planet. Survival might be fought on behalf of the parts rather than the whole of humankind. This choice looks like being the great social dialectic that will shape the unfolding of the current and future phases of the transition towards modernity, and the fate of our species itself. The mainly fractious global response to Covid-19 suggests that the learning curve ahead is still very steep. Having globalised the economy and the environment, the next task is to find a way of globalising humankind sufficiently to enable it to operate and survive at a high density on a planetary scale. That almost certainly cannot be done in opposition to the deeply embedded fragmentation of the species that is now being reinforced by contested deep pluralism. Any attempt to make a zero-sum game between a stronger sense of humankind and its obligations to future generations, on the one hand, and its historical legacy of multiple identities, on the other hand, looks doomed to fail. Either a way is found for both go forward in some kind of harmony, or neither will go forward.

Part IV

Conclusions

9   Conclusions

Introduction

This book started out by proposing to fill in the space between the detailed, event-driven, narratives of Global/World History, and the alluring, but oversimplified, grand abstractions of social science. It wanted to build bridges, and possibly a common project, connecting IR, Global Historical Sociology (GHS) and Global/World History. To do this, it set out an analytical framework drawn mainly, but not wholly, from the English School (ES). This framework aimed to deepen and expand the linkage between International Relations (IR) theory and history that has for long been a hallmark of the ES. It promised to provide a novel, middle-path form of history that combined the dry abstractions of social science with the rich descriptions and narratives of historians, while avoiding the limitations and extremes of both. Its trick was to deploy a middling level of abstraction in the form of primary institutions, which could sustain the narrative complexity that is the strength of historians, while avoiding the overabstractions of many social science approaches, and to do so over a very *longue durée*. The idea was to tell the story of humankind in terms of both general material conditions and social structures, and do this in a style that could convey a living sense of the continuities and changes that define the main eras of the human story.

So, after all of these pages, what has it delivered? In my view three things. First, it demonstrates that there is a global society constructed around a widely accepted, durable, but evolving, set of primary institutions. For most of its history, whether as smaller integrated world societies, or at planetary scale, this society has paradoxically embodied a dialectic between a variety of principles of legitimate fragmentation, on the one hand, and aspirations to universalism, on the other hand. Universal principles have ranged from religion and empire during the CAPE era, to human equality, the market, environmental stewardship, science, and sport under modernity. Second, the book gives a successful test-run of a novel form of history-telling that unfolds a familiar story in an unfamiliar way, opening up perspectives on that history that are not otherwise obvious. In that it puts the social organisation of humankind at the centre of the analysis, it is a fully global approach to both history and international relations. It is explicitly structured to minimise inappropriate Eurocentrism, or indeed any other form of civilisational centrism, other than one focused on humankind as a whole. And it is consciously aimed at facilitating the construction of a more Global IR discipline. Within that, it makes specific, and I think substantial, contributions both to periodisation and the definition of eras. It sharpens understanding of both the transition from the CAPE era to modernity, and the main phases of the transition towards modernity. The book's third contribution is to the fields and theories it addresses, and how they both see themselves and relate to each other. The book invites the ES to be more ambitious about what it conceives itself to be doing, and it invites IR, GHS and World/Global History to think differently both about how they might jointly fill in the space that separates them, and about how they understand modernity. Whether or not this aim will be realised, depends, of course, on who reads the book, how they receive it, and whether or not it inspires anyone to further that interdisciplinary project.

The next section elaborates these contributions in terms first of telling history, and second in terms of the implications for the fields and theories that are the targets of the argument.

History

The history told in this book is neither that of any particular civilisation, nor indeed of a comparative set of civilisations. It is the history of humankind, told through its material conditions and social structures, both of which are in general widely shared across the species throughout its history. The social structure story of humankind has been told in terms of an evolving set of primary institutions that are embedded in, and work across, a framework of three domains. Bringing in the three domains ensures that what is taken into account is not just what has gone on in the interpolity domain, which is often privileged over the other two, but also in the transnational and interhuman domains. None of these domains has been given any automatic privilege over the others, and the crossovers and interplays amongst them have been explored in depth. Unlike in most traditional ES approaches, the assessment here is that an integrated world society stretching across these three domains has been the normal social structure of humankind since at least the beginning of the CAPE era. The interpolity domain has never made sense by itself. Even from early in the CAPE era, the political side of humankind's social structure could not be understood without taking both merchants and trade (transnational), and religions (mostly interhuman), fully into account. The dynamics and dialectics of power, wealth and identity have always been closely interlocked ever since human societies became large enough, and complex enough to generate those differentiations in a meaningful way.

Approaching primary institutions through the three domains in this more balanced way has some signal advantages. Not least, it necessarily reintegrates a political economy perspective, repairing the damage that too much distancing from economics has done not just to the ES, but to IR more broadly (much less so to GHS and Global/World History). It also opens the way to a clearer view of how the dynamics of identity play across all three domains. The main historical story, therefore, has been about the intensification of integrated world societies, at first within a number of only lightly connected civilisational cores, and then with a fairly steady, but rather slow, expansion towards an integrated human society on a global scale. From the nineteenth century onward, intensification within that global society became the main story.

This book makes two more specific contributions to a historical perspective: first, generally, in terms of defining eras and periodisations; and second, more specifically, in applying that thinking to understanding the evolution of modernity since its take-off in the nineteenth century. In terms of the practice of periodisation generally, the approach through primary institutions offers a new and attractive set of criteria for identifying the benchmarks required for periodisation. When viewed in relation to material conditions, primary institutions work above the level of particular wars, empires, technologies and comparative civilisations that dominate most historical periodisations, and below the level of grand, abstract causes that mainly inspire social science. Primary institutions constitute an in-between approach that offers multiple causalities in complex formations to underpin claims to both durable continuities and deep and dramatic changes. Unsurprisingly, this approach does not entirely sweep away existing understandings that the really big patterns of continuity and change in the history of humankind fall broadly into three eras: nomadic hunter-gatherers, settled/agrarian civilisations and modernity. But it does sharpen up the definition of these eras, inserts the radical idea that there are distinct transition periods between them, and raises novel questions about modernity.

In material terms, each era added to the physical portfolio of humankind in terms of sources of energy, available materials, interaction capacity and types of technology. The hunter-gatherers added fire, wood, clay and stone. They had basic technologies related to these, but added little in the way of interaction capacity except for primitive water-craft. The CAPE era added animal muscle power, wind, a limited range of soft and hard metals, glass and elaborate machinery. They added very substantially to interaction capacity with wheeled vehicles, animal traction, wind- and oar-powered ships, and transportation infrastructure (ports, lighthouses, *caravanserais*). The modern era added essentially limitless sources of energy and materials, and a huge range of technologies that is still expanding fast. During the transition towards modernity, interaction capacity effectively shrank the planet in many respects to being a single space, while also generating a crisis of sustainability in relation to the carrying capacity of the planet.

In terms of social structure, there was a general trend towards larger scale, higher intensity of interaction, and greater differentiation and complexity, with each era having its own signature innovations. The hunter-gatherer era invented bands, kinship networks, trade and spiritualism. The CAPE era invented city-states and empires; 'universal' civilisations, gods and religions; professional merchants and market-places; and many forms of human inequality. The modern era is still shaping up, but it looks as if its contributions are states, nations, secular ideologies of progress, science, global sport, the modern limited liability company, and at least a significant degree of human equality in some respects.

As I have shown, these innovations were cumulative, both materially and socially. New eras do not necessarily, or even usually, replace the innovations of earlier ones, though some institutions do become obsolete. New eras mainly adapt them and add to them. This is the process by which global society has been built. Up until very recently all of these developments took place in an unconstrained and open way. They might encounter intrinsic limits: wooden ships can only be built up to a certain size before they exceed the structural strength of wood; CAPE empires and trading systems ran into the limits of interaction capacity and administration during that era. Or they might meet local environmental constraints such as soil exhaustion or drought. But basically, both material and social developments were able to unfold to their intrinsic limits in pursuit of human empowerment, and to do so without obviously threatening the carrying capacity of the planet. Since the CAPE era, labour, both human and animal, has always been ruthlessly exploited for this process, and while that often remains the case at the time of writing, a vista is opening up in which that might be diminishing as automation takes an increasing role in most aspects of human life. Even the reproductive labour of women is dwindling as fertility rates drop well below replacement level, with consequences that remain to be seen.

The analytical framework used in this book offers four substantial ways of sharpening up this general analysis. First, it highlights the place of transition periods between these eras, and offers quite fine-grained criteria for observing and assessing the process of transition. This is particularly valuable for modernity, where the framework is able to show in some detail the process of transition from CAPE to modern that took two centuries to work its way through, especially in terms of social structures. This transition process is not given the recognition it requires, and the ongoing contestation over the most appropriate start date for modernity (1500, 1648, late eighteenth/early nineteenth century) is still heavily entangled with Eurocentrism. The global society approach is able to nail down in good detail the material conditions and social structures that do and don't differentiate modernity from the CAPE era.

Second, the approach reveals the very impressive continuity and homogeneity of the CAPE era, emphasising the durable similarity of the material conditions and social structures that defined it. Notwithstanding Eurocentric claims for earlier onsets of modernity, those conditions remained robustly in place right up to the late eighteenth century. In the few centuries before that, Europe was in many political, economic and social respects, a backwater that was becoming more like the rest of the CAPE world. At the same time, it was also nurturing the take-off of modernity. The change towards a globally impacting modernity, as many have argued, only took off in the nineteenth century.

Third, by bringing in the idea that eras are separated by transition periods, this approach offers a coherent, yet unorthodox, way of approaching modernity. Modernity is a question around which there is much muddle and controversy, and a lot of Eurocentrism. It is not easy to get a clear perspective on it because the history is very recent. Not only do we lack the advantage of hindsight, but we are handicapped by living in the history we are trying to analyse. This book argues that there is much to be gained by questioning the assumption that modernity as a third era arrived sometime after the late eighteenth century, and has been unfolding ever since. It opens space for a period of transition separating the CAPE era from modernity, and assesses the material and social history in that light. Approaching the analysis in that way leaves open the question of when the modern era – modernity proper – might arrive, and how we would know.

I have argued that so far there are three clear phases in the transition towards modernity. The first phase was clearly transitional: definitely post-CAPE, but not yet fully modern. That phase ran from the late eighteenth century up to the 1970s. During it, the material profile of modernity developed quickly, but only in a narrow distribution. The social profile was a blend of old and new institutions, and the ongoing struggles amongst them. This phase of transition towards modernity was narrowly based in the sense that while it was certainly global, it was extremely unequal, hierarchical and structured in a core–periphery form of developed/underdeveloped. The handful of first-round modernisers took advantage of the opportunity to maximise their own interests in the pursuit of unrestrained human empowerment and the intensification of globalisation.

The second phase stretched from the 1970s to roughly 2020, and was also pretty clearly transitional. During this phase, the distribution of development became notably less uneven across humankind. The first-round modernisers began to lose their dominance as a second round of modernisers achieved access to wealth, power, and political and cultural authority. As a consequence, global society began to fragment into civilisational bunkers. At the same time, environmental constraints began moving to central place in defining the operating conditions for modernity. It raised the question of how a global society, highly committed at all levels to pursuit of unrestrained development, could operate sustainably within the limits of planetary carrying capacity, which were beginning to be reached and exceeded. This new factor opened an existential threat to the ruthless and unrestrained pursuit of material wealth and power, and the social structures built on it, that had dominated the first two phases.

The third phase, just beginning at the time of writing, I have called deep pluralism. From 2020 onwards, global society was clearly operating in a post-Western world order in the sense that the West and Japan, while still rich and powerful, were no longer dominant either materially or ideationally in global society. Deep pluralism quickly tipped into the second cold war that is remaking global alignments, and seems likely to endure for at least the rest of the 2020s, possibly longer. But the looming environmental crisis, and the broad contradiction between unrestrained human empowerment, and the limits of planetary carrying capacity, are intensifying alongside it. How the dialectic between political and civilisational fragmentation and contestation, and a rising shared fate from the environment, works out, is the big question for this third phase.

Because of this dialectic, the third phase of deep pluralism might still be thought of as part of the transition period from CAPE to modernity. The case for seeing it as still part of the transition, rests on two key points. First, the widening of modernisation is still far from even, and has a long way to go. It remains politically unstable in many places. Second is that modernity has not reached a point where it has a sustainable relationship with planetary carrying capacity. Until it does, it is not environmentally stable, and in a fundamental sense therefore not durable enough to form the basis for a new era. It could all too easily fall off the path of human empowerment, and crash into species suicide or regression. In this view, modernity proper will not arrive until humankind survives the present crisis of climate change, and finds a way of bringing the ongoing pursuit of human empowerment into line with planetary carrying capacity. Modernity will only become 'proper', if and when the development it embodies become sustainable. If these arguments prevail, then we are still in the transition from CAPE to modernity. We have no guarantee that we will get to modernity proper before the whole project of human empowerment comes off the rails. In this view, modernity proper still lies a few decades ahead, and only if humankind has considerable luck, and makes a lot of hard choices correctly, along the way. Modernity proper would be defined by sustainable development; a more even distribution of wealth and power; planetary management; a stronger sense of humankind, including future generations; and probably an expansion of the planetary sphere into space. All of those are imaginable, if far from certain, as features of the later twenty-first century. If they happened, the transition from the CAPE era to modernity would have lasted between two-and-a-half and three centuries.

But phase three deep pluralism could also be interpreted as the opening of modernity proper. The case for seeing it in this way rests on three arguments. First, the material condition of modernity is now a well-established pattern. Second, many of the contradictions between and among the social structure of the CAPE era, and the new institutions characteristic of modernity, have either been resolved (monarchy/dynasticism versus popular sovereignty, imperialism), or have reached a kind of stability or balance (e.g. human (in)equality, religion versus science, market versus economic nationalism). Third, modernity has now spread significantly beyond its original core, breaking down the unbalanced core–periphery system that defined the transition out of the CAPE era. On this basis it could be argued that modernity is now properly global. If these arguments prevail, then we have clear boundaries defining the transition period between the CAPE and modern eras: from 1776 to 2020. Everything from here on in will be modernity proper.

The fourth contribution of the analytical framework is to highlight the importance of environmental conditions to the human project. The CAPE era, and the transition to it, were very powerfully shaped by a warming and stabilising climate. The transition to modernity benefited from this, but has now resulted in a rising constraint on human empowerment that is a really big and profound change in the human condition. Climate change in particular changes the foundations on which human civilisation and development have rested since the beginning of the CAPE era. This point is of course made by much of the literature around the *Anthropocene* era. The contribution here is to show specifically how this change impacts on the material conditions and social structures of modernity. Rapacious exploitation of the natural world has been a central theme of human history since the dawn of civilisation. During the CAPE era, this rapaciousness was constrained by the quite tight limits on technology and energy sources, and the consequent relatively modest size of the human population, that defined the era. The transition towards modernity took the lid off those constraints. It opened a period of unprecedented increase not just in human numbers, but in human ability to extract energy and materials from the planet, to consume on an unprecedented scale, and to inject vast quantities of waste products into its ecosphere. That extraordinary unleashing has very quickly led to the environmental crisis that is already putting visible pressure on primary institutions such as development, human equality, sovereignty, territoriality, great power management, war and the market. The modernity project will either end, possibly quite soon, in a major derailment off the pathway of human empowerment; or continue with a diminished humankind that has undergone substantial changes to its institutional and material structures.

Fields and Theories

A key aim of this book is to develop a way of filling in the space that separates IR, GHS and Global/World History, and to inspire those interested within those fields to build bridges to each other's communities. That space might be defined as the history of how humankind has organised itself as a species. The academic space defined in that way is not entirely unoccupied. All three fields have a presence there already. IR is mainly a forward-looking field, and has also allowed itself (unwisely in my view), to be pulled towards a narrow sectoral view of humankind by seeing its subject matter principally as world politics. Its biggest contribution to explaining the story of humankind has been the extremely narrow (neo)realist theory that power politics is the main key to understanding humankind in all times and all places, and that what matters is the biggest concentrations of power. Only a small minority of people within IR have taken much interest in actually applying that idea to premodern times (e.g. Wohlforth et al., 2007). GHS has been much more interested in looking back, and has kept a wider, multi-sectoral, perspective. But it has tended to favour big, sometimes oversimplifying theories, often Marxian, to do so. Global/World Historians have been very thorough in looking back, and have also developed a multi-sectoral perspective. But its practitioners have found it methodologically more convenient to concentrate on particular times and/or places, and so end up focusing more on the trees than on the forest as a whole. Mann (1986) with his multi-sectoral 'IEMP' approach, and long view, has perhaps come closest to finding a way of filling this space, but by his own assessment it was too messy.

The approach offered here comes from IR, but is drawn principally from the ES, a minority taste within that field, and one that lies at the edges of its mainstream. The ES has several advantages as the framing for addressing the history of how humankind has organised itself as a species. Its societal approach has always been a bit marginal within an IR focused mainly in the military and political sectors, but it is very well-suited to the subject matter of humankind, and is potentially compatible with the sociological side of GHS approaches. The ES has always been more open to taking history seriously than most of the rest of IR, though this book extends that connection more deeply and widely than has been done before. The ES has also remained open to International Law. Its multi-disciplinarity has been slow to tie in with IPE, but that has been mainly because of a lack of relevant expertise rather than any principled incompatibility. The preceding chapters show how that link can be made. Thus, although the ES has until now occupied a modest niche within IR, it is better-constituted and better-positioned than any other theoretical approach within IR to play an interdisciplinary role beyond IR. There have already been some substantial ES moves into this interdisciplinary space, most notably Wight's (1977) and Watson's (1992) attempts at comparative civilisations stretching back into the CAPE era; Linklater's (2016) exploration of harm conventions within and between societies, also stretching back into the CAPE era; and Neumann's studies of steppe nomads (Neumann and Wigen, 2018) and diplomacy (Neumann, 2020).

This putting forward of the ES is absolutely not a call to merge or dissolve existing disciplines or fields. It invites those interested within these cognate neighbouring disciplines to consider a collaborative project about how to analyse and understand the organisation of humankind as a species. The invitation to GHS is to examine the analytical framework and method deployed here and evaluate to what extent and how it might enhance their own approaches. To Global/World History, the invitation is to consider the implications for their craft of telling a historical narrative based on a particular set of abstract, mid-level, social-structural concepts. Global/World historians are anyway required to resort to big themes in order to keep their work to manageable lengths, and in the process, they already stretch their relationship with formal historiography. To that extent, they are already somewhat open to the type of approach used here. To IR, the invitation is to become Global IR. That involves moving away from both the parochiality of West-centrism that has defined the field since its birth at the height of Western colonialism, and the narrow perspective on its subject matter defined by Political Science, state-centrism and positivist methods. IR needs to adopt a longer, wider and more multi-disciplinary view of what constitutes its subject matter. To accomplish that, it can use the ES as a bridge to adjacent bodies of work from which there is much to be learned, and with which there is much to exchange. This invitation will not be attractive to everyone in these fields, probably not even to a majority, who will be content to carry on as they are. But if the approach set out here is seen to have delivered what I have claimed for it, it should appeal at least to a substantial minority within these fields, and that would be enough to support a joint project amongst them.

That leaves the question of what implications all this has for the ES, and how it might respond? I am open to the charge that I have hijacked the School's ideas, and taken them, without permission, well outside its comfort zone. The invitation to the ES is therefore to consider both its internal structure and self-understanding, and its role within IR and the social sciences more broadly. The implications of this book for the ES are potentially quite substantial. Some might think that this book has moved beyond the ES, simply borrowing some of its elements, but basically moving into the realms of GHS. Others might think that it defines a possible future direction for the ES by building bridges that connect it, and IR more generally, to Global/World history and GHS. The comments that follow are aimed mainly at the latter group.

By focusing on global society as a concept that works across the interpolity, transnational and interhuman domains, the book exposes the limitations of the ES's division of things into international and world society. That foundational ES division was useful, and a key to the distinctiveness of the ES, in at least two ways. It opened a normative dimension through world society as an ethical referent point; and it opened the idea of second-order society – a society of societies – as a distinctive approach to analysing IR. But it also had three substantial downsides. First, it privileged the interstate domain, in the process somewhat sidelining other types of polity, particularly empires, and reinforcing a Eurocentric story of making a world of modern states. Second, it largely shut out the transnational domain, and with it a significant cast of non-state actors and institutions. This bias was in part responsible for marginalising the place of international political economy within international society. Third, it largely consigned the interhuman domain to a normative role resting on a universal, but abstract, positioning of humankind as a whole. As a consequence, the ES neglected the rich tapestry of non-universal identities there, and how they play into the other two domains. On this basis, at least some within the ES might want to reconsider the utility of its traditional framing.

The key to any such reconsideration is to use primary institutions in a global society perspective, opening a deeper structural view in which such institutions are normally, not exceptionally, embedded across the three domains. Without this quite radical repositioning, one cannot really understand how they work, how stable or not they might be, and what sort of global society they structure. The cross-domain character of primary institutions has to be made central to the analysis. Indeed, this global society approach inverts the normal assumption within the ES about integrated world society: Instead of integrated world society defining a possible future, it is set up as the core structural framing that defines both a long past and most probable futures. This move puts the nature, degree and scale of societal integration at the centre of the analysis.

Although the distinction between international and world society had its uses, it has unhelpfully masked the more important reality of a global society that structures not just states, but also non-state actors in the transnational domain, and peoples in the interhuman one. Global society is deeper than the old ES framing can easily see, and addresses the condition of humankind as a whole. A huge gain from making primary institutions the central focus, and looking at them across the three domains, is that it puts institutions such as religion, science, sport, the market/economic nationalism, development, nationalism and environmental stewardship squarely into the mainstream of ES analysis. Because primary institutions are no longer artificially tied to the interstate/polity domain, institutions that have their main roots in the transnational and interhuman domains can now get full play. Indeed, from the long historical analysis, it becomes crystal clear that while the interpolity/state domain is distinctive and important as a form of society, it has always stood alongside, and shared social structures with, the other two domains that are equally important. For example, during the CAPE era merchant diasporas, long-distance trade and religion were all substantially autonomous from the states/empires of the time while also being closely entangled with them. One cannot understand that history on the basis of interpolity society alone, and the same is true for the transition towards modernity, and for modernity proper whenever that arrives.

Another big gain from making primary institutions the central focus is that it gives the ES a distinctive approach to the analysis of polity-formation and reproduction. How different configurations of primary institutions underpin different types of polity, opens up a theory of the state. The shift from dynasticism to nationalism as one of the trilogy of institutions defining the dominant polity, for example, is massively important in understanding the transitions from the empires of the CAPE era, to the nation states of the modern one. Primary institutions can also be used in the same way to analyse non-state actors.

The global society approach thus puts the ES in a strong position to do big history. Using this toolkit, it can define eras, and the transitions between them, with considerable precision. It breaks away from the rather state-centric, and in part also Eurocentric, approach of the traditional ES. It can look both backwards and forwards across the range of human history to good effect, and without temporal limits or confinement to particular types of polity. It thereby becomes a method for presenting history at a high enough level of abstraction to reveal significant patterns for purposes of both constructing narratives, and making comparisons between eras. By transcending the unit level, and even the civilisational one, primary institutions and material conditions open up an analytical approach that is comprehensively systemic and global. Using an elaborated version of the ES's primary institutions as a meeting point between World/Global history and social science, positions the ES as a powerful voice with links to Global Historical Sociology. It offers a fairly fine-grained view of social structure, which, among other things, provides a neat way of analysing the political superstructure of the state, and understanding how it has evolved from CAPE towards modernity. Using primary institutions to address global history in this way has the signal benefit of providing a detailed account of how such institutions, and the interplay among them, have evolved over the *longue durée*.

These gains do not come at the expense of the foundational ES ideas that the composition and balance of global social structure is always changing (usually slowly); that this process is conditional and contingent rather than teleological; and that it is open to agency, and therefore also a vehicle for normative debate. Thus, although the approach put forward in this book makes quite radical changes to both the ES's 'three traditions' approach, and its state-centric understanding of primary institutions, it leaves intact most of the core thinking that has defined the ES and made it a distinctive body of theory within IR. For those scholars who see themselves as working within or alongside the ES, the choices are not difficult. Those who want to carry on with whatever they have been doing can, and those who find advantages in the global society approach can adapt it to their work to the degree they think appropriate. Some might want to take advantage of the opportunity to work on a larger scale of space and time, and some not. In my view, the global society approach extends the possibilities of what might be done under the ES banner, but offers that only to those who want to take it. It does not undermine or invalidate the work of those who want to carry on with a more traditional understanding of what the ES is about.

If the arguments in this book gain significant traction within the ES, then they open up a substantial research agenda. As noted at the beginning, I would be amazed, and disappointed, if mine was the last word on the issues raised here.

Perhaps most obviously, the global society approach raises a lot of questions about primary institutions. I have offered an empirical approach to validating such institutions, extended their number quite considerably, and repositioned them across the three domains. Is the empirical approach to identifying primary institutions good enough for the job, or could it be improved? Is the empirical approach the best, or only one, or have I missed a more theoretical approach that might do a better job? Is the particular set of primary institutions identified in this book correct? Should there be fewer? Or more? Might revolution, for example, be counted as a primary institution?[1] Or should some institutions be redefined? Was it a good idea, for example, to work with a broad institution such as human equality/inequality, rather than more specific ones such as human rights or democracy?[2] What are the implications of situating primary institutions across the three domains in terms both of understanding their roots, and how they operate and interact with each other? Some primary institutions are already well-researched, most obviously sovereignty, balance of power, diplomacy and nationalism. But many are not. There are big literatures on religion, sport, science, and the many forms of human (in)equality, for example, but not as primary institutions. How should the ES go about linking to these literatures, and would doing so change some of the arguments made here? Does the global society approach work for the regional/subglobal level of integrated world society, or does it require rethinking how to approach the society question at that level?

Another set of questions arises around secondary institutions. My own sense is that what I have argued here does not, with one exception, disturb the current moves within the ES to open up the processes of mutual constitution between primary and secondary institutions. The exception is my argument that states/polities should be seen as secondary

---

[1] Halliday (1999) and Lawson (2019) might be taken as starting points for thinking about this.
[2] Keister and Southgate (2021) use such an aggregation, though for a contemporary analysis, not a deep historical one.

institutions. The case for doing so is that it brings to the ES a theory of the state rooted in the set of primary institutions, and the interplay among them, that constitute polities/states. The demonstration case for this was how the shift from dynasticism to nationalism reconstituted the dominant form of polity during the first phase of the transition towards modernity. But is it valid to think of polities/states in this way? The advantage is that it puts all secondary institutions on common ground, and downgrades the privileging of the state. But should the state be privileged, and if so why? Is there an unworkable tension between continuing to deploy an interstate/polity domain while at the same time classifying the state as a form of secondary institution?

One of the conclusions I draw from this is that it might be time for the ES to drop the parochial-sounding and misleading label that has been its name-tag so far, and that was attached to it by someone calling for its closure (Jones, 1981). The ES, or parts of it, might want to consider moving to a more specific and more accurate name that would better define its place in the academic constellation. On the basis of this book, *Global Society Approach* is the obvious option (Buzan, 2022). But that is a choice to be made, or not, by the younger generation of ES scholars, who might well have other ideas of their own.

A final conclusion is that, in my view, something like a global society approach should inform, and indeed be the foundation of, the discipline of IR as a whole. This thought represents my long-standing view that IR is not, and should not be, merely international or world politics: that is, just a subdiscipline of Political Science. Most social sciences define themselves by a particular function or type of behaviour (political, legal, economic, etc.). History, uniquely, defines itself by time. IR needs to understand that what defines it is scale. IR should, and could (and sometimes does), stretch across, and integrate, the macro-end of all of the social sciences and History. It should be the study of how humankind as a whole organises itself. In my view, only that kind of approach can deliver the discipline from its Eurocentric legacy, and unfold the path towards a discipline of Global IR for long advocated by Amitav Acharya. The ES is the best available vehicle within IR to begin the journey towards not just that end, but also towards the making of an Earth System Social Science.

References

Acharya, Amitav (2004) 'How Ideas Spread, Whose Norms Matter? Norm Localization and Institutional Change in Asian Regionalism', *International Organization*, 58:2, 239–75.

(2009) *Whose Ideas Matter? Agency and Power in Asian Regionalism*, Ithaca, NY: Cornell University Press.

(2014) *The End of American World Order*, Cambridge: Polity.

Acharya, Amitav and Barry Buzan (2007) 'Why Is There No Non-Western International Relations Theory? An Introduction', *International Relations of the Asia-Pacific*, 7:3, 287–312.

Acharya, Amitav and Barry Buzan (eds.) (2010) *Non-Western International Relations Theory: Perspectives on and beyond Asia*, London: Routledge.

(2017) 'Why Is There No Non-Western International Relations Theory? Ten Years On', *International Relations of the Asia-Pacific*, 17:3, 341–70.

(2019) *The Making of Global International Relations*, Cambridge: Cambridge University Press.

Albert, Mathias and Barry Buzan (2011) 'Securitization, Sectors and Functional Differentiation', *Security Dialogue*, 42:4–5, 413–25.

(2013) 'International Relations Theory and the "Social Whole": Encounters and Gaps between IR and Sociology', *International Political Sociology*, 7:2, 117–35.

Albert, Mathias and Lena Hilkermeier (eds.) (2004) *Observing International Relations: Niklas Luhmann and World Politics*, London: Routledge.

Albert, Mathias, Barry Buzan and Michael Zürn (eds.) (2013) *Bringing Sociology to International Relations: World Politics as Differentiation Theory*, Cambridge: Cambridge University Press.

Alexandrowicz, C. H. (1967) *An Introduction to the History of the Law of Nations in the East Indies (16th, 17th, and 18th Centuries)*, London: Oxford University Press.

Allan, Bentley B. (2018) *Scientific Cosmology and International Orders*, Cambridge: Cambridge University Press.

Anderson, Benedict (1983) *Imagined Communities: Reflections on the Origin and Spread of Nationalism*, London: Verso.

Anderson, Fred (2000) *Crucible of War: The Seven Years' War and the Fate of Empire in British North America, 1754–1766*, New York: Vintage.

Andrade, Tonio (2016) *The Gunpowder Age: China, Military Innovation, and the Rise of the West in World History*, Princeton: Princeton University Press.

Anghie, Antony (2004) *Imperialism, Sovereignty and the Making of International Law*, Cambridge: Cambridge University Press.

Armstrong, David (1977) *Revolutionary Diplomacy: The United Front Doctrine and Chinese Foreign Policy*, Berkeley and Los Angeles: University of California Press.

(1998) 'Globalisation and the Social State', *Review of International Studies*, 24:4, 461–78.

(1999) 'Law, Justice and the Idea of a World Society', *International Affairs*, 75:3, 643–53.

(2006) 'The Nature of Law in an Anarchical Society', in Richard Little and John Williams (eds.), *The Anarchical Society in a Globalized World*, Basingstoke: Palgrave, 121–40.

Armstrong, Karen (2002) *Islam: A Short History*, New York: The Modern Library.

Arnaoutoglou, Ilias (2016) 'Hierapolis and Its Professional Associations: A Comparative Analysis', in Andrew Wilson and Miko Flohr (eds.), *Urban Craftsmen and Traders in the Roman World*, New York: Oxford University Press, 278–98.

Aydin, Cemil (2007) *The Politics of Anti-Westernism in Asia*, New York: Columbia University Press.

Azhar, Azeem (2021) *Exponential: How Accelerating Technology Is Leaving Us Behind and What to Do About It*, London: Penguin.

Bacevich, Andrew J. (2002) *American Empire: The Realities and Consequences of U.S. Diplomacy*, Cambridge, MA: Harvard University Press.

Bain, Ebenezer (1887) *Merchant and Craft Guilds: A History of the Aberdeen Incorporated Trades*, Aberdeen: J & JP Edmond and Spark.

Bain, William (2003) *Between Anarchy and Society: Trusteeship and the Obligations of Power*, Oxford: Oxford University Press.

(2010) 'The Pluralist–Solidarist Debate in the English School', in Robert A. Denemark (ed.), *International Studies Encyclopedia*, Blackwell Publishing for ISA, English School section editor Daniel M. Green.

Baldwin, James (2017 [1958]) 'Stranger in the Village', in *Notes of a Native Son*, London: Penguin.

Bayly, C. A. (2004) *The Birth of the Modern World 1780–1914: Global Connections and Comparisons*, Oxford: Blackwell.

(2018) *Remaking the Modern World 1900–2015: Global Connections and Comparisons*, Chichester: Wiley Blackwell.

Becker, Jeff (2021) 'A Starcruiser for Space Force: Thinking through the Imminent Transformation of Spacepower', *War on the Rocks*, 19 May, https://warontherocks.com/2021/05/a-starcruiser-for-space-force-thinking-through-the-imminent-transformation-of-spacepower/, accessed 28 May 2021.

Beeson, Mark (2009) 'Developmental States in East Asia: A Comparison of the Japanese and Chinese Experiences', *Asian Perspective*, 332, 5–39.

Bell, Duncan (2007) *The Idea of Greater Britain: Empire and the Future of World Order 1860–1900*, Princeton: Princeton University Press.

(2013) 'Race and International Relations: Introduction', *Cambridge Review of International Affairs*, 26:1, 1–4.

Bennison, Amira K. (2009) 'The Ottoman Empire and Its Precedents from the Perspective of English School Theory', in Barry Buzan and Ana Gonzalez-Pelaez (eds.), *International Society and the Middle East: English School Theory at the Regional Level*, Basingstoke: Palgrave, 45–69.

Bentley, Jerry H. (1993) *Old World Encounters: Cross-Cultural Contacts and Exchanges in Pre-modern Times*, Oxford: Oxford University Press.

(1996) 'Cross-Cultural Interaction and Periodization in World History', *The American Historical Review*, 101:3, 749–70.

Best, Jacqueline (2006) 'Civilising through Transparency: The International Monetary Fund', in Brett Bowden and Leonard Seabrooke (eds.), *Global Standards of Market Civilisation*, Abingdon: Routledge, 133–45.

Bjola, Corneliu and Marcus Holmes (2015) *Digital Diplomacy: Theory and Practice*, Abingdon: Routledge.

Blyth, Mark (2013) *Austerity: The History of a Dangerous Idea*, Oxford: Oxford University Press.

Bobbitt, Philip (2002) *The Shield of Achilles: War, Peace and the Course of History*, London: Penguin.

Bostrum, Nick (2014) *Superintelligence: Paths, Dangers, Strategies*, Oxford: Oxford University Press.

Bostrum, Nick and Milan M. Ćirković (eds.) (2008) *Global Catastrophic Risks*, Oxford: Oxford University Press.

Boulding, Kenneth E. (1966) 'The Economics of the Coming Spaceship Earth', in H. Jarrett (ed.), *Environmental Quality in a Growing Economy*, Baltimore: Johns Hopkins University Press, 3–14.

Bowden, Brett (2009) *The Empire of Civilisation: The Evolution of an Imperial Idea*, Kindle ed., Chicago: University of Chicago Press.

Bowden, Brett and Leonard Seabrooke (eds.) (2006) *Global Standards of Market Civilisation*, Abingdon: Routledge.

Branch, Jordan (2012) 'Colonial Reflection and Territoriality: The Peripheral Origins of Sovereignty', *European Journal of International Relations*, 18:2, 277–97.

Brand, Stewart (2010) *Whole Earth Discipline*, London: Atlantic Books.

Braudel, Fernand (1985) *The Perspective of the World: Civilization and Capitalism 15th–18th Century*, vol. III. London: Fontana Press.

(1994 [1987]) *A History of Civilization*, London: Penguin.

Breuilly, John (1993) *Nationalism and the State*, Manchester: Manchester University Press.

Brewin, Christopher (1982) 'Sovereignty', in James Mayall (ed.), *The Community of States: A Study in International Political Theory*, London: George Allen & Unwin, 34–48.

Bricker, Darrell and John Ibbitson (2019) *Empty Planet: The Shock of Global Population Decline*, London: Robinson.

Brodie, Bernard (1941) *Sea Power in the Machine Age*, Princeton: Princeton University Press.

Brodie, Bernard and Fawn M. Brodie (1973) *From Crossbow to H-Bomb*, Bloomington: Indiana University Press.

Brown, Chris (2004) 'Do Great Powers Have Great Responsibilities? Great Powers and Moral Agency', *Global Society*, 18:1, 5–19.

Brown, Jonathan A. C. (2020) *Slavery and Islam*, London: Oneworld Academic.

Buck, Philip W. (1974 [1942]) *The Politics of Mercantilism*, New York: Octagon Books.

Bukovansky, Mlada, Ian Clark, Robyn Eckersley, et al. (2012) *Special Responsibilities: Global Problems and American Power*, Cambridge: Cambridge University Press.

Bull, Hedley (1966) 'The Grotian Conception of International Society', in Herbert Butterfield and Martin Wight (eds.), *Diplomatic Investigations*, London: Allen and Unwin, 50–73.

(1977) *The Anarchical Society: A Study of Order in World Politics*, London: Macmillan.

(1979) 'Natural Law and International Relations', *British Journal of International Studies*, 5:2, 171–81.

(1980) 'The Great Irresponsibles? The United States, The Soviet Union and World Order', *International Journal*, 35:3, 437–47.

(1984) 'The Revolt against the West', in H. Bull and A. Watson (eds.), *The Expansion of International Society*, Oxford: Oxford University Press, 217–28.

(1990) 'The Importance of Grotius in the Study of International Relations', in Hedley Bull, Benedict Kingsbury and Adam Roberts (eds.), *Hugo Grotius and International Relations*, Oxford: Clarendon, 65–93.

Bull, Hedley and Adam Watson (eds.) (1984) *The Expansion of International Society*, Oxford: Oxford University Press.

Bull, Hedley, Benedict Kingsbury and Adam Roberts (eds.) (1990) *Hugo Grotius and International Relations*, Oxford: Clarendon.

Burbank, Jane and Frederick Cooper (2010) *Empires in World History: Power and the Politics of Difference*, Princeton: Princeton University Press.

Buzan, Barry (1993) 'From International System to International Society: Structural Realism and Regime Theory Meet the English School', *International Organization*, 47:3, 327–52.

(2001) 'The English School: An Underexploited Resource in IR', *Review of International Studies*, 27:3, 471–88.

(2002) 'South Asia Moving towards Transformation: Emergence of India as a Great Power', *International Studies*, 39:1, 1–24.

(2004a) *From International to World Society? English School Theory and the Social Structure of Globalisation*, Cambridge: Cambridge University Press.

(2004b) *The United States and the Great Powers*, Cambridge: Polity.

(2004c) '"Civil" and "Uncivil" in World Society', in Stefano Guzzini and Dietrich Jung (eds.), *Contemporary Security Analysis and Copenhagen Peace Research*, London, Routledge, 94–105.

(2007 [1991]) *People, States and Fear*, Colchester: ECPR Press.

(2008) 'A Leader without Followers? The United States in World Politics after Bush', *International Politics*, 45:5, 554–70.

(2010a) 'Culture and International Society', *International Affairs*, 86:1, 1–25.

(2010b) 'China in International Society: Is "Peaceful Rise" Possible?', *Chinese Journal of International Politics*, 3:1, 5–36.

(2011) 'A World Order without Superpowers: Decentred Globalism', *International Relations*, 25:1, 1–23.

(2014a) *An Introduction to the English School of International Relations*, Cambridge: Cambridge University Press.

(2014b) 'The Logic and Contradictions of "Peaceful Rise/Development" as China's Grand Strategy', *Chinese Journal of International Politics*, 7:4, 381–420.

(2017) 'Universal Sovereignty', in Tim Dunne and Christian Reus-Smit (eds.), *The Globalisation of International Society*, Oxford: Oxford University Press, 227–47.

(2018a) 'Revisiting World Society', *International Politics*, 55:1, 125–40. Follow up at http://www.e-ir.info/2018/03/16/the-english-school-world-society-debate-a-forum-article/

(2018b) 'China's Rise in English School Perspective', *International Relations of the Asia-Pacific*, 18:3, 449–76.

(2023) 'The Evolution of Global Society Theory', in Laura Horn Ayşem Mert and Franziska Müller (eds.) *The Handbook of Global Politics in the 22nd Century*, Basingstoke: Palgrave, 15–30.

Buzan, Barry and Amitav Acharya (2022) *Re-Imagining International Relations: World Orders in the Thought and Practice of Indian, Chinese, and Islamic Civilizations*, Cambridge: Cambridge University Press.

Buzan, Barry and Mathias Albert (2010) 'Differentiation: A Sociological Approach to International Relations Theory', *European Journal of International Relations*, 16:3, 315–37.

Buzan, Barry and Michael Cox (2013) 'China and the US: Comparable Cases of "Peaceful Rise"?', *Chinese Journal of International Politics*, 6:2, 109–32.

(2022) 'The End of Anglo-America?', in Cornelia Navari and Tonny Brems Knudsen (eds.), *Power Shifts in English School Perspective*, Basingstoke: Palgrave.

Buzan, Barry and Robert Falkner (2022) 'The Market in Global International Society: A Dialectic of Contestation and Resilience', in Trine Flockhart and Zachary Paikin (eds.), *Rebooting Global International Society: Change, Contestation, and Resilience*, Basingstoke: Palgrave.

(forthcoming) *The Market and Global International Society*.

Buzan, Barry and Evelyn Goh (2020) *Rethinking Sino-Japanese Alienation: History Problems and Historical Opportunities*, London: Oxford University Press.

Buzan, Barry and Ana Gonzalez-Pelaez (eds.) (2009) *International Society and the Middle East: English School Theory at the Regional Level*, Basingstoke: Palgrave.

Buzan, Barry and Lene Hansen (2009) *The Evolution of International Security Studies*, Cambridge: Cambridge University Press.

Buzan, Barry and Eric Herring (1998) *The Arms Dynamic in World Politics*, Boulder: Lynne Rienner.

Buzan, Barry and Hitomi Koyama (2019) 'Rethinking Japan in Mainstream International Relations', *International Relations of the Asia-Pacific*, 19:2, 185–212.

Buzan, Barry and George Lawson (2014a) 'Rethinking Benchmark Dates in International Relations', *European Journal of International Relations*, 20:2, 437–62.

(2014b) 'Capitalism and the Emergent World Order', *International Affairs*, 90:1, 71–91.

(2015) *The Global Transformation: History, Modernity and the Making of International Relations*, Cambridge: Cambridge University Press.

(2016) 'The Impact of the "Global Transformation" on Uneven and Combined Development', in Alexander Anievas and Kamran Matin (eds.), *Historical Sociology and World History: Uneven and Combined Development over the Longue Durée*, London: Rowman & Littlefield, 171–84.

(2018) 'The English School: History and Primary Institutions as Empirical IR Theory?', in William R. Thompson (ed.), *The Oxford Encyclopedia of Empirical International Relations Theory*, New York: Oxford University Press, 783–99.

(2020) 'China through the Lens of Modernity', *Chinese Journal of International Politics*, 13:2, 187–217.

(forthcoming) *Modes of Power: A Framework for Global History and International Relations*.

Buzan, Barry and Richard Little (2000) *International Systems in World History: Remaking the Study of International Relations*, Oxford: Oxford University Press.

Buzan, Barry and Laust Schouenborg (2018) *Global International Society: A New Framework for Analysis*, Cambridge: Cambridge University Press.

Buzan, Barry and Ole Wæver (2003) *Regions and Powers: The Structure of International Security*, Cambridge: Cambridge University Press.

Buzan, Barry and Yongjin Zhang (2014) *Contesting International Society in East Asia*, Cambridge: Cambridge University Press.

(2019) 'China and the Global Reach of Human Rights', *China Quarterly*, online first.

Buzan, Barry, Charles Jones and Richard Little (1993) *The Logic of Anarchy: Neorealism to Structural Realism*, New York: Columbia University Press.

Buzan, Barry, Ole Wæver and Jaap de Wilde (1998) *Security: A New Framework for Analysis*, Boulder: Lynne Rienner.

Cairncross, Frances (2001) *The Death of Distance 2.0*, London: Texere.

Caney, Simon (2022) 'Global Climate Governance, Short-Termism, and the Vulnerability of Future Generations', *Ethics and International Affairs*, 36:2, 137–55.

Cerny, Phil (1993) '"Plurilateralism": Structural Differentiation and Functional Conflict in the Post-Cold War World Order', *Millennium*, 22:1, 27–51.

Chaudhuri, K. N. (1985) *Trade and Civilization in the Indian Ocean*, Cambridge: Cambridge University Press.

Chevillard, Nicole and Sébastien Leconte (1986) 'Slavery and Women', in Stephanie Coontz and Peta Henderson (eds.), *Women's Work, Men's Property: The Origins of Gender and Class*, London: Verso, 156–68.

Chong, Ja Ian (2014) 'Popular Narratives vs. China's History: Implications for Understanding an Emergent China', *European Journal of International Relations*, 20:4, 939–64.

Christian, David (2004) *Maps of Time*, Berkeley: University of California Press.

(2019) *Origin Story: A Big History of Everything*, London: Penguin.

Clark, Ann Marie (1995) 'Non-governmental Organizations and their Influence on International Society', *Journal of International Affairs*, 48:2, 507–25.

Clark, Ian (1999) *Globalisation and International Relations Theory*, Oxford: Oxford University Press.

(2005) *Legitimacy in International Society*, Oxford: Oxford University Press.

(2007) *International Legitimacy and World Society*, Oxford: Oxford University Press.

(2009a) 'Towards an English School Theory of Hegemony', *European Journal of International Relations*, 15:2, 203–28.

(2009b) 'Bringing Hegemony Back In: The United States and International Order', *International Affairs*, 85:1, 23–36.

(2011) *Hegemony in International Society*, Oxford: Oxford University Press.

(2013) *The Vulnerable in International Society*, Oxford: Oxford University Press.

Cline, Eric H. (2014) *1177 BC: The Year Civilization Collapsed*, Princeton: Princeton University Press.

Coggan, Philip (2020) *More: The 10,000 Year Rise of the World Economy*, London: Profile Books.

Cohen, Raymond and Raymond Westbrook (eds.) (2000) *Amarna Diplomacy: The Beginnings of International Relations*, Baltimore: Johns Hopkins University Press.

Cohen, Robin and Paul Kennedy (2007) *Global Sociology*, 2nd ed., Basingstoke: Palgrave.

Conrad, Sebastian (2016) *What Is Global History?*, Princeton: Princeton University Press.

Coontz, Stephanie and Peta Henderson (1986) 'Introduction: Explanations of Male Dominance', in Stephanie Coontz and Peta Henderson (eds.), *Women's Work, Men's Property: The Origins of Gender and Class*, London: Verso, 1–43.

Cooper, Luke (2015) 'The International Relations of the "Imagined Community": Explaining the Late Nineteenth Century Genesis of the Chinese Nation', *Review of International Studies*, 41:3, 477–501.

Cowen, Tyler (2011) *The Great Stagnation*, New York: Penguin.

Cox, Michael (2016) 'Not Just "Convenient": China and Russia's New Strategic Partnership in the Age of Geopolitics', *Asian Journal of Comparative Politics*, 1:4, 317–34.

Cui, Shunji and Barry Buzan (2016) 'Great Power Management in International Society', *The Chinese Journal of International Politics*, 9:2, 181–210.

Curtin, Philip D. (1984) *Cross-Cultural Trade in World History*, Cambridge: Cambridge University Press.

Curtis, Simon (2016) *Global Cities and Global Order*, Oxford: Oxford University Press.

Cutler, Claire A. (1991) 'The "Grotian Tradition" in International Relations', *Review of International Studies*, 17:1, 41–65.

Dalby, Simon (2020) *Anthropocene Geopolitics: Globalization, Security, Sustainability*, Ottawa: University of Ottawa Press.

Dale, Stephen F. (2010) *The Muslim Empires of the Ottomans, Safavids and Mughals*, Cambridge: Cambridge University Press.

Darwin, John (2020) *Unlocking the World: Port Cities and Globalisation in the Age of Steam 1830–1930*, London: Penguin.

Davies, Thomas (2013) *NGOs: A New History of Transnational Civil Society*, London: Hurst.

Davis, John P. (1971 [1905]) *Corporations: A Study of the Origin and Development of Great Business Combinations and of Their Relation to the Authority of the State*, 2 vols., New York: Burt Franklin.

Davis, Mike (2002) *Late Victorian Holocausts*, London: Verso.

Davis, Robert C. (2003) *Christian Slaves, Muslim Masters: White Slavery in the Mediterranean, The Barbary Coast, and Italy, 1500–1800*, Basingstoke: Palgrave Macmillan.

De Ligt, Luuk (1993) *Fairs and Markets in the Roman Empire: Economic and Social Aspects of Periodic Trade in a Pre-Industrial Society*, Amsterdam: J.C. Gieben.

Der Derian, James (1992) *Antidiplomacy: Spies, Terror, Speed and War*, Cambridge: Blackwell.

(2003) 'The Question of Information Technology', *Millennium*, 32:3, 441–56.

Deudney, Daniel (2007) *Bounding Power: Republican Security Theory from the Polis to the Global Village*, Princeton: Princeton University Press.

(2020) *Dark Skies*, Princeton: Princeton University Press.

Devetak, Richard (1996a) 'Critical Theory', in Scott Burchill and Andrew Linklater (eds.), *Theories of International Relations*, Houndmills: Macmillan, 145–76.

(1996b) 'Postmodernism', in Scott Burchill and Andrew Linklater (eds.), *Theories of International Relations*, Houndmills: Macmillan, 179–209.

Diamond, Jared (1997) *Guns, Germs and Steel: The Fates of Human Societies*, New York: W.W. Norton.

(2005) *Collapse: How Societies Choose to Fail or Survive*, London: Allen Lane.

Dikötter, Frank (2011) *Mao's Great Famine*, Kindle ed., London: Bloomsbury.

(2016) *The Cultural Revolution: A People's History 1962–1976*, New York: Bloomsbury Press.

Donnelly, Jack (1998) 'Human Rights: A New Standard of Civilization?', *International Affairs*, 74:1, 1–23.

Dower, John W. (1986) *War without Mercy: Race and Power in the Pacific War*, New York: Pantheon Books.

Drezner, David W. (2012) 'The Irony of Global Economic Governance: The System Worked', Working Paper, Council on Foreign Relations, New York.

Duara, Prasenjit (1995) *Rescuing History from the Nation: Questioning Narratives of Modern China*, Chicago: University of Chicago Press.

Dunne, Tim (2003) 'Society and Hierarchy in International Relations', *International Relations*, 17:3, 303–20.

Dunne, Tim and Christian Reus-Smit (eds.) (2017) *The Globalisation of International Society*, Oxford: Oxford University Press.

Dunne, Tim and Nicholas Wheeler (1996) 'Hedley Bull's Pluralism of the Intellect and Solidarism of the Will', *International Affairs*, 72:1, 91–107.

Duvall, Raymond and Jonathan Havercroft (2008) 'Taking Sovereignty out of This World: Space Weapons and Empire of the Future', *Review of International Studies*, 34:4, 755–75.

Eichengreen, Barry (2019) *Globalising Capital: A History of the International Monetary System*, 3rd ed., Princeton: Princeton University Press.

Eisenstadt, Shmuel N. (2000) 'Multiple Modernities', *Dædalus*, 129:1, 1–29.

Engels, Friedrich (2010 [1884]) *The Origin of the Family, Private Property and the State*, London: Penguin Books.

Epple, Angelika (2021) 'Periodization in Global History: The Productive Power of Comparing', in Mathias Albert and Tobias Werron (eds.), *What in the World? Understanding Global Social Change*, Bristol: Bristol University Press.

Epple, Angelika, Walter Erhart and Johannes Grave (eds.) (2020) *Practices of Comparing: Towards a New Understanding of a Fundamental Human Practice*, Bielefeld: Bielefeld University Press.

Fadlan, Ibn (2012 [mid 12th century]) *Ibn Fadlan and the Land of Darkness*, Kindle ed., Penguin Books.

Fagan, Brian M. (1993) *World Prehistory: A Brief Introduction*, 2nd ed., New York: Harper Collins.

(2004) *The Long Summer: How Climate Changed Civilisation*, Cambridge, MA: Basic Books.

Falkner, Robert (2016) 'The Paris Agreement and the New Logic of International Climate Politics', *International Affairs*, 92:5, 1107–25.

(2021) *Environmentalism and Global International Society*, Cambridge: Cambridge University Press.

Falkner, Robert and Barry Buzan (2019) 'The Emergence of Environmental Stewardship as a Primary Institution of Global International Society', *European Journal of International Relations*, 25:1, 131–55.

Falkner, Robert and Barry Buzan (eds.) (2022) *Great Power Responsibility and Global Environmental Politics*, Oxford: Oxford University Press.

(forthcoming) *The Market and Global International Society*.

Falkner, Robert and Nico Jaspers (2012) 'Regulating Nanotechnologies: Risk, Uncertainty and the Global Governance Gap', *Global Environmental Politics*, 12:1, 30–55.

Ferguson, Yale and Richard Mansbach (1996) *Polities: Authority, Identities and Change*, Columbia: University of South Carolina Press.

Fidler, David (2000) 'A Kinder, Gentler System of Capitulations? International Law, Structural Adjustment Policies, and the Standard of Liberal, Globalized Civilization', *Texas International Law Journal*, 35:3, 387–413.

Findlay, Ronald and Kevin H. O'Rourke (2007) *Power and Plenty: Trade, War, and the World Economy in the Second Millennium*, Princeton: Princeton University Press.

Finley, Moses I. (1973) *The Ancient Economy*, Berkeley: University of California Press.

Flockhart, Trine (2016) 'The Coming Multi-Order World', *Contemporary Security Policy*, 37:1, 3–30.

Fôldeâk, Arpâd (1979) *Chess Olympiads 1927–1968*, translated from the Hungarian by Robert Ejury and Jenô Bochkor, translation revised by Peter H. Clarke, New York: Dover.

Frank, Andre Gunder (1990) 'A Theoretical Introduction to 5000 Years of World System History', *Review*, 13:2, 155–248.

Frank, Andre Gunder and Barry Gills (eds.) (1993) *The World System: 500 Years or 5000?* London: Routledge.

Frase, Peter (2016) *Four Futures: Visions of the World after Capitalism*, London: Verso.

Frieden, Jeffry A. (2006) *Global Capitalism: Its Fall and Rise in the Twentieth Century*, New York: W.W. Norton.

Frieden, Jeffry A., Michael Pettis, Dani Rodrik and Ernesto Zedillo (2012) *After the Fall: The Future of Global Cooperation*, Geneva: International Center for Monetary and Banking Studies, Geneva Reports on the World Economy 14.

Fry, Douglas P. and Patrik Söderberg (2013) 'Lethal Aggression in Mobile Forager Bands, and Implications for the Origins of War', *Science*, 341:6143, 270–3.

Fukuyama, Francis (1992) *The End of History and the Last Man*, London: Penguin.

Fukuzawa, Yukichi (2008 [1875]) *An Outline of a Theory of Civilization*, translated by David A. Dalworth and G. Cameron Hurst III, New York: Columbia University Press.

Galor, Oded (2022) *The Journey of Humanity: The Origins of Wealth and Inequality*, London: Penguin.

Galtung, Johan (1969) 'Violence, Peace and Peace Research', *Journal of Peace Research*, 6:3, 167–91.

Ganguli, Birendranath (1965) *Dadabhai Naoroji and the Drain Theory*, New York: Asia Pub. House.

Gardner, Richard N. (1969) *Sterling-Dollar Diplomacy: The Origins and Prospects of Our International Economic Order*, New York: McGraw-Hill.

Garver, John W. (2016) *China's Quest: The History of the Foreign Relations of the People's Republic of China*, New York: Oxford University Press.

Gaskarth, Jamie (ed.) (2015) *China, India and the Future of International Society*, London: Rowman and Littlefield.

Geertz, Clifford (1993 [1973]) *The Interpretation of Cultures*, London: William Collins.

Gehrke, Hans-Joachim (2020a) 'Introduction', in Hans-Joachim Gehrke (ed.), *Making Civilizations: The World before 600*, Cambridge, MA: Harvard University Press, 1–38.

Gehrke, Hans-Joachim (ed.) (2020b) *Making Civilizations: The World before 600*, Cambridge, MA: Harvard University Press.

Gellner, Ernest (1981) *Muslim Society*, Cambridge: Cambridge University Press.
  (1983) *Nations and Nationalism*, Oxford: Blackwell.
  (1988) *Plough, Sword and Book: The Structure of Human History*, London: Paladin.
  (1992) 'Nationalism Reconsidered and E.H. Carr', *Review of International Studies*, 18:4, 286–93.

Giddens, Anthony (1979) *Central Problems in Social Theory*, London: Macmillan.
  (1985) *The Nation State and Violence*, Cambridge: Polity.
  (1991) *The Consequences of Modernity*, Cambridge: Polity.

Gilpin, Robert (1981) *War and Change in World Politics*, Cambridge: Cambridge University Press.

(1987) *The Political Economy of International Relations*, Princeton: Princeton University Press.

Go, Julian and George Lawson (2017) 'Introduction: For a Global Historical Sociology', in Julian Go and George Lawson (eds.), *Global Historical Sociology*, Cambridge: Cambridge University Press, 1–34.

Goldenberg, Maya J. (2016) 'Public Misunderstanding of Science? Reframing the Problem of Vaccine Hesitancy', *Perspectives on Science*, 24:5, 552–81.

Goldthwaite, Richard A. (2011) *The Economy of Renaissance Florence*, Baltimore: Johns Hopkins University Press.

Gong, Gerrit W. (1984) *The Standard of 'Civilisation' in International Society*, Oxford: Clarendon Press.

(2002) 'Standards of Civilization Today', in Mehdi Mozaffari (ed.), *Globalization and Civilization*, New York: Routledge, 77–96.

Goody, Jack (2010) *The Eurasian Miracle*, Cambridge: Polity.

Graeber, David and David Wengrow (2021) *The Dawn of Everything*, Penguin Books.

Gray, Colin S. (2012) *War, Peace and International Relations: An Introduction to Strategic History*, 2nd ed., London: Routledge.

Gray, Jack (2002) *Rebellions and Revolutions: China from the 1800s to 2000*, Oxford: Oxford University Press.

Greely, Henry T. (2021) *CRISPR People: The Science and Ethics of Editing Humans*, Cambridge, MA: MIT Press.

Green, Daniel (2013) 'Not 1648, but How About 1689? Early Modern Europe after the 1680s and a Model of the "Eighteenth Century European System"', paper presented at the European International Studies Association Conference, Warsaw, 18–21 September.

Greenhill, Kelly M. (2010) *Weapons of Mass Migration: Forced Displacement, Coercion, and Foreign Policy*, Ithaca, NY: Cornell University Press.

Guillaume, Xavier (2021) 'Historical Periods and the Act of Periodisation', in Benjamin de Carvalho, Julia Costa Lopez and Halvard Leira (eds.), *Routledge Handbook of Historical International Relations*, Abingdon, Routledge, 562–70.

Habermas, Jurgen (1990) *The Philosophical Discourse of Modernity: Twelve Lectures*, Cambridge: Polity.

Haldén, Peter (2020) *Family Power: Kinship, War and Political Orders in Eurasia, 550–2018*, Cambridge: Cambridge University Press.

Hall, Ian (2002) 'History, Christianity and Diplomacy: Sir Herbert Butterfield and International Relations', *Review of International Studies*, 28:4, 719–36.

(2006) 'Diplomacy, Anti-diplomacy and International Society', in Richard Little and John Williams (eds.), *The Anarchical Society in a Globalized World*, Basingstoke: Palgrave, 144–61.

(2017) 'The "Revolt against the West" Revisited', in Tim Dunne and Christian Reus-Smit (eds.), *The Globalisation of International Society*, Oxford: Oxford University Press, 345–61.

Hall, Stuart, David Held, Don Hubert and Kenneth Thompson (eds.) (1996) *Modernity: An Introduction to Modern Societies*, Oxford: Wiley-Blackwell.

Halliday, Fred (1999) *Revolution and World Politics*, Basingstoke: Macmillan.

Hamalainen, Pekka (2019) *Lakota America*, New Haven: Yale University Press.

Hansen, Valerie (2012) *The Silk Road*, New York: Oxford University Press.

Harari, Yuval Noah (2011) *Homo Sapiens: A Brief History of Humankind*, London: Penguin.

(2016) *Homo Deus: A Brief History of Tomorrow*, London: Penguin.

Harrison, Mark (2013) *Contagion: How Commerce Has Spread Disease*, New Haven: Yale University Press.

Headrick, Daniel R. (2010) *Power over Peoples: Technology, Environment, and Western Imperialism, 1400 to Present*, Princeton: Princeton University Press.

Heckscher, Eli F. (1955 [1935]) *Mercantilism*, vol. 1, London: Allen and Unwin.

Heeren, A. H. L. (1834) *A Manual of the History of the Political System of Europe and Its Colonies*, Oxford: Talboys.

Held, David, Anthony McGrew, David Goldblatt and Jonathan Perraton (1999) *Global Transformations*, Cambridge: Polity.

Helleiner, Eric (1994) 'From Bretton Woods to Global Finance: A World Turned Upside Down', in Richard Stubbs and Geoffrey Underhill (eds.), *Political Economy and the Changing Global Order*, Toronto: McClelland and Stewart, 163–75.

Herz, John H. (1969) 'The Territorial State Revisited', in James N. Rosenau (ed.), *International Politics and Foreign Policy*, New York: Free Press, 76–89.

Hill, Christopher L. (2008) *National History and the World of Nations: Capital, State, and the Rhetoric of History in Japan, France, and the United States*, Durham: Duke University Press.

Hirst, Paul and Grahame Thompson (1996) *Globalisation in Question*, Cambridge: Polity.

Hjorth, Ronnie (2011) 'Equality in the Theory of International Society: Kelsen, Rawls and the English School', *Review of International Studies*, 37:5 , 2585–602.

Hobsbawm, Eric (1962) *The Age of Revolution, 1789–1848*, London: Abacus.

(1975) *The Age of Capital, 1848–1875*, London: Abacus.

(1987) *The Age of Empire, 1875–1914*, London: Abacus.

(1990) *Nations and Nationalism since 1780*, Cambridge: Cambridge University Press.

Hobson, John (2004) *The Eastern Origins of Western Civilization*, Cambridge: Cambridge University Press.

Hobson, John M. (2012) *The Eurocentric Origins of International Relations*, Cambridge: Cambridge University Press.

(2021) *Multicultural Origins of the Global Economy beyond the Western-Centric Frontier*, Cambridge: Cambridge University Press.

Hodgson, Marshall G. S. (1993) *Rethinking World History: Essays on Europe, Islam and World History*, Cambridge: Cambridge University Press.

Holsti, Kalevi J. (1991) *Peace and War: Armed Conflicts and International Order 1648–1989*, Cambridge: Cambridge University Press.

(2004) *Taming the Sovereigns: Institutional Change in International Politics*, Cambridge: Cambridge University Press.

Horn, Stephanie Malia (2013) 'On the Origins of Making Italy: Massimo D'Azeglio and "Fatta l'Italia, bisogna fare gli Italiani"', *Italian Culture*, 31:1, 1–16.

Howard, Michael (1966) 'War as an Instrument of Policy', in Herbert Butterfield and Martin Wight (eds.), *Diplomatic Investigations*, London: Allen and Unwin.

(1976) *War in European History*, Oxford: Oxford University Press.

Hsu, Cho-yun (2012) *China: A New Cultural History*, New York: Columbia University Press.

Hurd, Ian (1999) 'Legitimacy and Authority in International Politics', *International Organization*, 53:2, 379–408.

Hurrell, Andrew (2002a) '"There Are No Rules" (George W. Bush): International Order after September 11', *International Relations*, 16:2, 185–204.

(2002b) 'Norms and Ethics in International Relations', in Walter Carlsnaes, Thomas Risse and Beth A. Simmons (eds.), *Handbook of International Relations*, London: Sage, 137–54.

(2002c) 'Foreword to the Third Edition: *The Anarchical Society* 25 Years On', in Hedley Bull, *The Anarchical Society*, Basingstoke: Palgrave, vii–xxiii.

(2007) *On Global Order: Power, Values and the Constitution of International Society*, Oxford: Oxford University Press.

(2020) 'Cultural Diversity within Global International Society', in Andrew Phillips and Christian Reus-Smit (eds.), *Culture and Order in World Politics*, Cambridge: Cambridge University Press, 115–37.

Ikenberry, John G. (2001) *After Victory: Institutions, Strategic Restraint and the Rebuilding of Order after Major Wars*, Princeton: Princeton University Press.

Jackson, Gregory and Richard Deeg (2006) 'How Many Varieties of Capitalism? Comparing the Comparative Institutional Analyses of Capitalist Diversity', Discussion Paper 06/2, Max Planck Institute for the Study of Societies, Köln.

Jackson, Robert H. (2000) *The Global Covenant: Human Conduct in a World of States*, Oxford: Oxford University Press.

Jackson, Robert H. and Carl G. Rosberg (1982) 'Why Africa's Weak States Persist: The Empirical and the Juridical in Statehood', *World Politics*, 35:1, 1–24.

James, Alan (1984) 'Sovereignty: Ground Rule or Gibberish?', *Review of International Studies*, 10:1, 1–18.

(1986) *Sovereign Statehood: The Basis of International Society*, London: Allen and Unwin.

(1999) 'The Practice of Sovereign Statehood in Contemporary International Society', *Political Studies*, 47:3, 457–73.

James, C.L.R. (2001 [1938]) *The Black Jacobins: Toussaint L'Ouverture and the San Domingo Revolution*, London: Penguin.

Jansen, Marius B. (2000) *The Making of Modern Japan*, Cambridge, MA: Belknap Press.

Jones, Catherine (2014) 'Constructing Great Powers: China's Status in a Socially Constructed Plurality', *International Politics*, 51:5, 597–618.

Jones, Charles A. (2006) 'War in the Twenty-First Century: An Institution in Crisis', in Richard Little and John Williams (eds.), *The Anarchical Society in a Globalized World*, Basingstoke: Palgrave, 162–88.

Jones, E. L. (1987) *The European Miracle: Environment, Economies, and Geopolitics in the History of Europe and Asia*, 2nd ed., Cambridge: Cambridge University Press.

Jones, Geoffrey (2005) *Multinationals and Global Capitalism from the Nineteenth to the Twenty-First Century*, Oxford: Oxford University Press.

Jones, Lee and Shahar Hameiri (2021) *Fractured China: How State Transformation Is Shaping China's Rise*, Cambridge: Cambridge University Press.

Jones, Roy E. (1981) 'The English School of International Relations: A Case for Closure', *Review of International Studies*, 7:1, 1–13.

Jones, Terry L. and Mark W. Allen (2016) 'The Prehistory of Violence and Warfare among Hunter-Gatherers', in Mark W. Allen and Terry L. Jones (eds.), *Violence and Warfare among Hunter-Gatherers*, London: Routledge, 351–71.

Kaldor, Mary (1982) *The Baroque Arsenal*, London: Andre Deutsch.
    (2001) *New and Old Wars: Organized Violence in a Global Era*, Cambridge: Polity.

Karl, Rebecca (2002) *Staging the World: Chinese Nationalism at the Turn of the Twentieth Century*, Durham: Duke University Press.

Karns, Margaret P. and Karen A. Mingst (2010) *International Organizations: The Politics and Processes of Global Governance*, Boulder: Lynne Rienner.

Katzenstein, Peter J. (2012) 'Many Wests and Polymorphic Globalism', in Peter J. Katzenstein (ed.), *Anglo-America and Its Discontents: Civilizational Identities beyond West and East*, London and New York: Routledge, 207–47.

Kaufman, Stuart, Richard Little and William Wohlforth (eds.) (2007) *The Balance of Power in World History*, Basingstoke: Palgrave Macmillan.

Kaufmann, Chaim D. and Robert A. Pape (1999) 'Explaining Costly International Moral Action: Britain's Sixty-Year Campaign against the Atlantic Slave Trade', *International Organisation*, 53:4, 631–68.

Keal, Paul (2003) *European Conquest and the Rights of Indigenous Peoples: The Moral Backwardness of International Society*, Cambridge: Cambridge University Press.

Keene, Edward (2002) *Beyond the Anarchical Society*, Cambridge: Cambridge University Press.
    (2013) 'The Naming of Powers', *Cooperation and Conflict*, 48:2, 268–82.

Keister, Lisa A. and Darby E. Southgate (2021) *Inequality: A Contemporary Approach to Race, Class, and Gender*, 2nd ed., Cambridge: Cambridge University Press.

Kennedy, Hugh (2016) *The Caliphate*, London: Pelican.

Kennedy, Paul (1989) *The Rise and Fall of the Great Powers*, London: Fontana.

Keohane, Robert O. (1984) *After Hegemony: Cooperation and Discord in the World Political Economy*, Princeton: Princeton University Press.
    (1995) 'Hobbes' Dilemma and Institutional Change in World Politics: Sovereignty in International Society', in Hans-Henrik Holm and Georg Sørensen (eds.), *Whose World Order*, Boulder: Westview Press, 165–86.

Keohane, Robert O. and Joseph Nye (2000) 'Globalisation: What's New? What's Not? (And So What)', *Foreign Policy*, 118, 104–19.

Kerr, P.H. (1916) 'Political Relations between Advanced and Backward Peoples', in A. F. Grant, Arthur Greenwood, J. D. I. Hughes, P. H. Kerr and F. F. Urquhart (eds.), *An Introduction to the Study of International Relations*, London: Macmillan, 141–82.

Khadduri, Majid (1966) *The Islamic Law of Nations: Shaybānī's Siyar*, Baltimore: The Johns Hopkins Press.

Khaldun, Ibn (1969 [1370]) *Muqaddimah: An Introduction to History*, translated by Franz Rosenthal, Princeton: Princeton University Press/Ballinger.

Kim, Tung Dao and Peter A. G. van Bergeijk (2022) 'Winds from the East: Ancient Asian Views on International Trade', The Hague: International Institute of Social Studies, Working Paper No. 705.

Kindleberger, Charles P. (1973) *The World in Depression 1919–39*, London: Allen Lane.

(1984) *A Financial History of Western Europe*, London: Allen & Unwin.

Kissinger, Henry (2011) *On China*, London: Allen Lane.

Klotz, Audie (2017) 'Racial Inequality', in Tim Dunne and Christian Reus-Smit (eds.), *The Globalisation of International Society*, Oxford: Oxford University Press, 362–79.

Knudsen, Tonny Brems and Cornelia Navari (eds.) (2019) *International Organization in the Anarchical Society: The Institutional Structure of World Order*, Cham: Palgrave Macmillan.

Knutsen, Torbjørn (2016) *A History of International Relations Theory*, 3rd ed., Manchester: Manchester University Press.

Koskenniemi, Martti (2001) *The Gentle Civilizer of Nations: The Rise and Fall of International Law, 1870–1960*, Cambridge: Cambridge University Press.

Koyama, Hitomi and Barry Buzan (2019) 'Rethinking Japan in Mainstream International Relations', *International Relations of the Asia-Pacific*, 19:2, 185–212.

Krasner, Stephen (1976) 'State Power and the Structure of International Trade', *World Politics*, 28:3, 317–43.

(1999) *Sovereignty: Organized Hypocrisy*, Princeton: Princeton University Press.

Kratochwil, Friedrich (1989) *Rules, Norms and Decisions: On the Conditions of Practical and Legal Reasoning in International Relations and Domestic Affairs*, Cambridge: Cambridge University Press.

Kroeber, Arthur R. (2016) *China's Economy: What Everyone Needs to Know*, Oxford: Oxford University Press.

Kupchan, Charles A. (2012) *No One's World: The West, the Rising Rest, and the Coming Global Turn*, New York: Oxford University Press.

Kurzweil, Ray (2005) *The Singularity Is Near: When Humans Transcend Biology*, London: Duckworth Overlook.

Land, Nick (2013) The Dark Enlightenment. www.thedarkenlightenment.com/the-dark-enlightenment-by-nick-land (accessed 10 June 2019).

Landes, David S. (1969) *The Unbound Prometheus*, London: Cambridge University Press.

Lasmar, Jorge (2015) 'Managing Great Powers in the Post-Cold War World: Old Rules New Game? The Case of the Global War on Terror', *Cambridge Review of International Affairs*, 28:3, 396–423.

Lasswell, Harold (1935) *World Politics and Personal Insecurity*, New York: Free Press.

Lawson, George (2019) *Anatomies of Revolution*, Cambridge: Cambridge University Press.

LeBlanc, Steven A. (2016) 'Forager Warfare and Our Evolutionary Past', in Mark W. Allen and Terry L. Jones (eds.), *Violence and Warfare among Hunter-Gatherers*, London: Routledge, 26–45.

Lee, Kai-fu (2018) *AI Superpowers: China, Silicon Valley, and the New World Order*, Boston: Houghton-Harcourt.

Lenin, V. I. (1975 [1916]) *Imperialism: The Highest Stage of Capitalism*, Peking: Foreign Languages Press.

Lerner, Gerda (1986) *The Creation of Patriarchy*, New York: Oxford University Press.

Lieven, Dominic (2022) *In the Shadow of the Gods: The Emperor in World History*, n.l.: Penguin.

Lindblom, Charles E. (2001) *The Market System: What It Is, How It Works, and What to Make of It*, New Haven: Yale University Press.

Linklater, Andrew (2001) 'Marxism', in Scott Burchill, Richard Devetak, Andrew Linklater, Matthew Paterson, Christian Reus-Smit and Jacqui True (eds.), *Theories of International Relations*, 2nd ed., Basingstoke: Palgrave, 129–54.

(2016) *Violence and Civilization in the Western States-Systems*, Cambridge: Cambridge University Press.

Little, Richard (1995) 'Neorealism and the English School: A Methodological, Ontological and Theoretical Reassessment', *European Journal of International Relations*, 1:1, 9–34.

(2006) 'The Balance of Power and Great Power Management', in Richard Little and John Williams (eds.), *The Anarchical Society in a Globalized World*, Basingstoke, Palgrave, 97–120.

(2007) *The Balance of Power in International Relations: Metaphors, Myths and Models*, Cambridge: Cambridge University Press.

(2008) 'The Expansion of the International Society in Heron's Account of the European States System', SPAIS Working Paper No 07-08, University of Bristol.

Liu, Xinru (2010) *The Silk Road in World History*, New York: Oxford university Press.

Lorimer, James (1884) *The Institutes of the Law of Nations: A Treatise on the Jural Relations of Separate Political Communities*, Edinburgh and London: William Blackwood and Sons.

Lovell, Julia (2011) *The Opium War: Drugs, Dreams and the Making of China*, London: Picador.

Lustick, Ian S. (1997) 'The Absence of Middle Eastern Great Powers: Political "Backwardness" in Historical Perspective', *International Organisation*, 5:4, 653–83.

Luttwak, Edward N. (2012) *The Rise of China vs. the Logic of Strategy*, Cambridge, MA: The Belknap Press of Harvard University Press.

Mackinder, Halford (1996 [1904]), 'The Geographical Pivot of History', in Halford Mackinder (ed.), *Democratic Ideals and Reality*, Washington, DC: National Defence University, 175–94.

Mann, Michael (1986a) *The Sources of Social Power*, vol. 1, Cambridge: Cambridge University Press.

(1986b) *The Sources of Social Power*, vol. 2, Cambridge: Cambridge University Press.

Manning, C. A. W. (1962) *The Nature of International Society*, London: LSE; Macmillan.

Manning, Patrick (2020) *A History of Humanity: The Evolution of the Human System*, Cambridge: Cambridge University Press.

March, James G. and Johan P. Olsen (1998) 'The Institutional Dynamics of International Political Orders', *International Organization*, 52:4, 943–69.

Marx, Karl (1852) *The Eighteenth Brumaire of Louis Bonaparte*, www.marxists.org/archive/marx/works/1852/18th-brumaire/ch01.htm (accessed 22 April 2022).

Marx, Karl and Frederick Engels (1969 [1848]) *Manifesto of the Communist Party*, Marx/Engels Selected Works, vol. 1, Moscow: Progress Publishers, 98–137, www.marxists.org/archive/marx/works/download/pdf/Manifesto.pdf (accessed 24 May 2017).

Mayall, James (1984) 'Reflections on the "New" Economic Nationalism', *Review of International Studies*, 10:4, 313–21.

(1990) *Nationalism and International Society*, Cambridge: Cambridge University Press.

(2000a) *World Politics: Progress and Its Limits*, Cambridge: Polity.

(2000b) 'Democracy and International Society', *International Affairs*, 76:1, 61–76.

Maza, Sarah (2017) *Thinking about History*, Chicago, University of Chicago Press.

Mazower, Mark (2012) *Governing the World*, London: Allen Lane.

McMahon, Cian T. (2021) *The Coffin Ship: Life and Death at Sea during the Great Irish Famine*, New York: New York University Press.

McNally, Christopher (2013) 'How Emerging Forms of Capitalism Are Changing the Global Economic Order', East-West Center: Asia-Pacific Issues, No. 107.

McNeill, William (1963) *The Rise of the West: A History of the Human Community*, Chicago: University of Chicago Press.

(1976) *Plagues and Peoples*, London: Penguin.

McNeill, William H. (1982) *The Pursuit of Power*, Chicago: University of Chicago Press.

(1991) *The Rise of the West: A History of the Human Community*, 2nd ed., Chicago: University of Chicago Press.

Meadows, D. H. and D. L. Meadows (1972) *The Limits to Growth*, New York: New American Library.

Mearsheimer, John J. (2019) 'Bound to Fail: The Rise and Fall of the Liberal International Order', *International Security*, 43:4, 7–50.

Meier, Samuel A. (2000) 'Diplomacy and International Marriages', in Raymond Cohen and Raymond Westbrook (eds.), *Amarna Diplomacy: The Beginnings of International Relations*, Baltimore: Johns Hopkins University Press, 165–73.

Meijer, Fik and Onno van Nijf (1992) *Trade, Transport and Society in the Ancient World*, London: Routledge.

Meltzer, Milton (1993) *Slavery: A World History*, Boston: Da Capo Press.

Micklethwait, John and Adrian Wooldridge (2003) *The Company: A Short History of a Revolutionary Idea*, London: Weidenfeld and Nicolson.

Milanovic, Branko (2019) *Capitalism Alone: The Future of the System that Rules the World*, Cambridge, MA: Belknap Press.

Mills, David (2013) *Our Uncertain Future: When Digital Evolution, Global Warming and Automation Converge*, Pacific Beach Publishing.

Mishra, Pankaj (2020) *Age of Anger: A History of the Present*, New Delhi: Juggernaut Books.

Mithen, Stephan (2003) *After the Ice: A Global Human History*, London: Weidenfeld and Nicolson.

Moll-Murata, Christine (2008) 'Chinese Guilds from the Seventeenth to the Twentieth Centuries: An Overview', *International Review of Social History*, Supplement, 213–47.

Morris, Ian (2010) *Why the West Rules for Now*, London: Profile.

Morris, Justin (2005) 'Normative Innovation and the Great Powers', in Alex J. Bellamy (ed.), *International Society and Its Critics*, Oxford: Oxford University Press, 265–82.

Mulk, Nizam al (2002) *The Book of Government, or Rules for Kings*, Abingdon: Routledge.

Murphy, R. Taggart (2014) *Japan and the Shackles of the Past*, Oxford: Oxford University Press.

Nau, Henry R. (2001) 'Why "The Rise and Fall of the Great Powers" Was Wrong', *Review of International Studies*, 27:4, 579–92.

Navari, Cornelia (2000) *Internationalism and the State in the Twentieth Century*, London: Routledge.

(2007) 'States and State Systems: Democratic, Westphalian or Both?', *Review of International Studies*, 33:4, 577–95.

(2016) 'Primary and Secondary Institutions: Quo Vadit?', *Cooperation and Conflict*, 51:1, 121–7.

Neff, Stephen C. (2010) 'A Short History of International Law', in Malcolm D. Evans (ed.), *International Law*, 2nd ed., Oxford: Oxford University Press, 3–31.

Neumann, Iver B. (1996) *Russia and the Idea of Europe: A Study in Identity and International Relations*, London: Routledge.

(2001) 'The English School and the Practices of World Society', *Review of International Studies*, 27:3, 503–7.

(2003) 'The English School on Diplomacy: Scholarly Promise Unfulfilled', *International Relations*, 17:3, 341–69.

(2011) 'Entry into International Society Reconceptualised: The Case of Russia', *Review of International Studies*, 37:2, 463–84.

(2017) 'Introduction', in Filip Ejdus (ed.), *Memories of Empire and Entry into International Society: Views from the European Periphery*, Abingdon: Routledge, 1–15.

(2020) *Diplomatic Tenses: A Social Evolutionary Perspective on Diplomacy*, Manchester: Manchester University Press.

Neumann, Iver B. and Einar Wigen (2018) *The Steppe Tradition in International Relations: Russians, Turks and European State Building 4000 BCE–2017 CE*, Cambridge: Cambridge University Press.

Neumann, Iver B., Kristin Haugevik and John Harold Sande Lie (2018) 'Introduction and Framework', in Kristin Haugevik and Iver B. Neumann (eds.), *Kinship in International Relations*, London: Routledge, 1–20.

Nightingale Carl H. (2022) *Earthopolis: A Biography of Our Urban Planet*, Cambridge: Cambridge University Press.

Nye, Joseph S. (1986) 'Nuclear Winter and Policy Choices', *Survival*, 38:2, 119–27

O'Brian, Robert and Marc Williams (2016) *Global Political Economy: Evolution and Dynamics*, 5th ed., London: Palgrave.

Odgaard, Liselotte (2012) *China and Coexistence: Beijing's National Security Strategy for the Twenty-First Century*, Baltimore: Johns Hopkins University Press.

OECD (2015) *The Metropolitan Century: Understanding Urbanisation and Its Consequences*, Paris: OECD Publishing.

Ogilvie, Sheilagh (2011) *Institutions and European Trade: Merchant Guilds 1000–1800*, Cambridge: Cambridge University Press.

Olson, Mancur (1965) *The Logic of Collective Action: Public Goods and the Theory of Groups*, Boston, MA: Harvard University Press.

Onuf, Nicholas (2002) 'Institutions, Intentions and International Relations', *Review of International Studies*, 28:2, 211–28.

Onuma, Yasuaki (2000) 'When Was the Law of International Society Born? An Inquiry of the History of International Law from an Intercivilisational Perspective', *Journal of the History of International Law*, 2, 1–66.

Ord, Toby (2020) *The Precipice: Existential Risk and the Future of Humanity*, London: Bloomsbury.

Oreskes, Naomi and Erik M. Conway (2014) *The Collapse of Western Civilisation: A View from the Future*, New York: Columbia University Press.

Osterhammel, Jürgen (2014) *The Transformation of the World: A Global History of the Nineteenth Century*, translated by Patrick Camiller, Princeton: Princeton University Press.

Outram, Alan K. (2014) 'Animal Domestications', in Vicki Cummings, Peter Jordan and Marek Zvelebil (eds.), *The Oxford Handbook of the Archaeology and Anthropology of Hunter-Gatherers*, Oxford: Oxford University Press, locs. 19452–798.

Özkirimli, Umut (2010) *Theories of Nationalism*, New York: St Martin's.

Paine, Lincoln (2014) *The Sea and Civilisation: A Maritime History of the World*, London: Atlantic Books.

Paine, S.C.M. (2003) *The Sino-Japanese War of 1894–1895*, New York: Cambridge University Press.

Palliser, Michael (1984) 'Diplomacy Today', in Hedley Bull and Adam Watson (eds.), *The Expansion of International Society*, Oxford: Oxford University Press, 371–85.

Parzinger, Hermann (2020) 'Prehistory and Early History', in Hans-Joachim Gehrke (ed.), *Making Civilizations: The World before 600*, Cambridge, MA: Harvard University Press, 39–304.

Patterson, Orlanda (2018) *Slavery and Social Death: A Comparative Study*, Cambridge, MA: Harvard University Press.

Pauley, Louis W. (2017) '*The Anarchical Society* and a Global Political Economy', in Hidemi Suganami, Madeline Carr and Adam Humphreys (eds.), *The Anarchical Society at 40: Contemporary Challenges and Prospects*, Oxford: Oxford University Press, 179–97.

Pearson, Michael (2003) *The Indian Ocean*, London: Routledge.

Pearton, Maurice (1982) *The Knowledgeable State: Diplomacy, War and Technology since 1830*, London: Burnett Books.

Pejcinovic, Lacy (2013) *War in International Society*, Abingdon: Routledge.

Peterson, V. Spike (1992) 'Security and Sovereign States: What Is at Stake in Taking Feminism Seriously', in V. Spike Peterson (ed.), *Gendered States: Feminist (Re)Visions of International Relations Theory*, Boulder: Lynne Rienner, 31–64.

Phillips, Andrew (2011) *War, Religion and Empire: The Transformation of International Orders*, Cambridge: Cambridge University Press.

Phillips, Andrew and J. C. Sharman (2015) *International Order in Diversity: War, Trade and Rule in the Indian Ocean*, Cambridge: Cambridge University Press.
  (2020) *Outsourcing Empire: How Company-States Made the Modern World*, Princeton: Princeton University Press.

Pieke, Frank N. (2016) *Knowing China: A Twenty-First Century Guide*, Cambridge: Cambridge University Press.

Piketty, Thomas (2014) *Capital in the Twenty-First Century*, Cambridge, MA: Belknap Press.

Pines, Yuri (2012) *The Everlasting Empire: The Political Culture of Ancient China and Its Imperial Legacy*, Princeton: Princeton University Press.

Piscatori, James (1986) *Islam in a World of Nation-States*, Cambridge: Cambridge University Press.

Pohl, Frederik and C.M. Kornbluth (1960) *The Space Merchants*, London: Brown Watson.

Pomeranz, Kenneth (2000) *The Great Divergence*, Princeton: Princeton University Press.

Preston, Paul (2000) 'The Great Civil War: European Politics, 1914–1945', in T.C. W. Blanning (ed.), *The Oxford History of Modern Europe*, Oxford, Oxford University Press, 153–85.

Prestowitz, Clyde P. (2003) *Rogue Nation: American Unilateralism and the Failure of Good Intentions*, New York: Basic Books.

Prys-Hansen, Miriam (2022) 'Politics of Responsibility: India in Global Climate Governance', in Robert Falkner and Barry Buzan (eds.), *Great Power Responsibility and Global Environmental Politics*, Oxford: Oxford University Press.

Qin, Yaqing (2011) 'Rule, Rules, and Relations: Towards a Synthetic Approach to Governance', *Chinese Journal of International Politics*, 4:2, 117–45.

(2018) *A Relational Theory of World Politics*, Cambridge: Cambridge University Press.

Radner, Karen (2020) 'Early Civilizations of the Ancient Near East: Egypt and Western Asia', in Hans-Joachim Gehrke (ed.), *Making Civilizations: The World before 600*, Cambridge, MA: Harvard University Press, 307–476.

Rai, Shirin M. (2008) *The Gender Politics of Development: Essays in Hope and Despair*, London: Zed Books.

Ralph, Jason (2005) 'International Society, the International Criminal Court and American Foreign Policy', *Review of International Studies*, 31:1, 27–44.

(2010) 'War as an Institution of International Hierarchy: Carl Schmitt's Theory of the Partisan and Contemporary US Practice', *Millennium*, 39:2, 279–98.

Rees, Martin (2003) *Our Final Century*, London: Heinemann.

Ren, Xiao (2016) 'Idea Change Matters: China's Practices and the East Asian Peace', *Asian Perspectives*, 40, 329–56.

Reus-Smit, Christian (1996) 'The Normative Structure of International Society', in Fen Osler Hampson and Judith Reppy (eds.), *Earthly Goods: Environmental Change and Social Justice*, Ithaca: Cornell University Press, 96–121.

(1997) 'The Constitutional Structure of International Society and the Nature of Fundamental Institutions', *International Organization*, 51:4, 555–89.

(1999) *The Moral Purpose of the State*, Princeton: Princeton University Press.

(2014) 'Power, Legitimacy, and Order', *The Chinese Journal of International Politics*, 7:3, 341–59.

Reus-Smit, Christian and Tim Dunne (2017) 'The Globalization of International Society', in Tim Dunne and Christian Reus-Smit (eds.), *The Globalisation of International Society*, Oxford: Oxford University Press, 18–40.

Rice, Candace (2016) 'Mercantile Specialization and Trading Communities: Economic Strategies in Roman Maritime Trade', in Andrew Wilson and Miko Flohr (eds.), *Urban Craftsmen and Traders in the Roman World*, New York: Oxford University Press, 97–114.

Ripsman, Norrin M. and T. V. Paul (2010) *Globalisation and the National Security State*, New York: Oxford University Press.

Risso, Patricia (1995) *Merchants and Faith: Muslim Commerce and Culture in the Indian Ocean*, New York: Routledge.

Robinson, Kim Stanley (2020) *The Ministry for the Future*, London: Little, Brown Book Group.

Rosenau, James N. (1992) 'Governance, Order and Change in World Politics', in James N. Rosenau and Ernst-Otto Czempiel (eds.), *Governance without Government: Order and Change in World Politics*, Cambridge: Cambridge University Press.

Rosenberg, Justin (1994) *The Empire of Civil Society*, London: Verso.

(2010) 'Problems in the Theory of Uneven and Combined Development Part II: Unevenness and Multiplicity', *Cambridge Review of International Affairs*, 2:1, 165–89.

(2013a) 'Kenneth Waltz and Leon Trotsky: Anarchy in the Mirror of Uneven and Combined Development', *International Politics*, 50:2, 183–230.

(2013b) 'The "Philosophical Premises" of Uneven and Combined Development', *Review of International Studies*, 39:3. 569–97.

(2016) 'International Relations in the Prison of Political Science', *International Relations*, 30:2, 127–53.

(2020) 'Uneven and Combined Development: A Defense of the General Abstraction', *Cambridge Review of International Affairs*, online first.

Roumate, Fatima (ed.) (2021) *Artificial Intelligence and Digital Diplomacy: Challenges and Opportunities*, Cham: Springer.

Ruggie, John G. (1982) 'International Regimes, Transactions, and Change: Embedded Liberalism in the Postwar Economic Order', *International Organisation*, 36:2, 379–415.

Ruggie, John Gerrard (1983) 'Continuity and Transformation in the World Polity: Towards a Neo-Realist Synthesis', *World Politics*, 35:2, 261–85.

(1993) 'Territoriality and Beyond: Problematising Modernity in International Relations', *International Organisation*, 47:1, 139–74.

Sagan, Carl (1983/4) 'Nuclear War and Climatic Catastrophe', *Foreign Affairs*, 62:2, 257–92.

Sassen, Saskia (1996) *Losing Control? Sovereignty in an Age of Globalisation*, New York: Columbia University Press.

Sassoon, Donald (2019) *The Anxious Triumph: A Global History of Capitalism 1860–1914*, London: Penguin.

Scheidel, Walter (2017) *The Great Leveller: Violence and the History of Inequality from the Stone Age to the Twenty-First Century*, Princeton: Princeton University Press.

Schell, Jonathan (1982) *The Fate of the Earth*, New York: Alfred A. Knopf.

Schell, Orville and John Delury (2013) *Wealth and Power: China's Long March to the Twenty-First Century*, London: Little, Brown.

Schmidt, Brian C. (1998) *The Political Discourse of Anarchy: A Disciplinary History of International Relations*, Albany: State University of New York Press.

Scholte, Jan Aart (2000) *Globalisation: A Critical Introduction*, Basingstoke: Palgrave.

Scholz, Piotr O. (2001) *Eunuchs and Castrati: A Cultural History*, Princeton: Markus Wiener.

Schouenborg, Laust (2011) 'A New Institutionalism? The English School as International Sociological Theory', *International Relations*, 25:1, 26–44.

(2017) *International Institutions in World History: Divorcing International Relations Theory from Stage and State Models*, London: Routledge.

Schwarzenberger, Georg (1951) *Power Politics: A Study of International Society*, London: Stevens and Sons.

Scott, James C. (2017) *Against the Grain: A Deep History of the Earliest States*, New Haven: Yale University Press.

Segal, Gerald (1999) 'Does China Matter?', *Foreign Affairs*, 78:5, 24–36.

Senghaas, Dieter (1974) 'Towards an Analysis of Threat Policy in International Relations', in Klaus von Beyme (ed.), *German Political Studies*, London: Sage, 59–103.

Shambaugh, David (2013) *China Goes Global: The Partial Power*, Oxford: Oxford University Press.

Sharman, Jason (2019) *Empires of the Weak: The Real Story of European Expansion and the Creation of the New World Order*, Princeton: Princeton University Press.

Sharp, Paul (2003) 'Herbert Butterfield, the English School and the Civilizing Virtues of Diplomacy', *International Affairs*, 79:4, 855–78.

Shaw, Martin (1992) 'Global Society and Global Responsibility: The Theoretical, Historical and Political Limits of "International Society"', in *Millennium*, 21:3, 421–34; Also in: Rick Fawn and Jeremy Larkin (eds.) (1996), *International Society after the Cold War*, London, Macmillan.

Shimazu, Naoko (1998) *Japan, Race and Equality: The Racial Equality Proposal of 1919*, London: Routledge.

Simpson, Gerry (2004) *Great Powers and Outlaw States: Unequal Sovereigns in the International Legal Order*, Cambridge: Cambridge University Press.

Singer, Charles, E. J. Holmyard, A. R. Hall and Trevor I Williams (1954) *A History of Technology, Vol. I, From Early Times to the Fall of Ancient Empires*, Oxford, Clarendon Press.

Skidelsky, Robert (2009) *Keynes: The Return of the Master*, London: Allen Lane.
(2018) *Money and Government: A Challenge to Mainstream Economics*, London: Allen Lane.

Smith, Anthony D. (1991) *National Identity*, London: Penguin.
(1998) *Nationalism and Modernism*, London: Routledge.

Smith, Derek D. (2006) *Deterring America: Rogue States and the Proliferation of Weapons of Mass Destruction*, Cambridge: Cambridge University Press.

Sørensen, Georg (1999) 'Sovereignty: Change and Continuity in a Fundamental Institution', *Political Studies*, 47:3, 590–604.

Spandler, Kilian (2015) 'The Political International Society: Change in Primary and Secondary Institutions', *Review of International Studies*, 41:3, 601–22.

Spruyt, Hendrik (2020) *The World Imagined: Collective Beliefs and Political Order in the Sinocentric, Islamic and Southeast Asian International Societies*, Cambridge: Cambridge University Press.

Stavrianos, L. S. (1990) *Lifelines from Our Past*, London: I.B. Tauris.

Steffen, Will, Katherine Richardson, Johan Rockström, et al. (2020) 'The Emergence and Evolution of Earth System Science', *Nature Reviews Earth & Environment*, 1, 54–63.

Stevens, Tina and Stuart Newman (2019) *Biotech Juggernaut: Hope, Hype, and Hidden Agendas of Entrepreneurial BioScience*, New York: Routledge.

Stopford, John M., Susan Strange with John S. Henley (1991) *Rival States, Rival Firms: Competition for World Market Shares*, Cambridge: Cambridge University Press.

Strange, Susan (1988) *States and Markets*, London: Pinter.

Suganami, Hidemi (1989) *The Domestic Analogy and World Order Proposals*, Cambridge: Cambridge University Press.

Sun, Yat-sen (2017 [1922]) *The International Development of China*, n.l.: Andesite Press.

Suzuki, Shogo (2005) 'Japan's Socialisation into Janus-Faced European International Society', *European Journal of International Relations*, 11:1, 137–64.

(2008) 'Seeking "Legitimate" Great Power Status in Post-Cold War International Society: China's and Japan's Participation in UNPKO', *International Relations*, 22:1, 45–63.

(2009) *Civilisation and Empire: China and Japan's Encounter with European International Society*, London: Routledge.

Swope, Kenneth M. (2009) *A Dragon's Head and a Serpent's Tail: Ming China and the First Great East Asian War*, Norman: University of Oklahoma Press.

Sykes, Rebecca Wragg (2020) *Kindred: Neanderthal Life, Love, Death and Art*, London: Bloomsbury Sigma.

Sylvan, David J. (1981) 'The Newest Mercantilism', *International Organisation*, 35:2, 375–93.

Tagore, Rabindranath (1918) *Nationalism*, London: Macmillan.

Tainter, Joseph A. (1988) *The Collapse of Complex Societies*, Cambridge: Cambridge University Press.

Tang, Shiping (2013) *The Social Evolution of International Politics*, Oxford: Oxford University Press.

Temin, Peter and David Vines (2013) *The Leaderless Economy: Why the World Economic System Fell Apart and How to Fix It*, Princeton: Princeton University Press.

Thaplyal, Kiran Kumer (2001) 'Guilds in Ancient India (Antiquity and Various Stages in the Development of Guilds up to AD 300)', in G.C. Pande (ed.), *Life, Thoughts and Culture in India*, Delhi: Munshiram Manoharlal Publishers Pvt. Ltd, 995–1006.

Tilly, Charles (1990) *Coercion, Capital and European States, AD 990–1992*, Oxford: Blackwell.

Toler, Pamela D. (2019) *Women Warriors: An Unexpected History*, Boston: Beacon Press.

Tönnies, Ferdinand (1887) *Gemeinschaft und Gesellschaft*, Leipzig: Fues's Verlag.

Totman, Conrad (2005) *A History of Japan*, 2nd ed., Malden, MA: Blackwell.

Towns, Ann (2009) 'The Status of Women as a "Standard of Civilisation"', *European Journal of International Relations*, 15:4, 681–706.

(2010) *Women and States*, Cambridge: Cambridge University Press.

(2017) 'Gender, Power, and International Society', in Tim Dunne and Christian Reus-Smit (eds.), *The Globalisation of International Society*, Oxford: Oxford University Press, 380–98.

(2021) 'Gender in Historical International Relations', in Benjamin de Carvalho, Julia Costa Lopez and Halvard Leira (eds.), *Routledge Handbook of Historical International Relations*, Abingdon, Routledge, 153–61.

Toynbee, Arnold (1972) *A Study of History*, Oxford University Press and Thames and Hudson Ltd.

United Nations Department of Economic and Social Affairs (2019) 'World Population Prospects 2019: Data Booklet', 2–3:6, 10. https://population.un.org/wpp/Publications/Files/WPP2019_DataBooklet.pdf (accessed 11 July 2021).

Vamplew, Wray (2021) *Games People Played: A Global History of Sports*, Chicago: Chicago University Press.

Van Creveld, Martin (1991) *Technology and War from 2000 BC to the Present*, London: Brassey's.

Vernon, Raymond (1971) *Sovereignty at Bay: The Multinational Spread of U.S. Enterprises*, New York: Basic Books.

Vincent, R. John (1986) *Human Rights and International Relations: Issues and Responses*, Cambridge: Cambridge University Press.

Vitalis, Robert (2005) 'Birth of a Discipline', in David Long and Brian Schmidt (eds.), *Imperialism and Internationalism in the Discipline of International Relations*, Albany: SUNY Press, 159–81.

Wæver, Ole (1992) 'International Society – Theoretical Promises Unfulfilled?', *Cooperation and Conflict*, 27:1, 97–128.

Wæver, Ole, Barry Buzan, Morten Kelstrup, et al., *Identity, Migration and the New Security Agenda in Europe*, London: Pinter, 1993.

Wagar, Warren W. (1964) *H.G. Wells: Journalism and Prophecy, 1893–1946*, Boston: Houghton Mifflin.

Wagner, Peter (2012) *Modernity: Understanding the Present*, Cambridge: Polity.

Walker, R.J.B. (1990) 'Security, Sovereignty, and the Challenge of World Politics', *Alternatives*, 15:1, 3–27.

Wallace, Michael and J. David Singer (1970) 'Intergovernmental Organization in the Global System, 1816–1964: A Quantitative Description', *International Organization*, 24:2, 239–87.

Wallerstein, Immanuel (1979) *The Capitalist World Economy*, Cambridge: Cambridge University Press.

(1984) *The Politics of the World Economy*, Cambridge: Cambridge University Press.

(2004) *World Systems Analysis*, Durham NC: Duke University Press.

Waltz, Kenneth N. (1979) *Theory of International Politics*, Reading, MA: Addison-Wesley.

Walvin, James (2007) *A Short History of Slavery*, London: Penguin.

Wang, Gungwu (2019) *China Reconnects: Joining a Deep-Rooted Past to a New World Order*, Singapore: World Scientific Publishing.

Wang, Jisi (2011) 'China's Search for a Grand Strategy', *Foreign Affairs*, 90:2, 68–79.

Watson, Adam (1982) *Diplomacy: The Dialogue between States*, London: Routledge.

(1992) *The Evolution of International Society*, London: Routledge.

Watson, Matthew (2018) *The Market*, Newcastle: Agenda Publishing.

Weber, Eugen (1976) *Peasants into Frenchmen: The Modernization of Rural France*, Stanford: Stanford University Press.

Weiss, Thomas G. (2013) *Global Governance: Why? What? Whither?* Cambridge: Polity.

Wendt, Alexander (1999) *Social Theory of International Politics*, Cambridge: Cambridge University Press.

(2004) 'The Inevitability of a World State', *European Journal of International Relations*, 4:9, 539–90.

Westad, Arne (2007) *The Global Cold War*, Cambridge: Cambridge University Press.

Westbrook, Raymond (2000) 'International Law in the Amarna Age', in Raymond Cohen and Raymond Westbrook (eds.), *Amarna Diplomacy: The Beginnings of International Relations*, Baltimore: Johns Hopkins University Press, 28–41.

Wheaton, Henry (1866) *Elements of International Law*, 8th ed., London: Sampson Low, Son & Co.

Wheeler, Nicholas J. (1992) 'Pluralist and Solidarist Conceptions of International Society: Bull and Vincent on Humanitarian Intervention', *Millennium*, 21.3, 463–89.

Whitehouse, David (2012) *Glass: A Short History*, London: British Museum Press.

Wight, Martin (1966) 'Western Values in International Relations', in Herbert Butterfield and Martin Wight (eds.), *Diplomatic Investigations*, London: Allen and Unwin, 17–34.

(1977) *Systems of States*, edited by Hedley Bull, Leicester: Leicester University Press.

(1979) *Power Politics*, 2nd ed., edited by Hedley Bull and Carsten Holbraad, London: Penguin.

(1991) *International Theory: The Three Traditions*, edited by Brian Porter and Gabriele Wight, Leicester, Leicester University Press/Royal Institute of International Affairs.

Williams, Eric (1944) *Capitalism and Slavery*, Chapel Hill: University of North Carolina Press.

Williams, John (2002) 'Territorial Borders, Toleration and the English School', *Review of International Studies*, 28:4, 737–58.

(2005) 'Pluralism, Solidarism and the Emergence of World Society in English School Theory', *International Relations*, 19:1, 19–38.

(2010) 'Hedley Bull and Just War: Missed Opportunities and Lessons to Be Learned', *European Journal of International Relations*, 16:2, 179–96.

(2015) *Ethics, Diversity and World Politics: Saving Pluralism from Itself*, Oxford: Oxford University Press.

Wilson, Peter (2012) 'The English School Meets the Chicago School: The Case for a Grounded Theory of International Institutions', *International Studies Review*, 14:4, 567–90.

Wohlforth, William C., Richard Little, Stuart J. Kaufman, et al. (2007) 'Testing Balance-of-Power Theory in World History', *European Journal of International Relations*, 13:2, 155–85.

Wolf, Martin (2014) *The Shifts and the Shocks: What We've Learned – and Have Still to Learn – from the Financial Crisis*, London: Penguin.

Womack, Brantly (2014) 'China's Future in a Multinodal World Order', *Pacific Affairs*, 87:2, 265–84.

Woods, Ngaire (ed.) (2000) *The Political Economy of Globalisation*, Basingstoke: Macmillan.

Yao, Joanne (2021) 'Race and Historical International Relations', in Benjamin de Carvalho, Julia Costa Lopez and Halvard Leira (eds.), *Routledge Handbook of Historical International Relations*, Abingdon, Routledge, 192–200.

Yeophanton, Pichamon and Evelyn Goh (2022) 'China as a "Partial" Environmental Great Power', in Robert Falkner and Barry Buzan (eds.), *Great Power Responsibility and Global Environmental Politics*, Oxford: Oxford University Press.

Zacher, Mark (2001) 'The Territorial Integrity Norm: Internal Boundaries and the Use of Force', *International Organization*, 55:2, 215–50.

Zakaria, Fareed (2009) *The Post-American World and the Rise of the Rest*, London: Penguin.

Zarakol, Ayse (2011) *After Defeat: How the East Learned to Live with the West*, Cambridge: Cambridge University Press.

(2022) *Before the West*, Cambridge: Cambridge University Press.

Zhang, Feng (2009) 'Rethinking the "Tribute System": Broadening the Conceptual Horizon of Historical East Asian Politics', *The Chinese Journal of International Politics*, 2:4, 545–74.

(2015) 'Confucian Foreign Policy Traditions in Chinese History', *The Chinese Journal of International Politics*, 8:2, 197–218.

Zhang, Feng and Barry Buzan (2022) 'The Relevance of Deep Pluralism for China's Foreign Policy', *The Chinese Journal of International Politics*, online first.

Zhang, Yongjin (2001) 'System, Empire and State in Chinese International Relations', in Michael Cox, Tim Dunne and Ken Booth (eds.), *Empires, Systems and States: Great Transformations in International Politics*, Cambridge: Cambridge University Press, 43–63.

Zhang, Yongjin and Barry Buzan (2012) 'The Tributary System as International Society in Theory and Practice', *Chinese Journal of International Politics*, 5:1, 3–36.

(2019) 'China and the Global Reach of Human Rights', *China Quarterly*, online first.

Zürn, Michael (2010) 'Global Governance as Multi-level Governance', in Henrik Enderlein, Sonja Wälti and Michael Zürn (eds.), *Handbook of Multi-level Governance*, Cheltenham: Edward Elgar, 80–102.

Index

functional differentiation
 generally, 24
 economic inequality and, 205–6
 in hunter–gatherer era, 56, 67
 liberalism and, 205–6
 modernity, transition from
  stratificatory to functional
  differentiation in, 159
 sectors and, 27
 socialism and, 205–6
segmentary differentiation
 generally, 23–4
 in hunter–gatherer era, 55–6
 sequence in, 24–5
stratificatory differentiation
 generally, 24
 in CAPE era, 91
 in hunter–gatherer era, 65–7
 modernity, transition from
  stratificatory to functional
  differentiation in, 159
 in religion, 126
digital technology, 178–9, 304, 346–7
diplomacy
 Amarna system, 139–40
 in CAPE era
  generally, 239
  ambassadors, 141–2
  dynastic marriage and, 140–1
  foreign ministries, 142
  hierarchy and, 138–40
  historical evolution of, 138–40
  interhuman domain and, 143
  interpolity domain and, 142–3
  kinship and, 140–1
  merchants and, 143
  modern system, 141
  similarities in, 140
  transnational domain and, 143
 communication, impact of, 239–40
 community and, 140
 cross-domain nature of, 37–8
 decolonisation and, 242
 deep pluralism and
  generally, 359–60
  anti-hegemonism and, 360–2
  autism analogy, 360–1, 368
  colonialism, legacy of, 362–5
  digital diplomacy, 359
  firms and, 359, 366
  'forgetting' of colonialism and, 363–4
  INGOs and, 366–7
  interhuman domain and, 364
  interpolity domain and, 364
  non-state actors and, 365–7

regionalisation, 367–70
resentment against colonialism and,
 362–3
transnational domain and, 364
dynastic marriage and, 140–1
English School and, 142, 361
heteronomous structure of relations and,
 141
in hunter–gatherer era, 56
raison de système and, 142, 239, 358,
 361–2
raison d'état and, 142, 358, 361–2
in transition from CAPE era to modernity
 actors, increase in, 240–1
 agenda, widening of, 240
 antidiplomacy, 239
 communication, impact of, 239–40
 current status of, 243
 IGOs and, 241–4
 INGOs and, 240–1
 interhuman domain and, 243–4
 interpolity domain and, 243–4
 multilateralism and, 241–3
 nationalism, impact of, 239
 in postmodern international system,
  243
 transnational domain and, 243–4
 transportation, impact of, 239–40
 transportation, impact of, 239–40
disease
 antibiotics and, 169, 303
 in CAPE era, 85
 COVID-19 (See COVID-19)
 in hunter–gatherer era, 58
 monarchy/dynasticism and, 144
distribution of power
 associational balance of power and, 250
 diffuse nature of, 341
 great powers, 338
 IGOs and, 275
 international politics as driven by, 46–7
 international system and, 7–8
 regional powers, 338–9
 superpowers, 338
 World War I and, 310–11
divided sovereignty, 195–6, 232–3
Diwali, 148
DNA, 171
dollar as de facto global currency, 377
domains
 generally, 9–11
 interhuman domain (See interhuman
  domain)
 interpolity domain (See interpolity
  domain)

Cambridge Studies in
International Relations

For EU product safety concerns, contact us at Calle de José Abascal, 56–1°,
28003 Madrid, Spain or eugpsr@cambridge.org.

www.ingramcontent.com/pod-product-compliance
Ingram Content Group UK Ltd.
Pitfield, Milton Keynes, MK11 3LW, UK
UKHW020404140625
459647UK00020B/2640